The Road to Gettysburg

★ **Other Books by Donald S. (Don) Lowry** ★

The 1864 Series

*No Turning Back: The Beginning of the End
of the Civil War, March–June 1864* (1992)

*Fate of the Country: The Civil War
from June to September 1864* (1992)

*Dark and Cruel War: The Decisive Months of the
Civil War, September–December, 1864* (1993)

*Towards an Indefinite Shore: The Final Months of
the Civil War, December 1864–May 1865* (1995)

The 1863 Series

*Over the River: The Campaigns of Vicksburg and
Chancellorsville, March–May 1863* (2014)

THE ROAD TO GETTYSBURG

Lee's Invasion of Pennsylvania and Grant's Siege of Vicksburg, May—July 1863

Donald S. Lowry

The Road to Gettysburg
Copyright 2015 by Donald S. Lowry

All rights reserved. No part of this publication may be reproduced, stored in a retrieval system, or transmitted, in any form or by any means, electronic, mechanical, photocopying, or otherwise, without the prior written permission of the author.

ISBN-13: 978-1514609613
ISBN-10: 1514609614

Cover and maps by George Skoch, copyright 2015 by Donald S. Lowry

Designed and typeset by Catspaw DTP Services
http://www.catspawdtp.com/

Table of Contents

Prologue ... 1

Part One The Threat to Vicksburg ... 3
Chapter 1 "Vicksburg has not fallen" ... 4
Chapter 2 "The Valley of the Shadow of Death" ... 31
Chapter 3 "They Are About to Move Forward" ... 63
Chapter 4 "All I Want Now Are Men" ... 91
Chapter 5 "It Seems to Me Desperate" ... 119

Part Two Uncertainty ... 143
Chapter 6 "If the War Was a Tournament" ... 144
Chapter 7 "To Secure Peace Through Victory" ... 172
Chapter 8 "I Am Still Confident of the Final Result" ... 200
Chapter 9 "He Will Be Gobbled Up" ... 228
Chapter 10 "Nearly Everything Is Conjecture" ... 258
Chapter 11 "Get Us Information" ... 286
Chapter 12 "Hope Deferred Makes the Heart Sick" ... 319
Chapter 13 "High Expectations Formed" ... 347

Part Three Advances: North and South, East and West ... 371
Chapter 14 "Few Skirmishes Ever Equaled It" ... 372
Chapter 15 "The Rebels Are Coming!" ... 395
Chapter 16 "The Whole Rebel Army Is Marching Toward Harrisburg" ... 426
Chapter 17 "Tried and Condemned Without a Hearing" ... 458
Chapter 18 "Move in the Direction of Gettysburg" ... 495
Chapter 19 "The Best Opportunity We Have Had" ... 529
Chapter 20 "We Must Fight a Battle Here" ... 563

Epilogue ... 584
The Armies ... 589
Bibliography ... 614

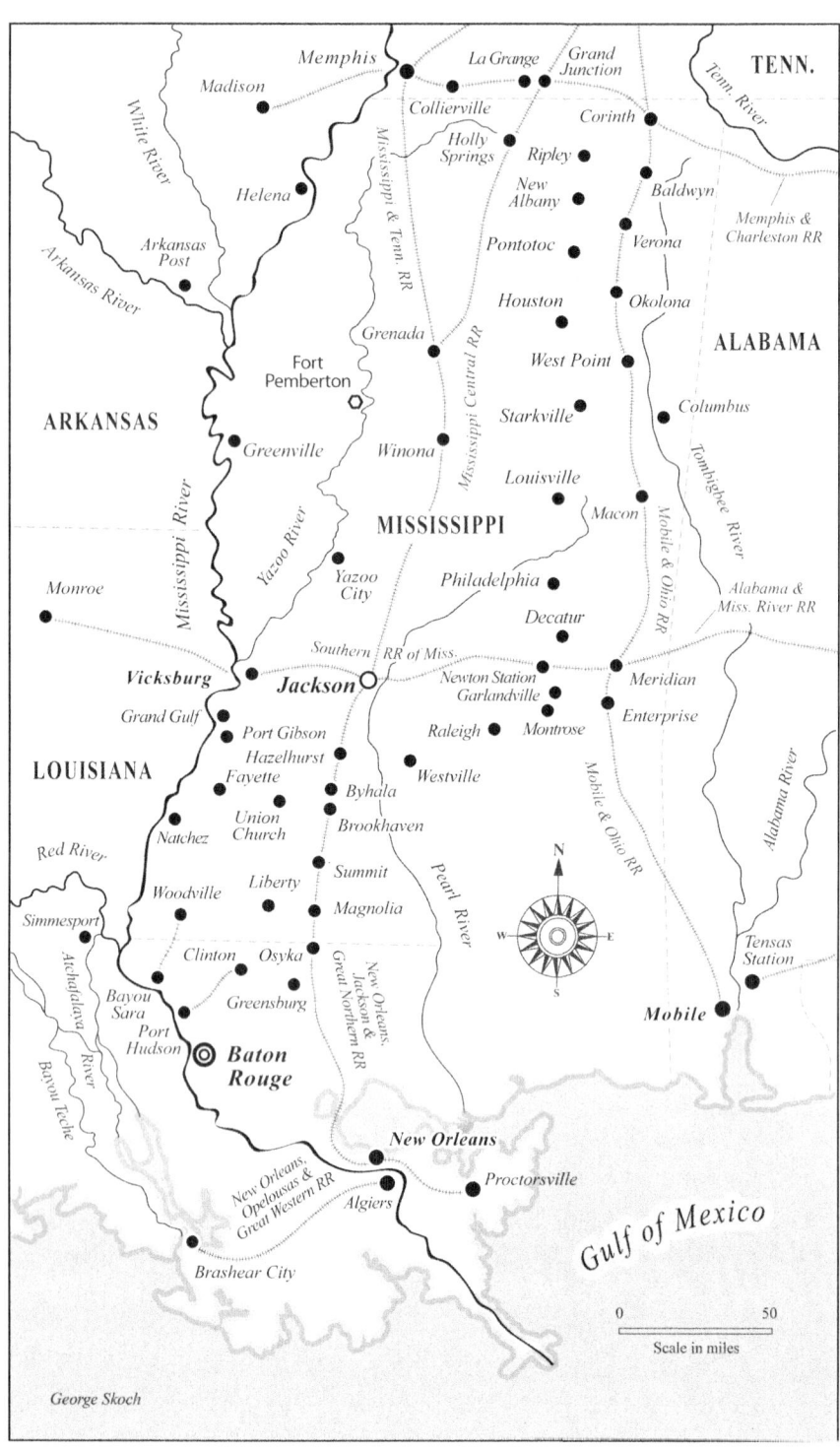

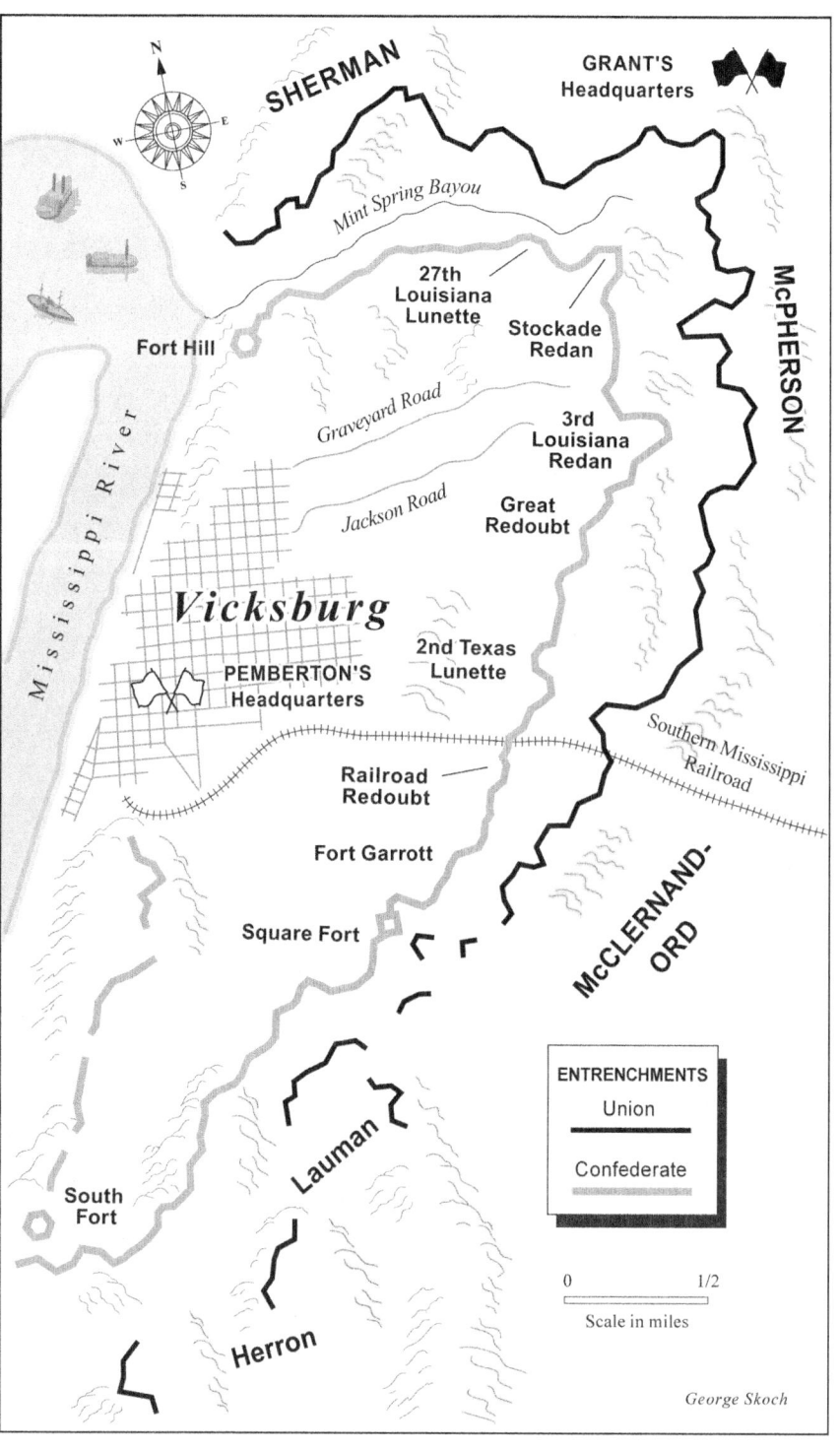

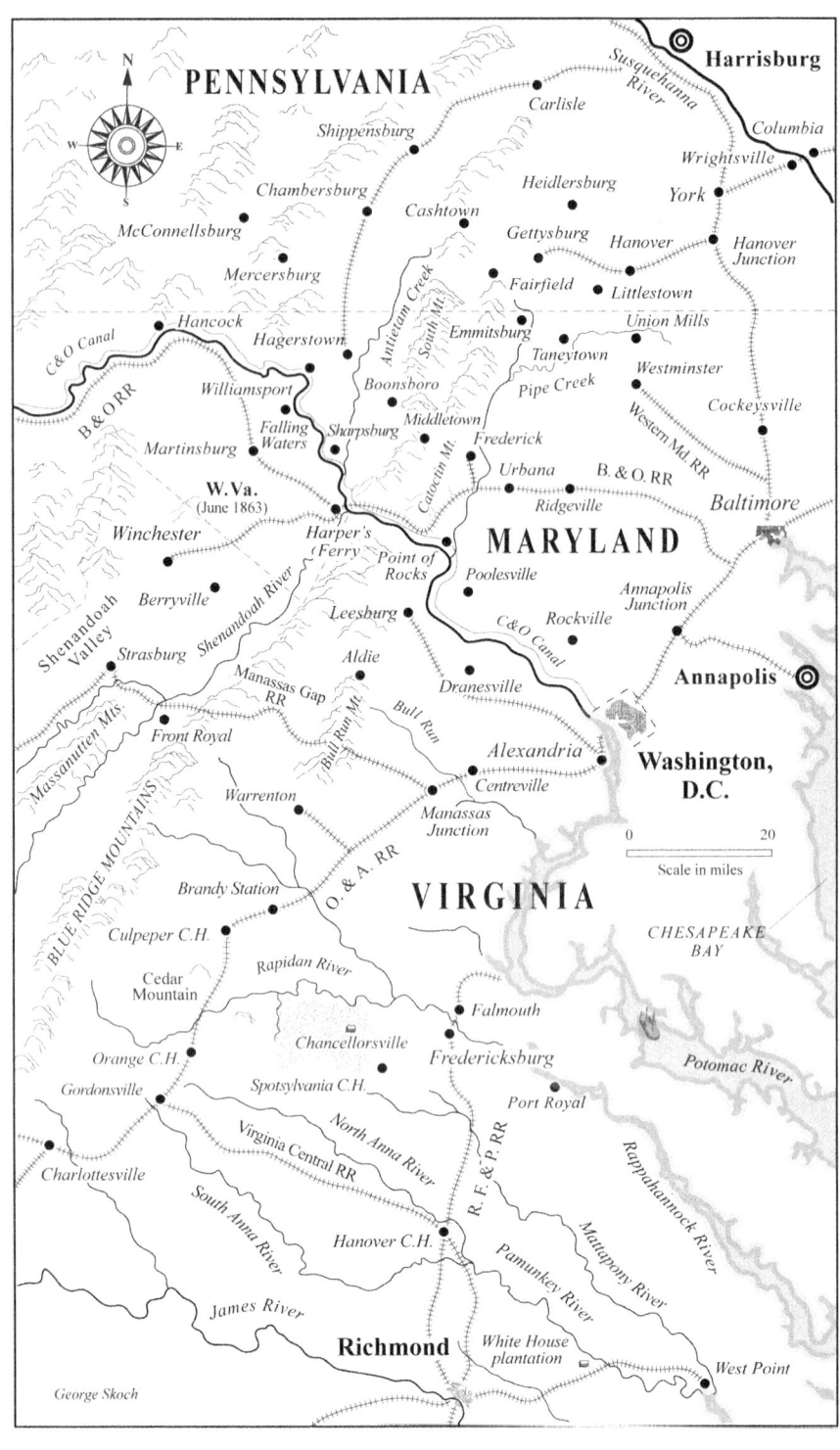

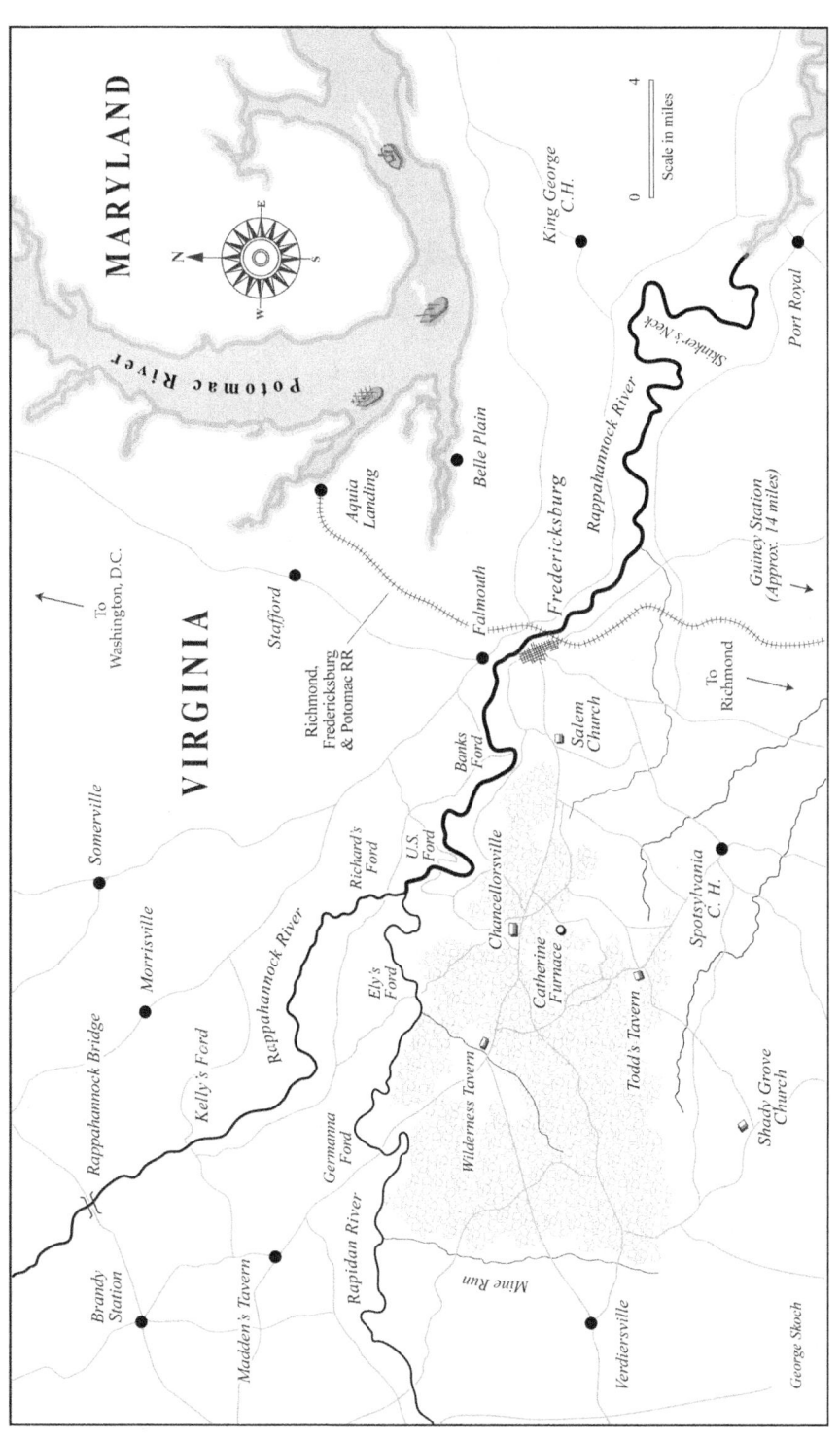

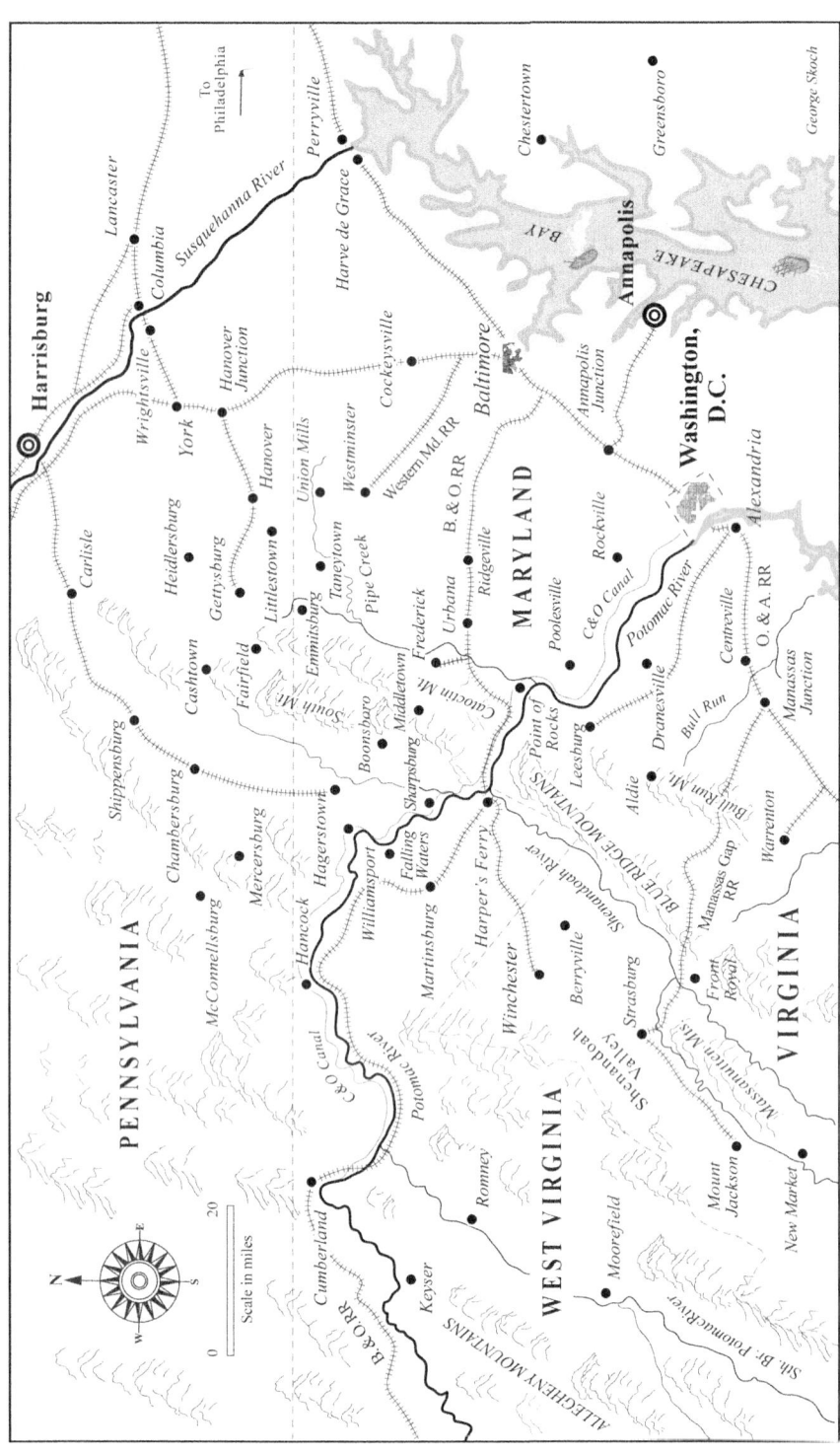

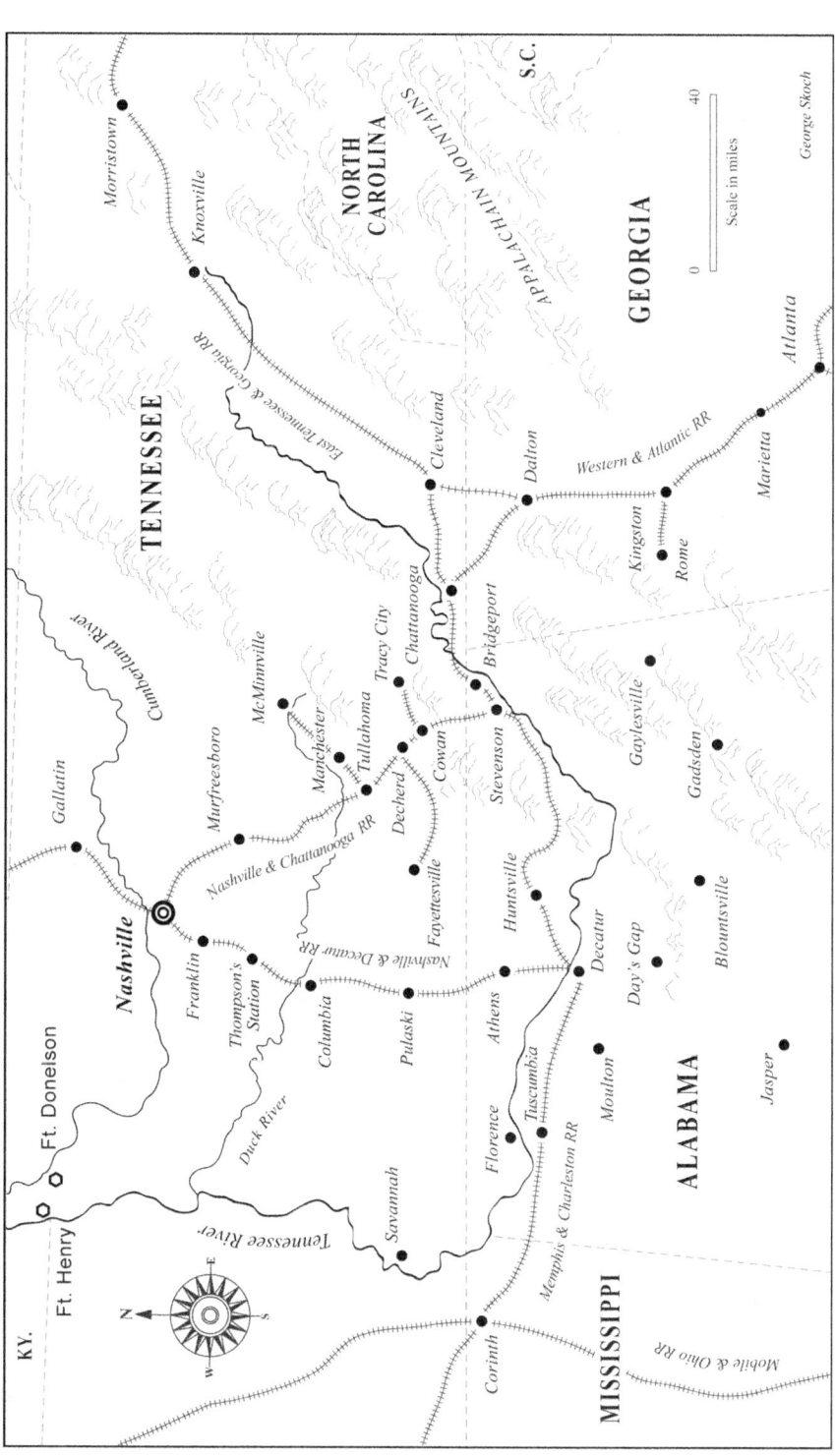

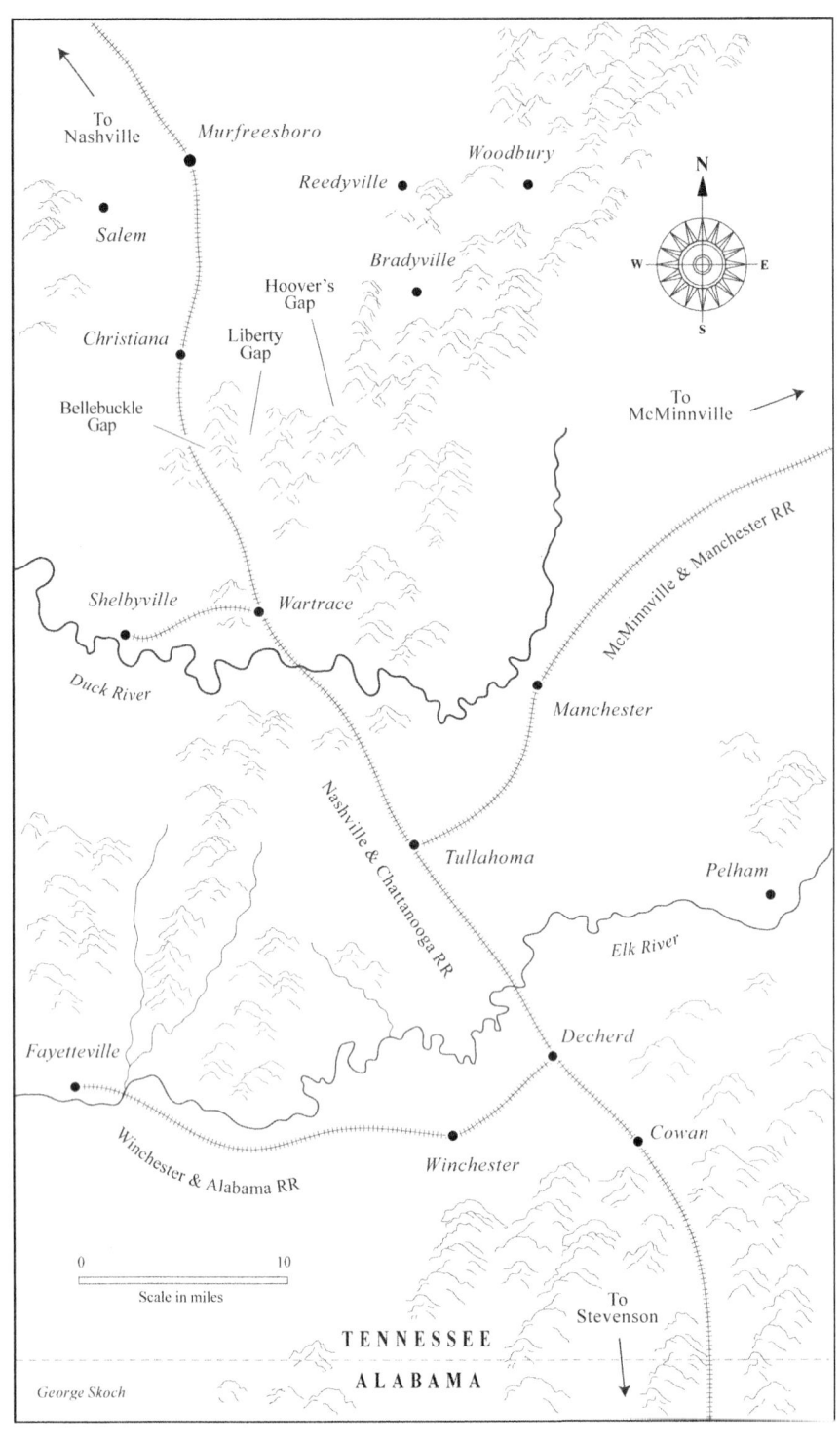

PROLOGUE

THIS BOOK IS THE SECOND VOLUME of a trilogy that covers the spring and early summer of the American Civil War's pivotal year, 1863. (Actually, I started out to write a single book, but it grew.) The first volume, *Over the River,* covered the campaign and battle of Chancellorsville in the East, General Grant's crossing of the Mississippi and his maneuvering thereafter that led to the siege of Vicksburg, and General Banks' campaign in western Louisiana that led to the simultaneous siege of Port Hudson. This volume covers almost the entirety of those sieges, as well as General Rosecrans' almost bloodless Tullahoma campaign, against which background it narrates General Lee's advance from the Rappahannock River in Virginia well into Pennsylvania and brings us to the brink of the battle of Gettysburg. That battle and its aftermath, as well as the final fall of those two fortified towns, will be the subject of the next volume, after which I hope, in some future work or works, to go on and narrate the rest of 1863 and connect this series with my previous four volumes that covered 1864-65.

That said, there is no reason why this volume could not stand alone as a narrative of an often overlooked or downplayed period of the Civil War. It is not necessary for the reader to have read the first volume in order to understand this one, although I have tried to hold the introductory material to a minimum so we can get right into it. While there are no great battles to write about in this short period of a little over a month, there is much to cover. And in the end I think much of what happened at Gettysburg can be better understood by a look at these weeks that led up to it.

As with my previous works, I follow a strictly chronological approach, which, I feel, helps us to see things as they were seen at the time and to understand how events in various places interacted with each other. I have provided endnotes to show the sources of all quotations in the text and have used, within the quotes, the spelling and punctuation found in those sources, although I have often changed the paragraphing in order to maintain a more consistent style. I place these notes at the end of each chapter, as I do not like the current fashion of placing them at the end of the book, where they are hard to find.

I'd like to express my appreciation for the aid of my son, James Lowry, in proof-reading this volume. A second pair of knowledgeable eyes are very helpful.

Part One
THE THREAT TO VICKSBURG

CHAPTER 1

"Vicksburg has not fallen"

22 – 23 May 1863

"VICKSBURG HAS NOT FALLEN – is not going to fall," the Richmond, Virginia, *Examiner* told its readers on the 22nd day of May 1863. "It is not in so much danger now as it has often been before, and the Federal army . . . is in a very dangerous situation."[1]

Vicksburg, Mississippi, was a small city sitting high on the bluffs overlooking a horseshoe bend of the Mississippi River. Numerous Confederate cannon placed on these bluffs that stretched along the east side of the river threatened any vessel attempting to descend the river from what was then called the Northwest – what we now call the Midwest – or coming upriver from Union-controlled New Orleans or Baton Rouge.

Although ironclad steamboats of the U.S. Navy and even unarmored warships and transports carrying supplies for the Union army had on a few occasions run past these Confederate guns without being sunk (though often with considerable damage; and some of the unarmored ones were sunk), no civilian boat owner on a purely commercial venture would dream of taking such a risk. Therefore the grain of Midwestern farmers and the products of Midwestern factories were cut off from their traditional route to their markets, not only in the South, but, via the Gulf and the Atlantic Ocean, to the East and even to Europe. Of course, a network of railroads had grown up in the last couple of decades to connect the Midwest with the East Coast, but their rates were higher than those for steamboats and their carrying capacity was not really sufficient for the job, so Midwesterners still looked upon the Mississippi River as their natural avenue of commerce.

Midwesterners tended to react to this blockade of their

commerce in two ways: either they joined or supported one of several anti-war organizations, known collectively as Copperheads, in the hope of ending the war or withdrawing their area from participation in it, followed by making a deal with the Confederacy (if not openly allying with it), or they joined or supported the Union army and navy in their attempt to open the Mississippi by clearing it of all Confederate bastions.

Union forces had gotten off to a good start, and by the summer of 1862 Federal military units controlled the river as far south as Memphis, Tennessee, and Helena, Arkansas. Others had come up the river from the Gulf and captured New Orleans and Baton Rouge, Louisiana. But before their control could be extended to the vital stretch of river between Helena and Baton Rouge, the Confederates had planted their big guns at Vicksburg and others at Port Hudson, Louisiana, just upriver from Baton Rouge. And sizable forces of Confederate infantry had been stationed at both places to protect the artillery. As long as the Rebels controlled these two vital points – Vicksburg and Port Hudson – they maintained a link with Texas, Arkansas, and the western portion of Louisiana, from which they had been drawing most of the food supplies needed for their troops in Mississippi as well as some manufactured goods imported from Europe by way of Mexican ports. And they prevented the Union forces, and Northwestern farmers and factories, from traversing the full length of the Mississippi.

The officer in charge of the Union forces coming up the river was Major General Nathaniel P. Banks, commander of the Department of the Gulf, whose troops were known as the 19th Army Corps, consisting of four divisions. Banks owed his high rank to his political importance, being a former Speaker of the House of Representatives and Governor of Massachusetts. His military experience was now considerable, but his skills were still somewhat limited.

Federal forces coming down the river were under Major General Ulysses S. Grant, commander of the Department of the Tennessee, a graduate of West Point and one of the Union's most successful generals in the war so far. Grant's army was much larger than Banks', consisting of four corps, each of three or more divisions. His 16th Corps, commanded by Major General Stephen Hurlbut, was defending Union-held territory in West Tennessee and western Kentucky, but Grant had with him, for use against Vicksburg, the 13th Corps, under Major General John A. McClernand, the 15th Corps, under Major General William Tecumseh Sherman, and the 17th Corps, under Major General James B. McPherson.

Grant's problem had been how to get at Vicksburg. Situated as it was on high bluffs lined with heavy guns overlooking the broad river, a frontal assault had been out of the question. Just north of the city another navigable river, the Yazoo, slanting in from the northeast, emptied into the Mississippi. In the narrow angle between the two rivers was the low-lying swampy area known as the Delta – too wet for the Army and too dry for the Navy. The eastern bank of the Yazoo was lined with a continuation of the bluffs that made Vicksburg so formidable.

Back in December, Grant had tried moving down the railroad that ran from Memphis, Tennessee, to Jackson, Mississippi, while Sherman, his favorite subordinate, had tried to assault the bluffs overlooking the Yazoo, but both efforts had failed. Then, all through the winter of 1862-63 Grant had tried numerous ways to get at Vicksburg without going all the way back to Memphis and coming down overland again. Water levels were high in the Mississippi and its numerous tributaries, so efforts were made to get gunboats and transports into the middle reaches of the Yazoo River via various bayous and streams in the Delta and to find similar connections between streams west of the Mississippi that could be used to bypass the Rebel guns at Vicksburg, but one by one all these attempts failed for one reason or another. They did, however, serve two useful purposes: they kept Grant's troops occupied, and they kept the Confederates busy trying to figure out what Grant was up to and how to stop him – too busy to get up offensives of their own.

One plan that had looked as though it was going to work

had been to use a series of bayous just west of Vicksburg to connect Grant's camps on the west bank of the river above Vicksburg with a village called New Carthage on the same bank south of Vicksburg. But in April, just as this route was about to prove useful, the winter rains ended, the water level in the river and bayous began to fall, and the connection was lost. However, with more dry land finally emerging on the west side of the river, Grant put his troops to work building roads, and soon he was able to haul supplies to New Carthage by wagon. This provided him with a way to get his army south of Vicksburg, but he was still on the wrong side of the Mississippi.

To solve this problem, several ironclad gunboats, commanded by Rear Admiral David Dixon Porter, and a few unarmored steamboats for use as transports, had successfully run past the Vicksburg batteries on the night of 16 April 1863. However, once the gunboats had run past Vicksburg they had discovered that the Rebels were implanting more big guns on the bluffs at a town called Grand Gulf, several miles downstream from Vicksburg and just south of another stream, the Big Black River, that also came slanting in from the northeast to empty into the Mississippi. The gunboats had attacked these batteries but could not subdue them, and so they had waited for night and had then run past them to get even farther downriver. Grant had marched his troops on down the west bank to keep pace. Then, while Sherman had been sent up the Yazoo River with part of his corps to try to make the Confederates think that he was going to attack the bluffs up there again, Grant had finally gotten some of his troops ferried across the big river at a place called Bruinsburg, not far south of Grand Gulf.

Grant's original intention had been, once he got a sizable force across the Mississippi, to send part of it down to help General Banks take Port Hudson. However, Banks had, meanwhile, found Port Hudson too well defended for him to take it alone. So, leaving a division to hold Baton Rouge and another to hold New Orleans, he had gone off to clear the Confederates out of western Louisiana. This he had done successfully, moving up the Atchafalaya River to the Red and up that river to Alexandria, Louisiana, and beyond.

Grant's first units across, most of McClernand's corps and part of McPherson's, had moved northeast along the high ground and defeated a Confederate division at Port Gibson, which had then retreated across the Big Black River toward Vicksburg, leaving Grand Gulf open for Grant's use in ferrying supplies and more troops across the river. While waiting for these to arrive via the circuitous route along the west side of the river, Grant had rounded up all the wagons, horses and mules his troops could find to carry the ample food supplies he found in the surrounding countryside and had begun edging his forces to the northeast, keeping the Big Black River between his army and the Rebels at Vicksburg.

Finding that Banks had gone off in a different direction, Grant then moved up the east side of the Big Black River to threaten not only Vicksburg but also Jackson, the state capital, and the vital railroad that linked the two towns. Especially vulnerable was the bridge where the railroad crossed the Big Black River about halfway between the two. The Confederate commander in the area, Lieutenant General John C. Pemberton, had spread his forces to hold Vicksburg, to watch the lower crossings of the Big Black, and to defend the vital bridge. He had also ordered the commander at Port Hudson to send troops to the town of Raymond, which was between Jackson and Grant's forces, to be joined there by reinforcements coming into Jackson from South Carolina and Tennessee. But, learning that Confederate reinforcements were expected at Jackson, Grant had decided, even before all his army had caught up with him, to take that city first, cutting these reinforcements off from Pemberton, after which he would turn west and deal with that general's main force. To make this move against Jackson, Grant had cut loose from his supply line – a bold, unconventional, and dangerous move that the Confederates had not expected.

The Rebels from Port Hudson and the first few reinforcements to arrive from South Carolina had been defeated at

Raymond on 12 May 1863 by McPherson and then driven from Jackson two days later by McPherson and Sherman, who, with two of his divisions, had just caught up with Grant. The Rebels at Jackson had been under the direct command of General Joseph E. Johnston, who was in charge of all Confederate forces between the Appalachian Mountains and the Mississippi River. He had just arrived at Jackson from Tennessee to take personal command in Mississippi only to find Grant was between him and Pemberton, preventing the concentration of their forces.

Johnston's small force had been driven off to the north, and Sherman had been left to destroy everything in Jackson that might be useful to the Confederate war effort – especially the railroads – while Grant had turned back to the west with McClernand's and McPherson's corps. Johnston had ordered Pemberton to bring all the troops he could quickly collect and come join him, but Pemberton had left two divisions to hold Vicksburg and with the rest had then run into Grant's army instead of Johnston's, at a place called Champion's Hill. There he had been soundly defeated by two of McPherson's division's and one of McClernand's while McClernand himself, with four more divisions, had done little more than make cautious probes of Pemberton's position.

One Confederate division, under Major General W. W. Loring, had been cut off during this battle and forced to retreat around to the south and east, eventually joining up with Johnston. Meanwhile, driven westward and cut off from Johnston, Pemberton had made a brief stand at the bridge over the Big Black River the next day, but an impetuous Union charge had driven his troops from their strong earthworks and across the Big Black. Pemberton had then retreated into the formidable defenses of Vicksburg, rejoining the divisions he had left there.

On 19 May, just twenty days after first crossing the Mississippi, Grant had Vicksburg invested on the north and east, with Porter's gunboats patrolling the river to the southwest and northwest, and a new supply line running to the very same bluffs on the Yazoo River that Sherman had tried to storm back in December – and from there down to the mouth of the Yazoo and up the Mississippi. Grant had tried to take Vicksburg by assault that day, and he had tried again on the 22nd, but the Confederate lines had held, and Grant had decided he would have to starve the Rebels out, or take it by the slow process of digging approach trenches to bring his lines closer to those of the defenders.

The repulse of these assaults, especially those of the 22nd, did much to improve Confederate morale, which had been very low since their defeats at Champion's Hill and the Big Black River Bridge. Margaret Lord, wife of a clergyman living in the surrounded city, called it the "reincarnation of our army – men who had been gloomy and despondent once more stood erect and hurled defiance at the foe!"[2] But a surgeon in the besieged army noted that day, "We are penned in two square miles and fighting all around. It is decidedly unpleasant to be cut off from the world and know that important movements are going on outside without being able to learn the nature of them. . . ."[3]

People elsewhere were just as interested in what was happening in Mississippi as the surgeon was in what was going on outside it. President Lincoln sent a telegram that same day, the 22nd, to General Hurlbut, at Memphis: "We have news here in the Richmond newspapers of 20th. & 21st. including a dispatch from Gen. Joe Johnson himself, that on 15th. or 16th. (a little confusion as to the day) Grant beat Pemberton and Loring near Edward's Station, at the end of a nine hours fight, driving Pemberton over the Big Black & cutting Loring off, & driving him South to Chrystal-Springs 25 miles below Jackson. Joe Johnson telegraphed all this, except about Loring, from his camp between Brownsville & Lexington, on the 18th. Another dispatch indicates that Grant was moving against Johnson on the 18th."[4]

It's interesting to note that Lincoln's first news of Grant's success came by way of a Southern newspaper. Enemy newspapers were a major source of information for both sides during that war, as there was very little in the way of censorship, and the papers were freely traded across the lines. However, the last sentence of his telegram also illustrates the unreliability of such information, as Grant had not gone after Johnston on the 18th or anytime since driving him from Jackson on the 14th. He was, instead, laying siege to Vicksburg, while Johnston was collecting what forces he could along the railroad north of Jackson.

Sherman's 15th Corps, three divisions, held Grant's right, north of the city. That day, the 22nd, after the second assault on the Rebel lines had failed, Sherman wrote to Grant: "If Admiral Porter will send two of his best gunboats along this shore, and with his heavy artillery at close range clear the hill in front of my right on the immediate bank of the river, we may secure that flank of the enemy's works, and thereby turn them."[5] That is, if the gunboats could drive the Confederates from the earthworks at the northwestern end of their line of defenses, Sherman could then get around on their flank and drives them from the rest of their line.

So, while the Richmond newspaper's statement was true that Vicksburg had not fallen – and it was indeed a long way from falling, as its garrison was large and well supplied – it was not true that Grant's army was in any great danger; at least, not yet. However, the longer the Rebels in Vicksburg held out, the greater the danger would become. Johnston had with him north of Jackson the troops Grant had run out of that city, plus Loring's division that had been cut off from Pemberton at the battle of Champion's Hill, and a few thousand other troops who had since arrived, and more were on the way from South Carolina and Tennessee. But so far his collected force was still smaller than Grant's, and he was very weak in artillery and lacking in wagons for hauling supplies. Further, coordinating his forces with Pemberton's for a joint attack would be extremely difficult. If he approached Grant's rear with his present small force, that general might turn, attack, and defeat him before Pemberton could even know about it. So Johnston was holding back and waiting, hoping that more reinforcements would allow him to build an army capable of driving Grant away from Vicksburg.

And, in fact, Confederate President Jefferson Davis wired General Braxton Bragg in Tennessee that same day, 22 May: "The vital issue of holding the Mississippi at Vicksburg is dependent on the success of General Johnston in an attack on the investing force. The intelligence from there is discouraging. Can you aid him? If so, and you are without orders from General Johnston, act on your judgment."[6] So there was this much danger for Grant: that the longer Pemberton's army held out in Vicksburg, the greater the chance that the Union army, busy watching the besieged city, would be attacked from the rear. In fact, Johnston really didn't need to attack Grant's army directly; he only had to interpose his own army between Grant's lines and his supply base at Haynes' Bluff on the Yazoo River. This would force Grant to attack him, possibly providing Pemberton with a chance to break out. So Johnston waited, just beyond Grant's reach, for reinforcements to swell his forces.

No reinforcement would be coming to Mississippi from the Confederacy's principal army, however. General Robert E. Lee, commander of the Army of Northern Virginia, had recently talked President Davis out of sending any of his troops west. Instead he was gathering strength and laying plans for a move he had long wanted to make: across the Potomac River into Union territory in Maryland and Pennsylvania. In early May, Lee had stymied a move by the Union's largest force, the Army of the Potomac. That army's commander, Major General Joseph Hooker, had managed to get better than half of his large army across two rivers and onto the flank of Lee's formidable position on the hills south and southeast of the town of Fredericksburg. But finding his movements restricted by the thickets of second-growth forest in an area called the Wilderness of Virginia, Hooker had contented himself with going on the defensive near a crossroads known as Chancellorsville, thinking that Lee had no choice but to retreat from Fredericksburg or attack him head-on.

Instead, Lee had sent half of his smaller army, under Lieutenant General Thomas J. "Stonewall" Jackson, via roads hidden by the Wilderness thickets, to attack Hooker's army from the rear, completely routing one corps of Hooker's army, the 11th. That night, while reconnoitering in advance of his troops, Jackson had been accidentally wounded by his own men – a wound that had eventually proven fatal. In the course of another day of heavy combat, Hooker had pulled back into a formidable defensive position guarding his bridgehead south of the Rappahannock River. Then another corps of his army, the 6th, under Major General John Sedgwick, that had been left near Fredericksburg, had captured the formidable but lightly manned Confederate defenses back of that city. However, Lee, who was between Hooker and Sedgwick, had then turned and attacked Sedgwick, and the latter had retreated back across the river. Lee had planned to turn again and attack Hooker's main force the next day, but, under the cover of a heavy rainstorm, Hooker had also retreated across the river. Both armies were bloodied, but neither felt themselves to be defeated, as they both settled back into the same camps they had occupied all winter.

However, Lee felt that this repulse of Hooker now gave him the chance he had been waiting for to move north again. He had crossed the Potomac the summer before, but that time his plans had been disrupted by the discovery that a sizable Union garrison at Harper's Ferry, Virginia – where the Shenandoah River joins the Potomac – had not been withdrawn as Lee had expected. Its presence there had threatened his tenuous supply line through the Shenandoah Valley, so he had sent much of his army by various routes to surround Harper's Ferry and capture its garrison. This would have been well enough except that a copy of his order detailing the positions to be taken by his forces surrounding Harper's Ferry had fallen into the hands of Union soldiers, who had passed it up the chain of command to Major General George B. McClellan, who had then been the commander of the Army of the Potomac. With this information in his position, McClellan had moved faster than his usual snail's pace to attack Lee before the Confederate could concentrate his forces again. The resulting battle on 17 September 1862 near the banks of Antietam Creek and the north bank of the Potomac, at Sharpsburg, Maryland, had been the bloodiest single day of combat in the war. Lee had stood his ground and fought off numerous poorly coordinated attacks, but had soon found it necessary to withdraw across the Potomac back to Virginia.

He had been wanting to cross back to the north of that river ever since, and now he thought the time had finally arrived. Such a move would relieve war-torn northern Virginia from the presence of the two hungry armies; break up any Union plans for another campaign against Richmond, the Confederate capital; and, by threatening Washington, Baltimore, Philadelphia, and other Northern cities, perhaps draw Union troops away from Vicksburg – if not those already there, at least perhaps some that would otherwise be sent there as reinforcements. He could also damage important Northern railroads and perhaps disrupt the mining and/or shipping of coal from the mines of northeast Pennsylvania – coal needed for Northern factories, railroads and homes, and the Union navy. Actual capture of one of those important cities, and/or any substantial victory over the Union army in its own territory might even lead to recognition of the Confederacy's independence by the great powers of Europe – which in turn might lead to direct aid from one or more of those powers. It would at least help offset the loss of Vicksburg and Port Hudson, if those important positions should fall.

And Port Hudson was now in just as much danger as Vicksburg. That same day, 22 May, General Banks' forces crossed the Mississippi from west to east to cut off the Confederate garrison there. Port Hudson was to the Union forces coming up the great river what Vicksburg was to Grant's forces coming down the river – an easily defensible strongpoint where Confederate heavy guns could block Union vessels from going past on the river. However, General Pemberton had recently ordered most of Port Hudson's infantry to march north and join the fight against Grant, and there remained only one over-sized brigade of infantry, numerous artillery units, and a few cavalry troopers – all in all about 6,800 men, commanded by Major General Franklin Gardner.

When Banks had finally learned that the garrison at Port Hudson had been greatly reduced since he had last been there, he had turned about, descended the Red River and then the Mississippi, and started landing his troops on the eastern bank at Bayou Sara, a few miles north of Port Hudson, on the 22nd. Meanwhile, his division from Baton Rouge, commanded by Major General Christopher C. Augur, reinforced by some of the troops from New Orleans, had moved up the river and had started reaching out east of the Rebel defenses to meet the troops coming down from Red River. Some of Augur's troops had had a sharp little fight the day before with some of Gardner's Confederates at a crossroads dominated by a two-story building known as Plains Store. Having heard the gunfire of that battle, Banks now hastened his forces from Bayou Sara southward through a driving rainstorm in an effort to link up with Augur.

Also on that same 22nd day of May, the United States War Department established a new bureau for the organization of units composed of escaped slaves. Everyone knew that slavery was somehow the root cause of the war, and shortly after the battle of Antietam Lincoln had given the Confederates fair warning that, unless they gave up their armed struggle against his duly elected government by 1 January 1863, all slaves in the territories still under Confederate control would be considered free thereafter. The Confederates had not been swayed by this threat, and so Lincoln was proceeding to the next logical step: recruiting former slaves to fight for their own freedom. The adjutant general of the U. S. Army, Brigadier General Lorenzo Thomas, had already been touring the areas of the South controlled by Union forces and had made speeches to Federal soldiers in Grant's department along the Mississippi River and its tributaries enjoining them to support this new policy of the government, and holding out the promise that all officers in the new regiments of "U. S. Colored Troops" would be recruited from white veteran soldiers. It meant promotions for many of them and new units to strengthen their armies, which were at that time losing many men whose enlistments were expiring.

In fact, a great many regiments in General Hooker's Army of the Potomac were going home just then, or soon would be, because their enlistments were ending. Most units in the Union army were composed entirely of volunteers. All the men of a given unit had been recruited at the same time, and all would go home at the same time – all who had survived. While most newer Union units were obligated to serve for three years, there were some units, raised at the beginning of the war, when no one had thought it would last very long, who had been enlisted for only two years; and their time was now up. There were also numerous units that had been recruited the previous summer and autumn, when things had been going badly for the Union, to serve for only nine months, and most of those were also now reaching the ends of their terms. General Lee knew about this sudden reduction in Hooker's manpower and saw that, and the necessity for Hooker to reorganize his remaining forces, as another reason why he should be able to steal a march on the Federals and launch his raid across the Potomac.

A recently passed Federal law now provided for a "draft" or lottery of conscripted men to fill the ranks whenever volunteering failed to meet the needs of the Army, but the machinery for running these drafts was not yet in place, and it would be months before they provided many men to the dwindling Union forces. Meanwhile, there was much resistance among the citizens of the Northern states to all these changes. No one wanted to be drafted, and many men claimed that while they might fight to preserve the Union they did not care to fight to free the slaves. In the old Northwest, especially, Copperheads were organizing to resist the draft, oppose the war in general, and, if the war could not be stopped, to even go so far as to take the Northwestern states out of the Union to make their own deal with the Confederacy.

    Hooker's recent retreat after the battle of Chancellorsville, was being seen in the North as one more failure of Union arms. At first, solace had been taken in what had appeared to be a successful raid on Lee's communications by Hooker's cavalry, then commanded by Major General George Stoneman. But as more information had come in about exactly what Stoneman had accomplished, or not accomplished, it became apparent that this too had been a failure. Stoneman had ignored Hooker's detailed instructions, scattered his forces in small packets to attack various bridges and rail lines, and thus had failed to strike a heavy blow anywhere. Most especially, he had not substantially damaged the Richmond, Fredericksburg & Potomac Railroad, which was the vital lifeline connecting Lee's army at Fredericksburg with the Confederate capital at Richmond. Thus, on that same 22nd day of May, Stoneman was relieved of command of the Cavalry Corps of Hooker's army and succeeded by Brigadier General Alfred Pleasonton, who, during the recent Chancellorsville campaign, had commanded the few Union cavalry units that had stayed with Hooker's main army.

    Although two years younger than Stoneman, Pleasonton had graduated from West Point two years ahead of him (in 1844 – one class behind Grant). He owed his new position primarily to three causes: he had not gone on Stoneman's ineffectual raid; he had managed to convince Hooker that he had played an important part in saving the latter's army from even worse defeat when Stonewall Jackson's Rebels had unexpectedly come bursting out of the thickets to rout the 11th Corps; and he was the senior remaining officer in the Cavalry Corps after Stoneman left. In fact, Pleasonton was not yet officially appointed to the position, he merely assumed temporary command of the corps that day as the senior officer present. Hooker later claimed that he would have preferred to have Brigadier General John Buford, then commanding the Reserve Brigade of cavalry, but Pleasonton had seniority.

Another change of command was being contemplated but had not yet been made. President Lincoln was disappointed with Hooker's performance in the recent campaign, but had not yet made up his mind whether to replace him, and if so, with whom. That general had done an excellent job of restoring his army's morale when he had taken command a few months before, and had planned a brilliant campaign and executed it well – until he came within reach of Robert E. Lee and the Army of Northern Virginia. After that, he had obviously lost confidence in himself, allowed Lee to bluff him and bully him, and then had meekly retreated back across the Rappahannock while trying to place all the blame on various subordinates. And those subordinates were even more disappointed with Hooker than Lincoln was. There was much grumbling and second-guessing going on among them, much of which was leaking out to their friends and families, and some of which was reaching the ears of powerful politicians and Lincoln himself.

On that same 22nd of May, in Washington, Lincoln met with Major General Darius Couch, commander of the 2nd Corps and the next-ranking officer in the Army of the Potomac after Hooker. Lincoln sounded him out on the possibility of his succeeding Hooker as commander of the Union's largest army, but Couch pleaded ill health and emphatically declined. However, he did not want to serve under Hooker any longer, either, and so he requested a transfer. He was relieved of command of the 2nd Corps that same day and replaced by Major General Winfield S. Hancock, that corps' senior division commander.

Couch recommended Major General George G. Meade, commander of the 5th Corps, as Hooker's replacement, and he might well have added that major generals Henry W. Slocum, commander of the 12th Corps, and John Reynolds, commander of the 1st Corps, endorsed the idea. In fact, after alienating the commanders of the 6th, 11th, and cavalry corps by blaming them for his recent retreat, Hooker's only remaining supporters among the higher officers of the Army of the Potomac were his chief of staff, Brigadier General Dan Butterfield, and perhaps Major General Dan Sickles, commander of the 3rd Corps, both being old proteges.

The next day, the 23rd, Treasury Secretary Salmon P. Chase, Hooker's political sponsor, warned that general that it was a mistake "to have the Chiefs of Corps come up here to tell their several stories . . . ," with each relating how the recent battle of Chancellorsville would have turned out so much better "if his counsel or his ideas had been followed."[7] Chase advised weeding out the malcontents, even if it meant making new generals out of captains or lieutenants, but Hooker, who had himself been one of the chief grumblers against his predecessor, and perhaps feeling secure in his cordial relationship with the President, seemed to think it better to let the discontent among his senior officers surface in the form of complaints to Lincoln than to let it fester. He probably knew that the morale of the men in the ranks was still pretty good. So, over the next couple of weeks most of Hooker's corps commanders did visit Washington, and the message most of them brought there was that they had lost all faith in Joe Hooker.

Also on the 23rd, Lincoln conferred with military and naval officers about a recent unsuccessful attempt by the Union Navy to force its way into the harbor at Charleston, South Carolina. As the city where the war had begun, with the firing of Confederate guns on the Federal garrison of Fort Sumter in the middle of the harbor, Charleston was a powerful symbol to both sides. It was also a port where fast blockade-running ships, often of British registration, slipped past Union blockaders to bring vital supplies and scarce luxuries to the embattled Confederacy. So, for both practical and symbolic reasons, Lincoln wanted that port closed and that city captured. On 7 April a squadron of Union ironclad gunboats had tried to pound now-Confederate Fort Sumter into submission, but had received the worst of the fight. One ironclad, the lightly armored *Keokuk*, had been sunk and others slightly damaged, and the naval commander, Rear Admiral Samuel Du Pont, had retreated; he had little confidence in the ironclads, and had no plans for renewing the contest.

The Union army had taken little part in that fight, and its local commander, Major General David Hunter, commander of the 10th Army Corps and the Department of the South, didn't think he could do much so long as he was under orders to co-operate with Du Pont; he had, the day before, sent one of his aides north with a long letter in which he suggested that, if not tied to the Navy, he could mount raids into the heart of Georgia, marching through counties where 75 percent of the inhabitants were slaves, and "destroy all railroad communication along the eastern portion of the State, and lay waste all stores which can possibly be used for the sustenance of the rebellion."[8] In addition, General Banks, down in Louisiana, wanted at least some of Du Pont's ironclads to be sent there to help him and Admiral Farragut take Port Hudson.

But Lincoln was not yet ready to give up on taking Charleston. That very day Brigadier General Quincy A. Gillmore, on leave in New York, wrote to his friend, Brigadier General G. W. Cullum, who happened to be chief of staff to the Union Army's General-in-Chief, Major General Henry W. Halleck. Gillmore said that he had heard that he was being considered for a command "in connection with the reduction of the forts in Charleston Harbor," and he wanted to say that, although not given to asking for special favors, he thought, with enough heavy rifled artillery, he could do it and that he would like to have the chance to prove it.[9] His confidence would carry considerable weight, because he had, the year before, blasted the Rebels out of Fort Pulaski, at Savannah, Georgia, proving for the first time that the pre-war masonry forts along the East Coast, of which Fort Sumter was one, were not able to withstand the new rifled artillery. Gillmore was soon summoned to Washington by Halleck to join a group of officers who would plan a new attack on Charleston.

Although Stoneman's recent raid had done little material damage to the Confederates, it had alarmed them a great deal, and it had demonstrated the large numbers and improved efficiency of Hooker's cavalry. Partly because of this, Lee had been trying to increase his own cavalry forces. From his headquarters near Fredericksburg, he was writing that day, 23 May, to his cavalry commander, Major General J. E. B. "Jeb" Stuart, who was now making his headquarters well to the west, at Culpeper Court-House, roughly midway between the Rappahannock and Rapidan rivers. From there Stuart could detect and intercept any repetition of Stoneman's raid or of Hooker's recent movement around Lee's left flank. He was also in position to lead or screen any move Lee might make toward the Shenandoah Valley and thence across the upper Potomac.

Lee told Stuart not to undertake any expeditions of his own for now, but to rest and recuperate his command in preparation for the summer campaign. After telling him that carbines for his men were being sent to him from Richmond and from the main army, and complaining that Stuart was increasing his artillery even as Lee was expecting to have to reduce his own for lack of horses to pull them, he informed him that he had directed Brigadier General W. E. "Grumble" Jones to bring his brigade of cavalry from the Shenandoah Valley to join Stuart's other three brigades at Culpeper just as soon as Jones's place in the Valley could be taken by a brigade under Brigadier General Albert Jenkins being sent up from southwest Virginia.

Stuart already knew that two regiments of cavalry were on their way to him from North Carolina under the command of Brigadier General Beverly Robertson. Neither Stuart nor Lee seemed to want Robertson himself, but they needed his troopers. Lee also wrote that day to Brigadier General J. D. Imboden, commander of a unit called the Northwestern Virginia Brigade. Imboden and Grumble Jones had both just returned from a joint raid into Union-held West Virginia. After telling Imboden what to do with the cattle, horses, and other items captured during this recent raid, Lee told him to bring his brigade into the Shenandoah Valley "where you can keep strict watch on the movements of the enemy, and refresh and rest the men and animals. I wish you to have your force ready for active operations as soon as possible, and to relax nothing in watchfulness, as the enemy will be very apt to endeavor to return the compliment which General Jones and yourself have paid them."[10]

And, a Union cavalry raid was proposed that very day, but it was not targeted on the Shenandoah Valley. Captain Ulric Dahlgren, an aide on Hooker's staff and son of Admiral John Dahlgren, then head of the Navy's Ordnance Bureau, addressed a letter to Hooker with an interesting plan. He said, "The rebel cavalry are again feeling along our lines, probably to find a weak point to enter at, as is their custom. If they should attempt a raid, this would offer a fine chance for a small body of our cavalry to penetrate their country. . . ." His thinking was that, with most of the Confederate cavalry on the move in the opposite direction, there would be none available to pursue a Union raid. He wanted to borrow the 6th U.S. Cavalry and lead it clear down to and across the James River somewhere near Richmond. "The object of the expedition would be to destroy everything along the route, and especially on the south side of the James River, and attempt to enter Richmond and Petersburg."[11] Nothing came of this plan at the time (the Union cavalry's horses had not yet recovered from Stoneman's recent raid), but Dahlgren would get a chance to do daring and important things a little later in this coming campaign and to play a controversial part in a large raid toward Richmond some ten months later.

However, he was not the only one on the Union side to notice that Lee's cavalry seemed to be preparing for something. Secretary of War Stanton addressed a note to General-in-Chief Halleck that same day asking some specific questions about how prepared the Army of the Potomac and the garrisons around Washington were, "In view of the possibility of an early raid by the enemy. . . ."[12] Halleck replied with a long letter saying that he thought the defenses of Washington were as prepared as could be expected and that a number of Union soldiers who had been captured, paroled, and were awaiting exchange were being moved to the north side of the Potomac to get them out of the way, since they could not legally fight until exchanged, but added, in regard to the Army of the Potomac, "I have not now, nor have had since General Hooker assumed the command, any information in regard to its intended movements other than that which I have received from the President, to whom General Hooker reports directly."[13]

Hooker, meanwhile, via Brigadier General Seth Williams of his staff, gave General Pleasonton instructions that day to keep at least one of his three divisions of his cavalry on the Orange & Alexandria Railroad and to thoroughly picket the crossings of the Rappahannock River to protect against Rebel cavalry raiding toward Washington. He added that, "The general desires that you will spare no labor to place the cavalry arm of the service in a high state of efficiency at the earliest practicable moment. He cannot but feel that the force of this arm has been greatly impaired from want of system, organization, and judicious employment."[14]

Specifically, Hooker wanted the cavalry officers to make sure that the men took better care of their horses. This was never easy, since every cavalryman knew that the easiest way to avoid having to fight was to make sure he didn't have a serviceable horse to ride. Add to the cowards those who were too lazy to groom, feed, and look after a dumb animal, as well as those who just didn't know how, not to mention unscrupulous civilians who would gladly sell the government an old, weak, or sickly horse for the price of a good one, and it was almost certain that a sizable percentage of the cavalry would be dismounted, especially after a raid or battle, which inevitably involved hard riding and little rest. No wonder that Union infantry would ask each other with considerable sarcasm, "Whoever saw a dead cavalryman?"

In the Confederate service the troopers had to provide their own horses, which gave them an incentive to take care of them. However, a Rebel who lost his horse was often allowed to go home to get another one, thus providing him with some incentive to lose his first mount. And whenever Confederate troopers with few prospects of securing remounts were transferred to the infantry, many of them would desert. So even in that army, where the mounted arm had garnered many laurels for daring raids in the first two years of the war, cavalrymen were viewed with considerable disdain by their compatriots of the infantry.

Out in Mississippi that day, the 23rd, General Grant, having decided to settle into a siege of Vicksburg, rather than to risk assaulting its defenses again, briefly considered moving against another enemy – this time an internal one – Major General John A. McClernand, commander of the 13th Corps. During the assaults of the 22nd, McClernand had made exaggerated claims about the success on his own front that had led to a renewal of the attack by all three corps, which had only served to lengthen the casualty lists. When they had learned of the real situation, Grant and many of his officers had been incensed with the political general. Charles A. Dana, an official of the War Department who was accompanying Grant's headquarters on this campaign, later said, "Grant had resolved on the 23d to relieve McClernand for his false dispatch of the day before stating that he held two of the enemy's forts, but he changed his mind, concluding that it would be better on the whole to leave him in command till the siege was concluded." McClernand, a former Democratic Congressman from Illinois, owed his general's stars to his political prominence, and hoped to gain fame and glory in the war to enhance his future political prospects. Dana said that "McClernand was merely a smart man, quick, very active-minded, but his judgment was not solid, and he looked after himself a good deal. . . . But from the circumstances of Lincoln's supposed friendship, McClernand had more consequence in the army than he deserved."[15]

On the other hand, Dana, a former journalist and confidant of Secretary of War Stanton, admired Grant and his other two corps commanders, Sherman and McPherson, for their competence and their selfless devotion to the good of the country. He was impressed with them not only individually but also by how well they worked together. "The utmost cordiality and confidence existed between these three men," he later wrote, "and it always seemed to me that much of the success achieved in these marches and battles was owing to this very fact. There was no jealousy or bickering, and in their unpretending simplicity they were as alike as three peas."[16]

Of those three, Dana had a favorite: "Sherman especially impressed me as a man of genius and of the widest intellectual acquisitions," he said.[17] McClernand, therefore, was the odd man out; he was not a team player but was trying to garner personal glory that would enhance his political career. Grant, himself, Dana described as "the most disinterested, and the most honest man I ever knew, with a temper that nothing could disturb, and a judgment that was judicial in its comprehensiveness and wisdom. . . . sincere, thoughtful, deep, and gifted with courage that never faltered. . . ."[18]

After Grant, Dana later said, he spent a lot of time with Lieutenant Colonel John A. Rawlins, Grant's chief of staff and assistant adjutant general. In a letter later written to Stanton, after the siege had ended, Dana said, Rawlins "is a very industrious, conscientious man, who never loses a moment, & never gives himself any indulgence except swearing & scolding. He is a lawyer by profession, a townsman of Grant's, and has a great influence over him, especially because he watches him day & night, and whenever he commits the folly of tasting liquor hastens to remind him that at the beginning of the war he gave him (Rawlins) his word of honor not to touch a drop as long as it lasted. Grant thinks Rawlins a first rate adjutant, but I think this is a mistake. He is too slow and can't write the English language correctly without a great deal of careful consideration. Indeed, illiterateness is a general characteristic of Grant's staff, and in fact of Grant's generals and regimental officers of all ranks."[19] Rawlins' concern about Grant's drinking stemmed from the fact that his own father had been an alcoholic, much to the detriment of his family. Grant seems not to have been actually addicted. Instead, he seems to have been one of those people who don't drink very often, but for whom a little is too much.

In that same letter Dana went on to describe the other officers on Grant's staff, some of whom he praised and others he dismissed as useless. He added: "If Gen. Grant had about him a staff of thoroughly competent men, disciplinarians, & workers, the efficiency & fighting quality of his army would soon be much increased. As it is, things go too much by hazard & by spasms; or when the pinch comes, Grant forces through by his own energy & main strength what proper organization & proper staff officers would have done already."[20]

One of Grant's staff officers who did impress Dana was James Harrison Wilson, a young lieutenant colonel of volunteers and an assistant inspector general who was also a captain of engineers in the Regular Army. Dana often rode out with him to inspect different parts of the army. "His leading idea," Dana later told Stanton, "is the idea of duty & he applies it vigorously and often impatiently to others. In consequence he is unpopular among all who like to live with little work. But he has remarkable talents & uncommon executive power, & will be heard from hereafter." (He certainly was that, for, in fact, in 1864 he became a general himself, and by 1865 was one of the Union's best cavalry commanders.)

Wilson had a run-in with General McClernand that same day. Grant sent him to deliver an order to McClernand to send some troops to guard the crossings of the Big Black River, now in the army's rear as it faced Vicksburg. McClernand's anger at being superceded in the campaign to open the Mississippi, which he had wanted to lead himself, finally boiled over. "I'll be God damned if I'll do it!" he told Wilson. "I am tired of being dictated to – I won't stand for it any longer, and you can go back and tell General Grant!" This was followed by a string of oaths to which Wilson took personal affront. He didn't care if McClernand outranked him, he wasn't going to stand for it. So saying, Wilson threatened to "pull you off that horse and beat the boots off you!" And he was young enough and fit enough to do it. Stunned and then sobered, McClernand said, "I am not cursing you. I could not do that. Your father was my friend and I am yours. I was simply expressing my intense vehemence on the subject matter, sir, and I beg your pardon!"[21]

Somewhat mollified, Wilson rode back to headquarters and reported the exchange to Grant and Rawlins. Grant, who never swore and seldom displayed any signs of anger, found the whole thing amusing. Throughout the rest of the campaign, whenever he heard anyone cursing – it was usually Rawlins – he would say, "He's not swearing – he's just expressing his intense vehemence on the subject matter."[22]

Dana also visited the Navy's gunboats from time to time. He later said that Admiral Porter was "a very active, courageous, fresh-minded man, and an experienced naval officer, and I enjoyed the visits I made to his fleet. His boats were pretty well scattered, for the Confederates west of the Mississippi were pressing in, and unless watched might manage to cross somewhere. Seven of the gunboats were south of Vicksburg, one at Haynes's Bluff, one was at Chickasaw Bayou, one at Young's Point, one at Milliken's Bend, one at Lake Providence, one at Greenell, one at Island Sixty-five, two were at White River, and so on, and several were always in motion. They guarded the river so completely that no hostile movement from the west ever succeeded, or was likely to do so."[23]

The admiral wrote to Grant that day, describing what he and his vessels had done the day before to support the army's assault on the Vicksburg defenses, noting that one of them was disabled by Confederate fire and that the others had been "cut between wind and water," forcing them to retire, but added that "I fought the batteries one hour and half longer than you asked me to." He went on to tell the general, "Depend that I am doing everything that can be done with my small means. . . . Hope you soon finish up this Vicksburg business, or these people may get relief. I wrote to General Hurlbut four days ago, telling him that I thought you would thank him for every man he or any one else could send you. General Banks is not coming here with his men. He is going to occupy the attention of Port Hudson, and has landed at Bayou Sara, using your transports for that purpose."[24]

Grant replied before the day was out: "I am satisfied that you are doing all that can be done in aid of the reduction of Vicksburg. There is no doubt of the fall of this place ultimately, but how long it will take is a matter of doubt. I intend to lose no more men, but to force the enemy from one position to another without exposing my troops. I have information that the enemy under Johnston, who have been threatening me, have gone back to Calhoun, on the Mississippi Central Railroad. There is but about 8,000 of them, much demoralized. A force is collecting at Yazoo City which numbers now about 2,000 men. Does this expose your boats now up the Yazoo? If so, I will send Lauman to disperse them, although I do not like to detach any troops until this job here is closed up. One week is as long as I think the enemy can possibly hold out."[25]

Brigadier General Jacob G. Lauman commanded the 4th Division of the 16th Corps, which Hurlbut had already sent to join Grant. It had been landed at Haynes' Bluff, on the Yazoo north of Vicksburg, and was now moving around behind Grant's other forces to take position at the left, or south end, of his lines. Charles Dana did not think much of Lauman. "This general got his promotion by bravery on the field & Iowa political influence," he later told Secretary Stanton. "He is totally unfit to command, a very good man, but a very poor general."[26]

Sherman's corps headquarters issued orders that day for his troops to begin regular siege operations, and added that "It is the duty of the quartermaster's department to look to roads and communications to the rear. . . ." This order gave these officers authority to impress any soldiers or escaped slaves they found lurking in the rear without orders or passes and to put them to work. "Sick soldiers must stay in their regimental camps or at their hospitals," it said. "If well enough to wander about, they can work on a road, or in loading wagons."[27]

Otherwise, both armies at Vicksburg did very little on the 23rd. "This day was unusually quiet," General Pemberton later reported, "with but little artillery firing until late in the afternoon. The sharpshooters of the enemy were more cautious, and he was evidently staggered by the severe repulse of the day previous. Many of his dead were still lying unburied in sight of our trenches. The fire from the mortar-fleet continued heavy and incessant. At night the engineers were again busily engaged in repairing the works . . . which were badly shattered."[28]

Jefferson Davis was, that same day, writing a brief telegram to be sent to Pemberton at Vicksburg. (He didn't seem to yet understand that Pemberton was virtually surrounded): "I made every effort to re-enforce you promptly, which I am grieved was not successful. Hope that General Johnston will join you with enough force to break up the investment and defeat the enemy. Sympathizing with you for the reverses sustained, I pray God may yet give success to you and the brave troops under your command."[29]

∽ Endnotes ∽

1   A. A. Hoehling, *Vicksburg: 47 Days of Siege* (New York, 1969, Fairfax Press edition, 1991), 35.
2   Ibid., 41.
3   Ibid., 38.
4   Roy P. Basler, editor, *The Collected Works of Abraham Lincoln* (New Brunswick NJ, 1953), VI:226. Lincoln, of course, meant Joe Johnston, not Johnson.
5   War Department, *War of the Rebellion: Official Records of the Union and Confederate Armies* (Washington, 1889), Series I, Vol. 24, Part III, page 341. Hereinafter cited as *OR* with series, volume, part (if any) and page.
6   Ibid., I:23:II:847.
7   Stephen W. Sears, *Gettysburg* (Boston/New York, 2003), 23.
8   *OR*, I:14:457.
9   Ibid., I:4:459.
10 Ibid., I:25:II:819.
11 Ibid., I:25:II:517-8.
12 Ibid., I:25:II:514.
13 Ibid., I:25:II:515-6.
14 Ibid., I:25:II:517.

15 Charles A. Dana, *Recollections of the Civil War* (First Collier Books edition, New York, 1963), 71-2.
16 Ibid., 71.
17 Ibid., 48.
18 Ibid., 73.
19 Ibid., 82.
20 Ibid., 84.
21 Edward G. Longacre, *Grant's Cavalryman: The Life and Wars of General James H. Wilson* (Mechanicsburg PA, 1972), 82.
22 Bruce Catton, *Grant Moves South* (Boston, 1960), 457.
23 Dana, *Recollections of the Civil War*, 93.
24 *OR*, I:24:III:342-2.
25 Ibid., I:24:III:343.
26 Dana, *Recollections of the Civil War*, 78.
27 *OR*, I:24:III:344.
28 Ibid., I:24:I:276.
29 Ibid., I:24:III:909.

CHAPTER 2

"The Valley of the Shadow of Death"

23 – 27 May 1863

GENERAL HURLBUT, UNION commander in West Tennessee, forwarded to his friend President Lincoln that day a message that had been sent to him by Rawlins, Grant's chief of staff, on the 20th: "The Army of the Tennessee landed at Bruinsburg on 30th April. On 1st May, fought battle of Port Gibson; defeated rebels under Bowen, whose loss in killed, wounded and prisoners was at least 1,500; loss in artillery, five pieces. On 12th May, at the battle of Raymond, rebels were defeated, with a loss of 800. On the 14th, defeated Joseph E. Johnston, captured Jackson, with loss to the enemy of 400, besides immense stores and manufactures, and seventeen pieces of artillery. On the 16th, fought the bloody and decisive battle of Baker's Creek [Champion's Hill], in which the entire Vicksburg force, under Pemberton, was defeated, with loss of twenty-nine pieces of artillery and 4,000 men. On the 17th, defeated same force at Big Black Bridge, with loss of 2,600 men and eleven pieces of artillery. On the 18th, invested Vicksburg closely. To-day General Steele carried the rifle-pits on the north of the city. The right of the army rests on the Mississippi River above Vicksburg." Hurlbut added that he had heard that there were from 15,000 to 20,000 Rebels in the defenses of Vicksburg and that "Grant has probably captured nearly all."[1]

In response to Jefferson Davis's request of the day before, General Braxton Bragg, commanding the Confederate Army of Tennessee, issued orders that day, 23 May, to send the division commanded by Major General John C. Breckinridge to reinforce Joe Johnston in Mississippi. Breckinridge was a Kentuckian, a former vice-president of the United States who had been the nominee of the Southern wing of the Democratic Party in the 1860 presidential election. He had no military education, but had served in the Mexican War and had commanded a division-sized Reserve Corps at Shiloh in the spring of 1862. It was he who had first fortified Port Hudson on the Mississippi after an unsuccessful attempt to recapture Baton Rouge and before being transferred to Middle Tennessee. He was to leave a brigade of Tennessee troops with Bragg, taking only his other three brigades, and there would still be a few days before any of them reached the railroad to even begin their long journey on the rickety railroads of the Confederacy.

Brigadier General Samuel B. Maxey's brigade, which had been ordered north from Port Hudson by Pemberton before the latter had retreated into Vicksburg, reached the city of Jackson, Mississippi, that day, the 23rd, from which it soon moved to join Joe Johnston's growing forces. Johnston received that day a message from General Gardner at Port Hudson saying Banks's Union army was approaching and that he needed reinforcements. But Johnston was already upset that Pemberton had allowed his troops to be cornered in Vicksburg, where he was in danger of losing both the place and the troops, and he feared that the same would soon happen at Port Hudson. He felt that Gardner's forces would be of more use joined to his own small army, and he had already sent orders to that effect. Now one of his staff officers replied: "Orders have been sent to you for the immediate evacuation of Port Hudson. You cannot be re-enforced. Do not allow yourself to be invested. At every risk save the troops, and if practicable move in this direction."[2]

But it was too late; Gardner would never receive this message, for that day Banks' forces that had landed at Bayou Sara, north of Port Hudson, linked up with Augur's division coming up from the south, completing the investment of the town and its defenders. Actually, the unit that Banks first linked up with was a small brigade of cavalry commanded by Colonel Benjamin Grierson, which, sent on a raid by Grant, had recently ridden the full length of the state of Mississippi and had met up with Augur near Baton Rouge. Now it served as the link between Banks' forces that had campaigned west of the Mississippi with those that had stayed behind to guard the Union lodgments on the east side of the river.

Federal troops from New Orleans, under Brigadier General Thomas W. Sherman (no kin to William T. Sherman, up at Vicksburg with Grant), landed at Springfield Landing, south of Port Hudson, that day and took position at the southwestern end of the Union line that now stretched around the east side of the town and back to the river north of the Rebel defenses. A road well within the Union lines now linked Banks' entire force with the Mississippi, where steamers connected him with his base at New Orleans, giving him a secure supply line. Gardner's Confederate garrison, had none; it was cornered, besieged by a superior force, and unable to join Joe Johnston. On the contrary, like Pemberton's troops at Vicksburg, they could only hope that that general would soon attack their besiegers and rescue them before they starved.

The next day, 24 May, up at St. Louis, Missouri, Major General John M. Schofield assumed command of the Department of the Missouri. This consisted at that time of the states of Missouri and Kansas, the territories of Nebraska and Colorado, and as much of Arkansas and the Indian Territory (now Oklahoma) as were in Union hands, except that Union forces around Helena in northeast Arkansas were in Grant's Department of the Tennessee. General Halleck had been trying for weeks to get the department's former commander, Major General Samuel Curtis, to send reinforcements to Grant or, more often, to General Rosecrans' Army of the Cumberland in Middle Tennessee, but Curtis had consistently refused on the grounds that he was desperately short of men himself. This was perhaps part of the reason for the change of command.

Halleck, who had commanded in Missouri the previous year, before being appointed general-in-chief, had written to Schofield on the 22nd giving him some general directions, and in that letter he had said "as soon as the Mississippi was opened to the Arkansas, the former became the true base and the latter the true line of operations. I endeavored to impress this upon

General Curtis. But he brought troops from Helena to operate from Pilot Knob, and again pushed forward a column into Western Arkansas. If, on the contrary, he had simply held two or three fortified points, like Springfield, Rolla, and Pilot Knob, and pushed his entire force from the Mississippi River to Little Rock, I think Missouri would have been freed from all fear of invasion and the enemy kept south of the Arkansas River. . . . [M]y dispatches to General Curtis will show that I have frequently urged upon him not to scatter his troops so much in the interior of the department, but to push them forward for the defense of the southern frontier, and send all who could be spared for such purpose down the Mississippi or to General Rosecrans; but it seems that the general has been under a serious apprehension of insurrections in the interior and northern counties."[3]

Schofield, who had served in that department throughout most of the war so far, except for a recent stint under Rosecrans in Tennessee, was a relatively young man for such an important command, but he had been chosen by President Lincoln himself, in spite of threats from a few older generals to resign rather than to serve under him. A few days later (the 27th) Lincoln would write directly to Schofield to explain his reasons. The letter is interesting for what it shows about Lincoln's political acumen, as well as his writing style:

"Having relieved General Curtis and assigned you to the command of the Department of the Missouri, I think it may be of some advantage for me to state to you why I did it. I did not relieve General Curtis because of any full conviction that he had done wrong by commission or omission. I did it because of a conviction in my mind that the Union men of Missouri, constituting, when united, a vast majority of the whole people, have entered into a pestilent factional quarrel among themselves, General Curtis, perhaps not of choice, being the head of one faction, and Governor Gamble that of the other. After months of labor to reconcile the difficulty, it seemed to grow worse and worse, until I felt it my duty to break it up somehow, and, as I could not remove Governor Gamble, I had to remove General

Curtis. Now that you are in the position, I wish you to undo nothing merely because General Curtis or Governor Gamble did it, but to exercise your own judgment, and do right for the public interest. Let your military measures be strong enough to repel the invader and keep the peace, and not so strong as to unnecessarily harass and persecute the people. It is a difficult role, and so much greater will be the honor if you perform it well. If both factions, or neither, shall abuse you, you will, probably, be about right. Beware of being assailed by one and praised by the other."[4]

Lincoln visited military hospitals in and near Washington on the 24th.

General Grant finally wrote a long report that day to General Halleck, bringing him up to date on the situation in Mississippi. After briefly outlining his present position and describing the failed assault of the 22nd that led to a loss of some 1,500 men, he said, regarding the latter, "General McClernand's dispatches misled me as to the real state of facts, and caused much of this loss. He is entirely unfit for the position of corps commander, both on the march and on the battle-field. Looking after his corps gives me more labor and infinitely more uneasiness than all the remainder of my department." But, ever the optimist, he went on to say, "The enemy are now undoubtedly in our grasp. The fall of Vicksburg and the capture of most of the garrison can only be a question of time. I hear a great deal of the enemy bringing a large force from the east to effect a raising of the siege. They may attempt something of the kind, but I do not see how they can do it. The railroad is effectually destroyed at Jackson, so that it will take thirty days to repair it. This will leave a march of 50 miles over which the enemy will have to subsist an army, and bring their ordnance stores with teams. My position is so strong that I could hold out for several days against a vastly superior force. I do not see how the enemy could possibly maintain a long attack under these circumstances. I will keep a close watch on the enemy, however."[5]

Major General Cadwallader C. Washburn, just put in charge of Grant's supply base at Haynes' Bluff, reported that day that he would send 250 cavalry across the Yazoo and between two of its tributaries, the Sunflower and Deer Creek, "to drive out the secesh who are gathering up stock, and to drive the stock into our lines."[6] A gunboat would also go up the Sunflower at the same time.

Charles Dana wrote a long letter to Secretary of War Stanton that same day (the 24th), as he would do nearly every day. He started by saying he had received, a few weeks before, a letter that Stanton had sent him saying that Grant had the full confidence of the government and the power and responsibility to remove anyone who hindered his operations. He said that Grant had come close to using that authority to remove McClernand the day before, but had instead concluded that "it would be better on the whole to leave McClernand in his present command till the siege of Vicksburg is concluded, after which he will induce McClernand to ask for leave of absence. Meanwhile he (General Grant) will especially supervise all of McClernand's operations, and will place no reliance on his reports unless otherwise corroborated. My own judgment is that McClernand has not the qualities necessary for a good commander, even of a regiment." After giving some details of the position of Grant's three corps and their prospects, he added that "One thousand cavalry have been sent north to dispose of bridges over Big Black [River] on the Memphis and Jackson Railroad, and to burn corn and forage in the Yazoo region, so as to impede the possible approach of enemy. General Banks has decided to attack Port Hudson at once instead of moving hither."[7]

General Pemberton later reported the events of the 24th: "At an early hour the mortar-fleet opened and kept up a continuous and heavy bombardment throughout the day. Just before dark the artillery from the rear opened a rapid and heavy fire, but not of long duration. In the afternoon the enemy attempted to mine our works on the Jackson road, but were soon driven off by the use of hand-grenades. During the night the engineers were engaged in increasing and strengthening our works. Before daylight our pickets captured a barge laded with coal, which was sunk, it being found impracticable to unload it. General Stevenson was ordered to have collected all the ammunition scattered in front of our trenches, and to have the cartridge-boxes of the enemy's dead emptied of their contents, it being important to add in any way to our limited supply of ammunition, and of musket-caps especially, of which latter we stood greatly in need, having one million more of cartridges than caps, without which latter, of course, the former could be of no possible value."[8]

The vast majority of muskets and rifles of that war were muzzle-loaders. The men carried cartridges made of paper that contained the lead bullet or ball and the requisite amount of gunpowder to propel it, but, once these were loaded, the powder was ignited by means of a "cap", which in most cases was a small bronze or brass cup containing a voluble substance known as fulminate of mercury, placed under the weapon's hammer. There was a small opening under the cap to let its flames reach the gunpowder at the bottom of the barrel. As Pemberton said, without caps to ignite the powder, the cartridges would be useless. The hand-grenades Pemberton referred to were mostly artillery shells with fuses cut very short that were more rolled than hurled onto Union soldiers below the parapets of the Rebel works. Even heavier devises were constructed of kegs filled with nails, rocks, etc., and enough gunpowder to hurl these objects about when ignited by a short fuse. These were also rolled down on any sizable body of Federals that got too close to the Confederate defenses.

The bombardment by Union guns, especially the huge mortars of Porter's fleet, was starting to drive the inhabitants of Vicksburg to burrow into the ground for protection. Caves were dug for the purpose into numerous hills. Lucy McRae, who was a young girl at the time, later remembered the elaborate cave her family took refuge in, cut into the side of a high hill in the northeastern part of the town: "It had four entrances, dug in the form of arched hallways, coming to a common center, at which point was dug a room which was curtained off. In this cave my mother took refuge with her three young children, my father having such an aversion for a cave that he would not enter one. My two older brothers were in the army, one in Vicksburg, the other with General Lee in Virginia."

One night a Union shell hit the top of their hill, bored six feet into the earth, and exploded, causing a large chunk of dirt to fall right on top of Lucy, burying all of her but one leg. Her mother managed to dig her head out with the help of a partially paralyzed woman and a clergyman with an injured leg, so she could breathe, and eventually some men were able to free her. Her mother decided to give up on this cave after another shell struck one of its entrances early the next morning. They moved into a tent pitched near the entrance to another cave that, while dug into a smaller hill, was deeper beneath the surface. From there they could listen for or watch the mortar shells as they came over and move into the cave if one seemed to be coming close. "They were beautiful at night," she said, meaning the shells.[9] No doubt they would trail sparks from their fuses, giving them the appearance of low-flying comets. On one occasion she and her mother just managed to scramble for safety in time when they heard a shell approaching, and it landed directly on the tent, demolishing the washstand they had been standing beside.

Another resident, middle-aged Emma Balfour, wife of a socially prominent doctor, and mother of six, told her diary on the 24th, "We have spent the last two nights in a cave, but tonight I think we will stay at home. It is not safe I know, for the shells are falling all around us, but I hope none may strike us." She described how shells and shell-fragments had struck the school and the houses of neighbors, literally tearing one of the houses to pieces, but said she had heard of only two persons being killed in the town, one of them a small child pinned to a wall by a piece of shell. But she added that "Today a shocking think occurred. In one of the hospitals where some wounded men had just undergone operations, a shell exploded and six men had to have limbs amputated. Some of them that had [already] been taken off at the ankle had to have the leg taken off to the thigh and one who had lost one arm had to have the other taken off. It is horrible and the worst of it is we cannot help it. I suppose there never was a case before of a besieged town when the guns from front and back met and passed each other. The other day while standing on Sky Parlor Hill a shell exploded and pieces struck in the flag near the steps. This was from a [Navy] mortar. Then a Parrott shell from the eastern [Army] side passed over us and into Washington Street. . . . A shot from a gun boat missed the house batteries and struck the hill just below where we were standing. At that moment there was firing all around us – a complete circle from the fortifications above all around to those below and from the river. . . ." She added that she had seen hundreds of mules driven beyond the Confederate lines because there was not enough food for them. "No corn is issued for horses, except those of officers in the field."[10]

The Union soldiers had also taken to digging, not caves but earthworks and approach trenches, known as saps. The latter were zig-zag affairs, constructed so as to provide cover for attacking troops until they could get close to the Rebels' defenses. These, as well as the gun emplacements, and trenches for the infantry, were buttressed by bottomless baskets, known as *gabions*. woven from small sticks and filled with dirt. As the approach trenches were dug the men working at the front of it were provided some protection by an object similar to a large gabion but laid horizontally so that it could be rolled along as the trench advanced. This was known as a sap-roller.

"The ground about Vicksburg is admirable for defence," Grant later wrote. "On the north it is about two hundred feet above the Mississippi River at the highest point and very much cut up by the washing rains; the ravines were grown up with cane and underbrush, while the sides and tops were covered with dense forest. Farther south the ground flattens out somewhat, and was in cultivation. But here, too, it was cut up by ravines and small streams. The enemy's line of defence followed the crest of a ridge from the river north of the city eastward, then southerly around to the Jackson road, full three miles back from the city; thence in a southwesterly direction to the river. Deep ravines of the description given lay in front of these defences. As there is a succession of gullies, cut out by rains along the side of the ridge, the line was necessarily very irregular. To follow each of these spurs with intrenchments, so as to command the slopes on either side, would have lengthened their line very much. Generally therefore, or in many places, their line would run from near the head of one gully nearly straight to the head of another, and an outer work triangular in shape, generally open in the rear, was thrown up on the point; with a few men in this outer work they commanded the approaches to the main line completely.

"The work to be done to make our position as strong against the enemy as his was against us, was very great. The problem was also complicated by our wanting our line as near that of the enemy as possible. We had but four engineer officers with us. Captain [Frederick E.] Prime, of the Engineer Corps, was the chief, and the work at the beginning was mainly directed by him. . . . To provide assistants on such a long line I directed that all officers who had graduated at West Point, where they had necessarily to study military engineering, should in addition to their other duties assist in the work." Grant's chief commissary officer, a short, heavy man, was a West Point graduate, but he begged off on the grounds that when it came to engineering he would be useless, unless Grant wanted to use him as a sap-roller. "As soldiers require rations while working in the ditches as well as when marching and fighting, and as we would be sure to lose him if he was used as a sap-roller," Grant said, "I let him off."

"The first thing to do," Grant wrote, "was to get the artillery in batteries where they would occupy commanding positions; then establish the camps, under cover from the fire of the enemy but near up as possible; and then construct rifle-pits and covered ways, to connect the entire command by the shortest route. The enemy did not harass us much while we were constructing our batteries. Probably their artillery ammunition was short; and their infantry was kept down by our sharpshooters, who were always on the alert and ready to fire at a head whenever it showed itself above the rebel works.

"In no place were our lines more than six hundred yards from the enemy. It was necessary, therefore, to cover our men by something more than the ordinary parapet. To give additional protection sand bags, bullet-proof, were placed along the tops of the parapets far enough apart to make loop-holes for musketry. On top of these, logs were put. By these means the men were enabled to walk about erect when off duty, without fear of annoyance from sharpshooters. . . . The enemy could not resort to our method to protect their men, because we had an inexhaustible supply of ammunition to draw upon and used it freely. Splinters from the timber would have made havoc among the men behind.

"There were no mortars with the besiegers, except what the navy had in front of the city; but wooden ones were made by taking logs of the toughest wood that could be found, boring them out for six or twelve-pound shells and binding them with strong iron bands. These answered as coehorns, and shells were successfully thrown from them into the trenches of the enemy.

"The labor of building the batteries and intrenching was largely done by the pioneers, assisted by negroes who came within our lines and who were paid for their work; but details from the troops had often to be made. The work was pushed forward as rapidly as possible, and when an advanced position was secured and covered from the fire of the enemy the batteries were advanced. . . . There were eight roads leading into Vicksburg, along which and their immediate sides, our work was specially pushed and batteries advanced; but no commanding point within range of the enemy was neglected."[11]

The next day, 25 May, the 7th Illinois Cavalry, one of Colonel Grierson's two regiments, now with Banks outside Port Hudson, captured two steamers on Thompson's Creek, a tributary of the

Mississippi. But the Universe seemed to want to keep such things in cosmic balance, for that same day in the far-off South Atlantic the Confederate commerce raider CSS *Alabama* took two prizes off Bahia, Brazil.

In Middle Tennessee that day a prominent Copperhead, Clement L. Vallandigham, was, under flag of truce, delivered into Confederate hands. A Democrat, he had been trying to gain his party's nomination for governor of Ohio by making inflammatory speeches denouncing the war when he had been arrested by Union soldiers for violating a standing order by Major General Ambrose Burnside against publicly expressing support for the enemy. Democrats had been outraged, but a military court had sentenced him to imprisonment for the remainder of the war. President Lincoln had feared that Vallandigham as a silent martyr in prison would be far more troublesome than as a maker of inflammatory, but rather silly, speeches. However, releasing him would signal weakness and carte blanche to all draft-resisters, deserters, and those who would encourage such. Lincoln neatly turned the problem over to Jefferson Davis by commuting Vallandigham's sentence to banishment to the Confederacy. It connected the Copperhead with his Confederate friends in the public mind, and, as he clambered to be returned to the country he had decried as tyrannous, he was soon being seen not as a martyr but as a figure of ridicule, at least by some.

In Mississippi that day, Grant's headquarters issued Special Orders No. 140, directing corps commanders to begin "the work of reducing the enemy by regular approaches. It is desirable that no more loss of life shall be sustained in the reduction of Vicksburg and the capture of the garrison. Every advantage will be taken of the natural inequalities of the ground to gain positions from which to start mines, trenches, or advance batteries."[12]

Rawlins, Grant's chief-of-staff, wrote to General Hurlbut, at Memphis, that day telling him to send a heavy cavalry force into northern Mississippi as far as Grenada and to send as much infantry to the Vicksburg front as he could possibly spare, with Brigadier General Nathan Kimball in command. "Contract everything on the line from Memphis to Corinth, and keep your cavalry well out south of there. By this means you ought to be able to send here quite a large force."[13] Unknown to Rawlins, Hurlbut was writing to Grant that same day to report that Joe Johnston had evidently called for all the Rebel troops from north Mississippi and that he, Hurlbut, had sent 1,700 cavalry and mounted infantry under Colonel Edward Hatch after them. (Hatch, commander of the 2nd Iowa Cavalry, had participated in the opening stages of Grierson's recent raid, his regiment being sent back to Tennessee to fool the Confederates into thinking that the entire brigade was turning back.) Hatch had encountered Rebels under Brigadier General James R. Chalmers in Senatobia swamp and had charged them, killing a few and driving the rest across the Tallahatchee River. "My cavalry will be at work all the time as far as I can reach," Hurlbut said.[14] He also said he was sending a transport loaded with ammunition to Grant.

Grant himself wrote that day to Major General Benjamin Prentiss, his commander at Helena, Arkansas, saying he needed more cavalry to watch Johnston's growing Confederate army. Prentiss was, therefore, to send some cavalry, that he had recently been ordered to send to Hurlbut, to Vicksburg instead. He added, "if you are certain that you can maintain your position with fewer forces than you now have, send me all the infantry and cavalry you can spare."[15]

Grant also wrote to General Banks that day, the letter to be delivered by Colonel John Riggin, Jr., of his staff, who, Grant said, could give Banks more information about the situation at Vicksburg than Grant could write in a letter. The main purpose of his communication was to discuss how the two could cooperate. "When I commenced writing this," Grant said, "it was my intention to propose sending you, if you will furnish the transportation, 8,000 or 10,000 men to co-operate with you on Port Hudson, but, whilst writing, a courier came in from my cavalry, stating that a force of the enemy are now about 30 miles northeast of here. They may be collecting there for the purpose of making an attack. At present, therefore, I do not deem it prudent to send off any men I have, or even safe, without abandoning some of the advantages already gained. I would be pleased, general, to have you come, with such force as you are able to spare. You can be supplied with everything from Young's Point. The road is now good across the point opposite Vicksburg, and, with your transports, the ferriage can be made. I am in hopes this letter will find you in possession of Port Hudson, and, therefore, of a much larger force to bring to this place than you could otherwise detach."[16] He closed with an appeal for the return of Colonel Grierson and his cavalry. It was neither his first such appeal nor fated to be his last.

Grant also wrote to Army headquarters in Washington that eight men had been arrested while attempting to get through his lines into Vicksburg with 200,000 percussion caps for the Confederate troops. They were also carrying a coded message to Pemberton from Joe Johnston, but "Having no one with me who has the ingenuity to translate it, I send it to Washington, hoping that some one there may be able to make it out," he said.[17] It was a note Johnston had written that day, the 25th, saying: "My last note was returned by bearer. Two hundred thousand caps have been sent. It will be continued as they arrive. Bragg is sending a division. When it comes, I will move to you. Which do you think the best route? How and where is the enemy encamped? What is your force?"[18]

Pemberton's report of that day's activities says: "The enemy appeared in force to-day on the Warrenton and Hall's Ferry roads. The firing was about as usual until 6 o'clock, when a cessation of hostilities was agreed upon, to permit the enemy to bury his dead, killed in the assault of Friday."[19] Confederate Colonel Ephraim Anderson, from Missouri, described this truce: "Flags were displayed along both lines, and the troops thronged the breastworks, gaily chatting with each other, discussing the issues of the war, disputing over differences of opinion, losses in the fight, etc. Numbers of the Confederates accepted invitations to visit the enemy's lines, where they were hospitably entertained and warmly welcomed. They were abundantly supplied with provisions, supplies of various kind, and liquors.... The foe were exultant, confident of success, and in high spirits; the Confederates defiant, undaunted in soul, and equally well assured of a successful defense."[20] Many of the men found old friends and even relatives in the opposing army.

After a talk with Brigadier General S. D. Lee, one of Pemberton's brigade commanders (distant kin to the Virginia Lees), Emma Balfour noted in her diary that "Conversations occur nightly between friends on the opposite sides. Two missionary brothers held a conversation, very friendly – one sent the other coffee and whiskey. Then they parted with an oath and an exclamation from one that he would 'blow the other's head off to-morrow.' How unnatural all this is. The commanders object to this intercourse, but it is impossible they say in two armies so near to prevent it altogether...."[21]

Major Samuel Lockett, Pemberton's chief engineer, was spotted by General Sherman during this truce, and recognizing him as an officer, invited him over for a chat. Sherman gave him some letters that had been intrusted to him by Northern friends for delivery to acquaintances or relatives in the Confederate army, saying he wanted to pass them on before they got too old. The major said they certainly would be old indeed if they had to wait for Sherman to bring them into Vicksburg himself. Sherman admitted that regular approaches, parallels and zigzags were a slow way of getting into a place, but a very sure one, "and I was determined to deliver those letters sooner or later," he said. The two officers sat on a log and discussed the situation, and Lockett later said, "Intentionally or not, his civility certainly prevented my from seeing many other points in our front that I as chief engineer was very anxious to examine."[22]

Brigadier General States Rights Gist, who commanded one of the brigades of reinforcements that had been sent to Mississippi from other Confederate forces, found himself in temporary command of six such brigades near Canton, Mississippi, while Joe Johnston went down to Jackson, the state capital, to look after Major General W. W. Loring's division, which had reached that city after being separated from the rest of Pemberton's army during the recent battle at Champion's Hill. Gist wrote that day to his previous commander, General P. G. T. Beauregard, whose headquarters were at Charleston, South Carolina. After giving a brief account of how things had been going in Mississippi, he said, "Pemberton, of course, is censured by everyone, particularly for making the first fight at Baker's Creek [Champion's Hill], without awaiting General Johnston, who was marching to join him. . . . It is said that the troops were badly handled by Pemberton, and other hard things are said about him. This we must expect if an officer is unsuccessful. I can form no opinion, as I have no reliable information about the matter. Vicksburg is completely invested by Grant's army, but we learn from scouts that Pemberton has signally repulsed, with great slaughter to the enemy, three several attempts to storm his defenses. He has provisions enough, and, if troops are sent us in time, we can yet save Vicksburg. We will move as soon as we are strong enough to be effective. Officers, men, and citizens have unbounded confidence in Johnston."[23]

Down at Port Hudson it was the Confederates who were doing the digging. They had always assumed that any Union attack there would come from the direction of Baton Rouge, so they had never bothered to build defenses on the north and northeast sides of the town. But most of Banks' forces had approached from the north by way of Bayou Sara and had invested Port Hudson on a full arc, from the river above the town to the river below. Only the very rough terrain in the northeast – woods, thickets, hills, and two swampy streams – and about 1000 Rebels under Colonel I. G. W. Steedman, had prevented Banks right wing, under Brigadier General Godfrey Weitzel, from detecting the town's vulnerability in that sector. On the night of the 25th Gardner sent all available tools and slaves to his chief engineer, Lieutenant Frederick Y. Dabney; by daylight Dabney had the defenses laid out; and all through the day of the 26th Steedman's men, now reinforced to about 2,100 infantry, one company of cavalry, and the equivalent of two batteries of field artillery, worked to improve the sketchy lines.

That same day, Tuesday, the 26th of May, as gold was being discovered at Alder Gulch, later renamed Virginia City, in what is now the state of Montana, Confederate President Jefferson Davis was meeting with his cabinet to discuss the situation in Mississippi and Lee's proposed raid north of the Potomac. He also wrote a long letter to General Lee about possible promotions and assignments of officers in Lee's army and the shuffling of brigades between North Carolina, Richmond, and Lee. In a brief passage showing that he did not fully understand the danger that Vicksburg was in, Davis said: "Our intelligence from Mississippi is, on the whole, encouraging. Pemberton is stoutly defending the intrenchments at Vicksburg, and Johnston has an army outside, which I suppose will be able to raise the siege, and, combined with Pemberton's forces, may win a victory."[24]

Lincoln, on the other hand, seems to have had a better grasp of the situation in Mississippi. In a letter written to an old friend that day, trying to explain why he could not at that time give important commands to generals Benjamin Butler, John Charles Fremont and Franz Sigel, he said: "Whether Gen. Grant shall or shall not consummate the capture of Vicksburg, his campaign from the beginning of this month up to the twenty second day of it, is one of the most brilliant in the world. His corps commanders, & Division commanders, in part, are McClernand, McPherson, Sherman, Steele, Hovey, Blair, & Logan. And yet taking Gen. Grant & these seven of his generals, and you can scarcely name one of them that has not been constantly denounced and opposed by the same men who are now so anxious to get Halleck out, and Fremont & Butler & Sigel in."[25]

In Mississippi on the 26th, approach trenches were being dug, or soon would be, from eight different places, and two more would be added later. "On the Jackson road," Grant's chief engineers later reported, "where it enters the enemy's line of defense, is a commanding hill, quite strongly salient, which had on it a redan for several guns. The ridge along which the Jackson road runs offered fair ground, and along it McPherson pushed his main approach – the one earliest begun and on which his corps did most work."[26] Captain Andrew Hickenlooper, chief engineer of the 17th Corps, kept a diary concerning his work on the siege. He had placed another captain in charge of constructing approaches in front of General Ransom's division and a third captain in charge of constructing defenses for batteries in front of General Quinby's division, and took personal charge of the central approach along the Jackson road. Not much had been accomplished on the 25th because of the truce to bury the dead. His entry for 26 May says: "Commenced on main sap with 300 men. Same number went on and relieved day detail at 7 p.m."[27]

After the war, Hickenlooper described in more detail his work on this approach. He said it began "on the Jackson road at a point about 150 feet south-east of a large frame plantation house, known as the White House, which for some unexplained reason had been left standing by the enemy. Up to this point troops could be marched in comparative safety under cover of the intervening hills, supplemented by the construction of parapets at exposed points. The line of the first section was selected during the night of the 23d under cover of an attack made upon the enemy's pickets. Upon this line the workmen were placed at intervals of about five feet, each equipped with a gabion, pick, and shovel, with instructions to cover themselves securely and dig a connection through to the adjoining burrow before daylight. The day relief was engaged in deepening and widening the sap thus commenced. . . ."[28]

Vicksburg resident Emma Balfour noted a 45-minute bombardment by Union guns that day and counted 65 shells fired during that time.

Grant was still concerned about the possibility of Joe Johnston attacking him from the rear. Brigadier General P. J. Osterhaus's division of the 13th Corps was guarding the crossings of the Big Black River behind McClernand's front – on the direct route from Jackson – with instructions from Grant that "All forage beyond Black River that can be reached should be destroyed. All negroes, teams, and cattle should be brought in, and everything done to prevent an army coming this way supplying itself."[29] But Johnston's position north of Jackson indicated a threat that he might cross the Big Black farther north and come down between that river and the Yazoo to attack Grant's supply base at Haynes' Bluff or interpose between the base and Grant's main lines. To guard against this, Grant ordered an expedition to be put together this day, consisting of six brigades drawn from the 15th and 17th Corps, under the command of Major General Frank Blair, one of Sherman's division commanders.

Blair was the son of Francis P. Blair, Sr., an influential publisher and politician, who had been an unofficial advisor of presidents since Andrew Jackson's day. Another son was Montgomery Blair, Postmaster General in Lincoln's cabinet. Frank Blair – Francis, Jr. – was himself a prominent political figure in Missouri and had done much in the early days of the war to prevent that state from joining the Confederacy. Both Grant and Sherman seem to have liked him, both as a friend and as a general. Grant later wrote, "I had known Blair in Missouri, where I had voted against him in 1858 when he ran for Congress. I knew him as a frank, positive and generous man, true to his friends even to a fault, but always a leader." Grant had worried about having another political general on his hands, looking for glory and self-advancement, like McClernand, but said he was agreeably disappointed. "There was no man braver than he, nor was there any who obeyed all orders of his superior in rank with more unquestioning alacrity."[30] Blair's new assignment was to move northeast between the Yazoo and the Big Black and see what, if anything, the Confederates were up to in that area and to drive them out of it if possible.

Farther down the river, at Port Hudson, at midnight of 25-26 May, Lieutenant Colonel Richard B. Irwin of Banks' staff wrote to Rear Admiral David Farragut, commander of Union naval forces in the lower Mississippi, giving the position of Banks' forces:

"[Thomas W.] Sherman on the left, in advance of the enemy's first line of rifle-pits, having his pickets at the front edge of a skirt of woods, separated from the enemy's main line of works by an open plain. His position is in front of the school-house. [Major General Christopher C.] Augur, next on the road from the Plains to Port Hudson, and well advanced. [Brigadier General Cuvier] Grover, on the Jackson road, holding the front edge of a wood which is within from 250 to 400 yards of the apparent center of the works, and in plain sight and easy range of them. [Brigadier General Godfrey] Weitzel, with his own brigade, [Brigadier General William] Dwight's, and [Brigadier General Halbert E.] Paine's (Emory's) division, reduced to about a brigade, on the right, near where the Telegraph road from Port Hudson to Bayou Sara crosses the Big Sandy Creek. This morning everybody except Grover has closed up, and Grover cannot close up without taking the works in front of him. Thus the place is completely invested."[31]

Banks himself wrote to Farragut about an hour later, saying, among other things: " To-day our artillery will be placed in position. We shall bring about ninety guns to bear upon the enemy. We shall replenish exhausted ammunition, bring up that which we need for the work before us, and prepare everything for the assault. At daylight to-morrow (27th), unless something unexpected occurs, I shall order the works carried by assault."[32]

As Banks said, his troops spent the day of the 26th making preparations: getting the men and guns into position, replenishing ammunition, building a pontoon bridge over swollen Big Sandy Creek; burning some plantation outbuildings that blocked a battery's line of fire; reconnoitering the Confederate position as best they could; and constructing bundles of sticks, known as fascines, for filling the ditch in front of the Rebel defenses. That night Banks called his principle officers together at a plantation house. Evidently three of his four division/wing commanders Augur, Weitzel, and Sherman, were not sanguine about making an assault, but Banks had made up his mind to try it. Joe Johnston was out there somewhere, gathering who-knew-how-many reinforcements from all over the Confederacy. He might attack Grant and drive him into the river and then come down and attack Banks', or he might bypass Grant and attack Banks' smaller army first. The two Union armies needed to be united for safety, but that could only happen when one of the Rebel bastions fell.

"Port Hudson must be taken to-morrow," said Colonel Irwin's written order for the attack. Unfortunately for Banks, while the order specified that Augur and Sherman were to open fire with their artillery at daybreak, and the heavy guns were to open up about 6 a.m., nowhere did it say when the infantry should advance. Weitzel was only to "take advantage of the attacks on other parts of the line to endeavor to force his way into the enemy's works on our right," and Grover was to "hold himself in readiness to re-enforce within the right or left, if necessary, or to force his own way into the enemy's works. . . ."[33]

Had Banks ordered an all-out assault for dawn on the 26th a breakthrough on his right, the Confederate left, where the Rebels were only starting to entrench, would have been fairly likely, but by waiting until the 27th he had given Gardner time to fortify and reinforce that critical sector. By that morning, rifle pits and breastworks of logs for the infantry and lunettes for the artillery protected all the most vulnerable points, and the Rebels started to work again at 5 a.m. to further improve these and the older defenses. Moreover, Weitzel, commanding on the Union right, was only supposed to attack after Augur and Sherman had attracted the Confederates' attention by assaulting the lines in their fronts.

In the Confederate lines, to Steedman's right, Brigadier General William N. R. Beall commanded the central part of Gardner's line, facing Grover and Augur with about 2,300 men and two batteries. On Beall's right, facing Tom Sherman, was Colonel William R. Miles with about 1,150 men and eight field guns. Most of the heavy artillery still faced the river, manned by about 300 cannoneers, but three rifled 24-pounders were stationed in Steedman's lines, including one sited to cover a road approaching along a ravine; two 24-pounder smoothbores were in position where the railroad running northeast to Clinton,

Louisiana, entered the defenses; a 4.62-inch bronze rifle nicknamed "The Baby" had been placed in a redan guarding the road to Jackson; and a 30-pounder Parrott rifle was at the extreme right end of the land defenses.

Just after dawn on the 27th, at about 5:30 a.m., the bombardment by Sherman's and Augur's artillery began. It was soon suicide for any Rebel to expose himself anywhere along the Confederate right or center. At about 7 a.m., Farragut's ships added the fire of their big guns, but, having only vague ideas of the Confederate positions, their fire was not very effective, and they ceased fire an hour later for fear of hitting the Federal infantry when it attacked. However, neither Sherman's nor Augur's men advanced.

Weitzel, however, perhaps figuring that their artillery fire was enough to keep the Rebels' attention, or perhaps because he had farther to go (his troops were not yet even within sight of Steedman's new defenses), began to advance at about 6 a.m. He had about 6,000 men, with two brigades under Dwight in front and two more under Paine following. Their first problem was to drive back about 500 Confederate skirmishers Steedman had sent out to buy more time for his men to improve their defenses. As the Federals advanced they tried to keep their right flank guided on Big Sandy Creek, which ran to the southwest, and dense woods and steep ravines up to thirty feet deep broke up the Union formations. Before long the leading brigade was dispersed and exhausted, so the second brigade passed through and took over the lead, and by the time it had gained the crest of a ridge north of Little Sandy Creek, a tributary of the Big Sandy, every regiment was pretty much on its own. In the course of this advance the Federals had killed, wounded or captured about 200 of the 500 Rebel skirmishers and had driven the rest into their defenses.

From this crest, the Union soldiers finally got a look at Steedman's new line, seen only as newly turned yellow dirt along the next ridge on the opposite side of the creek. In the valley between the two ridges, besides the creek itself, were more ravines, small hillocks, some dense stands of pine and magnolia trees, and the interlaced branches of felled trees forming a formidable barrier, known in military terminology as an *abatis*. Rebel sharpshooters sniped at them from the cover of trees and ravines. The first two Union regiments to advance were broken into small squads by the obstacles in the valley and took heavy casualties from a pair of 12-pounder howitzers in an advanced lunette and a battery stationed on an eminence known as Commissary Hill (because it was near there that the Confederates had placed their supply of rations and a mill for producing more, back when they had thought that no Yankee would ever approach Port Hudson from this direction). The impetus of the assault was broken, but the Federals took cover in the creek valley, using the same trees, ravines, etc., that had broken their formations as cover from the Rebels' fire. Some of them were within easy range of the Confederate rifle pits.

Meanwhile Union pioneers had followed the advancing infantry, and they quickly hacked out roads through the woods so that artillery could be brought forward. The Rebel cannoneers switched targets to hit the Union guns as they came up, taking advantage of range-markers they had placed in the trees on the opposite crest before the battle. Their fire quickly dismounted a couple of Union guns and killed several artillerists, five or six being taken out by a rammer that one Rebel gunner accidentally left in his gun when it fired. But the return fire of two Federal batteries soon silenced the two howitzers in the lunette, killing their commander and disabling one piece. Confederate infantrymen dragged the surviving howitzer away and stationed it where it could cover their flank and rear. Then the Union guns went on to knock out most of the cannon on Commissary Hill. Three companies of a Connecticut regiment drove the Rebel gunners to the safety of the infantry trenches and went on to occupy the ditch in front of the parapet. The Confederates tried to oust them but could not, but neither could these Federals advance farther.

Elsewhere a regiment of Alabamans broke up the charge of a New York regiment by firing a concerted volley with their smoothbore muskets loaded with "buck and ball" – paper cartridges containing one musket ball and three buckshot – at the deadly range of 40 yards. But the Alabamans took heavy casualties from a Union regiment, the 1st Louisiana – a unit of what the Rebels called "home-made Yankees" – firing from the opposite ridge.

Seeing Dwight's two brigades bogged down, Paine ordered his two brigades to charge. Some of these Federals met the same fate as Dwight's men, broken up by the terrain and bogged down outside the Rebel works. Others headed for a weakly held part of the Confederate line near what the Rebels called the "Bull Pen" because it was where their commissary slaughtered cattle for their rations. Taking casualties from Confederate artillery, these Federals made their way through the obstructions in what one of their officers called "the valley of the shadow of death," and a few of them reached the crest on the other side.[34]

However, Gardner had sent reinforcements from the unassailed sector in front of T. W. Sherman – three Arkansas regiments under Colonel O. P. Lyles – and these arrived in time to block this attack and drive the Federals back below the crest, where they went to ground and returned fire. Grover sent a few regiments in on Paine's right, and at about 10 a.m. one of them charged with a great shout, crashing through brush and over the abatis, to be stopped by a Rebel volley within 30 yards of the defenses. At about 10:30 a.m. another regiment from Grover's division, the 12th Maine, managed to plant its battleflag on the parapet of an earthwork on a hill that soon came to be known as Fort Desperate, as a desperate battle raged around it for hours, but the fort could not be taken.

Also at about 10 a.m. Dwight decided to make one more try and called upon two regiments that had been guarding the Union right flank. These were the 1st and 3rd Louisiana Native Guards. The 3rd regiment was composed mostly of former slaves with white officers; the 1st regiment, however, was unique in being composed mostly of free black or "colored" men from New Orleans. Even most of its officers were black. Many of these men were educated and some were wealthy. Neither regiment had ever seen combat, as Union generals had not quite been ready to trust them in critical situations – until now. Six companies of the 1st regiment and nine of the 3rd, accompanied by a couple of 6-pounder guns from a Massachusetts battery and a few dismounted troopers from the 1st Louisiana (U.S.) Cavalry, crossed the pontoon bridge and deployed among some willows in what had once been part of the riverbed before the Mississippi had made one of its frequent changes of course. Rebel artillery drove off the two Union guns after they had got off only one shot, but the infantry came on, the 1st Native Guards in front and the 3rd in support, both regiments in line of battle.

The sector of the defenses they were assaulting was held by about 300 Mississippians and several field pieces on a steep bluff overlooking Foster's Creek and flooded backwaters. A connected ridge, also a rugged bluff, projecting from the Rebel position, served as a formidable outwork. It was held by about 45 more Mississippians and 15 dismounted Louisiana cavalrymen. Fire from this ridge took the attackers in flank, causing disorder in the ranks, but the Federals pressed on toward the main Confederate line until within about 200 yards of it. At that point the Rebel guns to their front opened fire with a type of ammunition known as canister: cans full of iron balls, smaller than cannon shot but larger than musket balls, that turned the guns into giant shotguns. The Mississippians in the main line added their rifle fire as well. This sudden storm of fire stopped the advance. The 1st Regiment got off one volley in return, then fell back in great confusion, which soon spread to the 3rd Regiment, and both units fell back to the cover of some woods.

There their officers tried to rally them, while a few small bands resumed the advance. One group tried to wade through some of the backwater, but could not, another scaled the projecting ridge in an attempt to halt the flanking fire coming from there, but the entire group was either killed or captured. The Confederate guns bombarded the main formations with exploding shells and solid shot, which sent dangerous limbs and splinters flying from the surrounding trees. Colonel John A. Nelson, commander of the two regiments, sent an aide to ask Dwight for permission to withdraw, but Dwight said to tell Nelson, ". . . he has done nothing unless he carries the enemy's works." The aide pleaded that the two regiments had already lost half their men, but Dwight told him to "Charge again, and let the impetuosity of the charge counterbalance the paucity of the numbers."[35] Nelson had sense enough to disobey this order, but he didn't dare order a withdrawal, so the Native Guards stayed put, took more casualties, and returned fire as best they could. Shortly after noon Grover and Weitzel, having heard nothing of any fight on the Union left, gave up on trying to take the works in their fronts and asked for further orders.

The vagaries of the previous night's council and the written orders for the attack had prevented a truly coordinated assault by the Union divisions. Augur's men had been in position, ready to attack, all morning, while their commander waited for a signal from Banks. Banks either thought that no signal was necessary, orders having been given the night before, or was waiting for Sherman to attack on the Union left. At about noon, Banks rode over to Sherman's headquarters to learn why he had heard only cannon fire from that direction all morning, but no musketry. He was not happy with what he found. At 1:45 p.m. he wrote to Weitzel: "General Sherman has failed utterly and criminally to bring his men into the field. At 12 m. I found him at dinner, his staff officers all with their horses unsaddled, and none knowing where to find their command. I have placed General Andrews in command, and hope every moment to learn that he is ready to advance with Augur, who waits for him. Together they have 5,000 men."[36] Brigadier General George L. Andrews was Banks' chief of staff, who had to ride over from army headquarters, but when he arrived he found Sherman leading his men forward at last, so he did not assume command.

It was about 2 p.m. when the Confederates manning the center third of their line saw large Union formations forming along the Plains Store road. This being the sector from which Colonel Lyles' three Arkansas regiments had been withdrawn earlier to reinforce the left, there were only about 120 Rebel pickets manning the lines in this sector; about one man for every 20 yards of trench. General Beall sent to Colonel Miles, commanding the Confederate right, for help, but Miles had already observed the need, and extended his own units to the left. Miles had his men formed in pairs, one to fire and one to load, with each pair having extra muskets obtained from the arsenal and from the sick men in the hospital. To speed the reloading process, most of the men spread cartridges on the parapet within easy reach. An Arkansas lieutenant noted his men's expressions at they prepared to receive the attack. "Some were serious and silent," he said. "Others joked, danced, or sang short snatches of song, but there was an intense earnestness about it all." Miles told his men, "Shoot low, boys; it takes two men to take away a man who is wounded, and they never come back."[37]

The Federals soon emerged from some woods. There were two brigades of them, of four regiments each. Brigadier General Neal Dow's brigade advanced through the fields and passed the ruins of a house belonging to a family appropriately named Slaughter. His troops were preceded by former slaves carrying poles with which to bridge the ditch in front of the Rebel works; after them came 130 volunteers carrying heavy planks to lay across the poles. Then came the lead regiment, the 6th Michigan, the only Westerners in this division, followed by the other three regiments, one after the other. Within minutes a cannonball struck Tom Sherman's horse, causing it to lurch backwards and fall on his rider. Somewhat shaken, the general managed to proceed on foot until a shot shattered his leg below the knee. While he was carried from the field his troops continued to advance, although their formations were disrupted by the Slaughter house and four successive fences. They passed around the house and threw down all four fences, but as they struggled to get through an abatis of felled trees, whose entangled limbs shredded their uniforms, the Confederate artillery opened on them with a deadly fire.

Most of the Federals got through the abatis, reformed and

came on. One Union skirmisher glanced to his right and admired the long line in blue advancing with flying flags, but then he turned and saw above the Rebel defenses ". . . a dark cloud of slouched hats and bronzed faces; the next moment a sheet of flames. I glanced again to the right; the line of blue had melted away."[38] The Federals were now within about 200 yards of the Confederate lines, and at this point the Rebel gunners shifted from firing shells to firing canister. The Union line wavered, broke, and ran for the rear, but the officers soon got the men under control, and they advanced again. General Dow was hit in the arm by a spent bullet, which made it impossible for him to control his horse. Like Tom Sherman, he proceeded on foot and like him he was hit in the leg; in this case by a bullet that passed through his left thigh. He was also carried off the field. One of his regimental commanders was killed and two others were wounded.

Finally this attack petered out about seventy yards from the Rebel breastworks, and the Federals went to ground, seeking what cover they could find. Deadly fire of Union sharpshooters forced the Confederates to hunker down in their trenches, unable to reply. The Michigan regiment continued to take casualties, however, for the Easterners behind them were firing too low. (The old black-powder weapons, even when rifled, fired with such low velocity that medium and long-ranged shots had to be elevated considerably; this made correctly estimating the range critical for accuracy.)

Sherman's other brigade, under Brigadier General Franklin S. Nickerson, also advanced in a column of regiments, with one of its two Maine regiments out front as skirmishers, followed by the other, then two New York regiments. Rebel artillery shells tore gaps in their lines, and they had to scramble through bushes and a deep ravine choked with felled timber. By the time they finally emerged onto an open plain the 165th New York had passed to the front. This unit wore a kind of uniform modeled after the North African *zouave* units of the French Army (made famous by the recent Crimean War against Russia), including baggy bright red trousers, or breeches, which might have looked impressive but only made the men better targets. Three New Yorkers went down trying to advance their flag, and their lieutenant colonel was mortally wounded as he exhorted his men to pick up the fallen banner. At one point a Rebel commander ordered his men to cease fire out of respect for the gallantry of the New Yorkers, but as the Federals took this respite to renew their advance the firing was soon resumed. Lacking support from the other regiments, and losing 186 men out of 350, the zouaves eventually went to ground or crawled back to the safety of the woods behind them. Their flag was captured by a bold Rebel who sallied from the defenses long enough to snatch it from the ground. Learning that Sherman was disabled, General Andrews finally assumed command of the division, attempting to reorganize the shattered units while, like Weitzel and Grover, awaiting further orders that never came.

When Banks had finally heard the rattle of musketry from Sherman's division, he ordered Augur to attack as well. Augur had had his men ready to advance all day. They were formed in column near the edge of some woods about a quarter of a mile from the Confederate lines. While waiting for the word, he noticed some of his men jerking their heads as they heard bullets come whizzing past. Black-powder weapons had low velocity, but not that low. "No use boys to dodge them after you hear them," he said.[39] By the time you could react the bullet would be long gone. When the attack order finally came Augur's men moved along a road until clear of the woods and then deployed into lines of battle, with skirmishers out front, followed by 200 volunteers carrying bundles of fascines and bags of cotton with which to fill the ditch in front of the Rebel defenses, and by the five regiments of Colonel Edward P. Chapin's brigade, reinforced by half a regiment from the division's other brigade, and a battery of artillery following along to provide close-range support.

With a yell, they advanced through briars and vines and, like Sherman's men to their left, became entangled in the Confederate abatis under a deadly hail of musket and artillery fire from the front. They were also being raked by a pair of 24-pounders on their flank whose gunners were using rusty nails, broken chains, and scraps of railroad iron in lieu of canister ammunition. Colonel Chapin, conspicuous in a white Panama hat, took a slight wound in one knee, took a few more steps, and was shot in the face. Young Colonel William F. Bartlett, who had already lost a leg at Yorktown, Virginia, the year before, seized the flag of his 49th Massachusetts and rode with it at the head of the Union column until he was severely wounded and fell from his horse a mere sixty yards from the Rebel defenses. Despite his wound and fall he lifted the flag to wave his men on. Confederate officers, who thought this "the bravest and most daring thing we have yet seen done in the war" ordered their men not to shoot him.

But none of the Federals made it through the abatis alive. They lost all formation and took cover behind stumps and logs or whatever cover they could find. The supporting battery did its best but could not keep the defenders from maintaining their fire. On one part of the field, underbrush caught fire, adding yet another danger, especially for severely wounded men who could not move out of the way. Lieutenant Colonel James O'Brien suddenly jumped up, waving his sword, and yelled, "Charge! Boys, charge!"[40] But only about a dozen men followed him, and he was soon shot dead.

General Banks was about to order Augur's other brigade forward when he got word that Sherman's attack had stalled. It was clear that the assault had failed all along the line, and he did not send in the last brigade. The three brigades that did attack on the left lost over a thousand men, killed, wounded, and missing. When it was obvious that the attack was over, generous Confederates took water out to the wounded Federals, and they carried nine wounded zouaves to their hospital. But most of the attackers had to lie under a cruel Louisiana sun all afternoon. At about 5 p.m. one Union colonel raised a white handkerchief on a stick and asked for a truce to bury the dead. General Gardner refused the request as irregular and an unwarranted use of a white flag, it not having come from Banks himself. He ordered hostilities to resume in half an hour. However, many Federals had taken advantage of the brief truce to withdraw to safer positions.

Finally, that evening, stretcher bearers were able to remove the dead and wounded, and when his division commanders reported their losses that night Banks learned that the repulse was even worse than he had thought. He sent for reinforcements from other parts of his department, and arms for his negro pioneers, but the most important loss was in confidence. "It was long indeed," Colonel Irwin later wrote, "before the men felt the same faith in themselves, and it is but the plain truth to say that their reliance on the department commander never quite returned."[41]

∽ Endnotes ∽

1 *OR*, I:24:III:344.
2 Ibid., I:52:II:482.
3 Ibid., I:22:II:290-1.
4 Ibid., I:22:II;293.
5 Ibid., I:24:I:37-8.
6 Ibid., I:24:III:346.
7 Ibid., I:24:I:87-8.
8 Ibid., I:24:I:276.
9 Hoehling, *Vicksburg: 47 Days of Siege*, 49.
10 Ibid., 51-2.
11 Grant, *Personal Memoirs*, I:535-46
12 *OR*, I:24:III:348.
13 Ibid., I:34:III:350.
14 Ibid.
15 Ibid., I:34:III:349.
16 Ibid., I:24:III:346-7.
17 Ibid., I:24:I:39.
18 Ibid., I:24:I:278.
19 Ibid., I:24:I:276.
20 Hoehling, *Vicksburg: 47 Days of Siege*, 54-5.
21 Ibid., 56.
22 Ibid., 56-7.
23 *OR*, I:24:III:920.
24 Ibid., I:51:II:717.
25 Basler, ed., *Collected Works of Abraham Lincoln*, VI:230.
26 OR, I:24:II:171.
27 Ibid., I:24:II:199.
28 Andrew Hickenlooper, "The Vicksburg Mine" in *Battles and Leaders of the*

Civil War (Castle Books edition, New York, 1956), III:540.
29 *OR,* I:24:III:351.
30 Grant, *Personal Memoirs,* I:574.
31 *OR,* I:26:I:504.
32 Ibid., I:26:I:506.
33 Ibid., I:26:I:509.
34 Lawrence Lee Hewitt, *Port Hudson, Confederate Bastion on the Mississippi* (Baton Rouge and London, 1987), 146.
35 Ibid., 150.
36 *OR,* I:26:I:509-10.
37 Hewitt, *Port Hudson,* 158.
38 Ibid., 159.
39 Ibid., 162.
40 Ibid., 164.
41 Ibid., 166.

CHAPTER 3

"They Are About to Move Forward"
27 – 30 May 1863

AT VICKSBURG ON THE MORNING of the 27th, the Union navy moved to comply with William T. Sherman's request for help against the guns guarding the far left of the Confederate lines. The USS *Cincinnati*, one of the seven original ironclad gunboats on the Western rivers, approached from upstream. Dr. Richard R. Hall, an acting assistant surgeon, was aboard her and was writing a letter to his wife and mother at the time. "Today we are ordered to run down to Vicksburg and take a 200-pound English parrott (cannon with a rifled bore) that has been a great bar to our progress. It goes by the name of 'Whistling Dick,' a sobriquet given it by our boys from the peculiar noise its balls make as they hurtle through the air. We have also to destroy a masked battery that holds General Sherman in check and shells our rifle pits that bar his progress. This masked battery has destroyed a great number of his brave boys; they have made two charges and both times have been repulsed. He says that if the *Cincinnati* will take the battery and shell the pits that he and his men will go into Vicksburg. Well, we will do it for him and give him a chance . . ."[1] Although there were a few more lines, the letter was never finished, for the boat got under way before he was done.

"This combat was witnessed by hundreds of our ladies," a sergeant in the Confederate batteries noted, "who ascended on the summits of the most prominent hills in Vicksburg. There were loud cheers, the waving of handkerchiefs, amid general exultation . . .," he said.[2] And there was much for the ladies to cheer about. The *Cincinnati*, like her six sisters (one of whom, the *Cairo*, had been sunk up the Yazoo River the year before by a "torpedo," or mine) was protected by only 2.5 inches of iron on the front and part of the sides of the wooden casemate that covered the gun deck. On this occasion logs and hay bales had been added to give extra protection, but they were not enough.

Sherman was watching from a hill at the extreme right end of his line and later described what he saw in a letter to Admiral Porter (who was still with the part of his squadron that was below the city): "As the Cincinnati neared, she fired several of her bow guns, but as the current would have carried her below [the city], she rounded to, firing from her broadside guns, but soon presented her stern. The enemy's shot at first went wild, but soon got her range, and struck her several direct shots, and two right under her stern. She ran slowly up stream, keeping mid-channel, and, when about 1 ½ miles up, she steered directly to the shore in the bend. I saw that her larboard quarter-boat was shot away, and her flag-staff, but otherwise she appeared uninjured. She ran to the shore and soon sank; her bow appeared down and her stern up, her upper decks out of water. . . . I deplore the sad result as much as any man could. The importance of the object aimed to be accomplished, in my judgment, fully warranted the attempt."[3] Forty men on board were killed or wounded.

Emma Balfour was one of the ladies of Vicksburg who witnessed the brief contest. "In a very short time we perceived that the monster was disabled and a tug from above came to her relief," she told her diary. "Later, men were seen to leave her side. There she drifted over to the Mississippi shore, and then arose the glad shout: 'She is sinking!' Sinking indeed she was and there she lies under water except her chimneys and her horn!"[4] The Rebel artillery sergeant said, "A large number of articles from the sunken boat were picked up in the river, including hay, clothing, whisky, a medical chest, letters, photographs, etc. We often wonder if the surgeon of the *Cincinnati*, who so comfortably penned a letter to his affectionate wife as the boat neared our batteries, escaped unhurt."[5]

Perhaps by way of compensation for this Union loss, over in Georgia that same day the Confederate ironclad *Chattahoochee* blew up accidentally on the river for which she was named. Eighteen men were killed.

Meanwhile Grant's army continued to dig. General Pemberton noted that "The enemy still continued to work steadily in completing and strengthening his line of circumvalation. His fire of both musketry and artillery was continuous...."[6] Captain Hickenlooper, chief engineer of the Union 17th Corps, noted that, by the 27th, he had 380 feet of approach trench covered. "Same number [of men] engaged in deepening and widening trench. Made survey of our front. New battery on General Ransom's front completed, and line of rifle pits south of Jackson road being pushed rapidly."[7]

President Lincoln's mind was on Vicksburg that day. He wired General Rosecrans, commanding the Army of the Cumberland, near Murfreesborough, Tennessee, "Have you anything from Grant? Where is Forrest's headquarters?"[8] Secretary of War Stanton later explained to Rosecrans that the interest in Brigadier General Nathan B. Forrest, a renowned Confederate cavalry commander, was due to a rumor, said to have come from Forrest's headquarters, that some disaster had befallen Grant. At 10:15 p.m. Rosecrans replied that Forrest had just that same day moved his headquarters from Spring Hill, south of Nashville, to Riggs' Cross-roads, 18 miles southwest of Murfreesborough. "The latest from Grant we have is of the rebel dispatch last night, saying that Johnston had crossed the Big Black north of him with 20,000 men. They were not jubilant at 2 o'clock to-day, when our provost-marshal was on their front, talking to Dr. Avent, Bragg's chief surgeon."[9] At 11 that night Lincoln wired Hooker to ask if he had the Richmond newspapers of that morning and, if so, what news they contained. Hooker replied twenty minutes later that he had the Richmond papers of the day before, but they contained no news of interest.

In Virginia that day, the 27th, Colonel George H. Sharpe, who was, in effect, General Hooker's intelligence officer (his title was head of the bureau of information), presented that general a remarkably accurate assessment of Lee's dispositions. He noted that the Confederate lines on the other side of the Rappahannock were "much more contracted" than they had been during the winter, extending from Banks' Ford on Lee's left to near Moss Neck on his right, and named the divisions in their proper order. He also noted that Major General George Pickett's and Major General John B. Hood's divisions of Lieutenant General James Longstreet's Corps – both of which had been down in southern Virginia at the time of the recent battle of Chancellorsville – were now at Hanover Junction, north of Richmond, and near Louisa Court House and Gordonsville, farther west, respectively.

There were three brigades of cavalry near Culpeper Court House and Kelly's Ford on the upper Rappahannock, properly identified by their commanders' names, with 4,700 mounted effective troopers, who were being constantly reinforced as horses were recruited by the spring growth of grass in the pastures of the area. Another brigade of cavalry, 1,400 men and 12 guns under Brigadier General William "Grumble" Jones, was correctly located in the Shenandoah Valley, near the village of New Market, and Major John S. Mosby's 200 "partisans," who blended in with the local civilians, were known to be north of Warrenton. "The Confederate army is under marching orders," the report said, "and an order from General Lee was very lately read to the troops, announcing a campaign of long marches and hard fighting, in a part of the country where they would have no railroad transportation." It concluded with the caution that "All the deserters say that the idea is very prevalent in the ranks that they are about to move forward upon or above our right flank."[10]

Hooker immediately forwarded a copy of this report to General-in-Chief Halleck, but for some reason the latter did not receive it until 8 June. But that same day Hooker wrote to Secretary of War Stanton. His primary purpose was to request a copy of a report that Halleck had recently written for Stanton on the strength and location of the troops in and around Washington, but he added, "From information forwarded to the major-general commanding the army this a.m., it seems that the enemy will soon be in motion. It was derived from deserters, but I place a good deal of confidence in it."[11]

Lee wanted to put his army in motion, to and across the Potomac, but at the moment he was worried about a possible move by Hooker. Apparent reductions in the size of the Union camps across the Rappahannock River from Lee's army, plus the recent move of Hooker's cavalry corps far upstream, made the Rebel commander suspect that Hooker was up to something. Lee wrote that day to Major General Arnold Elzey, commanding the forces around Richmond: "From the reports of scouts, it is very probable that a large force of Federal cavalry is about to set out on an expedition to the interior of the State. A large body of cavalry has moved up from Aquia Creek toward Warrenton. Among the Federal soldiers two cavalry raids are spoken of, having in view the capture of Richmond. There are indications of a movement on the part of Hooker's army in front also. The number of tents is much diminished, the wagon trains coming from the depot are much smaller, and the camp-fires on the hills in the rear much lessened. Citizens and others across the Rappahannock speak of a change of base to the James River. . . . If you can take care of Richmond with the force which you now have, I will order Pickett's division up to join Hood, on the Rapidan, so as to have a force in the rear of the enemy should he cross that stream."[12]

Hooker, meanwhile, sent a wire that day to Major General Erasmus D. Keyes, commanding Union forces down on the peninsula east of Richmond. Two regiments of cavalry from Hooker's army had, during Stoneman's recent raid, taken refuge there after hitting the railroads north of Richmond. Hooker wanted to know if there was any Confederate force in position to keep the two regiments, commanded by Colonel Hugh Judson Kilpatrick, from moving up to Urbana on the lower Rappahannock, and whether Kilpatrick's horses were in shape to make the trip. From there the troopers could be ferried across the river under the cover of gunboats sent up from Chesapeake Bay. Back came a message from Keyes' boss, Major General John A. Dix, commander of the Department of Virginia, forwarding a report from Keyes that Kilpatrick's horses were in fair condition and that he knew of no force that could prevent his troopers from crossing at Urbana, but Dix added that there was a Rebel force on the Mattapony River, and that "About 200 of Colonel Kilpatrick's men are not mounted. I wish you would leave them with me at present. I need them very much at West Point [a plantation on the York River, east of Richmond], where I have only 200 cavalry."[13]

The next day, the 28th, Lincoln sent another brief wire to Rosecrans: "I would not push you to any rashness, but I am very anxious that you do your utmost, short of rashness, to keep Bragg from getting off to help Johnston against Grant."[14] Rosecrans' army had been stationary since the battle at Murfreesborough, back in January, while that general gathered strength for another push. He had been making constant demands on Halleck for more cavalry and more horses for the cavalry that he had, but was never satisfied with what he received. It is little wonder that Lincoln was worried that his inactivity would allow Bragg to slip away from him and go attack Grant. It wouldn't be the first time the Rebels had pulled off something of that sort; in fact, the very first battle of the war, the first battle of Bull Run, had resulted in a Federal defeat precisely because Joe Johnston had slipped away from a Union army in the Shenandoah Valley to join Beauregard at Manassas and turn the tide of battle. And similar moves had been made since. Rosecrans sent an even shorter reply: "Dispatch received. I will attend to it."[15] In fact, Rosecrans had been showing signs of stirring into life, alerting his largest corps the day before to be ready to march at a moment's notice, and negotiating with General Burnside, up in Kentucky, about the latter protecting his left flank when he advanced.

The reason why the Union camps across the river from Lee

seemed to be noticeably smaller was not that Hooker was moving his army but that much of it was going home. Quite a few of the regiments with expiring enlistments had already left, and more would soon be eligible to leave. Hooker wrote to Army headquarters in Washington that day listing all his regiments that had or would be discharged subsequent to 20 May, giving their current strengths. "It will be seen that between 20 May and the last of June we shall lose by expiration of service alone nearly 16,000 men," he said.[16] Not many new units were being formed; there was no mechanism for recruiting individuals to fill up old regiments, unless those units sent officers back to their home states to see if they could dig some up; and the draft had not yet started.

However, at 9 a.m. on the 28th one newly raised Union regiment got off the train at Boston, formed up, and, preceded by a band, marched through the city to the State House. This was the 54th Massachusetts, the first regiment of black soldiers raised in the Northeast. Some of its members had escaped from slavery in the South, but many had been born free in the North. Since the prejudices of the day did not allow black men to be commissioned, all of its officers were white. Governor Andrew had asked that at least some of the lieutenants be commissioned from among the educated free blacks, but the War Department had refused permission.

"All along the route," one of the white officers remembered, "the sidewalks, windows, and balconies were thronged with spectators, and the appearance of the regiment caused repeated cheers and waving of flags and handkerchiefs."[17] At the State House the regiment was greeted by the governor, a senator, the mayor of the city, two generals and many other prominent men. After a short rest, the regiment passed in review, marched down to Battery Wharf, and embarked on the steamer *De Molay*, bound for South Carolina. "To this Massachusetts Fifty-fourth," noted Horace Greeley's New York *Tribune*, "was set the stupendous task to convince the white race that colored troops would fight, – and not only that they would fight, but that they could be made, in every sense of the word, soldiers."[18]

Hooker also forwarded to Washington that day a report by his new Cavalry Corps commander, Alfred Pleasonton, complaining about the state he found his new command in after his predecessor's recent not-very-fruitful raid. He said that so many horses had been rendered unserviceable that, while the effective strength of the corps by the March returns was upward of 12,000 men and horses, "It is now one-third of that strength, and, so far as I can ascertain, is not fitted to take the field."[19] However, the figures in the same report show that his three divisions plus a reserve brigade actually added up to 6,677 serviceable horses. Then, for some reason, he *subtracted* 2,000 to represent Kilpatrick's two regiments, not yet rejoined, and other detachments; but since the original figure of 6,677 was a count of those men with horses actually with their commands at the time, a figure for Kilpatrick's detachment should have been *added*, not subtracted – though 2,000 was too high a figure for two veteran regiments, which Hooker's own chief of staff put at about 800. This would have made his total, counting Kilpatrick, close to 7,500 men with serviceable mounts, or almost *two* thirds of those shown on the March returns, not one third – even without Kilpatrick, still well over half. Nevertheless, a lot of horses would be needed.

Hooker's chief of staff, Brigadier General Dan Butterfield, fired off a message to Kilpatrick that day with orders to move with his command to Urbana, where gunboats and a small force of infantry would be waiting for him on the morning of 1 June to cover his crossing of that stream. "Your march will be through one of the richest portions of Virginia, and it is expected you will bring in a large number of horses and contrabands [slaves], and make your march tell."[20]

Meanwhile, Hooker responded to Pleasonton that same day by directing him to destroy the bridge at Rappahannock Station and leave as few of his men on picket duty as was absolutely necessary, so that the rest of his command could stay in camp and recruit their strength as much as possible. General Meade, commander of the 5th Corps, was directed to send one of his infantry divisions to guard the fords upstream from the main army, so the cavalry could be relieved of that duty. But Pleasonton reported that same day that Stuart had a large force of Confederate cavalry camped near Culpeper Court House, between the Rappahannock and its tributary farther south, the Rapidan. Pleasonton wanted to move the Reserve Brigade, commanded by the able Brigadier General John Buford, farther west to reinforce his 3rd Division, commanded by Brigadier General David Gregg, another good officer. He also thought the cavalry of the Department of Washington should be moved farther southwest along the Orange & Alexandria Railroad. "The rebels always mean something when their scouts become numerous," he warned.[21]

Hooker's assistant adjutant-general, Brigadier General Seth Williams, replied that Hooker agreed and wanted Buford, by virtue of his seniority, to take command of both units. "It is reported that the enemy's skirmishers have shown themselves on the north side of the Rappahannock, in the vicinity of Warrenton. If General Buford should find this to be the case, you will please direct that officer to force them to recross the river, and to keep them there; or, if he should find himself with sufficient force, to drive the enemy out of his camp near Culpeper and across the Rapidan, destroying the bridge at that point. The advance of the enemy's cavalry in the vicinity of Warrenton may have had for its object a concealment of a movement in force up the [Shenandoah] Valley. The commanding general desires that no labor be spared to ascertain the true object of the movement. At all events, they have no business on this side of the river."[22]

Hooker also wrote to Secretary Stanton, telling him briefly what orders he had given his cavalry and suggesting that Major General Julius Stahel, commanding the cavalry division of the Department of Washington, should scout into the Shenandoah Valley to see what was going on over there. "In the event a forward movement should be contemplated by the enemy, and he should have been re-enforced by the army from Charleston, I am in doubt as to the direction he will take, but probably the one of last year, however desperate it may appear. . . . If Stoneman had not almost destroyed one-half of my serviceable cavalry force, I would pitch into him in his camps, and would now, if General Stahel's cavalry were with me for a few days."[23]

Until the recent Chancellorsville campaign, Lieutenant General James Longstreet, commander of the 1st Corps of Lee's army, had been in temporary command of Confederate forces in Southside Virginia and North Carolina, to which he had taken two of his divisions – those of Hood and Pickett. The clash of Lee's and Hooker's armies had caused Longstreet and his two divisions to be recalled by Lee, leaving something of a command vacuum south of the James River. Lee had supervisory authority over that area, so, in accordance with his recently expressed wishes, the Confederate Adjutant and Inspector General's office issued orders on the 28th extending the Department of North Carolina to include Virginia south of the James River, with Major General D. H. Hill in command. Hill was already in command in North Carolina. He was a former division commander in Lee's army, and had been a good one, but as a department commander Lee was finding him somewhat hard to work with. The two generals were engaged in a long and detailed correspondence about what forces Hill could spare to reinforce Lee. Major General S. G. French, who had been commanding in Southside Virginia, and with whom Longstreet had been very displeased, was reassigned, by the same order, and sent to Mississippi, where Joe Johnston had been complaining about not having any major generals to command divisions in the army he was assembling there.

At Vicksburg, the Federals continued to dig. "The siege works progress satisfactorily," Charles Dana wrote that day, 28 May, to Secretary Stanton. (This message reached Cairo, Illinois, at 9 p.m. on 30 May and was received in Washington at 3:15 on 1 June.) "Sherman has his parallels completed to within 80 yards of the rebel fortifications. He is able to carry artillery and wagons with horses under cover to that point. McPherson's rifle-pits are at about the same distance from the forts in his front. On both these lines our sharpshooters keep the rebels under cover and never allow them to load a cannon. It is a mistake to say that the place is entirely invested. I made the complete circuit of the lines yesterday. The left is open in direction of Warrenton, so that the enemy have no difficulty in sending messengers in and out. Our force is not large enough to occupy the whole line and keep the necessary reserves and outposts at dangerous and important points; still, the enemy cannot either escape by that route or receive supplies."[24]

Captain Hickenlooper's notes for the day say, "Engaged in making sketch of our front, in accordance with orders received from the major-general commanding. Detail upon main trench reduced to 200 men. Enemy more active this morning. They placed a 6-pounder in position on Fort Hill, which was silenced by our guns in about 30 minutes."[25] There were two forts in the Confederate lines called Fort Hill. The one referred to here, which the Federals called Fort Hill, was known to the Rebels as the 3rd Louisiana Redan. (A redan is a V-shaped salient in the line, with the point facing the enemy.) It was positioned to help block the Jackson Road, along with the 21st Louisiana Redan, which was also known as the Great Redoubt. (A redoubt is an earthwork with right angles jutting out from the main line.) The Confederates, however, applied the name Fort Hill to a series of redans on a hill near the river, about a mile north of the town, which was probably the fort Sherman asked the Navy to attack.

Inside the Confederate defenses, soldiers and civilians alike endured an almost constant bombardment. "The mortars seldom ceased their work all day long, and through the still hours of the night spoke their thunder voices," a Rebel sergeant noted, "and the concussions of their explosions shook the buildings to their very foundations. There was a strange fascination in watching these huge missiles at night as they described their graceful curves through the darkness, exploding with a sudden glare, followed by the strange sounds of their descending fragments. The spectacle to the eyesight was quite agreeable, but to the other senses anything but pleasant."[26]

Another Confederate said, "The people had become familiar with the deafening thunder of the mortar-boats, and accustomed to the loud and terrific explosions of their monstrous and massive shells, many of which ornamented gate-posts of the citizens. The weight of these shells varied from a hundred and twenty-eight to two hundred and forty pounds; they were thrown high in the air from the distance of four miles, describing nearly a half-circle in the flight, and either bursted in large fragments hundreds of feet above the earth, or, failing to explode, buried themselves deep in its surface, where they frequently blew up and tore immense holes in the ground, or, the fuse having been extinguished, they remained whole and self-deposited in these silent and undisturbed recesses."[27]

General Blair's expedition up the peninsula between the Yazoo and Big Black rivers reached Mechanicsburg that day, the 28th, where it had a slight skirmish with a small party of Rebels, but could find no large body of the enemy between the two rivers. Colonel A. K. Johnson, who commanded the Union cavalry with this expedition, sent Blair word that a civilian claimed that Confederate General A. P. Hill had arrived at Jackson two days before and that he and Joe Johnston had, between them, some 45,000 men east of the Big Black at Jackson and Canton, giving details about where the reinforcements had come from. Blair reported to Grant that Colonel Johnson "has no doubt of the entire correctness of the statement, with the exception that he believes the numbers are greatly exaggerated," which they were. In actuality, Johnston had about 18,000 men so far, and A. P. Hill was still with Lee's army in Virginia. "If I determine to push on," Blair told Grant, "and it shall be found that the enemy are in the force represented, or anything like it, it will be necessary for me to go over to the Yazoo River and rejoin you by that route if you can send up transportation for me under convoy of a gunboat. If you hear nothing from me in the next few days, you may conclude that I have taken this course."[28]

Over in Kentucky, all the troops in Burnside's Department of the Ohio, except for two divisions of the 9th Corps, which Burnside had brought with him from Virginia, were being organized as a new 23rd Corps of the Union army, and Major General George L. Hartsuff assumed command of the new corps that day, the 28th. Burnside was just about ready to make a major advance with all the movable forces he could spare from garrisoning various important positions. President Lincoln had long been trying to get one general or another to advance into East Tennessee, where many, perhaps most, of the residents were pro-Union. Confederate authorities had clamped down on the area with draconian measures to suppress an incipient rebellion – or counter-rebellion – and the Unionists had been crying loudly for help from the Federal government. But it was a difficult area to reach from the north, being separated from Middle Tennessee and Kentucky by sparsely settled hills and mountains. The only railroad in the area came down from Confederate-controlled Virginia, screened by those mountains.

Burnside was going to try it, but in coordination with Rosecrans' larger army, which was at last contemplating an advance against Bragg's Confederates. Rosecrans wired Burnside from Murfreesborough on the 29th: "Please let me know exact position of your troops. When will they be at Carthage and Jamestown? My own movements are awaiting yours. The position of affairs in front may make it necessary for you to push on to McMinnville. Please hold your troops in readiness, should this be necessary."[29]

And yet Burnside was still distracted by other problems. He wired President Lincoln that day that he had heard from Governor Oliver P. Morton of Indiana, an ardent Republican, that Burnside's arrest of Vallandigham "was not approved by a single member of your cabinet," which convinced Burnside that his action had been "a source of embarrassment to you. . . . I should be glad to be relieved if the interest of the public service require it, but at the same time I am willing to remain & assume the responsibility of carrying out the policy which has been inaugurated if it is approved." Lincoln replied before the day was out: "When I shall wish to supersede you I will let you know. All the cabinet regretted the necessity of arresting, for instance, Vallandigham, some perhaps, doubting, that there was a real necessity for it – but, being done, all were for seeing you through with it."[30]

Meanwhile, Andrew Johnson, military governor of Tennessee, who was an East Tennessean himself and one of the most ardent advocates of sending military help to the region, wired Lincoln that day pleading that a third division of the 9th Corps that had been left behind in Virginia when Burnside had brought the other two to Kentucky (it was then part of the force defending Suffolk, Virginia, which had recently been threatened by Longstreet's forces in that region) should be sent to join Burnside. "We hope this can be done," Johnson said, "as it will enable him to prosecute with success the expedition into East Tennessee. This part of the State should be entered. The oppressions and inhumanity inflicted are indescribable, and must be redressed. If the Government does not give that protection guaranteed by the Constitution, the Tennessee forces should be massed and permitted to enter East Tennessee. This they will do though they perish to a man in the attempt." Lincoln replied, "General Burnside has been frequently informed lately that the division under General Getty cannot be spared. I am sorry to have to tell you this, but it is true, and cannot be helped."[31]

Down at Vicksburg, "On the morning of the 29th," General Pemberton later reported, "the enemy opened a terrific fire from the rear, and for four hours a storm of shot and shell was rained upon the city, seriously damaging many buildings, killing and wounding a large number of soldiers and citizens."[32] Emma Balfour said, "Sure enough, after passing a bad night, from the bursting of bombs all around us, we were roused this morning by the whistling of Parrott shells and I assure you we dressed hurriedly. They came so thick and fast that it seemed a miracle that none came in the windows or against the house."[33] Meanwhile, on the Union side, the digging continued. Captain Hickenlooper's notes for the 29th say: "Main trench completed up to a point 750 feet beyond white house, 8 feet wide by 7 feet deep, with beam and parapet."[34]

General Hurlbut wrote to Rawlins from Memphis that day that, in accordance with the instructions he had just received, four regiments of infantry from the defenses of Columbus, Kentucky, as well as all detached cavalry located there, and eight more regiments of infantry from Jackson, Tennessee, and Corinth, Mississippi, would all be sent forward as soon as boats were available to take them downriver. Because of this reduction in his force he would abandon the railroad from Jackson, Tennessee, to Bolivar. "I find many officers and some soldiers coming up from below," he added. "All that are not unfit for service, and not under orders from your headquarters, I order back, as I do not consider it a fit time for any indulgences."[35]

Grant, meanwhile, wrote a brief note to be sent up the Mississippi and telegraphed to General Halleck at Washington from Memphis: "The enemy under Johnston is collecting in large force to attack me and rescue the garrison of Vicksburg. I have had my cavalry and six brigades of infantry out looking after them, and they confirm the report of a large force being collected at Canton. The number is reported to be 45,000, but may not be so large. If Banks does not come to my assistance, I must be reenforced from elsewhere. I will avoid a surprise, and do the best I can with all the means at hand."[36]

Scrounging for every reinforcement he could find, he also wrote to Admiral Porter: "Will you have the goodness to order the Marine Brigade to Haynes' Bluff, with directions to disembark and remain in occupation until I can relieve them by other troops? I have also to request that you put at the disposal of Major Lyford, chief of ordnance, two siege guns, ammunition, and implements complete, to be placed to the rear of Vicksburg. After they are in battery, and ready for use, I should be pleased to have them manned by crews from your fleet."[37] The Mississippi Marine Brigade, commanded by Colonel Charles Ellet, was neither from Mississippi nor composed of U.S. Marines. It was an army unit – infantry, cavalry and light artillery – recruited mostly from men unfit for long marches, whose job it was to help the gunboats protect the navigation of the Mississippi River and its tributaries. Although raised by the Army, they were part of Admiral Porter's command.

Porter replied before the day was out: "The brigade will leave for Haynes' Bluff early in the morning. I have not a 9-inch gun here – not anything larger than a 32-pounder (long range), excepting one 10-inch gun with shell. This would require too much work to mount it, on account of pivot bolts, &c. I am fitting it on a mortar-boat, to throw shells into the pits in front of Sherman. I ordered two 9-inch guns sent to General McArthur at Warrenton. They are there now, on board the Tuscumbia, ready to be delivered. The difficulty will be in hauling them so far, though, perhaps, they may be in a better place for your purposes. I have six 8-inch guns on the Manitou, which vessel is now up at Yazoo City. The moment she arrives, I will direct her commander to land the guns, and send to Cairo at once for more 9-inch guns."[38]

Grant also asked Porter to send one or two gunboats up the Yazoo to assist Blair and wrote the latter: "It is so important that we should save all our troops to act together, that I would direct that you take no risks whatever, either of a defeat or of being cut off. If you are satisfied of the presence of a large force at Canton and north of there, return immediately, leaving Mower's brigade at Haynes' Bluff. If you deem Haynes' Bluff in danger of an early attack, you may also leave McArthur, with the brigade of his division. Returning, destroy all the forage and stock you can, and obstruct all roads behind you by burning bridges, felling timber, and in all possible ways. . . ."[39]

If Johnston wanted to move against the rear of his army, Grant wasn't going to make it easy for him. His headquarters issued

Special Orders No. 144 that day telling commanders of corps and detached forces to "take immediate steps to obstruct and render impassable for troops all roads leading into the rear of their respective commands and into Vicksburg, except the main Jackson road, via the Big Black Railroad bridge and the different roads to Haynes' Bluff."[40] To General Osterhaus, guarding the crossings of the Big Black River in rear of McClernand's corps, Grant wrote: "Burn up the remainder of the Big Black River bridge. Make details from negroes collected about your camp and also from the troops, and have as much of the [rail]road taken up, east of the river, as you can. Pile the ties up, and lay the rails across them and burn them up. Wherever there is a bridge or trestle work, as far east as you send troops, have them destroyed. Effectually destroy the road, and particularly the rails, as far east as you can."[41]

Grant also wrote another letter to be sent down the river to Banks: "I send Mr. C. A. Dana, inspector of the pay department, to urge the same suggestions made by me in the communication of which Colonel Riggin was bearer. I have nothing further to add since my last that Mr. Dana cannot communicate more fully than can well be done in a written statement. The enemy are now concentrating a force near Canton, Miss. With an additional force here, I could detach everything but about 25,000 men, and go with the balance and capture or disperse him, leaving the State of Mississippi an easy prize to our armies. Hoping, general, this may find you in possession of Port Hudson, and of all the Mississippi River below here, I am, with great respect, yours, truly, U. S. Grant."[42]

This crossed with a long letter from Banks to Grant asking for just the opposite form of cooperation: for Grant to send him at least 10,000 men so he could successfully assault the defenses of Port Hudson and avoid a prolonged siege. "My force is far less than you imagine," he said, "and, with such detachments from it as would be necessary to protect New Orleans, while Port Hudson, Mobile, and Kirby Smith are within a few days' movement of New Orleans, my assistance would be insignificant, not enough to counter-balance the disadvantage occasioned by such movements of the enemy in this quarter as would follow the withdrawal of my troops. . . . When I came to Port Hudson, it was with the understanding from General Dwight's report that you could assist us in its reduction, if it did not fall before my force alone. It is unexpectedly strong, not stronger than I had supposed, but stronger than anybody here would for a moment admit. We can reduce it, if uninterrupted, in the course of a week or ten days. With 10,000 men in addition, we could carry it in three days. If we hold Murfreesborough, Vicksburg, and Port Hudson at the same time, the enemy will beat us all in detail, and the campaign of the West will end like the campaigns of the East, in utter and disgraceful defeat before an inferior enemy. . . . Unless we succeed on the river, the war goes over to another year. By the concentration of our forces, even at some risk, we shall succeed. That concentration is absolutely dependent upon the fall of Port Hudson."[43]

A Confederate courier got through Grant's lines that evening with another copy of the same note from Joe Johnston to Pemberton of the 25th (the one that the Federals had previously intercepted, along with 200,000 percussion caps, but had been unable to decipher). This courier brought only 20,000 caps, though another had got through the day before with an additional 18,000 but no message. Pemberton wrote an immediate reply: "I have 18,000 men to man the lines and river front; no reserves; I do not think you should move with less than 30,000 or 35,000, and then, if possible, toward Snyder's Mill, giving me notice of the time of your approach. The enemy encompasses my lines from right to left flank, occupying all roads. He has three corps – Sherman on my left, McPherson center, McClernand on my right. Hurlbut's division from Memphis and Ellet's Marine Brigade, the last afloat. My men are in good spirits, awaiting your arrival. Since investment we have lost about 1,000 men – many officers. You may depend on my holding the place as long as possible. . . ."[44] Snyder's Mill was near Haynes' Bluff, where Grant's supplies were landed.

Another Confederate was also writing to Johnston that day.

This was Colonel John Logan of the 11th Arkansas, writing from Clinton, Louisiana. (Not to be confused with the Union general of the same name who commanded a division in Grant's army.) He wrote to say that dispatches Johnston had sent to General Gardner could not be delivered because Port Hudson was now completely invested by Banks' army, and had been brought to him instead. "I am at this place with a small command of cavalry and mounted infantry, 1,200 men," he said, "doing all I can to aid General Gardner by dashing upon the enemy's lines, destroying his wagons, &c., drawing the enemy's troops from Port Hudson. I cannot do a great deal, but am determined to do all that can be done with the means at my command." Like most other commanders on both sides, he asked for reinforcements. He had heard that Lieutenant General E. Kirby Smith, Confederate commander west of the Mississippi, was near the mouth of the Red River with 10,000 men. "If he would come down and cross at Port Hudson, under cover of our guns, Port Hudson would be relieved at once," he said.[45]

However, the Confederate force on the Red River was headed in another direction. The very next day, 30 May, Kirby Smith was writing to Pemberton from his headquarters at Shreveport, Louisiana, in reply to a letter Pemberton had written to him back on 22 April, just now reaching him: "It would be too late now to take any steps for co-operating with you in the vicinity of Vicksburg. I have, however, anticipated your demands, and [Major] General [Richard] Taylor is moving with his command on General Grant's communications between Young's Point and New Carthage. [Major] General [John G.] Walker's division was ordered on the 14th of April from the Arkansas River to Northern Louisiana. Owing to the distance and the difficulties encountered, they only arrived on Red River the 24th instant. General Taylor, with a force of less than 3,000 infantry, has been opposed to Banks' corps, nearly 30,000 strong. The withdrawal of Banks has made Taylor's command disposable, and, with Walker's division, he is ordered to operate on the Mississippi River opposite Vicksburg. A brigade of General Price's division at Little Rock has been ordered to Monroe, La., to co-operate in this movement...."[46]

In Virginia on 30 May, Lee's army was officially reorganized from two corps into three. The immediate cause of this change was the recent death of his most talented and trusted subordinate, Lieutenant General Thomas J. "Stonewall" Jackson, who had been severely wounded by his own men while reconnoitering the roads to his front the night after he routed the Union 11th Corps at Chancellorsville. He had died a few days later of pneumonia. Lee thought that half of his army was too large a force for one man to control effectively, especially in the wooded country it had been operating in so far. Smaller corps would be easier to handle, and it would be easier to find men capable of handling them. This also allowed for the promotion of two officers who had good claims as Jackson's successor instead of having to choose between them. One of these was A. P. Hill, whose large division was part of Jackson's 2nd Corps; he had been wounded at the same time as Jackson and had missed the rest of the battle of Chancellorsville, but had since recovered and taken command of Jackson's corps. The other was Richard Ewell, who had commanded a division under Jackson in the latter's brilliant Shenandoah Valley campaign of 1862, but had been severely wounded during the Second Bull Run campaign. Ewell had just returned to the army the day before, minus a leg but plus a bride: a widow whom he introduced to all as "my wife, Mrs. Brown." Both men had been promoted to the grade of lieutenant general, the appropriate rank for a Confederate corps commander.

Under the new arrangement, Ewell would command a reduced 2nd Corps of three divisions: the one that had been his own, commanded since his wounding by Major General Jubal Early; the one that had originally been Jackson's, now under Major General Edward "Allegheny" Johnson, another recently recovered officer who had served in Jackson's Valley Campaign;

plus what had been D. H. Hill's division, now under newly promoted Major General Robert Rodes, who had handled it brilliantly during the Chancellorsville fighting.

A. P. Hill's large "Light Division," named for a famous British unit of the Napoleonic wars, was taken from the 2nd Corps to form the nucleus of a new 3rd Corps, which Hill would command. The division would be commanded by Hill's good friend, Major General Dorsey Pender, but two of his six brigades were detached and combined with two brigades that were new to Lee's army to form a new division, to be commanded by Major General Harry Heth. To even out the corps at three divisions each, Major General Richard Anderson's division was transferred from Longstreet's 1st Corps to Hill's 3rd. This left Longstreet with the two divisions that he had brought back from Southside Virginia, Hood's and Pickett's, plus that of Major General Lafayette McLaws.

In another change, the brigade that Stonewall Jackson had commanded at the first battle of Bull Run (First Manassas, the Rebels called it), now part of Ed Johnson's division, was officially designated the "Stonewall Brigade." Jackson himself had requested this, saying the name properly belonged to the brigade, not himself.

The cavalry, though in the process of being enlarged by reinforcements from three brigades to six, was still organized as one division, under the highly effective Major General J. E. B. "Jeb" Stuart. As the only major general who had been on hand at the time Jackson and A. P. Hill were wounded, Stuart had taken temporary command of the 2nd Corps and had done a very good job with it during the succeeding days' combat around Chancellorsville, but out of Lee's sight. Colonel E. Porter Alexander, commander of a battalion of artillery, later said, "Had Gen. Lee been present on the left, during the Sunday morning attack, and seen Stuart's energy and efficiency in handling his reserves, inspiring men by his contagious spirit, and in the cooperation of artillery, with the infantry, he might have rewarded Stuart on the spot by promoting him to the now vacant command of Jackson's corps. Ewell, who did succeed Jackson, was always loved and admired, but he was not always equal to his opportunities...."[47]

However, transferring Stuart to the infantry would have left Lee with the problem of finding a new cavalry commander just as that arm was being doubled in size. A more logical step would have been to make the cavalry a corps of two or three small divisions, but this was not done until months later. Lee that same day turned down a proposal by Stuart, in order to give promotions to worthy and talented officers, to reorganize his cavalry from six brigades of about five regiments each to ten of three each.

One of Stuart's protege's, Captain John Singleton Mosby, who was organizing a force of "partisan rangers" (guerillas), pulled off a daring feat that very same final day of May. He and four dozen men, with a little mountain howitzer recently given him by Stuart, ambushed a Federal supply train near Catlett's Station on the Orange and Alexandria Railroad. The engine ran off the track due to a loosened rail, then the howitzer blew a hole in its boiler. The lieutenant commanding the train's guard (25 men from the 15th Vermont, a 9-months regiment in the outer defenses of Washington) ordered a retreat, and Mosby's men looted the train before the 5th New York Cavalry chased them off. In a running fight Mosby and most of his men escaped the pursuit under cover of the howitzer, which they abandoned after it ran out of ammunition.

Another officer who had served with Jackson in the Valley Campaign and who was also just recovered from a wound, was Major General Isaac R. Trimble. Both his wound and his age (he was older than Lee) made his usefulness in the field suspect, but on this day he was given command of the Valley District, meaning the Shenandoah Valley. His forces consisted merely of one small brigade of somewhat irregular cavalry, commanded by Brigadier General Albert G. Jenkins, just transferred from Southwest Virginia, plus small single Maryland battalions of infantry and cavalry. One of the jobs Lee hoped Trimble, a Marylander himself, could accomplish was to get more recruits for these Maryland units. There was also Brigadier General John

Imboden's Northwest Virginia Brigade nearby, and Lee authorized Trimble to use it in an emergency.

Yet another of Jackson's former subordinates who might have been in line for his command was Major General D. H. Hill (no kin to A. P. Hill, though he had been brother-in-law to Jackson himself). "He had done as much hard fighting as any other general," Colonel Alexander later wrote, "and had also displayed great ability in holding his men to their work by supervision and example. But at this time he was not with the army, and was in command of the important department south of the James. He was a North Carolinian, and very acceptable to the State authorities. . . . There was an earnestness about D. H. Hill's fighting which was like Jackson's at its best. Had opportunity come to him, he must have won greater fame. His individuality may be briefly illustrated by an official indorsement placed upon the application of a soldier to be transferred from the infantry to the band. 'Respectfully forwarded, disapproved. Shooters are more needed than tooters.'"[48]

In fact, Lee was finding it hard to work with D. H. Hill in his capacity as commander of the Department of North Carolina. "When in Richmond," Lee wrote to President Jefferson Davis that day, 30 May, "I gave General D. H. Hill discretionary instructions, stating my belief that the contest of the summer would take place in Virginia; to apportion his force to the strength of the enemy, and send me every man he could spare. He declined to act under those instructions, and requested positive instructions. He now offers objections, which, if previously presented, I should not have issued the latter." Lee did not like to give detailed instructions to his subordinates. He preferred to outline objectives and let them achieve them in their own way. This had worked well with Jackson and Stuart, but most other officers wanted a clearer idea of just what he expected, especially if they did not share Lee's views about the objective. He would soon have problems along these lines with both Ewell and Longstreet and even with Stuart.

The problem with Hill was, of course, that, being concerned primarily with the defense of his own department, he did not want to give up any more men that he had to; Lee, wanting to take the offensive, wanted every man he could get, but did not want to strip Hill's department of forces the local commander felt were absolutely necessary for its defense. "You will see," Lee told Davis, "that I am unable to operate under these circumstances, and request to be relieved from any control of the department from the James to the Cape Fear River. I have for nearly a month been endeavoring to get this army in a condition to move – to anticipate an expected blow from the enemy. I fear I shall have to receive it here at a disadvantage, or to retreat. The enemy will either make a combined movement to force me back, or transfer his army to the James River. If I was stronger, I think I could prevent either, and force him back."[49] An implied threat to retreat was one of Lee's favorite tactics with Davis, and it usually sufficed to get him what he wanted, but it was a bluff; in actuality he almost never retreated, at least not until after he had given battle.

Lee was, however, concerned that Hooker might be contemplating another move around his left flank, such as the one that had started the Chancellorsville campaign. So, that same day, Longstreet's headquarters sent orders to General Hood, whose division was camped along the Virginia Central Railroad, well to the southwest, to move up as soon as possible to Verdiersville, which was a small village on the Orange Turnpike south of the Rapidan River, well to the west of the Chancellorsville crossroads, near a small stream called Mine Run, where he was to take up the best camp he could find "for wood, water, and grass. . . . Major-General Stuart, commanding cavalry, has been directed to communicate to you information of the enemy's crossing below you, should the attempt be made; at the earliest receipt of which, you will put your command in motion for Guiney's Station, marching through Spotsylvania Court-House. . . . The information brought in by our scouts leads to the idea that the enemy is preparing for another crossing . . ."[50]

Lee was also puzzled by the presence of Federal troops at West Point, Virginia, east of Richmond, where the Pamunkey and Mattapony rivers come together to form the York. This force was too small to pose much of a threat to his right flank, but it could be the precursor to the landing of a larger force. It was one reason Pickett's division was being kept not far upstream at Hanover Junction, waiting to see what developed. In fact, the Union force, commanded by Major General George H. Gordon, had been landed there with no clear objective in mind, and now that Lee was not busily engaged with Hooker's army, General Dix, commander of the Department of Virginia, was getting nervous about having it stuck out there by itself. He wrote to Halleck that day: "I went with Major-Generals Peck and Keyes to West Point yesterday, and, on consultation with General Gordon, it was unanimously decided to withdraw the troops, throw them up the Peninsula and above the enemy at Diascund Bridge, which is as near Richmond as West Point. There are at West Point only 4,700 men, and they will be reduced to 4,000 shortly by the discharge of a regiment. General Keyes has only 5,000 men at Gloucester Point, Yorktown, and Williamsburg, and it is very desirable that he should have this re-enforcement. I have lost three regiments and shall lose fourteen more by expiration of service."[51]

At Vicksburg, General Pemberton, having reduced the meat ration for his troops by one half, increased the rations of sugar, rice and beans in compensation. To keep up morale, Pemberton also seized all chewing tobacco and had it issued to his troops. "This had a very beneficial influence," he reported. "The enemy kept steadily at work day and night," he said, "and taking advantage of the cover of the hills, had run his parallels up to within 75 yards of our works. He was also mining at different points, and it required the active and constant attention of our engineers to repair at night the damage inflicted upon our works during the day, and to meet his different mines by counter-mining. Orders were issued to prepare thunder barrels and petards for the defense of weak points, and every precaution was taken to check the enemy in his operations and to delay them as far as possible."[52]

However, much of the Federals' attention was being diverted at that time to protecting their rear against Joe Johnston's lurking force. Captain Hickenlooper recorded that day, 30 May: "In compliance with orders received from the major-general commanding, left at 3 a.m. for Big Black River, accompanied by 300 detailed men from General Ransom's command and pioneer company of Third Division. Arrived at Bridgeport, on Big Black River, at 11 a.m. At 3 p.m. commenced moving westwardly along Bridgeport road, obstructing the road by felling trees across same. From Tiffin I sent the pioneer company southwest, on Bovina Station road, with orders to return on Hebron road, obstructing said roads in same manner. Burned the bridges across Clear Creek, and small creek next west of Hebron road."[53]

Emma Balfour noted that "The shelling from the mortars was worse than usual last night. . . . I could hear the pieces falling all around us as the shell would explode, and once I thought our time had come." A newly married couple had a very close call. The husband had been standing by a window watching the trails left by the fuses of the shells when he saw one coming right at them. He yelled for his bride to run, which she did. "I was just within the door when the crash came that threw me to the floor," she told her diary. "It was the most appalling sensation I'd ever known. Worse than an earthquake, which I've also experienced."[54] Neither she nor her husband were hurt, but the room they had been in was now missing one wall.

However, the biggest bombshell that exploded at Vicksburg on 30 May was not one made of iron and gunpowder, but of paper and ink: General McClernand published his corps' General Orders No. 72, which was a long, bombastic harangue to be read to all his troops, congratulating them for their efforts in the campaign so far. It would take a few days, but the effects of this missive would eventually be deadly to his career.

∽ Endnotes ∽

1   Hoehling, *Vicksburg: 47 Days of Siege,* 64.
2   Ibid., 65.

3   OR, I:24:III:354.
4   Hoehling, *Vicksburg: 47 Days of Siege,* 63.
5   Ibid., 65.
6   OR, I:24:I:277.
7   Ibid., I:24:II:199.
8   Ibid., I:23:II:365.
9   Ibid., I:23:II:366.
10 Ibid, I:25:II:528.
11 Ibid., I:25:II:527.
12 Ibid., I:25:II:826-7.
13 Ibid., I:25:II:531.
14 Ibid., I:23:II:369.
15 Ibid.
16 Ibid., I:25:II:532.
17 Luis F. Emilio, *A Brave Black Regiment: History of the Fifty-fourth Regiment of Massachusetts Volunteer Infantry 1863-1865* (Bantom Books edition, New York, 1992), 33-4.
18 Ibid., x.
19 OR, I:25:II:533.
20 Ibid., I:25:II:538.
21 Ibid., I:25:II:536.
22 Ibid., I:25:II:537.
23 Ibid., I:25:II:542-3.
24 Ibid., I:24:I:90.
25 Ibid., I:24:II:199.
26 Hoehling, *Vicksburg: 47 Days of Siege,* 67.
27 Ibid., 68-9.
28 OR, I:24:III:354-5.
29 Ibid., I:23:II:372.
30 Roy P. Basler, ed., *The Collected Works of Abraham Lincoln* (New Brunswick NJ, 1953), VI:237.
31 OR, I:23:II:372.
32 Ibid., I:24:I:277.
33 Hoehling, *Vicksburg: 47 Days of Siege,* 71.
34 OR, I:24:II:199.
35 Ibid., I:24:III:363.
36 Ibid., I:24:I:40.
37 Ibid., I:24:III:361.
38 Ibid.
39 Ibid., I:24:III:361-2.
40 Ibid., I:24:III:363.
41 Ibid., I:24:III:362.
42 Ibid., I:24:III:359.
43 Ibid., I:24:III:359-60.
44 Ibid., I:24:I:278.

45 Ibid., I:26:I:180.
46 Ibid., I:24:III:935-6.
47 Edward Porter Alexander, *Military Memoirs of a Confederate* (Da Capo Press edition, New York, 1993), 360.
48 Ibid., 367, n. 1.
49 *OR,* I:25:II:832.
50 Ibid., I:25:II:839.
51 Ibid., I:25:II:567-8.
52 Ibid., I:24:I:278.
53 Ibid., I:24:II:200.
54 Hoehling, *Vicksburg: 47 Days of Siege,* 74-5. Both quotes.

CHAPTER 4

"All I Want Now Are Men"

30 May – 4 June 1863

General Hurlbut, at Memphis, was writing to General Halleck, at Washington, that day, Saturday, 30 May, passing on the latest rumors about the size and intentions of Johnston's force. He had heard that Johnston had received 20,000 men from Bragg's army in Middle Tennessee, 10,000 from Port Hudson, and 6,700 from Mobile. "This is undoubtedly incorrect," he said, "or it relates to the whole force drawn from these points instead of late re-enforcements. Two railroad engineers, who left Canton on Wednesday, and arrived at La Grange to-day, state that Johnston is at Jackson with 13,000 men. One of the men heard Johnston say that D. H. Hill was on the way from Virginia with 18,000 men; said that he would attack Grant in rear in five days. Crossings over Pearl River are being constructed." Hurlbut sent similar messages to Rosecrans and to Grant. To the latter he added, "I have informed Rosecrans for two weeks past that all my information pointed to heavy drafts from the force opposed to him. Up to this time he has refused to credit it."[1]

Rosecrans was busy, as he was finally preparing to advance, but he was having trouble coordinating with Burnside's forces coming down from south-central Kentucky. Burnside wrote to him that day: "I have one column concentrated at Columbia [KY], with the advance at Jamestown; one at Somerset, with the advance at Waitsborough; one at Crab Orchard, and one at London and Mount Vernon, with outposts at Barboursville, Cumberland Ford, and Manchester. Orders are now out for concentrating the first three columns for the movement you speak of, and I leave this place for the front on Tuesday. I am anxiously awaiting your letter, after the receipt of which I will start a bearer of dispatches to you at once. Hartsuff has great difficulty in concentrating his troops in consequence of lack of transportation. Your requisitions for mules and horses have been so great that we have not been able to organize our own trains. He will not be at the point we agreed upon with his troops in time to relieve the Tennessee regiments at Carthage; so that our first move will have to be made without them. We will not be able to use your pack-mule train unless they have panniers. The first column will move without reference to Hartsuff. If there is occasion for special haste in order to co-operate with you, let me know definitely."[2] One of Burnside's major defects as a general was that he never saw the need for "special haste." In this, he was certainly not unique. Rosecrans himself was another of the many generals on both sides who never, or at least seldom, saw the overwhelming value of time and speed.

Charles Dana, agent of the Union War Department, started on his way that day to carry Grant's latest message downriver to Banks. "The route for getting out from the rear of Vicksburg at that time," he later remembered, "was through the Chickasaw Bayou into the Yazoo and thence into the Mississippi. From the mouth of the Yazoo I crossed the Mississippi to Young's Point, and from there went overland across the peninsula to get a gunboat at a point south of Vicksburg. As we were going down the river [on 31 May] we met a steamer just above Grand Gulf bearing one of the previous messengers whom Grant had sent to Banks. He was bringing word that Banks could send no forces; on the other hand, he asked reinforcements from Grant to aid in his siege of Port Hudson, which he had closely invested. This news, of course, made my trip unnecessary, and I returned at once to headquarters, having been gone not over twenty-four hours."[3]

On his return he wrote a message for Secretary Stanton from Chickasaw Bayou about noon on the 31st: "General Banks is investing Port Hudson, and declines to send any forces here. He opened his lines May 21, with 12,000 men, and on the 27th assaulted the place ineffectually, losing 1,000 killed and wounded. He has ordered up 4,000 more troops from his own forces below, which will make his force 15,000, and desires that General Grant should also send him re-enforcements. Grierson's cavalry, which General Grant pressingly needs, General Banks retains on the plea of necessity. He says that if he were to raise the siege, in order to help General Grant, he would still be unable to send him any more than 5,000 troops, as he must retain the bulk of his army there as long as Port Hudson is unsubdued. The number of the garrison he estimates at 6,000. Of their supplies of food and ammunition he knows nothing positively, and does not say how long he thinks it will require to reduce the place."[4]

Four hours later he wrote again, from Grant's headquarters: "Blair reports there is no rebel force between the Yazoo and the Big Black, and that Johnston has now at Canton only 18,000 men, and does not intend to move until he has 40,000. Blair confirms his own previous report that three divisions have been withdrawn by Johnston from the army opposed to General Rosecrans, but these three divisions have not yet reported to Canton. This tallies with General Grant's information from other sources. Johnston says he shall have his 40,000 in time to save Vicksburg. Pardon me for again urging that re-enforcements be at once sent here from Tennessee, Kentucky, or Missouri in numbers sufficient to put our success beyond all peradventure. The same messenger who bears this to Memphis bears also General Grant's orders for 7,000 men from Hurlbut's forces to be sent here at once; but this will not meet all the requirements of the case. Our position here is infinitely more secure and the result incomparably more certain than our position and its results at Corinth last year. The place is far more important. Its ultimate possession ought to be assured by all the means in our power. Better retreat from Nashville than retreat from the hills of Vicksburg."[5]

Blair had been correct when he reported that there was no large force of Confederates in the area between the Yazoo and Big Black rivers, but just as he was withdrawing Johnston sent one in. On that last day of May, Major General W. H. T. Walker wrote to Johnston from Benton, some eight or ten miles east of Yazoo City, saying that he had arrived there at 9 a.m. He was on his way to Yazoo City with a division newly formed out of disparate units to plant some guns to protect that place and to interdict the Yazoo River. Walker was a highly competent officer, an 1837 graduate of West Point and later commandant of cadets there, but he had been severely wounded in the Mexican War and he had never fully recovered, so that he had been on and off duty since joining the Confederacy. He had just recently been promoted to major general upon Johnston's recommendation as the only brigadier then with him qualified to command a division.

Colonel Riggin – the messenger Dana had met coming back with Banks' reply to Grant – having brought Banks' letters of the 28th and 29th, Grant replied before the day was out: "While I regret the situation in which they left you, and clearly see the necessity of your being re-enforced in order to be immediately successful, the circumstances by which I am surrounded will prevent my making any detachments at this time. Concentration is essential to the success of the general campaign in the West, but Vicksburg is the vital point. Our situation is for the first time during the entire Western campaign what it should be. We have, after great labor and extraordinary risk, secured a position which should not be jeopardized by any detachments whatever. On the contrary, I am now and shall continue to exert myself to the utmost to concentrate. . . . My arrangements for supplies are ample, and can be expanded to meet any exigency. All I want now are men."[6]

As Dana told Stanton, the same messenger that carried his message upriver – Colonel William S. Hillyer of Grant's staff – also carried one from Grant to Hurlbut with an order to send more troops south. "I want your district stripped to the very lowest possible standard," Grant told him. "You can be in no danger for the time it will be necessary to keep these troops away. All points in West Tennessee north of the Memphis and Charleston [rail]road, if necessary, can be abandoned entirely. Western Kentucky may be reduced to a small garrison at Columbus and Paducah. If you have not already brought troops forward to

Memphis to send me, bring [Brigadier General William Sooy] Smith's, formerly Denver's, division. Add to this all other force you can spare. Send two regiments of cavalry also. If you have not received the cavalry last ordered from Helena, divert them to this place, instead of sending two other regiments. No boats will be permitted to leave Memphis, going north, until the transportation is fully provided for all troops coming this way. The quartermaster in charge of transportation and Colonel Hillyer are specially instructed to see that this direction is fully enforced. The entire rebel force heretofore against me are completely at my mercy. I do not want to see them escape by being re-enforced from elsewhere."[7]

To ease the transportation problem for his reinforcements, Grant also wrote to Admiral Porter that day: "Will you please direct the Marine Brigade to debark at Haynes' Bluff, and send all their steamers, or as many of them as possible, to Memphis to bring down re-enforcements? I have ordered the troops, but it is a difficult matter to get transportation. I would specially request that any of these steamers that can be spared be got off at the earliest possible moment."[8] Also, orders were issued for the garrison left at Grand Gulf to destroy the old Confederate river defenses there and to move up to Warrenton, just south of Vicksburg, where they could help cut the latter city off from all outside aid.

That same day, Sunday, 31 May, Banks was writing to Halleck in praise of Colonel Grierson and his cavalry: "The moral effect of that remarkable expedition upon a wavering and astonished enemy, and the assistance rendered us in breaking up the enemy's communications, in establishing our own, and in covering the concentration of our forces against this place, can hardly be overestimated. Their timely presence has supplied a want which you will remember I have frequently represented was crippling all our operations. I trust that the services of Colonel Grierson and his command will receive at the hands of the Government that acknowledgment which they so eminently deserve."[9]

Meanwhile, the siege was beginning to wear on the beleaguered Rebels in the trenches at Vicksburg. "Sunday brought with it no cessation of hostilities," Sergeant William Tunnard of the 3rd Louisiana wrote. "Fourteen long days and wearisome nights had passed away and still no prospects of relief to the defiant troops. The mortar fleet concentrated their fire on the courthouse, near the central portion of the city. The constant daily fighting, night work and disturbed rest began to exhibit their effects on the men. They were physically worn out and much reduced in flesh. Rations began to be shortened, and for the first time a mixture of ground peas and meal was issued. This food was very unhealthy, as it was almost impossible to thoroughly bake the mixture so that both pea flour and meal would be fit for consumption. Yet these deficiencies were heroically endured, and the men succeeded by an ingenious application of the culinary art in rendering this unwholesome food palatable, calling the dish 'cush-cush.'"[10]

Another Confederate, Colonel Ephraim Anderson of the 1st Missouri, explained that the peas in question were really small beans known colloquially as "cow peas." They were usually used to feed cattle. The peas were ground into meal, but turning pea meal into bread was a bad idea, for, he said, "It never got done, and the longer it was cooked, the harder it became on the outside, which was natural, but, at the same time, it grew relatively softer on the inside, and, upon breaking it, you were sure to find raw pea-meal in the centre."[11] In his unit, he said, they gave up after three days – during which it had already made some of the men sick – and just boiled the whole peas, which, he said, constituted about half of their rations.

Joe Johnston wrote that day to Kirby Smith, commanding all Confederate forces west of the Mississippi: "Port Hudson is invested by Major-General Banks; Vicksburg by Major-General Grant. I am preparing to aid Vicksburg, but cannot march to Port Hudson without exposing my little army to destruction. If you can do anything to succor Port Hudson, I beg you to do it."[12]

Smith, however, as he had written to Pemberton the day before, was sending what force he could muster not to help Port Hudson, but toward Vicksburg. Major General Richard Taylor, commander of the District of Western Louisiana in Smith's Trans Mississippi Department, arrived that day at Judge John Perkins' plantation on the west side of the river south of Vicksburg, with a division of Texans commanded by John G. Walker, no kin to the General W. H. T. Walker then leading a division in Johnston's army on the other side of the river. This plantation had been an important depot on Grant's supply line west of the river, but Taylor had arrived too late, for Grant had now abandoned that supply line in favor of his new base on the Yazoo, north of Vicksburg. Taylor did learn, however, that there were still Federals at Milliken's Bend, on his side of the river, north of Vicksburg, where they were recruiting and training escaped slaves.

In Virginia, Jefferson Davis was writing to Lee that last day of May: "I had never fairly comprehended your views and purposes until the receipt of your letter of yesterday, and now have to regret that I did not earlier know all that you had communicated to others. I could hardly have misunderstood you, and need not say would have been glad to second your wishes, confiding, as I always do, as well in your judgment as in your information." After going into a detailed discussion of the movement of various units between North Carolina, Richmond, and Lee's army, he said, "I note your request to be relieved of the command of the troops between the James River and the Cape Fear. This is one of the few instances in which I have found my thoughts running in the opposite direction from your own. It has several times occurred to me that it would be better for you to control all the operations of the Atlantic slope, and I must ask you to reconsider the matter." After a few other matters he turned to the news from the West: "General Johnston did not, as you thought advisable, attack Grant promptly, and I fear the result is that which you anticipated, if time was given. The last intelligence indicates that Grant's army is concentrating on the Yazoo, where he connects with his gunboats and river transportation, and threatens the line of communication between Jackson and Vicksburg. The position, naturally strong, may soon be intrenched, and, with the heavy guns which he can bring by water, will require to be reduced by some other means than a direct attack. . . . All the accounts we have of Pemberton's conduct fully sustain the good opinion heretofore entertained of him, and I hope has secured for him that confidence of his troops which is so essential to success."[13]

This shows that Davis still did not understand the situation at Vicksburg, for Grant was not "concentrating on the Yazoo" to merely threaten the line of communication between Jackson and Vicksburg; he was drawing his supplies via the Yazoo, but most of his army was investing the Vicksburg defenses, sitting solidly on the line of communication between those two cities, facing both ways, prepared to keep Pemberton's forces in, and everyone else out, of Vicksburg.

A staff officer wired Joe Johnston, at Canton, Mississippi, from the city of Jackson on 1 June: "General Breckinridge, with his division, excepting two batteries, which are expected tonight, have arrived. Division numbers about 5,200 effective; aggregate about 5,600."[14] This brought the total of Pemberton's and Johnston's forces to about 58,000 men, slightly more than Grant's 51,000; but Grant was between the two Confederates, who could only communicate by passing messengers through or around Grant's increasingly tight siege of Vicksburg.

Meanwhile, perhaps feeling vindicated by Lincoln's refusal to remove him over the arrest of Vallandigham, Burnside made another move that first day of June against what he perceived as treason in his department. His headquarters, at Cincinnati, issued General Orders No. 84 forbidding the circulation of the New York *World* in his department because of its "pernicious and treasonable influence." Also, "On account of the repeated expression of disloyal and incendiary sentiments, the publication of the newspaper known as the Chicago Times is hereby suppressed."[15] Vallandigham, meanwhile, had become a Confederate problem. The next day, 2 June, Jefferson Davis ordered him sent to Wilmington, North Carolina, and there put under guard as an enemy alien.

In Virginia on the second day of June, Lee was completing the reorganization of his army by redistributing his artillery. His batteries had already been grouped into larger formations, much like the brigades Hooker was instituting in his army, but called battalions by the Confederates. They were somewhat smaller, containing, on the average, about 16 guns in four batteries. But, in contrast to Hunt's large Artillery Reserve in the Army of the Potomac, Lee broke up his artillery reserve, until now commanded by Brigadier General William Nelson Pendleton, an Episcopal clergyman whose performance had proved to be less than stellar. Pendleton would remain the chief of artillery, but only as an officer on Lee's staff, where he could exercise his talents for administration.

Each of Lee's large divisions would continue to have one battalion of artillery attached, and each of the three corps would now have its own reserve of two more battalions. Thus each of his corps was a true "army corps" – a miniature army – except that they lacked any cavalry of their own, other than a company or so of escorts and couriers attached to each corps headquarters. And each of his divisions, having four or five brigades of infantry (which were larger on average than Union brigades) plus one battalion of artillery, was roughly equivalent (though slightly smaller) to one of Hooker's seven small corps, which were composed of six to ten brigades of infantry plus a brigade of artillery each. But Lee had three corps commanders to help him coordinate his nine infantry divisions, while Hooker had no intermediate commanders to help him handle seven infantry corps of unequal sizes, plus the cavalry corps and the artillery reserve.

Confederate Secretary of War Seddon wired Lee that day: "Reliable information informs that the enemy have evacuated West Point, and probably, to a great extent, Yorktown and Gloucester Point, and are marching in a column of 2,000 or 3,000 men on both sides of the Piankatank, northwest. This may be meant to cover some movement of Hooker's to the Lower Rappahannock and across, or up to the Piankatank, or it may be a mere diversion. You can best judge. I telegraph the above to the commander at Hanover Junction, for his information."[16] The Piankatank River is a relatively small stream that splits the peninsula between the Rappahannock and the York. The force moving along it was actually Kilpatrick's cavalry, on its way from Gloucester Point, opposite Yorktown, to rejoin Hooker's army. The Confederate high command confused this move with the sudden disappearance of the force at West Point. Lee was closer to the truth when he told Jeb Stuart that day, "They may be making for Urbana or Tappahannock, to cross to General Hooker, or to lend him a hand to cross. I have moved Collins and Pickett in that direction. I presume I shall hear to-morrow what it means."[17] (Major Charles R. Collins was commander of the 15th Virginia Cavalry Regiment, which watched the crossings of the Rappahannock downstream from Lee's main force.)

Major General John F. Reynolds, commander of the 1st Corps in Hooker's army, made a quick trip to Washington that day, 2 June. According to his sister, who saw him later that evening, but did not record her memory of the meeting until years later, "He told us he had been with the President that day, and that Mr. Lincoln had offered him the command of the Army of the Potomac, which he told the President he would accept, if he was not interfered with from Washington. *This* the President would not promise him...."[18] However, Reynolds' friend, Major General George Meade, commander of the 5th Corps, after talking with Reynolds ten days later, wrote his wife the next day: "He told me that being informed by a friend in Washington, that he was talked of for command of this army, he immediately went to the President and told him he did not want the command and would not take it."[19] This seems the more likely scenario. Reynolds was one of several officers who had already expressed their preference for having Hooker replaced by his friend Meade; it therefore seems likely that, hearing that he was being considered himself, he went to Washington to say he didn't want the job but wanted Meade to have it. However, Lincoln, at the time, seems to have been willing to keep Hooker. Meade added, in his account of what Reynolds told him, "He spoke, he says, very freely to the President about Hooker, but the President said he was not disposed to throw away a gun because it missed fire once; that he would pick the lock and try it again."[20]

Lincoln's mind, at that time, was more concerned with his armies in the West, which were active, than the quiet one along the Rappahannock, but his information was out of date. He telegraphed to Grant that day: "Are you in communication with Gen. Banks? Is he coming toward you, or going further off? Is there, or has there been any thing to hinder his coming directly to you by water from Alexandria?"[21]

What information had reached Washington about the situation on the Mississippi had made one thing clear, at least: Grant needed reinforcements to hold off Joe Johnston's growing army. Hurlbut sent another message to Halleck that second day of June outlining what a scout had learned on a recent foray inside Confederate lines. He correctly stated that two divisions of infantry and two brigades of cavalry had been sent from Bragg's army in Tennessee to reinforce Johnston. "They think if Pemberton can hold out two weeks Johnston will be able to relieve him. He is now at Jackson organizing and provisioning troops. They think General Grant's position very strong, and estimate his force very high."[22] He sent a similar message to Rosecrans. Halleck wired

General Schofield, the new commander in Missouri, that same day: "If you can possibly spare some troops, send them immediately to General Grant. They can be returned to you the moment Vicksburg is taken."[23] Similar messages were sent to Burnside – pointing out that much of Johnston's force was believed to be derived from Bragg's army, making it unlikely that the Rebels would be raiding into Kentucky any time soon – and to Rosecrans, saying, "If you can do nothing yourself, a portion of your troops must be sent to Grant's relief."[24]

Burnside made no reply that day, but Schofield answered: "I will send six regiments of infantry. I can spare three excellent batteries. Shall I send them also?" Halleck wired back: "Yes; send everything you can to General Grant. Send those nearest, and replace them from the interior. It is all-important that Grant have every assistance." Rosecrans sent back a long answer justifying his own recent lack of activity on the grounds that if he drove Bragg's army farther south it would just be that much more likely to go and join Johnston. He correctly estimated that Bragg had sent Breckinridge's and what had been J. P. McCown's divisions of infantry and W. H. "Red" Jackson's division of cavalry to Johnston so far. "The time appears now nearly ripe," he concluded, "and we have begun a movement, which, with God's blessing, will give us some good results."[25] Since he thus believed that he was doing something himself, or was about to, he sent no troops to Grant. He also wired Burnside: "Our movement has begun, and we want you to come up as near and as quickly as possible. It will not interfere with your East Tennessee movement, but will strengthen it."[26]

At Vicksburg the siege continued. "Through the entire siege," Charles Dana later remembered, "I lived in General Grant's headquarters, which were on a high bluff northeast of Sherman's extreme left. I had a tent to myself, and on the whole was very comfortable. We never lacked an abundance of provisions. There was good water, enough even for the bath, and we suffered very little from excessive heat. The only serious annoyance was the cannonade from our whole line, which from the first of June went on steadily by night as well as by day." In a letter written to his young daughter on 2 June Dana said, "Sometimes I wake up in the night and think it is raining, the wind roars so in the tops of the great oak forest on the hillside where we are encamped, and I think it is thundering till I look out and see the golden moonlight in all its glory, and listen again and know that it is only General Sherman's great guns, that neither rest nor let others rest by night or by day."[27]

If Dana thought the bombardment was bad from where he slept, he should have experienced it on the other side of the lines. Alexander Abrams, a reporter for the Vicksburg *Whig*, said: "Our line of works, as planned by Major General M. L. Smith, was as good as could be desired, but the execution of his plans was the most miserable ever performed by men claiming to be engineers. . . . So badly were the works erected, that three days after the siege commenced the enemy had enfiladed us, and a few days after that, opened a fire in reverse. We were thus subject to a continual fire from all quarters. The number of pieces of artillery brought to bear upon our defenses, could not have been less than from two hundred and fifty to three hundred of all descriptions and calibres. This large number of guns, keeping up a constant fire on our lines, naturally created an uproar almost deafening, and as a result thousands of shells were poured into our works. There was no portion of the space of ground in our lines but where whole shells and fragments of shells could be seen, while at the line, and about one hundred yards from it, thousands upon thousands of minie' balls covered the road and woods."[28]

Minié ball was the name for the bullet used in the rifled musket, invented by a Captain Minié of the French army. In fact, it was not really a "ball," such as older smoothbore muskets used, but pointed, like modern bullets, and its posterior end was concave, so that when the gunpowder exploded it forced the soft lead bullet to expand into the spiral grooves, called rifling, that lined the inside of the barrel. This imparted a spin to the bullet, which stabilized its flight and thus increased its range and accuracy compared to a round ball. In fact, a staff officer wrote to General Bowen, one of Pemberton's division commanders, that same second day of June, saying, "The amount of Minie cartridges on hand is so small that the Minie musket in the hands of our troops is utterly valueless. The practice of exchanging our own arms for those captured from the enemy must, therefore, by rigidly prohibited."[29]

Emma Balfour said, "I have almost made up my mind not to think of retiring at night. I see we are to have no rest. They are evidently trying to harrass our army into submission. All night they fired so that our poor soldiers have no rest, and as we have few reserves it is very hard on them."[30] And the firing, as Dana said, went on both day and night. "There was the usual heavy cannonading at early dawn, and dusk," Sergeant Tunnard wrote. "During the hottest portion of the day the enemy seemed content to seek shelter from the sun's scorching rays, but in the morning they exercised their skill by pouring a rapid and heavy fire into the breastworks."[31]

But while the artillery bombardment was loud and frightening, the Union riflemen were deadlier. "The enemy's sharpshooters were all splendid marksmen," Abrams, the reporter, said, "and effectually prevented any of our men from rising above the parapet on pain of certain death, while it was an utter impossibility for our cannoneers to load the guns remaining in position on our line, without being exposed to the aim of a dense line of sharpshooters."[32]

Meanwhile the Federal engineers continued to dig. Having returned to the front from obstructing roads in the army's rear, Captain Hickenlooper of the 17th Corps noted that day, 2 June: "Engaged on main trench. Detail reduced to 150 men. The Third Division pioneer company engaged in making gabions, fascines, &c."[33]

Sherman wrote a long letter to Grant that day suggesting that the latter use his influence with President Lincoln "to accomplish a result on which it may be the ultimate peace and security of our country depends. I mean his use of the draft to fill up our old regiments. I see by the public journals that a draft is to be made, and that 100,000 men are to be assigned to fill up the old regiments, and 200,000 to be organized as new troops. . . ." He pointed out that when new regiments had joined their army back in November and December they had contained about 900 men each, whereas now the regiments of their army averaged around 300. The loss of over two thirds of their men was due not so much to battle as to sickness. "All who deal with troops in fact instead of theory know that the knowledge of the little details of camp life is absolutely necessary to keep men alive. New regiments, for want of this knowledge, have measles, mumps, diarrhea, and the whole catalog of infantile diseases; whereas the same number of men, distributed among the older regiments, would learn from the sergeants and corporals and privates the art of taking care of themselves, which would actually save their lives and preserve their health against the host of diseases that invariably attack the new regiments. Also recruits, distributed among older companies, catch up, from close and intimate contact, a knowledge of drill, the care and use of arms, and all the instructions which otherwise it would take months to impart. . . . If a draft be made, and the men be organized into new regiments, instead of filling up the old, the President may satisfy a few aspiring men, but will prolong the war for years, and allow the old regiments to die of natural exhaustion."[34]

That same day Frank Blair was writing to Grant about the situation between the Yazoo and Big Black rivers. "Since seeing you on yesterday, the Fifth Illinois Cavalry, 750 strong, have reached this place, bringing with them carbines for the Fourth Iowa Cavalry, now here. The Fifth Illinois is armed with carbines, and also the detachment of the Second Illinois, now here. This gives about 1,200 well-armed cavalry. Colonel Johnson believes, with this force, properly supported with infantry and artillery, he can destroy the railroad bridge over the Big Black north of Canton. The plan is to move the whole cavalry force toward Mechanicsburg to-morrow morning by the three roads I pointed out to you, the main body moving by the central road, with flanking parties on the right and left hand roads, and at the same time to send Mower's brigade, with a full battery of artillery, by the Yazoo River to Satartia, to land at that point and push to Mechanicsburg. This will compel [Wirt] Adams' cavalry, the only force on this side of Black River, to cross the Big Black River at Kibby's or Cox's Ferry in order to escape capture, and prevent them from recrossing that river, while Johnson with his entire force can push forward and destroy the bridge with little risk or hazard; nor will Mower's brigade, provided with transports at Satartia convoyed by a gunboat, run any risk, especially if he keep out a few cavalry on the different roads to advise him of the enemy's movements." This was endorsed by Rawlins before the day was out: "Respectfully returned to Major-General Blair, commanding expeditionary corps, who will issue orders for the expedition against the Big Black railroad bridge north of Canton, in exact accordance with the plan within proposed."[35]

Brigadier General Joseph A. Mower was a good choice to command the infantry in this expedition. A brigade commander in Sherman's corps, he was not quite 36 years old that summer. He had been an enlisted man in the Mexican War and later commissioned in the Regular Army without passing through West Point; early in the Civil War he was appointed colonel of the 11th Missouri. Dana described him as "a brilliant officer, but not of large mental calibre," without explaining the apparent contradiction.[36] Sherman regarded him as "the boldest young soldier we have."[37] Grant himself wrote the instructions for Mower's part in the move and told the latter, "In a few days I will be able to send an entire division, or move to re-enforce you, when I think you will be able to make excursions up through the rich Yazoo bottoms, and keep me well informed of all information collected."[38]

Grant also ordered a brigade of Brigadier General Nathan Kimball's provisional division of the 16th Corps, just arrived from Memphis, to take over garrisoning Haynes' Bluff. By the next day, 3 June, the rest of Kimball's force had arrived, and Grant ordered it to proceed on its transports up the Yazoo to Satartia and then march over to Mechanicsburg, three miles away, where it would meet up with Mower's brigade and Colonel Johnson's cavalry. (Dana later described Kimball as "not so bad a commander as Lauman but he is bad enough, brave of course, but lacking the military instinct and the genius of generalship."[39]) Being the senior officer, Kimball was to take overall command of the expedition, following the instructions already given to Mower.

"The object of placing troops at Mechanicsburg," Grant told him, "is to watch the movements of the enemy, who are said to be collecting a large force in the vicinity of Canton. With your cavalry you will watch all the ferries over Big Black, north of Bridgeport. Obstruct all roads leading west from the river, not wanted by yourself, in every way possible. Collect all the forage, cattle, and provisions you can, and destroy what you cannot bring away. It is important that the country be left so that it cannot subsist an army passing over it. . . . It is desirable that all possible information should be acquired of the movements of the enemy, and sent promptly to these headquarters. You are therefore, authorized to employ spies. . . ."[40]

Blair was ordered, that day, to "proceed, with the five brigades temporarily under his command, to the left of the investing army. The position to be occupied by him will be designated by Lieutenant Colonel Wilson, assistant inspector-general." Once Blair's force was in position guarding its left, Lauman's division of the 16th Corps, which was, until now, at the left end of Grant's line, would move forward, "occupying as advanced a position as possible, intrenching the ground taken," but it was Blair who was "charged with making the investment of the south side of the city so perfect as to prevent the possible ingress or egress of couriers of the enemy. . . ."[41]

Grant wrote to Halleck that day, 3 June: "The approaches are gradually nearing the enemy's fortifications. Five days more should plant our batteries on their parapets. Johnston is still collecting troops at Canton and Jackson. Some are coming over the railroad, and all the country is joining his standard. The destruction of the enemy's artillery and ordnance stores was so complete that all these must be brought in from a distance. I sent a large force on the narrowest part of land between the two rivers, about 45 miles northeast, with the cavalry watching all the crossings of Big Black River. We shell the town a little every day, and keep the enemy constantly on the alert. We but seldom lose a man now. The best of health and spirits prevail among the troops."[42]

From Memphis, Hurlbut wired Halleck again that day, saying he was, on Grant's order, sending all possible reinforcements downriver, but that he thought at least another 10,000 men would be needed from outside Grant's department. Meanwhile, Burnside, at Cincinnati, finally replied to Halleck's order of the day before, saying, "Rosecrans is relying upon my advance into Tennessee, and I am all ready. If I do not go there, some 8,000 or 10,000 men might be spared for Grant. Rosecrans has just telegraphed me that he is moving, and wants me to push on. I leave for Hickman Bridge at daylight to-morrow. Telegraph me at Lexington." Halleck shot back: "You will immediately dispatch 8,000 men to General Grant at Vicksburg. Should it be found that General Grant will not require them, they will be stopped by the way or returned to you as early as possible." In a follow-up telegram, Halleck added: "You must hurry forward re-enforcements to General Grant. If you cannot hire river boats, you must impress them. Telegrams from Memphis say that Bragg is sending large re-enforcements to Johnston." Schofield wired Halleck from St. Louis that day: "I have concluded to send eight regiments and three batteries. The last will be off to-morrow. This leaves me very weak, but I will do it in view of the vast importance of Grant's success." Late that night he added, "My latest information is that [Confederate Major General Sterling] Price has still 10,000 or 12,000 infantry near Little Rock. If satisfied that this force has gone also, I can send more troops down the river. Shall I run the risk of sending them now?" Burnside replied to Halleck's first message from Lexington, Kentucky, that night: "The two divisions of the Ninth Army Corps go. Shall I go with them? Hartsuff is concentrating the troops, and can look out for matters here, and I will have nothing to do. I may be able to help Grant."[43] He also wired Rosecrans telling him what was going on, saying "My plans are all deranged."[44] With his best troops leaving his department, he gave up on any advance into Tennessee and personally returned to Cincinnati.

In a note written that day to Grant, Admiral Porter said that the Navy was picking up about 15 Confederate deserters a day and that, according to them, the fire of the Federal guns at night was not enough to prevent the Rebels from moving their heavy guns about after dark. He recommended that the artillery keep at it but regretted to say that he was out of ammunition for his mortars, although he hoped to receive more in a day or two. "I have sent six 8-inch guns up the Yazoo, with men to work them, to be placed where required, and two 9-inch at Warrenton. I will send plenty of hand-grenades if you want them. I have sent some already. They work beautifully."[45]

On the landward side of the city, Union soldiers continued to dig. A dozen or more approach trenches were now being worked on. Captain Hickenlooper's notes for that day, 3 June, say: "Detail on main trench reduced to 100 men. Trench finished up to and through advanced battery, with side rifle-pits, &c."[46]

Pemberton wrote a note to Johnston that day, to be smuggled through the Union lines somehow: "Have heard nothing from you since 29th. No important changes in that time. Enemy continues to work at his intrenchments, and very close to our line; is very vigilant. I can get no information from outside as to your present position and strength, and very little in regard to the enemy. I have heard that two messengers with caps have been captured. In what direction will you move, and when? I hope north of Jackson road."[47] That day the division of 3,000 cavalry under Brigadier General William "Red" Jackson, sent from Middle Tennessee by General Bragg, reached Canton and joined Johnston's army.

In Virginia that day, 3 June, Kilpatrick's cavalry rejoined the Army of the Potomac, having crossed the lower Rappahannock without incident. They brought in about 200 prisoners, 40 wagons and 1,000 escaped slaves. Lee, not knowing that these troopers were left-overs, as it were, from Stoneman's recent raid, assumed that they were on "a marauding expedition," and told Pickett, who had been sent out after them from Hanover Junction, "If you learn that the enemy has retired and is beyond your grasp, I desire you to return to your position."[48]

Meanwhile, Lee took the first tentative steps on his planned second move across the Potomac River that day. Hood's Division – the other of Longstreet's two divisions that had missed the battle of Chancellorsville – was ordered to move to Culpeper Court House, some thirty miles to the northwest, in the angle between the Rappahannock and Rapidan rivers. Longstreet's third division, McLaws', which had taken part in the Chancellorsville fight, also pulled out of its camps near Fredericksburg that same day and began marching west, as did the 1st Corps artillery.

"I recall the morning vividly," Colonel Porter Alexander, whose artillery battalion was now in the 1st Corps artillery reserve, later wrote. "A beautiful bright June day, & about 11 a.m. a courier from Longstreet's headqrs. brought the order. Although it was only to march to Culpeper C.H. we knew that it meant another great battle with the enemy's army...."[49] Lee's men could assume that they would be outnumbered again, and the move away from the excellent defensive position near Fredericksburg might seem risky, but they were quite willing to trust in Lee's judgment. "I am sure," Colonel Alexander said, "there can never have been an army with more supreme confidence in its commander than that army had in Gen. Lee. We looked forward to victory under him as certainly as to successive sunrises."[50]

Keeping the Rappahannock between him and Hooker, Lee was edging off to his left one corps at a time, hoping to break contact with the Union army and head off into the Shenandoah and the crossings of the upper Potomac, but he would not commit himself to a definite move until he saw how Hooker reacted. Two of Lee's objectives in invading the North again were to impress the British and the French, who might be induced to recognize Confederate independence if the Rebels could be seen to be winning the war, and to induce Northerners, especially those who opposed Lincoln's Republican administration, to give up on the idea of conquering the South. And there were reasons to hope for both results. At Sheffield, England, that same day, there was a meeting honoring "Stonewall" Jackson, the Confederate general who had recently died from wounds received at Chancellorsville. And at New York City there was a meeting of Democrats, led by Mayor Fernando Wood, urging peace – presumably even if it meant Confederate independence, since the Confederate government was not going to accept peace on any other terms so long as it controlled an army to fight with.

Major General David Hunter, commander of the Union Army's Department of the South, comprising several lodgments along the coast of South Carolina, Georgia, and Florida, wrote that day, 3 June, to the governor of Massachusetts: "I have the honor to announce that the Fifty-fourth Massachusetts (colored troops), Colonel Shaw commanding, arrived safely in this harbor this afternoon and have been sent to Port Royal Island. The regiment had an excellent passage, and from the appearance of the men I doubt not that this command will yet win a reputation and place in history deserving the patronage you have given them."[51]

Hunter, an old regular army officer (West Point class of 1822), was an enthusiastic supporter of the idea of recruiting "colored" regiments. In fact, he had been the first to recruit one, known as the 1st South Carolina, but he had done so without authorization and before the Lincoln administration had been prepared to risk alienating the slaveholding border states that had sided with the Union, and he had been forced to disband that unit. However, after such recruiting had finally been authorized he had raised the 2nd South Carolina, and he reported to Secretary of War Stanton that day that it had just successfully completed the first of his planned raids into the Southern interior. Colonel James Montgomery had taken 300 of his men, accompanied by a couple of artillery pieces from a Rhode Island battery, 25 miles into Rebel territory and destroyed a Confederate pontoon bridge over the Combahee River, as well as "a vast amount of cotton, rice, and other property, and brought away with him 725 slaves and some 5 horses. . . . Colonel Montgomery with his forces will repeat his incursions as rapidly as possible in different directions, injuring the enemy all he can and carrying away their slaves, thus rapidly filling up the South Carolina regiments in this department, of which there are now four."[52]

Hunter would have been pleased had he known that the Secretary of the Navy issued orders that day relieving Admiral Du Pont of his command along the Atlantic Coast, to be replaced by Rear Admiral Andrew H. Foote, who had proven to be an aggressive leader when in command of the gunboats on the Western rivers the year before. Foote had been wounded at Fort Donelson, and after helping General John Pope capture Island No. 10 in the Mississippi, had been given a desk job, in charge of the Bureau of Equipment and Recruiting. However, Hunter would not have been so pleased to learn that on the same day the War Department issued orders replacing Hunter, temporarily, as commander of the Department of the South, with Brigadier General Quincy Gillmore, the officer who had proclaimed himself ready to try his hand at battering the Confederate forts at Charleston into submission as he had Fort Pulaski, near Savannah, the year before. Gillmore was a much younger man, who had graduated at the top of his class at West Point in 1849 and had later taught there. He was an excellent engineer and the army's leading expert on the new rifled heavy artillery.

At Washington on 3 June, General Halleck was writing a brief note to General Banks. He said he had just received letters from the latter dated 5, 13, and 19 May, but not one of 12 May that was mentioned. "I cannot ascertain from your letters," he said, "whether you propose to re-enforce General Grant at Vicksburg or not. The newspapers state that your forces are moving on Port Hudson, instead of co-operating with General Grant, leaving the latter to fight both Johnston and Pemberton. As this is so contrary to all your instructions, and so opposed to military principles, I can hardly believe it true. I have so often pointed out what I thought ought to be done, and the peril of separate and isolated operations, that it would be useless to repeat them here."[53]

Unknown to Halleck, of course, Banks hoped that day to deal with the Rebel cavalry under Colonel John Logan that was lurking in his rear, so that morning Colonel Grierson with most of Banks' cavalry (about 1,300 troopers) and eight pieces of artillery, set out for Clinton, Louisiana. But they were ambushed just short of the town and then attacked in the flank and forced to retreat.

The next day, 4 June, Halleck wrote to Banks again, saying he had just received Banks' letters of 8, 11, 12 (four of them), 18, and 19 May. "These fully account for your movement on Port Hudson," he said, "which before seemed so unaccountable. General Grant was probably drawn so far north in pursuit of the enemy that he found it necessary to connect himself with his supplies above Vicksburg. As at Alexandria you were almost as near to Grand Gulf as to Port Hudson, we thought it exceedingly strange that you and General Grant should move in opposite directions to attack both places at the same time. I hope that you have ere this given up your attempt on Port Hudson and sent all your spare forces to Grant. The moment Vicksburg falls there will be no serious difficulty in taking Port Hudson. Moreover, both your armies can be supplied from the Upper Mississippi. If I have been over-urgent in this matter, it has arisen from my extreme anxiety lest the enemy should concentrate all his strength on one of your armies before you could unite, whereas, if you act together, you certainly will be able to defeat him."[54]

As it happened, Banks was writing to Halleck that same

fourth day of June, in reply to the latter's letter of 19 May. "I marched to Alexandria for the double purpose of dispersing the rebel army said to be concentrating there under Kirby Smith, and destroying the materials upon which an army could be organized or supported in that country. . . . Besides, my arrangement with Major-General Grant, upon his own proposition, was that I should join a corps of his force in the reduction of Port Hudson on May 25." Here, and even later in his official report of the campaign, Banks shows that he did not understand that when Grant had said he could send forces to help him, the intended date was 25 April, not 25 May, but the message took so long to reach Banks that it was by then already too late to arrange the rendezvous. Meanwhile, learning that Banks had gone up the Red River to Alexandria and beyond, Grant had given up on the idea and had proceeded independently. Banks then renewed his argument, and a good one, that he previously used in correspondence with Grant, that if he left Port Hudson alone he would have to leave most of his forces south of it to protect New Orleans and the rest of occupied Louisiana while leaving the Confederate garrison free to go join Joe Johnston's army, which would strengthen the latter by at least as many men as he could then send to Grant. "Under these circumstances, my only course seems to be to carry this post as soon as possible, and then to join General Grant. If I abandon it, I cannot materially aid him. I have now my heavy artillery in position, and I am confident of success in the course of a week. We can then render efficient aid to the army at Vicksburg. . . . I need not say what I have so many times urged, that the force placed at my disposal is inadequate to the duty imposed upon me, and yet I appreciate the impossibility of re-enforcing my command."[55]

Banks also wrote another message to Grant that day, saying pretty much the same thing and adding that there was a force of Rebels (Logan's) collecting in his rear, which he estimated at from 2,000 to 3,000 strong, "that will in a short time give us some trouble."[56] This gave him an excuse for hanging onto Grierson's cavalry.

Grant, meanwhile, was still worried about the Rebels operating in his rear (and probably wishing yet again to have Grierson and his troopers with him). He wrote that day to General Kimball, whose provisional division of the 16th Corps was being sent up the peninsula between the Yazoo and Big Black rivers: "I have just received information that a portion of Johnston's force has gone into Yazoo City. In penetrating north, therefore, the cavalry going in advance will be in danger of having their rear cut off by this force closing in behind them. The position of the enemy and his numbers must be well ascertained before going much beyond Mechanicsburg. I do not want to run any great risk of having any portion of the army cut off or defeated. If, therefore, your judgment is against reaching Big Black River Bridge with security, and getting back again, you need not attempt it."[57]

Also on 4 June, Halleck answered Schofield's offer to send even more troops to Grant and his worries about the Rebels at Little Rock: "I think you had better send no more at present. The moment General Grant succeeds on the Mississippi, an expedition will be sent up the Arkansas to drive out Price or take him in rear. Banks thinks most of Price's forces have been drawn south."[58] Halleck also replied to Burnside's query of the day before as to whether he should accompany the 9th Corps divisions he was sending down to Grant: "It would be obviously improper for you to leave your department to accompany a temporary detachment of less that one-quarter of your effective force. Morever, the organization of the Kentucky militia requires your immediate attention."[59] That same day the War Department informed Burnside that the President wanted him to revoke the order suspending the publication of the Chicago *Times*.

Meanwhile the siege of Vicksburg continued. Captain Hickenlooper's notes for 4 June say: "Engaged on advanced battery, putting in embrasures, revetments, &c. This work is irregular in shape, of 3,000 square feet, two embrasures on north and one on west face, and open to and covered by batteries to the rear."[60]

An Iowa woman visiting the Union hospitals outside

Vicksburg found that just getting to many of them was a highly dangerous exercise, nor were they very pleasant places once she reached them. "The ceaseless roar of artillery, and scream of shot and shell; the sharp whiz and whirr of small shot just over our heads, the June sun blazing down upon us with torrid heat, and no shelter for the sick but the white canvas tents, perched on the sides of the bluffs in places excavated for them, the bank cutting off the circulation of air – were almost unbearable. How the poor fever-racked heads and fainting hearts ached amid the ceaseless din and the dust and heat of these little camp hospitals!" Sitting in one of these she noticed the weeds nearby were constantly shaking and was informed that the cause was Rebel bullets falling among them. The doctors said it was safe, though, for all the bullets fell short. However, three days later an officer was killed while sitting in the very same chair she had used. She made lemonade for the patients, but noted that cool water was very scarce. "There were some springs, and a few wells were dug; but at points water had to be hauled long distances. Think of thousands of men to be supplied – of the thousands of horses and mules, the great burden-bearers of the army, that must have their thirst quenched. Most of the water for the use in camp was hauled up from the Mississippi River or the Yazoo, through the hot sun in barrels, and stood in camp all day."[61]

On the Confederate side of the lines, not just thirst but hunger was beginning to be a problem. "On this day all surplus provisions in the city were seized," wrote Sergeant Tunnard, "and rations issued to citizens and soldiers alike. To the perils of the siege began now to be added the prospect of famine."[62]

∽ **Endnotes** ∽

1   *OR,* I:24:III:366.
2   Ibid., I:23:II:373-4.
3   Dana, *Recollections of the Civil War,* 89.
4   *OR,* I:24:I:91.
5   Ibid., I:24:I:91-2.
6   Ibid., I:24:III:367.
7   Ibid., I:24:III:369.

8. Ibid., I:24:III:368.
9. Ibid., I:24:III:369.
10. Hoehling, *Vicksburg: 47 Days of Siege*, 77.
11. Ibid., 83.
12. *OR*, I:26:II:26.
13. Ibid., I:25:II:842-3.
14. Ibid., I:24:III:942.
15. Ibid., I:23:II:381.
16. Ibid., I:25:II:847.
17. Ibid., I:25:II:850.
18. Edward J. Nichols, *Toward Gettysburg: A Biography of General John F. Reynolds* (Pennsylvania, 1958), 220.
19. Ibid., 221.
20. Ibid., 184. Meade's account was written far closer to the event than was that of Reynold's sister and fits the known attitudes of both Lincoln and Reynolds better. Also it was written before Meade was given the command and before the death of Reynolds, both of which events soon lent interest to the question of whether or not Reynolds had been offered the command.
21. Basler, ed., *Collected Works of Abraham Lincoln*, VI:244.
22. *OR*, I:24:III:377.
23. Ibid.
24. Ibid., I:24:III:376.
25. Ibid., I:24:III:377.
26. Ibid., I:23:II:381.
27. Dana, *Recollections of the Civil War*, 88.
28. Hoehling, *Vicksburg: 47 Days of Siege*, 88.
29. *OR*, I:24:III:942. Many of Grant's men, however, must also have been armed with smoothbore muskets, for when the Confederates finally surrendered he allowed his regiments to exchange any obsolescent arms for superior ones yielded by the Rebels.
30. Hoehling, *Vicksburg: 47 Days of Siege*, 89.
31. Ibid.
32. Ibid., 87.
33. *OR*, I:24:II:200.
34. Ibid., I:24:III:372-3, also III:3:386-8.
35. Ibid., I:24:III:373-4.
36. Dana, *Recollections of the Civil War*, 77.
37. Edwin C. Bearss, *Forrest at Brice's Cross Roads and in North Mississippi in 1864* (Dayton OH, 1979), 328.
38. *OR*, I:24:III:375.
39. Dana, *Recollections of the Civil War*, 78.
40. *OR*, I:24:III:379.
41. Ibid., I:24:III:380.
42. Ibid., I:24:I:41.

43 Ibid., I:24:III:383-4.
44 Ibid., I:23:II:384.
45 Ibid., I:24:III:378.
46 Ibid., I:24:II:200.
47 Ibid., I:52:II:487.
48 Ibid., I:25:II:852-3.
49 Sears, *Gettysburg*, 58.
50 Ibid., 59.
51 *OR*, I:14:462.
52 Ibid., I:14:463.
53 Ibid., I:26:I:534.
54 Ibid., I:26:I:535.
55 Ibid., I:26:I:535-6.
56 Ibid., I:24:III:385.
57 Ibid., I:24:III:384.
58 Ibid.
59 Ibid., I:23:II:386-7.
60 Ibid., I:24:II:200.
61 Hoehling, *Vicksburg: 47 Days of Siege*, 98,
62 Ibid., 99.

CHAPTER 5

"It Seems to Me Desperate"

4 – 7 June 1863

In Virginia early in the morning of Thursday, 4 June, Rodes' Division of Ewell's 2nd Corps of Lee's army broke camp and took up the march for Culpeper Court House, followed by Early's Division. To avoid being spotted by the Union observation balloons, they marched to the southwest first, going by way of Spotsylvania Court House (to be made famous a year later) and through the cover of the Wilderness.

However, changes in Lee's camps had not gone unnoticed by the Federals across the Rappahannock. Major General Daniel Butterfield, Hooker's chief of staff, sent messages that day to generals Meade and Buford, watching the fords upstream, that some of Lee's troops seemed to have left their camps and to keep a sharp lookout and report anything that indicated a Confederate movement upriver. Hooker wired General Dix to see if anything he was doing might account for what Hooker called "the commotion observed this morning in the rebels camps opposite me." Dix replied that he had withdrawn his forces from West Point on 31 May and had not yet made his contemplated move up the peninsula between the York and James Rivers because his chief cavalry officer was sick. "I will advise you two or three days before I move. My force is small, and you must not count on anything more than a diversion. I expect, however, to create some disturbance at least."[1]

That evening Jeb Stuart held a ball at Culpeper Court House. Dignitaries and belles alike descended upon the little county seat for the festive occasion, and the next day, Friday, 5 June, the visitors were treated by a sight of martial splendor seldom witnessed on the North American continent. Stuart had picked out a huge open field up the railroad near Brandy Station where his entire newly enlarged Cavalry Division of the Army of Northern Virginia could be put on display. The troops were bivouacked on nearby Fleetwood Hill, there was a small hillock in the field he could use as a reviewing stand, and the field was close enough to the railroad tracks that his guests, male and female, could witness the entire spectacle from the cars that brought them from Culpeper if they so wished.

Stuart's men had been at some pains to improve the appearance of themselves and their mounts, and the general and his staff officers all wore new and splendid uniforms. In addition to wanting to put on their best front for the visiting ladies and dignitaries, they had expected General Lee to be on hand to review them, but he was still back at Fredericksburg and could not attend. Nevertheless, with his five brigades of cavalry and one large battalion of horse artillery drawn up in formation for inspection, Stuart and his staff rode down the line – it was a mile and half long – and as they passed each brigade its commander and his staff fell in behind. Upon reaching the far end, the enlarged party of generals and staffers turned and rode the length of the line again, this time behind the troopers.

It was 10 a.m. by the time Stuart took position on the little knoll that served as the reviewing stand. With a flourish of bugles, the units at one end of the line wheeled into a column of squadrons, advancing at the walk, and each unit fell into position as it was passed until every regiment had filed past their commander. Then the entire column – 8 to 10,000 men and horses – turned and came back by in the other direction at a trot, and, when within a hundred yards of the reviewing stand, they drew sabers, raised a Rebel yell, spurred to a gallop, and charged past Stuart straight for the guns of the horse artillery, which opened fire with blank charges that filled the air with billows of white smoke. Some of the female spectators were seen to swoon or faint, though, strange to say, only those who had a male companion near enough to catch them.

"It was a brilliant day," Major Henry B. McClellan of Stuart's staff remembered, " and the thirst for the 'pomp and circumstance' of war was fully satisfied."[2] That night there was another ball, this time held under the open sky to the light of huge bonfires on the same field where the troopers had charged. The enlisted men, of course, were not invited.

That same day the remaining division of Ewell's 2nd Corps also broke camp and marched west, leaving only A. P. Hill's new 3rd Corps to hold the old defenses around Fredericksburg. Lee, about to move west himself, gave written instructions to Hill. (A rarity for Lee, who usually gave only verbal directions to his corps commanders.) "I desire you to occupy the position of Fredericksburg with the troops under your command, making such disposition as will be best calculated to deceive the enemy, and keep him in ignorance of any change in the disposition of this army. Should the enemy make an advance upon you, you will endeavor to repel him, and, if not able to do so, or hold him in check, you must fall back along the line of the Fredericksburg Railroad, protecting your communications, and offering such resistance as you can to his advance toward Richmond. If you find it necessary, you can call up Pickett and Pettigrew, now at Hanover Junction. [Brigadier General J. Johnston Pettigrew commanded a brigade of North Carolinians recently brought of from that state and stationed near Hanover Junction. It was to become part of Heth's new division in Hill's new 3rd Corps.]

"Should you find that the enemy has evacuated his position opposite you, you will, after informing yourself of the fact by your scouts, &c., if practicable and in your opinion advantageous, cross the river and pursue him, inflicting all the damage you can upon his rear. I request that you will keep me informed of everything material relative to yourself, position, and of the enemy. Colonel [W. C.] Wickham, with his cavalry, is on your left, and Major [C. R.] Collins, commanding Fifteenth Virginia Cavalry, on your right. Captain [Richard E.] Frayser, signal officer, is at Port Royal. These officers have been instructed to report to you. There is a line of couriers to Culpeper Court-House. My headquarters will be there for the present. You are desired to open any official communications sent to me, and, if necessary, act upon them, according to the dictates of your good judgment."[3]

As with the move the day before, this latest Confederate movement did not go undetected by the Federals across the river. General Hooker sent a long message to President Lincoln at 11:30 a.m. reporting what had been noticed the last couple of days, including the fact that deserters from Hood's and Pickett's divisions had come into his lines.

"I concluded," he said, "that those divisions had been brought to the front from their late positions at Gordonsville and Taylorsville, and that this could be for no other purpose but to enable the enemy to move up the river, with a view to the execution of a movement similar to that of Lee's last year. He must either have it in mind to cross the Upper Potomac, or to throw his army between mine and Washington, in case I am correct in my conjecture. To accomplish either, he must have been greatly reenforced, and if making this movement, the fair presumption is that he has been by the troops from Charleston. Of this I have no evidence further than that furnished me by Major-General Dix, that they had come to Richmond. . . . As I am liable to be called on to make a movement with the utmost promptitude, I desire that I may be informed as early as practicable of the views of the Government concerning this army. Under instructions from the major-general commanding the army [Halleck], dated January 31, I am instructed to keep in view always the importance of covering Washington and Harper's Ferry, either directly or by so operating as to be able to punish any force of the enemy sent against them.'" Harper's Ferry was a small town where a Federal arsenal, manufacturing rifles, had been located, before the Confederates had moved its machinery farther south; its real importance was as the point where the Baltimore & Ohio Railroad crossed from the north to the south side of the Potomac. A sizable Union garrison, part of the Middle Department, occupied the town and the surrounding hills. Another Union force garrisoned Martinsburg, farther west on the B&O, and Winchester, to the southwest, up the Shenandoah Valley ("up" because it's upstream; the Shenandoah River runs southwest to northeast).

"In the event the enemy should move, as I almost anticipate he will," Hooker continued, "the head of his column will probably be headed toward the Potomac, via Gordonsville or Culpeper, while the rear will rest on Fredericksburg. After giving the subject my best reflection, I am of opinion that it is my duty to pitch into his rear, although in so doing the head of his column may reach Warrenton before I can return. Will it be within the spirit of my instructions to do so?

"In view of these contemplated movements of the enemy, I cannot too forcibly impress upon the mind of His Excellency the President the necessity of having one commander for all of the troops whose operations can have an influence on those of Lee's army. Under the present system, all independent commanders are in ignorance of the movements of the others; at least such is my situation. I trust that I may not be considered in the way to this arrangement, as it is a position I do not desire, and only suggest it, as I feel the necessity for concert as well as vigorous action."[4]

Three and a half hours later Halleck wired Hooker: "Prisoners and deserters brought in here state that Stuart is preparing a column of from 15,000 to 20,000 men, cavalry and artillery, for a raid. They say it will be ready in two or three days."[5] Sometime that afternoon Hooker forwarded to Secretary Stanton a report from General Buford, of the cavalry, saying that he had information that Stuart had collected five brigades of cavalry in Culpeper County, numbering 20,000 men, presumably for a raid. (The number of brigades was correct, of course, but the number of men was more than doubled.)

An hour after Halleck's wire, Lincoln replied to Hooker's message: "So much of professional military skill is requisite to answer it, that I have turned the task over to General Halleck. He promises to perform it with his utmost care. I have but one idea which I think worth suggesting to you, and that is, in case you find Lee coming to the north of the Rappahannock, I would by no means cross to the south of it. If he should leave a rear force at Fredericksburg, tempting you to fall upon it, it would fight in intrenchments and have you at disadvantage, and so, man for man, worst you at that point, while his main force would in some way be getting an advantage of you northward. In one word, I would not take any risk of being entangled upon the river, like an ox jumped half over a fence and liable to be torn by dogs front and rear, without a fair chance to gore one way or kick the other. If Lee would come to my side of the river, I would keep on the same side, and fight him or act on the defensive, according as might be my estimate of his strength relatively to my own. But these are mere suggestions, which I desire to be controlled by the judgment of yourself and General Halleck."[6]

Forty minutes later Halleck sent his answer: "My instructions of January 31, which were then shown to the President, left you entirely free to act as circumstances, in your judgment, might require, with the simple injunction to keep in view the safety of Washington and Harper's Ferry. In regard to the contingency which you suppose may arise of General Lee's leaving a part of his forces in Fredericksburg, while, with the head of his column, he moves by Gordonsville or Culpeper toward the Potomac, it seems to me that such an operation would give you great advantages upon his flank to cut him in two, and fight his divided forces. Would it not be more advantageous to fight his movable column first, instead of first attacking his intrenchments, with your own force separated by the Rappahannock? Moreover, you are aware that the troops under General Heintzelman are much less than the number recommended by all the boards for the defenses of Washington. Neither this capital nor Harper's Ferry could long hold out against a large force. They must depend for their security very much upon the co-operation of your army. It would, therefore, seem perilous to permit Lee's main force to move upon the Potomac while your army is attacking an intrenched position on the other side of the Rappahannock. Of course your movements must depend in a great measure upon those made by Lee.

"There is another contingency not altogether improbable – that Lee will seek to hold you in check with his main force, while a strong force will be detached for a raid into Maryland and

Pennsylvania. The main force of the enemy in North Carolina have probably come north, but I think all available troops in South Carolina and Georgia have been sent to re-enforce Johnston in Mississippi. Such is the information here. General Heintzelman and General Dix are instructed to telegraph directly to you all the movements which they may ascertain or make. Directions have also been given to forward military information which may be received from General Schenck's command [the Middle Department – Delaware, Maryland, and West Virginia]. Any movements you may suggest of troops in these commands will be ordered, if deemed practicable. Lee will probably move light and rapidly. Your movable forces should be prepared to do the same. The foregoing views are approved by the President."[7]

Meanwhile, a circular was sent by Hooker's headquarters to at least some of his corps commanders to have their troops ready to move on short notice, with three days' cooked rations on hand and all surplus baggage sent to the rear; no more leaves or furloughs would be granted and any that were to start that day were to be revoked. Then Hooker decided to lay a couple of pontoon bridges across the Rappahannock at Franklin's Crossing – one of the spots near Fredericksburg that had been used to bridge the river preliminary to both the Battle of Fredericksburg and that of Chancellorsville – and sent troops across to find out what the Rebels were up to on the south side of the river.

At 9:15 p.m. he telegraphed Lincoln again: "As soon as we got to work [on the bridge], they began to assemble in great numbers from all quarters, and the more remote are still arriving. I took about 50 prisoners, and they report that the changes remarked in their camps proceeded from the reorganization of their army, and the assignments of them to new camps. All of Longstreet's command are now with Lee, but no part of the Charleston forces. They have no infantry force higher up the Rappahannock than its junction with the Rapidan. Their cavalry is assembled around Culpeper, but the threat to make a crossing may cause them to return. I shall keep my bridges down a few days."[8]

Hooker was at least partially correct in his estimate of how

Lee would react to his bridging the Rappahannock. "On the afternoon of Friday, the 5th instant," Lee wrote to President Davis a couple of days later, "the enemy made open preparations to cross the Rappahannock at the old position at the mouth of Deep Run. After driving back our sharpshooters, under a furious cannonade from their batteries, by a force of skirmishers, they crossed a small body of troops, and occupied the bank of the river. It was so devoid of concealment, that I supposed the intention was to ascertain what forces occupied the position at Fredericksburg, or to fix our attention upon that place while they should accomplish some other object. I thought it prudent to send that night to General Ewell to halt his march until I could see what the next day would develop, and placed A. P. Hill's corps in position to meet any attack that might be made the next morning."[9]

Southeast of Lee's right flank and east of Richmond, a small Union expedition, consisting of four detachments of 100 men each drawn from four different infantry regiments, steamed up the Mattapony River on a transport escorted by three Navy gunboats and landed at the village of Walkerton at about 3 a.m. Their commander, Colonel C. Carroll Tevis of the 4th Delaware, knew that there was a large Confederate force ten miles to the south at White House plantation on the Pamunkey River (property of Lee's second son, Brigadier General W. H. F. "Rooney" Lee, who commanded a brigade in Stuart's cavalry), so he left detachments to watch the roads coming up from that place and marched ten miles upriver (northwest) to a village called Aylett's, which he reached at about 7 a.m. There he found his objective, a large iron foundry, where, as his instructions from General Keyes stated, "shot and shell, guns, and other instruments of rebellion are manufactured."[10]

"This," Tevis reported, "with a large machine-shop, a lumber-yard, a store-house filled with agricultural implements, tobacco, cotton, turpentine, and other articles, and five Government houses, containing several thousand bushels of corn, were, in obedience to orders, destroyed. On the retreat, a very large grist-mill belonging to Colonel [W. R.] Aylett, of the rebel army, with eight 'run of stone,' and containing 2,500 barrels of flour and 2,000 bushels of wheat, was burned. I also destroyed twenty barns and ten wheat stacks, containing in all 20,000 bushels of grain; also some stores of bacon (about 2,000 pounds), a quantity of tobacco, some cotton goods, and 80 gallons of whiskey. I captured 120 horses and mules, and 80 head of horned cattle, all of which were driven to the wharf at Walkerton, but of which only a portion was shipped on board the transport, owing to the refusal of Captain [Lieutenant Commander James H.] Gillis to delay his return, he having received intelligence that the enemy were posting batteries along the banks of the river. I also report the capture of 2 rebel soldiers, who are now in the guard-house at Yorktown. One of these, from papers taken on his person, . . . I believe to have violated his parole."[11]

This expedition caused some considerable consternation among the Confederate commanders in the area. Major General Arnold Elzey, in charge of the defenses of Richmond, sent a telegram to General Pettigrew, at Hanover Junction, almost due west of Tevis's raiders, to get word to General Pickett, whose division was also near there, that President Davis "wants the enemy captured or destroyed, if possible, and thinks if General Pickett will move or send a force rapidly to Walkerton or below it, with some artillery, and you send some down, the combined movement with Wise from White House would do the business."[12] But both Pickett and Pettigrew were slated to join Lee's army, they were both subject to being called upon by A. P. Hill, if he should be attacked, and there was some uncertainty about where Pickett was – it was thought at first that he had gone to Richmond – and by the time he was found it was too late to catch Tevis.

The Rebel with the best chance of catching him was Brigadier General Henry A. Wise, a former governor of Virginia, commanding the brigade stationed at White House plantation, only about ten miles south of Walkerton. His brigade had been stationed there to keep an eye on the Union forces that had been farther east at West Point, as well as those south of the York River in what was known as the Peninsula. But when Wise reported to Elzey about Federals moving up the Mattapony he had at first been forbidden to cross the Pamunkey River to go after them. By the time permission to do so finally came it was too late, although some cavalry he sent up managed to skirmish with Tevis's rearguard. "It was a daring and destructive raid," Wise reported, "and can be perpetrated again unless General Pettigrew can be ordered to picket and hold the upper ferries of the Mattapony, and unless I be allowed (at discretion) to cross the Pamunkey as emergency may require."[13]

Down at Port Hudson that fifth day of June, Banks, irritated about the ambush of Grierson's cavalry at Clinton two days before, started a large force of infantry, artillery and cavalry toward the same place that day, under the command of Brigadier General Halbert Paine.

In Mississippi that day, Joe Johnston telegraphed Confederate Secretary of War Seddon: "Grant still receives re-enforcements. Scouts near Friar's Point report 8 boats, loaded with troops, passed down Monday and Tuesday. Twelve empty transports passed up."[14] Those two had been exchanging short telegrams for some days, dealing mainly with the question of the size – or smallness – of Johnston's forces and whether any more troops could be sent to him from elsewhere. Johnston also wrote Seddon a long letter that day:

"I suppose, from my telegraphic correspondence with the Government, that all the troops to be hoped for have arrived," he said. "Our resources seem so small, and those of the enemy so great, that the relief of Vicksburg is beginning to appear impossible to me. Pemberton will undoubtedly make a gallant and obstinate defense, and hold out as long as he can make resistance; but unless we assemble a force strong enough to break Grant's line of investment, the surrender of the place will be a mere question of time. General Grant is receiving re-enforcements almost daily. His force, according to the best information to be had, is more than treble that which I command. Our scouts say, too, that he has constructed lines of circumvalation and has blocked up all roads leading to his position. The enterprise of forcing the enemy's lines would be a difficult one to a force double that at my disposal. If you are unable to increase that force decidedly, I must try to accomplish something in aid of the besieged garrison; and yet, when considering it, it seems to me desperate. . . .

"I beg you to consider in connection with affairs in this department that I have had not only to organize, but to provide means of transportation and supplies of all sorts for an army. The artillery is not yet equipped. All of Lieutenant-General Pemberton's supplies were, of course, with his troops about Vicksburg and Port Hudson. I found myself, therefore, without subsistence, stores, ammunition, or the means of conveying those indispensables. It has proved more difficult to collect wagons and provisions than I expected. We have not yet the means of operating for more than four days away from the railroads. That to Vicksburg is destroyed. We draw our provisions from the northern part of the State. The protection of that country employs about 2,500 irregular cavalry. It is much too small. I am endeavoring to increase it by calling for volunteers, but am by no means sanguine as to the result."[15]

Meanwhile, the bombardment of Vicksburg continued, with the Rebels working at night to repair as best they could whatever damage the Union guns did to their defenses. Colonel Bevier of the Confederate Missouri Brigade said, "No safe place in all the corporation could be found except behind some of the parapets where the soldiers lay, and in the deep holes which the citizens burrowed in the sandy soil and occupied as residences; even some of these were invaded by unwelcome messengers, scattering death and destruction all around."[16]

And the Federals continued to dig their way toward the Rebel lines. Captain Hickenlooper's notes for 5 June say: "Advanced battery finished, and main trench carried about 20 feet southwest, with lead sap down to the road. Detail reduced to 75 men."[17] Colonel Bevier saw the Union soldiers "approaching, like moles, through the ground, in parallels, pushing their sharpshooters to the front, who ensconced themselves in innumerable rifle-pits, and behind every stump and tree, and from the land-side kept up a constant discharge of hot shot, shrapnel, shell and grape, while 'Porter's Bombs,' from over the river, with hideous screeches, cleaved the upper air."[18] There was joy in the Union camps that day, occasioned by the arrival of new uniforms to replace the clothes the men had been marching, fighting and digging in for weeks.

In a letter to Secretary Stanton, written that day, Charles Dana said: "The expeditionary corps, under Blair's command, commenced its march yesterday morning to occupy fully the southern approaches to the city, but were called back about noon, and the brigades returned to their original divisions. This was a result of some new demonstrations of the enemy, thought to be indicative of a purpose to sally, and also of General Grant's unwillingness to scatter his troops. The cannonade from our whole line is now steadily maintained by night as well as by day. Some fifteen 8 and 9 inch Navy guns lent by Admiral Porter, with crews to fight them, are being put in position. General Grant is considering the subject of sudden attack in great force on the south, where there are no siege lines and where enemy expect nothing. From the drift of his remarks, however, I conclude he will not adopt the measure. Another brigade of N. Kimball's has arrived, and is now at Haynes' Bluff. Kimball has been ordered with his whole division to Mechanicsburg, to increase and to command the observing force previously sent there under Mower. Joe Johnston has sent some troops to Yazoo City, and appears to be occupying with small detachments the line thence to Canton."[19]

By chance, Stanton was writing to Dana that very same day: "Everything in the power of this Government will be put forth to aid General Grant. The emergency is not underrated here. Your telegrams are a great obligation, and are looked for with deep interest. I cannot thank you as much as I feel for the service you are now rendering. You have been appointed an assistant adjutant-general, with rank of major, with liberty to report to General Grant, if he needs you. The appointment may be a protection to you. I shall expect daily reports if possible."[20] Years later Dana explained that Stanton "was by nature a very anxious man. When he perceived from my dispatches that I was going every day on expeditions into dangerous territory, he became alarmed lest I might be caught by the Confederates; for as I was a private citizen it would have been difficult to exchange me [for a Rebel prisoner]. If I were in the regular volunteer service as an assistant adjutant general, however, there would be no trouble about an exchange, hence my appointment."[21]

The next day, 6 June, was a Saturday, and there was at Vicksburg what a Confederate chaplain in a Mississippi regiment considered "a shower of rain. I was curious to know whether the enemy would cease firing during the rain," he said. "Instead of that they rather increased it, no doubt getting a view of our men as they would arise to adjust their blankets. The harder it rained, the more frequent the fire."[22]

A lady from the Chicago office of the Sanitary Commission (a precursor of the Red Cross) considered it more than a shower. She called it a southern tornado. The sun was scorching hot on a bright clear day when she left a Union hospital in an ambulance wagon, at about 5 p.m., but, "Within twenty minutes after I left, I observed a cloud of inky blackness just above the horizon. As it rose and spread impetuously, its rim was exquisitely bordered with a pure white fringe that floated in graceful beauty from the edge of the towering masses of cloud that soon veiled the canopy with darkness. The artillery of heaven blazed and crashed till my heart almost ceased to beat." In fact, she found everything about the weather in Mississippi too extreme for her taste. "Here rains were torrents," she said, "and left rivers and ravines in their wake. The shimmering rays of the tropical sun melted, blistered, and licked up the moisture of the valleys and hillsides. . . . Winds were tornados, snapping the trunks of lofty pines and cedars as stems of pipe-clay."[23] She wasn't kidding about the latter: only a last-second burst of speed saved her ambulance from being crushed by a falling tree.

The shower or storm, or whatever it was, didn't stop the digging. Captain Hickenlooper's notes for 6 June say: "Two 24-pounder howitzers and one 6-pounder placed in advanced battery, within 100 yards of Fort Hill. Carried the main trench down to and lead-sap across the road."[24]

"On June 6th," Dana later remembered, "the reports from Satartia, our advance up the Yazoo, were so unsatisfactory that Grant decided to examine the situation there himself. That morning he said to me at breakfast: 'Mr. Dana, I am going to Satartia to-day; would you like to go along?' I said I would, and we were soon on horseback, riding with a cavalry guard to Haynes's Bluff, where we took a small steamer reserved for Grant's use and carrying his flag. Grant was ill and went to bed soon after he started. We had gone up the river to within two miles of Satartia, when we met two gunboats coming down. Seeing the general's flag, the officers in charge of the gunboats came aboard our steamer and asked where the general was going. I told them Satartia.

"'Why,' said they, 'it will not be safe. Kimball has retreated from there, and is sending all his supplies to Haynes's Bluff. The enemy is probably in the town now.' I told them Grant was sick and asleep, and that I did not want to waken him. They insisted that it was unsafe to go on, and that I would better call the general. Finally I did so, but he was too sick to decide. 'I will leave it with you,' he said. I immediately said we would go back to Haynes's Bluff, which we did. The next morning Grant came out to breakfast fresh as a rose, clean shirt and all, quite himself. 'Well, Mr. Dana,' he said, 'I suppose we are at Satartia now.' 'No, general,' I said, 'we are at Haynes's Bluff.' And I told him what had happened."[25]

One reason for reprinting this account in detail here is that there has been much suspicion that when Dana said Grant was "sick" he meant "drunk." This is a possibility. A letter written by Rawlins to Grant at 1 a.m. on 6 June complained that "I find you where the wine bottle has just been emptied, in company with those who drink and urge you to do likewise." But if Grant was drunk, it was not obvious, even to the ever-suspicious Rawlins, who could only cite as evidence Grant's "lack of your usual promptness and decision, and clearness in expressing yourself in writing." That he was far from certain can be seen from the fact that he added, "If my suspicions are unfounded, let my friendship for you and my zeal for my country be my excuse for this letter."[26]

Long after the war, newspaper correspondent Sylvanus Cadwallader, who had attached himself to Grant's headquarters, claimed to have gone along on this trip to Satartia; that Grant got drunk at the steamer's bar; that it was Cadwallader who had put the general to bed; that he had later seen Grant drinking again on the boat and again after going ashore; and that he had eventually procured an ambulance wagon with which he had delivered the inebriated general into Rawlins' hands. This story seems very unlikely. After the war Rawlins certified a copy of his 6 June letter as being accurate and added, "Its admonitions were heeded and all went well."[27] Anyway, had Grant really been that drunk, it would have been Dana's duty to report it to Stanton, but there is no hint of such a thing in his report of the trip upriver written as soon as he got back.

Instead, in that message, written from Haynes' Bluff on 7 June, Dana told Stanton: "On approaching to within 2 miles of Satartia last evening, we found that N. Kimball had retreated to Oak Ridge Post-Office, sending the commissary stores and baggage by the river to this place. The gunboats were also coming down, and General Grant returned here with them. The reason for Kimball's movement appears to be an extraordinary fall in the Yazoo, which caused him to fear that his supplies might become insecure at Satartia. His affair on the 4th was but a small skirmish, in which he took some 40 prisoners, with no loss to himself, as I am informed from Kimball. We have no official report. A rebel deserter reports that General W. H. T. Walker is at Yazoo City with eight brigades, and that Joe Johnston is advancing from

Canton to the Big Black with a large force."[28]

Down in Louisiana on 7 June, the force under General Paine that Banks had sent toward Clinton, Louisiana, two days before, finally reached that town, but the only Rebels it found there were twenty sick and wounded men, who were captured.

Pemberton was writing to Joe Johnston that same day: "I am still without information from you later than your dispatch of the 25th. The enemy continues to intrench his positions around Vicksburg. I have sent out couriers to you almost daily. The same men are constantly in the trenches, but are still in good spirits, expecting your approach. The enemy is so vigilant that it is impossible to obtain reliable information. When may I expect you to move, and in what direction? My subsistence may be put down for about twenty days."[29]

Johnston answered, perhaps coincidentally, before the day was out: "We are nearly ready to move, but don't know the best route. Co-operation is absolutely necessary. Tell us how to effect it, and by what route to approach." However, a note in Johnston's letter-book said this message was "Sent by Colonel Sprague's servant; not delivered."[30] Getting any messages in or out of Vicksburg was becoming increasingly difficult. One method used, apparently, was by way of the rivers. One courier, named Absalom Grimes, later claimed that he and a friend named Bob would paddle a small skiff up and down the Mississippi and Yazoo at night, wearing uniforms taken from captured Federals and carrying messages in water-proof tin boxes suspended out of sight below the water.

Captain Hickenlooper's notes for the seventh are short: "Have a constant detail of 70 men, under immediate charge of General Leggett or staff officer. Work progressing finely."[31] (Brigadier General Mortimer Leggett commanded the 2nd Brigade of the 3rd Division of McPherson's 17th Corps.) The seventh, a Sunday, was "very hot and clear," noted Sergeant Tunnard of the 3rd Louisiana – the unit that manned the very fort toward which Hickenlooper was digging – "the mortars after several hours' silence, opened fire again, very lively. This Sabbath-day finished the third week of the siege, and still no hopes of relief. The men did not lose heart, but still kept in fine spirits. The members of the regiment fought today with renewed vigor, and a reckless exposure of their persons, killing and wounding a large number of the enemy. Heavy firing was heard west of the Mississippi, afterward ascertained to have been an attack on the Yankee forces at Milliken's Bend by the troops of the Trans-Mississippi Department."[32]

On the west side of the Mississippi River, just above Vicksburg, the Federal government had seized several abandoned plantations and was leasing them to escaped slaves. To protect these and to recruit and train new regiments of former slaves, there were still small military camps at Milliken's Bend, Young's Point, and Lake Providence, where once three corps of Grant's army had camped before marching down the river to below Vicksburg. For the last couple of days, advance scouts of General Taylor's Confederates had been spying out this area, as his main force, consisting mostly of John Walker's division, approached from the southwest. Taylor, son of President Zachary Taylor, was a lawyer before the war, not a soldier, but he had learned his trade as commander of a brigade of Louisiana troops in Stonewall Jackson's Shenandoah Valley campaign of the previous year. He was a man of considerable talents and energy.

"At Lake Providence," Taylor later reported, "the enemy had a few companies (perhaps four), and a large number of negroes arriving. Below that point to Milliken's he had a number of plantations at work under the new system. At Milliken's there was a negro brigade of uncertain strength and four companies of the Tenth Illinois Cavalry. . . . Between Milliken's and Young's Point (opposite the mouth of the Yazoo), a distance of 11 miles, tents were scattered in large numbers, most of them empty or occupied by sick and convalescents. At Young's were some 500 or 600 men, detachments and convalescents."

So, Taylor decided, Colonel Frank A. Bartlett, with about 900 mounted men, would be sent to strike the post that was both the weakest and the farthest north, Lake Providence. The infantry would take on the other two posts. Because of the heat of the days at this time of the year, and to lessen "the risk of annoyance by gunboats," Taylor decided to approach these positions by a night march from the town of Richmond, Louisiana, some ten miles south of Milliken's Bend. "I instructed General Walker to send one brigade to Young's, one to Milliken's, and hold the third in reserve at a point 6 miles from Richmond." Twenty men from another cavalry battalion, who were supposedly familiar with the area, were sent with each of the attacking columns. Taylor also sent his signals officer, Lieutenant S. M. Routh, and some of his men with the brigade heading for Young's Point, from which place they were to try to communicate with the garrison of Vicksburg, across the great river. "The two columns," Taylor said, "after clearing the points aimed at, were to march up and down the river, respectively, to Duckport, nearly equidistant from Young's and Milliken's. . . ." clearing the river bank of all armed resistance.[33] Since only Walker's division would be engaged, Taylor left the actual execution of the plan to him. Walker elected to stay with the reserve brigade and left the actual attacks up to his two brigadiers. This turned out to be a mistake.

The troops were already an hour behind schedule when they left Richmond. The brigade of Brigadier General Henry E. McCulloch, a former Texas Ranger, was the one selected to attack Milliken's Bend. Having the shorter distance to travel, it was within about a mile and half of the Union camp when the attached cavalry scouts were fired on by Federal pickets. McCulloch's skirmishers drove the pickets back, and the brigade advanced about a quarter of a mile, until it was fired on by a sizable force from the cover of a large hedge. He formed part of his command into line of battle and it drove the Federals from this hedge to another, about 600 yards behind the first one, and from it to yet another. But the only way the Confederates could pass through these hedges was by means of small openings that had been left by the plantation owner for his own use, and this broke up their formations completely, after which the men had to be reformed into line under a galling fire. At last they got through the last hedge only to find themselves confronted by a levee, about 25 yards away, which the Union troops were using as a parapet. It was ten feet high and topped in many places with cotton bales.

Three of McCulloch's regiments charged this levee, behind which was a sizable Union camp, "carrying it instantly," McCulloch said, "killing and wounding many of the enemy by their deadly fire, as well as the bayonet. This charge was resisted by the negro portion of the enemy's force with considerable obstinacy, while the white or true Yankee portion ran like whipped curs almost as soon as the charge was ordered. There were several instances in this charge where the enemy crossed bayonets with us or were shot down at the muzzle of the musket."[34]

Brigadier General Elias S. Dennis, overall commander of the Union forces in the area, claimed that when the Rebels charged the levee they did so "with cries of 'no quarter!'" He said, "The African regiments being inexperienced in the use of arms, some of them having been drilled but a few days, and the guns being very inferior [old Austrian smoothbore muskets], the enemy succeeded in getting upon our works before more than one or two volleys were fired at them. Here ensued a most terrible hand-to-hand conflict of several minutes duration, our men using the bayonet freely and clubbing their guns with fierce obstinacy, contesting every inch of ground, until the enemy succeeded in flanking them, and poured a murderous enfilading fire along our lines, directing their fire chiefly at the officers, who fell in numbers. Not till they were overpowered and forced by superior numbers did our men fall back behind the bank of the river, at the same time pouring volley after volley into the ranks of the advancing enemy."[35]

Beyond the camp there was another levee at the river's edge, behind which the Federals made their final stand. Again the Rebels advanced, "using the bayonet freely," as Walker put it. "At the second levee, however, our men encountered the main force of the enemy, entirely covered from our fire, and, after a gallant effort to carry this position, were compelled to fall back behind the first levee, which we continued to hold until the wounded were sent to the rear, and the men, exhausted by the excessive heat of the day and want of water, were withdrawn in good order by General McCulloch." The reserve brigade and artillery was brought forward by Walker in answer to requests for reinforcements, "but did not reach the scene of action," he said, "until General McCulloch, having several times failed to carry the second levee, had drawn off his brigade. In the mean time the enemy's gunboats (four in number) had taken position so as to rake the open space between the second levee and the river with grape and canister. . . . Under such circumstances it would have been folly to have persisted in the attack. . . ."[36]

General Dennis said that when the Rebels fell back, "Our men, seeing this movement, advanced upon the retreating column, firing volley after volley at them while they remained within gunshot. The gunboat Lexington then paid her compliments to the fleeing foe in several well-directed shots, scattering them in all directions."[37]

Taylor complained in his report that there had at first been only one gunboat, mounting a single gun, plus some unarmed transports that the troops had taken for gunboats, but said, "General Walker reported to me that three additional gunboats, attracted by the firing, had arrived; that he could find no position from which to use his artillery, and that the prostration of the men from the intense heat prevented him from marching down to Duckport, as directed. It is true the heat was intense, the thermometer marking 95 degrees in the shade; but, had common vigor and judgment been displayed, the work would have been completed by 8 a.m. . . . In this affair General McCulloch appears to have shown great personal bravery, but no capacity for handling masses." He also complained, that, although a "very large number of the negroes were killed and wounded . . . unfortunately, some 50, with 2 of their white officers, [were] captured," and asked Kirby Smith what he should do with them.[38] Charles Dana later reported to Secretary Stanton that Union Colonel T. Kilby Smith, who witnessed the fight at Milliken's Bend, "certified in an official statement that the rebels carried a black flag bearing a death's head and cross-bones."[39]

Brigadier General J. M. Hawes' brigade of three Texas regiments had set out for Young's Point, twenty miles away, at 7 p.m. on the 6th. When about halfway to his objective he discovered that the bridge over Walnut Bayou had been destroyed, and the lieutenant commanding the cavalry scouts sent with him, who lived near there, said there was no other crossing. However, Hawes heard of another bridge some six miles away and sent an officer to find it. He came back about 4 a.m. on the 7th with word that the other bridge was in good order, and Hawes marched his column that way. By 10:30 a.m. it was within a mile and three quarters of the Union camp at Young's Point, and there it encountered and drove in the Union pickets. Hawes then formed two regiments in line of battle, with the third in reserve and approached the enemy camp through some woods and came to a large clearing in view of the camp and the river – a clearing that should not have been there according to what the cavalry scouts had told him. Hawes saw what he took to be three gunboats in the river and three regiments of Union reinforcements entering the camp and gave the order to fall back into the cover of the woods.

The gunboats began shelling the woods between him and the camp, and he discovered that over a third of his men were too exhausted to fight. Two hundred of these had to be carried to the rear. "Knowing that General McCulloch had withdrawn from Milliken's Bend without carrying the position, and had asked for re-enforcements, and that the general commanding division had marched to his assistance with Colonel Randal's brigade, and that I could not carry the camp and destroy the stores there without a useless sacrifice of life," Hawes later reported, "I determined to retire by the road I came."[40] Lieutenant Routh, Taylor said, "asked General Hawes if any attempt was to be made to communicate with Vicksburg (in sight with a good glass), and received a negative reply. Lieutenant Routh then attempted to make his own way down the Point, but, meeting some armed Yankees and negroes, was forced to return."[41]

General Walker was inclined to be forgiving of Hawes' lack of aggressiveness, saying, "I am satisfied that the conviction must have been overpowering that the attack would fail after a useless sacrifice of life, or he would not have taken the responsibility he did."[42] Taylor did not feel so generous, complaining that Hawes had "consumed seventeen hours in marching 19 miles over a good road without impediments," that the enemy had fired only two shots at his command, one killing a horse and the other wounding a cavalry scout, and that he had "returned to the junction of the roads in less time than he had taken to advance." In short, he was very unhappy with the whole command. "I discovered too late," he reported, "that the officers and men of this division were possessed of a dread of gunboats such as pervaded our people at the commencement of the war. To this circumstance and to want of mobility in these troops are to be attributed the meager results of the expedition."[43]

Admiral Porter would have been happy to concur in Taylor's accusations about fear of gunboats in the Confederate ranks. "Last night, or early this morning," he wrote to Grant, "the rebels, supposed to amount to 3,000 or 4,000 strong, attacked Milliken's Bend, and nearly gobbled up the whole party. Fortunately, I heard of it in time to get the Choctaw and Lexington up there just as the attack commenced. The rebels got into our camps and killed a good many negroes, and left about 80 of their number killed on the levee. Our troops (mostly negroes) retreated behind the banks, near the water's edge, and the gunboats opened so rapidly on the enemy that they scampered off, the shells chasing them as far as the woods. They got nothing but hard knocks. The moment I heard of it I went up in the Black Hawk and saw quite an ugly sight. The dead negroes lined the ditch inside of the parapet, or levee, and were mostly shot on the top of the head. In front of them, close to the levee, lay an equal number of rebels, stinking in the sun. There knapsacks contained four days's provisions. They were miserable looking wretches.... I think we want more force here, and everything at Young's Point moved over on the opposite side of the river, near the mouth of the Yazoo, where there is a good landing."[44]

"This engagement at Milliken's Bend became famous,"

Charles Dana said, "from the conduct of the colored troops. General E. S. Dennis, who saw the battle, told me that it was the hardest fought engagement he had ever seen. It was fought mainly hand to hand. After it was over many men were found dead with bayonet stabs, and others with their skulls broken open by butts of muskets. 'It is impossible,' said General Dennis, 'for men to show greater gallantry than the negro troops in that fight.' The bravery of the blacks in the battle at Milliken's Bend completely revolutionized the sentiment of the army with regard to the employment of negro troops. I heard prominent officers who formerly in private had sneered at the idea of the negroes fighting express themselves after that as heartily in favor of it."[45]

∽ Endnotes ∽

1 *OR*, I:27:III:6-7.
2 H. B. McClellan, *I Rode With Jeb Stuart* (Da Capo Press edition, New York, 1994), 261.
3 *OR*, I:27:III:859-60.
4 Ibid., I:27:I:30.
5 Ibid., I:27:I:31.
6 Ibid.
7 Ibid., I:27:I:31-2.
8 Ibid., I:27:I:32-3.
9 Ibid., I:27:II:293.
10 Ibid., I:27:II:778.
11 Ibid., I:27:II:779.
12 Ibid., I:27:III:861.
13 Ibid., I:27:II:784.
14 Ibid., I:24:I:225.
15 Ibid., I:24:I:224-5.
16 Hoehling, *Vicksburg: 47 Days of Siege*, 107.
17 *OR*, I:24:II:200.
18 Hoehling, *Vicksburg: 47 Days of Siege*, 107.
19 *OR*, I:24:I:93.
20 Ibid.
21 Dana, *Recollections of the Civil War*, 90.
22 Hoehling, *Vicksburg: 47 Days of Siege*, 116.
23 Ibid., 111.
24 *OR*, I:24:II:200.
25 Dana, *Recollections of the Civil War*, 90-1.
26 Catton, *Grant Moves South*, 463.

27 Ibid., 464.
28 *OR*, I:24:I:94.
29 Ibid., I:24:III:953.
30 Ibid.
31 Ibid., I:24:II:200.
32 Hoehling, *Vicksburg: 47 Days of Siege*, 119.
33 *OR.*, I:24:II:458.
34 Ibid., I:24:II:467.
35 Ibid., I:24:II:447.
36 Ibid., I:24:II:464.
37 Ibid., I:24:II:448.
38 Ibid., I:24:II:459.
39 Ibid., I:24:I:102.
40 Ibid., I:24:II:472.
41 Ibid., I:24:II:459.
42 Ibid., I:24:II:465.
43 Ibid., I:24:II:459-60.
44 Ibid., I:24:II:453-4.
45 Dana, *Recollections of the Civil War*, 93.

Part Two
UNCERTAINTY

CHAPTER 6

"If the War Was a Tournament"
7 – 9 June 1863

THAT SAME SEVENTH DAY OF JUNE, Union soldiers sacked and burned Jefferson Davis's plantation, south of Vicksburg. Much, much farther to the south, 40,000 French troops occupied Mexico City that day, knowing that the United States was too busy with its Civil War to enforce the Monroe Doctrine.

In Virginia that morning, Lee arrived at Culpeper Court House. The next step in his move to take the war across the Potomac would be a big one: to move into the Shenandoah Valley and clear it of Union troops. To prepare for this move, he wrote ahead to several commanders. One message went to Brigadier General John D. Imboden, who commanded the small mixed force known as the Northwestern Brigade. Lee wanted him, after leaving a guard at Shenandoah Mountain to protect his rear, to cross the mountains west of the Shenandoah Valley into the valley of the South Branch of the Potomac River as soon as possible to "attract the enemy's attention" away from the Shenandoah, "detaining whatever force they may have at New Creek, Cumberland, Cacapon, &c. . . . striking them a damaging blow at any point where opportunity offers, and where you deem most practicable. It will be important, if you can accomplish it, to destroy some bridges, so as to prevent communication and the transfer of re-enforcements to Martinsburg [in the Shenandoah]." After accomplishing this, he should, if possible, "co-operate with any troops that you may find in the Valley."[1]

To Brigadier General Albert G. Jenkins, who had recently been transferred from southwest Virginia to the Shenandoah

Valley with a part of his large cavalry brigade, Lee wrote, "I desire you to have your command ready to be concentrated at Strasburg or Front Royal, or any point in front of either by Wednesday, the 10th instant, with a view to co-operate with a force of infantry. . . . Send me all the information you have about the position and strength of the enemy at Winchester, Martinsburg, Charlestown, Berryville, and any other point where they may be. Keep your horses as fresh as you can, and have your whole command prepared for active service."[2] He also wrote to Jenkins' former boss, Major General Samuel Jones, commander of the Department of Western Virginia, informing him of what orders he had given to Imboden, so that Jones could watch for any move by the Federals from his area toward the Shenandoah, and asking him to send Jenkins any more of his cavalry that he could spare.

Samuel Jones, incidentally, had just received word that the Federals in Kentucky, under Burnside, were planning a move into East Tennessee, and he wrote to two of his brigade commanders that day warning them to be ready on short notice to move to reinforce Major General Simon Bolivar Buckner's Department of East Tennessee. (Word that Burnside's plans had been disrupted by the necessity of sending reinforcements to Grant had not yet been received by Jones.) Jones was also writing to Colonel A. L. Long, Lee's military secretary, that day, in answer to a letter from him of the 3rd, discussing the units of Jenkins' cavalry brigade that the latter had left behind in Jones's department: "I earnestly desired to contribute all that I could from this department to General Lee's army, and think I have done so. If I were to yield to the calls of General Lee on my right and General Buckner on my left, this department would soon be without troops. I must, therefore, decline – and I do it with reluctance – detaching any more troops from my command without an order from the War Department."[3]

Another message Lee sent was to Major General Isaac R. Trimble, who had recently been assigned to command in the Shenandoah Valley, telling him what orders had been sent to Imboden and Jenkins, and adding, "Not knowing whether you have yet reached Staunton, I have sent these orders direct to those officers, but should you have assumed command of the Valley District, I beg you to facilitate their execution. I have sent no special directions concerning the Maryland troops in the Valley, but if they can be serviceable with General Jenkins, they had better operate with him, or, at least, be so disposed as to guard the approaches up the Valley while General Jenkins is operating below. Should you have entered upon your duties in the Valley, and your health be sufficiently restored, you are, of course, at liberty to accompany the troops, and take part in their operations."[4]

On the north side of the Rappahannock, the Federals were busy preparing a move across that river to attack Stuart's concentration of cavalry in Culpeper Country. Captain Ulric Dahlgren of Hooker's staff brought that general's instructions to Pleasonton on this seventh day of June, as Hooker didn't want to entrust it to the telegraph wires. In these orders, Dan Butterfield, Hooker's chief of staff, told Pleasonton to "cross the Rappahannock at Beverly and Kelly's Fords, and march directly on Culpeper. For this you will divide your cavalry force as you think proper, to carry into execution the object in view, which is to disperse and destroy the rebel force assembled in the vicinity of Culpeper, and to destroy his trains and supplies of all description to the utmost of your ability."[5]

Pleasonton temporarily divided his cavalry corps into two commands: The Reserve Brigade and the 1st Division under Buford, and the 2nd and 3rd Divisions under Brigadier General David M. Gregg. Because the cavalry was still badly understrength, due to the condition of its horses, it would be reinforced by detachments of picked infantry assembled into two brigades, commanded by brigadier generals Adelbert Ames, from the 11th Corps, and D. A. Russell, from the 6th Corps. Messages were hurried back and forth between army headquarters, Pleasonton's headquarters, and the various subordinate units, as the forces quietly assembled near the river while trying not to give their presence away to the Confederates on the other side.

The following day, Monday, 8 June, General Richard Taylor wrote from Richmond, Louisiana, a long report on his unsuccessful attacks on Milliken's Bend and Young's Point (extensively quoted in the previous chapter). He said he had not heard from Colonel Bartlett – who had been sent against the Union camps at Lake Providence – since the 5th, at which time he had been about 25 miles from that place, building a bridge across Macon Bayou. "If he succeeds in the operations intrusted to him, the west bank of the Mississippi River from the mouth of Red River to the Arkansas line will be free from the presence of the enemy. I shall use every exertion by placing an adequate force of cavalry and light artillery on the bank of the river to annoy and interfere with the navigation of the stream by transports, upon which Grant is dependent for his supplies by way of the Yazoo River. As soon as Tappan's brigade can reach Richmond, I shall withdraw Walker's division to operate south of Red River. . . . I leave this evening for Monroe and Alexandria, to look after affairs in the southern portion of the State, which are every day increasing in interest."[6] With most of Banks' forces tied down at Port Hudson, Taylor saw opportunities to recover lost ground in the rest of the state.

That same day, Grant sent Mower's brigade, which had been between the Yazoo and the Big Black, across the Mississippi to help defend the camps there in case of another Confederate attack in that quarter. "He is sent merely for temporary service," he informed General Dennis, "to repel any threatened attack. With the force you will have with this accession, I think you can drive the enemy beyond the Tensas River. If, however, you think more force is required, let me know, and it will be promptly sent. If the enemy is in the neighborhood of Richmond, he should be driven from there, and our troops should push on to Monroe. Every vestige of an enemy's camp ought to be shoved back of that point. I am not fully advised of the force you are likely to meet, but cannot think it large. No such blind move could be made by an intelligent foe as to send more than a force for a raid into such a pocket. Let me hear what intelligence you have from the rebel forces concentrating on the peninsula." He added a P.S. "You understand that all the troops in the District of Northeastern Louisiana, both black and white, are subject to your orders. At lake Providence you have two white regiments that can join you in any movement toward Monroe."[7]

Also, Grant's headquarters issued orders that day assigning Major General Cadwallader C. Washburn "to the command of all the troops of the Sixteenth Army Corps now here and to arrive. He will establish his headquarters at Haynes' Bluff, and prosecute the defenses of that place with all possible dispatch."[8] Washburn, who was thus given a corps-sized command, was, despite the difference in spelling, a brother of Elihu Washburne, representative in Congress of the Illinois district where Grant had lived before the war, and who had been instrumental in getting Grant promoted from colonel to brigadier general early in the conflict. Cadwallader Washburn was, or had been, a politician as well, having served as a Republican Congressman from Wisconsin. (A third brother, Israel, had also been a Congressman and governor of Maine.) "I know Washburn very well," Charles Dana later wrote to Secretary Stanton, "both as a politician & a military man, and I say frankly that he has better qualifications for the latter than the former function. He is brave, steady, respectable; receives suggestions & weighs them carefully; is not above being advised, but acts with independence nevertheless. His judgment is good and his vigilance sufficient. I have not seen him in battle however, and cannot say how far he holds his mind there. I don't find in him, I'm sorry to say, that effort to learn the military art, which every commander ought to exhibit, no matter whether he has received a military education or not. Washburn's whole soul is not put into the business of arms, & for me that is an unpardonable defect. But he is a good man, and above the average of our generals, at least of those in Grant's command."[9]

Dana wrote a report to Stanton at 10 that morning: "I have just returned from the vicinity of Mechanicsburg, whither I went with a party of cavalry from Haynes' Bluff yesterday. There were no signs of any considerable force of the enemy, though Kimball had retreated from there the day before in a semi-panic. No doubt Johnston has moved some of his troops this side of the Big Black, but his main force yet stays at Canton. The idea of operating in that direction, both for devastation and for more direct military objects, General Grant has by no means abandoned. His intention has been to put C. C. Washburn in command there, but I now think he will send Sherman with a force of from 15,000 to 20,000 troops, including 2,500 cavalry. . . .

"Advices from Port Hudson to the 4th instant were brought yesterday by Col. J. Riggin, of General Grant's staff. The siege has not reached a decisive point. General Banks thinks if he had 10,000 troops more he could reduce the place in a few days, but we have not facts enough to understand the grounds of this opinion. So far as it is possible to judge at this distance, a regular siege is as indispensable there as it is here. The reason General Banks gives for not co-operating with General Grant is that he could not spare more troops from his own army and still hold New Orleans safe against any possible attack; then he would, by giving up the siege, liberate the enemy to join Johnston. Milliken's Bend and Young's Point were both attacked day before yesterday [sic] by a body of rebels reported at about 1,500. At Milliken's Bend the negro troops at first gave way, but hearing that those of their number who were captured were killed, they rallied with great fury and routed the enemy. The white troops at Young's Point also repulsed him decisively."[10]

Also that day, Grant answered President Lincoln's message of 2 June, about whether he was in touch with Banks, by sending him Banks' letter of the 4th, just received. "I am in communication with him," Grant assured the President. "He has Port Hudson closely invested." He used the same phrase in a message to Halleck written that same day: "Vicksburg is closely invested. I have a spare force of about 30,000 men with which to repel anything from the rear. This includes all I have ordered from West Tennessee. Johnston is concentrating a force at Canton, and now has a portion of it west of Big Black River. My troops have been north as far as Satartia, and on the ridge back of that point there is no force yet. I will make a waste of all that country I can between the two rivers. I am fortifying Haynes' Bluff, and will defend the line from here to that point at all hazards." In a follow-up note he said, "It is reported that three divisions have left Bragg's army to join Johnston. Breckinridge is known to have arrived."[11]

"Although the presence of Joe Johnston on the east, and the rumors of invasion by Kirby Smith from the west, compelled constant attention," Dana later remembered, "the real work behind Vicksburg was always that of the siege. No amount of outside alarm loosened Grant's hold on the rebel stronghold. The siege went on steadily and effectively."[12] Captain Hickenlooper's notes for 8 June said: "Captain [Adoniram J.] Merritt placed on duty as assistant engineer. Placed traverse over main trench, and built magazine immediately south of advanced battery."[13]

"The struggle raged with unabated fury," wrote Sergeant Tunnard of the 3rd Louisiana, watching Hickenlooper's men dig toward the fort his regiment defended. "The enemy's lines were slowly but surely approaching nearer to our own breastworks, and the struggle was daily becoming more fierce and deadly. The Federals procured a [railroad] car-frame, which they placed on wheels, loading it with cotton-bales. They pushed this along the Jackson Road in front of the breastworks held by our Third Regiment. Protected by this novel, movable shelter, they constructed their works with impunity, and with almost the certainty of eventually reaching our entrenchments. Rifles had no effect on the cotton-bales, and there was not a single piece of artillery to batter them down. They were not a hundred yards from the regiment, and the men could only quietly watch their operations, and anxiously await the approaching hand-to-hand struggle."[14]

The bombardment of the town and its defenses also continued. "They are plowing up the land with their deadly missiles and sowing it with gunpowder," Henry Ginder, a civilian engineer employed by Pemberton's army, wrote in a letter to his wife. "Sometimes the powder falls around us, and sounds like a shower of rain among the trees. We are lulled to sleep by a lullaby of roaring cannon and bursting shells, and in the morning the same sounds take the place to our ears of birds singing and chanticleer's clear ring." He added that "The weather is growing so hot it fairly makes one dizzy to remain in the sun long, particularly on these dusty, white-looking sands where I breathe nothing but dust which fills my ears, eyes, nose, hair, everything."[15]

Willie Lord, then a young boy living in the town, remembered later in life how near he came to death during the siege. A spent artillery shell, moving slowly enough that his mother could see it as it passed just over his head, came close enough "to stir my hair," just as he bent over to pick up something off the ground. But Willie thought there was something else even scarier than the artillery. "Rifle-bullets made of lead and shaped like miniature beehives occasionally found their way into our valley among the larger shot and shell," he remembered. "These little messengers were called 'Minié balls,' and as they whistled past made a peculiar beelike sound, strangely in keeping with their beehive form, and ending with a thud as they struck the hillside or a tree. The sound, as I recall it, was, b-z-z-z-z-z-z-ip; and of nothing were we more afraid, for when we heard it the bullet was beyond all question close at hand. One of these 'Minié balls' struck and wounded, but not dangerously, a young girl as she was sitting with her parents on the piazza of her home, which, sheltered by a hill at the rear of the hospital, was considered safe. The bullet was at once located and extracted, and a clever convalescent soldier at the hospital transformed it later into a set of Lilliputian knives and forks, to the girl's infinite pride and delight."[16]

Confederate Secretary of War Seddon wrote to General Johnston from Richmond that day: "Do you advise more re-enforcements from General Bragg? You, as commandant of the department, have power to so order, if you, in view of the whole case, so determine. We cannot send from Virginia or elsewhere, for we stand already not one to two."[17] Johnston, some months before, had been put in charge of a strange super-department, called the Department of the West, which included both Bragg's army in

Middle Tennessee and Pemberton's Department of Mississippi and Eastern Louisiana, as well as Buckner's Department of East Tennessee. Johnston had not liked the assignment, feeling that there was little he could do to coordinate the forces in Tennessee with those on the Mississippi, and, when he had been ordered to go to Mississippi and take direct charge there, he had thought of this as a new assignment, and had not realized that the Confederate War Department still regarded him as overseeing the forces in Tennessee as well. But, now, it obviously did. That same day the Confederate Adjutant and Inspector General's office issued Special Orders No. 136 creating yet another department "within the geographical command of General J. E. Johnston," to consist of Mobile, Alabama, an important port on the Gulf of Mexico, "and the country containing the approaches to it, as well as that immediately around it."[18]

In Tennessee that day, General Rosecrans' headquarters sent a confidential circular to all of his corps and division commanders: "In view of our present military position, the general commanding desires you to answer, in writing, according to the best of your judgment, the following questions, giving your reasons therefor:

1. From the fullest information in you possession, do you think the enemy in front of us has been so materially weakened by detachments to Johnston or elsewhere that this army could advance on him at this time, with strong reasonable chances of fighting a great and successful battle?

2. Do you think an advance of our army at present likely to prevent additional re-enforcements being sent against General Grant by the enemy in our front?

3. Do you think any immediate or early advance of our army advisable?"[19]

Most of them answered "no" to all three questions, with explanations of varying lengths. One, with the perhaps-unfortunate name, for a Union general, of Brigadier General Jefferson C. Davis, commander of the 1st Division of the 20th Corps, gave one of the shortest, and one of the few even partially positive answers: "I do not believe Bragg's forces in our front have been materially weakened by sending re-enforcements to Vicksburg. I do not think a great and successful battle could be fought with reasonable chances of success at present. In my judgment, the chances of victory would be about equal, and I do not, therefore, recommend an immediate advance under the circumstances. I am of opinion, however, that an advance would have the effect of preventing Bragg from sending further re-enforcements to Mississippi."[20]

Most of the others thought that forcing Bragg back would only encourage him to send troops to Johnston, while an advance would only lengthen their own supply line and make it even more vulnerable to raids by Rebel cavalry; some said an advance would not keep Bragg from sending more troops to Johnston because he had already sent all he could afford to send; one said it would be impossible to advance until some other Union force occupied East Tennessee, because Rebel forces there would threaten their flank and rear if they should do so; and more than one suggested that Bragg could not have sent away more troops than he could afford to because to do so would be foolish and make him vulnerable to attack – therefore he probably hadn't, and therefore they shouldn't attack.

Special Field Orders No. 156 of Rosecrans' Department of the Cumberland were published that same day, reorganizing the force that had been known as the Army of Kentucky into a new unofficial Reserve Corps, still under the command of Major General Gordon Granger. Several regiments were transferred from it to the 14th and 21st Corps, and what had been the 4th Division of the 14th Corps was transferred into the new Reserve Corps, which would be composed of three divisions and continue to hold the area due south of Nashville, down to and including the town of Franklin, on the Harpeth River.

Two men came into the lines at that very town at about dark

that evening, dressed in Union uniforms and claiming to be a colonel and a major – an inspector-general and his assistant. Colonel J. P. Baird, commanding the post, was almost fooled, but a couple of his officers were more suspicious, so Baird wired their names to Rosecrans' chief of staff, Brigadier General James Garfield (the future President), to see if any such officers existed. Garfield replied that they must be spies, as "no such men have been accredited from these headquarters." With this the two men admitted that they were Confederate officers, and Baird wired Garfield again to ask, "what shall I do with them? My bile is stirred, and some hanging would do me good."[21]

"It was not esteemed a matter of congratulation," wrote Major McClellan of Jeb Stuart's staff, "when on the 7th of June notice was received that the commanding general [Lee] desired to review the cavalry on the following day. The invitation could not be declined; and on the 8th of June the brigades were assembled on the same field, and passed in review before the great leader of the Army of Northern Virginia."[22]

Although Lee was now on hand, there were not be so many pretty young ladies and other civilians present this time. There would, however, be far more soldiers in attendance. Besides Lee and his staff there were Longstreet and Ewell and their staffs. And one of Stuart's brigade commanders, Brigadier General Fitzhugh Lee (Robert E. Lee's nephew), had issued an off-hand invitation to Major General John Bell Hood, whose division of Longstreet's corps was not far off, to "Come and see the review, and bring any of your people." Hood had taken him up on it, perhaps more literally than had been intended, for he brought with him his entire division of infantry. Good humored Fitz Lee took it well but was concerned about the Confederate infantrymen's habitual teasing of the cavalry, whom they didn't quite consider real soldiers. "Well, don't let them halloo, 'Here's your mule!' at the review," Fitz said (an insinuation that the mounted men were farmers searching for their lost livestock); his fellow cavalry brigade commander, Brigadier General Wade Hampton of South Carolina, added, "If they do, we will charge you!" When Stuart spotted a sergeant in the horse artillery actually riding a mule he managed to head him off before he came to where Hood's men could see it, and hustled him off the field. The sergeant didn't mind, but later added that "the mule looked a little bit surprised, and, I think, felt ashamed of himself and his waving ears, which cost him his prominent position in the grand cavalcade."[23]

"Much less of display was attempted on this occasion," Major McClellan said, "for General Lee, always careful not to tax his men unnecessarily, would not allow the cavalry to take the gallop, not would he permit the artillerymen to work their guns. He would reserve all their strength for the serious work which must shortly ensue.... Longstreet and Ewell had already reached Culpeper Court House, and he wished his cavalry to move across the Rappahannock on the following day, to protect the flank of these corps as they moved northward. In preparation for this movement the brigades were, on the evening of the same day, moved down toward the river."[24]

Although ready to begin his movement toward the Shenandoah and the Potomac, Lee was still trying to coax a few more reinforcements out of the authorities at Richmond while preparing them for the move he was about to make without spelling it out in detail. He wrote to Secretary Seddon from Culpeper Court House that day, and, after a long paragraph in which he hoped to demonstrate that Union strength in North Carolina could not be as great as D. H. Hill thought it was, he added, "As far as I can judge, there is nothing to be gained by this army remaining quietly on the defensive, which it must do unless it can be re-enforced. I am aware there is difficulty and hazard in taking the aggressive with so large an army in its front, intrenched behind a river, where it cannot be advantageously attacked. Unless it can be drawn out in a position to be assailed, it will take its own time to prepare and strengthen itself to renew its advance upon Richmond, and force this army back within the intrenchments of that city. This may be the result in any event; still, I think it is worth a trial to prevent such a catastrophe. Still, if the Department thinks it better to remain on the defensive, and guard as far as possible all the avenues of approach, and await the time of the enemy, I am ready to adopt this course. You have, therefore, only to inform me.

"I think our southern coast might be held during the sickly season by local troops, aided by a small organized force, and the predatory excursions of the enemy be repressed. This would give us an active force in the field with which we might hope to make some impression on the enemy, both on our northern and western frontiers. Unless this can be done, I see little hope of accomplishing anything of importance. All our military preparations and organizations should now be pressed forward with the greatest vigor, and every exertion made to obtain some material advantage in this campaign."[25]

Lee also wrote to A. P. Hill, back at Fredericksburg, that day, answering a message from him: "I think from what you state and other indications, that the mass of General Hooker's army cannot be very near Fredericksburg. Its exact position or intention I have not yet discovered. If Pickett leaves [Hanover] Junction, I do not think three companies sufficient guard for that point. You had better place there a regiment. I requested [Brigadier General John R.] Cooke's brigade to be advanced there, but do not know whether it will be, or where it is. . . . Should you find the enemy in your front leaving you and going north, so that you can diminish your own force, you had better begin by sending forward Anderson's division to this place. If going south, he must be sent back to the Junction. I have just received your dispatch of to-day in reference to the enemy reappearing at Walkerton. I fear Pickett did not go far enough at their last visit, and they therefore supposed that we had no troops in that direction. I have telegraphed to him that he must drive them back. I have heard nothing more of the movements of the enemy extending up the Rappahannock since I last wrote."[26]

Also, Lee wrote to Colonel Josiah Gorgas, chief of ordnance

of the Confederate Army, that day, saying that he had just reviewed Stuart's five brigades of cavalry: "My attention was thus called to a subject which I have previously brought to your notice, viz, the saddles and carbines manufactured in Richmond. I could not examine them myself, but was assured by officers that the former ruined the horses' backs, and the latter were so defective as to be demoralizing to the men."[27] He said it was desirable to improve the quality of the equipment, even if the quantity should suffer.

Union commanders, meanwhile, continued to worry about the build-up of Confederate cavalry in Culpeper County. The headquarters of the Middle Department (at Baltimore, Maryland) sent telegrams that day to Major General Robert Milroy, commanding a division at Winchester, in the Shenandoah Valley, Brigadier General Benjamin Kelley, commanding the garrison at Harper's Ferry, and Brigadier General William Averell, commanding at Weston, West Virginia, saying: "A dispatch just received from General Halleck states – That the enemy is massing 12,000 cavalry and artillery in Culpeper County for a raid. Deserters say that the men have been given to understand that it is to be a long and desperate one. We shall not probably know the direction or intention of this raid until it is actually in motion. Have a sharp lookout, and keep these headquarters well informed of any movements."[28]

Milroy's reply was in turn passed on to Halleck: "Jenkins is still above Strasburg, but the greater part of the rebel cavalry have left the Valley to join Stuart at Culpeper. I learn from various sources that Lee has mounted the whole of Hood's infantry division. Their cavalry force at Culpeper is probably more than twice 12,000. I would advise that the militia of Maryland, Pennsylvania, and Ohio be at once called out, as there is doubtless a mighty raid on foot. A number of foreigners just from Richmond speak of a great movement of troops through Richmond from the South."[29] Of course, Hood's division had not been mounted, and even the estimate of 12,000 Rebel cavalry was somewhat exaggerated, the true total of the brigades with Stuart probably being closer to

10,000.

Meanwhile, General Halleck saw opportunity as well as menace in this apparent concentration of Confederate strength in Virginia, and he wrote to Major General J. G. Foster, commander of the Department of North Carolina, that day, saying: "All our information here indicates that nearly all the rebel troops in Georgia and South Carolina have been sent west, to raise the siege of Vicksburg, and that those in North Carolina have been brought north to re-enforce General Lee. If such is really the case, it is suggested that your army corps could resume offensive operations, destroy railroads, &c."[30]

While Lee reviewed Stuart's cavalry and prepared to begin the next stage of his movement toward the Shenandoah, Pleasonton's Union cavalry and its two supporting detachments of infantry moved into position in the woods just north of the two fords they would use to cross the Rappahannock River the next morning. Their approaches had been timed so that they arrived after dark; campfires were forbidden, and their presence was not detected by the Confederates on the other side of the river. At about 4:30 a.m. on Tuesday, the 9th day of June, troopers of the 8th New York Cavalry splashed across Beverly Ford, led by young Captain George Armstrong Custer of Pleasonton's staff. The 8th's colonel, Benjamin Franklin "Grimes" Davis, was commander of the brigade to which it belonged, the 1st of the 1st Division of the Cavalry Corps. Colonel Thomas C. Devin of the 6th New York Cavalry commanded the division, which, along with the Reserve Brigade, commanded by Major Charles Whiting of the Regular Army, and the infantry under General Ames, all came under the command of Brigadier General John Buford. Buford, whose Confederate cousin, Abraham Buford, was the commander of a brigade in Loring's Division of Joe Johnston's army out in Mississippi, was a West Point graduate (class of 1848); a compact, soldierly man in his middle 30s, who wore a large, tawny mustache but no beard. A colleague described him as "straightforward, honest, conscientious, full of good common sense, and always to be relied on in any emergency...."[31]

Pleasonton chose to accompany Buford's column. He was slightly older than Buford and had graduated from West Point four years ahead of him; a short, slim, dapper bachelor whose primary talent seemed to be one for self-promotion, even at the expense of the truth. He had commanded what little cavalry Hooker had kept with his main army during the recent Chancellorsville campaign, while then-corps-commander Stoneman had taken most of it off on a fruitless raid. Pleasonton had claimed credit for saving Hooker's army in the wake of Stonewall Jackson's rout of the 11th Corps, when in fact the cavalry charge he claimed to have ordered was just an accidental collision of troopers riding along a blind road and Confederate infantry forming along the same path. One cavalry officer said, "It is the universal opinion that Pleasonton's own reputation, and Pleasonton's late promotions are bolstered up by systematic lying."[32] Another said, "He does nothing save with a view to a newspaper paragraph."[33] Nevertheless, he was bold and aggressive, which were traits then much needed by the Union cavalry, but he was more interested in fighting and gaining glory than in providing Hooker with information about Lee's movements.

About six miles downstream, the troopers of Brigadier General David M. Gregg would cross at Kelly's Ford. Gregg, an 1855 graduate of West Point, was also a highly competent cavalry commander, but, like Buford and unlike Pleasonton, he avoided publicity. His most notable characteristic was an unflappable calm. His command consisted of his own 3rd Division of the Cavalry Corps, the 2nd Division, commanded by Colonel Alfred N. Duffié, and Russell's infantry detachment. Duffié, 28-year-old colonel of the 1st Rhode Island Cavalry, had formerly been an officer in the French cavalry (he was a graduate of St. Cyr), but he never seemed to quite measure up as a division commander. For instance, his division was late getting into position this morning after having arrived late at its designated camping spot the night before.

Buford and Gregg each had about 4,000 cavalrymen, most of them trained to fight on foot with their breechloading carbines as well from horseback with sabers and revolvers; and each had about 1,500 infantry attached, plus two batteries of horse artillery. So far as Pleasonton knew, Stuart's troopers were still camped around Culpeper Court House. He didn't know that many of them had been moved closer to the river in anticipation of crossing it themselves in the morning. Therefore, his plan was for Buford's and Gregg's columns to converge at the little village of Brandy Station, on the Orange & Alexandria Railroad, before moving on to Culpeper. Gregg's own division and that of Duffié were to take different roads, the latter moving more to the west, via the village of Stevensburg, while Gregg's turned to the northwest, toward Brandy Station. And so, that morning, the two large cavalry forces, Union and Confederate, each in ignorance of the other's location and strength, moved toward a violent collision. It would be the largest cavalry battle of the war.

Beverly Ford was picketed by Company A of the 6th Virginia Cavalry, part of the brigade of Brigadier General William E. Jones, which had recently been transferred from the Shenandoah Valley. Jones had been in the same class at West Point as John Buford. There were so many Joneses in the army that many of them acquired nicknames to help keep them straight. This one was known as "Grumble" Jones, and very aptly so, for complaining was one of his major talents. He and Stuart never got along. At the review the day before his brigade had been out of place, with his men loitering around as though not part of the affair. A lieutenant sent over by Stuart to prod them into place had been met with an angry response, but Jones had finally got his men into position.

Neither Jones's brigade nor the other new additions to Stuart's command quite fit in with his older outfits yet. The three brigades that had been with Stuart for the last several campaigns were used to his ways, and had been trained to perform more or less in the tradition of European light cavalry – to raid and to fight, of course, but mostly to serve as the eyes and ears of the main army. They almost always preferred to fight from horseback, although they more often preferred the revolver to the saber as their weapon of choice. The brigades that had just recently been added to Stuart's division – Jones's and that of Brigadier General Beverly Robertson, just up from North Carolina, and that of Albert Jenkins still off in the Shenandoah – because they had seldom served with a large army, and had mostly fought in small formations in heavily wooded terrain – were more like partisans or guerillas than regular cavalry, and were used to fighting dismounted, using horses mostly as a means of transportation to and from a fight. In fact, Robertson's two regiments came armed with British Enfield Rifles, which were somewhat shorter than the rifle muskets of the infantry but, being muzzle-loaders, were totally unsuited for use while the men were mounted.

It was standard procedure in Stuart's cavalry that when troopers were on picket duty their horses, including those of any reserve, should be kept saddled. Perhaps Grumble Jones didn't know that, or perhaps he just didn't feel like complying, but for whatever reason the horses of his brigade, including those of the 6th Virginia Cavalry, had been unsaddled and turned out to pasture for the night some distance from the brigade's camps.

Grimes Davis's Federal column had no problem overwhelming Jones's lone company of pickets, and it advanced southward in column of fours because of the narrowness of the road, which was flanked by ditches and woods on both sides. Fighting dismounted, dodging from tree to tree, the 6th Virginia slowed the Federals some, and hit them with a mounted charge by about 100 troopers whose horses happened to be near to hand, although they had to ride bare-back.

The Confederate horse artillery had been parked for the night between the 6th Virginia and the rest of Jones's brigade, and only the charge of the 100 mounted men gave the gunners a chance to get their pieces limbered (hooked to 2-wheel carts called "limbers," to which the horses were harnessed) and hasten to the rear, while Jones brought up the 7th Virginia – some mounted, some not, some only half-dressed. The 7th and the 6th regiments then made a more organized fighting withdrawal, but two slow-moving howitzers were almost captured and were only saved by a desperate charges by more of Jones's regiments coming up. During this fight Grimes Davis was mortally wounded, and Captain Custer took temporary command of the brigade. One Confederate charge came close to capturing Custer, whose horse didn't want to leave the supposed safety of a roadside fence. But eventually Devin's other brigade charged through the disorganized units of what had been Davis's brigade and drove the Rebels back again.

However, all this gave time for more Confederates to arrive, for by then Stuart had been informed that Union cavalry was across the river at Beverly Ford in force, and he moved to concentrate against them. He sent orders for the two Lees (Fitzhugh and Rooney) to bring down their brigades, which were farther north, sent his supply wagons back towards Culpeper Court House, and sent two regiments, one from Fitz Lee's brigade and one from Hampton's, to the nearby village of Brandy Station to guard the rear, for he had received word that more Union cavalry was crossing at Kelly's Ford, where only Robertson's two North Carolina regiments opposed Gregg's column. He sent another of Hampton's regiments to reinforce Robertson, then, leaving Major McClellan at his headquarters on Fleetwood Hill to receive any messages meant for him, he rode off with the rest of Hampton's brigade to join Jones's regiments and the horse artillery, which had taken position behind a stone wall at St. James Church with a half-mile of open ground before them that the Federals would have to cross to get at them.

Hampton came up on Jones's right, and Rooney Lee took position on the left, also behind a stone wall. The order to Fitz Lee's brigade was greatly delayed because the courier carrying it took it to young Lee himself, who was not with his brigade but some distance away – he was suffering from a bout of rheumatism – instead of to the brigade's temporary commander, Colonel Thomas Munford. Munford moved farther south, but did not join the fight. A series of small mounted probes by the Federals were easily repulsed, the last one drawing a brief pursuit, by which time both Buford and Pleasonton had reached the front. It was obvious to them that the plan for the Union columns to converge at Brandy Station before attacking was now impossible to implement. At 7:40 a.m. Pleasonton sent a brief message to General Hooker from Beverly Ford: "The enemy is in strong cavalry force here. We have had a severe fight. They were aware of our movement, and were prepared."[34] He would have the two brigades of the 1st Division hold on where they were, crowded among some woods not far from the ford, while he brought up the Reserve Brigade, the horse artillery, and Ames's infantry, and sent word to Gregg.

But Stuart was not willing to let things stand as they were. The Rebel line curved forward at both ends, threatening both Union flanks, and at around 10 a.m. he sent part of Hampton's brigade forward dismounted against Buford's left and drove it back, threatening to flank the entire Union line. Buford countered with a mounted charge by the 6th U.S. and 6th Pennsylvania Cavalry, both from the vaunted Reserve Brigade. Until recently the 6th Pennsylvania, recruited from the gentry of Philadelphia, had been the only regiment in either army armed with the lance, a weapon that had been much favored by Napoleon a half-century before. This charge against dismounted Rebels would have been an ideal chance to use them, but after a year of campaigning in the heavily wooded countryside of eastern Virginia, the lances had recently been discarded, so the "Lancers" used their sabers.

Despite the fire of Hampton's dismounted troopers and the Rebel horse artillery, the Pennsylvanians soon outdistanced the Regulars, crossed three wide, deep ditches – or most of them did – and made for the point where Hampton's and Jones's brigades met. Their commander, Major Robert Morris, was among the men and horses who piled up in one of the ditches and was soon captured. "I didn't know that Morris was not with us," wrote his next in command, Major Henry Whelan, "and we dashed on, driving the Rebels into and through the woods, our men fighting with the sabre alone, whilst they used principally pistols. Our brave fellows cut them out of the saddle and fought like tigers, until I discovered they were on both flanks, pouring a cross fire of carbines and pistols on us. . . ." The regiment's supports fell back and so did many of its own men, but others, rallied by Captain Dahlgren of Hooker's staff, rode on and attacked the gunners of the Confederate horse artillery before being driven off by a mounted counterattack. At last even these Pennsylvanians turned and fled for their own lines in what Whelan called a "race for life."[35]

Their charge had been costly but it had restored the balance between the opposing forces, and there followed another lull in the fighting while Pleasonton and Stuart both shifted units about and removed the dead and wounded men that could be reached. About noon Stuart received a warning from Grumble Jones that the Federals who had crossed farther downstream at Kelly's Ford were advancing in their direction. Stuart, who had never liked Jones, told the courier who brought this message, "Tell General Jones, to attend to the Yankees in his front, and I'll watch the flanks." When this was relayed to "Grumble" he said, "So he thinks they ain't coming, does he? Well, let him alone; he'll damn soon see for himself."[36]

At Kelly's Ford, Duffié's tardiness had thrown the whole timetable off, for his intended route was the longest and he was supposed to cross first. Instead of arriving at 3:30 a.m., as ordered, it was past 7 a.m. when his division started to cross, and 8 a.m. by the time the tail of Gregg's command was over the river. Fortunately for the Federals, there had been almost no opposition. Duffié's small 2nd Division set out to the southwest for the village of Stevensburg, from which he was to send detachments to watch the nearby fords over the Rapidan River and protect the southern flank of Pleasonton's forces. Gregg's 3rd Division followed for a while but turned off before going halfway, heading northwest toward Brandy Station. A division of Meade's 5th Corps moved over to cover Kelly's Ford after the cavalry passed, and may have sent 500 men across the river.

Robertson's two large North Carolina regiments were posted just north of Kelly's Ford, blocking the most direct road (near the river) to the scene of the battle near Beverly Ford. However,

Robertson stuck to a literal interpretation of his orders and made no effort to interfere with the Union move so long as it did not come up that one road he had been ordered to defend. Gregg's official report, written three days later, says he ordered his attached infantry to move up that road, but General Russell seems to have thought his job was merely to hold the ford so the cavalry could return that way if necessary. Russell faced off against Robertson and the two forces kept each other out of the serious fighting for the rest of the day. Somewhere along the road north, Gregg was met by another courier from Pleasonton "informing me of the severity of the fight on the right and of the largely superior force of the enemy," and since he had already been informed that Duffié had reached Stevensburg without opposition, he sent an order to that officer to turn back and bring his division up the same road Gregg had followed.[37]

Between 11 a.m. and 12 noon, Gregg's division reached the Orange & Alexandria Railroad at Brandy Station and turned to the right – the east – toward Fleetwood Hill, which was actually a low ridge about two miles long running roughly north and south. It was the highest ground in the area, and thus the key to the battlefield, and it was behind Jeb Stuart's lines. At that moment it was manned only by Major McClellan of Stuart's staff and a handful of couriers, for the two regiments sent there earlier had later been sent down toward Stevensburg to oppose Duffié's division. When a scout brought McClellan word of Federals advancing upon the Confederate rear he had thought it impossible and sent the scout back for another look. "In less than five minutes the man reported what I could now see for myself. And so it was!" McClellan turned to the only help that was at hand: a single cannon that had retired from the fight against Buford's column, because it was almost out of ammunition, and had then halted near the bottom of the hill. The major ordered it brought up to the crest. "A few imperfect shells and some round shot were found in the limber chest," he said; "a slow fire was at once opened upon the marching column, and courier after courier was dispatched to General Stuart to inform him of the peril."[38] The presence and fire of this one gun was enough to give the Union column pause – where there was one there were probably more, so Colonel Percy Wyndham, commander of the leading brigade, stopped to bring up some horse artillery of his own before proceeding.

When McClellan's first courier reached him, Stuart was skeptical. "Ride back there," he told Captain James Hart of the horse artillery, "and see what this foolishness is about!" But before Hart had gone very far one of Stuart's most trusted headquarters clerks came galloping up to the general, crying, "The Yankees are at Brandy!"[39] This exclamation was punctuated by the sound of artillery fire in that direction, and Stuart suddenly became a believer. He ordered Jones to send two regiments back to Fleetwood Hill, and he soon followed to see for himself. When he came within sight of the ridge he saw that the Union force was far too large for a mere two regiments to handle, and he sent orders for Hampton to send a couple as well. Hampton soon followed with the rest of his brigade, and the fight now became a real cavalry melee, with regiments, squadrons, even small groups or individual troopers, charging and countercharging until almost all formation was lost on both sides. Fresh units, as they were fed into the fight, having more order, usually swept the more disorganized units before them until they too lost their cohesion and fell to some more recent arrival.

"The country about Brandy Station is open, and on the south side extensive level fields, particularly suited for a cavalry engagement," Gregg later reported. "Coming thus upon the enemy, and having at hand only the Third Division (total strength 2,400), I either had to decline the fight in the face of the enemy or throw upon him at once the entire division. Not doubting but that the Second Division was near, and delay not being admissible, I directed the commanders of my advance brigade to charge the enemy, formed in columns about Brandy House. The whole brigade charged with drawn sabers, fell upon the masses of the enemy, and, after a brief but severe contest, drove them back, killing and wounding many and taking a large number of prisoners. Other columns of the enemy coming up, charged this brigade before it could reform, and it was driven back. Seeing this, I ordered the First Brigade to charge the enemy upon the right. This brigade came forward gallantly through the open fields, dashed upon the enemy, drove him away, and occupied the hill. Now that my entire division was engaged, the fight was everywhere most fierce. Fresh columns of the enemy arriving upon the ground received the vigorous charges of my regiments, and, under the heavy blows of our sabers, were in every instance driven back. Martin's battery of horse artillery, divided between the two brigades, poured load after load of canister upon the rebel regiments. Assailed on all sides, the men stood to the guns nobly. Thus for an hour and a half was the contest continued, not in skirmishing, but in determined charges."[40]

Feeling himself heavily outnumbered (Pleasonton was still in the process of realigning Buford's forces and failed to keep the Rebels in his front busy), and Duffié still not having arrived (his division being engaged with the two regiments sent down from Brandy Station), Gregg finally pulled back. "Retiring about 1 mile south of the station," he reported, "I again formed my brigades, and discovered the Second Division some distance in the rear. Hearing that General Russell had gotten up to General Buford's left with his infantry, I moved my command in the direction of Rappahannock Bridge, and soon united with General Buford's left. On the hills near Brandy Station the enemy had artillery posted, the fire of which they directed upon my line in this new position. A few guns well served were sufficient to prevent any advance in that direction.... The field having been well contested and the enemy being re-enforced with infantry, which could be thrown in any force upon us from Culpeper, I received orders from Brigadier-General Pleasonton to recross my command at Rappahannock Ford."[41]

During Gregg's fight, Buford sent the 2nd U.S. Cavalry and the 6th Pennsylvania to charge the left flank of the Rebel line facing him, held by the 9th Virginia Cavalry of Rooney Lee's brigade. It was probably Rooney himself who briefly crossed sabers with young Captain Wesley Merritt, soon to be a general himself;

neither was badly hurt, though Merritt lost his hat. But Lee was later wounded severely in the leg. Here, as on Gregg's front, there was charge and countercharge as other units were drawn into the fight, including part of Fitz Lee's brigade that finally got into the battle, and eventually the Federals were driven off.

The Confederates there were preparing an attack of their own when they discovered that Buford's column, like Gregg's, was withdrawing across the river. Dan Butterfield had replied at 12:10 p.m. to Pleasonton's message of 7:40 a.m., saying, "If you cannot make head against the force in front of you, return and take position on the north bank of the river, and defend it. At this distance it is impossible for the general to understand all of your circumstances. Exercise your best judgment, and the general will be satisfied."[42] Pleasonton's best judgment was to withdraw across the river before any large force of Confederate infantry butted into the fight.

The Rebels did little to interfere with this move, and Pleasonton sent a message to Hooker at 8 p.m. in which he claimed that he had information "from letters and official reports captured in the enemy's camp, as well as from prisoners, that the enemy had upward of 12,000 cavalry (which was double my own force of cavalry) and twenty-five pieces of artillery. . . . To-morrow morning Stuart was to have started on a raid into Maryland, so captured papers state. You may rest satisfied he will not attempt it."[43]

Upon being notified of the Union attack, General Lee had sent infantry to Stuart's support – a division of Longstreet's corps toward Stevensburg and one of Ewell's toward Brandy Station – but, as Major Charles Venable of his staff wrote to Stuart, "As the whole thing seems to be a reconnaissance to determine our force and position, he wishes these concealed as much as possible, and the infantry not to be seen, if it is possible to avoid it."[44]   None of the infantry got into the fight. Pleasonton was happy to agree, however, that the whole thing had just been a reconnaissance to try to find Lee's infantry, and claimed to thus have fulfilled his mission, although he still could not have said just which Rebel infantry units were present around Culpeper. Soon it was forgotten that his instructions had actually been "to disperse and destroy the rebel force."

So, although Stuart's cavalry was far from destroyed or even dispersed, the Union troopers rode away feeling good about what they had accomplished. For the first time they had stood up to the vaunted Rebel horsemen in an all-out major fight and had fought them on even terms. They had surprised them, chased them out of their camps, and on more than one occasion, forced them to flee for their lives. That the Federals had also chosen to flee from more than one charge was not so important; nor the fact that their losses were heavier than those of the Rebels; even the fact that three guns of the Union horse artillery had been left in Confederate hands did not seem to so bad. They had given Jeb Stuart a hard knock, and perhaps now their infantry comrades would not be so inclined to ask sarcastically, "Whoever saw a dead cavalryman?" As Major McClellan later wrote: "One result of incalculable importance certainly did follow this battle, – it *made* the Federal cavalry."[45]

Stuart, on the other hand, was humiliated. After the pomp and posturing of his grand reviews, to have the enemy cavalry suddenly descend upon him, not only crossing the river before he knew they were there but coming unseen upon the very rear of his battle line, made him look incompetent. He must have known that the whole army would soon be abuzz with talk, and it was. Nor were the newspapers silent. The Richmond *Examiner*, which had not forgotten the recent depredations of Stoneman's raid, ran a long editorial a few days later about "the necessary consequences of negligence and bad management" in Stuart's cavalry, saying, among much else: "If the war was a tournament, invented and supported for the pleasure of a few vain and weak-headed officers, these disasters might be dismissed with compassion. But the country pays dearly for the blunders which encourage the enemy to overrun and devastate the land, with a cavalry which is daily learning to despise the mounted troops of the Confederacy."[46]

As Stuart's West Point classmate, Dorsey Pender, commanding a division in Hill's corps, remarked upon hearing the criticism, "I suppose it is all right that Stuart should get all the blame, for when anything handsome is done he gets all the credit."[47] Veteran Confederate artilleryman Colonel Porter Alexander, in a letter to his father written a few days later, pronounced the great cavalry battle "a great humbug. Twelve or fifteen thousand engaged all day," he said, "and loss on our side not four hundred. I rode over the field the next day and saw only about twenty dead Yankees – only two killed with the sabre."[48]

∽ Endnotes ∽

1 OR, I:27:III:865.
2 Ibid., I:27:III:865-6.
3 Ibid., I:27:III:867-8.
4 Ibid., I:27:III:866-7.
5 Ibid., I:27:III:27.
6 Ibid., I:27:II:460-1.
7 Ibid., I:24:III:390.
8 Ibid., I:24:III:391-2.
9 Dana, *Recollections of the Civil War*, 82.
10 OR, I:24:I:94-5.
11 Ibid., I:24:I:41.
12 Dana, *Recollections of the Civil War*, 94.
13 OR, I:24:II:200.
14 Hoehling, *Vicksburg: 47 Days of Siege*, 125.
15 Ibid., 123.
16 Ibid., 126.
17 OR, I:24:I:226.
18 Ibid., I:24:III:956.
19 Ibid., I:23:II:394-5.
20 Ibid., I:23:II:395.
21 Ibid., I:23:II:398.
22 McClellan, *I Rode With Jeb Stuart*, 261-2.
23 Douglas Southall Freeman, *Lee's Lieutenants* (New York, 1944), III:3-4.
24 McClellan, *I Rode With Jeb Stuart*, 262.
25 OR, I:27:III:868-9.
26 Ibid., I:27:III:869.
27 Ibid., I:27:III:872-3.
28 Ibid., I:27:III:35.
29 Ibid., I:27:III:36.

30 Ibid., I:27:III:37.
31 Edward G. Longacre, *The Cavalry at Gettysburg* (Lincoln NB, 1986), 49-50.
32 Ibid., 49.
33 Ibid., 48.
34 *OR*, I:27:III:38.
35 Longacre, *The Cavalry at Gettysburg.*, 72.
36 Freeman, *Lee's Lieutenants*, III:9.
37 *OR*, I:27:I:950.
38 McClellan, *I Rode With Jeb Stuart*, 270. McClellan calls this piece a 6-pounder howitzer, but no such type of cannon existed; the smallest howitzers in use in this war were 12-pounders; the fact that it used solid shot (round shot) is strong evidence that it was not a howitzer but a gun. McClellan was not an artilleryman.
39 Freeman, *Lee's Lieutenants*, III:9.
40 *OR*, I:27:I:950-1.
41 Ibid, I:27:I:951.
42 Ibid., I:27:III:39.
43 Ibid., I:27:I:903-4.
44 Ibid., I:27:III:876.
45 McClellan, *I Rode With Jeb Stuart*, 294.
46 Freeman, *Lee's Lieutenants*, III:19.
47 Ibid., III:18.
48 Edwin B. Coddington, *The Gettysburg Campaign* (New York, 1968), 66.

CHAPTER 7

"To Secure Peace Through Victory"

9 – 12 June 1863

Out of fear of a Confederate Cavalry raid, or, as Hooker had suggested, of Lee's entire army moving across the Potomac, the Union War Department created, that same ninth day of June, two new military departments: The Department of the Susquehanna would include all of Pennsylvania east of Johnstown and the Laurel Hill mountain range and would be commanded by Major General Darius Couch, former commander of the 2nd Corps in the Army of the Potomac, with headquarters at Chambersburg; the Department of the Monongahela would cover the western portion of Pennsylvania, with headquarters at Pittsburgh, and was to be commanded by Major General W. T. H. "Bully" Brooks, who had commanded the 1st Division of the 6th Corps in the recent Chancellorsville campaign.

So far neither department had much to work with in the way of troops, but Secretary Stanton issued an order that same day authorizing the raising of what he called the Army Corps of the Monongahela "for the protection and defense of the public property within that department," the troops of which would serve "during the pleasure of the President or the continuance of the war."[1] They would not, however, receive the enlistment bonuses being offered other volunteers, nor was there any guarantee that they would not have to serve beyond the boundaries of the new department. In fact, there was no provision to pay them until Congress, which was not in session, authorized it.

Out near the Kentucky-Tennessee line that day, a cavalry action was fought along Kettle Creek. A small brigade of

Union cavalry of Burnside's department surprised a battalion of Brigadier General John Hunt Morgan's Kentucky Confederates, overrunning its camp and, according to Morgan, "capturing two pieces of artillery, wagons and stores, $25,000 public funds, and many men and horses, scattering the entire command. . . . There is now no force on the Cumberland River, and the entire rear of this flank [of Bragg's army] is exposed to raids, which no doubt the enemy will attempt, and, if successful, with most disastrous results."[2]

At Franklin, Tennessee, the two Confederates captured posing as Union officers were executed that day. Colonel Baird's bile seems to have calmed down, for he asked to have them taken somewhere else to be hanged, but was ordered by Garfield to do it himself. "The officers I executed this morning, in my opinion, were no ordinary spies, and had some mission more important that finding out my situation," Baird wrote to Garfield. "They came near dark, asked no questions about forces, and did not attempt to inspect works, and, after they confessed, insisted they were not spies in the ordinary sense, and that they wanted no information about this place. Said they were going to Canada and something about Europe; not clear. We found on them memorandum of commanding officers and their assistant adjutant-generals in Northern States. Though they admitted the justice of the sentence and died like soldiers, they would not disclose their true object. Their conduct was very singular, indeed; I can make nothing of it."[3] Possibly the two Confederates were attempting to make their way through Union lines to contact Copperheads in the states north of the Ohio River, or to reach Canada and perhaps go on to Europe from there. Maybe both.

Down in Louisiana that day, 9 June, the 600 troops Taylor had sent to attack the Federals at Lake Providence finally tried to do so. They were composed of the Thirteenth Texas Cavalry and the Thirteenth Louisiana Battalion (mounted), and their fortune was no better than their numerical designations would lead any superstitious person to expect. Two companies of the 1st Kansas Mounted Infantry met them some six miles west of town, skirmished with them as they advanced to Bayou Tensas, and then retreated across that stream, destroying the bridge behind them. In the meantime, the local commander, Brigadier General Hugh T. Reid, brought up his main force, some 800 strong, including 300 men of the 8th Louisiana Volunteers "of African descent."

The Rebels formed line of battle and advanced skirmishers right up to the bayou and attempted to repair the bridge under the cover of a 6-pounder gun. "Our skirmishers from the First Kansas and Sixteenth Wisconsin were advanced from our main body," Reid reported, "under cover of the bank, to within close musket range of their gun, and soon compelled them to withdraw it, after firing only 5 rounds; then I sent forward a heavy force of skirmishers to meet their whole line on the bayou, and, after a brisk fire for an hour and a half, the rebels retreated. . . ." By then it was nearly dark, but the Confederates had left a few skirmishers in the underbrush near the bayou, so Reid brought up the 8th Louisiana to the bayou in line of battle – supposedly to give them some experience at little risk – and had them fire four volleys at these Rebels, "which cleared them out, and greatly encouraged the darkies."[4]

General Kirby Smith, at Shreveport, was writing a long letter to Adjutant and Inspector General Samuel Cooper, at Richmond, Virginia, that day, and in it he noted that he had not yet heard the results of Taylor's efforts to aid the defenders of Vicksburg: "I await with great uneasiness the result of military operations on the Mississippi; especially in the vicinity of Vicksburg does the magnitude of the stake contended for increase my anxiety. Not only the Valley of the Mississippi, but the fate of the Trans-Mississippi Department, is involved in the result. I would throw every man to those points were they disposable. This immense empire is without an army. Were all the troops concentrated, they would scarcely be more than sufficient for operating at any one point threatened; distances are so great that it takes the time of a campaign to re-enforce from one district to another. No effectual concentration can be made at any one point without the abandonment of all others."[5]

Meanwhile, on the other side of the Mississippi, the siege of Vicksburg continued. Captain Hickenlooper's notes for the ninth say: "Carried lead-sap across the road last night. Am confined to my bed by sickness this morning."[6] Because of this, he missed some excitement that night. Long after the war he wrote: "The sap-roller, used to protect the workmen from an enfilading fire during the opening of each section of the sap, was a wicker casing five feet in diameter by ten feet in length compactly filled with cotton. The roller was several times found to be on fire, and on the night of June 9th it was totally consumed; but through what agency was, at the time, a great mystery."[7]

The answer is provided by Sergeant Tunnard of the 3rd Louisiana. He said the men of his regiment had been trying to come up with some way to destroy the Union sap-roller, some even proposing a suicidal raid to go out and burn it, but a lieutenant finally came up with a safer method. They had Enfield rifles, imported from Britain, and the bullets these Enfields fired had a hollow base, which caused the bullet to expand when fired so it would tightly fit the spiral grooves in the barrel (called rifling); this caused the bullet to spin, giving it stability in flight. A lieutenant in his regiment came up with the idea of soaking some cotton in turpentine and stuffing it into the hollow base of a bullet. When the bullet was fired, the gunpowder would ignite the cotton, turning it into a miniature flying torch. A rifle was loaded with one of these inventions, Tunnard wrote, "and, amid the utmost curiosity and interest, fired at the hated object. The sharp report was followed by the glittering ball, as it sped from the breastworks straight to the dark mass of cotton-bales, like the rapid flight of a firefly. Another and another blazing missile was sent on the mission of destruction, with apparently no satisfactory results, and the attempt was abandoned amid a general disappointment. The men, save those on guard, sought repose, and all the line became comparatively quiet.

"Suddenly someone exclaimed, 'I'll be d-----d if that thing isn't on fire!' The whole regiment was soon stirring about, like a hive of disturbed bees. Sure enough, smoke was seen issuing from the dark mass. The inventive genius of Lieutenant [W. M.] Washburn had proved a complete success, and the fire, which had smouldered in the dense mass of cotton, was about bursting forth. The men seized their rifles and five companies were immediately detailed to keep up a constant and rapid fire over the top and at each end of ... the great point of attraction, which was soon reduced to ashes and a mass of smouldering embers. How the men cheered and taunted the foe can better be imagined than described."[8]

"Ere the gray dawn it began to rain," Tunnard said, "and soon poured down in torrents. There was no cessation of the rapid and heavy firing around the lines. . . . All day long the rain fell, filling the trenches with water, and thoroughly wetting the exposed, unsheltered troops." Although the storm added to the discomfort of the men on both sides, it wasn't all bad. Another Confederate, Hugh Moss, said, "The weather has been exceedingly dry and sultry, and the dust was almost unbearable on our lines, but today the heavens have poured forth a bountiful rain, refreshing vegetation and animals. Late in the evening the heavens began to frown and the lightning darted rapidly through the elements, dark and heavy clouds arose in frightening magnitude and the rumbling thunder – all combined to produce a sublime scene. Eight o'clock came and the rain fell in torrents. I was on guard and the lightning was so vivid that it seemed that the very atmosphere would turn to electricity. The rain has been a blessing to us, filling the cisterns with water."[9] Union Sergeant Osborn Oldroyd said, "We have been looking for rain to cool the air and lay the dust, and this afternoon we were gratified by a heavy shower."[10]

The reinforcements Halleck had ordered to Grant now began to arrive. The eight regiments sent down from Missouri reached Young's Point on this 10th day of June, organized as a division of two brigades under Major General Francis J. Herron.

"Herron was a first-rate officer," Charles Dana later said, "and the only consummate dandy I ever saw in the army. He was always handsomely dressed; I believe he never went out without patent-leather boots on, and you would see him in the middle of a battle – well, I can not say exactly that he went into battle with a lace pocket-handkerchief, but at all events he always displayed a clean white one. But these little vanities appeared not to detract from his usefulness. Herron had already proved his ability and fighting qualities at the battle of Prairie Grove, December 7, 1862."[11]

That same day, Grant wrote to Admiral Porter: "I sent you a dispatch by signal requesting you to send a gunboat to meet transports known to be on their way here loaded with troops. I have been informed of thirteen being loaded at Memphis, and expected them here last night. Their non-arrival causes me much uneasiness lest they may be interrupted some place by a battery of the enemy. I have information of 19,000 troops being on the way here besides those already arrived, and would request that, until they all get here, a gunboat ply about Island No. 65 and other dangerous points below it. I am aware, admiral, that heavy drafts have been made on your fleet above Vicksburg, but hope you will still be able to comply with the request made herein. I am fortifying Haynes' Bluff, and intend to hold it. At present I do not think the enemy are near there. All the forces coming to me now are being sent to Haynes' Bluff, and I need not tell you how anxious I feel for the arrival of those I know to have started."[12]

Hurlbut wrote a long letter to Rawlins that day, in which he said, "Everything is being pressed forward as fast as possible, but there is a terrible scarcity of boats, and it seems as if boats that go down to your parts never return. It is impossible to send anything down until some of the boats below are returned. Every boat from Saint Louis is in service. They should not be kept an hour after they are discharged of their cargoes. I am fully satisfied that Johnston cannot bring more than 35,000 men, of all arms, within the next ten days. Bragg is removing his stores to Atlanta, but Rosecrans will not believe any reports from this quarter, and I have ceased communicating with him, except through

Washington. He could now easily clear Middle Tennessee. . . ."[13]

Pemberton wrote to Johnston again that day: "The enemy bombard day and night, from seven mortars on opposite side of peninsula. He also keeps up constant fire on our lines with artillery and sharpshooters. We are losing many officers and men. I am waiting most anxiously to know your intentions. Have heard nothing of you nor from you since May 25. I shall endeavor to hold out as long as we have anything to eat. Can you not send me a verbal message by a courier crossing the river above or below Vicksburg and swimming across again opposite Vicksburg?"[14] Evidently this message never reached Johnston. But Johnston was writing to Secretary of War Seddon that day: "I have not at my [disposal] half the number of troops necessary. It is for the Government to determine what department, if any, can furnish the re-enforcements required. I cannot know here General Bragg's wants compared with mine. The Government can make such comparisons."[15]

Kirby Smith was writing to Johnston that day in reply to the latter's letter of 31 May that had asked him to do what he could to help save Port Hudson: "All the disposable infantry of the department is now opposite Vicksburg, under General Taylor's command; his force includes General Walker's division and Tappan's brigade, just ordered from Arkansas. [Brigadier] General [Alfred] Mouton, with his cavalry command and such infantry as could be collected within his district, has been ordered to operate opposite Port Hudson. General Taylor has instructions to spare no exertions in throwing supplies into Vicksburg; he was not to hesitate in crossing his force, if he could effect any good by so doing. I have but little hopes of affording any assistance to the garrison at Port Hudson; the enemy will draw their supplies by the Mississippi and from Baton Rouge by the opposite bank."[16]

Halleck was writing to General Banks that same day, saying he had received the latter's letters of 21 and 30 May: "Your account of the bravery and good conduct of your troops at Port Hudson has given great satisfaction, and it is hoped that you will succeed in capturing the place. Nevertheless, there is much anxiety on the subject, and much annoyance at the simultaneous attack on Port Hudson and Vicksburg, when it was expected that you and General Grant would act in conjunction."[17]

In Virginia on the tenth, a boatload of Confederate prisoners of war (being shipped from Fortress Monroe, at the tip of the York-James peninsula, to Fort Delaware) forced the steamer to shore and escaped.

Also, that day, even as Ewell's 2nd Corps began its move toward the Shenandoah Valley, Lee was writing a long letter to President Davis on a subject that was well beyond his purview as an army commander: "I refer to the manner in which the demonstration of a desire for peace at the North has been received in our country. I think there can be no doubt that journalists and others at the South, to whom the Northern people naturally look for a reflection of our opinions, have met these indications in such a wise as to weaken the hands of the advocates of a pacific policy on the part of the Federal Government, and give much encouragement to those who urge a continuance of the war." After a long exposition on why this was bad policy, and why the Confederacy should not make fine distinctions between Northerners who thought the two sections could be reunited after the shooting stopped and those who were for peace at any price, he summed it up this way: "Should the belief that peace will bring back the Union become general, the war would no longer be supported, and that, after all, is what we are interested in bringing about. When peace is proposed to us, it will be time enough to discuss its terms, and it is not the part of prudence to spurn the proposition in advance, merely because those who wish to make it believe, or affect to believe, that it will result in bringing us back to the Union."[18]

A question that Lee did not bring up in this letter was whether a movement into the Northern states by any sizable Confederate force would encourage the peace party or cause them to rally behind the Federal government for the protection of their homes. But he seemed to be hoping for – perhaps even counting on – the former, and didn't seem to consider the latter as a likely response. However, citizens north of the Potomac were already becoming alarmed, and the governor of Maryland called that day for his people to rally in defense of their state against an anticipated Confederate invasion.

Joe Hooker wrote a long message to President Lincoln that afternoon about what he should do next: "General Pleasonton, by telegram forwarded to the major-general commanding the army [Halleck] this morning, reports that he had an affair with the rebel cavalry yesterday near Brandy Station, which resulted in crippling him [Stuart] so much that he will have to abandon his contemplated raid into Maryland, which was to have started this morning. I am not so certain that the raid will be abandoned from this cause. It may delay the departure a few days. I shall leave the cavalry, which is all that I have mounted, where they are, near Bealeton, with instructions to resist the passage of the river by the enemy's forces. If to effect this he [Lee] should bring up a considerable force of infantry, that will so much weaken him in my front that I have good reason to believe that I can throw a sufficient force over the river to compel the enemy to abandon his present position. If it should be the intention to send a heavy column of infantry to accompany the cavalry on the proposed raid, he can leave nothing behind to interpose any serious obstacle to my rapid advance on Richmond.

"I am not satisfied of his intention in this respect, but from certain movements in their corps I cannot regard it as altogether improbable. If it should be found to be the case, will it not promote the true interest of the cause for me to march to Richmond at once? From there all the disposable part of this army can be thrown to any threatened point north of the Potomac at short notice, and, until they can reach their destination, a sufficiency of troops can be collected to check, if not to stop, his invasion. If left to operate from my own judgment, with my present information, I do not hesitate to say that I should adopt this course as being the most speedy and certain mode of giving the rebellion a mortal blow. I desire that you will give it your reflection. At present the enemy has one corps of infantry at Gordonsville, with the advance at Culpeper, with the manifest tendency of other corps to drift in that direction. I now have two bridges across the Rappahannock, ready to spring over the river below Fredericksburg, and it is this, I believe, that causes the enemy to hesitate in moving forward.

"Major-General Dix informs me that he intends moving two columns up James River to-morrow; but if organized to correspond in numbers to troops as they have of late been posted, neither column will be successful. The one on the north side of the river will be too small, and on the south side, with his whole column, I question if Richmond can be taken at all, provided that 2,000 or 3,000 men could be assembled to defend it. The columns should unite at City Point, or below, and move on the north bank of that river. From information, which I deem reliable, the only troops remaining in Richmond is the provost-guard, 1,500, and all the troops between here and there are brought well to the front.

"It would be of incalculable service to this army to be transferred to some more remote point from Washington and Alexandria. The stampedes in those towns, gotten up, no doubt, by people in the rebel interest, have their influence on my men, for many of them have no means of knowing whether they are with or without cause. They think there must be some fire where there is so much smoke."[19]

In this letter Hooker revealed a great deal about himself. He was shrewd enough to realize that Pleasonton's battle of the day before had not hurt Stuart enough to prevent him from making a raid. And he had discerned Lee's movements enough to know that most of the Confederate army was sidling to its left, up the Rappahannock. He surmised, based on these facts, that Lee might well send not only Stuart's cavalry but a sizable part of his infantry north of that river in order to either get at Hooker's own flank, or to threaten Washington directly, or, more likely, to move across the Potomac into Maryland and even Pennsylvania. And he was probably correct that a good counter to such a move might be for him to march straight on Richmond. He was also correct in surmising that Dix's two small columns were no great threat to Richmond, but then Dix knew that as well – he only intended to draw Confederate attention, and troops, toward defending their own capital instead of threatening Union territory.

But Hooker did not anticipate the move that Lee was actually making, even as he was writing to Lincoln about it: not across the Rappahannock but into the Shenandoah Valley while keeping the Rappahannock between him and Hooker. However, the real weakness Hooker's letter reveals is that he wrote it at all. If he was going to have to discuss every move with Lincoln before making it, he would always be moving far too late or too slowly to counter Lee. Had he, instead of writing for instructions, just moved most of his army across the Rappahannock below Fredericksburg that day he would have put tremendous pressure on Lee to call off his movement north in order to protect Richmond or to come to the aid of A. P. Hill's lone corps.

Lincoln answered that evening: "If left to me, I would not go south of Rappahannock upon Lee's moving north of it. If you had Richmond invested to-day, you would not be able to take it in twenty days; meanwhile your communications, and with them your army, would be ruined. I think Lee's army, and not Richmond, is your sure objective point. If he comes toward the Upper Potomac, follow on his flank and on his inside track, shortening your lines [of supply] while he lengthens his. Fight him, too, when opportunity offers. If he stays where he is, fret him and fret him."[20] This was excellent advice as well, but such a policy left the initiative in Lee's hands, forcing Hooker to react instead of acting, and it required that Hooker maintain a sure knowledge of where Lee's forces were and in which direction they were moving – something that he did not yet have.

Lee was not the only Confederate general contemplating a raid or invasion of the North. That night, down in Tennessee, General Morgan gathered his officers together and informed them that they were going to make another raid. Morgan was a native of Kentucky – a state with divided loyalties, although it never seceded – and had made himself a high reputation by conducting daring raids deep into his home territory. But this time they would pass clear through Kentucky, cross the Ohio River, and sweep through southern Indiana and Ohio. Their first problem would be to get across the Cumberland River into Kentucky, their second would be to get across the wide Ohio, and their third would be to avoid Cincinnati, the largest Northern city west of the Appalachians; it would be well defended. Their fourth problem would be getting back again after stirring up every Union garrison and militia unit in three states. Maybe they would even ride all the way to Virginia, Maryland or Pennsylvania and link up with Lee. His officers, although a bit apprehensive, liked the idea. What Morgan didn't tell them (except Colonel Basil Duke, his brother-in-law, who was his division's logistics expert and senior brigade commander) was that to make such a raid they would have to disobey General Bragg, who wanted them to merely threaten Louisville, or capture it and its supplies if weakly defended, but to stay close enough to his main army that they could always be recalled to it in case of need.

Confederate Adjutant and Inspector General Cooper wired Beauregard at Charleston that day: "Northern papers report the reduction of Hunter's forces by sending troops to the Gulf. If this be true, you will, with such force as you can properly withdraw from your defensive line, proceed to Mobile, to resist an attack, if one should be designed at that place, but if the purpose of the enemy be to send his re-enforcements to the Mississippi, you will go on and co-operate with General Johnston in that quarter."[21] However, the report was not true – the Federals still had designs on Charleston – and Beauregard did not go.

That same evening Colonel James Montgomery of the 2nd South Carolina (one of Hunter's regiments of escaped slaves) led an attack on the Georgia coast with five companies of his own regiment and eight from the new 54th Massachusetts (the regiment of free black men from the North), plus a section of artillery. Under the protection of gunboats, they moved up the Altamaha River on transports and landed on the afternoon of the 11th near the beautiful town of Darien, shaded with huge oak and magnolia trees. Near the riverbank there were storehouses and mills for rice and resin. After the gunboats drove off some Rebel pickets, the infantry systematically plundered the town for food, livestock, lumber, and anything else they could use; then they burned the town.

Colonel Shaw of the 54th was horrified by this sort of warfare, but Montgomery said that since the Confederates had outlawed the Union regiments of colored troops they were therefore not bound by the ordinary rules of war; if the Rebels wanted them to behave like ordinary troops they would have to treat them as such. "But," Shaw later complained, "that makes it none the less revolting to wreak our vengeance on the innocent and defenseless."[22] Montgomery also had a reason for picking on Darien in particular: one of his white officers had lived there and had been run out of town for his pro-Union views, with the loss of all his property. Not all of the town was burned; a church, a few houses, and some lumberworks belonging to a Northern man were spared. Eighty bales of cotton were captured on a flatboat and a schooner near the town, the latter being loaded for a run to Nassau in the Bahamas. Colonel Shaw soon wrote to the governor of Massachusetts to complain, who in turn wrote to Hunter, who replied that these raids "compel the rebels either to lay down their arms and sue for restoration to the Union or to withdraw their slaves into the interior, thus leaving desolate the most fertile and productive of their counties along the Atlantic seaboard."[23] But the 54th was not sent on any more such raids.

That same day, 11 June, Admiral Foote left his home in New

Haven, Connecticut, to go down the coast and take command of the squadron operating against Charleston, but he stopped for the night at New York City, where he became seriously ill.

General Halleck wired Hooker at 12:40 on the afternoon of the 11th: "The President has just referred to me your telegram and his reply of yesterday, with directions to say to you whether or not I agree with him. I do so fully."[24] Hooker wired Halleck at 9 that night: "I have just been reliably informed that Pettigrew's and Darnell's [Davis's] brigades from North Carolina are in Heth's division, near Hamilton's Crossing. I have no information concerning the residue of the forces drawn from North Carolina. A. P. Hill's corps is on the right, opposite to Franklin's Crossing; Ewell's is in rear of Fredericksburg, and Longstreet's corps and the cavalry are at Culpeper. I have to-day dispatched the Third Corps to picket the river from Meade's right, at Kelly's Ford, to Beverly Ford, in order to relieve the cavalry in aid of Pleasonton, who is looking after the district of country from Beverly to Sulphur Springs. Pleasonton is weak in cavalry compared with the enemy."[25]

He was, of course, mistaken about Ewell's corps still being back of Fredericksburg, when, in fact, it was that day about halfway between Culpeper Court House and the Shenandoah Valley. In a message to Dan Butterfield that day, Pleasonton did, at least, place both Longstreet and Ewell around Culpeper, which was more accurate than what Hooker told Halleck, but at 7:15 that evening Pleasonton told Butterfield: "Deserters state that the enemy have 60,000 infantry at Culpeper – Pickett's, Anderson's, Hood's, and McLaw's. General Lee is also there. Ewell is at Fredericksburg with Jackson's corps. A. P. Hill is on the heights [behind Fredericksburg]."[26] Sixty thousand men would come close to covering all the infantry in Lee's army.

Hooker asked Meade that day, as he had frequently in the past, what Rebel forces were across the river from him, but

Meade replied: "It is very difficult to ascertain anything of the enemy's movements from this side, as he keeps his forces concealed."[27] Hooker's headquarters sent a circular that day to each of his corps commanders telling them to "hold your command in readiness to move at very short notice. The movement to be made [will be] of a nature to require the greatest possible mobility. Every article of every kind and description in excess of the allowance in orders, to be turned in to the quartermaster's department without delay."[28] Reynolds' 1st Corps was ordered that same day to move up the river, where it would serve as a support for the 3rd and 5th Corps, which were guarding the crossings of the Rappahannock.

General Order No. 18 of the Cavalry Corps, published that day, formally reorganized that corps into two divisions, to be constituted from the two commands that had fought at Brandy Station: the 1st Division, under Buford, to be composed of the old 1st Division plus the Reserve Brigade; the 2nd Division, under Gregg, to be composed of the units that had made up both the 2nd and 3rd divisions. Both new divisions were to be composed of three brigades, to be organized however the division commanders saw fit.

Major John S. Mosby's Confederate partisans raided across the Potomac into Maryland that day, which caused the chief of staff of the Department of Washington to tell Major General Julius Stahel, commander of that department's cavalry division – which was then guarding the railroad between Pleasonton's troopers and Washington – to send a force to intercept Mosby while another force, under Colonel Charles Russell Lowell, tried to do the same on the north side of the Potomac.

General Dix wired Hooker that day: "The movement up the [York-James] Peninsula is in progress. I left Williamsburg this morning to see about General Peck's movement [up the south side of the James], which, I am sorry to say, is for the present suspended by a movement of the enemy and other inevitable causes here. It is, however, only suspended."[29]

Generals Couch and Brooks assumed command of their new

departments that day, and from his headquarters at Chambersburg Couch called upon the "the citizens of Pennsylvania to furnish promptly all the men necessary to organize an army corps of volunteer infantry, artillery, and cavalry, to be designated the Army Corps of the Susquehanna" on identical terms as those for the corps it was hoped to be formed in Brooks' new department.

That same day, the eleventh, Richard Taylor wrote another long dispatch to his boss, Kirby Smith, from Alexandria, Louisiana: "I reached this place last night, having left Richmond [La.] forty-eight hours previously. I shall leave in a few minutes for Morgan's Ferry, on the Atchafalaya River. As Banks is reported to be using the west bank of the Mississippi for the transportation of his supplies, &c., I deem it of great importance that the most vigorous movement should be made by a portion of our forces against the enemy opposite Port Hudson, and it is necessary that I should give my personal supervision to the arrangements, and perhaps take command of the expedition. . . . As there are troops enough in the lower portion of the State for the expedition against the enemy, who is opposite Port Hudson, it is not necessary at this moment to withdraw General Walker's division, as I contemplated at the time of my report from Richmond. I shall either take command in person of the expedition against Banks' army, opposite Port Hudson, or, if the enemy attempts to cross below Vicksburg, of the forces in Madison Parish. My experience of the past few weeks satisfies me that it is necessary that I should rely upon myself not only to devise the plans, but also to execute them, in order to insure their being carried out vigorously. On my arrival here I received several reports from Brigadier-General [Alfred] Mouton . . . which are exceedingly unsatisfactory, and indicate that no movements commensurate with the forces under his command have been made, and that little activity has been displayed by that officer. While an excellent officer in the field, of great gallantry and fair qualifications, he is, I fear, unequal to the task of handling and disposing of any large body of troops, and I shall, therefore, at the earliest practicable moment, give my personal supervision to that command. From General Mouton's reports I am quite in the dark as to the condition of affairs on the Lower Teche, and as to the presence or absence of the enemy's troops on this side of Berwick Bay."[30]

At Port Hudson that day General Gardner sent Captain Robert Pruyn out of his lines with a message for Joe Johnston, saying he was closely invested and short of both provisions and ammunition. At 9:30 that night Pruyn, dressed in civilian clothes, slipped into the river on a crude raft buoyed by empty canteens and made his way down river, passing right through the Union fleet.

Banks launched a reconnaissance in force that same day for the purpose, as Colonel Irwin of his staff later put it, "of harassing the enemy, of inducing him to bring forward and expose his artillery, acquiring a knowledge before the enemy's front, and of favoring the operations of pioneers who may be sent forward to remove obstructions if necessary."[31] Since the assaults of 27 May, Banks had reorganized his forces: Dwight was now in command of what had been Tom Sherman's division; Paine's small division, which had been to the right of Grover's division was now on his left; Grover now commanded the entire right wing of the besieging forces; and Augur commanded the left. However, the reorganization did not improve the coordination of the various units. When Weitzel's and Joseph S. Morgan's brigades advanced there were blunders in transmitting the orders to the regiments, so that they went in piecemeal and their attack was soon broken up. In addition to enduring the Confederate fire, they were also caught in a sudden thunderstorm, which lasted for about an hour, after which the Federals returned to their own lines. About the only thing accomplished was that two Confederate cannon revealed themselves in helping to repulse the attack, and they were soon disabled by the fire of Union artillery.

Joe Johnston's headquarters issued orders that day placing Colonel Hylan B. Lyon in temporary command of all troops in the vicinity of, but outside of, Port Hudson, including Colonel John L. Logan's cavalry. "You will use every exertion," he was told, "to interrupt the progress of the siege of Port Hudson, and to harrass the enemy by intercepting his supplies, cutting off his communications, attacking his detachments, or in any manner you may deem practicable."[32]

Johnston was finally about to make a move, and his headquarters also published orders that day forbidding all leaves or furloughs in the army he had assembled "on any pretext whatever;" and Johnston wrote to General W. H. T. Walker, whose division was at Yazoo City: "As the preparations to move toward the enemy are nearly completed, and your division will have a longer distance to march than the others, please move as soon as practicable to some point on or near the Big Black, whence the distance will be nearly equal to that from Jackson; Vernon, for instance, or its neighborhood. As it is important that the baggage train should be as small as possible, the allowance of brigade wagons will be one for each hundred men (aggregate) for transportation of cooking utensils, ammunition, and of officers' baggage, one for medical supplies, one for each general officer and staff. I need not suggest to you to load with provisions all above this allowance. Should you be detained near Vernon, the neighborhood can supply."[33]

Grant was still working at improving his defenses against an attack by Johnston, and, as the Big Black River served as a moat to the east of his lines, he was still primarily concerned about the corridor to the northeast, between the Big Black and the Yazoo, especially since that was where his supplies landed. He wrote to Sherman that day: "Washburn, who is in command at Haynes' Bluff, reports that a division of rebel cavalry is encamped 2 miles beyond Mechanicsburg, and [W. H. T.] Walker, with an infantry force, is at Yazoo City. General W. S. Smith's division, from West Tennessee, is beginning to arrive, and, I suppose, will all be here to-day. This force goes to Haynes' Bluff, and will make a force of from 13,000 to 14,000 at that place. I have also received information that two brigades from Missouri are on their way, and have passed Memphis, and 8,000 are coming from Burnside's department. These latter I propose to land at Young's Point, and send across to Warrenton to close up the south side of Vicksburg. With the cavalry we have at Haynes' Bluff, when required, two brigades from your corps, and three from McPherson's, to be further relieved if it should become absolutely necessary, by taking all the troops to the left of McClernand [sic]. In case this has to be done, you will be detached temporarily from the command of your corps here, to take command at Haynes' Bluff whilst it may be besieged. The order then intended to be conveyed is, that two brigades from the Fifteenth Army Corps be held in readiness to march to Haynes' Bluff at the shortest notice."[34]

Since the detachment of Mower's brigade had left Brigadier General James M. Tuttle's division with only two brigades, and one of the other two was already in reserve, Sherman issued orders that day for that division to be held in reserve and for Blair's division to take over the part of the lines then held by Tuttle's remaining brigade. He also wrote to Rawlins that he would reconnoiter the ground north of Haynes' Bluff "and therefore be prepared for further orders at once."[35] Rawlins sent a note to McPherson, telling him to have three brigades ready to go to Haynes' Bluff on short notice.

Grant also wrote to General Dennis, on the west side of the Mississippi, that day: "In view of present danger of attack upon your command, it is advisable that every precaution be taken to hold all Government stores and the troops, at least, secure from capture. If the Government farms can be held, they should be held also, but not at the expense of sacrificing Government troops and stores first and the plantations afterward in detail. . . . General Mower's brigade was sent to you merely for an emergency. As soon as the emergency ceases, I want them returned to their division. With the cavalry you have, the mounted men General Reid has, and by mounting part of one negro regiment, they can scout out every road from Lake Providence to Young's Point, so as to keep you advised of the approach of any force in time to prepare for them. Have you learned what has become of the force that attacked you a few days since? They should not be allowed to remain about Richmond."[36]

General Hurlbut had expressed some concern that Johnston might, for lack of an easier target, come north against him, and Grant wrote to him that day: "I do not hear of the enemy running cars north of Water Valley. If this is so, they cannot send any large force against you without your cavalry being able to give timely notice of their approach. Should Johnston disappear from my flank, I will have a much larger force than is required, and would at once relieve you, either by sending troops back by way of the river, or sending them up in the rear of any force that might be advancing on you, or both. I may, however, be deceived by the enemy showing all the time a force at Yazoo City and across to Canton, while he will have the main body moving north. You will have to keep a good lookout for this with your cavalry and through scouts. It is now evident the enemy have brought large re-enforcements from Bragg's army, and I cannot think it is with any other design than to raise the siege of Vicksburg. It would only be after despairing of success here that they would attempt a northern move. Keep me well informed of all you learn of the movements of the enemy."[37]

Charles Dana wrote to Secretary Stanton again that day: "General Herron has just reported. His eight regiments are ordered to take position south of Vicksburg, between Lauman's troops and Mississippi River, completely closing the lines, and rendering egress and ingress absolutely impossible. . . . Deserters from Vicksburg last evening report corn-meal getting short, so that the ration of bread is one-half of pea flour. Hovey's artillery have destroyed one of their mills and injured the remaining one. They are also out of fresh beef, and have begun to issue bacon, of which some deserters were told by their officers that they have thirty days' supply. The re-enforcements yet to arrive will be concentrated at Haynes'. C. C. Washburn reports that place of such strength on the land side that 10,000 can hold it against 30,000. The engineers report the artificial defenses there will require little labor. General Grant thinks the demonstration of the enemy west of Mississippi River more serious than we have supposed. Of course, every means in their power on that side will be directed to hindering his operations here. Our forces at Milliken's Bend, including Mower's brigade, will not be sufficient for aggressive purposes toward Natchez, but will be ample for defense. The gunboats are judiciously placed – one at Haynes' Bluff, one at Chickasaw Bayou, one at Young's Point, one at Milliken's Bend, one at Lake Providence, one at Greenville, one at Island 65, two at White River, besides others in motion. The seven gunboats below Vicksburg are also stationed where most needed; but the line is long, and the rebels west of Mississippi River may manage to cross somewhere. It is my duty to report that the Marine Brigade, with its seven large steamers and its varied apparatus of artillery, infantry, and cavalry, is a very useless as well as a very costly institution."[38]

Grant was writing to Halleck that day: "I have reliable information from the entire interior of the South. Johnston has been re-enforced by 3,000 troops from Mobile and other parts of Georgia; by [J. P.] McCown's and Breckinridge's divisions (9,000 men), and 4,000 of Forrest's cavalry, from Bragg's army; 9,000 men from Charleston, and 2,200 from Port Hudson. Orders were sent the very day General Banks invested Port Hudson, to evacuate it. Garrison there now 8,000. Lee's army has not been reduced; Bragg's force now 46,000 infantry and artillery and 15,000 cavalry. Everything not required for daily use has been removed to Atlanta, Ga. His army can fall back to Bristol or Chattanooga at a moment's notice, which places, it is thought, he can hold, and spare 25,000 troops. Mobile and Savannah are now almost entirely without garrisons, further than men to manage large guns. No troops are left in the interior to send to any place. All further re-enforcements will have to come from one of the great armies. There are about 32,000 men west of the Mississippi, exclusive of the troops in Texas. Orders were sent them one week ago by Johnston. The purport of the order not known. Herron has arrived here, and troops from Burnside looked for to-morrow."[39]

Meanwhile, the siege continued. After the rain storm of the

day before, this day was relatively cool and pleasant. Captain Hickenlooper was still sick and confined to bed, but the digging continued. In front of the 3rd Louisiana the Federals had positioned two of the 9-inch Dahlgren naval shell guns that Admiral Porter had provided, "scarcely a hundred yards distant from the lines," Sergeant Tunnard said (although he thought they were 10-inch Columbiads, a similar type of gun designed for use in coastal defenses). "These terrible missiles, with their heavy scream and tremendous explosion, somewhat startled the boys, being a new and unexpected feature of the siege, and necessarily increasing the already accumulated dangers of their situation. After knocking the breastworks to pieces, and exhibiting their force and power, the enemy commenced a systematic method of practice so as to make the shells deadly missiles of destruction. So skillful and expert did they soon become in handling these huge siege-pieces that they loaded them with powder, producing force sufficient to only propel the shells over the breastworks, and they rolled among the men, producing a general scramble to escape the force and danger of the explosion."[40] Charles Dana was no doubt referring to the same battery when he wrote to Stanton the next day, although he mentioned only one gun and said the range was longer: "Fired at 300 yards, its shells penetrate the rebel parapet some 10 feet and then explode, clearing the parapet away as if by a mine."[41]

In Middle Tennessee all remained quiet. Halleck wired General Rosecrans from Washington that day: "I deem it my duty to repeat to you the great dissatisfaction that is felt here at your inactivity. There seems to be no doubt that a part of Bragg's force has gone to Johnston."[42] Rosecrans replied with a long dispatch. First he reminded the general-in-chief that he had said before that "a necessary condition of success" was "an adequate cavalry force," and he happily reported that he had only about 300 troopers that remained without mounts. "My preliminary infantry movements have nearly all been completed," he said, "and I am preparing to strike a blow that will tell; but, to show you how differently things are viewed here . . ." he passed on the results of his recent polling of his corps and division commanders about the desirability of advancing against Bragg. "Not one thinks an advance advisable until Vicksburg's fate is determined. . . . I therefore counsel caution and patience at headquarters. Better wait a little to get all we can ready to insure the best results, if by so doing we, per force of Providence, observe a great military maxim, not to risk two great and decisive battles at the same time. We might have cause to be thankful for it; at all events, you see that, to expect success, I must have such thorough grounds that when I say 'forward,' my word will inspire conviction and confidence, where both are now wanting. I should like to have your suggestion."[43]

In Ohio that day the banished Copperhead Clement L. Vallandigham was nominated for governor of Ohio by the Peace Democrats, even though he was then an unwelcome guest of the Confederacy and subject to arrest if he should return to Ohio. The next day, 12 June, at Washington, President Lincoln was writing a long, long letter to a number of Democrats who had sent him, back in May, the resolutions of a public meeting held in Albany, New York, to protest the arrest of Vallandigham. "The resolutions, as I understand them," he wrote, "are resolvable into two propositions – first, the expression of a purpose to sustain the cause of the Union, to secure peace through victory, and to support the administration in every constitutional, and lawful measure to suppress the rebellion; and secondly, a declaration of censure upon the administration for supposed unconstitutional action such as the making of military arrests.

"And from the two propositions a third is deduced, which is, that the gentlemen composing the meeting are resolved on doing their part to maintain our common government and country, despite the folly or wickedness, as they may conceive it, of any administration. This position is eminently patriotic, and as such, I thank the meeting and congratulate the nation for it. My own purpose is the same; so that the meeting and myself have a common object, and can have no difference, except in the choice of means or measures, for effecting that object. . . ."

He then pointed out that the Constitution provides for the suspension of the writ of *habeas corpus* "when, in cases of Rebellion or Invasion, the public Safety may require" it, and that even the resolutions of that assembly admitted that there was a rebellion in progress – "in fact, a clear, flagrant, and gigantic case of Rebellion," he said. "This provision plainly attests the understanding of those who made the constitution that ordinary courts of justice are inadequate to 'cases of Rebellion' – attests their purpose that in such cases, men may be held in custody whom the courts acting on ordinary rules, would discharge. . . . Indeed, arrests by process of courts, and arrests in cases of rebellion, do not proceed altogether upon the same basis. The former is directed at the small percentage of ordinary and continuous perpetration of crime; while the latter is directed at sudden and extensive uprisings against the government, which, at most, will succeed or fail, in no great length of time. In the latter case, arrests are made, not so much for what has been done, as for what probably would be done. The latter is more for the preventive, and less for the vindictive, than the former. In such cases the purposes of men are much more easily understood, than in cases of ordinary crime. The man who stands by and says nothing, when the peril of his government is discussed, can not be misunderstood. If not hindered, he is sure to help the enemy. Much more, if he talks ambiguously – talks for his country with 'buts' and 'ifs' and 'ands.'" He gave as an example how much the Rebel cause would have been weakened if various of their present leaders, such as Robert E. Lee and Joseph E. Johnston, had been arrested when it was known that they intended to join the Confederate army. "But no one of them had then committed any crime defined in the law. Every one of them if arrested would have been discharged on Habeas Corpus, were the writ allowed to operate. In view of these and similar cases, I think the time not unlikely to come when I shall be blamed for having made too few arrests rather than too many."

Then he took up one of the resolutions that insisted that, while military arrests might be constitutional in localities where rebellion actually exists, but were unconstitutional when made "outside of the lines of necessary military occupation, and the scenes of insurrection." He pointed out that the Constitution makes no such distinction and only requires that the arrests be necessary for the public safety. "I insist that in such cases, they are constitutional *wherever* the public safety does require them – as well in places to which they may prevent the rebellion extending, as in those where it may be already prevailing – as well where they may restrain mischievous interference with the raising and supplying of armies, to suppress the rebellion, as where the rebellion may actually be – as well where they may restrain the enticing men out of the army, as where they would prevent mutiny in the army – equally constitutional at all places where they will conduce to the public Safety, as against the dangers of Rebellion or Invasion."

He then turned to the specific case of Vallandigham, noting that the resolutions claimed that he had been arrested "for no other reason than words addressed to a public meeting, in criticism of the course of the administration, and in condemnation of the military orders of" General Burnside. "Now, if there be no mistake about this – if the assertion is the truth and the whole truth – if there was no other reason for the arrest, then I concede that the arrest was wrong. But the arrest, as I understand, was made for a very different reason. Mr. Vallandigham avows his hostility to the war on the part of the Union; and his arrest was made because he was laboring, with some effect, to prevent the raising of troops, to encourage desertions from the army, and to leave the rebellion without an adequate military force to suppress it. . . . He was warring upon the military; and this gave the military constitutional jurisdiction to lay hands upon him. . . .

I understand the meeting, whose resolutions I am considering, to be in favor of suppressing the rebellion by military force – by armies. Long experience has shown that armies can not be maintained unless desertion shall be punished by the severe penalty of death. The case requires, and the law and the constitution, sanction this punishment. Must I shoot a simple-minded soldier boy who deserts, while I must not touch a hair of a wiley agitator who induces him to desert? This is none the less injurious when effected by getting a father, or brother, or friend, into a public meeting, and there working upon his feelings, till he is persuaded to write the soldier boy, that he is fighting in a bad cause, for a wicked administration of a contemptable government, too weak to arrest and punish him if he shall desert. I think that in such a case, to silence the agitator, and save the boy, is not only constitutional, but, withal, a great mercy."[44] He went on for several more pages, but that was the gist of his argument, and his most telling point.

Halleck replied that day to Rosecrans' answer to him of the day before: "I do not understand your application of the military maxim 'not to fight two great battles at the same time.' It will apply to a single army, but not to two armies acting independently of each other. Johnston and Bragg are acting on interior lines between you and Grant, and it is for their interest, not ours, that they should fight at different times, so as to use the same force against both of you. It is for our interest to fight them, if possible, while divided. If you are not strong enough to fight Bragg with a part of his troops absent, you will not be able to fight him after the affair at Vicksburg is over and his troops return to your front. There is another military maxim, that 'councils of war never fight.' If you say that you are not prepared to fight Bragg, I shall not order you to do so, for the responsibility of fighting or refusing to fight at a particular time or place must rest upon the general in immediate command. It cannot be shared by a council of war, nor will the authorities here make you fight against your will. You ask me to counsel them 'caution and patience.' I have done so very often; but after five or six months of inactivity, with your force all the time diminishing, and no hope of any immediate increase, you must not be surprised that their patience is pretty well exhausted. If you do not deem it prudent to risk a general battle with Bragg, why can you not harass him, or make such demonstrations as to prevent his sending more reinforcements to Johnston? I do not write this in a spirit of fault-finding, but to assure you that the prolonged inactivity of so large an army in the field is causing much complaint and dissatisfaction, not only in Washington, but throughout the country."[45]

∽ Endnotes ∽

1. *OR*, I:27:III:44.
2. Ibid., I:23:I:369.
3. Ibid., I:23:II:416. A fuller account of this incident can be found in William Gilmore Beymer, *Scouts and Spies of the Civil War* (Lincoln NB, 2003), 28-53.
4. Ibid., I:24:II:449.
5. Ibid., I:26:II:41.
6. Ibid., I:24:II:200.
7. Hickenlooper, "The Vicksburg Mine" in *B&L* III:540.
8. Hoehling, *Vicksburg: 47 Days of Siege*, 128-9.
9. Ibid., 132-3.
10. Ibid., 134.
11. Dana, *Recollections of the Civil War*, 94.
12. *OR*, I:24:III:396.
13. Ibid., I:24:III:397.
14. Ibid., I:24:I:278 and I:24:III:958.
15. Ibid., I:24:I:226.
16. Ibid., I:26:II:43.
17. Ibid., I:26:I:545.
18. Ibid., I:27:III:881-2.
19. Ibid., I:27:I:34-5.
20. Ibid., I:27:I:35.
21. Ibid., I:24:III:958.
22. Emilio, *A Brave Black Regiment*, 46.
23. Stephen R. Wise, *Gate of Hell* (Columbia SC, 1994), 53.
24. *OR*, I:27:I:35.
25. Ibid., I:27:I:35-6.

26 Ibid., I:27:I:62.
27 Ibid., I:27:I:61.
28 Ibid., I:27:I:67.
29 Ibid., I:27:I:66.
30 Ibid., I:24:II:461-2.
31 Edward Cunningham, *The Port Hudson Campaign, 1862-1863* (Baton Rouge LA, 1963), 77.
32 *OR*, I:24:III:961.
33 Ibid., I:24:III:960.
34 Ibid., I:24:III:402.
35 Ibid.
36 Ibid., I:24:III:403-4.
37 Ibid., I:24:III:404-5.
38 Ibid., I:24:I:96-7.
39 Ibid., I:24:I:42.
40 Hoehling, *Vicksburg: 47 Days of Siege*, 141-2.
41 *OR*, I:24:I:97.
42 Ibid., I:23:I:10.
43 Ibid., I:23:I:8.
44 Basler, ed., *Collected Works of Abraham Lincoln*, VI:261-7.
45 *OR*, I:23:I:8.

CHAPTER 8

"I Am Still Confident of the Final Result"

12 – 14 June 1863

O N THAT TWELFTH DAY OF JUNE, a Friday, the CSS *Clarence*, (herself a prize of the CSS *Florida* captured off the coast of Brazil and armed with two boat howitzers) captured the civilian bark *Tacony* off Cape Henry by feigning distress. It was the Rebel raider's sixth prize that week. The Confederate crew destroyed their own ship after transferring their howitzers to the captured one to continue raiding in the North Atlantic.

Also that day, Ewell's 2nd Corps of Lee's army descended from the Blue Ridge mountains into the Shenandoah Valley, passing through the town of Front Royal, and at the town of Cedarville it was met by Jenkins' cavalry brigade. It was also met there by a wagon train hauling enough pontoons to lay a bridge across the Potomac River. Ewell dispatched Rodes' Division, with most of the cavalry and the pontoons, down the road to the northeast, "to capture, if possible, a force of 1,800 men, under Colonel [A. T.] McReynolds, reported at Berryville, and thence to press on to Martinsburg."[1]

The Union high command had some idea that Federal forces in the Valley were in danger, but was being indecisive about what to do about it. A telegram from the chief of staff of the Middle Department, Lieutenant Colonel Donn Piatt, was received by General Milroy, commanding the 2nd Division of the 8th Corps, at Winchester, at midnight of 11-12 June, saying, in accordance with orders from Halleck, for him to "immediately take steps to remove your command from Winchester to Harpers Ferry. You will, without delay, call in Colonel McReynolds and such other outposts not necessary for observation at the front. Send back your heavy guns, surplus ammunition, and subsistence, retaining only such force and arms as will constitute what General Halleck designates as a lookout, which can readily and without inconvenience fall back to Harper's Ferry."

However, Milroy immediately telegraphed General Schenck: "I have the place well protected, and am well prepared to hold it, as [Brigadier] General [Daniel] Tyler and Colonel Piatt will inform you, and I can and would hold it, if permitted to do so, against any force the rebels can afford to bring against me, and I exceedingly regret the prospect of having to give it up. It will be cruel to abandon the loyal people in this country to the rebel fiends again." An hour later Schenck replied: "Lieutenant-Colonel Piatt, as I learn by copy of dispatch sent me, which he forwarded to you from Harper's Ferry, misunderstood me, and somewhat exceeded his instructions. You will make all the required preparations for withdrawing, but hold your position in the meantime. Be ready for movement, but await further orders. I doubt the propriety of calling in McReynold's brigade at once. If you should fall back to Harper's Ferry, he will be in part on the way and covering your flank; but use your discretion as to any order to him."[2]

That night Milroy received a telegram from Schenck forwarding an explanation that Piatt had sent him, saying that he had interpreted Halleck's message as a positive order for Milroy to fall back, and that he didn't think Milroy had enough wagons to move all his supplies in the face of an enemy force. Milroy immediate replied: "I can at any time, if not cut off from Martinsburg, have sufficient transportation to take all public stores from here in six hours." Later that night he reported that his cavalry had skirmished with a few hundred Confederate horsemen that day. "The enemy is probably approaching in some force. Please state specifically whether I am to abandon this place or not."[3] He received no reply, although a message was starting to come in the next day when the telegraph line suddenly went dead.

Hooker still did not have a clue that Ewell had moved to the

Valley; in fact he was still worried about a Confederate move to the north side of the upper Rappahannock. He wired Halleck at 7 that morning: "It is reported to me from the [observation] balloon that several new rebel camps [near Fredericksburg] have made their appearance this morning. There can be no doubt but that the enemy has been greatly re-enforced." At 8:30 a.m. he wired again to say: "General Pleasonton, without additional cavalry, I fear will not be able to prevent the rebel cavalry from turning his right. I have not been able to ascertain his precise strength, but know that it is near 7,500, while that of the enemy is certainly not less than 10,000. He now pickets beyond Sulphur Springs. He will, however, do the best he can. If he should be turned, you will perceive that I shall be constrained to abandon the Aquia Creek line of operations." At the same hour he ordered Major General Oliver O. Howard to march his 11th Corps for Catlett's Station on the Orange & Alexandria Railroad, about halfway between the Rappahannock and Manassas Junction. At 1:15 p.m. he finally got around to reporting to Halleck Pleasonton's fight of three days before. Fifteen minutes after that, Halleck replied to the previous message: "There is no possibility of sending you more cavalry. Horses will be sent as fast as they can be procured."[4]

At noon General Dix wired Hooker: "The force sent from Williamsburg yesterday morning was 12 miles out last night, with an advance some 3 miles farther. The plan was changed at Suffolk, and a large force will be near the Blackwater [River] tonight. A small force was to cross the Chickahominy [River] near the mouth this morning. All these movements will be known in Richmond to-night. The first must have been known there last night. Can you tell me where Lee's and Longstreet's forces are?"[5] Hooker replied at 1:30: "All of Lee's army, so far as I know, is extended along the immediate banks of the Rappahannock, from Hamilton's Crossing to Culpeper. A. P. Hill's corps is on his right, below Fredericksburg. Ewell's corps joins his left, reaching to the Rapidan; and beyond that river is Longstreet's corps, with not less than 10,000 cavalry, under Stuart. These bodies have been much swollen in numbers of late, the enemy's divisions corresponding with our corps."[6]

At 2 p.m. Lincoln wired Hooker: "If you can show me a trial of the incendiary shells on Saturday night, I will try to join you at 5 p.m. that day." Hooker replied at 6:20 that evening: "If I am not very much mistaken, I shall be constrained to move my army on to the Orange and Alexandria Railroad before that time. I have three corps there at this time." But at 9 p.m. he wired again saying he had had his days mixed up: "It will give me great pleasure to have the gun on exhibition at 5 p.m. tomorrow. I have some good targets in the shape of rebel camps which the gun will enfilade."[7]

Meanwhile, Hooker continued to worry that Lee was going to cross the Rappahannock and get around his right flank. At 3:20 p.m. Dan Butterfield wired Pleasonton, who was at Warrenton Junction: "The general wishes every possible information with regard to enemy's movements. He desires you to lose no opportunity and neglect nothing possible to be done to obtain it. Look sharply to your right. By no means allow the enemy to turn it. Though he may be crippled by your gallant attack of the 9th, he will use the more exertion to get you or us at a disadvantage. Be watchful, vigilant, and let nothing escape you."[8] At 3:45 p.m. Seth Williams wired Pleasonton to return the infantry under Russell and Ames to their respective corps.

At 6 p.m. Pleasonton replied to Butterfield: "There is no news of the enemy's movements. I have parties out to the right on the lookout. I am inclined to believe they will not send off their cavalry or make a move until they are satisfied of ours. The information I receive is, that they will play the defensive until we make a false step. The most serious loss to the enemy has been horseflesh. . . . Assure the general I shall do everything I can to keep him advised and carry out his views." At 7:45 p.m. Butterfield wired Pleasonton again: "The general desires to know how far beyond Sulphur Springs and in what portion of the Valley your scouts have penetrated; what reports and what you know positively regarding enemy's movements in that direction. This is of importance, and information is desired as soon as possible. Inform General Reynolds also. He is at Deep Run to-night;

Bealeton to-morrow." Pleasonton replied at 10 p.m.: "My scouts to-day have been beyond Waterloo. Saw no signs of the enemy. Have scouts out on the way to Luray and Chester Gaps [in the Blue Ridge]. Will report as soon as I hear from them."[9]

Sometime during that day, Butterfield sent confidential orders to Reynolds: "In view of the position of affairs on the right, the absence of any specific information as to the objects, movements, and purposes of the enemy, the necessity for the presence of the commanding general here, he directs me to say to you that you will assume command of the right wing of the army until such time as he may arrive there. You will move with your corps up to the vicinity of Bealeton to-morrow. General Howard, with the Eleventh Corps, is at Catlett's, or should be to-morrow afternoon. He left here at 12 to-day. The positions of Meade and Birney [3rd Corps] you are advised of by previous letters. General Pleasonton, with all the cavalry, is on the right, and will, of course, be subject to your orders. The enemy must not be permitted to cross the river to make his intended raid. Circumstances may make it proper for you to attack him. Of this you must judge. Use all possible endeavors to get information."[10]

To Major General John Sedgwick, commander of the 6th Corps, part of which was still across the Rappahannock at Franklin's Crossing, Butterfield wrote sometime that day: "The major-general commanding directs that, upon receipt of this order, you quietly withdraw your forces to the north bank of the Rappahannock. When your forces are over, notify General Benham [of the engineers], that he may take up the bridges. You will cover the withdrawal of the bridges. The withdrawal not to commence until after dark. The general suggests that you cover the bridges with hay or boughs, to conceal any noise of artillery or troops in crossing."[11]

The governor of Pennsylvania, Andrew G. Curtin, issued a proclamation that day calling on the people of his state to enlist in the two new corps being specially raised for their defense. But he wrote to Secretary of War Stanton saying that, in order to facilitate this, he thought it advisable to postpone recruiting new

3-years regiments in his state. Stanton wired back a strong disapproval of this idea and wired General Couch "to give his neglect no countenance or assent, but, on the contrary, do everything in your power to promote the three years' recruiting."[12] No one wanted to volunteer for the new corps, as there was no bounty for enlisting in it, no guarantee that they'd ever get paid, and no apparent limit to how long they might have to serve.

At Murfreesborough, Tennessee, that day, 12 June, Rosecrans' chief of staff, General Garfield, wrote a long memorandum for his commander summarizing in considerable detail the responses of his corps and division commanders to his questions about advancing against Bragg. Then he went on to consider the current strength of Bragg's army, showing how he arrived at his figures. After all the additions, subtractions and explanations, he came up with a remarkably accurate figure for Bragg of 30,000 infantry, 9,500 cavalry, and 2,120 artillerymen (twenty batteries), or a total of 41,680. Then, he went on: ". . . assuming these to be correct, and granting, what is still more improbable, that Bragg would abandon all his rear posts, and entirely neglect his communications, and could bring his last man into battle, I next ask what have we to oppose to him?" After deducting for numerous garrisons, convalescents on light duty, headquarters types, and reinforcements not yet integrated into the main army, he came up with an estimate of "65,137 bayonets and sabers to throw against Bragg's 41,680." A ratio of over 3:2. He then enumerated several very telling points:

"1st. Bragg's army is now weaker than it has been since the battle [of Stones River] or is likely to be again for the present, while our army has reached its maximum strength, and we have no right to expect further re-enforcements for several months, if at all.

"2d. Whatever may be the result at Vicksburg, the determination of its fate will give large re-enforcements to Bragg. If Grant is successful, his army will require many weeks to recover from the shock and strain of his late campaign, while Johnston will send back to Bragg a force sufficient to insure the safety of Tennessee.

"3d. If Grant fails, the same result will inevitably follow, so far as Bragg's army is concerned. No man can affirm with certainty the result of any battle, however great the disparity in numbers. Such results are in the hands of God. But viewing the question in the light of human calculation, I refuse to entertain a doubt that this army, which in January last defeated Bragg's superior numbers, cannot overwhelm his present greatly inferior force. The most unfavorable course for us that Bragg could take would be to fall back without giving us battle, but this would be very disastrous to him. Besides the loss of material of war, and the abandonment of the rich and abundant harvest now nearly ripe in Central Tennessee, he would lose heavily by desertion. It is well known that a widespread dissatisfaction exists among his Kentucky and Tennessee troops. They are already deserting in large numbers.

"4th. A retreat would greatly increase both the desire and the opportunity for desertion, and would very materially reduce his physical and moral strength. While it would lengthen our communications, it would give us possession of McMinnville, and enable us to threaten Chattanooga and East Tennessee, and it would not be unreasonable to expect an early occupation of the former place.

"5th. But the chances are more than even that a sudden and rapid movement would compel a general engagement, and the defeat of Bragg would be in the highest degree disastrous to the rebellion.

"6th. The turbulent aspect of politics in the loyal States renders a decisive blow against the enemy at this time of the highest importance to the success of the Government at the polls, and in the enforcement of the conscription act.

"7th. The Government and the War Department believe that this army ought to move upon the enemy; the army desires it, and the country is anxiously hoping for it.

"8th. Our true objective point is the rebel army, whose last reserves are substantially in the field, and an effective blow will crush the shell, and soon be followed by the collapse of the rebel Government.

"9th. You have, in my judgment, wisely delayed a general movement hitherto, till you army could be massed and your cavalry could be mounted. Your mobile force can now be concentrated in twenty-four hours, and your cavalry, if not equal in numerical strength to that of the enemy, is greatly superior in efficiency and *morale.*

"For these reasons I believe an immediate advance of all our available forces is advisable, and under the providence of God will be successful."[13]

Garfield thus showed a considerably better grasp of the strategic situation than was demonstrated by any of Rosecrans' corps or division commanders (including the highly competent General George Thomas and the normally very aggressive Phil Sheridan), and this memorandum might well have been the most valuable piece of work Garfield ever did for the United States, before or after becoming President.

Down on the South Carolina coast that day, General Gillmore assumed command of the Department of the South. Admiral Foote, however, was still in New York, too ill to travel. A wound he had received while commanding the river ironclads at Fort Donelson had become infected.

At Vicksburg that twelfth day of June, Pemberton wrote another note that he would try to smuggle out to Johnston: "Courier Walker arrived this morning with [percussion] caps. No message from you. Very heavy firing yesterday from mortars and on lines."[14]

Johnston, meanwhile, was writing to Secretary Seddon again that day: "Your dispatch of the 8th imperfectly deciphered and partially answered on the 10th. I have not considered myself commanding in Tennessee since assignment here, and should not have felt authorized to take troops from that department after having been informed by the Executive that no more could be spared. To take from Bragg a force which would make this army fit to oppose Grant, would involve yielding Tennessee. It is for the Government to decide between this State and Tennessee."[15]

Meanwhile, General Halleck was writing to Grant from Washington that day: "I hope you fully appreciate the importance of time in the reduction of Vicksburg. The large re-enforcements sent to you have opened Missouri and Kentucky to rebel raids. The siege should be pushed night and day with all possible dispatch."[16]

Charles Dana wrote another report to Secretary Stanton that day: "Col. E. W. Gantt [Confederate], of Arkansas, who commanded a brigade at Island No. 10, was exchanged, and has since lived in retirement, came in yesterday from within the enemy's lines, and surrendered himself to General Grant, who has sent him to Memphis at his own wish as a prisoner. He gives information of the greatest importance. His motive is desire to bring the war to a close. The rebellion, he says, is near its end, and, if it should not perish by our arms, must fall from its own administration and general corruption into mere military despotism. Slavery, he thinks, is also ended forever. According to his report, Bragg has sent all his material to Atlanta, and is ready with his unincumbered troops to fall back to Bristol and Chattanooga as soon as ordered, so that he may hold those places, while he detaches 25,000 men, in addition to those he has already sent, to swell the forces here under Johnston. From Mobile and Savannah all the troops, except enough to man the heavy guns, have already been withdrawn, so that a small force could take either place. Johnston's present army amounts to 37,000 men, exclusive of the garrison of Vicksburg, which is 25,000, including sick and wounded. The order to evacuate Port Hudson arrived there the very day General Banks opened his lines before it. West of the Mississippi, exclusive of Texas, is Kirby Smith's command (32,500 men). He has been ordered to leave every object, except the relief of Vicksburg. Lee's army has not been reduced; on the contrary, it is stronger and more concentrated than ever. What supples of provisions Pemberton has he does not know, but he knows that percussion caps have been got to him, and that Johnston and he have daily communication.

"Herron will to-day take his position on the Warrenton road, taking care, of course, that the garrison at Vicksburg shall see the whole of his march from Young's Point across the point just below Vicksburg, where his troops will be ferried across the Mississippi. General Grant has also determined to place the whole of Burnside's re-enforcements in that part of the lines, and to put the whole, from McClernand's left, including Lauman's, Herron's, and Burnside's troops, under command of Ord, whose arrival is constantly expected. The siege works have been checked for twenty-four hours by violent storms, but were resumed yesterday. . . . Should General Grant think it advisable to assault again, we are now in position to do it with effect; but, unless Johnston becomes very pressing, he will rather trust to time and general compression."[17] Major General E. O. C. Ord was a favorite of Grant's. He had graduated from West Point four years ahead of him, and in the early days of the war he had commanded a brigade in the famous Pennsylvania Reserve Division of the Army of the Potomac (as had Meade and Reynolds). Later he had commanded a division under Grant, but he had been severely wounded in October of 1862 while pursuing the Confederate retreat from Corinth, Mississippi. He was now recovered from his wound and on his way back to Grant's army.

The division of the 16th Corps under General W. Sooy Smith reached Grant that day, but it was slated to join the forces accumulating around Haynes' Bluff to guard the army's rear.

Meanwhile, the siege continued. "About this time," Pemberton later noted in his report, "our provisions, particularly of meat, having become almost exhausted, General Stevenson was instructed to impress all cattle in the city, and the chief commissary directed to sell only one ration per diem to any officer. He was also instructed to issue for bread equal portions of rice and flour, four ounces of each."[18] Slaves working for Henry Ginder, a civilian engineer employed by Pemberton's army, fared even worse. Ginder, in writing to his wife, mentioned that they got only a small piece of cornbread for breakfast and another, plus a very small piece of bacon, for dinner. Personally, he was doing better, for, as he told his wife, even though he ate only two meals a day, "We live with a man who has a vegetable garden and keeps our table pretty well supplied." He casually mentioned that one of his carpenters had been struck by lightning the night of the storm but not seriously hurt. "I pitied our poor soldiers the night of the rainstorm," he said, "lying in it all night and unable to do anything else the next morning for fear of Yankee sharpshooters, who expend more ammunition in one day than we have on hand. If they don't get this place, it will have been a most unprofitably costly job to them; if they do get it, it will be a very cheap bargain."[19]

The next day, 13 June, the provost marshal of McClernand's corps sent a report to Grant on what had been learned from Confederate deserters: "We came out because we are starving," they said. "We get one-quarter pound of bacon, 9 ounces meal, made of ground peas and corn, *sometimes* a cupful of beans and a little sugar or molasses, as rations. The men are all weak, and about one-fourth of them sick, mostly with diarrhea. Don't think we could march 5 miles in a day in regular marching order. We are, according to common report, from 15,000 to 20,000 strong, not over 20,000. Some are killed and wounded every day, but we cannot say how many. Minie balls do the most execution. The mortar-boat shells mostly fall between the town and the fortifications, where there are not many persons. The forts are considerably damaged by the Federal artillery, and have to be repaired every night after being fired upon.

"All that I am acquainted with are getting very dissatisfied, officers now as well as men. Our only dependence is in General

Johnston, and we are losing all faith in him. We think that Vicksburg can hold out two weeks yet, if the men don't get tired before that time. We do not believe that many would be willing to try to cut their way out; it might be half would try it, if ordered, but doubt it. Rumor says you (Federals) have 100,000 men, but cannot be re-enforced, as Price has taken Helena [untrue]. We think the main body of your men is at Black River. More of the men would come over, but the Federal pickets fire too much for us. A great many are expecting that the place will be surrendered in a few days, and would prefer to be taken prisoners than run the risk of deserting. The town is pretty well used up, but the citizens stay in caves when you are shelling, and not many are killed. We don't like General Pemberton at all, and think General Grant is too sharp for him. . . . We have had no reliefs in the trenches until the last few days, and now they are put on because the men are getting so weak."[20]

General Hurlbut wrote to Grant that day, the 13th, from Memphis to warn that, because he had stripped his district of so many defenders, the Confederates were already up to mischief there. Rebel cavalry had crossed the Tennessee River and been seen around Jackson, Tennessee, recently abandoned by the Federals; other Confederates, under General S. A. M. Wood, were lurking near Corinth. "Rosecrans does not seem to press forward his right, which I think he should do, and this leaves my flank and rear open to any attack by way of Tennessee River," he complained, "and it will not be difficult for them, as they contract their line, to send a force of 6,000 or 10,000 in rear of Corinth. The demonstrations in that quarter have compelled me to countermand a strong expedition, intended to operate below the Tallahatchee. I hope in a few days to clear that part of the line and reach below."[21]

Joe Johnston reported to Richmond that day that scouts had spotted 23 transports loaded with Union infantry and artillery going down the Mississippi to Grant in the last few days. In response, evidently, to a question to his own chief of staff about whether Grant was receiving reinforcements from Rosecrans,

Johnston wired Bragg's chief of staff that day: "We have no means of knowing whence Grant's re-enforcements come. You ought to know if Rosecrans has sent away troops. If he has, the rest of Hardee's corps should come here. Ask General Bragg the question you put to Colonel Ewell."[22]

In Virginia on that Saturday, the 13th day of June, Lee was writing to Secretary Seddon: "You can realize the difficulty of operating in any offensive movement with this army if it has to be divided to cover Richmond. It seems to me useless to attempt it with the force against it. You will have seen its effective strength by the last returns. I grieve over the desolation of the country and the distress to innocent women and children, occasioned by spiteful excursions of the enemy unworthy of a civilized nation. It can only be prevented by local organizations and bold measures. As regards the cavalry, I have not half as much as I require to keep back the enemy's mounted force in my front. If I weaken it, I fear a heavier calamity may befall us than that we wish to avoid. . . . I believe the expedition reported to General Elzey as marching up the Peninsula is one of those raids. . . . I think the enemy had been mystified as to our movements until the publication of my dispatch to the Department of the cavalry fight on the 9th, and the comments and assertions of some of our Richmond papers. The day after the fight everything subsided to their former lines. Yesterday movements were discovered up the Rappahannock, and pickets report they continued all night."[23]

However, the Federals were still "mystified" about Lee's movements. General Pleasonton wired Hooker at 8 a.m. that one of his informants told him "that Ewell left Culpeper last Sunday morning, 7th, and Longstreet on Monday and Tuesday, for the Valley. Have parties over the river, and expect to know more today. Would it not be well for General Stahel to send out toward the Valley and see?"[24] There ensued a tremendous exchange of messages between Pleasonton, Dan Butterfield, John Reynolds, and other Union officers throughout that day, trying to figure out where the Rebels were, and what they were up to, and what to do about it. As Butterfield put it in one message to Reynolds, "In view of the lack of information concerning their movements, the position is a delicate one, requiring energy and vigilance.... The enemy must on no account be permitted to get on the line of retreat of your wing by Manassas to Alexandria, or a position in front of Washington."[25] In other words, try to avoid a repetition of the Second Bull Run campaign.

Lincoln wired Hooker at 11:30 a.m. about his proposed visit to witness a demonstration of a new incendiary shell: "I was coming down this afternoon, but if you prefer I should not, I shall blame you if you do not tell me so." Hooker replied, "It may be well not to come."[26] For that afternoon Hooker finally decided to abandon his position opposite Fredericksburg and move farther west. This necessitated breaking up his supply depot at Aquia Landing, on the Potomac River, and opening a new base at Alexandria. Consequently there was an additional flurry of messages between various quartermasters and other officers involved in this change, as well as instructions to the various corps commanders as to where and when to move and how to cover the movement from any pursuit while still watching the upper fords of the Rappahannock.

At 7:45 p.m. Hooker wired Halleck: "All my sources of information confirm the statement that Longstreet's and Ewell's corps have passed through Culpeper and Sperryville, toward the Valley. The instructions of the President, approved by yourself, and your original letter of instructions, compel me, in view of this movement of the enemy, to transfer the operations of this army from the line of the Aquia to the Orange and Alexandria Railroad. Accordingly, directions have been given for the First, Third, Fifth, and Eleventh Corps to rendezvous at Manassas Junction with the cavalry. The Second, Sixth, and Twelfth, with the Reserve Artillery, after covering the withdrawal of Government property from depots, have been directed to march to Dumfries, and from thence to be governed by the movements of the enemy, the object being to bring the two wings together as far in advance on that line as the movements of the enemy will justify. The corps will be withdrawn from their positions on the river to-night, the line being held by pickets until the proper time arrives for their withdrawal. To-morrow p.m. my headquarters will be at Dumfries."[27]

At 2:45 p.m. Governor Andrew Curtin of Pennsylvania wired General Halleck at Washington: "If the rebel cavalry move across the Potomac, will the cavalry of General Hooker's army pursue them, or be used to retard their movements? My object in asking is to know whether my duty as Executive of this State, under direction of the President, may not require an immediate call of the militia to resist invasion." Halleck replied, "I respectfully suggest the impropriety of my advising otherwise than through my official superiors, the Secretary of War and the President."[28]

Meanwhile, Ewell's 2nd Corps of Lee's army suddenly made its presence felt in the Shenandoah Valley that 13th day of June. With two of his divisions, his reserve artillery, and one regiment of Jenkins' cavalry (and the Maryland infantry battalion and artillery battery that had been stationed in the Valley previously), Ewell approached Winchester, which was held by General Milroy with two brigades of his 2nd Division of the 8th Corps/Middle Department. Ed Johnson's Confederate division, preceded by the cavalry regiment, took the road running from Front Royal to Winchester, drove in the Union pickets, and formed line of battle some two miles from the town while engaging in some long-range artillery dueling. Jubal Early's division moved west to get onto the macadamized Valley turnpike south of Winchester, then moved northward on it, skirmishing with some Federals near Kernstown, and halted for the night just within artillery range of the Union position at Winchester. "On examining the enemy's fortifications from General Johnson's position," Ewell later reported, "I found they had put up works on the hills I had intended gaining possession of, and were busy strengthening them."[29]

In the mean time, Rodes, with what had once been D. H. Hill's division plus most of Jenkins' cavalry, approached Berryville, ten miles east of Winchester, that day, where he was supposed to overwhelm a mixed brigade of Union infantry, cavalry and artillery (the 3rd Brigade of Milroy's division). "But before reaching Millwood," Rodes later reported, "the advance of the infantry was discovered by some of the enemy's cavalry who had come up from Berry's Ferry (apparently *en route* to Berryville), a result which would have been avoided had General Jenkins occupied Millwood during the night before, as he was ordered to do. Finding our movements discovered, the division was marched with the utmost celerity through Millwood upon Berryville, where Jenkins' brigade, after driving in the enemy's cavalry, was found held at bay by the Federal artillery."[30]

Actually, Colonel McReynolds, the Union brigade commander, had been informed the night before by his cavalry patrols of the Confederates' approach. He had sent off his supplies and wagons to Bunker Hill, on the Valley Turnpike about halfway between Winchester and Martinsburg, escorted by one company of infantry and one of cavalry. Most of Jenkins' cavalry followed this detachment and caught up with it at Bunker Hill, "losing several men in a gallant attack upon a party of the latter," Rodes reported, "who had thrown themselves into two stone houses, well provided for defense, with loop-holes and barricades fixed for that purpose. He captured here about 75 or 100 prisoners, and drove the balance toward Martinsburg."[31]

In reality, McReynolds' wagons and their escort had been warned by a scout that the Rebel cavalry was approaching and had hitched up again and moved out before Jenkins arrived, moving on to Martinsburg and joining the garrison there. The prisoners Jenkins took came from two companies of infantry regularly stationed at Bunker Hill who, instead of remaining in the pair of abandoned churches (not houses) they used for blockhouses, went out to fight in the open and got overrun by Jenkins' cavalry. Only then did the survivors hole up in their blockhouses, fighting off the Rebels until the latter gave up and decided to move on to the north, bivouacking for the night a few miles short of Martinsburg.

A signal of four guns being fired at Winchester meant that McReynolds was supposed to march his brigade to that town, but he found that part of the Rebel infantry was moving across the direct road between him and it, so he sent most of his command by a round-about route to the north, through Summit Point, while he, with six companies of infantry, 150 cavalrymen, and two guns, fought to delay pursuit, which he did for about 45 minutes before taking up the march himself. The Confederates followed but never brought him to bay, although one battalion of Jenkins' cavalry, which had remained with Rodes main force, managed to charge the Federals as they were crossing Opequon Creek. A countercharge by Union cavalry and a few blasts from a single cannon soon drove them back. Rodes then gave up the pursuit, for his men had already marched over 20 miles that day, and put his division into camp at Summit Point. McReynolds reached Winchester at about 9 p.m. in a heavy rain. There he found that the town itself was being abandoned and the Federal troops were moving into the fortifications on the hills northwest of town that Ewell had spotted. His command was placed in a work called, because of its shape, the star fort.

Milroy's boss, General Schenck, commander of the 8th Corps and the Middle Department, was ill at that time, but he had sent his chief of staff, Lieutenant Colonel Piatt, to Harper's Ferry to check on things in the Shenandoah Valley. Schenck telegraphed Piatt at 2:55 p.m. that day: "Instruct General Milroy to use great caution, risking nothing unnecessarily, and to be prepared for falling back, in good order, if overmatched. I rely on your having support afforded him as far as may be practicable."[32] And that same day 8th Corps headquarters issued orders for Brigadier General Daniel Tyler to "proceed immediately to Harper's Ferry and Martinsburg, confer with Brigadier-General Kelley, and assume command of all forces, including brigade at Martinsburg, which can be sent to the support of Major-General Milroy, and cover the march of that general's forces to Harper's Ferry. The general commanding Eighth Army Corps leaves much of the conduct of this important mission to the discretion of Brigadier-General Tyler, and only suggests Bunker Hill, 9 miles from Winchester, on the Martinsburg pike, as a suitable position on which to make a stand in case he should find the rebels in force between him and Major-General Milroy."[33] This was a good idea, but rather late, and no one had yet told Milroy that he should actually retreat to Harper's Ferry. He had only been told to prepare.

Although his troops had been skirmishing with the Confederates all day, up until about 6 p.m. Milroy had assumed that he was only confronted by the usual Confederate troops that operated in and around the Valley, "or," he later said, "that the anticipated cavalry raid of General Stuart was in progress, against either or both of which combined I could have held my position. I deemed it impossible that Lee's army, with its immense artillery and baggage trains, could have escaped from the Army of the Potomac, and crossed the Blue Ridge. . . . The movement must have occupied five or six days, and notice of its being in progress could have been conveyed to me from General Hooker's headquarters in five minutes, for telegraphic communication still existed between Baltimore and Winchester."[34]

However, at about 6 p.m. some of his troops recaptured a picket post that had been overrun by some Confederates, and they took a prisoner, "from whom I learned," Milroy later reported, "that he belonged to Hays' Louisiana brigade, which was a part of Ewell's corps, the whole of which, and part of Longstreet's, was in our immediate vicinity. A deserter who came in shortly afterward confirmed his statement. This was the first intimation that I received that Lee's army had quietly retired before the lines of the Army of the Potomac, and performed a five or six days' march." Then, about three hours later, McReynolds' brigade had shown up with its tale of being attacked and pursued from Berryville by a large Rebel force. "At this time it was evident," Milroy said, "that at least two corps of Lee's army, numbering not less than 50,000 men, and abundantly supplied with artillery, were in my immediate vicinity, and that my retreat by the Martinsburg and Berryville roads was cut off. I still hoped that there had been some corresponding action of the Army of the Potomac, and that if I could sustain myself for twenty-four hours I would be relieved."[35] Actually, of course, it was only one corps of Lee's army, of about 25,000 men, but that would prove more than enough, since it outnumbered Milroy's division by about 3 to 1, and the Army of the Potomac was still far to the east.

At 9 p.m., just before McReynolds' arrived, Milroy tried to telegraph word to Schenck about the men captured from Ewell's corps, but the storm then in progress was interfering with the telegraph wires, and the operator thought perhaps the Rebels had cut them. Milroy asked for volunteers to take the message to Martinsburg or Harper's Ferry. Captain William H. Boyd, a company commander in the 1st New York Cavalry, in McReynolds' brigade, offered to carry it if he could take his whole company along as an escort, considering the number of Rebels lurking in the area, and Milroy agreed.

Out in Tennessee that day, the 13th, General Forrest was wounded in an altercation with one of his own officers. A lieutenant in a battery of artillery attached to Forrest's cavalry shot him during a heated discussion about why the lieutenant was being transferred to another command. Forrest then stabbed his assailant with a pocket knife. The lieutenant's wound proved fatal; the general's did not, although doctors at first thought it might be.

Down in Louisiana at 11:15 a.m. on the 13th, every gun and mortar in Banks' army and Farragut's fleet opened fire on the Confederate defenses of Port Hudson. For an hour shells rained down upon the Rebel positions at the rate of about one per second. The silence that followed served to dramatize the appearance of a flag of truce, and a message from Banks to General

Gardner was sent into the Confederate lines demanding the surrender of the garrison. Gardner replied, "I have to state that my duty requires me to defend this position, and, therefore, I decline to surrender."[36] When this answer was received, Banks ordered the bombardment to start again, and it continued throughout the night. That evening Banks and his division commanders met at his headquarters to make final plans for an assault to be made the next day. During the night an unaccountable tidal wave, six feet high, swept up the Mississippi, and one of the Confederate river batteries collapsed, one of its guns being lost in the muddy water.

To make sure everyone would follow the planned time-table, watches of Union division and brigade commanders had been set by a telegraphic signal sent from Banks headquarters. By 1 a.m. on the 14th, a Sunday, the final orders for the assault had been distributed, which didn't leave much time for any final arrangements, for, as planned, at 3 a.m. the Union artillery opened fire again, and, although a thick fog had settled over the entire area, at 3:45 a.m. General Augur launched a feint – a fake attack – on the work called the Citadel at the extreme right, or southern end, of the Rebel defenses. At 4 a.m. the bombardment stopped, and men from General Dwight's division tried to pass up the river bank, below the bluffs upon which the Citadel sat. First there was a detachment of 50 men who were to race through this narrow gap, under the cover of Augur's feint, and capture Gardner's headquarters. Following them was a detachment of 200 men who were to get around behind the Citadel and take it from the rear, which would be a signal for two regiments to charge forward and roll up the Rebel line. However, the two detachments found that it was impossible for them to get past the Citadel, and the whole idea had to be abandoned. Dwight sent forward a few regiments to attack the Citadel from the front, but they only got to within about 300 yards of it before being forced by Rebel artillery to take cover in a gully. The fight on this end of the line then turned into a day-long sniping contest.

Much farther up the line, also at 4 a.m., two regiments of

Paine's 3rd Division of the 19th Corps advanced, deployed as skirmishers. They were followed by several companies carrying hand grenades as well as their rifles. Then came the 31st Massachusetts, carrying bags full of cotton with which to fill the ditch in front of the Rebel parapet, followed by the rest of the division, one brigade at a time. Their objective was a small salient in the Confederate line not far from Commissary Hill called the Priest Cap.

Since the unsuccessful assault on 27 May, the Confederates had not only greatly strengthened their works but had sent men out to gather up arms and ammunition left on the field by dead and wounded Federals. Now almost every Rebel had a rifle for long-range firing and a musket loaded with buckshot for close-range work. When the Union skirmishers were within 90 yards of the Confederate lines, General Paine yelled out the order to charge, but almost immediately the Rebels opened fire, and scores of Federals went down, including Paine, whose leg was broken below the knee by a rifle bullet. Nevertheless the 31st Massachusetts managed to reach and partially fill the ditch with their bags of cotton, and troops from several Union regiments climbed over the parapet and entered the Rebel fort.

However, the bulk of the division could not or would not advance, and, with Paine out of action, his units were getting all mixed up and becoming unmanageable. General Grover sent Colonel Henry W. Birge to take command of Paine's division, but by the time he arrived the assault had lost its momentum. The 1st Mississippi counterattacked the Federals who had entered the Confederate works and, although taking heavy casualties in the process, drove them out. The Federals reformed and tried again, making repeated assaults on the Rebel works, in many cases getting close enough to lob grenades into the defenses, but could not again breach the Confederate line. Birge threw in his other two brigades, but they could do no better. The colonel of the 133rd New York was wounded while clambering up the Rebel breastworks, but the Federals never got inside them again. By 8 a.m. this attack was finished.

Weitzel's 4th Division was supposed to have attacked

simultaneously with Paine's, but various complications had delayed it until 7 a.m., and even then things did not go smoothly. This assault was also supposed to be led by two regiments of skirmishers, followed by one carrying grenades and one carrying 30-pound bags of cotton. But one of the regiments meant to serve as skirmishers had been guided in the wrong direction by a staff officer, and the other one, the 75th New York, moved out alone. The Rebels heard them approaching along their covered way, a sunken road, and opened fire as they emerged within 80 yards of the Confederate lines. The other regiment of skirmishers, the 12th Connecticut, was further delayed by wounded New Yorkers using the sunken road to make for the rear, but it finally emerged only to be instantly driven to cover by enemy fire, as the New Yorkers had been before them. The officer in command of the two skirmishing regiments went down with a wound, but the two regiments stayed in place, returning the Rebel fire as best they could from whatever cover they could find, within 20 to 50 yards of the defenses.

Under cover of their fire, the 91st New York moved up to the edge of the ditch in front of the parapet and hurled their 5-pound grenades, then, unslinging their rifles, started crossing the ditch, only to have many of their grenades tossed back at them by the Confederates. Nevertheless these New Yorkers stormed up the outer face of the parapet, led by their color-bearer, a Union-loyal Southerner, who, in one of those crazy coincidences of this fraternal struggle, was shot by his Confederate brother as he attempted to plant his flag on top of the parapet. The regiment was driven back and soon replaced by others as they emerged from the sunken road, but the 24th Connecticut had failed to fill the ditch with their bags of cotton, which lay scattered on the ground, some being used as cover by Federals firing at the Confederates who exposed themselves above the parapet. The colonel commanding the leading brigade went down with a wound, and soon, here too, units lost all cohesion in the face of an almost continuous fire of rifles and muskets. Any Rebel artillery that attempted to join in, however, was almost immediately silenced by the overwhelming fire of Union guns.

An order arrived from Banks telling Weitzel to storm Port Hudson no matter what the cost, and that general sent for another brigade. Its commander yelled to his men, "All I ask of you is to follow me! Will you follow me?" Fifty men shouted, "Yes," but the rest declined to answer and remained sitting on the ground.[37] The next brigade, coming up in support, was more responsive, and the colonel led the two units forward, only to have his brains blown out. His men, demoralized by this and disorganized by the rough terrain they had to cross, soon lost their momentum, but many of them reached a ravine only a few yards from the Confederate works, and by 10 a.m. between 500 and 1000 Federals had taken shelter there. Several Union officers conferred at a point only 30 yards from the Rebel defenses and decided that to attack again would merely increase the casualty list. "If General Banks wants to go in there," one colonel said, "let him go and be damned. I won't slaughter my men that way."[38] Banks sent an order for a storming party of 200 men to be organized, promising promotions to all who volunteered. The volunteers were found easily enough, but the regimental commanders agreed that to send them forward was stupid, and eventually Banks rescinded the order.

By 11 a.m. the battle was over, but the Federals in advanced positions had to lie in the sun for the rest of the day, waiting for darkness to cover their movements. Over a thousand of them were wounded. General Paine lay between two rows in a field of cotton, afraid to even cover his face with his cap for fear that the movement would draw fire. Several soldiers who tried to come to his aid were shot. Finally a private from the 12th Connecticut crawled to him, took him on his back, and carried him to safety.

Banks wrote to Admiral Farragut: "As you will have readily perceived, the attack did not succeed, though the merest accident separates success from failure. We hold advanced positions, and shall intrench them to-night. The enemy made one or two attempts on the center and right to open with his artillery, but was almost instantly silenced. It required a little longer to silence some troublesome guns on the left, but it was done. We shall hold the advanced positions we now have, and throw up rifle-pits to cover them to-night. I believe our loss has not been heavy, excepting in officers, and the men are in tolerable good spirits. I am still confident of the final result."[39]

Up at Vicksburg that day, 14 June, Charles Dana was writing another report to Secretary Stanton. (It took from 3 to 5 days for them to reach him.) He obviously thought his work there would soon be done. "All the indications point to the speedy surrender of this place," he said. "Deserters who came out yesterday say that the Tennessee and Georgia regiments have determined to stack their arms within three days and refuse to continue the defense on the ground that it is useless, and that it is impossible to fight on the rations they receive. . . . These deserters also say that fully one-third of the garrison are in hospital, and that officers, as well as men, have begun to despair of relief from Johnston. The troops of General Herron got into position yesterday. The advance of the Ninth Army Corps is also believed by General Grant to have arrived at Young's Point, though he has no positive report. . . . All of W. S. Smith's division are now at Haynes' Bluff, where I saw them yesterday working upon the intrenchments with admirable zeal. . . . From Joe Johnston there is no news since my last dispatch. . . . He has made no new movements in this quarter. . . . Please inform me by telegraph whether you wish me to go to General Rosecrans after the fall of Vicksburg, or whether you have any other orders for me."[40]

That day General Pemberton wrote another note to be smuggled out to Johnston: "Last night Captain Sanders arrived with 200,000 [percussion] caps, but brought no information as to your position or movements. The enemy is landing troops in large numbers on Louisiana shore, above Vicksburg. They are probably from Memphis, but it may be from Yazoo; I cannot ascertain positively. On the Graveyard road [Sherman's front] the enemy has run his saps to within 25 yards of our works. He will probably attempt to sink a mine. I shall try to thwart him. I am anxiously expecting to hear from you, to arrange for co-operation." Johnston wrote to Pemberton that same day: "All that we can attempt is, to save you and your garrison. To do this, exact co-operation is indispensable. By fighting the enemy simultaneously at the same point of his line, you may be extricated. Our joint forces cannot raise the siege of Vicksburg. My communication with the rear can best be preserved by operating north of railroad. Inform me as soon as possible what point will suit you best."[41] Johnston's chief quartermaster wired General Breckinridge, at Jackson, that day that, in order to move their army they would have to seize horses or mules from civilians to pull the supply wagons. "General Johnston is absent," he said. "One day is important. I propose you send me a cavalry company or two, and let us take them right up. . . . Time is blood now."[42]

Meanwhile, the siege continued. Captain Hickenlooper was finally well enough to resume his duties that day and found that mistakes had been made in his absence. His notes for the 14th say: "Visited the work this morning. I find the trench was not carried far enough across the road before making the turn, and was then run too far to the right. Corrected it by cutting away south side and putting up two traverses."[43]

Although a Sunday, the 14th was not a day of rest for either army. "I wish we had one day in seven for rest and freedom from care," said Sergeant Osborn Oldroyd of McPherson's corps; "but there is no such thing now for the soldier. It is shoot, shoot, dodge, dodge, from morning to night, without cessation, except when we are asleep. When the time comes, we can lie down and sleep soundly all night, right under our cannon, firing over us all the time, without disturbing us in the least. . . . Sunday is general inspection day, and the officers passed through our quarters at 10 a.m., finding our guns and accoutrements bright and clean. If any young lady at the North needs a good housekeeper, she can easily be accommodated by making a requisition on the 20th Ohio. In fact we can all do patchwork, sew on buttons, make beds, and sweep.... We are so close to the Third Louisiana redan that a hardtack [cracker] was tossed into it by one of our boys, and then held up on a bayonet there to satisfy us of its safe arrival. Some of the boys have become reckless about the rifle-pits, and are frequently hit by rebel bullets. Familiarity breeds a contempt of danger."[44]

Sharpshooters took their toll of the Rebels as well. Sergeant Tunnard of the 3rd Louisiana mentioned one member of his regiment, William McGuinness, who "was shot through the right eye as he was looking through one of the pipes planted in the earthworks to observe the effects of his shooting. He was seen by one of the enemy, who fired at him with deadly aim. This incident is given to show how close the combatants were to each other, and with what certainty each party used their rifles upon the smallest-sized object exposed to their aim. McGuinness recovered, but lost his eyesight and a piece of the bone from the side of his face."[45]

The most famous, or notorious, sharpshooter on either side was 2nd Lieutenant Henry C. Foster of the 23rd Indiana, in McPherson's corps. "He was an unerring shot," according to a later newspaper account, "and wore a cap made of raccoon fur. From this he was called 'Coonskin' the Seventeenth Corps through, and wherever he was, woe to the Confederate head that appeared above a parapet. 'Coonskin' went out once in the nighttime, crept up toward the Confederate defenses and built himself a burrow in the ground, with a peep-hole in it. There he would frequently take provisions with him, and stay several days at a time, watching for Confederates. At length he built 'Coonskin's Tower.' The Jackson and Vicksburg railway had been torn up for miles in the rear of Vicksburg, and railway iron and cross-ties lay all about. Taking advantage of the night hours, Coonskin built himself a tower of the loose railroad ties. Learned in backwoods lore, he knew how to construct the genuine pioneer log-cabin. Working several nights, he at length built the tower so high that by climbing toward its top he could actually look over the Confederate parapets. He could see the men inside the works.

Then, taking aim through the chinks of the logs, he would pick off the enemy. The tower was a terror to the Confederates. They could not use their artillery against it, that having been already quite silenced by the Union batteries. All they could do was to fire musket-balls at it, which whistled around its corners or buried themselves in the logs."[46]

Endnotes

1 OR, I:27:II:440.
2 Ibid., I:27:II:49-50. The first of these messages, with unimportant differences, is also found in I:27:III:50-1, where it is dated 10 June. This is obviously wrong, because the message from Halleck that caused this message to be sent is dated, in I:27:II:50 and I:27:II:171, on the 11th. Milroy's reply and Schenck's reply to him, modifying the order, do not appear in I:27:III at all (nor in III:3) but only in Milroy's report (I:27:II). Since Milroy was later the scapegoat for what befell him, it is possible that someone tampered with the files of messages to make it look like he had been ordered to retreat in plenty of time to do so.
3 Ibid., I:27:II:50-1.
4 Ibid., I:27:I:36-7.
5 Ibid., I:27:III:76.
6 Ibid., I:27:III:70.
7 Ibid., I:27:I:37.
8 Ibid., I:27:III:70.
9 Ibid., I:27:III:71.
10 Ibid., I:27:III:72-3.
11 Ibid., I:27:III:73.
12 Ibid., I:27:III:77.
13 Ibid., I:23:II:420-4.
14 Ibid., I:24:III:961.
15 Ibid., I:24:I:226.
16 Ibid., I:24:I:42.
17 Ibid., I:24:I:97.
18 Ibid., I:24:I:279.
19 Hoehling, *Vicksburg: 47 Days of Siege*, 148.
20 OR, I:24:III:407.
21 Ibid., I:24:III:408-9.
22 Ibid., I:24:III:961-2.
23 Ibid., I:27:III:886.
24 Ibid., I:27:III:80.
25 Ibid., I:27:III:87.
26 Ibid., I:27:I:37.

27 Ibid., I:27:I:38.
28 Ibid., I:27:III:97.
29 Ibid., I:27:II:440.
30 Ibid., I:27:II:547.
31 Ibid., I:27:II:548.
32 Ibid., I:27:III:96.
33 Ibid., I:27:III:96-7.
34 Ibid., I:27:II:43.
35 Ibid., I:27:II:45.
36 Ibid., I:26:I:553.
37 Cunningham, *The Port Hudson Campaign*, 89.
38 Ibid.
39 *OR*, I:26:I:556.
40 Ibid., I:24:I:98-9.
41 Ibid., I:24:III:963.
42 Ibid., I:24:III:964.
43 Ibid., I:24;II:200.
44 Hoehling, *Vicksburg: 47 Days of Siege*, 155-6.
45 Ibid. 155.
46 Johnson and Buel, editors, *Battles and Leaders of the Civil War*, III:541 n.

CHAPTER 9

"He Will Be Gobbled Up"

14 – 15 June 1863

O<small>N THAT SAME</small> 14<small>TH</small> <small>DAY</small> of June, Federals burned Eunice, Arkansas, on the Mississippi River, in retaliation for guerillas firing into the USS *Marmora* from near there.

Up in Middle Tennessee that day, young Major General Joseph Wheeler, commander of the Cavalry Corps of Bragg's Army of Tennessee, went to army headquarters to seek approval for the raid that Morgan, one of his three division commanders, wanted to make into Kentucky. Wheeler didn't know that Morgan intended to go far beyond Kentucky, and with Burnside's best troops now gone, it looked like a good time to re-enter the Blue Grass State. And, as far as the Confederates could tell, Louisville, an important Union supply depot, was defended by only 300 men. Bragg was not anxious to diminish his cavalry, since he had already sent off much of his infantry to Joe Johnston. But, on the other hand, a raid into Kentucky – especially the destruction of a major supply base – might disrupt any Union plans for an offensive against him. He compromised and authorized Morgan to go, but with only 1,500 out of his 2,750 men, plus whatever artillery he thought appropriate. Bragg wanted only Kentucky units sent, so that they could recruit their strength while in their native state. He also stipulated that if Morgan should learn of a Union advance, he was to turn and fall upon the Federals' rear.

In fact, a Union raid in the opposite direction set out that very day, as Colonel William P. Sanders of the 5th Kentucky Cavalry started out from Mount Vernon, Kentucky, with 1,500 cavalry and mounted infantry and two pieces of artillery, headed for East Tennessee. A train of supply wagons would accompany the expedition as far as the Cumberland River. A pair of small Confederate raids were already under way, as well. A detachment of Rebel Kentuckians out of East Tennessee, under Captain P. M. Everett, was near Mount Sterling, east of Lexington, that day, headed for the Ohio River, and a detachment of Morgan's own command, under Captain Thomas H. Hines, had already crossed the Green River and, near Elizabethtown, had burned two railroad cars and taken 100 horses from a train that day. These raiders also captured a Federal paymaster and what Hines later described as "a large sum of money, in greenbacks."[1]

At 11 a.m. that same day, the 14th, Secretary Stanton wired General Dix, at Fort Monroe, to "please forward immediately to Aquia every transport not indispensable to your safety."[2] An hour later General Halleck wired the same officer saying, "Lee's army is in motion toward the Shenandoah Valley. All your available force should be concentrated to threaten Richmond, by seizing and destroying their railroad bridges over the South and North Anna Rivers, and do them all the damage possible. If you cannot accomplish this, you can at least find occupation for a large force of the enemy. There can be no serious danger of an attack on Norfolk now." Dix answered Halleck that afternoon: "All the transports I have are ordered to Aquia Creek, and some of them have gone. If you will order them back as soon as they can be spared, I will concentrate all my force at West Point, and move toward Richmond. I have now no means of bringing the troops at Suffolk here, and my force up the Peninsula is too small to produce much disturbance."[3]

All day and all that Sunday evening Hooker, Halleck, Stanton, and Lincoln remained in the dark about just what was going on in the Shenandoah Valley and where Lee's army was. It should have been Pleasonton's job to keep track of the latter, but Hooker had many of his troopers scattered up and down the

Rappahannock guarding fords so the infantry could be pulled away from the river, and one of his cavalry brigades guarding Thoroughfare Gap in the Bull Run Mountains, a relatively low range to the east of the Blue Ridge, through which Lee had moved to descend upon the Union rear the previous summer, during the Second Bull Run campaign. Sometime that day, General Halleck wired General Schenck, commander of the Middle Department: "I have so repeatedly urged you to withdraw your main forces from Winchester, and so recently (the 11th) directed it, that I cannot understand how Milroy could have been left there to be invested. I repeat, you must concentrate on Harper's Ferry, not on Winchester or Martinsburg. If General Milroy does not obey your orders, remove him from command."[4] What Halleck had failed to take into account was that Schenck was basically a politician in uniform; he probably never heard of the military dictum that a commander's suggestions and advice were the same as orders. At 1 p.m. President Lincoln telegraphed Schenck in words that even he could understand: "Get Milroy from Winchester to Harper's Ferry if possible. He will be gobbled up if he remains, if he is not already past salvation."[5]

Fifteen minutes later Lincoln wired General Hooker: "Do you consider it possible that 15,000 of Ewell's men can now be at Winchester?"[6] Hooker did not answer right away, probably because he didn't know. Besides, he was busy getting his army withdrawn from the position across from Fredericksburg that had been its home for many months, and there was much message traffic between his headquarters and those of the various corps as they tried to coordinate their movements. His army was moving into a well-fought-over area of Northern Virginia that formed a rough square, with the Potomac River forming the north and east sides, the Rappahannock River the south, and the Blue Ridge mountains the west; Aquia Landing was at the southeast corner, and Washington at the northeast corner. Major General Gouverneur K. Warren, Hooker's chief engineer, was in charge of dismantling the supply base at Aquia Landing and making sure that nothing valuable was left behind.

Like Hooker, Union generals in the Valley were of little help in explaining the situation to Washington. Sometime that day Lincoln telegraphed to General Tyler at Martinsburg: "Is Milroy invested so that he cannot fall back to Harper's Ferry?" No reply. At 1:27 p.m. Lincoln wired Brigadier General Benjamin Kelley at Harper's Ferry: "are the forces at Winchester and Martinsburg making an effort to get to you?" Kelley at least answered: "I am not advised that the forces at Winchester, under General Milroy, are falling back to this place. The forces of my command at Martinsburg are ordered to fall back on me, if assailed by overpowering numbers."[7] He didn't say whether they were being "assailed" or not.

At 2:20 p.m. Halleck telegraphed General Brooks at Pittsburgh: "Lee's army is in motion toward the Shenandoah Valley. Pittsburgh and Wheeling should be put in defensible condition as rapidly as possible."[8] No similar message was sent to General Couch, who had now set up his headquarters at Harrisburg, the capital of Pennsylvania. However, sometime that day Schenck wired Couch: "Ewell, with Jackson's old division, and in force, has been fighting us since last night at Winchester, and is pressing on to Martinsburg. I have not the means to check him at the Baltimore and Ohio Railroad or at the Potomac River. I shall concentrate all I can to hold Maryland Heights."[9] Maryland Heights were the high hills just across the Potomac from Harper's Ferry. At 4:30 p.m. Governor Curtin of Pennsylvania wired Stanton that the telegraph line had been down between Winchester and Martinsburg since about 11 o'clock that morning, and that escaping slaves coming into Maryland and Pennsylvania from the Shenandoah all indicated that Martinsburg was under attack.

At 5:30 p.m. Hooker telegraphed Secretary Stanton: "Have received dispatch from General Milroy, dated yesterday. Will act on it as soon as I can hear from the column on the Orange and Alexandria Railroad. Instructions were given for Thoroughfare Gap to be taken possession of and held by my cavalry last night. If the enemy should be making for Maryland, I will make the best dispositions in my power to come up with him."[10] Twenty minutes later Lincoln himself replied: "So far as we can make out here, the enemy have Milroy surrounded at Winchester and Tyler at Martinsburg. If they could hold out a few days, could you help them? If the head of Lee's army is at Martinsburg and the tail of it on the Plank road between Fredericksburg and Chancellorsville, the animal must be very slim somewhere. Could you not break him?"[11] This was an excellent question, but if it was meant to be a suggestion, Lincoln should have remembered that he had already told Hooker not to cross to the south side of the Rappahannock. Since Lee's army, except for "the head" in the Shenandoah Valley, was all still south of that river, Hooker could not "break" it without crossing.

At 6:05 p.m. Stanton received a message, sent to him as well as to Hooker, by Pleasonton: "A negro just in states that he left Gaines' Cross-Roads last night, and the enemy's column passed there for Harper's Ferry on Friday morning [the 12th]. Expected to reach Harper's Ferry by Saturday night. States that Lee was in command; that the whole army was in the column. Saw Ewell in his carriage; also Longstreet and Early. The column was two days passing Gaines' Cross-Roads. Few troops were left at Fredericksburg, and few, excepting cavalry, at Culpeper, as a blind. The whole army was destined for Harper's Ferry, and thence across into Maryland. I believe this man's report."[12] Most of it was wrong. Lee himself and Longstreet's corps were still around Culpeper Court House, and A. P. Hill's corps was still at Fredericksburg.

Stanton replied to Governor Curtin at 6:30 p.m.: "We have this afternoon intelligence from General Tyler, at Martinsburg, that the enemy have appeared there, but in what force he does not state. They are also at Winchester. It is certain now that there is a general movement toward Pennsylvania, although the rear of Lee's army is still south of the Rappahannock."[13] At 7 p.m. General Tyler wired Lincoln: "As soon as night sets in, we will fall back to Williamsport [on the Potomac]; thence to Harper's Ferry." The befuddled President replied: "If you are besieged, how do you dispatch me? Why did you not leave before being besieged?"[14]

At 7:10 p.m. Hooker finally answered Lincoln's question of some six hours before: "In answer to your dispatch concerning General Ewell, I must refer you to that of General Pleasonton, dated 6.05 p. m. to-day."[15] At 7:15 p.m. Pleasonton answered a query from the War Department: "Gaines' Cross-Roads is on the road from Culpeper to Chester Gap [in the Blue Ridge]. I have information that the rebel column passed through Chester Gap on Thursday [the 11th] and Friday. Fifteen thousand infantry and artillery and a good deal of cavalry were left at Culpeper, and are now there. My scouts just in from Barbee's Cross-Roads and Chester Gap. No signs of enemy between this and those points. Shots were heard to-day a long distance off, in the direction of Harper's Ferry."[16] At 8 p.m. Dan Butterfield wired Pleasonton: "General says if enemy are near Harper's Ferry, his cavalry is with him. He would not think of crossing the Potomac with 15,000 artillery and infantry."[17]

At 8:30 p.m. Hooker wrote again to Lincoln: "I have reason to believe that Longstreet's and the greater part of Ewell's corps marched from Culpeper, on the Sperryville road, on Sunday last [7th], and that a column, which occupied four hours in passing, followed on Thursday. If this was the case, the head of the column has had time to reach Winchester, and if it is a movement for invasion, it is a fair presumption to conclude that the bulk of his cavalry is with him. The enemy has in this column not less than between 70,000 and 80,000 men. A. P. Hill's corps, of about 30,000, is still on the south side of the Rappahannock, and General Hancock has just informed me that present appearances indicate that he intends to force the passage of the river in the morning. . . . My [wagon] trains are all this side of Stafford Court-House, and the public property, I am informed, will be removed from Aquia to-morrow – the sick to-night. The First Corps is at Kettle Run; the Second on the Rappahannock; the Third and Fifth at Catlett's Station; the Sixth at Potomac Creek; the Eleventh at Centreville; and the Twelfth at Dumfries to-night. The Second will probably withdraw, the First march to Manassas, and the Sixth to Stafford Court-House during the night."[18]

At 9 p.m. General Kelley at Harper's Ferry wired Secretary Stanton: "Nothing from Winchester to-day, neither from the enemy nor General Schenck. Heavy firing at Martinsburg heard for one and a half hours, ceasing at dusk. Telegraphic communication ceased at 7 p.m., and result not known. Enemy reported at Berryville and Smithfield. My force here is not as large as it should be, yet the troops are in good spirits, and will give a good account of themselves."[19]

At around 9:30 that night Governor Curtin wired Lincoln that he was sending Colonel T. A. Scott, an official of the Pennsylvania Railroad, to Washington to see Lincoln and Stanton to "present you my request to authorize a call for 50,000 troops, which we feel very confident will prove successful."[20] The plan to raise two special corps for the new departments in his state was going to take too long to meet the emergency looming upon them. It was time to call out the militia. Curtin didn't want to do it on his on, because it would hurt him politically and he was running for re-election. He wanted Lincoln to make the call and take the heat.

At 9:45 p.m. Butterfield wired Reynolds: "The general directs me to say Pleasonton can withdraw at 1 to-night from the Rappahannock without reference to Hancock [2nd Corps]. All cavalry, excepting that necessary for correct information, [should be] concentrated at Centreville [25 miles west of Washington], and gotten ready for vigorous service. It will be strengthened by every mounted man that can be sent."[21] It didn't seem to occur to Hooker that it would take Pleasonton's entire corps, to get "correct information." Nor would even that insure that Pleasonton would recognize correct information if he saw it.

At 11:15 p.m. Hooker wired Lincoln again: "Has anything further been heard from Winchester? Will the President allow me to inquire if it is his opinion that Winchester is surrounded by the rebel forces? I make this inquiry for the reason that [Confederate] General Trimble was recently assigned, in orders, to the command of that district, and it is not known what command he had, unless his old one, which had Louisiana regiments in it, and it was in Jackson's, now Ewell's corps. I do not feel like making a move for an enemy until I am satisfied as to his whereabouts. To proceed to Winchester and have him make his appearance elsewhere, would subject me to ridicule. With this feeling, unless otherwise directed, I feel it my duty to proceed to execute the movement indicated on yesterday. I will not, however, issue my order of march until the last moment, in the hope that further information may be received."[22] Worrying about not becoming the subject of ridicule instead of worrying about the best way to defeat the enemy is not the sign of a first-rate commander.

Lincoln answered forty minutes later: "You have nearly all the elements for forming an opinion whether Winchester is surrounded that I have. I really fear, almost believe, it is. No communication has been had with it during the day, either at Martinsburg or Harper's Ferry. At 7 p.m. we lost communication with Martinsburg. The enemy had also appeared there some hours before. At 9 p.m. Harper's Ferry said the enemy was reported at Berryville and Smithfield. If I could know that Longstreet and Ewell moved in that direction so long ago as you stated in your last, then I should feel sure that Winchester is strongly invested. It is quite certain that a considerable force of the enemy is thereabout, and I fear it is an overwhelming one compared with Milroy's. I am unable to give you any more certain opinions."[23]

At 11:45 p.m. Pleasonton sent Hooker some more bad information: "A prisoner, belonging to Breathed's battery, Stuart's artillery, says that Lee's army is divided into three corps, of 30,000 each, commanded by Ewell, A. P. Hill, and Longstreet; that Ewell is above Sulphur Springs, Longstreet is to cross [the Rappahannock] at United States or Banks' Ford, and that Hill is to cross in the vicinity of Fredericksburg. Three days' rations were issued yesterday morning to Ewell's corps. He thinks Ewell will be heard from before to-morrow night."[24] That last sentence, at least, was true.

"As early as Saturday evening," Milroy later reported, "after

I learned of the presence of Lee's army in force, I made up my mind to act on the defensive, economize my forces, wait until the enemy had massed himself for the final attack, and then, unless relieved, force my way through what might appear to be the weakest portion of his lines."[25]

Milroy was an interesting character. Then about 47, he was tall and lithe with an aquiline nose and a thick shock of gray hair that led his troops to sometimes call him their "Old Gray Eagle."[26] He was an abolitionist, a graduate of a Vermont university/military academy with a law degree from Indiana University, and had served as a captain in the Mexican War. He had begun this war as colonel of the 9th Indiana and had earned his stars by good service in the liberation of West Virginia the year before. "No braver warrior than Gen. Milroy ever buckled on a sword," one of his soldiers said.[27] But he was also impulsive and intolerant. Another of his soldiers said he "was of the extremely nervous, excitable kind. He was generally out of patience with something or other, and when in such a mood it seemed difficult for him to treat one civilly."[28] Naturally enough, subordinates tend to avoid superiors with such dispositions whenever possible; consequently such superiors don't get told everything they may need to know.

Early that Sunday morning, the 14th, after the storm of the night before had passed, Milroy sent out detachments of cavalry to scout around, while some of his troops skirmished with some of Ewell's east of Winchester. But, Milroy said, "In consequence of the overwhelming masses of the enemy about me, I kept my forces during the day well in hand and in immediate connection with the forts."[29] These forts were on the hills northwest of town, part of what the Federals called Apple Pie Ridge: two well-built earthworks straddling a road running west to Pughtown. North of the road was the Star Fort, so called because of its five-pointed shape, in and around which McReynold's two infantry regiments and one battery had taken position the night before. South of the road was a four-sided work of similar size, referred to by the Confederates as the Main Fort or Flag Fort. Both works were connected to more extensive, but less formidable, earthworks. About a mile west of these two forts was another string of hills knows at Flint Ridge, and there was a line of earthworks under construction there as well, sometimes called the West Fort, defended by one regiment plus one company of another and a battery of artillery, under Colonel J. Warren Keifer.

At about 9 a.m. Ewell and Early had a look at the Union defenses from another height southwest of town, called Bowers' Hill, and agreed that taking them would not be simple. One of his men said, "We all began to feel as if we had caught the elephant, but could not tell what to do with it."[30] But the two generals eventually agreed that the best point of attack was the unfinished works on Flint Ridge. Once those were taken, they would be in position to dominate the forts on Apple Pie Ridge. Therefore Early's division was sent by a round-about route, so as to remain out of view, to come at the Union defenses from the west. Johnson's division was used to threaten the Federals from the east and keep their attention focused in that direction. The Maryland battalion and one brigade of Early's division, under Brigadier General John B. Gordon, as well as two batteries of artillery, were left at Bowers' Hill to serve as a connecting link between the two divisions and to further divert the Federals' attention.

General Dan Tyler had stepped off the train at Martinsburg at about 8 a.m., under orders to take command of the garrison there: namely two regiments of infantry (one of which had just been called in from North Mountain Depot, farther west), a battery of artillery and a company of Maryland cavalry – in all, about 1,200 men. This small force was the 1st Brigade of the 1st Division of the 8th Corps. To this force had been added the one company of infantry and one of cavalry that had brought in McReynolds' wagons the night before. Martinsburg's importance lay in the fact that it was where the Valley Turnpike crossed the Baltimore & Ohio Railroad, an important lifeline of Washington. The garrison's primary job was to protect the railroad from small Confederate raids. Unfortunately for Tyler, just as he arrived so did the Rebels, in the form of Jenkins' cavalry brigade – or at least word arrived that Confederate cavalry was approaching from the south. Not having had a chance to acquaint himself with the area or the circumstances, he declined to take command, and left the current commander, Colonel B. F. Smith, to confront the Confederates in his own way, saying only that he would be on had to offer advice, if needed.

The two Union commanders were a study in contrasts. Tyler, old enough to be Smith's father, had graduated from West Point way back in 1819, had left the Army in 1834 to be a civil engineer and, eventually, a railroad president, and had commanded a division at the first battle of Bull Run. Since then he had been in and out of the Army a couple of times. Smith had graduated from West Point in 1853, had been a captain in the Regular Army when the war began, and had commanded a regiment at Shiloh before being transferred to the East. Besides the difference in their backgrounds, they were working under different orders. Tyler had been told to hold the door open so Milroy could retreat, but Smith had been told to fall back to Harper's Ferry if attacked by a superior force. He didn't yet know if the force approaching him was large enough to fit that description, so he went out to see. Between 9 and 10 a.m. he deployed his own 126th Ohio (short two companies) behind some stone fences south of town, sent out skirmishers and brought up his battery of six guns, then finally called forward his other regiment, the 106th New York, which deployed straddling the Valley pike, sending out skirmishers of its own. The Rebels did not attack, but lurked about, seemingly wary of his artillery. Their force seemed somewhat larger than his, but not necessarily overwhelming.

Within a few minutes Captain Boyd and his company of the 1st New York Cavalry reached town with the message that Milroy wanted sent to Schenck. Riding to the post headquarters he thus missed Smith but found Tyler and delivered his message. This was the first real indication that Tyler had that there was a large Confederate force in the Valley. When he had stopped at Harper's Ferry early that morning General Kelley had assured him that his scouts had no indication of any Rebels other than the usual ones of Imboden, Grumble Jones and Jenkins (Tyler mistakenly called the latter Jackson). At 10 a.m. Tyler wired Colonel Piatt at Baltimore: "A scout has just arrived with a dispatch from Milroy, whose headquarters he left at 11 o'clock last night. Milroy reports Ewell's entire corps in and around Winchester, June 13, 15,000 to 18,000 strong, with Jones' and Imboden's forces; that they fought yesterday with success; quite a loss on both sides. Milroy advises Smith, at Martinsburg, to be on his guard, as he apprehends a raid on Martinsburg and Harper's Ferry."[31]

About 11 a.m. Smith's quartermaster reported to Tyler that, all the supplies having been sent off to Harper's Ferry by rail, he was ready to leave with the brigade's wagons and those of McReynold's brigade, which had come in the night before. Tyler told him to take the wagons north as quickly as possible to Williamsport, where they could cross the Potomac on a ferry, after which they were to continue on into Pennsylvania. Boyd, having nothing to do now that he had delivered his message, decided to take his company of cavalry along with the wagons as an escort.

Milroy's message convinced Tyler that Smith would have to retreat. He had inspected Milroy's defenses only a few days before, and knew that they were good, but "it was apparent that the attack was made by one of the most efficient army corps of Lee's army, and the inference was fair that this corps was not alone in the Valley."[32] He also figured that the capture of Bunker Hill indicated that a sizable Rebel force had bypassed Winchester. Smith's force was even smaller than McReynolds', and Tyler soon was convinced that the only thing keeping the Rebels from attacking Smith was the Union artillery, for so far the Confederates didn't seem to have any of their own. "Up to this time," Tyler later reported, "I had been counting on assistance from the railroad, if deemed necessary to move the troops to Harper's Ferry, but, on applying to the agent at the station, was surprised to find that every car and engine had been sent away from the depot, and that there were neither cars nor engines in either direction that could be made available in the exigency."[33]

About noon he notified Smith that a retreat was inevitable, but he wanted to give the wagons plenty of time to get away and to get out of the way, for he wanted the troops to also move toward Williamsport when they went. Sure that it was impossible, or suicidal, for Smith's small force to advance to Bunker Hill, as had been suggested in his orders, he decided that the thing to do "was to hold on at Martinsburg until the last moment, in order to cover any men who might escape in that direction from Winchester, and for that object, and for the security of the Martinsburg baggage train, I proposed, if possible, to hold Martinsburg until sundown, by which time I supposed the baggage train would be safe, and the troops escaping in the way of Martinsburg would have arrived."[34]

By noon Smith, fearing that he could easily be outflanked where he was, had withdrawn his forces from their first position and moved to a hill just southeast of the town where the local cemetery was located. Not far behind this hill a road ran southeastward toward Shepherdstown, another place where the Potomac could be crossed. At about 1 p.m. Jenkins sent in a demand for the surrender of the town. "Should you refuse," it said, "you are respectfully requested to notify the inhabitants of the place to remove forthwith to a place of safety. Small-arms only will be used for one hour upon the town after your reception of this note. After that, I shall feel at liberty to shell the town, if I see proper. Should you refuse to give the necessary notification to the inhabitants, I shall be compelled to hold your command responsible." Smith replied: "Martinsburg will not be surrendered. You may commence shelling as soon as you choose. I will, however, inform the women and children of your threats."[35] When Smith did, indeed, pass Jenkins' threat to the town's inhabitants large numbers of them hastily departed. But Jenkins had been bluffing; he never did shell the town, and evidently had no artillery with him.

Down at Winchester, one of the cavalry patrols Milroy had sent out returned at about 2 p.m. after having gone west as far as Pughtown, returning by way of the road to Romney, and had seen no signs of any Confederates to the west. This report, Milroy later said, "relieved me from all apprehension of an immediate attack in that direction, and induced me to turn my attention to the approaches in other directions."[36] Instead of a moving patrol, what Milroy needed was a line of videttes or some lookout posts to watch the approaches from the west, for the patrol had come and gone by the time the Rebels arrived. Milroy, who spent a lot of his time in a basket hoisted by block and tackle up the flagpole at the Main Fort, scanning the countryside with a powerful glass, evidently believed that the skirmishing of the day before had convinced the Rebels that it would be too costly to assault his position and that most of them had gone off to the north, leaving only part of their force to keep him on the defensive. Sounds of gunfire coming from Martinsburg helped to support this conclusion.

One of the problems of defending Winchester, whichever side tried to hold it, was that each ridge west of town was dominated by the next ridge to the west of it. By 4 p.m. Early had reached a wooded ridge west of, and overlooking, the works on Flint Ridge, without being detected. There he let his men rest a while and began to make his arrangements for taking the first earthwork. At about 5 p.m. (Ewell said 6 p.m.) twenty pieces of Confederate artillery were suddenly wheeled into place in an orchard and a cornfield and opened fire on the West Fort, "completely surprising the enemy," Ewell said, "whose entire attention at this point was engrossed by Gordon."[37] (Gordon's Brigade held Bower's Hill, and some of his men even entered the town of Winchester, but were driven out.) The lone Union battery of six guns responded, but eventually (accounts vary from a half-hour to an hour and a half) it was silenced by the superior number of Confederate guns. Then the artillery subsided, and it was the infantry's turn. The five Louisiana regiments of Brigadier General Harry Hays' brigade, supported by Early's other two brigades, who had been working their way forward through some woods, charged forward through an abatis of brushwood and easily captured the works and the six guns, two of which were turned upon the fleeing defenders, who were, until then, rallying as if to counterattack.

"Hurrah for the Louisiana boys!" Ewell was heard to cry as he watched through his field glasses. "There's Early! I hope the old fellow won't be hurt."[38] However, it wasn't Early but Ewell who was hurt, for no sooner had he spoken than he was hit in the chest by a spent bullet. It knocked the one-legged general off-balance, but otherwise did no more harm than to produce a bad bruise. The corps surgeon tried to get him to lie down and relax for a while, going so far as to confiscate his crutches, but the general was too excited to rest and was soon up and stumping about on his wooden leg. "It was by this time too late to do more than prepare to improve this important advantage promptly in the morning" Ewell later reported. "This result established the correctness of General Early's views as to the point of attack, and rendered the main fort untenable." He figured that Milroy would realize his forts' vulnerability as well and try to escape, so he sent Johnson, with two of his brigades, half of another, and eight pieces of artillery "to proceed to a point on the Martinsburg pike about 2 ½ miles from Winchester, so as to intercept any attempt to retreat, or be ready to attack at daylight if the enemy held their ground."[39]

Up at Martinsburg, General Rodes arrived that afternoon, well ahead of his troops. His men, he reported, had "a very fatiguing march of 19 miles. . . . I found General Jenkins with his command before the enemy, skirmishing with him occasionally. . . . Before the infantry came up, I ordered General Jenkins to move most of his force to the left [west] of the town, to dismount it, and send it forward as skirmishers, to endeavor to get possession of the town, thus cutting off the enemy's retreat toward Hedgesville and Williamsport, and to report to me what force, if any, he discovered in and to the left of the town. At the same time, Lieutenant-Colonel [Thomas H.] Carter was directed to take the best position for his artillery to enable him to silence the opposing battery, which was annoying us."[40]

When the Federals saw Jenkins cavalry moving around to

the west of town and more Rebels approaching from the south, they divided their artillery, one section (two guns) were moved back about 150 yards and faced to the west to take on the cavalry, while the other four guns remained in their original position, facing south. The sun was sinking fast as Rodes' infantry began to arrive, and he immediately began forming the leading brigades for attack. While the infantry was forming, Carter's artillery battalion of 16 pieces opened fire. Its opening salvo fell among the limbers of the two Union guns facing west and the sight of it blowing the artillery horses to pieces caused about half of the 106th New York to run down the back side of the hill, where they were rallied by General Tyler and several other officers. Seeing the stir in the Union ranks, Rodes was afraid they would all retreat before he could surround them. He ordered his leading brigade "and each of the others in turn to advance with speed upon the enemy's position."[41] But his infantry had to cross two miles of rough ground, broken up by bushes and stone fences, which gave the Federals enough time to get away.

It being near the time set for the retreat, Smith had already called in his skirmishers and ordered the artillery to limber up when the Rebel artillery opened fire, which act added considerable urgency to the withdrawal. With his 126th Ohio, Smith set out on the road to Shepherdstown instead of the one to Williamsport, probably because it was nearer or because the other road would take them too close to Jenkins' cavalry. The colonel of the 106th New York sent his adjutant to ask if it should follow the same road and was told "yes." Tyler went with them, as did one piece of artillery; they soon caught up with Smith, and they all reached Shepherdstown by midnight and forded the Potomac there, following the towpath of the Chesapeake & Ohio Canal to Maryland Heights. One piece of artillery got stuck in a ditch, and, apparently, the other four were abandoned by the artillerymen, who retreated northward to Williamsport. One company of infantry that had been manning a blockhouse guarding the railroad also tried to retreat that way, but was cut off and forced to surrender. Smith's report cites his small cavalry force for "contending for every inch of ground" as Jenkins' men occupied the town, but it doesn't say what became of them after that.[42]

Again, as at Berryville, the team of Rodes and Jenkins had failed to bag the Union garrison or to capture many of their supplies. (At Martinsburg he did find about 400 rounds of artillery ammunition and some 6,000 bushels of grain, and, of course, the five abandoned cannon.) Most of the blame would seem to belong to Jenkins. At Martinsburg he had almost all day in which to cut off the Federals' retreat by circling around to the north and east and yet contented himself with long-range skirmishing from the south until Rodes came up.

That evening Rodes told Jenkins to march north early enough the next morning to reach Chambersburg, Pennsylvania, that day. His mission would be to gather horses, cattle, and anything else useful to the Confederate army that would soon follow him across the Potomac. Jenkins had reveille sounded in his camps at 2 a.m. on the 15th and set out to follow these orders.

At Winchester, at about 9 p.m. on the 14th, Milroy convened his brigade commanders for a council of war. As Ewell had foreseen, they felt that, with Flint Ridge in Rebel hands, they could no longer hold their position. Having only one day's rations on hand – or so Milroy now claimed – and very little artillery ammunition left, and finding themselves up against, so far as they knew, Lee's entire army, but unwilling to surrender, the commanders decided that their only reasonable course was to cut their way out. To make it easier for them to move, all wheeled vehicles, including the artillery, would be left behind, but the quartermasters would bring out the horses, which could carry sick and slightly wounded men. The three brigades set out, in numerical order, at about 1 a.m. on the 15th after spiking the cannon and chopping their wheels and throwing much of the excess ammunition into the cisterns of the forts. Two companies that were out on picket duty got left behind, their regimental commander neglecting to call them in. The Federals avoided the town by going through a ravine that came out on the Martinsburg pike after about a mile.

About four and a half miles northeast of Winchester, near

Stephenson's Depot, the leading brigade, under Brigadier General Washington Elliott, ran into Johnson's Confederates. There followed a confusing fight in the dark, a rare thing in this war, when it was hard enough to control large units under fire even in the daytime. Johnson only had about a brigade and half in position when the fight started, the Stonewall Brigade having received faulty directions, but he had the advantage of being already in position with those, plus the cover of some woods and a cut for the Winchester & Potomac railroad. Also, the Rebels were the only ones with artillery, which seemed to demoralize some Union units, as did an incident of one Union regiment accidentally firing into the backs of another. (In the dark, it had not realized anyone was in front of it but Rebels. General Milroy bravely rode out between the two regiments to stop the firing.)

A signal from a few troops left at Winchester then notified Milroy that the Confederates had taken the forts and possibly were now approaching his rear, and he gave instructions for all his forces not yet engaged, as well as the quartermasters with the horses, to continue the retreat under cover of the brigade that was engaged. Several units took the wrong road, which led over the mountains to the town of Bath, near the Potomac; other units and individuals scattered in various directions, and numerous staff officers sent to McReynolds could not find him or his brigade. About then Milroy's horse was shot out from under him, and it took him some time to find a new mount, during which time he lost whatever control he had had over the fighting.

Not realizing, in the dark, that his division was actually winning the battle, Milroy ordered the units still fighting to break off and join the withdrawal. By the time he was remounted, the retreat was well under way, and he rode to the head of the column. However, his 2nd Brigade was in the midst of a charge when the order came to break off, and it was easier said than done. And just then the quartermasters, gunless artillerymen, and other noncombatants mounted on the unemployed horses and mules panicked and stampeded right through several Union regiments, breaking up their formations and adding to the general air of fear and confusion. When the wayward Stonewall Brigade finally showed up, Colonel Ely, commander of Milroy's 2nd Brigade, believing himself surrounded, waived a white blanket in token of surrender.

McReynolds, at the tail of the Union column, coming up before the fight was quite ended, saw (it was growing light by then) that the Rebel artillery was, as he told the colonel of the 13th Pennsylvania Cavalry, "mowing down our infantry!"[43] He ordered this regiment, temporarily attached to his brigade, to charge some guns near the left end of the Confederate line, which it did, losing about half its men in the process, and the survivors fell back out of range, turned off to the east, and eventually reached Harper's Ferry. While this was going on, McReynolds sent his two infantry regiments along a side road to gain a position from which they could attack the Confederate left. The lead regiment, the 67th Pennsylvania, upon coming to a farmhouse, broke ranks and went in search of water. The other regiment, the 6th Maryland, maintained its formation and advanced against the enemy, but was soon confronted by two Louisiana regiments and a Rebel battery. Finding themselves all alone, the Marylanders decided the situation was hopeless; they turned back, picking up some stragglers from the 67th Pennsylvania, turned to the east, and also headed for Harper's Ferry, using small country roads and avoiding all large towns.

McReynolds, meanwhile, had gone in search of his own regiment, the 1st New York Cavalry, supposed to be bringing up the rear, but couldn't find it. It had been about to charge into the confused situation on Colonel Ely's front, just before the latter surrendered, when a staff officer from General Milroy had showed up and led it off to the northwest and to safety along the road to Bath. McReynolds turned back to join his infantry but couldn't find it either. Having lost his entire command, except for two orderlies, he too headed for Harper's Ferry.

Meanwhile, General Johnson led a pursuit of some Federals who had fled by way of the road to Charlestown, leading only about a dozen infantrymen and one piece of artillery. He claimed to have personally captured 30 Federals at the crossing of Opequon Creek with nothing more deadly than his opera glass. (One of them was kind enough to rescue his hat for him when it fell into the creek). Hundreds of other Federal stragglers were rounded up by the Confederate Maryland cavalry battalion. Altogether, over a third of Milroy's division was captured that day. Part of Early's division arrived in time to take charge of the prisoners, and a regiment was detailed to march them south to Staunton, from which they could be sent via railroad to Richmond. Johnson's men, having marched and fought all night, went into camp right on the battlefield to rest for the remainder of the day. Early's division bivouacked in a large field three miles north of Winchester.

At Winchester, Ewell captured 23 pieces of artillery, their barrels spiked and wheels chopped, but they were easily repaired. Some of these were issued to the Maryland battery that had been serving in the Valley, which was then attached to Jenkins' cavalry brigade. Ewell also came into possession of 300 wagons loaded with the baggage of Milroy's command and a large quantity of quartermaster and commissary supplies.

That morning of the 15th Jenkins' troopers stopped for breakfast at Williamsport, where the local people set out tables of meat, bread and milk for them. Then they crossed the Potomac into Maryland at a nearby ford. There they were delayed by Captain Boyd's company of cavalry, which was armed with Spencer repeating rifles. His small force took advantage of each successive low ridge to open fire at long range and force some of Jenkins' men to deploy for an attack, which consumed time; but, before the Rebels could charge, the Federals would fade back to the next ridge and do it all over again. It was some time between 10 a.m. and noon before Jenkins managed to cover the six miles from Williamsport to Hagerstown, Maryland.

Here the Rebels also received a hearty welcome from the pro-Confederate elements of the population. Someone warned Jenkins that there was a superior Union force just across the Pennsylvania line at Greencastle. Apparently impressed by this, which wasn't true, and still skirmishing with Boyd's New Yorkers, Jenkins took ten hours or more to ride the 22 miles to that place. Upon approaching it, he divided his brigade, deployed on both sides of the highway, and advanced cautiously, but there were no Federals there. The Rebels had, however, passed several partially burned wagons from the train that had left Martinsburg, which by now was twenty miles ahead of them but moving at such a frantic pace that it was exhausting its animals and thus losing wagons that couldn't keep up.

Hordes of refugees were also fleeing before the Rebel cavalry, many of them free blacks and runaway slaves. Many of these had already reached Chambersburg when the Union wagon train arrived there about midmorning. It had started out with at least 80 vehicles and was now down to about 50. Lieutenant Charles A. Palmer, commanding a small detachment of Maryland cavalry (Union), saw them come hurrying into town, their drivers whipping their teams for more speed and telling all who would listen that the Rebels were right behind them. Palmer stopped the column with drawn revolver and forced the teamsters to slow to a walk as they proceeded on to Philadelphia. Nevertheless they spread panic all along the Cumberland Valley – the extension north of the Potomac of Virginia's Shenandoah Valley.

Early's and Johnson's divisions remained in camp that day, the 15th. General Rodes let his men rest until 10 a.m., when he finally got word from Ewell of what had taken place at Winchester. He also learned that Milroy's forces had already gone too far toward Harper's Ferry for him to intercept them, so he didn't try. He then ordered his pioneers put to work at destroying the B&O Railroad all that day and the next, left one regiment to occupy the town, and marched the rest of his division to Williamsport, which he reached about dark "after the most trying march we had yet had," he said; "most trying because of the intense heat, the character of the road, and the increased number of barefooted men in the command. Three brigades . . . with three batteries of artillery, were ordered across the Potomac at once."[44] Lee's pontoon train was still with Rodes, and it was used to bridge the river downstream from Williamsport at a spot called Falling Waters. However, Rodes didn't wait for the bridge to be laid, but had three of his five brigades wade the river by way of the ford at Williamsport, leaving the other two on the West Virginia side. Then he put his men in camp to await the arrival of the rest of the corps.

Lee wrote a brief report to President Davis at 7 a.m. on the 15th. Only now did he mention that he had sent Ewell to the Valley five days before. Since he didn't yet know the result himself, he could only report that Rodes had driven the Federals out of Berryville and that Ewell had driven Milroy into his defenses. "According to our understanding," he said, "I presume he has advanced toward the Potomac, leaving a division in front of Winchester. General A. P. Hill reported yesterday that the Federal force in front of him withdrew from the south side of the Rappahannock on the night of the 13th, and by morning had nearly all disappeared, leaving strong pickets on the river. One division was seen going over the Stafford Hills, in the direction of Aquia, and he supposes the main body to have taken that route. Our scouts report a general movement of the enemy up the Rappahannock, but I have got no certain information on that point; I know a large force has been thrown toward Warrenton. The uncertainty of the reports as to threatened expeditions of the enemy along the coast of North Carolina, and between the Rappahannock and James Rivers in Virginia, has caused delay in the movements of this army, and it may now be too late to accomplish all that was desired. I am still ignorant as to the extent of the expedition said to be moving up the Peninsula, and hesitate to draw the whole of A. P. Hill's corps to me. Two of Pickett's brigades are at Hanover Junction and Richmond, so that I am quite weak."[45]

Nevertheless, that same day, Longstreet's 1st Corps of Lee's army left the vicinity of Culpeper Court House. Its orders were to march northward along the eastern slope of the Blue Ridge – not through the Shenandoah Valley but in the smaller Loudon Valley to the east – posing a threat to Hooker's army and to Washington, D.C. Jeb Stuart was under orders, as he later reported, "to leave a sufficient force on the Rappahannock to watch the enemy in front, and move the main body parallel to the Blue Ridge and on Longstreet's right flank." He left Hampton's brigade on the Rappahannock, ordered Fitz Lee's brigade, still under Colonel Munford, to lead Longstreet's march, Grumble Jones's to bring up the rear, and sent Rooney Lee's (now under Colonel John R. Chambliss) and Robertson's brigades to cross the Rappahannock farther downstream. "The movement was not interrupted," Stuart reported, "the enemy having disappeared from our front during the night, and our march continued to within a few miles of Salem, to bivouac for the night. Scouting parties were sent to Warrenton, where it was ascertained the enemy had withdrawn his forces to Centreville the day previous."[46]

At 8:30 that night Lee, still back at Culpeper, wrote to Longstreet: "A dispatch from Ewell, dated 5 a.m. to-day, stated that Early's division stormed the enemy's works at Winchester, capturing their cannon, &c., with little loss on our side. He was pushing on. . . ." He also advised him that A. P. Hill's corps had started moving west. "Anderson encamped this evening 2 miles this side of Germanna, and will pass beyond this place to-morrow evening. Heth left Fredericksburg to-day. Hill wrote that Pender was ready, and would move as soon as he heard from his scouts that he had sent north of the Rappahannock. As far as heard from, the enemy had all gone."[47]

It was 11 p.m. when advanced scouts of Jenkins' cavalry reached Chambersburg. Two Rebel lieutenants rode into the town square, then illuminated by a single gaslight. They shouted for the town's mayor to come out, but there was no response from the darkened homes and businesses. As they moved away from the light into the shadows they were set upon, one at a time, by a pair of burly but unarmed civilians who had just recently mustered out of the Union Army. The Confederates were relieved of their weapons, horses, and equipment, and escorted to the local jail. However, when a larger group of Confederates rode in, the two lieutenants were hastily released, and their two captors rode quickly out of town eastward, on the road to Gettysburg. Jenkins left a provost guard in the town and led the rest of his brigade a mile farther north to make camp on the estate of Colonel Alexander McClure. McClure wasn't home, but his wife served the Rebel general and his staff a bountiful late supper. Later she turned one of her farm buildings over to them for use as an infirmary for their sick and helped to care for them herself.

Colonel McClure was a prominent publisher, lawyer and politician who had been appointed an assistant adjutant general in the state forces and assigned to supervise the enrollment for the draft in Franklin County. He was also running a clandestine scouting and intelligence operation for Governor Curtin, using several employees of the Pennsylvania Railroad and a few members of the Union Army's Military Telegraph Corps who had portable keys they could use to tap into the lines anywhere. On the 14th, McClure had been visited by a former client who now lived in Virginia, come to warn him that the Rebels would soon be in Pennsylvania and would arrest him if they found him. McClure had turned over his intelligence function to Judge F. M. Kimmell and taken the next train for Harrisburg.

Colonel Scott wired Governor Curtin of Pennsylvania at 2:30 a.m. on the 15th that Lincoln would issue a call for 100,000 militia to serve six months, unless sooner released. Half would be from Pennsylvania, with the rest from Ohio, Maryland and West Virginia. Twelve hours later Stanton sent telegrams to most of the other Northern governors, telling them about that call and adding: "It is important to have the largest possible force in the least time, and if other States would furnish militia for a short term, to be credited on the draft, it would greatly advance the object," and asked them to inform him immediately how many men they could provide.[48]

Stanton had already wired Governor Horatio Seymour of New York at 11:10 a.m. a similar message, asking if he could provide 20,000 men. New York, unlike most of the other states, including Pennsylvania, had militia regiments already organized and ready to mobilize. Seymour, a Democrat, replied: "I will spare no effort to send you troops at once. I have sent orders to the militia officer of the state."[49] Stanton and Seymour continued to exchange messages throughout that day, deciding to send about 8,000 or 10,000 men in the regiments from New York City and Brooklyn (then a separate city) to Philadelphia right away, where they were to report to General Couch. Seymour said he also had about 2,000 volunteers (as opposed to militia) who had just enlisted and that he would organize them into companies and regiments and send them on at once. Most of the other governors said they could organize a few troops in 30 to 60 days, but only Massachusetts had any ready to call out immediately, and only a few.

Although Stanton wired Hooker at midnight 14-15 June that "No doubt is entertained here that Milroy is surrounded at Winchester," Hooker made no move to go to his rescue, but continued to move closer to Washington. At 9:15 a.m. on the 15th he wired Halleck: "The First, Third, Sixth, and Eleventh Corps, with the cavalry, will be assembled at Manassas and Centreville to-night. They have instructions to replenish their forage and rations, which I trust they will be able to do to-day. The Second Corps will be at Dumfries, the Sixth at Wolf Run Shoals, and the Twelfth at Fairfax Court-House to-night. Major-General Hancock reports that the rebel forces about Fredericksburg have moved in the direction of Culpeper this morning. To-night my headquarters will be at Fairfax Station. If your information from the Upper Potomac should be of a character to justify a movement in that direction, I request that I may be informed of it at the earliest practicable moment."[50]

Meanwhile, Pleasonton continued to pepper both Hooker and Stanton with reports mixing good and bad information about Lee's army – the worst part of which was repeated assertions that Ewell's corps was still south of the Rappahannock River. He was also still pushing the idea of Stuart making a big cavalry raid and warned Stanton to put "several batteries and a good force" at the point where the Monocacy River flows into the Potomac, on the north side of the latter, west of Washington, as Stuart would attempt to cross there and under the culvert that carried the Chesapeake & Ohio Canal across the Monocacy.[51] How he "knew" this he didn't say.

Fortunately for Hooker, Pleasonton was not his only source of information about the enemy. At 10:20 a.m. Dan Butterfield wired Halleck: "Two of our best scouts returned from the interior, above Fredericksburg, yesterday (Sunday) morning. They report A. P. Hill, with sixty guns and 20,000 men, left on the heights about Fredericksburg. On Saturday p.m. 4,000 of this force moved toward Culpeper. On the same day, General Lee's headquarters were on the Lacy farm, between Brandy Station and Culpeper Court-House. Citizens say that the cavalry expedition was intended for Alexandria, while Lee was to go up the Valley. They believe that a great cavalry raid is now given up as the cavalry is divided, a considerable part being still near Brandy Station.... The Richmond papers of the 13th blame Stuart much for allowing himself to be surprised in his camp by Pleasonton, and call upon him to do something to retrieve his reputation. Anxiety expressed concerning the movements on the Peninsula. Will send the papers to you."[52]

At 12:20 p.m., Tyler wired Schenck: "Officers and men just in from General Milroy show that he is wiped out. I doubt if 500 will escape." Twenty minutes later he wired Schenck again: "Colonel McReynolds has just come from the front. He reports that Generals Milroy and Elliot are within an hour's march of this city. He thinks that 2,000 will cover his loss. Not nearly so bad as I had feared."[53]

Evidently this news was not immediately forwarded to Halleck for, at 2 p.m., Halleck wired Hooker: "Garrison of Martinsburg has arrived at Harper's Ferry. Milroy did not obey orders given on the 11th to abandon Winchester, and probably has or will be captured. Harper's Ferry ought to hold out some time. Pleasonton's telegrams to you contain all the information we have of the enemy's movements. They are very contradictory.

Your army is entirely free to operate as you desire against Lee's army, so long as you keep his main army from Washington. It is believed that Longstreet and Stuart are crossing the Potomac above and below Harper's Ferry. They certainly should be pursued. The force used for that purpose must depend upon your information of the movements or position of the remainder of Lee's army. Leesburg [west of Washington, south of the Potomac] seems about the best point to move on first. The information sent here by General Pleasonton is very unsatisfactory. His suggestions to send batteries from here to the mouth of the Monocacy cannot be adopted. If we had them to send, they would only be lost."[54]

Halleck received a message from Schenck at 5:35 p.m. saying: "General Milroy has cut his way through, and arrived at Harper's Ferry. His losses are reported considerable, with great damage to the enemy. He will telegraph soon. Tyler brought troops from Martinsburg to Maryland Heights, and is in command there. Have sent Kelley around to New Creek, to concentrate troops on western portion of railroad. Ordered [Brig. Gen. W. W.] Averell to concentrate at Grafton, with a view to covering approaches to Wheeling, and to come eastward, perhaps also to New Creek, to hold as much as possible of the railroad eastward toward Martinsburg."[55] Halleck wired Schenck (whether before or after receiving the above is not clear): "Do not give General Milroy any command at Harper's Ferry. We have had enough of that sort of military genius. If you have not already done so, send all your small posts and available troops there. That place must be held."[56] Piatt wired Milroy at Harper's Ferry in Schenck's name: "You will turn over your command for the present to Brigadier-General Tyler, and report in person to these headquarters."[57]

At 8:30 p.m. Lincoln wired Hooker: "The facts are now known here that Winchester and Martinsburg were both besieged yesterday. The troops from Martinsburg have got into Harper's Ferry without loss. Those from Winchester are also in, having lost in killed, wounded, and missing about one-third of their number. Of course, the enemy holds both places, and I think the report is authentic that he is crossing the Potomac at Williamsport. We have not heard of his yet appearing at Harper's Ferry or on the river anywhere below. I would like to hear from you." Hooker replied: "It seems to disclose the intentions of the enemy to make an invasion, and, if so, it is not in my power to prevent it. I can, however, make an effort to check him until he has concentrated all his forces. I may possibly be able to prevent the junction, and commence the movement during to-morrow. On so short reflection, I am not prepared to say this is the wisest move, nor do I know that my opinion on this subject is wanted. A. P. Hill moved up toward Culpeper this morning, indicating his intention to re-enforce their forces on the Upper Potomac."[58]

Why wouldn't Lincoln want Hooker's opinion on what he should do next? Although what Lincoln really wanted was not opinions or consultations, but action. Hooker, on the other hand, seems to have wanted Lincoln or Halleck to tell him what they wanted him to do.

Hooker wrote to Lincoln again at 10 p.m.: "With regard to the enemy, your dispatch is more conclusive than any I have received. I now feel that invasion is his settled purpose. If so, he has more to accomplish, but with more hazard, by striking an easterly direction after crossing than a northerly one. It seems to me that he will be more likely to go north, and to incline to the west. He can have no design to look after his rear. It is an act of desperation on his part, no matter in what force he moves. It will kill copperheadism in the North. I do not know that my opinion as to the duty of this army in the case is wanted; if it should be, you know that I will be happy to give it. I have heard nothing of the movements of the enemy to-day, excepting that he has not attempted to follow me across the Rappahannock. I have only heard that all of A. P. Hill's forces moved up the river this morning, in the direction of Culpeper. If it should be determined for me to make a movement in pursuit, which I am not prepared to recommend at this time, I may possibly be able to move some corps to-morrow, and can reach the point of the enemy's crossing in advance of A. P. Hill. If I should move at once, he would probably wait until his forces are concentrated. If they are moving toward Maryland, I can better fight them there than make a running fight. If they come up in front of Washington, I can threaten and cut their communications, and Dix can be re-enforced from the south to act on their rear. I could not sit still and have them turn my right. My sources of information could not successfully cover such an extent of country as their movements indicate. I add these as suggestions for your consideration."[59] Actually the last two statements, about not sitting still and his sources of information, sound more like explanations of what he had done, and not done, so far.

Stanton received a message at 10:50 p.m. from General Couch, at Harrisburg: "The enemy are following my pickets 9 miles south of Chambersburg, and apparently moving north in three columns; one to Chambersburg, one to Gettysburg, and the other in the direction of the coal mines. Infantry reported with them. I shall have but little to resist them, I fear."[60]

Endnotes

1 James D. Horan, *Confederate Agent* (New York, 1954), 25.
2 OR, I:27:III:110.
3 Ibid., I:27:III:111.
4 Ibid., I:27:II:171.
5 Ibid., I:51:I:1055.
6 Ibid., I:27:I:38.
7 Ibid., I:27:III:108.
8 Ibid., I:27:III:113.
9 Ibid., I:51:I:1055. The same message is in I:27:III:95 but dated 13 June. The 14th seems more logical.
10 Ibid., I:27:I:38.
11 Ibid., I:27:I:39.
12 Ibid., I:27:III:101.
13 Ibid., I:27:III:112.
14 Ibid., I:27:III:109.
15 Ibid., I:27:I:39.
16 Ibid., I:27:III:103.
17 Ibid., I:27:III:104.
18 Ibid., I:27:I:39.
19 Ibid., I:27:III:109.

20 Ibid., I:27:III:113.
21 Ibid., I:27:III:106.
22 Ibid., I:27:I:39-40.
23 Ibid., I:27:I:40.
24 Ibid., I:27:III:107.
25 Ibid., I:27:II:46.
26 W. Hunter Lesser, *Rebels at the Gate* (Naperville IL, 2004), 251.
27 Ibid.
28 Sears, *Gettysburg*, 77.
29 *OR*, I:27:II:46.
30 Sears, *Gettysburg*, 78.
31 *OR*, I:27:II:33.
32 Ibid., I:27:II:34.
33 Ibid., I:27:II:18. Tyler, here, makes it sound like this discovery came after Jenkins demanded the surrender of the town, but, obviously it must have come before he told Smith that they would retreat by way of Williamsport, which he says he did at about noon.
34 Ibid., I:27:II:34-5.
35 Ibid., I:27:II:38.
36 Sears, *Gettysburg*, 46.
37 *OR*, I:27:II:441.
38 Freeman, *Lee's Lieutenants*, III:23.
39 *OR*, I:27:II:441.
40 Ibid., I:27:II:548-9.
41 Ibid., I:27:II:549.
42 Ibid., I:27:II:39.
43 Wilbur Sturtevant Nye, *Here Come the Rebels!* (Baton Rouge LA, 1965), 119.
44 *OR*, I:27:II:550.
45 Ibid., I:27:II:295.
46 Ibid., I:27:II:687-8.
47 Ibid., I:27:III:890.
48 Ibid., I:27:III:137.
49 Ibid., I:27:III:138.
50 Ibid., I:27:I:40-1.
51 Ibid., I:27:III:115.
52 Ibid., I:27:I:41.
53 Ibid., I:27:III:124.
54 Ibid., I:27:I:41-2.
55 Ibid., I:27:III:126.
56 Ibid., I:27:III:124.
57 Ibid., I:27:III:127.
58 Ibid., I:27:I:43.
59 Ibid., I:27:I:43-4.
60 Ibid., I:27:III:131.

CHAPTER 10

"Nearly Everything Is Conjecture"

15 – 17 June 1863

IN INDIANA, THAT 15TH DAY of June, a Federal officer enrolling men for the draft was surrounded by 25 or 30 hostile men and pelted with eggs by the women of Whitestown, in Boone County.

Off the east coast, the U.S. Navy sent ships after the recently captured *Tacony*.

In England the House of Lords debated what to do about the seizure of British ships by the U.S. Navy.

Near Port Hudson, Confederate cavalry attacked a Union cavalry camp at Newport, Louisiana, at dawn. Many of the Federals (14th New York Cavalry) were still asleep, others were out picking blackberries for breakfast, and four companies and most of another were all captured without a shot being fired. The Rebels then attacked the pickets of a company of Massachusetts cavalry and drove them headlong for two miles until they reached the protection of Banks' main force. The Confederates also captured a house being used as a hospital by the Federals, and escaped before a counterattack could be launched, making off with some 800 sabers, twice that many pistols, and a great deal of ammunition.

At Port Royal, South Carolina, General Gillmore, the new commander of the Union Army's Department of the South, was writing to Halleck that day saying that he had made a personal reconnaissance of the coastal islands south of Charleston, the most important of which was Morris Island, the north end of which faced the south side of the channel leading into Charleston harbor, at which point the Confederates had an earthwork called Battery Gregg. These islands were separated from the mainland and from each other not by large stretches of open water but merely by narrow, sluggish streams and large low swampy areas that were neither sea nor land. Heavy guns in Battery Gregg and others at and near Fort Moultrie on the northern edge of the channel, and still others at Fort Sumter (built on shoals near the middle of the harbor entrance), effectively closed the harbor to any Union force.

Back in April several ironclads of the U.S. Navy had tried to batter Sumter into submission, but had received most of the battering themselves. Now Gillmore wanted to land troops at the south end of long, narrow Morris Island and capture Battery Gregg from the rear, so as to make it easier for the Navy's next attempt to enter the harbor. But the Rebels also had guns planted at the south end of Morris Island to prevent a Union landing there. However, the Federals had troops on Folly Island, the next island south of Morris Island, and separated from it only by a narrow body of water called Lighthouse Inlet.

"General [Israel] Vogdes is in command on Folly Island," Gillmore told Halleck. "All his arrangements thus far have been defensive. He will openly continue in that attitude; but I have directed him to plant behind the sand-hills on the north end of Folly Island (secretly and without being seen by the enemy) batteries that will be able to dismount, in one hour, all the enemy's guns on the south end of Morris Island. . . . I have not fully sounded the navy as to the co-operation that may be expected from them in getting upon Morris Island. Probably nothing will be done by them offensively until the arrival of Admiral Foote. Colonel Montgomery, with 1,500 colored troops and some artillery, now occupies Saint Simon's Island, and will be directed to make raids from that point, and occupy the enemy in that direction. He will be able I think, to keep many, if not all, of the

Georgia troops in that quarter. As nearly as I can ascertain, there are about Charleston, for its defense, some 10,000 or 12,000 troops (mostly South Carolina militia), and there are about an equal number of Georgia militia available for the defense of Savannah."[1]

That very evening Vogdes' men began to construct earthworks to hold the guns for the masked batteries. To prevent the Rebels from learning of their presence, only the officers were allowed to speak, and they only in whispers, and all work was performed at night and as quietly as possible. "Not a rattle of a chain," one officer said, "nor the creak of a wheel told the enemy of our designs."[2]

At Vicksburg, Charles Dana later remembered, "By the middle of June our lines were so near the enemy's on Sherman's and McPherson's front that General Grant began to consider the project of another general assault as soon as McClernand's, Lauman's, and Herron's lines were brought up close. Accordingly, Sherman and McPherson were directed to hold their work until the others were up to them. Herron, of course, had not had time to advance, though since his arrival he had worked with great energy. Lauman had done little in the way of regular approaches. But the chief difficulty in the way was the backwardness of McClernand. His trenches were mere rifle-pits, three or four feet wide, and would allow neither the passage of artillery nor the assemblage of any considerable number of troops. His batteries were, with scarcely an exception, in the position they apparently had held when the siege was opened."[3]

All this was written long after the war. In a report to Stanton on the same 15th of June, he was not quite so critical: "McClernand is pressing his approaches, but is still much farther off than either of the others. He has some heavy 24-pounders in position and is getting up some 8-inch navy guns." He added, in that report, that "General Grant has determined to issue an order extending the command of Sherman so as to include Haynes' Bluff. Sherman, whose lines already touch those of Washburn, will thus have the chief command in all that region, and can be there in person and move re-enforcements there from his own corps whenever it may be necessary."[4]

Grant was writing a long message to McClernand that day, telling him that the 9th Corps, commanded by Major General John G. Parke, sent down by Burnside, would be placed at the south end of the Union lines, allowing Herron's division, from Missouri, to move to its right, which in turn would allow McClernand to shorten his lines. However, near the end of the long note, Grant said: "after writing the foregoing, and after General Parke had moved one division of his command to opposite Warrenton, I had to change my plan and send him to Haynes' Bluff. From information received, the enemy have 12,000 infantry and artillery at Yazoo [City], with orders to move south; four thousand cavalry already between the Yazoo and Big Black River, and Loring ordered to cross. This made it necessary to send the extra force up the Yazoo River. You will assume command of Lauman's division at once, Herron taking up part of the ground occupied by Lauman. The latter can better spare a regiment to garrison Warrenton than any one else."[5]

Pemberton wrote another note to be smuggled out to Johnston that day: "The enemy has placed several very heavy guns in position against our works, and is approaching them very nearly by sap. His fire is almost continuous. Our men have no relief; are becoming much fatigued, but are still in pretty good spirits. I think your movement should be made as soon as possible. The enemy is receiving re-enforcements. We are living on greatly reduced rations, but I think sufficient for twenty days yet."[6]

Johnston was writing to Secretary Seddon again that day, having finally gotten the latter's dispatch of the 8th completely deciphered: "I cannot advise in regard to the points from which troops can best be taken, having no means of knowing, nor is it for me to judge which is best to hold – Mississippi or Tennessee; that is for the Government to determine. Without some great blunder of the enemy we cannot hold both. The odds against me are much greater than those you express. I consider saving Vicksburg hopeless."[7]

Meanwhile, the siege continued. Captain Hickenlooper's notes for the 15th say: "Work progressing as usual. Captain Powell's (General Ransom's front) work being pushed forward. He commenced advance work on hill north of advanced battery."[8]

"By the middle of June," wrote Alexander Abrams, a reporter for the Vicksburg *Whig*, "Vicksburg was in a deplorable condition. There was scarcely a building but what had been struck by the enemy's shells, while many of them were entirely demolished. The city had the appearance of a half-ruined pile of buildings, and on every street unmistakable signs of the fearful bombardment it had undergone presented themselves to the observer."[9]

"The day was cloudy," Sergeant Tunnard of the 3rd Louisiana noted, "and threatened rain. The firing was very rapid, and shot and shells flew into and over the place in every direction. The enemy seemed to feel in a particularly lively humor." Chaplain W. L. Foster of the 35th Mississippi noted that the short rations were beginning to make noticeable changes in the Confederate troops: "The cheeks became thin, the eyes hollow and the flesh began to disappear from the body and limbs and the whole appearance was haggard and careworn. Yet they were cheerful and did not complain."[10]

The Union soldiers's might have fared better, so far as quantity of food is concerned, but the quality wasn't a lot better. One Union soldier, in writing to his sister that day, said: "I have just finished my dinner. It consists of hard crackers and two or three pieces of fried mess pork. For breakfast we had coffee and crackers and supper is boiled beef, coffee, and crackers. Sometimes we get potatoes and codfish, but seldom."[11]

Up in Tennessee that day, 15 June, General Morgan acknowledged receipt of General Wheeler's message telling him he could make his raid into Kentucky with 1,500 men, but he objected that this was too few: "Can accomplish everything with 2,000 men and four guns. To make the attempt with less, might prove disastrous, as large details will be required at Louisville to destroy the transportation, shipping, and Government property. Can I go? The result is certain."[12]

A few of Morgan's men – those led by Captain Thomas Hines – were already far up in Kentucky. These were the raiders who had robbed a Union paymaster the day before. On this day they were taking a swim when their pickets reported a large force of Federals approaching. They managed to escape by leaving their clothes behind, which they soon replaced at a small crossroads village.

And General Bragg wrote to President Davis that day: "A reliable agent from Kentucky reports nearly all Burnside's forces, Ninth and Twenty-third Army Corps, removed, part sent to Nashville to re-enforce Rosecrans and part to Vicksburg. A Louisville telegram of 10th to Cincinnati paper, just received, gives same report. I send an expedition to feel. Could not Buckner and Preston do the same?" Davis wrote to Joe Johnston that same day: "General Bragg has intelligence from West Tennessee and Missouri that the forces there have been sent to Grant; also, from Louisville, that since 1st instant the Twenty-third and Ninth Army Corps, Burnside's command, have been sent to same destination. The arrival of these re-enforcements must necessarily be anticipated by you in such manner as circumstances shall indicate to you."[13] The next day, the 16th, Johnston wrote to Bragg: "May not Kentucky now be invaded by all the troops of Tennessee? I suggest it to the Government and that East Tennessee should be added to your command."[14]

A small party of Confederate cavalry raided Maysville, Kentucky, on the south bank of the Ohio River, that day, the 16th, where it captured about 50 government horses, 25 pistols, and 330 rifles or muskets; among the latter were 150 British Enfield rifles belonging to a Union company then being recruited. There was also one piece of artillery, a 12-pounder, that the Federals had captured from the Confederates the year before. The cannon was spiked, the small-arms broken up, and the horses taken to replace broken-down mounts. But at sundown these Rebels encountered a larger force of Union cavalry and artillery that inflicted about 30 casualties on them and captured as many more, along with about 100 of their horses. Nevertheless, the raid proved that, with the 9th Corps gone to help Grant and most of the 23rd Corps concentrating in the southern part of the state to help Rosecrans, much of Kentucky was open to raids.

In the states just north of the Ohio, where the Copperheads were strong, there was continuing resistance to the draft. In Holmes County, Ohio, several hundred men were said to have assembled for the purpose of resisting the enrollment, and the governor of the state had issued a proclamation ordering them to disperse. Brigadier General Jacob D. Cox, commander of the District of Ohio in Burnside's Department of the Ohio, ordered the commander of the post at Columbus to send out a battalion of infantry and a section of artillery to deliver the governor's proclamation and arrest any of the men that the provost marshal wanted arrested.

General Burnside wrote to Secretary Stanton that day: "There is very great trouble in many counties in Indiana in carrying out the enrollment, and the force under my command is constantly called upon to aid the enrolling officers, notwithstanding the representations made to you that the exercise of military authority by me was unnecessary. I am more than ever satisfied that it is out of the power of the civil authorities to maintain the peace by prompt arrests and punishment. Can I have the authority to declare martial law at such times as I shall think necessary? Depend upon it, I can restore the whole department to perfect quiet if my policy is adopted."[15]

There was also strong opposition to the draft in the coal-mining areas of Pennsylvania. The provost marshal of the tenth district of that state wrote to the acting assistant provost marshal general of Pennsylvania on 16 June: "I have enrolling officers at work in all my sub-districts except six, and the greater number of them will, I think, finish their work this week. In two of the six I have enrolling officers, but they are so threatened that they do not dare to begin their work without a military force to attend them. In the remaining four I have not been able yet to get any person to accept the office of enroller. I learn from reliable sources that in some of these four meetings are held twice a week in opposition to the enrollment, and that the feeling against the enrollment is violent in them all. Several persons in these four to whom I have offered the enrolling have declined on the ground that their property would be destroyed and their lives be unsafe it they were to undertake it. . . . I see no method of making these enrollments except to march through the sub-districts with a military force. . . . Capt. J. Orr Finnie has reported to me here this afternoon with fifty men. I am glad for these; but to make the campaign of these subdistricts safely I ought to have at least 200 more and two pieces of artillery. The miners are organized and armed with guns and revolvers, and have appeared heretofore in large bodies, and give out that they can summon 1,500 to 2,000 men at a call, and will do so to prevent an enrollment and draft."[16]

Down at Vicksburg, Tuesday, the 16th, "dawned pleasant," as Sergeant Tunnard of the 3rd Louisiana put it, "light summer clouds floating gently across the empyrean. The firing had continued all night, and there was no diminution in its rapidity and volume. The place, as usual, was full of rumors of succor. The rations furnished the men were still good; sufficient to keep away actual starvation, but not to satisfy the voracious appetites of the troops. How the other troops felt, we know not, but the boys of the Third Regiment were *always hungry*."[17]

Henry Ginder, the civilian engineer who had found a place with a vegetable garden, said, "Our vegetables are disappearing fast, being stolen by our soldiers. The worst of it is, as they come at night, they cannot tell whether anything is ripe and they take them away green; so they do no good to them or us. (Since the rain the weather has not been so intolerably warm as it was before.) ... We have frequent displays of lightning at night all around our horizon, so that it is sometimes difficult to tell whether a gun has fired or a cloud has discharged its superabundant electricity."[18]

Admiral Porter was writing to General Grant that day: "Rather than be idle, and thinking it a good plan not to let the rebels be enjoying themselves too much at Richmond [La.], I dispatched General Ellet [and the Marine Brigade] to the commanding officer, to see if he would not lend a hand to drive the rebels away. So they started yesterday morning at early daylight, with about 2,000 men, all told, and found the rebels strongly posted at Richmond, with 4,000 men and six pieces of artillery. After an hour's fight, in which nobody was badly hurt (I believe) on our side, the rebels cleared out, and Richmond was burned in the row. Eleven prisoners fell into our hands. From them we learn that there are 6,000 men at Delhi, but without transportation. They left their wagons in Alexandria. From all I can learn, they expect more troops to join them, more field pieces, and their wagons. ... My idea is that this force is intended to co-operate with Vicksburg at the proper time. With the boats, flats, and coal barges they have they can transport their whole force to this side from Vicksburg in six hours, and if this party should suddenly seize the Point we could not prevent it. I am keeping a strong force of gunboats here, and shall keep the [Marine] brigade ready to land at a moment's notice. ... I do not know what else would bring these fellows here in such a hurry, and why they avoid a fight so. ... I tell you what I suppose to be their plans; you may see something else in the movement. ... Everything is quiet up the river. Hearing that [Confederate Major General Sterling] Price was advancing on Helena, I sent a force of gunboats there."[19]

Charles Dana wrote another report to Stanton that day, in which he reported Grant's decision to send the 9th Corps to Haynes' Bluff instead of the army's left flank. He also relayed complaints about the poor quality of the ammunition being supplied to Grant's forces, both for artillery and for small-arms.

"The days here are hot," he said, "thermometer sometimes rising to ninety at noon, but the nights are very cool. Showers have laid the dust for a week past. The army has hitherto got water from some springs in the ravines, but this source is running out. Some brigades are digging wells; others haul water from distance. Health of troops is excellent."[20]

General Sherman had promptly acted upon Grant's order placing him in command of the reverse lines guarding against an attack by Johnston, and that evening he wrote a report addressed to Rawlins: "Last night, in company with Colonel Wilson, I rode up to Snyder's Bluff, and this morning examined the line of pits and batteries in course of construction. They appear to me well adapted to the end in view, and will enable the two divisions of Kimball and Smith to hold any force coming from the north and northeast. I examined, in company with Generals Washburn, Kimball, and Smith, also Colonel Wilson, the valley of the Skillet-goliath, and have advised that General Parke dispose his force along that valley. . . . General Parke had not arrived at the hour of my starting back (4 p.m.), but I saw steamboats coming, which I think contained his troops. The accounts of the enemy brought in from the front were very conflicting, and my inference was that Loring is feeling his way cautiously down with cavalry, and a moderate force of infantry, as far as Post Oak Ridge. It seems the cavalry pickets drew in from that point last night, but General Washburn assured me he would replace them to-day. The Fourth Iowa Cavalry have moved, by my orders, to Wixon's, with orders to watch the approaches from Bush's and Birdsong's Ferries. With arrangements now completed, the enemy cannot come down the Valley road or the Ridge road via Snyder's. If he comes, he must come across the head of Clear Creek, debouching near Marshall's. That ground cannot well be obstructed, but it is advantageous to us, and could be rendered more so by constructing two or three detached forts. . . . If you deem it prudent, I will cause the ground to be more closely examined, and works laid off and begun. As you know, my corps has done much labor, but I will do anything and everything in human power to achieve final success."[21]

On the lines facing Vicksburg, the Union soldiers continued to dig. Captain Hickenlooper's notes for the 16th say: "Detail at work on main trench and rifle-pits leading from last angle south along crest of hill. The advanced batteries of General Quinby were completed to-day. Began another trench running south, 32 degrees west, along front of curtain of Fort Hill, commencing at a point on main trench, about 25 yards from ditch of Fort Hill. Constructing battery for 9-inch guns near General Logan's headquarters."[22] Alexander Abrams, the reporter for the Vicksburg *Whig*, said: "The enemy, by means of their sappers and miners, had gradually approached until they had erected powerful works within thirty yards of some portions of our line. On the left of the Jackson Road they had occupied [a] hill and erected a large fort on it. . . . It was a very high and strategic position, entirely overlooking our works. . . ."[23]

"It was difficult for the sharp-shooters to reach the Confederates by direct firing," Hickenlooper later wrote, "and the artillerymen found it impossible to gauge their shells so as to cause the explosion immediately behind the Confederate parapets. To overcome this latter difficulty, when the sap reached the vicinity of the fort we caused 'Coehorn mortars' to be made from short sections of gum-tree logs bored out and hooped with iron bands. These novel engines of warfare, being accurately charged with just sufficient powder to lift six or twelve pound shells over the parapet and drop them down immediately behind, proved exceedingly effective."[24]

Secretary Seddon responded on the 16th to Johnston's message of the day before: "Your telegram grieves and alarms me. Vicksburg must not be lost without a desperate struggle. The interest and honor of the Confederacy forbid it. I rely on you still to avert the loss. If better resources do not offer, you must hazard attack. It may be made in concert with the garrison, if practicable, but otherwise without, by day or night, as you think best."[25] But, before receiving this, Johnston wrote another message to Pemberton that day, saying: "I am too weak to save Vicksburg;

can do no more than attempt to save you and your garrison. It will be impossible to extricate you unless you co-operate and we make mutually supporting movements. Communicate your plans and suggestions, if possible."[26]

At Port Hudson that evening, the Federals attacked the extreme left of the Confederate line but were easily repulsed. After that, things settled down into a routine siege, and the troops of both sides observed a series of informal truces, during which they would often visit each other's positions or meet in the open ground between them.

At 2 p.m. on the 16th, Halleck wired General Rosecrans at Murfreesborough, Tennessee: "Is it your intention to make an immediate movement forward? A definite answer, yes or no, is required." Rosecrans replied at 6:30 p.m.: "In reply to your inquiry, if immediate means to-night or to-morrow, no. If it means as soon as all things are ready, say five days, yes."[27]

In Virginia that 16th day of June, Joe Hooker and the authorities at Washington were still in the dark about the true location and movements of Lee's army and at cross-purposes as to what to do about it. Much of the blame for this could be laid at Pleasonton's door; neither he nor Hooker seemed to understand that it was the cavalry's job to find Lee's army and keep track of it. Hooker, in the dark about Lee, continued to hope someone would tell him what they wanted him to do, while Halleck and Lincoln continued to hope that Pleasonton or Hooker or Schenck or someone would provide enough information about the Confederates to base a strategy upon. Several times that day Couch indicated that Rebels had occupied Chambersburg the night before, but Schenck kept saying such reports probably stemmed from over-excited civilians who had seen Milroy's troops retreating or perhaps the wagons escaping from Martinsburg. No one seems to have thought to send a unit or even an individual to Chambersburg to find out.

At 1:15 that morning, Lincoln received a message Hooker had sent at midnight from his new headquarters at Fairfax Station, not far southwest of Washington: "The Army of the Potomac is in this vicinity, excepting the Second and Sixth Corps, and, as they are marching in rear of all the trains, they will not be up before some time to-morrow. Perhaps the Second Corps will not be here until some time during to-morrow night. The First and Eleventh Corps were first to arrive on this line, but I have not yet learned whether they have drawn their supplies in readiness to march to-morrow morning or not. As soon as they are provided, they, as well as the others, will be put *en route*. I have been informed that the enemy nowhere crossed the Rappahannock on our withdrawal from it, but General Hill's troops moved up the river in the direction of Culpeper this [Monday] morning, for the purpose, I conclude, of re-enforcing Longstreet and Ewell, wherever they may be. I request that I may be informed what troops there are at Harper's Ferry, and who is in command of them, and also who is in command in this district."[28]

At 7 a.m., Hooker wrote to Lincoln again: "It appears to me from General Couch's dispatch of last night, received this a.m., that nearly all the cavalry of the Army of the Potomac should at once be sent into Maryland by the most direct route. General Stahel has an abundance to perform all cavalry duty that will be required south of the Potomac. I merely make the suggestion. If any considerable body of enemy's infantry should be thrown across the Potomac, they will probably take the direction of his advance pickets, and in that event it seems to me that a heavy column of ours should be thrown as speedily as possible across the river at Harper's Ferry, while another should be thrown over the most direct line covering Baltimore and Philadelphia. I only speak with reference to this army, as I know nothing of the location or numbers of troops at the disposal of the Government elsewhere."[29]

This was a pretty good reasoning, but, in the absence of any firm information of Lee's movements, no one wanted to turn this suggestion into an order. Hooker's final sentence underlines one of the reasons for the problems the Union command was having just then: Lee was moving into an area where several Union departments met: Hooker commanded only the Army of the Potomac; the District of Columbia and the neighboring parts of Northern Virginia were in the Department of Washington; the Shenandoah Valley was part of the Middle Department, whose headquarters were at Baltimore, far from the scene of action; southern Pennsylvania was part of Couch's new Department of the Susquehanna, which had almost no troops and was not really up and running yet. Hooker considered himself to be working directly under Lincoln, while Halleck was theoretically in charge of all these other departments (as well as those farther west and south), and Stanton stuck his nose in whenever and wherever he pleased.

Lincoln replied, "Your dispatches of last night and this morning are just received. I shall have General Halleck to answer them carefully. Meanwhile, I can only say that, as I understand, Heintzelman commands here in this District; that what troops, or very nearly what number, are at Harper's Ferry I do not know, though I do know that Tyler is in command there. Your idea to send your cavalry to this side of the river may be right – probably is; still, it pains me a little that it looks like defensive merely, and seems to abandon the fair chance now presented of breaking the enemy's long and necessarily slim line, stretched now from the Rappahannock to Pennsylvania."[30]

At 11 a.m. Hooker wrote the President again: "Please accept my suggestions in regard to what should be done in the spirit with which they were given. They were suggestions merely, for I have not the data necessary to form an enlightened opinion on the case. Upon general principles, I thought those were the movements to take. You have long been aware, Mr. President, that I have not enjoyed the confidence of the major-general commanding the army [Halleck], and I can assure you so long as this continues we may look in vain for success, especially as future operations will require our relations to be more dependent upon each other than heretofore. It may be possible now to move to prevent a junction of A. P. Hill's corps with those of Ewell and Longstreet. If so, please let instructions to that effect be given me. As will appear to you, the chances of my doing this are much smaller than when I was on the Rappahannock, for, if he should hold the passes [of the mountains] stoutly, he can cause me delay. You may depend upon it, we can never discover the whereabouts of the enemy, or divine his intentions, so long as he fills the country with a cloud of cavalry. We must break through that to find him."[31]

A half-hour after that, Halleck wrote to Hooker, evidently in response to his midnight and 7 a.m. messages to Lincoln: "I do not think there is reliable information that the enemy has crossed the Potomac in any force. Where his main corps are, is still uncertain, and I know of no way to ascertain, excepting through your cavalry, which should be kept near enough to the enemy to at least be able to tell where he is. My suggestion of yesterday, to follow the enemy's advance, by moving a considerable force first to Leesburg, and thence as circumstances may require, is the best one I can make. Unless your army is kept near enough to the enemy to ascertain his movements, yours must be in the dark or on mere conjecture. Tyler is in command at Harper's Ferry, with, it is said, only 9,000 men, but, according to returns of the 11th, he should have at least 13,600. Heintzelman, as you must be aware, commands this department [of Washington]. Besides the divisions of Abercrombie and Stahel, near you, he has little or no movable troops. Telegraph direct to him in all matters connected with the use of his troops."[32]

As a West Point-trained officer, Hooker surely knew that a superior's suggestions carried the weight of orders, but since he felt that he worked directly for Lincoln he evidently did not consider Halleck as his superior. Consequently he continued to ignore the "suggestion" that he move to Leesburg, which would have put him closer to Harper's Ferry and the Shenandoah Valley.

Meanwhile, Lincoln answered Hooker's 11 a.m. message, which had evidently been delivered by Captain Dahlgren, for it was he who carried the reply: "When you say I have long been aware that you do not enjoy the confidence of the major-general commanding, you state the case much too strongly. You do not lack his confidence in any degree to do you any harm. On seeing him, after telegraphing you this morning, I found him more nearly agreeing with you than I was myself. Surely you do not mean to understand that I am withholding my confidence from you when I happen to express an opinion (certainly never discourteously) differing from one of your own.

"I believe Halleck is dissatisfied with you to this extent only, that he knows that you write and telegraph ("report," as he calls it) to me. I think he is wrong to find fault with this; but I do not think he withholds any support from you on account of it. If you and he would use the same frankness to one another, and to me, that I use to both of you, there would be no difficulty. I need and must have the professional skill of both, and yet these suspicions tend to deprive me of both.

"I believe you are aware that since you took command of the army I have not believed you had any chance to effect anything till now. As it looks to me, Lee's now returning toward Harper's Ferry gives you back the chance that I thought McClellan lost last fall. Quite possibly I was wrong both then and now; but, in the great responsibility resting upon me, I cannot be entirely silent. Now, all I ask is that you will be in such mood that we can get into our action the best cordial judgment of yourself and General Halleck, with my poor mite added, if indeed he and you shall think it entitled to any consideration at all."[33]

Lincoln might not have known that Halleck and Hooker had disliked each other since their days in California just after the Mexican War. One story has it that Hooker borrowed money from Halleck and never repaid it. This has the ring of truth, for then, logically, he, as the "sinning" party, would try to avoid dealing with the "victim." Also, Lincoln obviously did not understand the principal of command that says each officer should have one and only one boss and report directly to him; if someone further up the chain of command wants to communicate with him it should only be done through the intermediate commander. By communicating directly with Hooker, Lincoln bypassed Halleck, and Halleck therefore felt that Lincoln had removed the Army of the Potomac from his area of responsibility and made Hooker his equal, not his subordinate. And Halleck was bound to have been hurt or offended by this, especially when it involved a should-be subordinate whom he didn't like to start with.

Halleck wrote to Hooker again at 3:50 p.m.: "There is now no doubt that the enemy is surrounding Harper's Ferry, but in what force I have no information. General Schenck says our force there is much less than before reported, and cannot hold out very long. He wished to know whether he may expect relief. He can hope for none, excepting from your army."[34] Hooker replied ten minutes later: "Just received your telegram. Please inform me whether our forces at Harper's Ferry are in the town or on the heights, and, if the latter, whether we hold Bolivar, Loudoun, or Maryland Heights, and which, if any; what bridges at Harper's Ferry, and where; from what direction is the enemy making his attack? I suppose it is a couple of long marches from here for the troops without trains, but this, of course, will depend upon the position of the enemy."[35]

Apparently Hooker took Halleck's message to be the positive orders he had been trying to get for days now, and at 7:30 p.m. he wrote to Halleck again: "In compliance with your directions, I shall march to the relief of Harper's Ferry. I [shall] put my column again in motion at 3 a.m. to-morrow. I expect to reach there in two days, and, if possible, earlier. The partial rest of to-day was not lost, being necessary to recruit from forced and heavy marches and fill up supplies."[36]

At 8:20 p.m., Halleck responded to Hooker's message of 4 p.m.: "Information of enemy's actual position and force in front of Harper's Ferry is as indefinite as that in your front. Nearly everything is conjecture. The only position of the enemy mentioned is Halltown. The bridges across both rivers [Shenandoah and Potomac] at Harper's Ferry are believed to be intact, and most of Tyler's troops on Maryland Heights. Loudoun Heights [east of the town] are not fortified, but swept by Maryland batteries. Your questions have been sent to Tyler, and his answer will be forwarded as soon as received. Any troops you can send to his relief should be in motion. A few of the enemy have shown themselves at Poolesville and Point of Rocks. No definite information of his movements from any place."[37]

Hooker wrote to Lincoln again at 9:40 p.m.: "My orders are out to march at 3 o'clock to-morrow morning. It will be likely to be one of vigor and power. I am prepared to move without communications with any place for ten days. I hope to reach my objective point before the arrival of Hill's corps, should it be moving in that direction. If I do not know this fact, I will shortly, but of information to the north of the Potomac I really have nothing. I wish that it might be made the duty of some person in the telegraph office in Washington to keep me informed of the enemy's movements in Maryland." The reply this drew from Lincoln, at 10 p.m., was just about the last thing Hooker wanted to hear: "To remove all misunderstanding, I now place you in the strict military relation to General Halleck of a commander of one of the armies to the general-in-chief of all the armies. I have not intended differently, but as it seems to be differently understood, I shall direct him to give you orders and you to obey them."[38]

Fifteen minutes after that, Halleck wrote to Hooker again, just now responding to the latter's message of 7:30 p.m.: "I have given no directions for your army to move to Harper's Ferry. I have advised the movement of a force, sufficiently strong to meet Longstreet, on Leesburg, to ascertain where the enemy is, and then move to the relief of Harper's Ferry, or elsewhere, as circumstances might require. With the remainder of your force in proper position to support this, I want you to push out your cavalry, to ascertain something definite about the enemy. You are in command of the Army of the Potomac, and will make the particular dispositions as you deem proper. I shall only indicate the objects to be aimed at. We have no positive information of any large force against Harper's Ferry, and it cannot be known whether it will be necessary to go there until you can feel the enemy and ascertain his whereabouts."[39]

His correspondence with Lincoln and Halleck not having gone to his liking, Hooker wired Secretary Stanton that night: "If General Cadwalader has gone to Pennsylvania, please request him to send me information of the rebel movements to the south of there. Also please have the newspapers announce that I am moving on to the James River line. I[t] will mask my real movements in these parts." (Major General George Cadwalader, then about 60 years old and a lawyer by vocation, had been a general in the Mexican War and had served in the Shenandoah Valley early in this war, but for some months had been a member of a board revising military laws and regulations.) Stanton replied: "General Cadwalader has not gone to Pennsylvania, but is here waiting for orders. You shall be kept posted upon all information received here as to enemy's movements, but must exercise your own judgment as to its credibility. The very demon of lying seems to be about these times, and generals will have to be broken for ignorance before they will take the trouble to find out the truth of reports."[40] It is not known whether Hooker realized that he might be one of the generals that needed to be broken. The fact that he evidently continued to believe Pleasonton's reports indicates that he probably did not.

Couch's reports about Chambersburg, at least, were not lies. Not only had Jenkins' cavalry spent the night of 15-16 June just north of there, but that morning he sent most of it about four miles northeastward on the road leading to Harrisburg. There, near a slight immanence called Shirk's Hill, the road crossed over Conococheague Creek. Meanwhile, Jenkins ordered his pioneers to move farther to the northeast to destroy the railroad bridge over the creek with cans of gunpowder while he, his staff, and a small foraging party went back into Chambersburg, where he set up headquarters in a hotel and sent for the mayor and town council. When these worthies arrived he demanded the return of the horses and equipment taken from his two lieutenants the night before, threatening to burn the town. This they were unable to do, but they agreed to pay for them with $900 and several pistols. Jenkins agreed, probably not aware, until it was too late to argue, that the locals would pay him in Confederate money that his men had been spending freely around the town – which would be useless to the locals anyway, once the Rebels left. Anyway, Jenkins could hardly refuse to accept legal tender issued by his own government.

His foraging party spent the rest of the day ransacking stores, stables and warehouses and gathering up horses, cattle, clothing, food and medicine, most of which was sent south to meet Lee's oncoming infantry. Parties were sent several miles to the east and west to do the same throughout the area. Any unattached negroes that could be caught were also rounded up and divided amongst the Confederate officers, to be sent south and sold into slavery, without regard to whether they were runaway slaves or free men (or women). However, several officers refused to take part in this trade and voluntarily released their share of the captives.

There was a "perfect panic" at Harrisburg on the 16th, according to a newspaper reporter, over the news of Confederates having occupied Chambersburg. Civilians there were sure their city would be next. "Every woman in the place seemed anxious to leave," the reporter said, and the outbound trains were crowded with people and their luggage.[41] At the state capitol building, papers, books, and other valuables were being packed up and prepared for shipment.

However, Jenkins cavalry came no closer that day, and Rodes' infantry remained in camp at Williamsport, straddling the Potomac, resting, bathing, and washing their clothes, while pioneers were set to work doing what damage they could to the Chesapeake & Ohio Canal. The division quartermaster purchased over two tons of leather from a tannery there, for repairing shoes, while the ordnance officer bought 35 kegs of gunpowder. Early's division remained around Winchester, and Johnson's marched to Smithfield, near Bunker Hill. General Ewell moved his headquarters to the latter place, but not before attending a celebration at Winchester, when a Confederate flag was raised over the main Union fort there, now renamed Fort Jackson in honor of the recently deceased "Stonewall." Pro-Confederate ladies in attendance called for a speech from Ewell, but the recently married general responded, in his lisping falsetto voice: "I can't make speeches to ladies. I never made a speech to but one lady in my life."[42] He tried to get General Early to do the honors, but Early, a lifelong bachelor, also declined, saying he had never been able to make a speech to even one lady.

Longstreet's 1st Corps of Lee's army continued moving northeastward along the eastern foot of the Blue Ridge on the 16th. Stuart's cavalry had been delayed by the infantry filling the roads, but that night his headquarters, plus Robertson's and Chambliss's (Rooney Lee's) brigades were at Salem; three regiment's of Munford's (Fitz Lee's) brigade were at Piedmont and two at Upperville. Hampton and Grumble Jones were still patrolling the upper Rappahannock to screen A. P. Hill's column, which was closing in on Culpeper Court House.

Lee, whose headquarters were still at that village, wrote to Hill that day: "I have received your two dispatches of yesterday, and conclude that the enemy has entirely disappeared from your front. General Anderson's division arrived here this morning. It will be supplied with provisions and forage, and will resume its march to-morrow. Heth, I hope, will reach here to-morrow, and as I have not yet heard of Pender being in motion, I presume he will not reach here until the next day. I wish your corps to follow Longstreet as closely as you can, and, keeping your divisions in supporting distance, your reserve artillery, heavy batteries, and reserve trains might advantageously take the Sperryville road as far as Woodville, and there turn off for Chester Gap to Front Royal, and so down the Valley.... Your divisions as they come up will be furnished with all the provisions and forage which they can take from this place. This being the last point where we will be in railroad communication with Richmond, I recommend that everything which may be found surplus in the baggage of your troops should be sent back from this place. If not here, I will be found in the advance with General Longstreet."[43]

And, in fact, Lee did leave Culpeper Court House the next day, Wednesday, the 17th, and rode to Markham, on the Manassas Gap Railroad just east of the Blue Ridge. The 17th was a scorching hot day. After six weeks without rain, water was scarce, and dust was kicked up with every step. Men of both armies died of thirst and heat stroke that day. Johnson's Division of Ewell's Corps marched to Shepherdstown, on the Potomac, that day. Rodes' Division was still at Williamsport, his last two brigades crossing to the north side of the river that day, and Early's Division was near Winchester.

Evidently, the head of Longstreet's corps turned west toward the gaps in the Blue Ridge on the 17th, for at 3:30 p.m. Lee wrote to his 1st Corps' commander: "I have heard nothing of the movements of General Hooker either from General Stuart or yourself, and, therefore, can form no opinion of the best move against him. If a part of our forces could have operated east of the mountains, it would have served more to confuse him, but as you have turned off to the Valley, and I understand all the trains have taken that route, I hope it is for the best. At any rate, it is too late to change from any information I have. You had better, therefore, push on, relieve Ewell's division as soon as you can, and let him advance into Maryland, at least as far as Hagerstown. Give out it is against Harper's Ferry. I will send back for A. P. Hill to move by Chester Gap.... I shall go from here to the Valley."[44]

He also wrote a note to Ewell, also dated at 3:30 p.m.: "I think the reports which you have of the forces in Harper's Ferry must be exaggerated. I wish you to move Rodes' division on as far as Hagerstown, and operate in the enemy's country according to the plan proposed. Give out that your movement is for the purpose of enveloping Harper's Ferry. Repress marauding. Take what is necessary for the army, and give citizens of Maryland Confederate money or certificates. Do not expose yourself. Keep your own scouts."[45]

The 35th Virginia Cavalry Battalion, commanded by Lieutenant Colonel E. V. White, part of Grumble Jones's brigade, was guarding the passes of the Blue Ridge between Snicker's Gap and the Potomac River. But at about 9 that morning, after leaving a few men to watch the passes, White took about 125 of his men across the Potomac at a point some three miles above Point of Rocks. Late that afternoon he split his command into two parts, each of which surprised and defeated larger Union formations. "We broke the telegraph wires, tore up some of the railroad track, and recrossed the Potomac River about 10 p.m.," he reported.[46]

Hooker and the Union high command remained in the dark about where Lee's army was and what it was up to, but at least their own chain of command had been clarified. Sometime on the morning of the 17th Hooker wrote to Halleck: "Your dispatch of 10 p.m. received by me at 1 a.m. Will make the dispositions of my forces to comply with the objects aimed at in your dispatch. The advices heretofore received by telegraph from Washington have stated successively that Martinsburg and Winchester were invested and surrounded; that Harper's Ferry was closely invested, with urgent calls upon me for relief; that the enemy were advancing in three columns through Pennsylvania, and had driven in General Couch's pickets. Now I am informed, in substance, that General Schenck thinks it all arises from one of his wagon trains; that General Tyler, at Harper's Ferry, whose urgent calls, as represented to me, required under my instructions rapid movements in this direction, seem to think that he is in no danger. Telegraph operator just reports to me that Harper's Ferry is abandoned by our forces. Is this true? . . . I should very much like to have reliable and correct information concerning enemy on the north side of the Potomac."[47] However, at 2:10 p.m. Halleck replied: "I regret equally with you that reports from north side of the Potomac are so unreliable and contradictory, but they are given to you as received. What is meant by abandoning Harper's Ferry is merely that General Tyler has concentrated his force in the fortifications on Maryland Heights. No enemy in any force has been seen below [down the Potomac from] Harper's Ferry, north of the river, and it is hoped that Tyler's cavalry may get something reliable above. So far, we have had only the wild rumors of panic-stricken people."[48]

At Chambersburg that morning, Jenkins' pickets on Shirk's Hill, north of town, spotted a thin line of Union horsemen watching them from another hill about a mile farther north and, behind those, a dark mass of people that they took to be at least a brigade of Federal troops, perhaps the advance guard of a whole corps said to be assembling on the Susquehanna River. Word of this development was hastened to Jenkins, who rounded up his foragers and shoppers, sent his horses south of town out of the way, and formed his brigade in dismounted line of battle between the town and Shirk's Hill. Several buildings in the town were commandeered for use as hospitals, but they weren't needed, for around noon the entire brigade marched south through the town, saddled up, and rode clear down to Greencastle, near the Maryland-Pennsylvania line (the famous Mason-Dixon Line), where foraging parties were again sent out to the east and west. None of the Rebels ever went close enough to the Federals north of Chambersburg to discover that most of them were just civilians come to stare at the Confederates who had invaded their country.

Imboden's small brigade was causing some of the confusion among Federal commanders. Messages were flying between the various commands in West Virginia and Pennsylvania trying to anticipate his movements and worrying that he represented the advanced guard of the long-expected giant Confederate cavalry raid. At 6 o'clock that morning Brigadier General B. F. Kelley, commander of the 1st Division of the 8th Corps (Middle Department), left Cumberland, Maryland, on the upper Potomac, heading southwest on the Baltimore & Ohio Railroad, but 10 miles out of town he found the track had been torn up by the Rebel raiders. His train then carried him back toward Cumberland, but he found the place to now be invested by Imboden's entire brigade. With an escort of 50 cavalry, which he found outside

Cumberland, he made his way on to New Creek, West Virginia – his original objective – from which place he reported by telegraph to General Schenck at Baltimore.

Schenck passed the report on to Halleck and also informed him that Colonel James A. Galligher of the 12th Pennsylvania had reached Hancock, Maryland (on the Potomac east of Cumberland and due north of Winchester, Virginia), with about 1,000 cavalry and 2,000 infantry of Milroy's division. He had contacted Kelley and asked for rations and ammunition. Kelley had agreed to supply them and ordered him to fall back on New Creek, but, as he reported to Schenck, "on account of the subsequent occupation of Cumberland by Imboden's forces, I directed him to retreat north into Pennsylvania." Schenck forwarded this to Halleck also, and added, "I have informed General Couch of this. He may be able, I hope, to communicate with these men, supply them, and use them to whip Jenkins' cavalry at Chambersburg, who, I have ascertained, certainly were less than 1,400 when they passed Hagerstown [Md.], and without artillery."[49]

Schenck's headquarters issued orders that day for General Milroy to proceed to Pennsylvania to take charge of these troops of his division and prepare them for use against "any smaller or equal force of rebels now supposed to be at Chambersburg or in that neighborhood, or will conduct them to Harrisburg . . . or, if found more expedient and advisable, . . . he may . . . use them to observe, pursue, or interrupt the movements and operations of any rebel force at Cumberland or proceeding westward."[50] In the latter case he was to communicate with Kelley at New Creek, and in any event to confer with Couch at Harrisburg. Schenck also suggested to Halleck that "Imboden, with his forces, may intend to push across through Uniontown, Pa., by the National road to Wheeling. I am looking to that, among other contingencies. There should be a gunboat at Wheeling, one also at Parkersburg, and one on the Kanawha."[51]

Meanwhile, forces were being scraped up for the defense of Pennsylvania. The first troops to reach Harrisburg arrived on the 17th: a company of the Invalid Corps from the hospital at

York, Pennsylvania. The Invalid Corps was an organization of wounded soldiers who were no longer fit for service in the field but could still perform light duties. The light duty they were now assigned was to protect the state of Pennsylvania from Robert E. Lee's army. General Couch put them on a train that day and sent them down to Shippensburg, some ten miles up the tracks from Chambersburg. The 20th Pennsylvania Militia Regiment, from Philadelphia, also reached Harrisburg that day, but they were unorganized, untrained and poorly equipped, so Couch did not dare send them to the front. Instead he sent them down to Wrightsville, on the lower Susquehanna, where they could build some earthworks while absorbing some rudimentary training.

The governor of New Jersey issued a proclamation that day calling on its citizens to come to the aid of their neighboring state, and at 10:25 that night Secretary Stanton received a telegram from the colonel of the 27th New Jersey, then at Cincinnati, Ohio: "My regiment, 800 strong, is on its way home for muster-out. I have offered their services, with their unanimous consent, to you for Pennsylvania's defense, through General Burnside." Stanton replied 25 minutes later accepting with gratitude and directing the colonel to "proceed with your regiment as rapidly as possible to Pittsburgh, by the way of the Ohio Central Railroad, in order that you may stop at Wheeling, if your services should be required there by General Brooks."[52]

The commander of New York's militia wired Halleck that day that he had organized two infantry brigades out of nine regiments of New York National Guards and that he could add 400 artillerymen if the Federal government could provide the guns, caissons and horses. Governor Curtin of Pennsylvania wired Stanton that same day that the 172nd Pennsylvania, then at Yorktown, Virginia, had offered to re-enlist for six months for the defense of its home state, asking if such an arrangement could be made. "I think the example would lead to similar offers from other regiments."[53]

Speaking of Yorktown, not much was being accomplished down that way by forces of the Union's Department of Virginia.

The general in command at Suffolk wrote General Dix that day to say that his forces had not been able to cross the Blackwater River, between that place and Petersburg; the fords were barricaded and strongly picketed. And General Keyes wrote from his camp near Williamsburg to say that there were no supplies on the Peninsula, so that "if we advance farther we must establish depots, and guard them. This we could not do with my present force, and our means of transportation are very limited. . . . Under such circumstances, it appears to me all our spare troops here should be sent north upon the track of the enemy, or to build forts and hold points, &c., with as little delay as practicable."[54]

Endnotes

1. OR I:28:II:5.
2. Wise, *Gate of Hell*, 40.
3. Dana, *Recollections of the Civil War*, 95-6.
4. OR, I:24:I:99-100.
5. Ibid., I:24:III:410.
6. Ibid., I:24:III:964, also I:24:I:279.
7. Ibid., I:24:I:227.
8. Ibid., I:24:II:200.
9. Hoehling, *Vicksburg: 47 Days of Siege*, 164-5.
10. Ibid., 159.
11. Duane Schultz, *The Most Glorious Fourth* (New York, 2002), 121.
12. OR, I:23:I:818.
13. Ibid., I:52:II:495-6.
14. Ibid., I:52:II:496.
15. Ibid., III:3:371.
16. Ibid., III:3:382.
17. Hoehling, *Vicksburg: 47 Days of Siege*, 169.
18. Ibid., 172-3.
19. OR, I:24:II:454-5.
20. Ibid., I:24:I:101.
21. Ibid., I:24:III:415.
22. Ibid., I:24:II:200.
23. Hoehling, *Vicksburg: 47 Days of Siege*, 171.
24. Hickenlooper, "The Vicksburg Mine," *B&L* III:540.
25. OR, I:24:I:227.
26. Ibid., I:24:III:965-6.
27. Ibid., I:23:I:10.
28. Ibid., I:27:I:44.

29 Ibid.
30 Basler, ed., *The Collected Works of Abraham Lincoln*, VI:280.
31 *OR*, I:27:I:45.
32 Ibid.
33 Basler, ed., *The Collected Works of Abraham Lincoln*, VI:281.
34 *OR*, I:27:I:45-6.
35 Ibid., I:27:I:46.
36 Ibid.
37 Ibid.
38 Ibid., I:27:I:47.
39 Ibid.
40 Ibid., I:27:I:47-8.
41 E. B. Long with Barbara Long, *The Civil War Day by Day* (Garden City NY, 1971), 367.
42 Freeman, *Lee's Lieutenant's*, III:26-7.
43 *OR*, I:27:III:896.
44 Ibid., I:27:III:900.
45 Ibid., I:27:III:900-1. This source adds, "Note in letter-book says: 'Copy from memory; draught mislaid.'"
46 Ibid., I:27:II:771.
47 Ibid., I:27:I:48.
48 Ibid., I:27:I:49.
49 Ibid., I:27:III:183.
50 Ibid., I:27:III:190.
51 Ibid., I:27:III:184.
52 Ibid., I:27:III:184-5.
53 Ibid., I:27:III:187.
54 Ibid., I:27:III:189-90.

CHAPTER 11

"Get Us Information"

17 – 19 June 1863

Halleck's order to Hooker the previous evening to "ascertain something definite about the enemy" had at last stirred the army commander to make a real effort to do just that. Sometime on the 17th, General Seth Williams, Hooker's assistant adjutant general, wrote to Pleasonton: "Since you were here last night, the character of the telegraphic information received would indicate that not as much has been seen of the enemy in Maryland as we supposed. This, like all other, is rumor. The telegraph operator at Harper's Ferry announces that General Tyler, commanding there, has withdrawn all his forces to Maryland Heights, evacuating Harper's Ferry. The infantry forces, instead of being ordered as when you were here, are directed – the Twelfth Corps to camp at Dranesville to-night; First Corps on Goose Creek; Eleventh Corps at Guilford Station; Fifth Corps at Gum Springs; Third Corps at Centreville; Second Corps at Sangster's Station; Sixth Corps at Fairfax Station; and headquarters remain to-night at Fairfax Station.

"Verbal orders have been sent you by Captain Dahlgren, some time since, instead of moving with your whole command, as directed last night, to make easy marches, put the main body of your command in the vicinity of Aldie, and push out reconnaissances toward Winchester, Berryville, and Harper's Ferry. The commanding general relies upon you with your cavalry force to give him information of where the enemy is, his force, and his movements. You have a sufficient cavalry force to do this. Drive in pickets, if necessary, and get us information. It is better that we should lose men than to be without knowledge of the enemy, as we now seem to be. Captain McEntee, of Colonel Sharpe's [intelligence] department, thoroughly understands the whole organization of the rebel army, and is sent out to join you. After you have examined any prisoners, deserters, or contrabands [slaves] brought in, the general desires you will give him [McEntee] a chance to examine all of them, and desires that all information may be communicated with great promptness, and directs that you leave nothing undone to give him the fullest information."[1]

Aldie, toward which Pleasonton was thus directed to move, was a small village where the Little River Turnpike from Alexandria reached the Bull Run Mountains. There the road split, with one fork running northwest to cross the Blue Ridge at Snicker's Gap and, after crossing the Shenandoah River, going on to Berryville and Winchester; the other fork, running more nearly due west, ran through Middleburg, Upperville, and Paris, to cross the Blue Ridge at Ashby's Gap before turning to the northwest and Winchester. All this was only a few miles northeast of Markham, which General Lee reached that afternoon, and the two gaps – Ashby's and Snicker's – were the very ones Longstreet's infantry was heading for. This land between the Bull Run Mountains and the Blue Ridge was known as the Loudoun Valley – about 15-20 miles wide. It was horse country, composed of beautiful rolling hills and the bottom lands bordering Goose Creek and its tributaries – all covered with pastures and wood lots and dotted with small, neat, picturesque villages and farms. And Aldie, right on the eastern edge of all this, with two fine roads leading toward the Blue Ridge, would serve as an excellent base for scouting the Loudoun Valley – a fact which was as obvious to Jeb Stuart as it was to the Federals, if not more so.

Stuart was moving across the Loudoun Valley that day with three of his brigades to secure the passes of the Bull Run Mountains and keep the Federals from spotting Longstreet's infantry. He sent Munford, with Fitz Lee's brigade, toward Aldie, Chambliss, with Rooney Lee's brigade, toward Thoroughfare Gap, and kept Robertson's two large, but inexperienced, North Carolina regiments near Rectortown to serve as a reserve. Stuart made his headquarters at Middleburg, where, as one of his staff officers noted, so many pretty girls surrounded him that "the scene looked like a dance around a maypole."[2]

At 4:15 p.m., Pleasonton wrote to Hooker from near Aldie: "Upon arriving at this place, a short time since, I found at least one brigade of the enemy's cavalry; how much more I have not ascertained. I have engaged them, and will send you further particulars as soon as I obtain them. Some prisoners were taken, who say that Fitz. Lee's brigade is here, and that Stuart is at Middleburg." He added, in a postscript, that "A scout of Captain McEntee says there is no infantry on this side the Blue Ridge, and that this is all the cavalry."[3]

For Pleasonton, this was a pretty accurate report, but he failed to mention the real significance of Stuart being at Middleburg, which was that Colonel Duffié (who, since his poor showing at Brandy Station and the reorganization of the cavalry into only two divisions, had been reduced to the command of his single regiment) had been sent to that same village, by way of Thoroughfare Gap, southwest of Aldie. His regiment, the 1st Rhode Island Cavalry (total strength: 275 men, plus officers), was supposed to camp there that night (the 17th). Duffié should have known his orders would put him in a dangerous position when he encountered part of Chambliss's brigade at Thoroughfare Gap. But, by around 11 a.m., Duffié was able to pass around the Rebels, and he proceeded on his way to Middleburg, leaving a dangerous force in his rear. The Confederates followed behind him for a while, then disappeared. (Chambliss, thinking that Duffié's regiment was only the vanguard of a larger force, chose to hold Thoroughfare Gap against the presumed greater threat.)

Meanwhile, the rest of Gregg's 2nd Division, accompanied by Pleasonton himself, made for Aldie. In the lead was a brigade commanded by Hugh Judson Kilpatrick, just promoted to brigadier general three days before. It reached the village around noon or a little after, where its advance regiment, the 2nd New York Cavalry, came upon a company of Munford's (Fitz Lee's) brigade, serving as pickets. Munford, with two of his five regiments, was still a couple of miles from Aldie, approaching along the Snicker's

Gap road, but he had sent these pickets on ahead. Two more of Munford's regiments plus his attached battery of horse artillery, all under Colonel William Wickham of the 4th Virginia Cavalry, had just stopped at Dover Mills, about a mile and a half west of Aldie on the road to Middleburg, to water their horses in Little River.

The leading squadron of New Yorkers charged Munford's pickets and chased them through Aldie, but about halfway to Dover's Mills they were charged in turn by Munford's remaining regiment, the 5th Virginia Cavalry, led by young Colonel Tom Rosser, who had overtaken and passed Wickham's two regiments and gone on ahead to select that night's campsite for the brigade. The leading Union squadron briefly crossed sabers with Rosser's Virginians, but, being badly outnumbered, soon fell back on the rest of its regiment. (A cavalry squadron consisted of two troops, or companies, but some sources seem to confuse the terms company and squadron. Union cavalry regiments had 12 companies = 6 squadrons = 3 battalions; Confederate regiments had 10 companies = 5 squadrons but no battalion organization. However, to make things more confusing, the Confederates had some independent battalions, which simply meant any units with fewer than 10 companies. At this point in the war, cavalry regiments would rarely field more that 300-400 men, so a squadron would be around 50-80.)

Both sides now halted to get reorganized, and in the meantime Kilpatrick's battery of horse artillery took position on a hill north of Aldie, supported by the 4th New York Cavalry, while the 1st Massachusetts Cavalry formed column of squadrons in a small field near the town. Kilpatrick and his staff soon arrived, and he ordered the commander of the 1st Massachusetts to send a squadron up the Snicker's Gap road to see if there were any Rebels in that direction. There were.

The first Confederates to arrive were a lieutenant and fifteen men sent ahead by Munford. They dismounted and took cover behind a stone wall on the north side of the road, just beyond the point where a side road came in from Dover Mills; they had orders to hold on until the 2nd and 3rd Virginia, coming down the Snicker's Gap road, could reach the field. Munford himself, after posting the pickets behind their stone wall, went down to Dover Mills to bring the 4th and 5th Virginia up to the Snicker's Gap road. The lead squadron of the 4th Virginia scouted down the road toward Aldie.

Kilpatrick told the captain commanding the advancing squadron of the 1st Massachusetts to drive these Rebels back but not to go beyond a house that was less than a quarter-mile up the road. However, when the Virginians gave way, the Federals followed and kept going right past the designated house. Finally, having gone about a mile up the road, the squadron was hit by the fire of the pickets behind their stone wall and charged in the flank by parts of the 4th and 5th Virginia, which, along with half the horse artillery, were just coming up the connecting road from Dover Mills. The Union squadron rallied and counter-charged, but, finding itself cut off, broke off the fight and escaped along a wood-cutter's road to the east.

The 1st Virginia Cavalry and half the horse artillery were left to block the road to Middleburg and cover the connecting road. Also, Rosser left one squadron of his 5th Virginia in a forward position, near where he had first encountered the Federals – too far forward, as it turned out. One squadron of the 2nd New York Cavalry charged this advanced position but was repulsed, but then the rest of the same regiment hit the Rebel squadron on its left flank while the 6th Ohio Cavalry charged down the road and hit it on the other flank. After losing a third of its men, the entire Confederate squadron, or what was left of it, surrendered.

This ended the fighting along the Middleburg road, for the Federals did not choose to attack the 1st Virginia, and again the fighting shifted to the Snicker's Gap pike. There the 1st Massachusetts twice again sent single squadrons to attack up the road, which, near the Confederate position, was narrow and crowded by embankments, so that there was no room to deploy in a broad formation. The charge of a fourth squadron of the 1st Massachusetts was met by a squadron of the 2nd Virginia, for that regiment and the 3rd had finally arrived. The two formations collided, but Munford had deployed one squadron of each of the two newly arrived regiments as dismounted sharpshooters, and these poured a deadly fire into the Federals. Then two more Confederate squadrons hit the Federals, one on each flank, and most of this squadron of the 1st Massachusetts was killed or captured, as was part of another squadron that tried to advance dismounted to its aid. Kilpatrick ordered the 4th New York to attack, but this charge was also repulsed, and the regiment's colonel and color-guard were captured.

A charge by the 3rd Virginia, supported on the flanks by the 2nd and 5th, then scattered what little was left of the 1st Massachusetts, but this charge's momentum carried it almost as far as Aldie, where it was charged in turn by a squadron of the 1st Maine Cavalry, part of the next Federal brigade, just coming up, and the reformed 4th New York, and they chased the Rebels back to their starting place. Among the chasers was Tom Rosser's friend and West Point classmate, George Custer, a captain on Pleasonton's staff. He had lost control of his horse, which galloped right into the Confederate ranks. Custer cut down two Rebels with his saber and passed clear through the Confederate formation. Then, finally regaining control of his mount, he circled back to Kilpatrick's headquarters. Newspaper correspondents witnessing the young captain's antics, not realizing that they weren't entirely voluntary, depicted him as the hero of the day.

About then Mumford received an order from Stuart to fall back toward Middleburg, which he did in good order, bringing off his dead and those wounded who could be moved. The 1st Maine followed for about a half-mile beyond the crossroads the Rebels had been defending, then let them go. By then it was about dark, and Munford established his pickets another half-mile down the road and put his men into bivouac for the night.

The reason for Stuart's order for Munford to fall back was the appearance of Duffié's regiment at Middleburg, at about 4 p.m. Stuart had no troops with him except an escort squadron, part of which was deployed as pickets around the town. When these were driven in by Duffié, Stuart and his staff made what one staff officer called "a retreat more rapid than was consistent with dignity and comfort."[4] Stuart retired toward Rector's Cross Roads, about halfway to Upperville, and sent orders for his three brigades to converge on Middleburg. Under orders to camp at Middleburg for the night himself, Duffié made no effort to escape, even though he knew that there was a superior Rebel force back on the road to Thoroughfare Gap and another due east of him at Aldie. He did have sense enough to know, however, that he was in a dangerous spot, and he barricaded all the roads leading into town and sent a captain and two men with a dispatch to Kilpatrick, his brigade commander, at Aldie, asking for help.

"At 7 o'clock," Duffié later reported, "I ascertained that the enemy was approaching in force from Aldie, Union, and Upperville. Determined to hold the position if possible, I dismounted one-half of my regiment, placing them behind stone walls and the barricades. The enemy surrounded the town and stormed the barricades, but were gallantly repulsed by my men with great slaughter. They did not, however, desist, but, confident of success, again attacked, and made three successive charges. I was compelled to retire on the road by which I came, that being the only one open to retreat. With all that was left of my command, I crossed Little River northeast of Middleburg, and bivouacked for the night, establishing strong pickets on the river.... At 10 p.m., having heard nothing from my dispatch sent to General Kilpatrick, I sent 20 men, under an officer, with a second dispatch. I have heard nothing from either party, and believe that both have been captured."[5]

The bearers of the first dispatch had not been captured, however, merely ignored. The captain who led that party reported two narrow escapes but said: "I reached Aldie, and delivered my dispatch to General Kilpatrick at 9 p.m. General Kilpatrick informed me that his brigade was so worn out that he could not send any re-enforcements to Middleburg, but that he would report the situation of our regiment to General Gregg. Returning, he said that General Gregg had gone to state the facts to General

Pleasonton, and directed me to remain at Aldie until he heard from General Pleasonton. I remained, but received no further orders."[6]

Meanwhile, Hooker remained in the dark about what Lee was up to. Sometime that evening, Dan Butterfield wrote to Brigadier General Rufus Ingalls, Hooker's quartermaster, who was in Washington: "Try and hunt up somebody from Pennsylvania who knows something, and has a cool enough head to judge what is the actual state of affairs there with regard to the enemy. Seven or eight thousand men are reported at Williamsport. Couch reports his pickets driven in. Enemy reported to have appeared at Poolesville, and everywhere else in Maryland, Pennsylvania, and Western Virginia. Cavalry enough is reported to have appeared to fill up the whole of Pennsylvania and leave no room for the inhabitants. Since we were not allowed to cross and whip A. P. Hill, while Longstreet and Ewell were moving off through Culpeper and Sperryville, we have lost the opportunity of doing a thing which we knew to a certainty we could accomplish. My impression now is that there is not a rebel, excepting scouts, this side of the Shenandoah Valley; that Lee is in as much uncertainty as to our whereabouts and what we are doing as we are as to his; that his movement on the Upper Potomac is a cover for a cavalry raid on the north side of the river, and a movement of his troops farther west, where he can turn up at some weak spot.... We cannot go boggling round until we know what we are going after."[7]

At 9:20 p.m. Hooker wrote to Halleck: "I am in constant receipt of copies of dispatches from General Couch with regard to enemy at Chambersburg. Is there, in you opinion, any foundation for the reports? All my cavalry are out, and I have deemed it prudent to suspend any farther advance of the infantry until I have information that the enemy are in force in the Shenandoah Valley." After a brief account of Pleasonton's battle at Aldie he added: "Has it ever suggested itself to you that this cavalry raid may be a cover to Lee's re-enforcing Bragg or moving troops to the West?"[8]

Brigadier General Marsena Patrick, provost marshal general

of the Army of the Potomac (in other words, the head of Hooker's military police), wrote that day that Hooker "acts like a man without a plan and is entirely at a loss what to do, or how to match the enemy, or counteract his movements. Whatever he does is the result of impulse, now, after having failed so signally, at Chancellorsville. His role now is that of Micawber, 'waiting for something to turn up,' and when something turns up, he plays like a gambler."[9]

Blockading Savannah, Georgia, might have been a fairly easy assignment for the U.S. Navy except for the fact that the Savannah River and the estuary at its mouth, called Tybee Roads, was not the only mouse-hole to watch. Twenty-some miles west of Tybee Roads the Great Ogeechee River, the Little Ogeechee River, and the Vernon River flow together to form Ossabaw Sound. The area between Tybee Roads and Ossabaw Sound (as well as the coast above the one and below the other) was cut up by numerous interconnecting streams that divided the land into numerous islands, similar to those up by Charleston. One of these streams, which connected with the Savannah River, was the Wilmington River, and it emptied into Wassaw Sound, another estuary about halfway between the other two. The USS *Weehawken*, an ironclad of the Monitor class, was anchored in Wassaw Sound on 17 June, when, at 4:10 a.m., a lookout spotted a Confederate ironclad approaching.

The *Weehawken* closely resembled the original USS *Monitor*, which is to say there was nothing showing above the waterline but an armored cylindrical revolving turret, which housed two guns. One modification had been moving the pilot house from the deck to atop the turret, which both gave better visibility for the pilot and got it out of the way of the guns. And, whereas the original *Monitor* had carried two 11-inch Dahlgren smoothbore shell-guns (named for their designer, Rear Admiral John A. Dahlgren, now temporarily in command of the South Atlantic

Blockading Squadron and father of Captain Ulric Dahlgren of General Hooker's staff), the *Weehawken* carried one 11-inch and one 15-inch Dahlgren. The *Weehawken* was commanded by Captain John Rodgers, scion of an illustrious naval family, and she had a veteran crew. She had led the Union Navy's attack on Fort Sumter, at Charleston, back in April, coming away with only minor damage. Also, there was another Monitor, the USS *Nahant*, nearby.

The approaching Confederate ironclad was the CSS *Atlanta*, which had been converted at Savannah from a Scottish-built iron-hulled merchant steamer. She followed the usual Confederate layout for ironclads: Her hull was cut off near the waterline and decked over; above that rose a sloping wooden casemate covered with iron armor and pierced for guns. In the *Atlanta*'s case, her casemate sloped even more than usual (29 degrees to horizontal) and had two layers of 2-inch iron laid over 15 inches of pine, and she carried a 7-inch rifle at each end that could be pivoted to fire to either side or abeam, plus a 6.4-inch rifle on each side, giving her broadsides of three guns in either direction. Since rifles fired shot of about twice the weight of smoothbores of comparable caliber, these three guns would have thrown even more total weight than the *Weehawken*'s two Dahlgrens. And, like most Confederate ironclads, she was also fitted with a ram, so that she could simply use her steam engine to run down an enemy vessel and stove in its hull. A novel feature was what was called a spar torpedo – a can of gunpowder (with a percussion-cap primer) fitted to the end of a pole that could be raised or lowered remotely – at the ship's bow. If simply ramming failed to sink an enemy ship, the torpedo could be dropped on it or shoved against it. Also unlike most other Confederate ironclads, she had relatively new machinery – probably the best propulsion unit of any of them – and, even with the weight of her armor and guns, she could make about 6 knots. She did have two problems, however: She drew a lot of water (16 feet), meaning that she could not go into shallow places; and she leaked, for the job of converting her had been done hastily and with a shortage of skilled workmen.

Technically, the *Atlanta* was commanded by Lieutenant George T. Sinclair, but the senior officer on board was the commander of the Savannah squadron, Commander William A. Webb. Since the only formidable vessel in his command, so far, was the *Atlanta*, Webb took direct control of her. His objective was to take advantage of a full tide to slip past the two Monitors, sink or chase away any wooden blockaders, go attack the Union base at Port Royal, South Carolina, and then come back and blockade Union-held Fort Pulaski in Tybee Roads. Confederate Secretary of the Navy Stephen Mallory had suggested that Webb wait for the completion of another ironclad, the CSS *Savannah*, so he could use the two together, but Webb had replied, "I assure you the whole abolition fleet has no terror for me, though the co-operation of the *Savannah* would be of great assistance."[10] Mallory had recently appointed Webb to this command because he was confident and aggressive, two characteristics that his predecessor had lacked, so he could hardly complain when Webb showed signs of aggressive confidence.

The Federals knew about the *Atlanta*, of course – it had been in commission for months – which is precisely why there were Monitors on hand to protect the blockading ships. When the Confederate ship was spotted heading his way, Rodgers at first ran downstream to give time for his vessel to get up a full head of steam while the crew took action stations, and the *Nahant* followed in his wake, doing the same. But, after about ten minutes, the *Weehawken* turned about and headed for the *Atlanta*. At the range of about a mile and a half, the Rebel ship opened fire; the shot passed over the *Weehawken* and fell short of the *Nahant*. But Rodgers was puzzled by the fact that the Confederate no longer seemed to be trying to get to the open sea. In fact, she seemed to be stopped and lying crosswise in the channel.

The reason for this was that the *Atlanta* had run aground on a sandbar. Not only was she thus unable to maneuver (rendering her torpedo and ram useless) but it also caused her to list slightly, making it difficult to bring her guns to bear on the closing *Weehawken*. Although she got off seven shots, she did no damage to the Union vessel. Rodgers waited until he had closed to within 300 yards, then opened fire with his big smoothbore guns. The first shot missed. Then a 15-inch shell struck the *Atlanta's* casemate, and, although it failed to penetrate the armor, it sent splinters of iron and wood flying around the gun deck, wounding several men and laying out 40 or 50 more just from the concussion. The third shot slightly damaged the small bit of non-sloping armor just above the waterline, known as the knuckle. The fourth glanced off the armored porthole shutter of the starboard gun just as it was being raised so that the gun could be run out to fire, wounding over half of the gun crew. The fifth shot carried away the top of the pilot house and wounded two of the pilots. Webb surrendered after only fifteen minutes of battle.

This brief fight ended the danger to the wooden blockaders and freed the Monitors to return to Charleston Harbor. It would also soon earn Rodgers the thanks of Congress and a promotion to commodore. The *Atlanta* was repaired and taken into the U.S. Navy and later served in its James River flotilla. But perhaps the most important result was that, when news of this battle crossed the Atlantic, Britain and France were alarmed to learn that a vessel bearing as much armor as their own best ironclads had been so easily pounded into submission by an American Monitor. This helped to spike any thoughts of interfering in the war.

Captain Tom Hines' small band of raiders from Morgan's cavalry crossed the Ohio River on the 17th, sixty miles downstream from Louisville. Hines told his men that they would now pretend to be a unit of home guards and call themselves the Indiana Grays. Not far away that same day, a U.S. marshal, backed up by 50 Union soldiers, was arresting some of the men who had taken part in the egging of an enrollment officer two days before. The women who had actually thrown the eggs were not arrested.

Meanwhile, the Union raid under Colonel William Sanders was proceeding in the opposite direction. It reached the vicinity of Montgomery, Tennessee, that evening, and Sanders learned that there was a small party of Rebels about a mile away, so he sent about 400 men of the 1st East Tennessee (mounted) Infantry – a unit of what the Confederates called "home-made Yankees" – to surprise and capture them, which they did – a total of 2 officers and 102 enlisted men, several horses, 60 boxes of ammunition, 6 wagons with their mule teams, 500 spades, 100 picks, and lots of bacon, salt, flour, meal, and corn. "The prisoners were paroled and the property destroyed," Sanders reported.[11] A few Confederates got away and carried word of the raid to Knoxville, Kingston, Loudon, and other places.

East Tennessee was on Jefferson Davis's mind that day, for he was writing to General Bragg about Joe Johnston's idea of extending Bragg's command to include Major General Simon Bolivar Buckner's Department of East Tennessee. Johnston had been supposed to coordinate both those commands as well as Pemberton's, but since going to Mississippi he was no longer supervising Bragg and Buckner. To Bragg, Davis wrote: "The arrangement made of several departments in a geographical district, to the command of which General Johnston was assigned, was intended to secure the fullest co-operation of the troops in those departments, and at the same time to avoid delay by putting the commander of each department in direct correspondence with the War Office. Under this view of the case the Department of East Tennessee, &c., was created, because of the delay which would attend the transmission of reports and orders, if they must need past from Southwestern Virginia to Middle Tennessee, and thence to Richmond, Va. Your telegram of the 15th, suggesting orders for co-operative movement by General Buckner, manifests the defeat of the existing arrangement while General Johnston's attention is absorbed by the operations in Mississippi. I would be glad to have from you such suggestions as you may please to make in relation to the proper remedy for the existing evil. Your command could be extended to embrace that of General Buckner by extending the limits of the Department of Tennessee. You will know better than myself how far the means of communication and your own leisure would permit you to direct the operations, especially in the eastern portion of General Buckner's department. You can also judge better than myself how far co-operation can be relied upon without the exercise of other command than that which arises after the junction of forces in camp, marches, &c."[12] Davis sent Buckner a copy of this letter and invited his comments as well.

That same day, Confederate Adjutant and Inspector General Samuel Cooper was writing to Buckner: "General Bragg learns that nearly all of Burnside's forces have been sent to Nashville and to Vicksburg. He proposes an expedition to feel the enemy, and suggests that you do the same on the right of your department. To insure co-intelligence and co-operation, you will communicate frequently and fully to General Bragg."[13]

At Port Hudson, on the 17th, Major David C. Houston, Banks' chief engineer, broke down under the strain of supervising the siege and was replaced by Captain John C. Palfrey, who soon decided that the key to the Rebel defenses was the area known as the Priest Cap. He wanted to extend an approach trench to the left of that position and erect "cavaliers" – platforms for sharpshooters – above the lines, from which the Confederate works could be enfiladed while he ran a zigzag approach trench to their ditch.

At Vicksburg that day, as Charles Dana later remembered, "The enemy laid aside his long-standing inactivity and opened violently with both artillery and musketry. Two mortars which the Confederates got into operation that day in front of General A. J. Smith particularly interested our generals. I remember going with a party of some twenty officers, including Sherman, Ord, McPherson, and Wilson, to the brow of a hill on McPherson's front to watch this battery with our field glasses. From where we were we could study the whole operation. We saw the shell start from the mortar, sail slowly through the air toward us, fall to the ground and explode, digging out a hole which looked like a crater. I remember one of these craters which must have been nine feet in diameter. As you watched a shell coming you could not tell whether it would fall a thousand feet away or by your side. Yet nobody budged. The men sat there on their horses, their reins loose, studying and discussing the work of the batteries, apparently indifferent to the danger. It was very interesting as a study of human steadiness."[14] General Ord had just arrived that day, as had the last of the 9th Corps.

Such fire was sometimes as dangerous to friend as to foe. Young Willie Lord, son of the local Episcopal priest, remembered his father telling about seeing a Confederate orderly, holding an officer's horse, decapitated by a shot from one of the Rebels' own river batteries that was trying to fire over the town at the Federals beyond. On the other hand, he marveled at how relatively little death and destruction actually resulted from the Union bombardment. "When we think of this iron hail," he wrote, "estimated at 60,000 shells every twenty-four hours, descending upon the town by night and by day, the mortality among the citizens, even considering the protection of the caves, was wonderfully small. But while comparatively few non-combatants were killed, all lived in a state of terror."[15]

Meanwhile, the digging continued. Captain Hickenlooper's notes for the 17th say: "Building platforms for 30-pounder Parrotts in advanced battery, the enemy having opened with two 20-pounder Parrotts on Ransom's front. Work on trench and rifle-pits progressing as usual."[16]

But the most import event at Vicksburg that day and the next came about because of the congratulatory order McClernand had issued to his corps after the unsuccessful assault on 22 May. Being a politician at heart, he was, of course, fond of publicity, and this "order" had soon found its way into the newspapers. When papers containing the order reached the troops at

Vicksburg, members of the other corps present took great umbrage at McClernand's account of events, and soon complaints made their way to Grant. He received a letter from Sherman on the 17th saying that Frank Blair had shown him a copy of the Memphis *Evening Bulletin* containing a copy of the order "with a request that I should notice it, lest the statements of fact and inference contained therein might receive credence from an excited public. It certainly gives me no pleasure or satisfaction to notice such a catalogue of nonsense – such an effusion of vainglory and hypocrisy; nor can I believe General McClernand ever published such an order officially to his corps. I know too well that the brave and intelligent soldiers and officers who compose that corps will not be humbugged by such stuff.

"If the order be a genuine production and not a forgery, it is manifestly addressed not to an army, but to a constituency in Illinois, far distant from the scene of the events attempted to be described, who might innocently be induced to think General McClernand the sagacious leader and bold hero he so complacently paints himself; but it its barely possible the order is a genuine one, and was actually read to the regiments of the Thirteenth Corps, in which case a copy must have been sent to your office for the information of the commanding general.

"I beg to call his attention to the requirements of General Orders, No. 151, of 1862, which actually forbids the publication of all official letters and reports, and requires the name of the writer to be laid before the President of the United States for dismissal. The document under question is not technically a letter or report, and though styled an order, is not an order. It orders nothing, but is in the nature of an address to soldiers, manifestly designed for publication for ulterior political purposes. . . ."[17] There was much more, but that is the gist of it. Grant immediately wrote to McClernand: "Inclosed I send you what purports to be your congratulatory address to the Thirteenth Army Corps. I would respectfully ask if it is a true copy. If it is not a correct copy, furnish me one by bearer, as required both by regulations and existing orders of the Department."[18]

McPherson wrote a letter to Grant the next day, the 18th, making complaints similar to Sherman's. And McClernand answered Grant's note on the 18th, saying, "The newspaper slip is a correct copy of my congratulatory order, No. 72. I am prepared to maintain its statements. I regret that my adjutant did not send you a copy promptly, as he ought, and I thought he had."[19] McClernand was a lawyer, but if he had been a good one he would have realized that, while the content of the order was the reason the officers in the other corps were upset – which in turn was what would force Grant to take action now instead of awaiting the fall of Vicksburg – it was not its content but its publication and his failure to send a copy to Grant's headquarters that provided the technicality that would do him in. No doubt John Rawlins enjoyed signing Special Orders No. 164 of the Department of the Tennessee that day: "Maj. Gen. John A. McClernand is hereby relieved from the command of the Thirteenth Army Corps. He will proceed to any point he may select in the State of Illinois, and report by letter to Headquarters of the Army for orders. Maj. Gen. E. O. C. Ord is hereby appointed to the command of the Thirteenth Army Corps, subject to the approval of the President, and will immediately assume charge of the same. By order of Maj. Gen. U. S. Grant."[20]

Colonel Wilson, still smarting about being cursed by McClernand on a previous occasion, happily volunteered to immediately deliver the order to McClernand, even though it was near midnight by the time that he saw it. He put on his best uniform, got the provost marshal and a sergeant with a squad of four men, and rode over to McClernand's headquarters and demanded that the general be awakened. McClernand must have had a suspicion about the purpose of Wilson's visit, for, after a bit of delay, he received the colonel wearing full uniform, with his sword lying on the table in front of him. Wilson handed him the order and stated that he was instructed to see that McClernand read it and understood it. The general did so and then exclaimed, "Well sir! I am relieved!" then added, "By God sir, we are both relieved!"[21]

It's doubtful that he meant Wilson; he no doubt meant that Grant would be relieved from his own command once McClernand could tell his side of the story to his friend Lincoln. He immediately wrote a reply to Grant: "Your order, relieving me and assigning Major-General Ord to the command of the Thirteenth Army Corps, is received. Having been appointed by the President to the command of that corps, under a definite act of Congress, I might justly challenge your authority in the premises, but forbear to do so at present. I am quite willing that any statement of fact in my congratulatory [order] to the Thirteenth Corps, to which you think just exception may be taken, should be made the subject of investigation, not doubting the result."[22]

Even if such an investigation had been held, and even if it had backed up McClernand's version of events, it would have done him no good. As Charles Dana explained in a report to Stanton, "Though the congratulatory address in question is the occasion of McClernand's removal, it is not its cause, as McClernand intimates when he says incorrectly that General Grant has taken exceptions to this address. That cause, as I understand it, is his repeated disobedience of important orders, his general insubordinate disposition, and his palpable incompetence for the duties of his position. As I learned by private conversation, it was, in General Grant's judgment, also necessary that he should be removed, for the reason, above all, that his relations with other corps commanders rendered it impossible that the chief command of this army should devolve upon him, as it would have done were General Grant disabled, without most pernicious consequences to the cause."[23]

McClernand probably didn't know that Grant was armed with Secretary Stanton's dispatch to Charles Dana saying that Grant had full powers to remove anybody that he thought was a hindrance to his operations. And Grant had the backing of Dana, Halleck, Sherman and McPherson. But what really made it impossible for McClernand to challenge Grant's decision was the fact that Grant was already by far the most successful of the Union's army commanders. If forced to choose between Grant and McClernand, there was little doubt which one Lincoln would choose. So McClernand was gone, and many others were "relieved" in a different sense of the word. Sherman said that it "was a relief to the whole Army."[24]

In the mean time, the siege proceeded. Thursday, 18 June, was "Cloudy and very warm," Sergeant Tunnard wrote. "The Vicksburg *Whig* published an extra [edition], containing a few items concerning the siege of Port Hudson. This paper, published at intervals, was printed on one side of wallpaper, taken from the sides of rooms. It was very small, and a great curiosity in the way of a relic. . . . The river began to rise, and the boats had disappeared. . . . Cannonading brisk and very rapid, in fact, terrific in the afternoon. The day was unusually sultry. Another Columbiad [a type of heavy smoothbore gun] opened on the regiment at close range, and the enemy's lines were now so near that scraps of paper could be thrown by the combatants into each other's ranks. Thus, a Yankee threw a hardtack biscuit among the men of the regiment, having written on it 'starvation.' The visitor was immediately returned, indorsed as follows, 'Forty days rations, and no thanks to you.'"[25] But Sergeant Osborn Oldroyd, on the Union side of the lines, wrote: "If what they say is true, the garrison over there is already familiar with mule meat and scanty meal rations. If they have had to eat mules such as we have killed in the trenches, I pity them, for they are on a tough job."[26]

Captain Hickenlooper's notes for the 18th say: "Sap-roller burned last night. The working party leaving it alongside cottonbale, the rebels threw over fire-balls, setting cotton on fire, which communicated to sap-roller before it could be removed. Detail increased to 150 men. The night detail was taken off during my sickness, and, in consequence of near approach to enemy's works, it is not considered advisable to put it on again."[27]

Grant wrote that day to General Parke, commander of the just-arrived 9th Corps, at Haynes' Bluff: "I want the work of intrenching your position pushed with all dispatch, ready to receive an attack, if one should be made, and to leave the troops free to move out should the enemy remain where he is." He then outlined what he knew of Johnston's forces, but added, "Keep your cavalry well out, and collect all the information you can of the movements of the enemy. Report all that you learn promptly. No order has been published assigning you to the command of all the forces at Haynes' Bluff, but being isolated from the general command, and being the senior officer, you necessarily command the whole."[28]

Johnston, meanwhile, wrote to Secretary Seddon that day: "Dispatch of 16th received. I think that you do not appreciate the difficulties in the course you direct nor the probabilities or consequences of failure. Grant's position, naturally very strong, is intrenched and protected by powerful artillery, and the roads obstructed. His re-enforcements have been at least equal to my whole force. The Big Black covers him from attack, and would cut off our retreat if defeated. We cannot combine operations with General Pemberton from uncertain and slow communication. The defeat of this little army would at once open Mississippi and Alabama to Grant. I will do all I can, without hope of doing more than aid to extricate the garrison."[29]

Up in Tennessee on the 18th, General Wheeler approved Morgan's request to take 2,000 of his men on his proposed raid instead of the 1500 authorized by Bragg. Wheeler's order to Morgan also specified that, "In addition to accomplishing the work which he has proposed, he will, as far as practicable, break up and destroy the Louisville and Nashville Railroad. He will, if practicable, destroy depots of supplies in the State of Kentucky, after which he will return to his present position."[30]

Captain Hines, who, with a few of Morgan's men, had slipped across the Ohio River into Indiana the day before, came upon a large force of real Home Guards on the 18th, but was able to pass himself and his men off as fellow Federals "hunting deserters and absentees from the Army."[31] The two outfits, one genuine and one not, rode together to the nearby town of Paoli, Indiana, where the townspeople set up a long table in the town square full of food for the troops. The meal was interrupted, however, when more Union troopers rode in and informed the mayor that some of his guests were Rebels in disguise. Hines managed to get his men out of town, and that night he bluffed another Union unit into surrendering to him by having his men ride around among the trees, firing their weapons, to give the impression that his command was far larger than it really was. He took the Federals' parole not to fight again until exchanged, and took their best horses as well. But other Home Guard units were on their trail all night, giving them little chance to rest. It was dawn before they finally eluded their pursuers.

Down in Louisiana, another Confederate raid was under way. Colonel James P. Major, with three small regiments of cavalry and a battery of artillery, was working his way south along the west side of the Mississippi. On the 18th, one of his regiments made a dash into the town of Plaquemine and took 87 prisoners, "burning 3 fine steamers, 2 steam flats, 100 bales of cotton, and capturing a large quantity of commissary stores."[32]

In Virginia, during the wee hours of the 18th, Colonel Duffié – bivouacked with his 1st Rhode Island Cavalry just northeast of Middleburg – learned that "the roads in every direction were full of [Rebel] cavalry, and that the Aldie road was commanded by a brigade, with four pieces of artillery." He then abandoned all thought of achieving his mission of advancing to the town of Union and concentrated on extricating his lone regiment from the midst of Stuart's much larger force. "I directed the head of my column on the road to Aldie," he reported, "when an engagement commenced at once, the enemy opening on both flanks with heavy volleys, yelling to us to surrender. I at once ordered

Captain [A. H.] Bixby, the officer commanding the advance, to charge any force in his front, and follow the Aldie road to the point where it connects with the road to White Plains. This order was executed admirably. Captain Bixby's horse was shot and he himself wounded. My command was in a most hazardous position, the enemy being in front, rear, and on both flanks, and we were intermixed with them for more than an hour, until we struck the road leading to Hopewell Gap."[33]

Duffié finally reached his old camp near Centreville at 1:30 p.m., accompanied by only 4 officers and 27 men. Four other groups that had managed to slip through the Confederates, totaling 61 men, eventually came in, but the rest of the regiment had been killed or captured, whole or wounded. The survivors were sent to Alexandria to recuperate and refit. Duffié was soon promoted to brigadier general. "When I do well, they take no notice of me," the Frenchman complained. "When I go make one bad business, make one fool of myself, they promote me."[34]

Before Duffié's fate was known, Pleasonton did send some help for the surrounded unit early on the morning of the 18th, but it was far too late. Part of the 1st Pennsylvania Cavalry was sent to Thoroughfare Gap, but went no farther that day, and Colonel J. Irvin Gregg's 3rd Brigade of David Gregg's 2nd Division (they were cousins) moved directly to Middleburg, not so much to rescue Duffié as to continue the move toward the Blue Ridge begun the day before. This brigade pushed aside elements of Robertson's and Chambliss's Rebel brigades and took over Middleburg, taking position behind the barricades Duffié had built, until 6 p.m. when it was recalled to Aldie. Colonel William Gamble's 1st Brigade of Buford's 1st Division moved toward Snicker's Gap, but at Philomont it ran into Munford's brigade. Gamble decided he was outnumbered and fell back.

A member of Major John Mosby's Partisan Rangers had reached Stuart at Middleburg about dawn on the 18th with a dispatch that had been found on a couple of Union officers that Mosby had captured the night before. Among the information revealed in this dispatch was the fact that much of Hooker's infantry was in camps not far beyond the Bull Run Mountains, waiting to see what Pleasonton's cavalry could find out about Lee, and that Pleasonton had been directed to concentrate at Aldie. With this, Stuart gave up on the idea of taking and holding the gaps of the Bull Run Mountains; he would, instead, try to keep the Union cavalry from getting to, or at least beyond, the gaps of the Blue Ridge. The dispatch also informed Stuart that two regiments from Stahel's cavalry division of the Department of Washington were being sent to Warrenton to make sure no Rebels were crossing the Rappahannock on what was now Hooker's left-rear, so he sent orders for Hampton's Brigade, on its way to join him, to take care of these Federals.

The loss of the dispatch was soon known at Hooker's headquarters, and Dan Butterfield suggested to General Meade, commander of the 5th Corps, that day that he "Catch and kill any guerillas, then try them."[35] However, another source of leaking information was on Hooker's mind that day. At 10:45 a.m. Butterfield wired the agent of the Associated Press at Washington and asked him to confidentially forward a request from Hooker to the editors of newspapers throughout the country: "1. Under no circumstances should be published the location of any corps, division, brigade, or regiment, and especially is the location of my headquarters never to be named excepting during a fight. 2. That official reports, when furnished without the sanction of the War Department, may never be published. After any fight the reporters can open their fire as loudly as they please, but avoid, unless it is a general battle, giving the designations of forces engaged. Require all reporters' signatures to their published letters. These rules being observed, every facility possible will be given to reporters and newspapers in this army, including the license to abuse or criticise me to their heart's content."[36]

As the dispatch captured by Mosby indicated, most of Hooker's infantry did indeed remain in place that day, resting and waiting for more information about Lee's position and movements. The only major exception was Major General Henry Slocum's 12th Corps, which was ordered to Leesburg, at the north end of the Bull Run Mountains, with orders to hold that point and the nearby fords of the Potomac. A pontoon train, guarded by a couple of regiments, had been ordered to cross to the north side of the Potomac at Washington and go northwest to the mouth of the Monocacy River, nor far northeast of Leesburg. The commander of that force was told to guard a couple of fords as well. Howard's 11th Corps was ordered to support Slocum if called upon. Meade's 5th Corps was to do the same for Pleasonton's cavalry.

Although Hooker at times expressed some dissatisfaction with Pleasonton, at this point he was impressed enough to wire Halleck at 10:07 a.m. that day: "I have to request that Brigadier-General Pleasonton, for his gallant conduct at Chancellorsville, his services there, and his attack and surprise of Stuart's forces, superior in numbers, on the Rappahannock, June 9, may be made major-general, and assigned to [permanently] command the cavalry corps."[37] Meanwhile, Dan Butterfield wrote to Pleasonton that night acknowledging the latter's brief report of his fight at Aldie and the fate of Duffié. After informing him of Slocum's location and orders, he again told the cavalry commander, "The general says your orders are to find out where the enemy is, if you have to lose men to do it."[38]

On the Confederate side of the Blue Ridge, Early's division of Ewell's corps advanced to Shepherdstown that day, the 18th, and Ed Johnson's division left there, crossed the Potomac at Boteler's Ford, and camped at Sharpsburg, Maryland, site of the Battle of Antietam the previous September (which had ended Lee's previous foray north of the Potomac). Johnson's headquarters were at the home of one his staff officers, Major Henry Kyd Douglas. "I could not get over the feeling," Douglas later remembered, "that an invasion of the enemy's territory, however tempting, was the wrong policy for us; but at the same time I believed that General Lee must know better than I did."[39] Perhaps Albert Jenkins agreed with him, for his cavalry was moving in the opposite direction that day, falling back across the Mason-Dixon Line to Hagerstown, Maryland, while his plunder from both states was sent on down to Williamsport and turned over to General Rodes. Lee met with Stuart and Longstreet that day at Paris, just a mile east of Ashby's Gap.

There was much telegraphing that day between Couch, Schenck, Stanton, and others about the threat to Pennsylvania, but that state had still not raised many troops for its own defense. And most of the arms available were being sent to Brooks at Pittsburgh, instead of to Couch, since the Federals were still of the opinion that a great Confederate raid was headed in that direction. However, the adjutant-general of New York wired Stanton that day that 12,000 of his militiamen were on their way to Harrisburg, or soon would be. In fact, two New York regiments, the 8th and 71st New York State National Guard, actually reached that city before daylight that very day and were immediately hastened across the Susquehanna River to garrison a new earthwork called Fort Washington. However, it was raining, and there were no tents available yet, so the New Yorkers slept in the cattle cars that had brought them to Pennsylvania. Some of these men, especially the sergeants and junior officers, could be accounted veterans, for both regiments had fought at the first battle of Bull Run.

That afternoon, the 23rd New Jersey also reached Harrisburg, riding in open coal cars. This was a 9-months regiment that was due to go home after serving in Bully Brooks' division of the 6th Corps, but had volunteered to delay mustering out in order to lend a hand to their Pennsylvania neighbors. Couch sent it to guard a ford over the Susquehanna near the Cumberland Valley Railroad Bridge, as the river was very low and the Confederates might try to cross there if the two bridges in town were burned. The regiment went to work preparing a rifle pit in Harris Park, masked by a fence along the river. However, the local citizens refused to give them water, charged them outrageous prices for food, and even got into fist fights with the soldiers, so, after a few days they changed their minds about extending their enlistments and went home.

The Union War Department that day authorized the governor

of Rhode Island to raise "one company of artillery to be composed of colored men, to be mustered into the U.S. service for three years or during the war. To these troops no bounties will be paid."[40] The governor of Ohio was authorized to raise an infantry regiment under the same terms. General Couch sent orders to a subordinate in Philadelphia to organize a regiment of "colored troops" there, "mustering in as offered by companies," rather than waiting for the entire regiment to be recruited.[41]

There was continued resistance to the draft in the Northern states, however. Brigadier General T. G. Pitcher wrote to the provost marshal general from Vermont that day to say: "There is serious resistance to the enrollment among the Irish laborers in the marble quarries at Rutland. Captain [C. R.] Crane, the provost-marshal of the district, the enrolling officer, the deputy sheriff of the county, and surgeon of the Board were yesterday about 3 p.m. violently attacked by a party of about 500 men. The provost-marshal reports that they are organized, and that they are armed to a great extent, and that they can raise now 1,000 men. A strong military force will be necessary to arrest them. There is none in the State. They have all, except about seventy-five, been enrolled from their employers' pay-rolls."[42]

The provost marshal for the seventh district of Indiana reported that day the murder of one of the enrolling officers for Sullivan County, shot in the road near his home that morning, and "unless some step is taken promptly in reference to it the enrollment of that county cannot be completed. I have a letter already from there in which I am informed that the Union citizens almost consider themselves as abandoned to the mercy of bands of outlaws who are led by desperate men, and that it will be impossible, if things remain in their present condition, to get anybody to undertake the work left unfinished by Mr. [Fletcher] Freeman, who was enrolling two townships, as in one of them no other person could be found to undertake it. . . . That the men who murdered Freeman belong to those who have been lately in the habit of meeting in Sullivan and Greene Counties for military drill, there can be no doubt. These men have resolved at their public meetings that the enrollment should not take place, and have notified the enrolling officers that if they went on with it they must do so at their peril. . . . I . . . have no doubt, from all the information I can get, that their numbers exceed 1,000 – possibly reach from 1,200 to 1,500 – armed with squirrel rifles, guns, and pistols, and knives. These men are generally exceedingly ignorant and are completely under the control of a few leaders, who keep them excited and inflamed to an intense degree by all sorts of stories about Government oppression, outrage, &c. . . . The [enrollment] papers (completed) were stolen in one township of Owen County a few nights ago. Also one in Clay, and in many places they have resolved that they shall never leave the counties."[43]

Down in the Union's Department of Virginia, the emphasis was shifting from the move up the Peninsula to another move to the Pamunkey River. General Dix wired Halleck from Fort Monroe that day: "I am moving troops from Suffolk up the York. I had no transportation till yesterday. Part of a brigade went up this morning. Gordon, with 5,000 men, is between Diascund Bridge and White House."[44]

Lee wrote to Ewell at 7 a.m. the next day, the 19th, acknowledging receipt of two letters from the latter: "Hood's division was sent yesterday from Upperville to replace Early's, in order that you might have with you your whole corps to operate with in Maryland and Pennsylvania, but later in the day the reports from General Stuart indicated that the enemy were moving up the roads concentrating at Snickersville, with the view of forcing a passage through the mountains to get into your rear, and Hood was directed to cross Snicker's Ferry, and hold Snicker's Gap, as we had only cavalry on that route. Longstreet's corps has been operating with a view to embarrass the enemy as to our movements, so as to detain his forces east of the mountains, until A. P. Hill could get up to your support. But should the enemy force a passage through the mountains, you would be separated, which it is the object of Longstreet to prevent, if possible. Anderson's division ought to be within reach to-day, and I will move him toward Berryville, so as either to relieve Early or support Hood, as circumstances may require. I very much regret that you have not the benefit of your whole corps, for, with that north of the Potomac, should we be able to detain General Hooker's army from following you, you would be able to accomplish as much, unmolested, as the whole army could perform with General Hooker in its front. Not knowing what force there is at Harper's Ferry, or what can be collected to oppose your progress, I cannot give definite instructions, especially as the movements of General Hooker's army are not yet ascertained. You must, therefore, be guided in your movements by controlling circumstances around you, endeavor to keep yourself supplied with provisions, send back any surplus, and carry out the plan you proposed, so far as in your judgment may seem fit. If your advance causes Hooker to cross the Potomac, or separate his army in any way, Longstreet can follow you. The last of Hill's divisions had, on the evening of the 18th, advanced a few miles this side of Culpeper Court-House, *en route* to the Valley. I hope all are now well on their way. As soon as I can get definite information as to the movements of General Hooker and the approach of General Hill, I will write to you again."[45]

Why Lee did not feel he had definite information on Hooker's movements in hard to say. By now he should have received the Federal dispatch Mosby had captured, or the information it contained. And Hooker complained to Halleck that day: "I have just been furnished with an extract from the New York Herald of yesterday concerning the late movements of this army. So long as newspapers continue to give publicity to our movements, we must not expect to gain any advantage over our adversaries. Is there no way of stopping it? I can suppress the circulation of this paper within my lines, but I cannot prevent their reaching it to the enemy. We could well afford to give millions of money for like information of the enemy." Halleck replied a couple of hours later: "I appreciate as fully as yourself the injury resulting from newspaper publication of the movements, numbers, and position of our troops, but I see no way of preventing it as long as reporters are permitted in our camps. I expelled them all from our lines in Mississippi. Every general must decide for himself what persons he will permit in his camps."[46] Perhaps, with the two armies out of contact, and thus no longer trading newspapers, Lee had not seen the article that Hooker complained of.

Hooker, too, still felt he lacked accurate information about his enemy, but Marsena Patrick, his top cop, did not agree. He wrote that day: "We get accurate information, but Hooker will not use it and insults all who differ from him in opinion. He has declared that the enemy's forces are larger than his own, which is all false & he knows it – He knows that Lee is his master & is afraid to meet him in fair battle."[47]

Rodes' Division broke camp that day and, in obedience to orders from Ewell, marched for Hagerstown, Maryland. Further instructions diverted it to the southeast, toward Boonsborough – a move that the Federals were sure to perceive as a threat to Harper's Ferry and Maryland Heights. However, the division marched only about two miles on the road to Boonsborough and went into camp. Lee's pontoon bridge was still at Falling Waters, guarded now only by a small detachment of infantry plus the teamsters who drove the wagons that were used to carry the pontoon boats.

Early that afternoon, Brigadier General Rufus Ingalls, chief quartermaster of the Army of the Potomac, wrote to the quartermaster general, in Washington: "The loss of cavalry horses in battle and on scouts is already beginning to be heavy. Probably 500 have been thus lost within as many days [5 days?]. Our cavalry is doing splendid service, and must be kept well mounted at this juncture."[48] More horses would be lost that day.

A sudden shower hit Pleasonton's troopers at Aldie before dawn on the 19th, but David Gregg's 2nd Division saddled up and moved into the Loudoun Valley again that morning, the brigade of Irvin Gregg leading, followed by Kilpatrick's brigade, then Gamble's from Buford's division. An hour's ride down the muddy road brought the column back to Middleburg. A few Rebel pickets were easily driven beyond the town, and the main force of Confederate cavalry was found about a mile west, barring the way to the Blue Ridge gaps. Gamble's brigade was sent off to the right to bypass or outflank the opposing Rebels. To keep Stuart busy, David Gregg ordered a charge straight down the Middleburg-Upperville road. Irvin Gregg proceeded cautiously, however. He could see Robertson's North Carolinians deployed on high ground south of the road and Chambliss's sharpshooter squadrons dismounted behind a stone wall on the other side, supported by a battery of horse artillery on a higher ridge. Behind these forces was the rest of Chambliss's brigade, mounted, ready to countercharge any attack on the front line. It was a formidable position.

However, Irvin Gregg was taking so long in his preparations that his cousin, the division commander, decided to spur him on, declaring, "The attack *must* be made, and at once!"[49] He did, however, bring up a battery of horse artillery to counter the Confederate guns that were hampering the Federals' deployments. At first this didn't help much. The Rebel guns and dismounted troopers broke up some of the advancing Union formations. But then the Union gunners got the upper hand and silenced the Confederate battery, and the 1st Maine and 4th and 16th Pennsylvania charged up and over the wooded ridge and Stuart's front line.

Chambliss's mounted reserve, however, then countercharged and drove them back. Irvin Gregg sent in two battalions of the 10th New York, but the first one was shot up by Chambliss's dismounted sharpshooters, and the second one was overwhelmed by the Rebel's mounted squadrons. Chambliss then dismounted his entire brigade and led it forward, supported by Robertson's and Munford's brigades, causing Stuart to boast to one of his staff officers that "I shall be in Middleburg in less than an hour!"[50] But a mounted counterattack by the third battalion of the 10th New York and all of the 2nd New York sent the Rebels running back for their horses, and, after a brief fight, Stuart withdrew to another ridge about a half-mile west of the first one he had defended. The Federals made no attempt to attack him there, and after dark he pulled back even closer to Upperville, where it would be easier to guard the approaches to the Blue Ridge. Both sides lost about 100 men in that day's fight.

Meanwhile, Gamble's brigade ran into Rosser's 5th Virginia of Munford's brigade and part of Grumble Jones's brigade, just coming up from the Rappahannock line, along the road to the inappropriately named town of Union. The Rebels launched uncoordinated mounted attacks that were driven off by Union skirmishers dismounted behind stone fences. Part of the 7th Virginia, of Jones's brigade, was dismounted to flush them out, only to find that the Federals had fallen back to another fence line, where their carbine fire was strengthened by cannister fire from half a battery of horse artillery and their line was backed up by Gamble's mounted squadrons ready to counterattack. The Rebels recovered their mounts and fell back to Union, content to block the Federals' way toward the Blue Ridge. Gamble did not pursue but held his position as a stepping stone for any later advance. That day Hampton's brigade joined Stuart after easily defeating the two regiments Stahel had sent to Warrenton. That night the rains came again in the form of a thunderstorm that stampeded some of the Union horses.

∽ Endnotes ∽

1   OR, I:27:III:171-2.
2   Longacre, *The Cavalry at Gettysburg*, 110.
3   OR, I:27:III:173.
4   McClellan, *I Rode With Jeb Stuart*, 303-4.

5   OR, I:27:I:963.
6   Ibid., I:27:I:965.
7   Ibid., I:27:III:174-5.
8   Ibid., I:27:I:50.
9   Coddington, *The Gettysburg Campaign*, 84.
10 William N. Still Jr., *Iron Afloat* (Nashville, 1971), 135.
11 OR, I:23:I:387.
12 Ibid., I:52:II:496-7.
13 Ibid., I:23:II:876.
14 Dana, *Recollections of the Civil War*, 95. This source indicates a date of 15 June, but Dana's reports to Stanton (OR, I:24:I:101-2) show that it must have been on 17 June.
15 Hoehling, *Vicksburg: 47 Days of Siege*, 177.
16 OR, I:24:II:200.
17 Ibid., I:24:I:162.
18 Ibid., I:24:I:159.
19 Ibid., I:24:I:162.
20 Ibid., I:24:I:164-5.
21 Catton, *Grant Moves South*, 467.
22 OR, I:24:I:166.
23 Ibid., I:24:I:103.
24 John F. Marszalek, *Sherman* (New York, 1993), 227-8.
25 Hoehling, *Vicksburg: 47 Days of Siege*, 184.
26 Ibid., 188.
27 OR, I:24:II:200-1
28 Ibid., I:24:III:418.
29 Ibid., I:24:I:227.
30 Ibid., I:23:I:817.
31 Horan, *Confederate Agent*, 26.
32 OR, I:26:I:271.
33 Ibid., I:27:I:963-4.
34 Longacre, *The Cavalry at Gettysburg*, 112.
35 OR, I:27:III:194.
36 Ibid., I:27:III:192.
37 Ibid., I:27:I:51.
38 Ibid., I:27:III:195.
39 Henry Kyd Douglas, *I Rode With Stonewall* (Mockingbird Books pocket edition, Atlanta, 1974), 235.
40 OR, III:3:383.
41 Ibid., III:3:381.
42 Ibid., III:3:383.
43 Ibid., III:3:393-4.
44 Ibid., I:27:III:206.
45 Ibid., I:27:III:905.
46 Ibid., I:27:I:52.

47 Coddington, *The Gettysburg Campaign*, 84.
48 *OR*, I:27:III:212.
49 Longacre, *The Cavalry at Gettysburg*, 122.
50 Ibid., 123.

CHAPTER 12

"Hope Deferred Makes the Heart Sick"

1 – 2 May

IN THE WEE HOURS OF 19 JUNE, while his men made camp in the woods, Captain Hines rode alone into the village of French Lick, Indiana. There the Rebel raider went to the home of Dr. William A. Bowles, a prominent Copperhead, to confer about a possible uprising in the states of the old Northwest Territory, which would form a new Confederacy of their own, in alliance with the Southern Confederacy. This conference was the main purpose of Hines' foray across the Ohio, and was probably meant to at least test the waters and lay the groundwork for Morgan's later raid into the same area. It is quite conceivable that Hines gave Bowles all or part of the money he had captured on a train down in Kentucky, for Bowles claimed to be raising an army of Copperheads, saying "he could command ten thousand men in twenty-four hours."[1] This meeting, like the dinner at Paoli the day before, was soon cut short, however, when one of Bowles' followers rode in to inform them that a provost marshal's patrol was on the way to arrest Hines.

The Captain rejoined his men and they headed south. They captured a small tugboat near an island in the Ohio River and began crossing back to Kentucky, but were soon interrupted by about 100 Union troops on an armed steamboat sent down from Louisville. Hines divided his force between those who wanted, with him, to try to swim from the island to the Kentucky shore and those who didn't want to risk it. He stripped to his long underwear, put his money and his revolver in his hat, and with 12 of his men, under the cover of the fire of the others, took to the water. Three of his swimming troopers were shot by the Federals, but he and the other nine made it across. Those left behind then broke their weapons and marched down to the water's edge under a white flag and surrendered.

That same day, General Halleck wrote to General Burnside, whose department included the states just north of the Ohio River, to say that northern governors and prominent citizens were complaining about Burnside's practice of appointing generals to command districts within those states. "They say that it conveys to the people an idea that they are being subjected to military constraint; that difficulties are multiplied between the civil and military authorities, the former taking offense at the assumption of the latter; that the public feeling is becoming strong that these military commanders, with their numerous staffs, had much better be in the field fighting the enemy than in exercising unnecessary military authority in the loyal States. . . . I think it would be well for you to consider this matter and the propriety of withdrawing these district commanders and leaving the control, as much as possible, in the hands of the Governors and civil authorities. . . . Moreover, there are daily applications for more generals in the field, with recommendations innumerable to make new ones, for which there are no vacancies." However, with his usual lack of forcefulness, he added, "I write this simply as a suggestion for your consideration."[2]

Colonel James B. Fry, provost marshal general of the Union army, wrote that day to his old friend General John M. Schofield, commander of the Department of the Missouri: "The only force I have in many places to enforce the enrollment and draft will be the Invalid Corps. I wish you would do all you can to facilitate the creation of this corps. It is the intention to put into it only those who are unfit for field service; thus the rolls of troops in the field will be relieved of these absentees and their places can be filled with drafted men. All men now necessarily kept about hospitals will thus come on the rolls of Invalid Corps instead of being on detached service from their various companies. Those required as attendants, &c., about general hospitals should be put into companies together and kept where they are under their new company officers, and all others sent to Colonel Alexander to be organized into companies for provost-guards in the different

Congressional districts. . . . I want to make up all the available companies I can to send to those Congressional districts which are likely to be troublesome in the draft. Can't you help me in this? I know you have your own troubles and labors, but you can bear 'em."[3]

In East Tennessee, also in Burnside's department – or prospectively in it – Colonel Sanders' raid continued. "At daylight on the 19th," he later reported, "I was within 3 miles of Loudon, and about the same distance from Lenoir's [Station]. I here learned that a force of three regiments was at the Loudon Bridge, with eight pieces of artillery, and that they had been for two weeks strengthening the works at that place, digging rifle-pits, ditches, &c.; and having captured a courier from the commanding officer, with dispatches ordering the forces from Kingston to follow in my rear, and stating that the troops from Lenoir's had been ordered to join them, I determined to avoid Loudon, and started immediately for Lenoir's Station, which place I reached about 8 a.m., arriving there about thirty minutes after the departure of the rebel troops. At this station I captured a detachment of artillerymen, with three 6-pounder iron guns, 8 officers, and 57 enlisted men. Burned the depot, a large brick building, containing five pieces of artillery, with harness and saddles, two thousand five hundred stand of small arms, a very large amount of artillery and musket ammunition, and artillery and cavalry equipments. The depot was entirely occupied with military stores, and one car filled with saddles and artillery harness. We also captured some 75 Confederate States mules and horses. There was a large cotton factory and a large amount of cotton at this place, and I ordered that it should not be burned, as it furnished the Union citizens of the country with their only material for making cloth, but have since learned that it was burned by mistake or accidentally. I had the telegraph wire and railroad destroyed from here on to Knoxville, at points about 1 mile apart. We met the enemy's pickets at Knoxville about 7 p.m. on the 19th, and drove them to within a mile of the city. Leaving a portion of the First Kentucky Cavalry on this side of the town, I moved the rest of the command as soon as it was dark by another road entirely around to the other side, driving in the pickets at several places, and cut the railroad, so that no troops could be sent to the bridges above."[4] Burnside justifiably described this as "one of the boldest raids of the war."[5]

Down at Vicksburg on 19 June, General Pemberton was writing to Joe Johnston again: "The enemy opened all his batteries on our lines about 3.30 this morning, and continued the heaviest fire we have yet sustained, until 8 o'clock, but he did not assault our works. Artillery is reported to have been distinctly heard about 2 a.m. toward east of Snyder's Mill, supposed to have been an engagement with your troops. On the Graveyard road the enemy's works are within 25 feet of our redan; also very close on Jackson and Baldwin's Ferry road. I hope you will advance with the least possible delay. My men have been thirty-four days and nights in trenches without relief, and the enemy is within conversation distance. We are living on very reduced rations, and, as you know, are entirely isolated. What aid am I to expect from you?"[6]

"Our men began to show signs of discouragement," a Confederate chaplain remembered. "They have waited for Johnston so long that hope deferred makes the heart sick. Often they imagine that they can hear his cannon in the rear. News is brought in that he has crossed the Big Black; that they had an engagement with the enemy and defeated them. But so many false reports have been circulated that our men are slow to credit any."[7]

"If the rebels are short of provisions," noted Sergeant Oldroyd, on the Union side of the lines, "their ammunition seems to hold out, for they are quite liberal in their distribution of it." He also observed that "The weather is getting altogether too hot for comfort. A few sunstrokes have occurred, but without proving fatal so far. One poor fellow even dropped at midnight, when I presume the surgeon's diagnosis must have been – moonstruck." He added that "Our artillerymen have had such good practice during the siege that they can generally drop a shell wherever they want to."[8]

Captain Hickenlooper's notes for the 19th say: "Work progressing as usual. Captain Merritt in charge of working party of left sap, which is a side cut, covered by our guns in the rear, and running almost parallel with parapet of Fort Hill."[9] His approach was one of ten that were underway by then, and many of these were now very close to the Confederate works. However, as Grant's chief engineers later reported, "The enemy resisted our approach here more strongly than at any other point, burning sap-rollers, using mines [tunnels], and throwing grenades."[10]

General Grant sent a very brief notice that day to Halleck that he had relieved McClernand and replaced him with Ord. Charles Dana sent a much longer and more detailed account, and justification, to Secretary Stanton that same day. He also told Stanton: "The siege works here are steadily progressing on the right and center, rather in the way of enlargement of covered ways and strengthening of the lines than of direct advances. On the front of the Thirteenth Corps and the extreme left, our works constantly approach those of the enemy. On the right of our center, however, an important advantage was this morning gained by General Ransom, who during the night pushed his trenches so that at daylight his sharpshooters were able to take in reverse the whole right flank of the main rebel fort in his front, called Fort Hill. He soon drove out the enemy, killing and wounding many, and will be able to crown the rebel parapet with his artillery whenever the order is given. The rebels are constructing an interior battery to cover the works they have thus virtually lost. . . . Weather is hot; thermometer at 95 degrees. The springs from which we get water are becoming bad. They are full of lime from decayed shells."[11]

The approach trench Dana mentions here, in front of Ransom's division of the 17th Corps, was the next one to the right, or north, of the one Captain Hickenlooper was in charge of.

"This approach," Grant's chief engineers later reported, "would have been very important in an assault, as the ground here in rear of the enemy's line was seen by our artillery, and it would have been difficult for him to mass troops to resist an assault."[12]

Also, Grant forwarded to President Lincoln that day the letter Sherman had written to him on 2 June about the wisdom of putting new recruits and drafted men into the old regiments instead of forming them into new regiments. "I would add," he said, "that our old regiments, all that remains of them, are veterans equaling regulars in discipline, and far superior to them in the material of which they are composed. A recruit added to them would become an old soldier, from the very contact, before he was aware of it. Company and regimental officers, camp and garrison equipage, transportation and everything are already provided. He would cost Government nothing but his pay and allowances, and would render efficient services from the start. Placed in a new organization all these things must be provided. Officers and men have to go through months of schooling, and, from ignorance of how to cook and provide for themselves, the ranks become depleted one-third before valuable services can be expected. Taken in economic point of view, one drafted man in an old regiment is worth three in a new one."[13] Neither he nor Sherman mentioned – perhaps did not know – that the Confederates were already using and benefitting from such use of their conscripted men.

Before the day was out, Grant's headquarters issued Special Orders No. 165 directing that "At 4 a.m. on the 20th instant, a general cannonading will be commenced from all parts of the line on the city of Vicksburg. Firing will continue until 10 a.m., unless otherwise directed. . . . All the rifle-pits will be filled with as many men as can be accommodated in them. Troops will be held under arms from 6:30 a.m., ready to take advantage of any signs the enemy may show of weakness, or to repel an attack should one be made. . . . It is not designed to assault the enemy's works, but to be prepared. Should corps commanders believe a favorable opportunity presents itself for possessing themselves of any portion of the lines of the enemy, without a serious battle, they will avail themselves of it, telegraphing immediately to headquarters of other corps and to general headquarters what they are doing, and suggesting any assistance or co-operation they may require."[14]

The guns – about 200 of them, counting the Navy's contribution – opened fire, as ordered, the next morning. "At early dawn every gun along the line suddenly opened," Sergeant Tunnard, on the receiving end, wrote, "keeping up a rapid and continuous fire. All concurred in the opinion that such a tremendous cannonading had never been equaled in their experience, and the volume of sound surpassed anything yet heard. It seemed as if heaven and earth were meeting in a fearful shock, and the earth trembled under the heavy concussions."[15]

"During the attack no Confederates were visible," Charles Dana said, "nor was any reply made to our artillery. Their musketry fire also amounted to nothing. Of course, some damage was done to the buildings of the town by our concentrated cannonade, but we could not tell whether their mills, foundry, or storehouses were destroyed. Their rifle-pits and defenses were little injured. At ten o'clock the cannonade ceased. It was evident that the probabilities of immediate success by assault would not compensate for the sacrifices."[16]

So the digging continued. Hickenlooper's notes for the 20th say: "Work on main trench progressing as usual. Placed new sap-roller on work to-day. In evening commenced work on Navy (9-inch) battery with a detail of 100 men, putting up heavy parapet, with embrasures reveted with gabions. The enemy have opened with a large mortar in hollow south of Fort Hill, with which they are shelling the Navy battery."[17]

West Virginia officially became the 35th state of the Union on that 20th day of June, 1863 (still counting those states who thought they were no longer part of the Union). Many of its citizens had desired a separation from the Old Dominion since long before the war. A mountainous region, it was totally unsuitable for large plantations and therefore contained few slaves; it was more concerned with mining and industry, and many of its inhabitants felt more connected with the other states along the Ohio River and its tributaries than to the counties east of the mountains, which, being more populous, dominated the government of Virginia. When the war had come, many – probably most – of the residents of what became the new state had supported the Union cause, or at least did not support the Confederate one. Union forces under the overall command of George McClellan, with such able assistants as Rosecrans, Kelley and Milroy, had advanced into the area in the opening months of the war and in several small battles had run the Rebels back over the mountains.

Even as the new state was born, however, Imboden's Confederate brigade was doing its best to destroy its assets. Lee wrote to that general on the 20th from Berryville, in the Shenandoah Valley: "Your letter of the 18th, from French's Depot, reporting the destruction of the important bridges on the Baltimore and Ohio Railroad over Evitt's Creek, Patterson's Creek, North and South Branches of the Potomac, with the depots, water-tanks, and engines between little Cacapon and Cumberland, has been received. I am very much gratified at the thorough manner in which your work in that line has been done. General Kelley's [Union] force at New Creek, I hope, is exaggerated, or that at any rate you will be able to disperse it in some way. I am also gratified at the cattle and horses that you have already captured for the use of the army, and hope that your expectations of obtaining similar supplies will be realized. They are not only important but essential, and I request that you will do all in your power to obtain all you can. At this time it is impossible to send a mounted brigade to your assistance, as the whole of the cavalry are required to watch the enemy and guard our movements east of the Blue Ridge and in Maryland. Should you find an opportunity, you can yourself advance north of the Potomac, and keep on the left of this army in its advance into Pennsylvania, but you must repress all marauding, take only the supplies necessary for your army, animals and provisions through your regular staff officers, who will account for the same, and give receipts to the owners, stating the kind, quantity, and estimated value of the articles received, the valuation to be made according to the market price in the country where the property is taken."[18]

Lee also wrote to General Samuel Jones, commander of the Confederate Department of Western Virginia, farther south, that day. After giving him a very brief rundown of the accomplishments of Ewell, Imboden, and White, he added: "I think the present offers to you a favorable time to threaten Western Virginia, and, if circumstances favor, you might convert the threat into a real attack. A more favorable opportunity will probably not occur during the war, and, if you can accomplish nothing else, you may at least prevent the troops in that region from being sent to re-enforce other points. I would recommend, therefore, that you unite all your available forces, and strike at some vulnerable point."[19] Jones, however, had his own problems. Buckner, in the neighboring Department of East Tennessee was looking to him for help against Union efforts to invade his area, and some Union forces in Kentucky were moving closer to his own department.

Lee wrote to President Davis that day as well, giving him a detailed account of the destruction wrought by Imboden and White. "General Ewell's corps is north of the Potomac," he added, "occupying Sharpsburg, Boonsborough, and Hagerstown. His advance cavalry is at Chambersburg, Pa. The first division of General A. P. Hill's corps will reach this vicinity today; the rest follow. General Longstreet's corps, with Stuart's cavalry, still occupy the Blue Ridge, between the roads leading through Ashby's and Snicker's Gaps, holding in check a large force of the enemy, consisting of cavalry, infantry, and artillery. The movement of the main body of the enemy is still toward the Potomac, but its real destination is not yet discovered. . . . If any of the brigades that I have left behind for the protection of Richmond can, in your opinion, be spared, I should like them to be sent to me."[20]

However, the movement of Union troops in the Department of Virginia was keeping the authorities at Richmond worried enough to hang on to all the troops Lee had left behind. Adjutant and Inspector General Cooper wrote to D. H. Hill that same day saying that President Davis wanted one brigade sent to Drewry's Bluff, on the James River just southeast of Richmond, and another one to Petersburg, "to be held in readiness to follow."[21] There were only three Confederate brigades plus a few smaller units left in all of North Carolina. Brigadier General M. D. Corse, commander of a brigade of Pickett's Division that had been left at Hanover Junction, notified Major General Arnold Elzey, commanding at Richmond, that day, "My scouts report a raiding party, 300 strong, at King and Queen Court-House, burning and destroying; their destination said to be Walkerton; also report a gunboat at West Point."[22]

On the morning of the 20th, a Union captain of engineers reached Harrisburg. General Couch had requested one a week before, to oversee the construction of fortifications on the southwest side of the Susquehanna to protect the state capital. By the time this officer arrived so much work had already been done in that regard that he decided not to make any changes, even though they had not been done the way he would have done them. Also arriving at Harrisburg that day was a brigade of three regiments of New York militia, the 11th, 22nd, and 37th New York State National Guard, with their own militia general, Brigadier General John Ewen, in command. They crossed the Susquehanna on what was known as the Camelback Bridge, which one militiaman said was built like an old barn and smelled like one too.

Also that morning, about 800 New York militiamen got off the cars of the Cumberland Valley Railroad at Shippensburg, northeast of Chambersburg. These were the two regiments that had seen some fighting at Bull Run (and had served a later 90-days term of enlistment, although without seeing combat during that time). Being the best troops he had, Couch had sent them down the night before from their camp opposite Harrisburg with orders to slow any Confederate advance, "but under all circumstances to avoid an engagement, but if pressed to retire slowly and harass the enemy as much as possible."[23] They were accompanied by a battery of boat howitzers that had been reluctantly lent to Couch by the Navy for the present emergency, complete with a naval officer to command them. When these troops had arrived the evening before, a heavy rain had been falling, and they had spent the night in the shelter of their railroad cars again. Although a steady rain continued to fall, the senior colonel marched this small brigade to the edge of town that morning and put it in position straddling the turnpike coming up from Chambersburg.

Soon thereafter a new brigade commander arrived in the person of 40-year-old Brigadier General Joseph F. Knipe, a resident of Harrisburg who had been at home recovering from a wound received at Chancellorsville (where he had commanded a brigade of the 12th Corps) until he volunteered his services to Couch. Knipe spent the day dealing with various administrative problems, such as getting Couch's quartermaster to send his troops something to eat and figuring out what to do with the company of the Invalid Corps, which had preceded the militia here (answer: nothing), as well as a company of cavalry recruits sent down from Carlisle Barracks. He received a telegram from Couch telling him to go forward with one regiment to Scotland, a village about two-thirds of the way to Chambersburg, where Jenkins had destroyed the railroad bridge a few days before, followed at 9 p.m. by another telling him to send at least a half-regiment all the way to Chambersburg.

Not yet acquainted with his new command or the situation around him, Knipe decided to wait for daylight. However, he received a small but valuable reinforcement in the form of Captain Boyd's company of the 1st New York Cavalry, which had been resting since escorting Milroy's and Tyler's wagons to Harrisburg. So Knipe attached the company of cavalry recruits to Boyd's veteran company and sent them off to the south through the still-falling rain. These troopers passed right through Chambersburg without seeing any Rebels and rode on to the southwest to Mercersburg, where local civilians informed them that Confederates had been in that town earlier that day.

This was because Jenkins had sent one of his regiments northwestwards from Greencastle over Cove Mountain through Mercersburg to McConnellsburg on the night of 19-20 June. These Rebels had arrived at the latter place at 4 a.m. and had forced the locals to open their stores and "sell" them shoes, hats, medicine, food, and everything they might find useful, paying in Confederate money or just giving receipts. Their plunder included 120 horses, $12,000 worth of cattle, and several potential slaves. On their way back through Mercersburg they had expected to meet opposition, since the locals there had had time to get organized and/or call for help, but there was none. They did less plundering there, because they already had about all they could carry. And they were gone when Boyd's troopers arrived that night. One resident of Mercersburg, a professor of theology, said, "The Rebels were very poorly and miscellaneously dressed, and equipped with pistols, rifles, and sabers, hard looking and full of fight, some noble but also some stupid and semi-savage faces. Some fell asleep on their horses. The officers were quite intelligent and courteous, but full of hatred for the Yankees."[24]

Meanwhile, Milroy wired Couch that day from Bloody Run, Pennsylvania, about 50 miles west of Shippensburg and Chambersburg: "Arrived here to-day. It is a better point for concentration than Bedford. It is at the terminus of the railroad, 9 miles east of Bedford. Find about 2,500 of my troops here and at Bedford. Will have them all here to-night. Two-thirds have arrived. All badly supplied with ammunition, and no rations. It is reported that the enemy are at McConnellsburg advancing on this place." Couch replied: "I think your selection good for the present. Rations will be up to-morrow or before. Send for ammunition. One hundred and fifty rebels were at McConnellsburg to-day. Our mountain men took some prisoners. General Kelley occupies Cumberland, and says that [Imboden's] rebels are all along the south of the Potomac. I trust that you can prevent any force they may send from penetrating the country." Later he added: "Move your cavalry to McConnellsburg. When in the passes there, you can determine from information what course to take.

Report to me when you arrive at Chambersburg." Milroy replied: "We have information here that the enemy, after passing through McConnellsburg, turned toward Hancock via Mercersburg. General Schenck directs that I concentrate my command as soon as possible at Harper's Ferry. There is no enemy near here, and, if you do not need my force, I will move toward Harper's Ferry as soon as I can get my command gathered together."

Schenck, meanwhile, worried about reports of Confederates north of the Potomac, and, busy building fortifications to protect Baltimore, fired off a telegram addressed to Milroy at "Bedford, Pa., or wherever he may be: You have not reported to me since you left Harrisburg. You will at once inform me where you are, with what force, how engaged, and the condition of the troops you have found." However, Couch wired back to Milroy: "You will not obey the orders of any general but myself, no matter what may be his rank. You have received my orders about watching and taking care of the rebels." Milroy replied to this: "Certainly, general, as long as I am in your department it will be my duty and my pleasure to obey your orders strictly. I have ordered the 12th Pennsylvania Cavalry to McConnellsburg, as they are acquainted with the country, and kept the First New York to picket the various roads south from this. Regret that the report of the rebels being at Flint Stone is confirmed beyond a doubt." Couch replied at 5:20 p.m.: "Have scouts to find out the presence of the enemy. Have your force so as to concentrate on Bloody Run or vicinity, or move on McConnellsburg, as circumstances may determine. You must not be scrupulous about taking horses so as to move rapidly; put two men on one horse. Should they pass Bedford, force their rear guard, and compel them to stand. Your well-known activity will suggest a thousand means to harass and scatter them. Brooks said that he would look after the passes west of the county; he may not hurry."

Halleck then added to the confusion about Milroy's command by wiring to Schenck: "Major-General Milroy will be placed in arrest, and the members of his staff sent to Harper's Ferry, to report to General Tyler." To this Schenck replied: "Your order as to General Milroy will be obeyed as soon as practicable. I relieved him of command at Harper's Ferry, and ordered him to report here. I then sent him back to Harper's Ferry, to assist in collecting and reorganizing those of his troops who were to serve under General Tyler. The railroad communication being interrupted, he had to return from Monocacy. In the meantime, I heard of a large body of his men, who, having turned up in their retreat at Hancock, had gone up into Pennsylvania. I ordered him to proceed by Harrisburg to Bedford, to find and take charge of them. He went with his staff, and, at last accounts, was in command of that portion of his division, about 1,800 infantry and cavalry, at Bedford, or Bloody Run." Schenck also telegraphed Couch: "Where is General Milroy, and how engaged? I will comply with request to order him only through your headquarters. But General Halleck has directed that he be placed in arrest, and the members of his staff sent to Harper's Ferry."[25] The division of responsibility between departments was obviously still a problem for the Union command.

In a rare show of unselfishness by a department commander, Major General J. G. Foster, commander of the Union's Department of North Carolina, wrote to Halleck that day: "I have just received papers of the 18th instant, containing news of Lee's advance. I am anxious to render all the assistance in my power. . . . I can send either to Baltimore or Fort Monroe ten regiments immediately upon the receipt of your order to do so. These are nine-months' men, whose term of service has nearly expired, and whose places I am making arrangements to fill as best I can. I can as well spare them now as a few weeks hence. Six of these regiments are from Massachusetts, well drilled, and good fighting men, having all been in several successful affairs. The other four regiments are from Pennsylvania, and are good, serviceable troops. If you want these men, I will send them under good officers."[26]

Hooker, meanwhile, was still trying to find a source of good information about what was going on north of the Potomac. At 10:10 a.m. that day he wrote a telegram to John C. Babcock, then at Frederick, Maryland. Babcock was a former architect who, as a mere private in McClellan's bodyguard during the latter's Peninsula Campaign the year before, had produced some invaluable maps for that general – much better than those produced by the Army's topographical engineers. Now a civilian, he was an important member of Hooker's intelligence service, known as the Bureau of Military Information. "Employ and send persons on to the heights of South Mountain," Hooker told him, "to overlook the valley beyond, and see if the enemy have camps there. Direct them to avoid the roads, and employ only such persons as can look upon a body of armed men without being frightened out of their senses. Tell me whether it is infantry, cavalry, or artillery they have seen. If they take a position in the forest, they can even count them, as they pass on the road, with impunity. Send me no information but that which you know to be authentic. It is necessary for me to know if the enemy has any considerable number of his forces on the north side of the Potomac. Be vigilant and active. Use money, and it shall be returned to you."[27]

Babcock replied at 3:10 p.m. with information obtained from a doctor who had left Williamsport at 2:30 p.m. on his way to Baltimore. After giving several details, somewhat out of date, he said, "In short, a division of infantry, under General Rodes, and some 1,200 cavalry, under Jenkins, together with mounted infantry, comprise all the force at or near Williamsport, the majority of the infantry being at Charlestown. The main body of Lee's army is not in the vicinity or within supporting distance of this force. No artillery has crossed the river. The scouts sent to Elk Ridge will return to-morrow."[28] At 5:30 p.m. Babcock wired Colonel G. H. Sharpe, head of Hooker's Bureau of Military Information, from Frederick: "Signal corps just driven in, and are flying through the town. Report that the rebels are advancing three miles out. Everything in uproar, and everybody leaving. I suppose I must go, too. If I have to leave, I will go to Monocacy, and return here when I can. It is only a raid, and may prove beneficial to me, as I can learn much on returning after they have left."[29]

But the U.S. War Department was more concerned that day

about getting accurate information about its own forces than about Lee's. At the direction of Secretary Stanton, Halleck wrote instructions that day for Brigadier General W. Scott Ketchum, a headquarters officer there in Washington, to proceed to Harper's Ferry and check into a large discrepancy between the number of men Tyler said he had for the defense of that place and the official returns of units in that district as previously reported by General Schenck. "You will report how these statements conform to the results of your inspection, what has become of the missing men, and also, so far as you can ascertain, the facts in relation to General Milroy's retreat from Winchester."[30] Ketchum was provided copies of Halleck's messages to Schenck of 8 and 11 June telling him to concentrate his forces and leave only an outpost at Winchester.

Lee was in error, in his letter to Davis, in saying that Longstreet's infantry still occupied the passes of the Blue Ridge. "On June 20," Longstreet later reported, "I received a dispatch from general headquarters, directing that I should hold myself in readiness to move in the direction of the Potomac, with a view to crossing, &c. As I was ready, and had been expecting an order to execute such purpose, I supposed the intimation meant other preparation, and, knowing of nothing else that I could do to render my preparations complete, I supposed that it was desirable that I should cross the Shenandoah. I therefore passed the river, occupied the banks at the ferries opposite the Gaps, and a road at an intermediate ford, which was practicable for cavalry and infantry."[31] In other words, he left the passes and descended into the Shenandoah Valley, leaving Stuart on his own without immediate support.

Pleasonton, meanwhile, sent off a dispatch to Hooker's headquarters at 7 that morning, filled with his usual mix of correct, incorrect, and outdated information about Lee's army. It included the revealing statement that "I have been attacking Stuart to make him keep his people together, so that they cannot scout and find out anything about our forces." He was still missing the point that his current mission was just the opposite: to find out about Lee's forces. He went on to say: "Their cavalry force is very numerous; a great deal of it mounted infantry. [Only Robertson's brigade, armed with Enfield rifles, could be so described.] Lee is playing his old game of covering the gaps and moving his forces up [actually down] the Shenandoah Valley. [In that valley north, or northeast, is "down" because the river runs downstream in that direction.] Chester Gap has been the gap they passed through. The infantry on this side is simply to assist Stuart. We cannot force the gaps of the Blue Ridge in the presence of a superior force."[32] That much, at least, was correct, but was the force still superior?

At 5:20 p.m. Dan Butterfield wrote to Pleasonton, in reply to a message from the latter not found in the records: "Your dispatch of 12.30 p.m. of this date has been received and laid before the major-general commanding, who authorizes you, in accordance with your request, to move to-morrow morning with your entire corps against the enemy's cavalry. Major-General Meade will be instructed to detach two brigades of infantry from his corps to support this movement, to march at 3 a.m. to-morrow. The commanding general is very anxious that you should ascertain, at the earliest possible moment, where the main body of the enemy's infantry are to be found at the present time, especially A. P. Hill's corps. The commanding general thinks you cannot have more than 4,000 of the enemy's cavalry in your vicinity, and he suggests that you make your attack in front with a very small force, and turn the enemy's position with your main body."[33]

Pleasonton passed this on to David Gregg at 11:15 p.m., garbling it somewhat in the process: "A division of infantry will leave at 2 o'clock [sic] in the morning to join you, to support an attack by my whole force upon the enemy in your front. The infantry had best pass to the left of Middleburg, and operate by the left, occupying the stone fences and woods. General Hooker recommends an attack in front with a small force, and turn the enemy's position with your main body. I shall, therefore, send Buford to the right, let the infantry take the left, and you the center; a brigade of your command and one of the infantry to act as reserve, and occupy your present position at Middleburg."[34]

Out in Tennessee on the 20th, Morgan's raid was getting under way, but was soon aborted. After being ordered by Bragg to take only 1500 men and begging permission from Wheeler to take 2000 he was actually taking 2460 men of his division – nine cavalry regiments in two brigades, plus two 10-pounder Parrott rifles and two 12-pounder howitzers – leaving behind only 280 men of the 9th Kentucky Cavalry. His move was quickly detected by the Federals. Rosecrans wired General Hartsuff, commander of the 23rd Corps in Burnside's department, that same day: "Morgan is reported 9 miles from Lebanon, probably on his way into Kentucky, or perhaps to Carthage. His forces reported 4,000 and one battery."[35] The Rebels crossed the upper Cumberland River that day and went into camp near the town of Carthage, where there was a Union force that Morgan planned to attack the next day. However, a courier brought him orders to turn back and intercept Sanders' Federals, who were then approaching Knoxville.

General Buckner was in the process of concentrating his forces at Clinton, northwest of Knoxville, so all that was left to defend the latter city were two regiments of infantry, 37 cavalrymen, and some artillery pieces in an ordnance depot. Upon the Federals' approach the night before, the guns had been issued to the ranking artillery officer on hand, and civilians were called upon to come to the defense of their city. Only about 200 volunteered, since many of them would have been happy to see the Confederates defeated.

Sanders later reported: "At daylight I moved up to the city, on the Tazewell road. I found the enemy well posted on the heights and in the adjacent buildings, with eight or nine pieces of artillery. The streets were barricaded with cotton bales, and the batteries protected by the same material. Their force was estimated at 3,000, including citizens who were impressed into service. After about one hour's skirmishing, I withdrew, capturing near the city two pieces of artillery – 6-pounders – the tents, and all the camp equipage of a regiment of conscripts, about 80 Confederates States horses, and 31 prisoners.

"I then started [northeastwards] for Strawberry Plains, following the railroad, and destroyed all the small bridges and depots to within 4 miles of the latter place, at Flat Creek, where I burned a finely built covered bridge, and also a county bridge. The guard had retreated. I left the railroad 3 miles below the town, and crossed the Holston River, so as to attack the bridge on the same side the enemy were. As soon as we came in sight they opened on the advance with four pieces of artillery. I dismounted the infantry and sent the Forty-Fourth Ohio, under Major [Alpheus S.] Moore, up the river, and the rest, under Colonel [R. K.] Byrd and Major [Tristam T.] Dow, to get in their rear. After about an hour's skirmishing, the enemy were driven off, and having a train and locomotive, with steam up, in waiting, a portion of them escaped, leaving all their guns (five in number), 137 enlisted men and 2 officers as prisoners, a vast amount of stores, ammunition, and provisions, including 600 sacks of salt, about 70 tents, and a great quantity of camp equipage, in our possession. I remained at this place all night, and destroyed the splendid bridge over the Holston River, over 1,600 feet long, build on eleven piers. The trestle-work included, this bridge was 2,100 feet in length."[36]

At Port Hudson, the Federals completed on the 20th a new work, known as Battery No. 24, on top of a bluff opposite the Confederate position known as the Citadel, at the southern end of the defenses. This new Union work contained seventeen pieces of artillery of various types and calibers, including two 10-inch mortars, and was less than 200 yards from Confederate Battery XI, but the Rebels did not seem to be concerned, having even offered to send over some of their officers to aid in the construction. The guns opened fire that day but did so little damage to the Citadel that General Dwight authorized the start of a series of zigzag trenches to approach Battery XI.

Farther down in Louisiana that day, one regiment of Colonel Major's Confederates attacked a Union force at the town of Donaldsonville, where Bayou Lafourche meets the Mississippi River west of New Orleans, and reported taking 140 prisoners and a large quantity of supplies. Major, meanwhile, was pushing on down the Lafourche. At 3:30 a.m. on the 21st he reached the town of Thibodeaux, near which the railroad from New Orleans to Brashear City crossed the Lafourche. There he encountered Federal troops rushed out from Brashear City on the railroad, amid "one of the heaviest rains I ever saw fall."[37] He said he had only about 30 rounds of ammunition per man to start with and by 5 p.m., when the rains stopped, so much of it was wet that he estimated he was down to about 3 rounds per man that was usable. He ordered one of his regiments to strengthen its pickets and feel out the Union force, but that regiment got a little over-eager and charged the Federals, capturing some, driving the rest into their earthworks, and capturing four guns. But that night another train brought in about 300 more Federals, and Major withdrew. Meanwhile, the telegraph wires were busy carrying messages back and forth between Banks' army outside Port Hudson, Admiral Farragut, General Emory in command at New Orleans, and various subordinate Union commanders. Emory was now stripped down to about 400 men to hold New Orleans, by far the largest city in the entire South, and Major was squarely across the railroad between there and Brashear City, where there was a small Federal garrison and numerous supplies.

Confederate Secretary of War Seddon was wiring Joe Johnston that 21st day of June, saying he had received the latter's message of the 19th complaining of the difficulties and dangers of attacking Grant: "Consequences are realized and difficulties are recognized as very great, but I still think, other means failing, the course recommended should be hazarded. The aim, in my judgment, justifies any risk and all probable consequences." He followed that with a more personal dispatch: "Only my conviction of almost imperative necessity for action induces the official dispatch I have just sent you. On every ground I have great deference to you superior knowledge of the position, your judgment and military genius, but I feel it right to share, if need be to take, the responsibility, and leave you free to follow the most desperate course the occasion may demand. Rely upon it, the eyes and hopes of the whole Confederacy are upon you, with the full confidence that you will act, and with the sentiment that it were better to fail nobly daring than through prudence even to be inactive. I look to attack in last resort, but rely on your resources of generalship to suggest less desperate modes of relief. I can scarce dare to suggest, but might it not be possible to strike Banks first and unite the garrison of Port Hudson with you or to secure sufficient co-operation from General [Kirby] Smith, or to practically besiege Grant by operations with artillery from the swamps now dry on the north side of the Yazoo below Haynes' Bluff? I rely on you for all possible [efforts] to save Vicksburg."[38]

Colonel E. J. Harvie, Johnston's inspector general, wrote a long letter that day to Joseph R. Davis, Jefferson Davis's older brother, a prominent citizen of Mississippi, explaining Johnston's position. After covering the current situation around Vicksburg, and why his present force was too small to take on Grant, he said, "Now, suppose General Bragg's army was at once ordered to Mississippi. The bulk of it could be gotten here in three weeks. General Johnston with this re-enforcement could not only succor the garrison in Vicksburg, but disperse Grant's army and save the city itself. Why, you will ask, has this not been done before? I anticipate and answer your question frankly. It has not been done by General Johnston for two reasons: 1st. Until the 10th instant, he had no idea that he possessed the power to make such an order, all his antecedent correspondence with the Government having excluded the conclusion that such control over General Bragg's troops was within the chart of his authority in the department. 2d. When, on the 10th instant, the President, by implication, conferred on him the power to make such a disposition of General Bragg's army, it was very late, and what might have before been a clear military proposition, had then assumed political proportions, which made General Johnston unwilling to take a responsibility involving the possible abandonment of States. General Johnston thought then, and so telegraphed the President, that it was a political question between Middle Tennessee and the Mississippi Valley, which he, as the head of the Government, ought to decide. This is the point on which the order failed. Should it fail on such a point? If it is right; if it is exigent; if it alone can save the Mississippi Valley, and, above all, render certain the release from possible captivity of 25,000 of our gallant troops, to say nothing of maintaining our hold on the river and communications with the country beyond it, ought it not to be done by somebody? If so, by whom more properly than the President of the Confederacy, the center of all executive power? He ought to decide the question and take the responsibility. It may be that his decision involves the very fate of the Republic itself."[39] But President Davis gave no such order, his strategy seeming to be little more than hoping for the best, and Johnston refused to take the responsibility for doing what he knew needed to be done.

Pemberton wrote to Johnston again that day: "Your dispatches of the 14th and 16th received. If it is absolutely impossible, in you opinion, to raise the siege with our combined forces, and that nothing more can be done than to extricate the garrison, I suggest that, giving me full information in time to act, you move by the north of the railroad, drive in the enemy's pickets at night, and at daylight next morning engage him heavily with skirmishers, occupying him during the entire day, and that on that night I move by the Warrenton road, by Hankinson's Ferry, to which point you should previously send a brigade of cavalry, with two field batteries, to build a bridge there, and hold that ferry; also Hall's and Baldwin's, to cover my crossing at Hankinson's. I shall not be able to move with my artillery or wagons. I suggest this as the best plan, because all the other roads are too strongly intrenched and the enemy in too heavy force for a reasonable prospect of success, unless you move in sufficient force to compel him to abandon his communications with Snyder's, which I hope we may be able to do. I await your orders."[40]

Two different couriers had brought Pemberton the messages he was thus replying to. One was a St. Louis man, an acquaintance of some young Confederate ordnance officers known to the Lord family of Vicksburg. Young Lida Lord said these officers "described him as a most daring man, but when cross-questioned admitted some doubts as to his being very reliable. He had passed the gunboats on the Yazoo, dressed as a fisherman, in a skiff full of lines and bait; but at the mouth of the river he saw so many men and boats that he had taken to the woods, and finally had floated down the Mississippi after dark on a plank canoe. He stated that he had been sworn to secrecy, but when eagerly questioned he replied: 'Now, boys, *don't*! I can only tell you that in three or four days you will hear the biggest kind of cannonading, and will see the Yanks skedaddling up the Yazoo.' He also said that Johnston's army consisted of the very flower of the South Carolina, Virginia, and Kentucky troops. This was corroborated by a courier, who came in the same day, and reported himself only three days absent from Johnston's camps. Joseph E. Johnston was our angel of deliverance in those days of siege, but alas! We were never even to touch the hem of his robe."[41]

"Pemberton is a fool!" a Union doctor wrote, "or he would surrender. The rebs in Vicksburg must suffer terribly, nothing to eat and nothing for their sick and wounded. And what will they gain by holding out any longer? I do not believe they expect aid from Johnston any more."[42] But Mary Loughborough, a Confederate officer's wife living in the town, noted, "I had often remarked how cheerfully the soldiers bore the hardships of the siege. I saw them often passing with their little sacks containing scanty rations, whistling and chatting pleasantly, as around them thickly flew the balls and shell. Poor men, yet so badly used, and undergoing so many privations."[43] Young Lucy McRae noted, "Our provisions were becoming scarce, and the Louisiana soldiers were eating rats as a delicacy, while mules were occasionally being carved up to appease the appetite."[44] On the other side of the lines Sergeant Oldroyd was watching a recently captured Rebel. "We gave him all he could eat," he said, "and that was no small amount. But he was certainly a very hungry man, and if he is a fair sampling of those remaining in Vicksburg, Uncle Sam's commissary will have to endure quite a burden, for after the surrender, no doubt, Grant will have to feed them all."[45]

Grant was contemplating ways that the Confederates defending Vicksburg might try to escape their fate. He wrote that day to Admiral Porter: "Information received from Vicksburg last night confirms your theory of the probable method Pemberton will take for escaping in the last extremity. One of our pickets and one of the enemy, by mutual consent, laid down their arms, met half way, and had a long conversation. The rebel said that our cannonading killed and wounded a great many in the rifle-pits; otherwise did no great damage. They fully counted upon an assault as being intended and were prepared for it. Finding that no assault was made, the feelings of the troops were canvassed to see if they could be got out to attack the Yankees. They not only declined this, but those on the right (our left) almost mutinied because their officers would not surrender. They were only reassured and persuaded to continue on duty by being told that they had provisions enough on hand to last seven days. In that time they would have two thousand boats finished, and they could make their escape by the river. The rebel said they were tearing down houses to get the materials out of which to build boats.

"I will direct General Mower to keep a strong picket in the river in front of Vicksburg at night; to place his battery behind the levees or hold it in some good position, to be used if an attempt should be made to escape in that way. If possible, fix up material to light and illuminate the river, should a large number of boats attempt to cross. I will direct General Mower to call on you and consult as to the best plan for defeating this method of escape. You will find General Mower an intelligent and gallant officer, capable of carrying out any plan that may be adopted."[46]

"Work on trenches progressing as usual," Captain Hickenlooper's notes for the 21st say. "The enemy are using hand-grenades (6 and 12 pound shells) with effect. Being within a few feet of the ditch of Fort Hill, I made a call for all the miners in the command to report to me in person. General Ransom has completed his advanced work, and General Quinby has commenced building Battery Archer for Navy guns."[47]

The campaign to capture Charleston, South Carolina, was still on hold, awaiting the recovery and arrival of Admiral Foote. On 21 June, Secretary of the Navy Welles reluctantly decided to go ahead without him and told Admiral John Dahlgren to assume full command of the naval forces involved, even though there would be grumbling among more senior officers who would think themselves more entitled to the command. Dahlgren had been a desk officer in the ordnance bureau throughout much of his career and had designed the heavy shell-guns that bore his name. He was the father of Captain Ulric Dahlgren of General Hooker's staff. He had been involved in much of the planning in Washington for the next attack at Charleston, which made him a logical choice to assume the command, but Welles still hoped for Foote to recover in time to take over.

In Tennessee that day, Morgan's Confederate cavalry crossed back to the south side of the Cumberland River in obedience to orders to go after Sanders' Federals, who had been working all night at destroying bridges northeast of Knoxville. "At daylight on the 21st," Sanders later reported, "I started up the railroad for the Mossy Creek Bridge, destroying the road at all convenient points. At Mossy Creek, New Market, and vicinity I captured

120 prisoners and destroyed several [railroad] cars, a large quantity of stores, several hundred barrels of saltpeter [an ingredient of gunpowder], 200 barrels of sugar, and a large amount of other stores. The bridge burned at Mossy Creek was a fine one, over 300 feet in length. Near this place I also destroyed the machinery of a gun factory and a saltpeter factory. I determined to leave the railroad here and endeavor to cross the mountains at Rogers' Gap, as I knew every exertion was being made on the part of the enemy to capture my command. I forded the Holston, at Hayworth's Bend, and started for the Powder Springs Gap, of Clinch Mountain. Here a large force was found directly in my front, and another strong force overtook and commenced skirmishing with my rear guard. By taking country roads, I got into the gap without trouble or loss, and had all this force in my rear.

"On arriving within a mile and a half of Rogers' Gap, I found that it was blockaded by fallen timber, and strongly guarded by artillery and infantry, and that all the gaps practicable were obstructed and guarded in similar manner. I then determined to abandon my artillery, and move by a wood path to Smith's Gap, 3 miles from Rogers' Gap. The guns, carriages, harness, and ammunition were completely destroyed, and left. I had now a large force both in front and rear, and could only avoid capture by getting into the mountains, and thus place all of them in my rear, which I succeeded in doing, after driving a regiment of cavalry from Smith's Gap. The road through this pass is only a bridle-path, and very rough. I did not get up the mountain until after night. About 170 of my men and officers got on the wrong road, and did not rejoin the command until we reached Kentucky. Owing to the continual march, many horses gave out and were left, and, although several hundred were captured on the march, they were not enough to supply all the men."[48]

General Rosecrans wrote to Halleck on the 21st: "In your favor of the 12th instant you say you do not see how the maxim of not fighting two great battles at the same time applies to the case of this army and Grant's. Looking at the matter practically, we and our opposing forces are so widely separated that for Bragg to materially aid Johnston he must abandon our front substantially, and then we can move to our ultimate work with more rapidity and less waste of material on natural obstacles. If Grant is defeated, both forces will come here, and then we ought to be near our base. The same maxim that forbids, as you take it, a single army fighting two great battles at the same time (by the way, a very awkward thing to do), would forbid this nation's engaging all its forces in the great West at the same time, so as to leave it without a single reserve to stem the current of possible disaster. This is, I think, sustained by high military and political considerations. We ought to fight here if we have a strong prospect of winning a decisive battle over the opposing force, and upon this ground I shall act. I shall be careful not to risk our last reserve without strong grounds to expect success."[49]

∽ Endnotes ∽

1 Horan, *Confederate Agent*, 27.
2 *OR*, III:3:385.
3 Ibid., III:3:385-6.
4 Ibid., I:23:I:387.
5 Ibid., I:23:I:13.
6 Ibid., I:24:III:967.
7 Hoehling, *Vicksburg: 47 Days of Siege*, 192.
8 Ibid., 190.
9 *OR*, I:24:II:202.
10 Ibid., I:24:II:173.
11 Ibid., I:24:I:103-4.
12 Ibid., I:24:II:172.
13 Ibid., III:3:386.
14 Ibid., I:24:III:418-9.
15 Hoehling, *Vicksburg: 47 Days of Siege*, 193.
16 Dana, *Recollections of the Civil War*, 97.
17 OR I:24:II:202.
18 Ibid., I:27:III:905-6.
19 Ibid., I:27:III:906.
20 Ibid., I:27:II:297.

21 Ibid., I:27:III:907.
22 Ibid.
23 Nye, *Here Come the Rebels*, 238.
24 Ibid., 252-3.
25 All these messages from, to, and about Milroy are in *OR*, I:27:III:235-8.
26 Ibid., I:27:III:242.
27 Ibid., I:27:III:225. For further information on Babcock, and Hooker's Bureau of Military Information, see Edwin C. Fishel, *The Secret War for the Union* (Boston and New York, 1996).
28 Ibid., I:27:III:227.
29 Ibid., I:27:III:228.
30 Ibid., I:27:III:234.
31 Ibid., I:27:II:357.
32 Ibid., I:27:III:224.
33 Ibid., I:27:III:227-8.
34 Ibid., I:27:III:229-30.
35 Ibid., I:23:II:440.
36 Ibid., I:23:I:387-8.
37 Ibid., I:26:I:218.
38 Ibid., I:24:I:228.
39 Ibid., I:24:III:970-1.
40 Ibid., I:24:III:969.
41 Hoehling, *Vicksburg: 47 Days of Siege,* 206.
42 Ibid., 204.
43 Ibid., 203.
44 Ibid., 201.
45 Ibid., 204.
46 *OR*, I:24:III:423-4.
47 Ibid., I:24:II:202.
48 Ibid., I:23:I:388.
49 Ibid., I:23:I:9.

CHAPTER 13

"High Expectations Formed"

21 – 23 June 1863

In Virginia on that 21st day of June, Confederate Major General Isaac Trimble, who had arrived to take command in the Shenandoah Valley just as Ewell's corps had cleared it of all enemies, talked with General Lee at Berryville, and the latter told him "We have again outmaneuvered the enemy, who even now does not know where we are or what our designs are. Our whole army will be in Pennsylvania day after tomorrow, leaving the enemy far behind and obliged to follow us by forced marches. I hope with these advantages to accomplish some signal result and to end the war, if Providence favors us."[1]

Major General George Pickett was writing from his division's camp near Berryville to Lee's adjutant and inspector general that day: "I have the honor to report that in point of numerical strength this division has been very much weakened. One brigade (Jenkins') was left on the Blackwater. Corse was left at Hanover Junction as a guard by my own order, upon the receipt of a telegram from the general commanding this army to bring up my division to Culpeper Court-House if I could leave the Junction. Being anxious to carry out his wishes, I marched immediately with three brigades, leaving Corse with orders to follow as soon as relieved, and sent a staff officer to Richmond to report the circumstances to the Adjutant-General, and reported the fact by telegraph and letter to the commanding general. I have now only three brigades, not more than 4,795 men, and unless these absent troops are certainly to rejoin me, I beg that another brigade be sent to this division ere we commence the campaign. I ask this in no spirit of complaint, but merely as an act of justice to my division and myself, for it is well known that a small division will be expected to do the same amount of hard service as a large one, and, as the army is now divided, my division will be, I think, decidedly the weakest."[2] These were prophetic words, considering the role this division would play at the climactic point of the coming campaign. However, no brigades were transferred to Pickett, even though a couple of divisions in Lee's army had five brigades, probably because Lee kept hoping that one or both of the brigades he had left behind would eventually be sent to him.

Pickett was a dapper widower of 38, who wore his hair in long, perfumed ringlets, and who was now engaged to a teen-aged girl who had had her eye on him since she was four. He had graduated at the very bottom of the famous West Point class of 1846, which had included George McClellan, "Stonewall" Jackson, and many others who were now generals on both sides of this war. He had secured his appointment to West Point from Illinois, with the help of Abraham Lincoln, but he was always a Virginian at heart. He had fought well in the Mexican War and had almost started a war with Britain over the San Juan Islands in what is now the state of Washington when that was disputed territory. He and Longstreet had served together in the regular army before the war, and they were good friends. As a division commander he was competent but not gifted. Neither fate nor history would be kind to him.

Secretary Seddon, at Richmond, and General D. H. Hill, at Petersburg, were exchanging messages that day about the situation in that area, which involved some of the units Lee longed for, including the brigade of Brigadier General Micah Jenkins from Pickett's Division (not to be confused with Albert Jenkins, no relation, whose cavalry brigade was leading – sort of – the advance into Pennsylvania). Seddon telegraphed Hill that the Federals had withdrawn from Suffolk, Virginia, and were concentrating as many as 20,000 men at Yorktown for an advance on Richmond. "Suffolk has not been evacuated," Hill replied. "Up to Thursday last, fourteen [Union] regiments of infantry, two of cavalry, and some twenty pieces of artillery were on the Blackwater. They had been there for six days, apparently trying to cross both day and night, but making very feeble efforts. This looks very much like evacuation, as they usually cover their retreats by feigned attacks. Still, I have no idea that they will fall back farther than Bowers' Hill, 8 miles from Portsmouth, if, indeed, they go back that far.

"In regard to an advance upon the capital, we have but two things to apprehend. A direct advance will not be made. They will either move upon Hanover, and cut the railroad and canal, or they will land at City Point, and isolate Petersburg, crossing the Appomattox between its mouth and this city. The former movement can be met by an attack in flank and rear. The latter would be a very serious one for us. It is entirely practicable for the Yankees, and cannot be resisted by us.

"Brig. Gen. Matt. Ransom is with his brigade at Drewry's Bluff, and five batteries of field artillery have been sent over there also. Brigadier-General Jenkins' troops will reach here from the Blackwater to-night and to-morrow. This is the only force to guard Petersburg and this long line of railroad. A front of 300 miles, containing an infinite number of approaches, is feebly guarded by three regiments of cavalry. We are obliged to meet with disaster at some point, if the Yankees show any enterprise.

"Now, this brings me to the object of this letter. I would most respectfully make two suggestions. I learn from General Jenkins that General Beauregard has more cavalry than he can use. Could not one of those regiments be ordered to this department?" His other suggestion was that recently exchanged prisoners, instead of being returned to their units in the West, be used to help defend Richmond and Petersburg until it was ascertained what the Federals were up to. "The exchanged men will get back too late to be of any service at Vicksburg," he said, "and will be on the road when they might be saving the capital of the Confederacy."[3]

Hill's analysis of the possible moves the Federals could make was very perceptive. In the event, they chose the move against Hanover Junction this year; the move against Petersburg and the area between it and Richmond was not tried until the following year.

In northern Virginia, on the 21st, Union engineers completed a 1340-foot pontoon bridge across the Potomac near Edward's

Ferry. And some good information about Lee's position finally started coming into Hooker's headquarters that day. Slocum wrote to Butterfield that evening from Leesburg: "A deserter from Pickett's division, Longstreet's corps, came in this evening. Longstreet's corps is near Snicker's Gap. McLaws' division is at Ashby's Gap. He says the rebel soldiers think Ewell's corps is in Maryland, and that Hill's corps is in rear of Longstreet's, but is to follow on; that the whole army is to go into Maryland."[4]

Milroy reported to Couch that day: "One of my most reliable scouts, sent yesterday morning toward Hagerstown, sent back a dispatch this morning, stating that the rebel infantry force at Hagerstown is estimated at 40,000, with eighteen pieces of artillery. There were 300 rebel cavalry at Mercersburg yesterday, gathering horses and cattle."[5]

Schenck wrote to Couch that day that he had reported to Halleck Couch's desire to hang onto Milroy but had been told that the order for the latter's arrest would not be suspended, "but that, being in your department, you are to place him at once in arrest."[6] Secretary Stanton also interfered with Couch's efforts to build up a defense of Pennsylvania that day by telling the governor of New York to send all the militia he could raise to Baltimore. This was at least partly Couch's own fault, for he telegraphed Halleck that evening that "Rebel cavalry have crossed South Mountain, and are at Middletown. Seem to be moving east, but not north."[7]

Babcock reported to Colonel Sharpe from Monocacy Junction that day, with a copy going to the War Department, that: "At 4 p.m. 40 of the First Maryland [Union] Cavalry routed the enemy in Frederick, leaving soon after. A force of 150 rebel cavalry immediately occupied the town, and are there now. The force to defend the railroad bridge here is insufficient, and an attempt to destroy it may be made to-night."[8] The Rebel cavalry were also Marylanders, being the battalion that had been in the Shenandoah Valley. From Frederick they went south with the idea of destroying a bridge over the Monocacy River, but finding it was made of iron they gave up and returned to South

Mountain, the Maryland extension of Virginia's Blue Ridge.

At Shippensburg, General Knipe had his men up before dawn on the 21st. He soon had them on the road, dropping off the 71st New York at Greene Village, about halfway to Chambersburg, and taking the 8th New York on to that town. They passed through it so early that there were still very few civilians up and about, and a mile out of town on the road to Hagerstown they made camp in a grove of trees and began constructing a roadblock while the boat howitzers took position on a low ridge. Knipe rode back into Chambersburg and wired Couch news of what he had done. Back came orders for him to leave the 8th New York in place and take the 71st to the village of Scotland, on the railroad northeast of Chambersburg. Another message informed him that his naval battery would soon be replaced by a military one, but difficulties with the railroad authorities caused the replacement battery to be taken only as far as Carlisle that day. The 71st reached Scotland at about 3 p.m. and went into camp. The railroad bridge Jenkins had destroyed at Scotland was being repaired but was not yet functional, and so the rations Knipe had ordered for his men got only that far that day. The 8th New York at Chambersburg, therefor, received none, but they were not exactly starving. The colonel of that regiment sent to Knipe to ask for a surgeon because many of his men were sick from eating too many stolen cherries.

At 3 a.m. on the 21st, Pleasonton wrote to Seth Williams, Hooker's assistant adjutant general, and the quality of his information was improving. He correctly stated that Longstreet's corps was in the Shenandoah Valley and that A. P. Hill's was either guarding the upper Rappahannock or moving into the Valley. "My opinion is, that Stuart's force is kept in our front as a blind until their main force is thrown across the Potomac. . . ." Then he spoiled it all by adding, "they will then turn westward toward Pittsburgh."[9] At 8:30 a.m., Williams told General Stahel, commanding the cavalry division of the Department of Washington, to make a reconnaissance in force in the direction of Warrenton and the upper Rappahannock and to "make every effort to ascertain the whereabouts of the enemy's forces, and particularly of the corps commanded by A. P. Hill."[10]

At around 7 a.m., Pleasonton began advancing again. Stuart now had all of his cavalry on hand (Neither Jenkins' brigade, with Ewell, nor Imboden's, off in West Virginia, was considered part of his division at this time). He had Munford's brigade near Snickersville, to cover the approaches to Snicker's Gap, and two brigades, Hampton's and Robertson's, west of Middleburg guarding the turnpike leading to Ashby's Gap. The remaining two brigades, Jones's and Chambliss's, were near Union, roughly halfway between the other two forces.

In accordance with his request for infantry, Pleasonton had been reinforced by the 1st Division of the 5th Corps, commanded by Brigadier General James Barnes. Two of its brigades were left to hold Middleburg and form a reserve and rallying point. The 3rd Brigade, commanded by Colonel Strong Vincent, with a battery of horse artillery, advanced to clear some dismounted Rebels from what Stuart called "a position previously chosen, of great strength against a force of ordinary size, or against cavalry alone."[11] Vincent, a few days short of his 26th birthday, had only risen from regimental to brigade command about a month before, and this was his first fight in his new position. He sent three of his regiments straight at the dismounted Rebels while his other regiment, his own 83rd Pennsylvania, disappeared into some woods to emerge on the Confederate flank. The Rebels pulled out, heading west, with the Union cavalry hot on their tails, and Vincent's men decided that their new commander knew his business.

Kilpatrick's brigade led the Union cavalry's advance again, although he was down to only three regiments, since the previous battles had chewed up the 1st Rhode Island and 1st Massachusetts. From a ridge, a battery of Confederate horse artillery slowed his pursuit, but his own horse battery soon returned fire, blowing up a Rebel ammunition chest and breaking the axle on one of the Confederates' guns, a nice British-made rifle, and almost hitting Wade Hampton in the process. After half an hour of this, Stuart withdrew again, leaving the damaged gun behind. (He claimed in his report that this was the first gun his horse artillery had ever lost.)

Stuart leap-frogged his units to the rear, taking up position after position to force the Federals to consume time in deploying for attack before he would pull out again. Along Goose Creek the Rebels held up Gregg's advance for an hour and a half, the horse battery firing from another ridge overlooking the stream. Finally one of Vincent's regiments, the 16th Michigan, rushed the stone bridge under a hail of fire and charged up the hill beyond, capturing several Confederates, and the Rebels fell back again, passing beyond Upperville rather, Stuart said, than have the town's women and children caught in the center of a battle. Feeling no such compunctions, Kilpatrick's three regiments charged and caught the last Confederate regiment, the 5th North Carolina of Robertson's Brigade, in the confining street of the town (it only had one, the pike) and routed it, but was counter-charged in the flank by Hampton's Brigade. After a brief melee, the Federals retreated to the east, reformed, and came on again. Meanwhile the Rebel guns poured fire into the Union ranks, shooting the horse out from under David Gregg. After several minutes, the two sides broke contact, each falling back on their own side of the town to reform.

Vincent's infantry had been left far behind but could still see the cavalry fighting up ahead. "The charges of the cavalry," he wrote the next day, "a sight I had never before witnessed, were truly inspiring, and the triumphant strains of the bands, as squadron after squadron hurled the enemy in his flight up the hills and toward the gap, gave us a feeling of regret that we, too, were not mounted and could not join in the chase."[12] His brigade did eventually catch up and was used to support the Union artillery, until it was replaced at about 6 p.m. by another brigade of infantry.

Meanwhile, Kilpatrick had been loaned two regiments from Irvin Gregg's brigade, and at about 5:30 p.m. he led them forward. Two squadrons of the 1st Maine, out ahead of the rest, overran a Confederate howitzer withdrawing through the town, and the rest of the regiment dismounted and charged up a hill where part of Robertson's Brigade was posted behind a stone wall. The 5th North Carolina, bent on atoning for its earlier rout, charged the second of the two leading squadrons, overrunning it and temporarily capturing Kilpatrick without knowing who he was. But the leading Maine squadron had turned back and was firing into the Carolinians from a roadside wall, and more Federals were still coming up the road. The Rebel colonel was just turning to lead his men back the way they had come when he was badly wounded. He, his lieutenant colonel, and several of his men were captured, and he died soon after being taken to a house in the town.

This attack by Gregg and Vincent up the road to Upperville had been designed merely to hold Stuart's attention while Buford's 1st Division got around the Rebel cavalry to hit their flank or rear. There had been so little time between Buford's receipt of the order to advance and the time set for it, that his men had to mount up and ride away from Aldie into a drizzling rain without any breakfast for man or horse, even though they started two hours late. At about 7 a.m. they passed through Middleburg, turning north for a couple of miles, and then followed the south bank of Goose Creek to the west. There was no road there, the fields were muddy, and where a couple of small tributaries came in from the south they got even worse. These Federals could see the flank of Stuart's line but couldn't get at it, so Buford turned back to where the road crossed Goose Creek, but there the head of his column, as it crossed and turned west then southwest, came under fire from pickets of Grumble Jones's brigade.

News of Buford's approach reached Jones at about the same time that he got word that Stuart wanted his and Chambliss's brigades to join up with Hampton's and Robertson's at Upperville. Jones used a couple of regiments to slow Buford's advance and moved with the rest to comply with Stuart's order. The two regiments, under Colonel Lundsford Lomax, used the same delaying tactics that Stuart had used against Gregg, falling back a mile, then another, then two more, but forcing the Federals to deploy each time before he would move on. Buford finally reached some high ground a mile and a half northeast of Upperville, from which he could see Gregg's division faced off against what appeared to be a larger Confederate force. Resolving to go to Gregg's aid, Buford set out across the fields again at a fast trot, but mud plus numerous gulches and stone walls dividing the fields slowed his move and tired his horses. Still a half-mile from Gregg's position, he reached some high ground from which he could see, off to the west, a column of Confederate troops and wagons on a road that would take them into Ashby's Gap. He turned his column in that direction, and, after advancing a mile, his leading brigade, three western regiments under Colonel William Gamble, came under artillery fire. (Gamble's own horse was blown to pieces.)

Gamble's men charged the Rebel battery, driving its gunners to cover with the fire of their revolvers. But they couldn't capture the guns, which were behind a stone wall that was six feet tall except where the Confederates had knocked down small sections to fire through. These troopers were then charged by some of Jones's men who emerged from some woods on their flank. The Federals charged to meet these Rebels but were driven back a few hundred yards, where they reformed behind another stone wall. Meanwhile the battery limbered up and moved to a low knoll, and Jones posted a regiment on each side of it, while leading the rest of his brigade to attack Gamble. However, the latter's troopers, dismounting to better use their carbines and revolvers, drove him back and were soon joined by a section (2 guns) of horse artillery and another brigade of cavalry, that of Colonel Thomas C. Devin. Seeing these Union reinforcements, and even though he had been reinforced himself by the arrival of Chambliss's brigade, Jones withdrew into Ashby's Gap. Buford followed at a distance, but found four Rebel batteries deployed in the gap, supported by the two Rebel brigades, so at sundown he turned back. A few scouting parties did manage to climb the ridge and look down into the Shenandoah Valley in the twilight and see the camps of McLaws' Division of Longstreet's corps.

Buford's third brigade, still calling itself the Reserve Brigade, had been diverted by Pleasonton to reinforce Gregg. With two regiments temporarily detached, this brigade was down to three regiments of regulars, and was commanded by Major Samuel H. Starr. But, when it advanced dismounted across the fields south of Upperville, Hampton took it for more Union infantry. He deployed a regiment as rear guard and withdrew the rest of his brigade at a walk beyond the town. Stuart was convinced by the dismounted regulars, and the earlier participation of Vincent's brigade, that a sizable body of Union infantry was present and so decided to pull back all the way to Ashby's Gap, where he could be reinforced by some of Longstreet's infantry coming up the other side. Pleasonton followed for a couple of miles, but not far enough to see any of Longstreet's men, although some slaves told him about their presence. That night Gregg's men bivouacked just east of Upperville. Both sides felt that they had done well in the day's fighting, but a Confederate officer said that, while the Federals' horsemanship was still not quite as good as the Rebels', the improvement in the Union cavalry "became painfully apparent in the fights around Upperville."[13]

But before the battle had even finished, Pleasonton wrote to Seth Williams, and, after passing on information confirming what Slocum had already reported about Lee's positions, said: "I shall return to-morrow to Aldie. My command has been fighting almost constantly for four days, and must have a day or two to rest and shoe [horses] and get things in order."[14] The next day, Monday the 22nd, he did in fact withdraw almost all the way back to his starting point, followed by Stuart, whose troopers reoccupied most of their old positions. Pleasonton's assistant adjutant general wrote to Seth Williams that evening "that the enemy followed us to-day in strong force, and that [Pleasonton] thought it best to concentrate his force in a strong position. He has, therefore, withdrawn from Middleburg, and now occupies a position in advance of Dover, about 2 ½ miles in front of [Aldie]. He has lost no men to-day."[15]

In a dispatch written earlier that day Pleasonton commended generals Gregg and Kilpatrick "for their gallant zeal and efficiency throughout the day. I desire to inform the general commanding that the losses my command has sustained in officers require me to ask for the promotion of good commanders. It is necessary to have a good commander for the regular [Reserve] brigade of cavalry, and I earnestly recommend Capt. Wesley Merritt to be made a brigadier-general for that purpose. He has all the qualifications for it, and has distinguished himself by his gallantry and daring. Give me good commanders and I will give you good results."[16] He also told Seth Williams he needed at least 1,500 horses to replace his losses of the last two weeks.

Stuart wrote to Longstreet on the morning of the 22nd with, as he later reported, a plan "of leaving a brigade or so in my present front, and passing through Hopewell or some other gap in Bull Run Mountains, attain the enemy's rear, passing between his main body and Washington, and cross into Maryland, joining our army north of the Potomac."[17] Stuart had been contemplating some such move for a while and had already dispatched one of his best scouts to check the fords of the Potomac for a good crossing place, but the scout had not yet returned, and, in fact did not until after Stuart had already started his move, and in trying to catch up with him was captured by Union cavalry.

Lee wrote back that day: "I judge the efforts of the enemy yesterday were to arrest our progress and ascertain our whereabouts. Perhaps he is satisfied. Do you know where he is and what he is doing? I fear he will steal a march on us, and get across the Potomac before we are aware. If you find that he is moving northward, and that two brigades can guard the Blue Ridge and take care of your rear, you can move with the other three into Maryland, and take position on General Ewell's right, place yourself in communication with him, guard his flank, keep him informed of the enemy's movements, and collect all the supplies you can for the use of the army. One column of General Ewell's army will probably move toward the Susquehanna by the Emmitsburg route; another by Chambersburg. Accounts from him last night state that there was no enemy west of Frederick. A cavalry force (about 100) guarded the Monocacy Bridge, which was barricaded. You will, of course, take charge of Jenkins' brigade, and give him necessary instructions. All supplies taken in Maryland must be by authorized staff officers for their respective departments – by no one else. They will be paid for, or receipts for the same given to the owners. I will send you a general order on this subject, which I wish you to see is strictly complied with."[18]

At 7 p.m. Longstreet wrote to Stuart: "General Lee has inclosed to me this letter for you to be forwarded to you, provided you can be spared from my front, and provided I think that you can move across the Potomac without disclosing our plans. He speaks of your leaving, via Hopewell Gap, and passing by the rear of the enemy. If you can get through by that route, I think that you will be less likely to indicate what our plans are than if you should cross by passing to our rear. I forward the letter of instructions with these suggestions. Please advise me of the condition of affairs before you leave, and order General Hampton – whom I suppose you will leave here in command – to report to me at Millwood, either by letter or in person, as may be most agreeable to him." In a postscript he added: "I think that your passage of the Potomac by our rear at the present moment will, in a measure, disclose our plans. You had better not leave us, therefore, unless you can take the proposed route in rear of the enemy."[19]

The dilemma facing Lee was that most of his army had passed behind Stuart's screening cavalry and gotten across, or closer to the Potomac than the horsemen, while now he really wanted most of his cavalry out front, up in Pennsylvania, screening the advance. So how could the cavalry get there? If it took the same route as the infantry was taking, it would be at the rear of the army, delayed by long columns of wagons, guns and infantry, instead of up front where it was needed. Longstreet, moreover, was afraid that, if the cavalry moved by way of the Shenandoah Valley fords before the infantry crossed, it would make it evident to Hooker that Lee's whole army was going to cross.

However, Major John Mosby, having discovered that the

various Union corps were rather widely dispersed, had told Stuart, and Stuart had told Lee, that there was enough room between the Federal camps for Stuart to pass behind the westernmost corps – between those and others back around Fairfax – and cross the Potomac at Seneca Ford before the Federals could do much to stop him. He could then head straight north up into Pennsylvania to link up with Ewell. This plan also had the virtue of appealing to Stuart's penchant for doing the bold and the unexpected, while affording possible opportunities of wreaking havoc on poorly defended rear areas of Hooker's army and diverting his attention from what Lee's other forces were doing. As Mosby later put it, when Stuart learned of "the scattered condition of Hooker's corps, he determined, with the approval of General Lee, to pass around, or rather through, them, as the shortest route to reaching Ewell."[20]

Lee also wrote to Ewell that day: "If you are ready to move, you can do so. I think your best course will be toward the Susquehanna, taking the routes by Emmitsburg, Chambersburg, and McConnellsburg. Your [wagon] trains had better be, as far as possible, kept on the center route. You must get command of your cavalry, and use it in gathering supplies, obtaining information, and protecting your flanks. If necessary, send a staff officer to remain with General Jenkins. It will depend upon the quantity of supplies obtained in that country whether the rest of the army can follow. There may be enough for your command, but none for the others. Every exertion should, therefore, be made to locate and secure them. Beef we can drive with us, but bread we cannot carry, and must secure it in the country. . . . I am much gratified at the success which has attended your movements, and feel assured, if they are conducted with the same energy and circumspection, it will continue. Your progress and direction will, of course, depend upon the development of circumstances. If Harrisburg comes within your means, capture it. General A. P. Hill arrived yesterday in the vicinity of Berryville. I shall move him on to-day, if possible."

In a second note to Ewell, written at 3:30 p.m., Lee said: "After dispatching my letter, learning that the enemy had not renewed his attempts of yesterday to break through the Blue Ridge, I directed General R. H. Anderson's division [of Hill's 3rd Corps] to commence its march toward Shepherdstown. It will reach there to-morrow. I also directed General Stuart, should the enemy have so far retired from his front as to permit of the departure of a portion of the cavalry, to march with three brigades across the Potomac, and place himself on your right and in communication with you, keep you advised of the movements of the enemy, and assist in collecting supplies for the army. I have not heard from him since. I also directed Imboden, if opportunity offered, to cross the Potomac, and perform the same offices on your left."[21]

Ewell's forces were already on the move that same day. Early's Division marched through Boonsborough to Cashtown, Maryland, that day, [not Cashtown, Pennsylvania], where it was joined by the 17th Virginia Cavalry of Jenkins' Brigade – the regiment that had gone to Mercersburg and McConnellsburg. Ewell's other two divisions marched up the center of the Cumberland Valley, heading for Greencastle.

At Scotland, Pennsylvania, the railroad bridge was repaired by 4 a.m. on the 22nd. The 71st New York broke camp about 8 a.m. and reached Chambersburg at 11, where the citizens gathered to cheer the soldiers and set out tables of food for them. It was, therefore, well after noon when the 71st took position on the Waynesborough road a mile southeast of the town. A civilian scout had warned General Knipe that Rebel cavalry had been in Waynesborough the day before – a detached company of Jenkins' Brigade. Knipe sent two of the naval guns to join the 71st but took position himself with the 8th New York on the road running south to Greencastle and Hagerstown. He issued some extra arms that had been brought along to civilian volunteers and attached these men to the 8th, whose colonel then sent them out to serve as advanced pickets for his regiment. That afternoon a woman dressed in mourning attire came into the Union camp, asking a lot of silly questions. Some of the home guard suspected she was really a man in disguise and a Rebel spy; they wanted to arrest her, but the colonel of the 8th declined to do so, and eventually she went off to the south. By mid-afternoon Knipe began receiving messages from Captain Boyd's cavalry, now almost as far south as Greencastle, that the Confederates south of there were beginning to stir.

This was because Jenkins was in the process of concentrating most of his brigade in the area between Greencastle and Hagerstown. And at 10 a.m. his troopers were overtaken by Rodes' infantry division, moving north at last, followed by Johnson's Division. Jenkins took over the lead and sent one company up the road to see what lay ahead. Its orders were, if it should meet any Federals, to fake a panicked retreat and lure them onto the main body of the brigade, which would ambush them. Not far out of Greencastle the lone company was spotted by some of Boyd's cavalry, who promptly charged, and the Rebels feigned retreat as ordered. The ambush might have worked, for the rest of Jenkins' men were out of sight, lying in a wheatfield just around a bend in the road, but Boyd, already suspicious, spotted Rodes' infantry in the distance and did not follow any farther. Rodes' men were tearing down fences to clear the way for the artillery to go into position for a major fight, because a local farmer had told Rodes that General McClellan was marching south to meet him with 40,000 men – a claim lent some verisimilitude by the fact that some Northern politicians and newspapers had been clamoring for the return of McClellan in the present emergency.

After an exchange of fire with Jenkins' troopers, Boyd fell back to the north, reaching Chambersburg at about 3 p.m., where he informed Knipe of the large Confederate force he had seen near Greencastle. Knipe sent orders for half the 71st New York to come to the support of the 8th, but at about 3:30, having seen no signs of the Rebels, he decided to go looking for them, riding south with his staff, with the 8th New York following behind. Two and half miles farther south he came to a slight rise, where he stopped to study the area ahead. There he asked a passing civilian whether there were any other roads by which the Confederates at Greencastle could approach Chambersburg and was informed that there were two others. Fearing for his flanks, he pulled back again, and at Chambersburg received an order from Couch to get his railroad train safely back across the bridge at Scotland. Not willing to be left alone in front of Lee's entire army (for all he knew) without a train to retreat on, he ordered his little brigade to get on the train now and withdraw to Carlisle, halfway back to Harrisburg. In their rush to leave, his men left behind their tents, their rations, and some extra clothes as well as some weapons, including two of the naval howitzers. But the home guards, being left behind, managed to save the guns and put them on the train before it left. The company of the Invalid Corps, now calling itself the Patapsco Guards, was also left behind, as was the other half of the 71st New York. The latter set out to march for Shippensburg.

That detached company of Jenkins' Brigade – Company D of the 14th Virginia Cavalry – encountered the first real Union resistance in Pennsylvania that day. While riding eastward on the Chambersburg Pike, near a village called Monterey, they came upon some Federal cavalry which seemed inclined to fight. The Rebel commander, Captain Robert B. Moorman, deployed his men and engaged in a brief fire-fight, in which no one was hurt on either side, and eventually decided he was outnumbered. (In fact he was up against a company of local militia cavalry, a company of mounted home guards, and part of the 1st Troop of the Philadelphia City Cavalry, a famous militia outfit dating back to the Revolutionary War.) Not wanting to risk losing the livestock he had rounded up, he turned back to rejoin Jenkins.

Meanwhile, at 10 that morning Couch had wired Schenck: "Your dispatch about arresting Milroy is received. He cannot be relieved at this moment." At 5:30 p.m. he wired Secretary Stanton: "Rodes' division of infantry are reported as entering Greencastle at 12:30 p.m. this day. Their cavalry advancing upon Chambersburg."[22] He also sent a letter to Stanton that day, in which he said: "In case the rebels advance in large force, I believe from my present knowledge of the Susquehanna that we can prevent them crossing from its junction with the Juniata to the

Maryland line. You will readily understand what kind of a force I have, when a few regiments, with a sprinkling of nine-months' men in them, are the veterans. The New York troops look very well, but are without much confidence in themselves. My little artillery is raw; my cavalry the same. I now have two New York regiments [Knipe's], 800 men, at Carlisle; one Pennsylvania regiment near Gettysburg, to harass the enemy, and, if possible, to hold the mountains there. I speak of the quality and condition of my troops, in order that you may not wonder why I do not boldly face them against the rebels in the Cumberland Valley. Milroy is at Bedford and vicinity, with perhaps 2,800 of his old force and 1,000 Pennsylvania militia. He there serves as a threat to any advance in this direction from Chambersburg, besides holding the country. Of course, I would like some old regiments, batteries, &c., but you know if they can be spared from other points. In case Hooker advances, no doubt I might move in co-operation with him and Schenck."[23]

Confederate naval raiders in the captured ship *Tacony* took five fishing schooners off New England that 22nd day of June.

From Richmond, Secretary Seddon wrote to D. H. Hill that day saying he was still sure the Federals had evacuated Suffolk but nevertheless found it hard to believe that they could have even 20,000 men at Yorktown and thought that the most they would do was make a feint toward Richmond and take it if they found it defenseless. To advance on the south side of the James they would have to expose their defenses and supply base at Yorktown. "The prisoners returned by the truce-boat," he added, "have, I fear, through the atrocious barbarity of the enemy, been so infected with small-pox as to render it unsafe to mix them with other troops. You had better have them separated and examined. As far as you deem safe to employ them, act on your suggestion, which is approved."[24]

And, down in Mississippi, General Johnston was writing to Pemberton again. The two Confederates were still able to communicate, but the time required to get messages in and out of the besieged city made it very difficult for them to coordinate their efforts: "General Taylor is sent by General E. K. Smith to co-operate with you from the west bank of the river," he said; "to throw in supplies and to cross with his force, if expedient and practicable. I will have the means of moving toward the enemy in a day or two, and will try to make a diversion in your favor, and, if possible, communicate [directly] with you, though I fear my force is too small to effect the latter. I have only two-thirds of the force you told Messenger Sanders to state to me as the least with which you think I ought to make an attack. If I can do nothing to relieve you, rather than surrender the garrison, endeavor to cross the river at the last moment, if you and General Taylor communicate."[25]

Among Johnston's other worries, Hurlbut kept sending raiding parties from West Tennessee into northern Mississippi to keep the Rebels there too busy to invade his district. A captain of scouts wrote to Johnston that day from Panola describing the situation: "Scout Weaver reported last night the 700 [Federals] from Pocahontas whipped by General [Daniel] Ruggles and driven back toward Memphis and Charleston Railroad. Scout from near Memphis just reports General [James R.] Chalmers engaged enemy near Hernando Saturday, killed 8 or 10, captured 100, and drove the remainder back toward Memphis. Chalmers was on the west side of Coldwater this morning, and [Union] Colonel [Edward] Hatch crossed at Matthews' Ferry late last evening, in pursuit of him, with about 800; burned the bridge after him. Colonel [Green L.] Blythe was following this morning after the enemy; he will be delayed somewhat in crossing Coldwater, but will be in time to render assistance to General Chalmers, if required. Colonel [Robert] McCulloch was in pursuit of another column of the enemy that went through Luxahoma toward LaGrange. The remaining column of the enemy crossed at Hernando Ferry and went toward Memphis."[26]

Although Johnston was at that time only planning to start a move in a few days, the Federals, seeing signs of his preparations, thought he was already making his move. As Charles Dana reported to Secretary Stanton that day and a few days later, the report of a spy and a small cavalry fight at Bridgeport, on the Big Black River north of Vicksburg, were the immediate causes of Union suspicions that Johnston was coming. Grant wrote to Sherman that day: "Information just received indicates that the enemy are crossing Big Black River, and intend marching against us by way of Bear Creek. They probably will start out to-morrow. I have ordered Parke to move out with four brigades to support his cavalry and hold the enemy as near Big Black River as possible until their position is clearly defined, when we can draw all our forces from Snyder's Bluff and the forces previously indicated here to their support. Tuttle's division [of Sherman's 15th Corps] should be marched out within supporting distance of Parke at once. You will go and command the entire force. Your wagon train can move from wherever you may be to Lake's Landing or Snyder's Bluff, whichever may be the most convenient for supplies and ordnance stores. When on the ground you can draw troops from Snyder's Bluff and the three brigades designated from McPherson's corps directly, without communicating through headquarters. Should any [further] forces become necessary, I can take them from our left by leaving that in the same condition it was before the arrival of Lauman and Herron."[27]

Grant followed up his initial order to Parke – which was to "Move out early to-morrow morning, or sooner, if you can" – saying: "Sherman goes out from here with five brigades and Osterhaus' division [of the 13th Corps], subject to his orders, besides. In addition to this, another division, 5,000 strong, is notified to be in readiness to move on notice. In addition to this,

I can spare still another division, 6,000 strong, if they should be required. We want to whip Johnston at least 15 miles off, if possible."[28]

He told Admiral Porter: "There is every indication of Joe Johnston making an attack within the next forty-eight hours. I have given all the necessary orders to meet him some 25 miles out, Sherman commanding. As Johnston undoubtedly communicates with the garrison at Vicksburg and the troops west of the Mississippi, there is probably an understanding by which there may be a simultaneous attack upon Young's Point, our lines here, and by Johnston on the outside. I will direct General Dennis to be vigilant, and not allow the enemy to approach without timely notice to his troops. Milliken's Bend, in such case, may come in for a visit also. I would think it advisable, therefore, to keep one gunboat there. My hands will be very full here in case of an attack. I will direct General Dennis, therefore, to consult with you in all matters relating to defenses on the west side of the river."[29]

Dana wrote to Stanton that morning and, besides informing him of Grant sending Sherman out to meet Johnston, said: "Ord is working very hard to bring up the lines where McClernand left them behind, but it will take some time to remedy the disorder which that incompetent commander produced in every part of the corps he has left."[30]

Captain Hickenlooper's notes for the 22nd say: "We reached the rebel fort to-day at 10 o'clock with main trench, and cleared away a place to commence mining operations. Experienced considerable annoyance to-day from rebel hand-grenades thrown among the workmen."[31] After the war he wrote: "The general plan of conducting the work with flying-sap by night and deepening and widening by day was pushed forward with the utmost energy until June 22d, when the head of the sap reached the outer ditch surrounding the fort. A few days previous an order had been issued for all men in the corps having a practical knowledge of coal-mining to report to the chief engineer. Out of those reporting thirty-six of the strongest and most experienced were selected and divided into two shifts for day and night duty, and each shift was divided into three reliefs. On the night of the 22d these men, properly equipped with drills, short-handled picks, shovels, etc. . . . commenced the mining operations by driving a gallery, four feet in width by five feet in height, in at right angles to the face of the parapet of the fort. Each relief worked an hour at a time, two picking, two shoveling, and two handing back the grain-sacks filled with earth, which were deposited in the ditch until they could be carried back."[32]

"On the night of the twenty-second of June," Sergeant Tunnard wrote, "a couple of Georgia regiments charged a Federal breastwork, about fifty yards in their front, which had been thrown up the night before, and contained a regiment of the enemy. They succeeded in dislodging this force at the point of the bayonet and captured a number of prisoners with very slight loss. The work was filled up and the spades and shovels of the enemy were taken and brought in."[33] The lieutenant colonel of the Federal regiment tried to avoid capture by playing dead, which worked until the Rebels started filling in the ditch, at which point he decided he didn't want to be buried alive. "Thus passes the fifth week of the dreadful siege," a Confederate chaplain wrote. "No relief yet. Our men are discouraged, though some are yet hopeful. . . ."[34]

Up in Middle Tennessee, General Bragg wrote a friendly letter to Joe Johnston that day, indicating that he was at last well from a prolonged illness brought on by "the long-continued excitement of mind and body" he had been subjected to, not only as commander of the Army of Tennessee but because his wife had been dreadfully ill. He said that, as far as he could tell, Rosecrans' army had not been weakened by any detachments but that most of Burnside's forces had been sent to Grant. "Hearing [of] the evacuation of Kentucky, I ordered Morgan's division at once to move into that State, and asked Buckner to let [Brigadier General John] Pegram co-operate. Morgan, as usual, was not ready; wanted a week, but was refused and ordered off. He did not get off, however, as he never has obeyed any order to move in less time. Before he crossed the Cumberland I hear of Pegram's rapid retreat before an inferior force – a mere raid – and in a short time the enemy appear at Loudon bridge – about 2,000 mounted infantry." After telling more about Sanders' raid and negotiations with Buckner over who should garrison the southern part of East Tennessee, he complained of the latter general (complaining was one of his major talents), "It seems he has been to Richmond and arranged matters his own way." Then he added, "I feel most acutely for you, general, in the position in which you find yourself. Great ends to be secured, high expectations formed, and most inadequate means furnished."[35]

Word of Morgan's intended raid had already reached Union authorities, for Burnside wired General Hartsuff, commander of his 23rd Corps, that day: "Keep all your cavalry ready to move at a moment's notice. If Morgan attempts to enter Kentucky he must be pursued and broken to pieces, if possible."[36] Also, Captain Hines had evidently returned to Indiana, for Burnside was also writing to Halleck that day: "The rebel raid of Friday and Saturday into Indiana, which was pretty well broken to pieces by our troops, has been followed by one much more formidable, which crossed yesterday, and was last heard from within 5 miles of the Ohio and Mississippi Railroad. I have sent troops both from Indianapolis and Louisville, but can hardly hope to prevent the burning of some of the important bridges on the railroad. These people are conducted by the sympathizers of Southern Indiana. Kentucky is to-day a more loyal State than either Indiana, Ohio, or Illinois. Within the last two or three weeks, rebel spies, recruiting officers, and mail-couriers, who have been before effectually checked, have been in full operation. I can see no reason why a stringent policy should not extend over these three States as well as Kentucky."[37]

Clement Vallandigham, the Copperhead politician from Ohio who had been banished to the Confederacy, reached Bermuda that day, a way point in a roundabout return to his home state, where he was a Democratic candidate for governor.

At Port Hudson, on the 22nd, the 28th Maine attacked the Confederate center but was repulsed. Before dawn the next day, two Union regiments tried to take a Rebel sally port on the Plains Store road by surprise, but the Rebels detected them in time and drove them back.

Farther down in Louisiana that next day, 23 June, the Confederates were moving against positions that had been left weakly defended while Banks was besieging Port Hudson. Brashear City – where the railroad crossed Berwick Bay and from which Banks had begun his campaign against Port Hudson two months before – still held an immense store of Union supplies. But when most of its garrison had been rushed over to Thibodeaux to defend the railroad from Major's raiders, only about 300 men had been left to defend it plus as many more convalescent wounded, mostly unarmed. The Federals who had fought off Major's attack near Thibodeaux were trying to get back to Brashear, but Major's force was in their way. The Union commanders did not realize that there were other Rebels in the area also, but during the night of 22-23 June about 325 Rebels under Major Sherod Hunter rowed a flotilla of small boats down Grand Lake and landed in the thick swamps behind Brashear City while newly promoted Brigadier General Thomas Green moved other units into the woods just across Berwick Bay from the city. On the morning of the 23rd, Green's artillery opened fire while Hunter's men waded through swamps up to their waists to attack the city's rear. The town's defenses all faced the water and were open on the inland side, so the Federals soon surrendered, and over two million dollars of supplies fell into Confederate hands.

∽ **Endnotes** ∽

1   Scott Bowden and Bill Ward, *Last Chance for Victory* (Conshohocken PA, 2001), 138.
2   *OR*, I:27:III:910.
3   Ibid., I:27:III:911.

4   Ibid., I:27:III:249.
5   Ibid., I:27:III:251.
6   Ibid., I:27:III:252.
7   Ibid., I:27:III:253.
8   Ibid., I:27:III:248-9.
9   Ibid., I:27:III:244.
10 Ibid., I:27:III:245.
11 Ibid., I:27:II:690.
12 Ibid., I:27:I:615.
13 Stephen Z. Starr, *The Union Cavalry in the Civil War* (Baton Rouge, 1879), I:410.
14 *OR*, I:27:I:912.
15 Ibid., I:27:III:258.
16 Ibid., I:27:I:913.
17 Ibid., I:27:II:692.
18 Ibid., I:27:III:913.
19 Ibid., I:27:III:915.
20 Bowden and Ward, *Last Chance for Victory*, 103.
21 *OR*, I:27:III:914-5.
22 Ibid., I:27:III:263.
23 Ibid., I:27:III:264.
24 Ibid., I:27:III:917.
25 Ibid., I:24:III:971-2.
26 Ibid., I:24:III:972.
27 Ibid., I:24:III:428.
28 Ibid.
29 Ibid., I:24:III:429.
30 Ibid., I:24:I:106.
31 Ibid., I:24:II:202.
32 Hickenlooper, "The Vicksburg Mine," in *B&L* III:540-1.
33 Hoehling, *Vicksburg: 47 Days of Siege*, 212.
34 Ibid., 208.
35 *OR*, I:52:II:500.
36 Ibid., I:23:I:443-4.
37 Ibid., I:23:I:397-8.

Part Three
ADVANCES: NORTH AND SOUTH, EAST AND WEST

CHAPTER 14

"Few Skirmishes Ever Equaled It"

23 – 24 June 1863

In Mississippi on the 23rd, Pemberton was finally considering the possibility of giving up his position at Vicksburg in order to save his troops for further use – something he should have thought of before allowing himself to be besieged, and every day since – and he wrote to Johnston that day: "If I cut my way out, this important position is lost, and many of my men, too. If I cannot cut my way out, both position and all my men are lost. This we cannot afford. Should suggest the probability of Grant's being open to terms that can result more to our advantage than either of the above actions. Not knowing your force or plans, he may accede to your proposition to pass this army out with all its arms and equipage. This proposal would come with greater prospects of success and better grace from you, while it necessarily could not come at all from me. You could make the showing of my ability and strength to still hold out for several weeks longer, which, together with his impression regarding your strength, might operate upon him to comply with your terms. While I make this suggestion, I still renew my hope of your being, by force of arms, enabled to act with me in saving this vital point. I will strain every nerve to hold out, if there is hope of our ultimate relief, for fifteen days longer."[1]

Grant was writing to Sherman that day: "In addition to the troops with you and at Snyder's, I have notified Herron's and A. J. Smith's divisions to be in readiness to move at a moment's notice. In addition to this, two more brigades can be taken from your corps without breaking the line investing Vicksburg. Should Johnston come, we want to whip him, if the siege has to be raised to do it. Use all the forces indicated above as you deem most advantageous; and should more be required, call on me, and they will be furnished, to the last man here and at Young's Point."[2] But Sherman wrote to Grant that "I hear nothing of Johnston at all; no trace of him or signs of his approach.... After satisfying myself that there is, or is not, a purpose on his part to cross over, I will communicate the fact; but, no matter what his strength, he must come by narrow roads, and I have as many men as can be handled on such grounds. If I conclude he does not design to come in by Birdsong Ferry or the ford above, I will blockade it, so as to force him to come on the main ridge within striking distance of Haynes' Bluff, so that we won't care if he comes or not. ... On the best evidence now procurable, he is not coming this way, or at this time."[3]

Another threat to Grant's rear, this time his supply line via the Mississippi River, was made known to him that day in a message from General Dennis on the west bank of the river. This informed him that four boats coming down the river had been fired upon by a Rebel battery of 6-pounder guns, as well as musketry, as they came down the river, and that Confederate deserters had been picked up who said they belonged to the command of Major General Sterling Price, last known to be in command at Little Rock, Arkansas. They said that all of Price's force except one brigade was on the move, probably heading for Helena, on the west bank of the river in the northeast part of Arkansas, where there was a Union garrison belonging to Grant's department. They said the battery firing at boats belonged to Price's command and would soon be joined by another. They also said that one of Price's brigades, from Missouri, consisted of volunteers, but that the rest were conscripts from Arkansas and that "it takes as many men to keep them in [the ranks] as to do the fighting.... They say that if the people of Arkansas could vote, they would vote the State into the Union by two-thirds majority."[4] Hurlbut was writing to Rawlins that day from Memphis that he had heard that Price was at Jacksonport, Arkansas, far to the northwest of Helena; he wrote the same to Halleck and added that "he meditates an attack on New Madrid," Missouri, another town along the river, north of Memphis and south of St. Louis.[5]

The weather at Vicksburg turned bad again that day, as clouds that had been gathering all the day before let loose a driving rain. A Confederate officer's wife recorded how the cave she was living in was suddenly inundated with water and how her husband told her, "with a grave face, of the poor soldiers he had seen in the rifle pits that morning, standing in water – some with little pieces of carpet drawn around them; others with nothing but their thin clothes, which were saturated; and there they would lie through the day, with only the meal of yesterday to sustain them."[6]

Captain Hickenlooper's miners were soon underground and out of the rain that morning, and they dug twelve feet into the hillside under Fort Hill on this their first day of work. "Today is the 37th since we have been surrounded," a Confederate doctor noted, "and no improvement in the situation, except that the mortars have ceased firing. I think they must have worn out, as the last shots fired all fell short. The shelling from the lines continued. . . . Rations very short. We are all in good spirits and look for help *one of these days.*"[7]

General McClernand reached Cairo, Illinois, that day and wired President Lincoln a message of two sentences: "I have been relieved for an omission of my adjutant. Hear me."[8]

Lee wrote again to Jeb Stuart that day: "If General Hooker's army remains inactive, you can leave two brigades to watch him, and withdraw with the three others, but should he not [sic] appear to be moving northward, I think you had better withdraw this side of the mountain to-morrow night, cross at Shepherdstown next day, and move over to Frederickstown [Frederick, Maryland]. You will however, be able to judge whether you can pass around their army without hinderance, doing them all the damage you can, and cross the river east of the mountains. In either case, after crossing the river, you must move on and feel the right of Ewell's troops, collecting information, provisions, &c. Give instructions to the commander of the brigades left behind, to watch the flank and rear of the army, and (in the event of the enemy leaving their front) retire from the mountains west of the Shenandoah, leaving sufficient pickets to guard the passes, and bringing everything clean along the Valley, closing upon the rear of the army. As regards the movements of the two brigades of the enemy moving toward Warrenton [Stahel's], the commander of the brigades to be left in the mountains must do what he can to counteract them [in fact, Stahel was ordered that day to return to Fairfax Court House that night, leaving one less worry for Stuart or whoever he left behind], but I think the sooner you cross into Maryland, after to-morrow, the better. The movements of Ewell's corps are as stated in my former letter. Hill's first division will reach the Potomac to-day, and Longstreet will follow to-morrow. Be watchful and circumspect in all your movements."[9] Lee's military secretary, who composed this message, said later that he had told Lee he didn't think it was necessary to so repeat his orders to Stuart, but Lee had said he was anxious about the matter and wanted to guard against any error.

"The season is now so far advanced," Lee wrote to President Davis that day, "as to render it improbable that the enemy will undertake active operations on the Carolina and Georgia coast before the return of frost. This impression is confirmed by the statements contained in Northern papers, that part of General Hunter's force has gone to re-enforce General Banks, and that Admiral Foote, the successor of Admiral DuPont in the command of the South Atlantic fleet, lies dangerously ill, a circumstance that will tend further to embarrass any designs the enemy may entertain of operating against the cities of the seaboard. Federal papers of the 19th allude to the frequent arrival or departure of troops and munitions at Old Point [Fort Monroe], and those of the 20th announce the arrival of General Peck and staff in Washington, without indicating the object of his visit, further than it may be connected with the movements just referred to. At this distance, I can see no benefit to be derived from maintaining a large force on the southern coast during the unhealthy months of the summer and autumn, and I think that a part, at least, of the troops in North Carolina, and those under General Beauregard, can be employed at this time to great advantage in Virginia.

"If an army could be organized under the command of General Beauregard, and pushed forward to Culpeper Court-House, threatening Washington from that direction, it would not only effect a diversion most favorable for this army, but would, I think, relieve us of any apprehension of an attack upon Richmond during our absence. The well known anxiety of the Northern Government for the safety of its capital would induce it to retain a large force for its defense, and thus sensibly relieve the opposition to our advance. Last summer, you will remember, that troops were recalled from Hilton Head, North Carolina, and Western Virginia for the protection of Washington, and there can be little doubt that if our present movements northward are accompanied by a demonstration on the south side of the Potomac, the coast would be again relieved, and the troops now on the Peninsula and south of the Potomac be withdrawn.

"If success should attend the operations of this army, and what I now suggest would greatly increase the probability of that result, we might even hope to compel the recall of some of the enemy's troops from the west.

"I think it most important that, whatever troops be used for the purpose I have named, General Beauregard be placed in command, and that his department be extended over North Carolina and Virginia. His presence would give magnitude to even a small demonstration, and tend greatly to perplex and confound the enemy. Of course, the larger the force that we can employ the better, but should you think it imprudent to withdraw a part of General Beauregard's army for the purpose indicated, I think good results would follow from sending forward, under General Beauregard, such of the troops about Richmond and in North Carolina as could be spared for a short time.

"The good effects of beginning to assemble an army at Culpeper Court-House would, I think, soon become apparent, and the movement might be increased in importance as the result might appear to justify. Should you agree with me, I need not say that it is desirable that the execution of the plan proposed should immediately begin. The enemy will hear of it soon enough, and a proper reticence on the part of our papers will cause them to attribute greater importance to it. I need not mention the benefit that the troops themselves would derive from being transferred to a more healthy climate."[10] Other than this repetition of Lee's oft-voiced, oft-disproved theory that the Southern coast was too unhealthy to operate in during the summer, this was not a bad idea – a phantom army of only a few brigades in the Culpeper area might have kept some Union units on the defensive that were soon sent to the Army of the Potomac while remaining close enough to Richmond to be rushed to its defense if necessary – but it was rather late to be bringing it up now.

However, Lee wanted to have his cake and eat it too, or at least to have a new army and yet have returned to him all his detached units, from which one might have been created. He wrote that same day to General Cooper at Richmond: "Upon leaving Fredericksburg, a regiment of General Pettigrew's brigade was sent to relieve General Corse's brigade, at Hanover Junction, to enable the latter to rejoin his division. General Corse was subsequently ordered to remain at the Junction, and I have not heard whether he has yet been sent forward. If not, I think the regiment will suffice for a guard at that point, and wish Corse's brigade to be ordered to rejoin its division under General Pickett as soon as possible. He will march by Culpeper Court-House, and thence through Chester Gap to Winchester, where he will be instructed by what route to proceed. I wish to have every man that can be spared, and desire that Cooke's brigade may [also] be sent forward by the same route, if it is not needed at Richmond. I think there will be no necessity for keeping a large number of troops at that place, especially if the plan of assembling an army at Culpeper Court-House under General Beauregard be adopted."[11]

Moreover, taking units away from Richmond to assemble at Culpeper Court House would be difficult when Federal forces were threatening Richmond just then. General Dix, commander of the Union's Department of Virginia, telegraphed Halleck from

Fort Monroe at 8 p.m. on the 23rd: "I have moved a considerable force up the York, and am just leaving to join it. I will communicate with you daily henceforth. I hope to land at the White House [plantation] to-morrow. It was known at Richmond, as I learn through our flag-of-truce boat, that we were sending troops from Suffolk the evening of the day the first regiment left. It is no doubt known now that we are going up to the White House or West Point."[12] Dix sent a force of about 1,000 cavalry and two howitzers, under Colonel Samuel P. Spear, with orders to disembark at White House, if possible, and proceed up the south, or Richmond side of the Pamunkey River and attack the railroads running north out of Richmond. Dix's infantry had to wait for the return of the transports that carried the cavalry.

More good information on the positions of Lee's various units reached Hooker that day, from Colonel Sharpe and General Stahel, but, of course, having accurate information and knowing that it is accurate are two different things. His army remained static, facing west toward the Blue Ridge while officers checked the fords of the Potomac near Leesburg in case a move to the north side of that river became necessary. Engineers had a pontoon bridge laid near there by then and more pontoons on the way from Washington, but Hooker made no move to send any sizable body of troops to the Maryland side of the river. He did send orders to Brigadier General S. W. Crawford, who commanded about the only veteran infantry force in the Department of Washington, to be ready to move on short notice. Crawford commanded a unique outfit, the Pennsylvania Reserve Division. In the early days of the war, Pennsylvania had raised even more troops than the Federal government had wanted, so it had formed the excess thirteen regiments into a division of its own. After the Union's disastrous defeat at the first battle of Bull Run, this division had been taken into Federal service after all, the only unit of that size in the Army of the Potomac composed completely of troops from a single state. Meade and Reynolds had originally been brigade commanders in that division (Ord, now down in Mississippi with Grant, had commanded the other brigade), and each had commanded the division at different times. It had served in both the 1st and 5th Corps, and after the battle of Fredericksburg it had been transferred to the Department of Washington to rest and refit. Now it was being called upon again.

Hooker also laid claim to another unit in the Department of Washington that day, though in this case not veterans. Brigadier General George Stannard, commander of the 2nd Vermont Brigade, consisting of five large regiments (about 700 men each) of nine-months volunteers, all from the Green Mountain state, received orders that day attaching his brigade to the Army of the Potomac. He was currently guarding the line of the Occoquon River, south of Washington, and its tributary, Bull Run, and, as an aide recorded, "He was to hold his line till all the rest of the army has passed on; and then he was to follow the column to the north, and report to General Reynolds, commanding the First Corps." [13] However, these regiments' enlistments would be ending in a few weeks.

Schenck's headquarters issued orders that day for Milroy to collect his troops and bring them to Baltimore. But General Couch wired Milroy that same day: "A force of the enemy's cavalry occupy Chambersburg. Keep your scouts well out in that direction, in order to cut them off in case they advance too far."[14] Jenkins' cavalry did, in fact, return to Chambersburg that day, and again it took up positions on Shirk's Hill, north of town. One-legged General Ewell passed through Greencastle that day riding in a carriage. A newspaperman spotted him, "closely examining a map. He appeared pale and delicate."[15] Early's Division continued to follow a road farther east, which took it through Smithburg (or Smithsburg) and Ringgold to Waynesborough, Pennsylvania, that day.

Colonel Sanders' raid into East Tennessee ended that day as his brigade reached Boston, Kentucky. But the Confederates in Tennessee immediately had something even more serious to worry about, for Rosecrans' Army of the Cumberland finally began its long-awaited advance on 23 June.

It had been resting, reorganizing and generally getting ready for almost half a year, since the bloody and indecisive Battle of Stones River, fought near Murfreesborough, some 30-odd miles southeast of Nashville. Failing to drive Rosecrans back to Nashville, the Confederates had retreated after that battle another 40 miles or so to the southeast. "Their main base of supplies was at Chattanooga," Rosecrans later explained in his report, "but a vastly superior cavalry force had enabled them to command all the resources of the Duck River Valley and the country southward. Tullahoma, a large intrenched camp, situated on the 'Barrens,' at the intersection of the Nashville and Chattanooga Railroad with the McMinnville branch, was their main depot.... Its front was covered by the defiles of Duck River – a deep, narrow stream, with but few fords or bridges – and a rough, rocky range of hills which divides the 'Barrens' from the lower level of Middle Tennessee. Bragg's main army occupied a strong position north of Duck River, the infantry extending from Shelbyville to Wartrace, and their cavalry on their right to McMinnville, and on their left to Columbia and Spring Hill, where Forrest was concentrated and threatening Franklin. The position of Bragg's infantry was covered by a range of high, rough, rocky hills, the principal routes passing southward [through it] from Murfreesborough toward Tullahoma and [the] line of the enemy's communications."

He then went on to enumerate and evaluate the various routes by which he could have approached Bragg's position. Starting on his own left, Bragg's right, he could have gone by way of McMinnville, but dismissed that route as too long (75 miles). And other roads between McMinnville and Manchester he dismissed as "so difficult as to be regarded as unsuited for the movement of an army." There was, however, a paved turnpike that led through the intervening range of hills by way of Hoover's Gap "and ascending to the 'Barrens' through a long difficult can[y]on called Matt's Hollow" to Manchester. The road to Wartrace ran through Liberty Gap and connected to a road running beside the railroad through Bellbuckle Gap. The road to Shelbyville ran through Guy's Gap. Then there was a dirt road through Middleton and another through Versailles that connected to the Shelbyville-Triune road, "both of which avoid passes and have few defiles. The enemy held all these passes, and his main position in front of Shelbyville was strengthened by a redan line extending from Horse Mountain, on the east, to Duck River, on the west, covered by a line of abatis."[16]

Bragg's Army of Tennessee at that time consisted of two army corps and two cavalry corps. Unlike in the Union Army, where corps were numbered in one sequence for the entire country, in the Confederate service they were numbered separately for each army. So, while there was a 1st, 2nd and 3rd Corps in Lee's army, there was also a 1st and a 2nd Corps in Bragg's. His 1st Corps was commanded by Lieutenant General Leonidas Polk, then aged 57, a graduate of West Point who had soon resigned his commission to enter the ministry. When the war broke out he had been an Episcopal bishop, but he was a good friend of Jefferson Davis, who had been one class behind him at West Point, and soon after the outbreak of war Davis had made him a general in the Confederate Army. However, nobody but Davis seemed to think much of his military talents. As one Rebel solider put it, "He was a very nice man, but of not much use to the army."[17] His major talent was for causing dissension in the ranks of the Army of Tennessee, for he combined his close association with Davis with a penchant for finding fault with General Bragg. The fact that Bragg had many real faults to find made it that much easier for him. But, while Davis liked Polk, he also liked Bragg – although nobody else did – and could not bring himself to remove or reassign either one of them. Back when Grant had first crossed the Mississippi to get at Vicksburg, three of Polk's brigades had been sent to Mississippi, where they now formed part of Joe Johnston's army. This left him with two divisions of four brigades each.

The 2nd Corps of the Army of Tennessee was commanded by William J. Hardee, then 48 years old, a graduate of West Point in the class of 1838 – the same year as Beauregard and eleven years behind Polk. But while Polk had left the army shortly after graduating, Hardee had stayed in the service – reaching the rank of lieutenant colonel – right up until the time he had resigned to join the Confederacy. He had been, at one time, commandant of cadets at West Point and an instructor of tactics there, and his manual of light infantry tactics was the standard text from which many of the officers of both sides learned their trade. He disliked Bragg as much as Polk did but was more subtle in his efforts to undermine his commander – although no less effective at it. Hardee's corps had consisted of two divisions, but one of them, Breckinridge's, had been sent to Mississippi. A new division had been put together for him from a brigade left behind by Breckinridge and some other odds and ends.

Of the two cavalry corps, one, which had been commanded by Van Dorn, was now defunct for all practical purposes, as Van Dorn was dead and one of his two divisions – under William H. "Red" Jackson – had been sent to join Johnston in Mississippi, leaving only Forrest's Division of two brigades to cover the Confederate far left flank. The other cavalry corps, commanded by Joe Wheeler, consisted of three divisions of two brigades each, but Morgan's Division was off chasing Sanders' raiders, after which it would start its own raid, so in practice there were two divisions, of two brigades each, to cover the Confederates' far right.

Forrest and Wheeler were opposites in almost every respect, and did not get along. Forrest, then almost 42, was an uneducated self-made millionaire slave dealer who, after briefly serving as a private, had raised a regiment at his own expense and had risen to his present position by virtue of a true talent for raiding and fighting. Wheeler was only 26, a graduate of the West Point class of 1859, who had impressed Bragg with his fighting qualities, although he also showed a preference for raiding over scouting and fighting. As Rosecrans said, Forrest's division covered Bragg's far left, a fertile area around Columbia, Tennessee, from which Bragg drew some supplies. He could have drawn much more except that the railroad leading south into Alabama and connecting with lines running to Chattanooga was not completely intact. Wheeler's corps extended Bragg's right as far as McMinnville with occasional forays as far as the upper reaches of the Cumberland River. It had the advantage of the branch railroad connecting Tullahoma to McMinnville. Despite all these railroads, Bragg's army was chronically short of supplies, especially forage for its artillery and wagon teams. The area it occupied was not called "The Barrens" without reason.

Although it would seem logical to have expected Rosecrans to advance – if he ever did – along the line of the Nashville & Chattanooga Railroad, to ease his own supply problems, Bragg did not center his two army corps on that line. Instead he stationed only Hardee on the railroad, at Wartrace (with detachments holding Hoover's, Liberty, and Bellbuckle gaps), but Polk's corps was stationed farther west, at the end of another, shorter, branch railroad, at Shelbyville. Bragg's plan, if he ever really had one, seems to have been that, if and when Rosecrans came down the railroad, he would be delayed by Hardee long enough for Polk to attack his right flank. If this was Bragg's plan, he seems to have neglected to inform either Polk or Hardee of it, although some of his staff seems to have been in on it. "Polk's corps was generally estimated by intelligent rebels and Union men at about 18,000, infantry and artillery," Rosecrans said; "Hardee's at 12,000, infantry and artillery – making a total of 30,000 of these arms, and probably 8,000 cavalry."[18] Actual returns show that Polk and Hardee each had about 15,000 infantry, Forrest about 4,000 cavalry and Wheeler about 7,000, not counting Morgan's division.

Rosecrans' Army of the Cumberland, named for the river that runs through Nashville, then consisted of four army corps and one cavalry corps, but two of the three divisions of Major General Gordon Granger's Reserve Corps (an unofficial unit) were garrisoning Nashville and other points it was necessary to hold, leaving only one of its divisions able to maneuver. Rosecrans' largest corps was the 14th (the original designation of his entire army, just as Grant's entire army had once been designated the 13th Corps), commanded by Major General George

H. Thomas. It had four divisions (a fifth having recently been transferred to Granger's corps). The other two corps had three divisions each; they were the 20th Corps, commanded by Major General Alexander McCook, and the 21st, commanded by Major General Thomas L. Crittenden. All these divisions had three brigades each except for one of the divisions of the Reserve Corps on garrison duty, which had only two. The Cavalry Corps had recently been organized to consist of two divisions of two brigades each and was commanded by Major General David S. Stanley. Thomas had about 23,000 infantry, McCook about 14,000, Crittenden about 15,000, Granger about 6,000 in his one movable division, and Stanley about 10,500 cavalry. So while the two armies were roughly equal in cavalry, Rosecrans had almost a 2:1 advantage in infantry.

Virginia-born Thomas, then almost 47, was one of several Southern-born officers in the Union Army; he had graduated from West Point in 1840 – the same class as Sherman. Charles Dana, who accompanied this army in a later campaign, said of Thomas, "He was certainly an officer of the very highest qualities, soldierly and personally. He was a man of the greatest dignity of character. He had more the character of George Washington than any other man I ever knew. At the same time he was a delightful man to be with; there was no artificial dignity about Thomas. . . . He was very set in his opinions, yet he was not impatient with anybody – a noble character."[19] McCook, 33, was one of 17 "Fighting McCooks" in the Union Army (two brothers and their numerous sons) and an 1852 graduate of West Point. Crittenden, just turned 44, was the son of Senator John J. Crittenden of Kentucky (like many Union soldiers from that state, he had a brother in the Confederate army); his education and experience before the war was in the law and business, not the military. Granger was then 40 and had graduated from West Point in 1845, serving in the Regular Army right up to the outbreak of the war; he was inclined to speak his mind and do as he pleased, odd habits for a career soldier. Stanley had just turned 35 on the first of June; he had graduated from West Point in 1848 and been in the Army ever since, mostly in the cavalry branch; although of Northern birth (Ohio) he had been offered, but had refused, a commission in the Confederate Army.

The two army commanders were an interesting study in contrast. Bragg was then 46, Rosecrans 43; Bragg had graduated from West Point in 1837, Rosecrans in 1842 (one year ahead of Grant). Bragg had recently been confirmed in the Episcopal church; Rosecrans was a devout convert to Roman Catholicism. Like many of the senior officers of this war, Bragg had served as a junior officer in the Mexican War, when he had commanded a battery of field artillery (his three lieutenants had been George H. Thomas, John F. Reynolds and D. H. Hill), but he had afterwards taken to civilian life as owner of a Louisiana plantation; Rosecrans had left the Army soon after graduating, to enter business as an architect and civil engineer.

Bragg had succeeded to the command of what was then called the Army of the Mississippi in the spring of 1862, shortly after the battle of Shiloh, when Beauregard had been incapacitated by illness, moving it by a roundabout route to Middle Tennessee, then into Kentucky and back. Rosecrans had provided much of the brains and energy that had liberated West Virginia in the war's first year, though McClellan, his superior there, had received most of the credit; then he had briefly served under Grant before being awarded, in the fall of 1862, the command of what had previously been known as the Army of the Ohio. Bragg was a strict disciplinarian, which did not go over well with his highly democratic citizen-soldiers, and a quarrelsome nit-picker with his subordinates. It was said that, in the old pre-War Regular Army, he had even quarreled with himself on paper while simultaneously holding down the jobs of company commander and post quartermaster, denying his own request for supplies and then complaining about the unjust denial. Rosecrans, on the other hand, Charles Dana said, "abounded in friendliness and approbativeness, [but] was greatly lacking in firmness and steadiness of will."[20] Yet, at Stones River, he had proven Gordon Granger's dictum that "The battle is neither to the swift nor the strong but to him that holds on to the end," outlasting Bragg in a contest of wills after both sides had been badly battered.[21]

"Positive information from various sources," Rosecrans said, "concurred to show the enemy intended to fight us in his intrenchments at Shelbyville, should we advance by that route, and that he would be in good position to retreat if beaten, and so retard our pursuit through the narrow, winding roads from that place which lead up to the 'Barrens,' and thus inflict severe loss without danger to their own line of retreat to the mountains toward their base. I was determined to render useless their intrenchments, and, if possible, secure their line of retreat by turning their right and moving on the railroad bridge across Elk River. This would compel a battle on our own ground or drive them on a disadvantageous line of retreat. To accomplish this it was necessary to make Bragg believe we could advance on him by the Shelbyville route, and to keep up the impression, if possible, until we had reached Manchester with the main body of the army, as this point must be reached over a single practicable road passing through Hoover's Gap, a narrow way 3 miles in length between high hills, and then through Matt's Hollow, a gorge 2 miles long, with scarce room anywhere for wagons to pass each other. These passes were occupied by the enemy but 8 miles from Hardee's headquarters, not more than 16 miles from their left at Shelbyville.

"The plan was, therefore, to move General Granger's command to Triune, and thus create the impression of our intention to advance on them by the Shelbyville and Triune pikes, while cavalry movements and an infantry advance toward Woodbury would seem to be feints designed by us to deceive Bragg and conceal our supposed real designs on their left, where the topography and the roads presented comparatively slight obstacles and afforded great facilities for moving in force. . . . On the 23rd of June, Major-General Granger, under orders, sent [Brigadier] General [Robert B.] Mitchell, with his cavalry division, on the Eagleville and Shelbyville pike, to make a furious attack on the enemy's cavalry and drive in their infantry guards on their main line, while

General Granger, with his own troops and [Brigadier General John M.] Brannon's division [of the 14th Corps], moved, with ten days' rations, to Salem [southwest of Murfreesborough], sending his sick and baggage to the camps at Murfreesborough. On the same day, Palmer's division [of the 21st Corps] and a brigade of cavalry were ordered to move, via Cripple Creek and Readyville, to the vicinity of Bradyville [southeast of Murfreesborough]; his advance to seize the head of the defile leading up to the 'Barrens' by an obscure road leading them to Manchester, by Lumley's Station. All the other troops were ordered to be in readiness to march, with twelve days' rations of bread, coffee, sugar, and salt; six days' meat on the hoof, and six days' pork or bacon. General Mitchell accomplished his work, after a sharp and gallant fight. ... General Granger arrived and took position at Salem, in pursuance of orders. The corps commanders met at headquarters in the evening, when the plan of the movement was explained to them, and each received written orders for his part...."[22]

The plan for the next day, the 24th, involved a complex choreography of moves, the important points of which were: McCook's 20th Corps would move toward Shelbyville but then turn two of its divisions toward Wartrace to seize and hold Liberty Gap; Crittenden's 21st Corps, leaving one division to hold Murfreesborough, would concentrate at Bradyville, threatening McMinnville; Thomas's 14th Corps would advance on the Manchester pike and seize and hold Hoover's Gap. One brigade of cavalry would accompany Crittenden and the rest would attack the Rebel cavalry. "All these movements were executed with commendable promptitude and success," Rosecrans reported, "in the midst of a continuous and drenching rain, which so softened the ground on all the dirt roads as to render them next to impassable. General McCook's taking of Liberty Gap was very gallant and creditable.... General [J. J.] Reynolds had the advance in the Fourteenth Corps, Wilder's mounted brigade leading."[23]

Wilder's four mounted infantry regiments, about 1,500 men, plus a battery of six 3-inch rifles and four little mountain howitzers, were on the road by about 3 a.m., leaving their camp a few miles north of Murfreesborough. They passed through the town and the camps of the foot-bound infantrymen, where bugles and drums were just calling these units into formation, and rode on south. The rain had already started, and as one soldier put it, this was no Presbyterian sprinkle, "but a genuine Baptist downpour."[24] General Stanley of the cavalry later said, "That day the rain set in . . . which, converting the whole surface of the country into a quagmire, has rendered this one of the most arduous, laborious, and distressing campaigns upon man and beast I have ever witnessed."[25]

Wilder's orders were to drive in the Confederate pickets, clearing the way for the rest of the 14th Corps, as far as some Rebel entrenchments at the narrowest part of Hoover's Gap, but he made up his own mind not to stop until forced to. The Rebels, perhaps thinking, logically enough, that if Rosecrans ever did advance it wouldn't be in the middle of a downpour, were not prepared. "We soon came into the camp of a regiment of cavalry," Major James A. Connolly of the 123rd Illinois later remembered, "which was so much surprised by our sudden appearance that they scattered through the woods and over the hills in every direction, every fellow for himself, and all making the best time they could bareback, on foot, and every other way, leaving all their tents, wagons, baggage, commissary stores and indeed everything in our hands."[26] The Confederates had even left behind a cannon, their embroidered silk flag, a signal station, and, most importantly, their line of entrenchments on a hill overlooking the gap. "Learning," Wilder later reported, "that a regiment of cavalry . . . were stationed at the Garrison Fork of Duck River, 1 mile farther on, and that a brigade of infantry were encamped 2 miles to the right, I determined to take the entire gap, and, if possible, hold it until the arrival of the infantry column, now some 6 miles behind us. . . ."[27]

The Confederate regiment that had abandoned its position, the consolidated 1st/3rd Kentucky Cavalry, managed to put together a rear guard of about a dozen men who tried to delay the advancing Federals, but it was about all they could do to stay ahead of Wilder's men. It was, Major Connolly said, "a mad race of pursuers and pursued down that Tennessee road, through mud and rain until exhausted horses and men were glad to stop, but not until we . . . raced after the enemy through the formidable Hoover's Gap and seized it as our own."[28] Part of the 72nd Indiana even went a couple of miles beyond the gap, capturing some wagons and cannon and stopping near the village of Beech Grove to get some tobacco from a store. The sound of drums from a nearby Rebel infantry camp, however, soon informed them that they had gone too far, and they fell back to join the rest of the brigade at the gap.

The drums had come from the camp of Brigadier General William B. Bate's brigade of A. P. Stewart's division of Hardee's corps. About 2 p.m. Bate received an order from Stewart to send two regiments and a battery over toward Beech Grove. Bate soon came upon the colonel of the Kentucky cavalry regiment and was told that Federal "cavalry" had occupied the gap, so he sent back for the rest of his brigade to move up in support. His skirmishers almost cut off two companies of the 72nd Indiana, and his artillery opened fire on them, but they escaped by a circuitous route.

Wilder, meanwhile, deployed his brigade straddling the gap, with the horses held to the rear and the guns of Captain Eli Lily's 18th Indiana Battery covering the road, and sent a courier back to his division commander to report that he held Hoover's Gap. Bate deployed his infantry (3 regiments and 2 battalions) in line of battle with his battery in support, and an artillery duel soon began. "Our regiment lay on the hill side in mud and water," Major Connolly wrote, "the rain pouring down in torrents, while each shell screamed so close to us as to make it seem that the next would tear us to pieces." Then Bate sent forward the 20th Tennessee to take the Union battery, and the 123rd Illinois rose and gave them a volley. The Rebels were staggered but came on again "thinking to reach the battery before our guns can be reloaded," Connolly said. They didn't know, of course, that Wilder's men were all armed with Spencer repeating rifles, and, as Connolly put it, "their charging yell was answered by another terrible volley, and another and another without cessation, until the poor regiment was cut to pieces."

Bate then sent what was left of the 20th Tennessee plus the 37th Georgia behind the cover of some hills to get around the Union right flank. Wilder countered with parts of the 17th Indiana and the 98th Illinois, which he had held in reserve. The division's adjutant then arrived with orders from Reynolds for Wilder to fall back immediately. The foot-sloggers were still miles behind and had stopped to repair a bridge. "I told him," Wilder said later, "I would hold this position against any force, and to tell General Reynolds to come on without hurrying." The adjutant threatened to arrest Wilder for disobeying an order, but Wilder refused to be arrested and told him again to go to Reynolds and say he "could not be driven by any forces that could come at us."[29]

Bate, thinking himself outnumbered 5:1, gave up even trying to drive Wilder away and settled for just preventing him from advancing farther. At about 7 p.m. another brigade of Stewart's Division arrived, commanded by Brigadier General Bushrod Johnson, but, within a half-hour, Wilder also received reinforcements. Major Connolly saw the arrival of "a weary, jaded regiment of infantry, trying to double quick, but it was all they could do to march at all; we greeted them with such lusty cheers as seemed to inspire them with new vigor, and they were soon in position; then came two more regiments of infantry, weary and footsore, but hurrying the best they could."[30] And darkness soon put an end to the fighting.

Generals Thomas and Rosecrans soon arrived, and Thomas grasped Wilder's hand. "You took the responsibility to disobey the order, did you. Thank God for your decision. It would have cost us two thousand lives to have taken this position if you had given it up." J. J. Reynolds soon arrived and didn't seem to be so happy about having his order disobeyed, but Rosecrans told him, "Wilder has done right. Promote him. Promote him."[31] Wilder never was promoted, although eventually he was breveted to brigadier general for his service throughout the war. However, his troops were awarded the name Lightning Brigade in official orders, and soon the Federal government decided it would pay for their Spencer repeating rifles, which Wilder had bought with a bank loan after the men had pledged to repay him in monthly installments. It was a good investment.

At Liberty Gap, the next pass west of Hoover's, Brigadier General Richard Johnson's 2nd Division of McCook's 20th Corps was led by five companies of the 39th Indiana Mounted Infantry. At about 2 p.m. on the 24th these mounted companies ran into solid resistance from about 800 Confederates, so the foot-infantry of Brigadier General August Willich's 1st Brigade took over the lead, pushing the Rebels back to the northern entrance of the Gap. "There," Willich reported, "the enemy had a very strong, and, in front, easily defended position. The hills are steep, to half their heights open, then rocky and covered with woods. I felt the enemy in front to ascertain whether he would make a decided resistance, and found him in force and determined."

Willich deployed his regiments and felt for the Confederate flanks. The Rebels almost outflanked his own left first, but he sent the mounted infantry companies there at the gallop and they arrived just in time "to drive back about 200 infantry, who were advancing toward our flank." In the meantime, one of his regiments, reinforced by two companies of another, "advanced straight up the hill, and, under a murderous fire, drove the enemy before them." The mounted infantry hit the Rebel defenders in the flank, and Willich sent a regiment loaned to him from the next brigade to his own right "to find the weak point, or the end of the enemy's line, then to take the crest of the hill, to swing round toward the left, and advance in the direction of the gap." This move was decisive, for, as Willich reported, "As soon as he had changed front to the left, I advanced with my two reserve regiments through the gap without being further resisted."[32] Johnson's 3rd Brigade then followed up, held off some Confederate reinforcements just coming up – the rest of the brigade to which the defenders belonged – and established a picket line at the south end of the gap. "The affair at Liberty Gap will always be considered a skirmish," Johnson said, "but few skirmishes ever equaled it in severity."[33]

General Sherman wrote to Grant on the 24th from Bear Creek, in the peninsula between the Big Black River and the Yazoo: "Not the sign of an enemy from Post Oak Ridge Post-office to Birdsong Ferry. Every point has been examined to-day, and nothing seen. No sign of an intention to cross anywhere near Bear Creek. I hear Port Hudson is taken; please telegraph me the whole truth."[34] Grant replied: "There is no news of importance from Port Hudson. Garrison still holds out, and have nothing to eat but parched corn to live on. Kirby Smith is trying to relieve them by attacking the point opposite. Banks had two repulses. Loss in killed and wounded, 4,000. The rebels have about 3,000 in the fort, so say deserters."[35]

Grant also wrote to Admiral Porter that day: "I have just received information that the rebel Bledsoe has gone from Yazoo City to a point on the Mississippi shore about 6 miles above Greenville. He has with him about 15 cavalry and a battery of light artillery. My cavalry and spare troops are now out with Sherman, looking for Johnston, so that I cannot well attend to him. Can you send the Marine Brigade up to clean Bledsoe out? and they might land at Greenville and dash in behind them, so as to secure the artillery, if nothing more."[36]

Grant's soldiers continued to dig, and work progressed rapidly on Captain Hickenlooper's mine under a Confederate fort. The Rebels knew what he was up to and were digging down themselves, trying to intercept his mine with a counter-mine, but they didn't go deep enough. His notes for the 24th say: "Captain Merritt sick and confined to his tent. Driving the gallery as rapidly as possible. Have penetrated to a distance of 40 feet, and commenced on branch gallery to left. Can hear the rebels at work on counter-mine very distinctly. Appear to be above and to the left of our gallery."[37]

Meanwhile, things were happening east of Richmond that day. A Confederate Signal Corps officer wired General Wise, at Chaffin's Farm, southeast of Richmond: "The enemy re-enforcing the Peninsula from Suffolk. Thirteen steamers left Suffolk loaded with infantry and cavalry. They were bound for the White House [plantation] or Yorktown. Women and children are ordered to leave Suffolk. The enemy say they intend to burn it. . . . Keyes with only 6,000 men at Fort Magruder, Yorktown, and Williamsburg. Large force went to Hooker from here last week." And Colonel W. P. Shingler, commanding the cavalry battalion of the Holcombe Legion, forwarded a message to Wise's adjutant that day saying, "Captain [J. K.] Littleton informs me that there are seven [Union] gunboats and transports at West Point, and apparently they are about to effect a landing."[38]

∽ Endnotes ∽

1 *OR*, I:24:III:974.
2 Ibid., I:24:III:430-1.
3 Ibid., I:24:II:245-6.
4 Ibid., I:24:III:432.
5 Ibid., I:24:III:433.
6 Hoehling, *Vicksburg: 47 Days of Siege*, 215.
7 Ibid., 213. Italics in the source.
8 *OR*, I:24:I:158.
9 Ibid., I:27:III:923.
10 Ibid., I:27:III:925.
11 Ibid., I:27:III:925-6.
12 Ibid., I:27:III:277.
13 Howard Coffin, *Nine Months to Gettysburg* (Woodstock VT, 1997), 170.
14 *OR*, I:27:I:277.
15 Nye, *Here Come the Rebels!*, 257.
16 *OR*, I:23:I:404.
17 James Lee McDonough and James Pickett Jones, *War So Terrible* (New York, 1987), 176.
18 *OR*, I:23:I:404.
19 Dana, *Recollections of the Civil War*, 122.
20 Ibid., 121.
21 Patricia Faust, editor, *Historical Times Illustrated Encyclopedia of the Civil War* (New York, 1986), 319.
22 *OR*, I:23:I:404-5.

23 Ibid., I:23:I:406.
24 Margaret L. Stuntz, "Lightning Strike at the Gap" in *America's Civil War*, July 1997, 52.
25 *OR*, I:23:I:538.
26 Stuntz, "Lightning Strike at the Gap," *ACW*, July '97, 53.
27 *OR*, I:23:I:458.
28 Stuntz, "Lightning Strike at the Gap," *ACW*, July '97, 53.
29 Ibid., 55.
30 Ibid., 56.
31 Peter Cozzens, *This Terrible Sound* (Urbana IL and Chicago, 1992), 18.
32 *OR*, I:23:I:486-7.
33 Ibid., I:23:I:485.
34 Ibid., I:24:II:246.
35 Ibid., I:24:III:435.
36 Ibid.
37 Ibid., I:24:II:202.
38 Ibid., I:27:III:928, both messages.

CHAPTER 15

"The Rebels Are Coming!"

24 – 25 June 1863

THE REVEREND DR. PHILIP SCHAFF, the professor at the theological seminary in Mercersburg, Pennsylvania, who had commented on the appearance of Jenkins' troopers, was just sitting down for the noon meal with his family on the 24th when one of his children came running in exclaiming, "The Rebels are coming, the Rebels are coming!"[1] A brigade from Ed Johnson's division of Ewell's Corps, commanded by Brigadier General George H. "Maryland" Steuart, soon came marching in with fifes and drums playing – over 2,000 infantrymen plus a company of field artillery armed with guns captured at Winchester. The brigade's provost marshal, like Steuart a Marylander, assembled the town's leading citizens and announced that all goods must be surrendered, although they would be paid for. Hams, sides of bacon, and large quantities of sugar, molasses, and flour all disappeared into captured wagons still marked "U.S.", while nuts, candy and cigars were consumed on the spot. About sundown, the Rebels marched out again, heading west toward McConnellsburg. At the top of the intervening mountains they were overtaken and joined by the Maryland cavalry battalion, under Major Harry Gilmor.

The town of McConnellsburg had acquired a few defenders since the first time the Confederates had visited it: There was the 12th Pennsylvania Cavalry Regiment, part of Milroy's force sent over from Bedford; a new regiment of "emergency" infantry; and an independent company of similar material. But there was no overall commander for these forces, and no overall plan for how to defend the town. Colonel Jacob Szink, commander of the infantry regiment, put half of his men in each of two mountain passes east of the town, but constructed neither barricades nor earthworks. The cavalry camped between the mountain and the town, where roads from the two passes met, and the independent company stayed in town.

Late on the 24th, from his mountain pass, Colonel Szink could see the Confederates start out from Mercersburg, heading his way. He fired a signal gun to let the others know. The independent company was commanded by Captain W. W. Wallace, a veteran of Antietam and Chancellorsville, and at the signal he led his men and several elderly volunteers up the road to help, but was soon met by the cavalry regiment rushing in the opposite direction to rejoin Milroy at Bloody Run. At the foot of the mountain he met Szink's regiment, also making good time toward the west. He tried to get the colonel to turn around and go back, but failed, so his little company went on alone, taking up a hidden position halfway up the mountain.

Pretty soon, Major Gilmor's Confederate cavalry came rushing past, chasing a couple of Union scouts. Wallace's company fired into the rear of Gilmor's battalion and then Wallace told his men to scatter and escape. The Maryland Rebels turned back to attack them but it was soon dark and they all got away. No one was killed on either side; one Federal was wounded. The Confederates rode on into McConnellsburg, where they found no opposition, and, when Steuart's infantry arrived, the cavalrymen were peacefully feeding their horses. Steuart sent the Maryland infantry battalion, now also attached to his brigade, to occupy the town and had his Virginia and North Carolina regiments camp outside of it. They stayed there for two days gathering supplies.

Meanwhile, General Knipe's small brigade, which had reassembled at the fair grounds in Carlisle, had been advised by Captain Boyd that Jenkins' Rebels were at Shippensburg. Carlisle had raised two companies of home guards, and they had laid out a defensive line atop Rocky Ridge, about a mile west of the town. It wasn't much of a ridge and not much of a defense, but it was better than nothing, consisting of a barricade in the road and some rifle pits nearby that had been dug by some free blacks who had been "drafted" from the streets of Carlisle. Knipe moved his two regiments of New York militia into these trenches, and the new Philadelphia Battery he had received, to replace his naval howitzers, was split up, with two guns supporting each regiment, their positions partially masked with tree limbs. A new addition to his command was a company of militia cavalry from Harrisburg that called itself the Curtin Guards. Part of it was held in reserve in the town and part sent out to scout. The militiamen were on the alert for several hours, but no Rebels came their way, and they slept on their arms that night, expecting a fight in the morning.

The rest of Johnson's Division continued to follow Rodes' Division on the 24th, which, Rodes said, "made 14 miles, passing through Chambersburg, which had been reoccupied by General Jenkins that morning, and bivouacked on the Conococheague, 2 ½ miles beyond the town."[2] One regiment was left in the town to guard it, and the businessmen were given a requisition for an enormous quantity of clothing, food, harness, and other items useful for an army, which they were able to fill only in part. Ewell, riding with Rodes, sent Jenkins' cavalry on ahead to Shippensburg. From there the latter found that there were three roads leading on to Carlisle, and he spread his brigade to cover all three, but, shortly before midnight, some of his pickets were fired on by Captain Boyd's small Union cavalry force, and Jenkins promptly sent a messenger galloping to Chambersburg asking for help.

Meanwhile, Early's Division marched that day through Quincy and Altodale to Greenwood, east of Chambersburg and about halfway between it and the Cashtown Gap in South Mountain. Hill's 3rd Corps began crossing the Potomac that day at Shepherdstown, marching for Boonsborough, Maryland. Longstreet's 1st Corps, now bringing up the rear, began marching north at early dawn on the 24th, moving through Berryville and Martinsburg to Williamsport.

Jeb Stuart, as suggested in Lee's instructions to him, was preparing to move around the Union Army – as he had done spectacularly on previous occasions – on his way to join Ewell's corps in Pennsylvania with three of his five brigades. Major Mosby had just returned from another foray into Union lines and confirmed that the Union army remained stationary in its widely separated camps, so the way was still open for the Confederate horsemen to pass between them and on across the Potomac. Mosby would again penetrate Union lines and meet the cavalry column near Gum Springs to lead it on to the river crossing. However, Stuart did not intend, as Longstreet had expected, to put Hampton in charge of the two brigades he would leave behind. He wanted to take with him his three old reliable brigades, including Hampton's; so he would leave behind the two that had recently been added to his command, those of Beverly Robertson and "Grumble" Jones.

One rationalization for this move was that, according to Major McClellan of his staff, Stuart considered Jones "the best outpost officer" in his command.[3] This may have been so, but the more obvious reason is that Stuart and Jones could not get along personally. There had been some argument between them back in the fall of 1861 which had never been resolved, and Jones certainly lived up to his nickname on all occasions. Therefore, Stuart did not want to take Jones along on his coming operation. Nor did he want Robertson, whose ability as an organizer he respected but not his ability on the field of battle. And the greatest problem he left behind him when he assembled his three older brigades at Salem on the night of the 24th was that, of the two brigadiers he was leaving behind, Robertson had seniority, and would thus be in command, even though Jones was the more experienced and capable officer and had the larger brigade.

Stuart wrote Robertson a long letter of instructions that day, in which he said, "Your object will be to watch the enemy; deceive him as to our designs, and harass his rear if you find he is retiring. Be always on the alert; let nothing escape your observation, and miss no opportunity which offers to damage the enemy. After the enemy has moved beyond your reach, leave sufficient pickets in the mountains, withdraw to the west side of the Shenandoah, place a strong and reliable picket to watch the enemy at Harper's Ferry, cross the Potomac, and follow the army, keeping on its right and rear."[4] There was a lot more, but that was the important part. Stuart sent separate instructions to Jones, but sent them through Robertson with orders for the latter to read them first before sending them on.

President Lincoln wired General Couch at 8:55 that morning: "Have you any reports of the enemy moving into Pennsylvania? And, if any, what?" Couch replied at 9:30: "Rebel cavalry are this side of Chambersburg. Scouts from Gettysburg report 7,000 at Greencastle. Deserters say A. P. Hill and Longstreet are across the Potomac; 40,000. Ten deserters in at McConnellsburg from Ewell's forces, say the latter is at Greencastle, with 30,000 men and thirty pieces of artillery. Two lieutenants taken prisoners say that Lee's headquarters are at Millwood, 12 miles from Winchester."[5] A copy of this was forwarded to Hooker at 12:25 that afternoon.

A company of 16 veterans of the War of 1812 (ages 68-76) marched through the streets of Harrisburg that day, and told Governor Curtin that they would cheerfully attempt any service he wanted to put them to. He accepted their service and used them for guards. They asked to be armed with old-style flintlock muskets, such as they had used in their youths, and they marched to old-fashioned tactics that seemed strange to their younger counterparts. But, a newspaper reporter wrote, "They kept their places, and kept step and obeyed orders with a precision that showed that the drill they had gone through in those stirring times had gone not merely to the ear, but to the heart."[6]

Several other reports reached Hooker and Halleck that day about large formations of Confederates crossing the Potomac into Maryland and some penetrating into southern Pennsylvania. The Federal War Department, realizing that this move by Lee effectually cut off General Schenck, at Baltimore, from much of his Middle Department, issued General Orders No. 186 that day creating a new Department of West Virginia, consisting of "that part of the Middle Department west of Hancock [Md.], including the adjacent counties of Ohio...."[7] General Kelley was named as commander of the new department. The same order finally made it official that Major General Winfield Scott Hancock was now the commander of the 2nd Corps, in Hooker's army; he had been the acting commander of it since Couch had been transferred to his new department. Halleck wired the governor of Ohio at 1 p.m. requesting that new regiments from that state be sent to Parkersburg, West Virginia, to report to Kelley but added, "Should it be found necessary, they can afterward be moved up the Ohio River to Wheeling or Pittsburgh."[8]

That same day, Hooker had Brigadier General G. K. Warren, his chief engineer, write out the reasons why the latter thought the Army of the Potomac should move at once to the neighborhood of Harper's Ferry (something Halleck had "suggested" he do a week before). Warren enumerated six reasons: "1. The whole of Lee's army is reported to be on the Potomac, above that place, part of it across the river, and threatening an advance upon Harrisburg. 2. There we can protect Washington as well, and Baltimore better than here, and preserve our communications and routes of supply. 3. It is the shortest line to reach Lee's army; will enable us to operate on his communications, if he advances; to throw overwhelming forces on either portion of his army that he allows the river to divide; and is too strong a position for him to attack us in, even if we make heavy detachments. 4. It will enable us to pass South Mountain without fighting for the passes, if we wish to move upon him, and will thus destroy any advantages these mountains would give as a protection to his right flank. 5. It will prevent Lee from detaching a corps to invade Pennsylvania with, as it would expose the rest of his army to our attack in superior force. 6. These opinions are based upon the idea that we are not to try and go round his army, and drive it out of Maryland, as we did last year, but to paralyze all its movements by threatening its flank and rear if it advances, and gain time to collect re-enforcements sufficient to render us the stronger army of the two, if we are not so already."[9]

But Hooker decided not to make such a move, not yet at any rate. Instead, he was sending Major General William H. French, a division commander in the 2nd Corps (without his division), to take command at Harpers Ferry. Seth Williams, of Hooker's staff, wrote instructions for French that day, saying: "He desires that you will closely observe the movements of the enemy, and keep informed of all that is transpiring in the vicinity, especially as to what relates to the movements of the enemy.... He has this day ordered Major-General Stahel with his division of cavalry to report to you. With this force, and the cavalry now at Harper's Ferry, it is believed that you will be able to drive away and destroy any rebel force of cavalry now on the north side of the Potomac. If practicable, it is also of importance to ascertain whether or not the passes over South Mountain are held by the enemy, and also, from the Union people of Maryland, what force of the rebel army has crossed the Potomac, their whereabouts, and destination. With the free use of the cavalry at your command, it is believed that you will be able to gather information of incalculable value, determining the future movements of this army."[10]

Hooker wrote to Halleck: "The aspect of the enemy is not much changed from yesterday. Ewell, I conclude, is over the river, and is now up the country, I suppose, for purposes of plunder. The yeomanry of that district should be able to check any extended advance of that column, and protect themselves from their aggression. Of the troops that marched to the river at Shepherdstown yesterday, I cannot learn that any have crossed, and as soon as I do I shall commence moving, myself, and, indeed, am preparing my new acquisitions for that event; the others are ready. General French is now on his way to Harper's Ferry, and I have given directions for the force at Poolesville [Md.] to march and report to him, and also for all of Stahel's cavalry, and, if I can do it without attracting observation, I shall send over a corps or two from here, in order, if possible, to sever Ewell from the balance of the rebel army, in case he should make a protracted sojourn with his Pennsylvania neighbors. If the enemy should conclude not to throw any additional force over the river, I desire to make Washington secure, and, with all the force I can muster, strike for his line of retreat in the direction of Richmond.

"I cannot learn the strength of Heintzelman's and Schenck's commands, nor where they are stationed, and hence I send my chief of staff to Washington and to Baltimore to ascertain, and also to start out a column of about 15,000 men on the National road as far as Frederick City. In any contingency, whether of an advance or retreat of the enemy, the defense of Washington or Baltimore, this amount of force should be there, and they should be held in readiness to march, which fact I will not be able to know until I put them on the road. I will send the best officers I have to command this body. I desire that instructions may be given Generals Heintzelman and Schenck to direct their commands to obey promptly any orders they may receive from me. Last evening the colonel commanding at Poolesville [A B. Jewett] responded to his orders to march that he did not belong to my command, but would refer his orders to General Heintzelman. Such delays may bring us reverses. When these instructions are given, I shall not be necessitated to repeat orders to any part of my command to march on the enemy. Allow me to suggest that the new troops arriving in Baltimore and Washington be at once put in the defenses, and the old ones, excepting those serving with the artillery, be put in marching condition. If this should be done quickly, I think that we may anticipate glorious results from the recent movement of the enemy, whether he should determine to advance or retreat. I request that my orders be sent me to-day, for outside of the Army of the Potomac I don't know whether I am standing on my head or feet."[11]

At 2:30 that afternoon, Halleck wired Hooker: "General Schenck has been notified that the troops of his department in Harper's Ferry and vicinity would obey all orders direct from you, and that he would obey your orders in regard to the other troops of his command. They, however, are nearly all militia."[12] At 2:45 Butterfield wired Hooker from Washington: "Just arrived. General Halleck informs me that there is not an available man for such purposes as my orders call for in Washington. Arrangements made to arm the Department clerks, so as to relieve the guards for storehouses, and put them [in the lines] between the forts. I now go to see Heintzelman's returns; then to the President."[13]

Schenck wired Halleck at 4:45 p.m. "I knew Tyler was mistaken. He has now at Maryland Heights 8,494 effective men for duty. Quite enough."[14] Sometime that day General Couch received a telegram from Brigadier General W. F. "Baldy" Smith, whom he had sent to check on Milroy's troops at Bloody Run: "McConnellsburg is in possession of the enemy. I think General Milroy had better [move] toward Mount Union, to cover that bridge, and be near you if you want his troops at Harrisburg." Baldy Smith was a West Point graduate (class of 1845) and had been a major general and corps commander for a while, but his complaining to the President about Burnside's incompetence after the Battle of Fredericksburg had led the Senate to refuse to confirm his promotion, causing him to revert to the one-star rank. He was slated by Couch to take command of the 1st Division of the new corps being raised for his department. But, instead of taking Smith's advice, Couch wired Milroy: "Send 400 or 500 old infantry on horse, if possible, to hold the gaps near McConnellsburg and the one toward Hancock. Push this matter right through without delay. Use horses to move rapidly. The troops there are not reliable."[15]

Speaking of horses, Seth Williams wrote to Pleasonton that day and, after discussing several minor subjects, said: "The general desires me to inquire if anything can be done with the rebel cavalry in your front by detaching an infantry force, either from the Second or the Twelfth Corps, and cutting their line of retreat." Pleasonton replied at 6:30 p.m.: "Stuart's cavalry is so situated, and the country is so open, that their retreat cannot be cut off by either infantry or cavalry. We were as near doing it on Sunday last as it can be done."[16] This seems to have ended all thought of trying to get at Lee by crossing the Blue Ridge or of making further attacks on Stuart in the Loudoun Valley for any other purpose.

General Howard reported to Williams that day that: "My entire corps [the 11th] is encamped on the south bank of Goose

Creek, near Edwards Ferry, as ordered. Headquarters close to the pontoon bridge." Williams replied at 7:30 p.m.: "The commanding general directs that, until otherwise ordered, you guard the bridge and depots at Edwards Ferry, on the north side of the Potomac at that place." But at 11:35 p.m. he sent new orders: "The commanding general directs that your corps take up the line of march early to-morrow morning for Sandy Hook, in the vicinity of Harper's Ferry, reaching that place to-morrow afternoon. You will take your entire command with you. Other troops will arrive in the course of the day, to guard the bridge and depots at Edwards Ferry."[17]

At 11:30 p.m., Butterfield, then at Baltimore, began a long report to Hooker about what reinforcements he had been able to scrape up from Schenck and Heintzelman. "The substance of what I have been able to accomplish thus far," he reported, "is a promise of a brigade of about 1,800 men from this point, to move to-morrow for Monocacy Bridge (3 miles this side of Frederick). . . . I may hunt out something more to-morrow morning. A portion of these will be militia. . . ." Then he gave a complete rundown of all the troops in the Middle Department and what they were used for, winding it up with: "Schenck guards the important bridges from here toward Philadelphia over the Gunpowder, Susquehanna, and Back Rivers. Also the Northern Central [RR] line to the Pennsylvania State line, where Couch meets him, the great fear seeming to be on all parts that, if these roads and bridges are not guarded, secessionists and enemies within will destroy them and interrupt communications.

"The total to be raised out of Schenck's command, including those at Harper's Ferry, would seem to be about 11,000; from Heintzelman – Abercrombie, say 7,333; Crawford, 3,613; Jewett (Poolesville), 1,221; Stahel (cavalry), 3,742. Total of all re-enforcements, 26,909. With our own cavalry, infantry, and artillery, as per our last returns, say 80,000, leaves us 106,919, when all are gotten together. . . . I had little to say (not having time, on account of anxiety to get here) to the President about putting all in one command, and concentrating all the forces, instead of scattering all over Pennsylvania and creation. . . . I send a few good maps . . . will try and arrange about guides, spies, &c., with other things, to-morrow. . . ."[18] It was 1:15 a.m. on the 25th by the time he finished his report, and then he added a long postscript detailing just what forces were guarding the railroad and bridges. He had been interrupted by a dispatch from Hooker, to which he replied at 12:30 a.m.: "I will leave on the first train. Shall I let the column under Lockwood proceed under their orders and report to Harper's Ferry or to some corps? . . . Think we had better keep them, now they are ordered and ready to march this p.m."[19] Brigadier General Henry H. Lockwood (West Point 1836) was the officer in command of the brigade that Butterfield mentioned at the beginning of his report.

Hooker at last decided, on the 25th, to move at least part of his army, not to Harpers Ferry, as both Halleck and Warren advised, but north of the Potomac. A second pontoon bridge, requiring 65 boats, was constructed at Edwards Ferry that day, although it didn't get started as early as Hooker had expected, and at 7:20 that morning Seth Williams wrote to General Slocum, whose 12th Corps was still at Leesburg: "The commanding general directs that you hold your command in readiness to march in the direction of Edwards Ferry. The First, Third, and Eleventh Corps will cross the river to-day."[20] The army's Artillery Reserve and Pleasonton's cavalry had already been ordered to march for Edwards Ferry but were not expected to cross the river yet.

At 8:10 a.m., Williams wrote to General Reynolds, commanding the 1st Corps: "Orders were telegraphed you early this morning to assume command of the Third and Eleventh Corps, in addition to your own. At the same time, directions were given for a brigade of [Stahel's] cavalry to report to you, with two sections of artillery. All of these troops are under orders to cross the Potomac to-day, at or near Edward's Ferry, all but the Third Corps being convenient to that crossing at this moment. The cavalry and sections are ordered to report to you, that you may take possession of Crampton's Pass, and what is called South Mountain Gap, as speedily as possible – if practicable, to-night;

and that each cavalry column be closely followed by a brigade of infantry and a battery, and all instructed to hold those passes until further orders. Late last night the enemy had no force at either point. As their possession may be of great importance in determining the future operations of this army, the general desires that you will take and hold them. You will direct your column in the direction of Middletown [Md.], on two lines, should you find it practicable, and there encamp, should you receive no orders to the contrary. Please keep the general informed of all your movements and those of the enemy as soon as you learn them, and especially advise him the moment we are in possession of the Gaps."[21] Colonel Sharpe wired John Babcock, at Frederick, to report to Reynolds "and remain with his advance."[22]

The five big nine-months regiments of the 2nd Vermont Brigade pulled in their pickets from the Occoquan and Bull Run and assembled at Union Mills that day. As one member of the 13th Vermont recorded, "The most of our regiment had prepared for a long march and discarded everything that we could get along without, experience having taught us that guns, forty rounds of cartridges, haversacks stuffed with rations, with canteen and shelter tent, rubber blanket, and extra shirt and pair of socks, letter paper, testaments that had been given us before we left home, needles, thread, etc., etc., tucked away in our knapsacks would be quite enough to carry." However, some of the men, thinking that they were on their way home via Washington, brought along everything they could carry. General Stannard's aide wrote, "Our men . . . were not inured to marching. Some were poorly shod, for in view of the speedy termination of their service they had not been allowed to exchange old shoes for new, but they marched well. With sore and bleeding feet, in some cases barefoot, they pushed along." The men were beginning to realize that they might yet be involved in a major battle before the end of their nine-months enlistments. One corporal wrote to his wife: "If I should get killed perhaps it would be as well for you. You would draw a pension of $8 a month and have a chance to get a younger and better husband."[23] Although some of its regiments had already made long marches that day, the brigade set out at 3 p.m., passed through Centreville and camped two miles beyond it, in the rain and the mud. "All the regiments did well," General Stannard recorded in his diary. "Came in closed up in good shape."[24]

Williams wrote to Brigadier General R. O. Tyler, commanding the Artillery Reserve, in the form of an official order: "The Fifth Corps (Aldie) will march at 4 a.m. to-morrow, crossing Goose Creek at Carter's Mill; thence to Leesburg, crossing the Potomac at the upper bridge at Edwards Ferry and the Monocacy at its mouth, and follow the river road in the direction of Frederick City. The Reserve Artillery will cross on the lower bridge at Edwards Ferry, and follow the Fifth Corps."[25]

Hancock's 2nd Corps started moving north that day, but, at 9:10 a.m., Seth Williams wrote to Pleasonton: "General Hancock reports that the enemy have appeared in the direction of New Baltimore [Va.], with a force estimated as from four regiments to 6,000 men, with one battery of artillery. The commanding general directs that you at once send a brigade of cavalry to report to General Hancock. He is marching to-day from Thoroughfare Gap to Gum Springs." Cavalry Corps headquarters passed this job to David Gregg's 2nd Division, saying that, "Inasmuch as the Eighth Pennsylvania Cavalry is already there [Thoroughfare Gap], it is suggested that you send the brigade to which it belongs."[26] That was Gregg's 2nd Brigade, commanded by Colonel Pennock Huey.

The Confederate force that Hancock had discovered was Jeb Stuart's three brigades on his intended ride through the Union army on his way to join Ewell in Pennsylvania. The Rebels had set out just after midnight, riding southeast from Salem, and early that morning had brushed aside a few Union pickets to pass through the Bull Run Mountains at Glasscock's Gap, south of Thoroughfare Gap, before turning to the northeast. Stuart intended to pass to the east of Hancock's Union 2nd Corps, known to be camped near Thoroughfare Gap, then cross the Manassas Gap Railroad near Haymarket, and Bull Run at Sudley Springs, turn north to Gum Springs, which was southeast of Meade's 5th Corps (camped near Aldie) and Howard's 11th Corps (camped along Goose Creek), and go on to Frankville, east of Leesburg (where Slocum's 12th Corps was camped) and then turn farther east to probably cross the Potomac at or near Seneca Ford.

However, near Haymarket, Stuart found his way blocked by Hancock's 2nd Corps, not in camp but marching in the same direction, in obedience to Hooker's orders, and taking up the road that Stuart wanted to use. Stuart diverted his cavalry farther south to get around this obstacle while deploying the one battery of horse artillery that he had brought along to blast the Union infantry column. Its first shot disabled a Union artillery caisson. The Federals swung into defensive formations, sent skirmishers forward, and brought up artillery of their own to return fire. Then Stuart had his guns limber up and follow the cavalry, and Hancock's infantry resumed its northward march.

Fitz Lee's brigade – that officer was back in command of it – camped that night near Gainesville, while Hampton's and Chambliss's made camp farther west, near Buckland, moves that were made to deceive the Federals about his intentions. An early stop was needed in order to let the horses graze, since they had not brought along enough grain to feed them; Stuart was taking no wagons except ambulances. He sent word to Lee, garnered from captured Federals, that Hancock's corps was headed for Gum Springs, but Lee never received it, although a copy did reach the Confederate War Department in Richmond. Stuart was supposed to meet Mosby near Gum Springs that night himself, for the latest word on the crossings of the Potomac; now that meeting was impossible. "It rained heavily that night," Stuart later reported. "To carry out my original design of passing west of Centreville, would have involved so much detention, on account of the presence of the enemy, that I determined to cross Bull Run lower down, and strike through Fairfax for the Potomac the next day."27

Butterfield wrote to Hooker from Baltimore again at 11 a.m., saying, "Another regiment, about 600, will be armed and gotten ready to-day; start to-morrow; are to join General Lockwood's command. This will bring him up to 2,700 with the Sixth New York Militia; 2,100 without. . . . The 2,200 of Milroy's command at Bedford, disorganized, and parts of new regiments and companies at Harper's Ferry have been ordered here by General Schenck, to be armed and sent forward. They could reach here in thirty-six hours by rail, be put in shape, and sent out in as many more. General Couch detains them with Milroy; says he must have them. As they are, they cannot be of much service. . . ."[28] But Hooker was writing to Butterfield at the same hour: "The small body of troops you speak of will be of more bother than use, in my opinion. You had better abandon all hope of getting assistance from that quarter. There are good reasons why you should return to-night."[29] Hooker ordered fourteen of his batteries to Washington that day, since he felt that he had more artillery than he needed in proportion to his infantry. As he explained to Butterfield in a message timed 3:45 p.m., "I have had artillery for 200,000 men, and have but 75,000 at all reliable. In my opinion, Milroy's men will fight better under a soldier. I have telegraphed General Halleck for men until I will do so no longer."[30]

The tug-of-war between Schenck and Couch over Milroy's force at Bedford and Bloody Run continued that day – even heated up. As Butterfield's comments show, Schenck was trying to get these men to Baltimore so they could be resupplied and reunited with the other refugees from Winchester, but Couch felt, as he told Schenck, "It is impossible, at the moment, to withdraw Milroy from his post in the mountains. He has to remain and fight where he is."[31] Schenck insisted; Couch regretted but still refused. Schenck sent an aide-de-camp to deliver orders directly to Milroy, but Couch still refused to let him go. Finally Schenck referred the whole question to Halleck, saying, "I think General Couch is wrong. Will you, if you think it advisable, order him to let Milroy and his troops come on?" He pointed out that a fifth of Milroy's men were without arms and many of them without shoes. "Parts of the same regiments and companies are with General Tyler. If I had those with Milroy back here, I could get the fragments together, strengthen Tyler, if necessary, and at the same time add at least 1,500 organized troops to those sent for General Hooker to the Monocacy."[32]

Butterfield's trip to Washington and Baltimore in search of reinforcements indicates Hooker's frustrations at dealing with Halleck, Heintzelman and Schenck. However much those three might (or might not) have been willing to help, the division of forces, in and around the area being invaded, among different departments with different missions and priorities, made it next to impossible to coordinate their efforts. Only Halleck had the power to do so, but he was also in charge of all the other armies and departments and could not give his complete attention to this area, nor was he at all inclined to micro-manage, but left each commander on his own with only broad guidelines to follow, plus the occasional snide comment when something irritated him, although he did sometimes get involved in small details.

For instance, that day he wrote to the captain commanding a company of (Union) Virginia Rangers at the Relay House on the B&O Railroad to "proceed to the region threatened by the rebel forces, and take possession of and drive off into the nearest depot all horses suitable for cavalry, artillery, or baggage trains, which are in any danger of falling into the hands of the enemy. Give receipts to the owners of these horses."[33] He went on to give details on what the receipts should say, advised the captain not to take any horses in the immediate vicinity of a railroad for fear that disgruntled owners might retaliate by obstructing the track, and finally informed him that a quartermaster's officer would be sent along with him to take charge of the horses.

All this was a good idea, but it seems, at this distance, a rather minor thing to absorb the attention of the general-in-chief of the Army. But horses were one of Halleck's sore subjects, since his generals (especially Rosecrans) were always complaining of a need for more, no matter how many they were sent. He wrote to Hooker that day: "The immense loss and destruction of horses in your army, and the difficulty of supplying this loss, render it necessary that you should impress every serviceable animal likely to fall into the hands of the enemy. There are many animals in Loudoun County [Va.] and the adjacent parts of Maryland. These should be seized, to save them from the enemy, as well as to supply yourself."[34] Loudoun County was, of course, the area that Pleasonton and Stuart had recently been fighting over and Hooker had already given up on the idea of driving Stuart out of it.

The Army of the Potomac had been shrinking drastically for weeks due to the two-years regiments and the nine-months regiments going home, while Hooker knew that Lee's army had been reinforced, and he was frustrated by his standing orders to protect Washington and Harper's Ferry when what he wanted to do was to march on Richmond while Lee was out of the way. The assignment of Reynolds to take three corps and part of Stahel's cavalry to seize the gaps in South Mountain (actually a long high ridge, an extension of the Blue Ridge north of the Potomac) was both defensive and offensive, as it would keep the Confederates from coming to the east side of the ridge while leaving Hooker the option of moving to the west side to attack Ewell's corps and any other Rebels in the Cumberland Valley. But he was also keeping his options open about attacking whatever part of Lee's army was still south of the Potomac. He wrote to General French, at Harper's Ferry, that day: "Please order your men to have three days' rations cooked and kept on hand for the present, supplied with ammunition, prepared to march at a moment's notice. I have not heard a word from your post to-day. If there should be any considerable [enemy] force remaining there, I should like to make a dash at them. By feeling, if not without, can you find out if they are there, or that they continue to cross? I should like to learn this to-morrow. My headquarters will be at Poolesville [Md.] 9 a.m. to-morrow." [35]

Some of Hooker's frustrations about dealing with commanders of other departments show through in a message he sent to Halleck that day. General Crawford, commander of the Pennsylvania Reserve Division, had written to Butterfield to say: "A dispatch has been received during the night from General

[John P.] Slough, military governor of Alexandria, informing me that the commanding officer of the Second Brigade, Pennsylvania Reserve Corps, has been instructed by him not to recognize the orders sent to him to prepare to join the division, as directed in your dispatch of June 23." Hooker forwarded this to Halleck that morning, saying: "Subjoined is a dispatch this moment received. It speaks for itself. I request that General Slough be arrested at once, and charges will be forwarded as soon as I have time to prepare them. You will find, I fear, when it is too late, that the effort to preserve department lines will be fatal to the cause of the country." Halleck checked with Heintzelman and then replied at 2 p.m.: "The Second Brigade, to which you refer in your telegram, forms no part of General Crawford's command, which was placed at your orders. No other troops can be withdrawn from the Defenses of Washington."[36]

Hooker, of course, was not the only commander unhappy with the division of troops among the departments. Heintzelman had replied to Halleck's inquiry with a long defense, saying in part: "The two regiments of Pennsylvania Reserves are a portion of the garrison of Alexandria, and, if removed, will leave but 776 men, much too small a command to garrison so important a point as the depots of Alexandria, as, from the withdrawal of all the troops along the Occoquan [Stannard's], there is no force whatever to prevent an enemy from advancing as far as the range of the guns of Fort Lyon. Two more regiments, composing the guard of the convalescent camp, also ordered to move, are within the lines of the Defenses, and are the guards for some 8,000 paroled prisoners, stragglers, and convalescents, and if these are withdrawn there will be nothing to prevent these men from straying all over the country. Should any of these troops be withdrawn, I have not another regiment to replace them. . . . As all my cavalry [Stahel's] has been taken from the other side, should the Army of the Potomac move from my front [which it was in the process of doing], the first indication of the approach of the enemy would be their appearance at our works."[37] This comment gives a glimpse of what the effect might have been had

Lee's suggestion to Jefferson Davis to form a phantom army under Beauregard at Culpeper Court House been carried out. At the very least Heintzelman would have called for the return of the troops he was giving to Hooker, and Halleck might well have agreed.

Lee was still pushing that idea. In a letter to Jefferson Davis written that day, the 25th, he said: "You will see that apprehension for the safety of Washington and their own territory has aroused the Federal Government and people to great exertions, and it is incumbent upon us to call forth all our energies. In addition to the 100,000 troops called for by President Lincoln to defend the frontier of Pennsylvania, you will see that he is concentrating other organized forces in Maryland. It is stated in the papers that they are all being withdrawn from Suffolk, and, according to General Buckner's report, Burnside and his corps are recalled from Kentucky. It is reasonable to suppose that this would be the case if their apprehensions were once aroused. I think this should liberate the troops in the Carolinas, and enable Generals Buckner and Bragg to accomplish something in Ohio. It is plain that if all the Federal Army is concentrated upon this [army], it will result in our accomplishing nothing, and being compelled to return to Virginia. If the plan that I suggested the other day, of organizing an army, even in effigy, under General Beauregard at Culpeper Court-House, can be carried into effect, much relief will be afforded. If even the brigades in Virginia and North Carolina, which Generals Hill and Elzey think cannot be spared, were ordered there at once, and General Beauregard were sent there, if he had to return to South Carolina, it would do more to protect both States from marauding expeditions of the enemy than anything else. I have not sufficient troops to maintain my communications, and, therefore, have to abandon them. I think I can throw General Hooker's army across the Potomac and draw troops from the south, embarrassing their plan of campaign in a measure, if I can do nothing more and have to return. I still hope that all things will end well for us at Vicksburg. At any rate, every effort should be made to bring about that result."[38]

Before the day was out he sent another letter to Davis, saying: "So strong is my conviction of the necessity of activity on our part in military affairs, that you will excuse my adverting to the subject again, notwithstanding what I have said in my previous letter of to-day. It seems to me that we cannot afford to keep our troops awaiting possible movements of the enemy, but that our true policy is, as far as we can, so to employ our forces as to give occupation to his at points of our selection.

"I have observed that extracts from Northern journals, contained in Richmond papers of the 22d instant, state that the yellow fever has appeared at New Berne [N.C.], and that, in consequence, the Federal troops are being moved back to Morehead City. If, in fact, the fever is in New Berne, it would tend of itself to prevent active operations from that point. But as I have never heard of the disease being in that city, and as it does not generally break out so early in the season, even in localities which are subject to it, I am disposed to doubt the truth of the statement, and regard it as a cover for the withdrawal of the enemy's forces for some other field. The attempt to conceal their movements, as in the case of the withdrawal of the troops from Suffolk, coupled with the fact that nothing has up to this time been undertaken on the North Carolina coast, convinces me that the enemy contemplates nothing important in that region, and that it is unnecessary to keep our troops to watch him.

"If he has been waiting until this time for re-enforcements, the probability of their being furnished is greatly diminished by the movements now in progress on our part, and they must at least await the result of our operations. The same course of reasoning is applicable to the question of the probability of the enemy assuming the offensive against Richmond, either on the Peninsula or south of the James. I feel sure, therefore, that the best use that can be made of the troops in Carolina, and those in Virginia now guarding Richmond, would be the prompt assembling of the main body of them, leaving sufficient to prevent raids, together with as many as can be drawn from the army of General Beauregard, at Culpeper Court-House, under the command of that officer. I do not think they could more effectually prevent aggressive movements on the part of the enemy in any other way, while their assistance to this army in its operations would be very great.

"If the report received from General Buckner of the withdrawal of General Burnside from Kentucky be correct, I think there is nothing to prevent a united movement of the commands of Generals Buckner and Sam. Jones into that State. They could render valuable service by collecting and bringing out supplies, if they did not do more, and would embarrass the enemy and prevent troops now there from being sent to other parts. If they are too weak to attempt this object, they need not be idle; and I think that if the enemy's forces have, in fact, been so far weakened as to render present active operations on his part against them improbable, they should go where they can be of immediate service, leaving only a sufficient guard to watch the lines they now hold. They might be sent with benefit to re-enforce General Johnston or General Bragg, to constitute part of the proposed army of General Beauregard at Culpeper Court-House, or they might accomplish good results by going into Northwestern Virginia. It should never be forgotten that our concentration at any point compels that of the enemy, and his numbers being limited, tends to relieve all other threatened localities.

"I earnestly commend these considerations to the attention of Your Excellency, and trust that you will be at liberty, in your better judgment, and with the superior means of information you possess as to our own necessities and the enemy's movements in the distant regions I have mentioned, to give effect to them, either in the way I have suggested, or in such other manner as may seem to you more judicious."[39]

However, moving troops away from Richmond, if not from the other places Lee named, seemed a bad idea just then. Secretary Seddon wired D. H. Hill at Petersburg that day: "We have news, relied on, that the enemy are landing in considerable force from seventeen vessels – gunboats and transports – at White House, 25 miles from the city. Another force believed to be advancing on the Peninsula. You had better move [Micah] Jenkins' brigade, and such other force as you can spare, either to this city, or in supporting distance, say at Drewry's Bluff." Hill replied: "The only force here is Jenkins' brigade and two weak battalions. It will not do to send all of Jenkins' brigade until the movement be more fully developed. Shall I send half of it to Drewry's Bluff? [Brigadier General Matthew] Ransom's brigade is at the Bluff."[40] Before the day was out Hill wrote again, giving details of the Union forces in North Carolina, and added, "I have made arrangements quietly to throw every available man in North Carolina to Richmond, in case of an emergency. . . ."[41] He also added that a Union advance north of the James was far preferable to one south of it, as the defenses of Petersburg were not yet complete, whereas he thought they could hold off 40,000 Federals without difficulty at Richmond. He also added a plea that, if the Federals did advance against Richmond north of the James, that he not be kept south of it.

General Dix reported to Halleck that day: "For want of transportation, I could not land at White House, as I hoped, last evening or this morning. I sent up a cavalry force, which probably landed and moved on immediately. I am waiting for the return transports, to send the infantry. Keyes' column will reach White House by land to-morrow, with Getty's artillery, and I expect to be there with my whole force to-morrow night. I shall occupy West Point to-day, and hold it with a small force. My advices are that Pickett's division, 8,000 strong, is at [Hanover] Junction, between the North and South Anna [rivers]. I fear the bridges over the latter are strongly guarded, and that my cavalry cannot get at them. They have some howitzers, and will do all that is practicable. The force in Richmond is small, but if Pickett gets down, they can collect enough from the Blackwater, Petersburg, and other points, including laborers and mechanics in their large workshops, who have all been organized, to make their whole force nearly, if not quite, equal to mine. I shall make a rapid movement. I have not men enough for a siege, and take no heavy artillery." He added, in a post script: "Dispatch just received from

White House. Cavalry landed. The enemy, with two companies of cavalry and small infantry force, burned a store-house, and fled. They were surprised."[42] Of course, Pickett's division, or most of it, was far away by that time, once more proving that outdated information is sometimes worse than none at all.

White House plantation belonged to Rooney Lee (inherited from his maternal grandfather, George Washington Parke Custis, adopted son of George Washington). The Union cavalry, commanded by Colonel Samuel P. Spear, consisted of 1,050 men, mostly from Spear's own 11th Pennsylvania Cavalry, but included some 250 Massachusetts and Illinois troopers under Lieutenant Colonel Hasbrouck Davis, who had led one of the more successful detachments in General Stoneman's raid during the Chancellorsville campaign. In his report, written a couple of days later, Spear said: "I proceeded direct from White House to Tunstall's Station [on the railroad leading to Richmond], where I found a picket of 12 men (cavalry), captured 1, cut the telegraph wires, burned the sutler's store and other Confederate buildings; continued on south side of the Pamunkey to Hanover Court-House, at which point I found a large quartermaster's depot; captured a train of 35 wagons, 6 mules to each team, covers, bows, &c., complete, and ready for the road. I also captured about 100 good mules belonging to the Confederate States. I burned about 35 wagons, 300 sets of harness, complete; stables, blacksmith's and wheelwright's shops, office, books, and papers, and everything pertaining to the depot at this point. I used every means to open a large (Confederate States) safe, but failed (too strong)."[43]

General Halleck wired the commanding officer at Fort Monroe that day: "Until further orders, all troops arriving [there] from North Carolina will report to General Dix, and be subject to his orders."[44] This, of course, referred to the 9-months and 2-years regiments on their way home and was Halleck's way of reinforcing Dix and encouraging him to move aggressively against Richmond.

Pleasonton sent Seth Williams some more out-of-date information that evening, indicating that Longstreet's corps was guarding the passes of the Blue Ridge and not allowing even civilians to cross into the Shenandoah Valley. He also expressed the fear that the Confederates would use horses they captured in Maryland and Pennsylvania to mount infantry for a raid "unless they are closely looked after." He added that, "The rebels are packing off supplies from Loudoun Valley. This does not look as if they intend to attack us, but that they are disposed to remain in the Shenandoah, and steal from Maryland and Pennsylvania as long as they are permitted."[45] At 9:30 p.m., he wrote to Williams again, saying that he had just then received a message over 24 hours old from the latter, as well as a more recent one, and that he would send a brigade of cavalry for army headquarters as ordered and would have the rest of his command "in readiness to move at a moment's notice. Have recalled the brigade of cavalry from Hancock, as it was evidently a mistake. Cannot the Eighth Pennsylvania Cavalry return to me from General Hancock?"[46]

The plea for help that Jenkins had sent to Rodes, when Boyd's cavalry fired on some of his men, had led to an order that reached Brigadier General Junius Daniel at about midnight of 24-25 June, telling him to take his brigade of Rodes' Division to Shippensburg. He had his men on the road by 1 a.m. and reached the town at about 5 on the morning of the 25th, where he assumed command as the senior officer.

All day on the 25th, Knipe's men, west of Carlisle, worked to improve their defenses. But, that night, Captain Boyd advised Knipe that the Rebels had advanced to Stoughstown, eight miles east of Shippensburg, and the general decided that this was too close for comfort. He wired Couch at 9:20 p.m. that he would fall back to Kingston and send the home guards home; he had his men on the road within five minutes. There were only enough horses to pull two of his guns, so the other two were loaded onto a railroad flatcar and shipped, along with the brigade's baggage, to Bridgeport, just across the Susquehanna from Harrisburg.

It was a 12-mile march to Kingston, where the brigade arrived during another downpour and, being without tents or blankets, which were part of the baggage, crowded into as many churches, houses, barns and shops as would take them, or slept in the open. The garrison at Carlisle Barracks, the Army's cavalry training post, some 250 men and four guns, also evacuated and headed for Harrisburg.

Soldiers were certainly not the only people on the road that day. The approach of the Confederates had also put many civilians to flight, as well as herds and flocks of animals. "The roads along the valley were crowded with horses, cattle, sheep and hogs," a young Methodist minister later remembered. "They were mixed up with long lines of wagons loaded with grain and many articles deemed of especial value. During the last week of June one steady procession passed through Carlisle from early morning till late at night."[47]

Jubal Early left his division camped at Greenwood that day, gathering supplies, and rode over to Chambersburg to confer with Ewell on the next stage of their advance. Ewell instructed him to march east the next day, passing through the crossroads town of Gettysburg heading for York, at which point he would be squarely across the direct rail link between Harrisburg and Baltimore. He was then to go on east and destroy the bridge across the Susquehanna River at Wrightsville, southeast of Harrisburg. After that he would move to the northwest and rejoin the rest of the corps at Carlisle, and then the entire corps would move on and capture Harrisburg. Besides his own division of infantry and its attached battalion of artillery, Early would have the 17th Virginia Cavalry of Jenkins' Brigade and Lige White's cavalry battalion, still detached from Grumble Jones's brigade. One of Early's officers wrote home that, although he pitied the poor civilians: "Pigs, chickens, geese, etc., are finding their way into our camp; it can't be prevented, and I can't think that it ought to be. We must show them something of war."[48] Hill's 3rd Corps marched to Hagerstown that day, and Pickett's Division and the reserve artillery of the 1st Corps crossed the Potomac at Williamsport.

Only Hood's and McLaws' divisions remained south of that river, and they were closed up and ready.

More Rebels visited Mercersburg that day, a party of guerillas from Virginia and Maryland. Unlike the regular troops, they robbed the civilians without making any pretense of payment, and they conducted a slave hunt. The Reverend Dr. Schaff described this as "the worst spectacle I ever saw. The raiders proclaimed first that they would burn every house that harbored a fugitive slave. They searched every house, capturing several contrabands, among them a woman with two little children. A most pitiful sight, sufficient to settle the slavery question for every humane mind. The guerillas left with horses, cattle, 500 sheep, two wagons full of store goods, and 21 Negroes. They claimed all the Negroes as Virginia slaves, but I was positively assured that two or three were born and raised in this neighborhood."[49] A detachment of the 1st New York Cavalry, part of Milroy's force at Bloody Run, attacked Maryland Steuart's pickets at McConnellsburg that day and drove them into the town, "creating," Milroy later reported, "great commotion in a large force of the enemy, mostly infantry – about 2,000."[50] But Milroy made no attempt to drive the Rebels away.

Lee, himself, crossed the Potomac into Maryland that rainy day, where he was met by a delegation of women who presented him with a wreath of flowers. He made camp in a hickory grove three miles from Williamsport, where he was visited by a young boy who had met him the previous year on his first foray north of the Potomac. The boy brought him some raspberries, and Lee invited the lad to dine with his mess, along with generals Longstreet and Hill.

In Middle Tennessee that day, the 25th, General Bragg's attention was primarily fixed on Liberty Gap, for McCook's position there threatened Polk's corps at Shelbyville, where Bragg expected Rosecrans to make his main attack. He saw Wilder's seizure of

Hoover's Gap and Crittenden's advance farther east as attempts to divert his attention. Rosecrans' plan, meanwhile, continued to unfold. "As it was not yet certain," he later reported, "whether the enemy would advance to test our strength on McCook's front, or mass on the flank of the Fourteenth Corps, near Fairfield, the orders for June 25 were as follows: Major-General Crittenden to advance to Lumley's Stand, 6 miles east of Beech Grove [at the south end of Hoover's Gap], and open communication with General Thomas. General Thomas to attack the rebels on the flank of his advance position at the forks of the road, and drive the rebels toward Fairfield. General McCook to feign an advance, as if in force on the Wartrace road, by the Liberty Gap passes. General Stanley, with his cavalry, to occupy their attention at Fosterville, and General Granger to support him with his infantry at Christiana." However, "the incessant rain," as Rosecrans termed it, slowed these movements to little more than a crawl. Thomas's advance was held up waiting for Brannan's division to return from its foray with Granger. Rosecrans said J. J. Reynolds' division did advance toward Fairfield, "but did not attack the enemy, who appeared to show a disposition to contest our advance by that route."[51] But Reynolds' report shows that this "advance" consisted only of bringing up reinforcements from other divisions and deploying more artillery. "Skirmishing was going on all day," Reynolds said, "more or less actively, between the regiments supporting the batteries and the enemy's pickets. Near sundown on the 25th, the enemy opened quite vigorously on our batteries, and for nearly an hour an active cannonade was kept up, which resulted in very slight damage to us."[52]

The only sizable combat that day was at Liberty Gap, where elements of Major General Patrick Cleburne's division – arguably the best in Bragg's army – tried to dislodge the Federals. General Willich's Union brigade took over the picket line at that gap early that morning, but Willich strengthened it to the point that it was a regular skirmish line, composed of two regiments, complete with support companies and reserves. Confederate probes by a few skirmishers, backed up by cavalry well to the rear, were easily repulsed in the morning. At around 2 p.m. the attacks became more serious as strong skirmish lines advanced but were also beaten off. "He repeated his attack," Willich later reported, "bringing up lines of battle, even columns, and planting one battery in front of our left and two small pieces [of artillery] in the center, but was not able to break our picket line, which was re-enforced by our support companies, who charged repeatedly against the forward pressing lines of the enemy, and drove him as often as he advanced."[53]

"The advancing enemy was exposed to the fire of our well-sheltered men," Willich said. "The fire was often given at from 30 to 50 yards, and our men fired coolly and deliberately." That was very close range for rifled muskets; even an individual is an easy target that close, let alone a whole battle line. At about 3 p.m. the two regiments on the skirmish line began to run out of ammunition, so Willich sent a third regiment forward, which shared its ammunition with the first two. "This, with the ammunition taken from the wounded and killed, enabled these three regiments to resist the repeated desperate efforts of the enemy," Willich said. He then sent another regiment to serve as a reserve behind the center of his line and posted a battery on a hill, although the latter had to fire over the heads of some of his infantry. As a result, as often happened in that war, some of the battery's shells fell on their own infantry. As Willich pointed out, "The powder used for the cartridges is of different [*i.e.* variable] quality, so much so that the best officers, with the most superior arms, and served by the most skillful men, can never become certain of the exact range of their guns."

Between 5 and 6 p.m. ammunition on the front line was nearly exhausted again, so Willich ordered his reserve to charge. "The Forty-ninth Ohio Volunteers advanced in splendid style, through the open woods, received with cheers by the rest of the brigade. The men of these regiments who had a few rounds left, and even many that had none, advanced bravely with the Forty-ninth Ohio. When coming under the enemy fire, Colonel [William H.] Gibson gave the order, 'Advance, firing.' The regiment formed in four ranks. The first rank delivered a volley, then the fourth, third, and second in succession took the front and delivered their fire, but already to the third volley the enemy did not answer. He had precipitately left his position." Advancing in this way allowed three ranks to be in various stages of reloading while one was firing, each rank advancing a short distance to the front before delivering its own volley. It made for a slow advance but one covered by an almost-continuous fire. Willich eventually halted his men at a fence bordering an open field, not wanting to expose them in the open to cannister fire from the Rebel artillery and feeling that his men could not follow the enemy "as quick as he ran."[54] Another brigade then came up and took over the front, but there were no more Confederate attacks that day.

General Buckner, commanding in East Tennessee, wired that day in response to a dispatch from Bragg's chief of staff, "I can send you two batteries and nearly 3,000 infantry. I will accompany them on your summons."[55] Buckner then wired General Sam Jones, Confederate commander in Western Virginia, saying he might soon again need to borrow the regiment from that department that he had recently borrowed during Sanders' raid.

At Port Hudson that day, Corporal L. H. Skelton of the 1st Mississippi crawled out of the Confederate position known as the Priest Cap and, in broad daylight, made his way to the head of the Union sap, set fire to the cotton bales being used as a sap roller, and safely returned to his regiment's defenses. However, he soon saw the Federals extinguish the fire, so he went back and lit it again, this time holding off the Federals with two captured Enfield rifles until the cotton was burning fiercely, and again he made it safely back to his lines. After that the Federals covered their cotton bales with dirt and erected a cavalier made of huge casks, called hogsheads, filled with dirt and covered with sandbags, from which sharpshooters could pick off anyone attempting to repeat Skelton's feat.

∽ **Endnotes** ∽

1. Nye, *Here Come the Rebels!*, 253.
2. *OR*, I:27:II:551.
3. McClellan, *I Rode with Jeb Stuart*, 319.
4. *OR*, I:27:III:927.
5. Ibid., I:27:III:295.
6. Cooper H. Wingert, *The Confederate Approach on Harrisburg* (Charleston, 2012).
7. *OR*, I:27:III: 299.
8. Ibid., I:27:III:301.
9. Ibid., I:27:III:292.
10. Ibid., I:27:III:291.
11. Ibid., I:27:I:55-6.
12. Ibid., I:27:I:56.
13. Ibid., I:27:III:285.
14. Ibid., I:27:III:295.
15. Ibid., I:27:III:296, both messages.
16. Ibid., I:27:III:288-9, both messages.
17. Ibid., I:27:III:289-291, all 3 messages.
18. Ibid., I:27:III:301-3.
19. Ibid., I:27:III:305.
20. Ibid., I:27:III:307.
21. Ibid.
22. Ibid., I:27:III:312.
23. Coffin, *Nine Months to Gettysburg*, 170-2. All three quotes.
24. Ibid., 177.
25. *OR*, I:27:III:318.
26. Ibid., I:27:III:309, both messages.
27. Ibid., I:27:II:693.
28. Ibid., I:27:III:311.
29. Ibid., I:27:III:312.
30. Ibid., I:27:III:317.
31. Ibid., I:27:III:324.
32. Ibid., I:27:III:325.
33. Ibid., I:27:III:317-18.
34. Ibid., I:27:I:57.
35. Ibid., I:27:III:317.
36. Ibid., I:27:I:56-7, all 3 messages.
37. Ibid., I:27:III:323.
38. Ibid., I:27:III:931.
39. Ibid., I:27:III:931-3.
40. Ibid., I:27:III:933, both messages.
41. Ibid., I:27:III:936.
42. Ibid., I:27:II:793.

43 Ibid., I:27:II:796.
44 Ibid., I:27:III:333.
45 Ibid., I:27:III:321.
46 Ibid., I:27:III:322.
47 Nye, *Here Come the Rebels!*, 263-4.
48 Ibid., 269.
49 Ibid., 255.
50 *OR*, I:27:II:280.
51 Ibid., I:23:I:406.
52 Ibid., I:23:I:456.
53 Ibid., I:23:I:487.
54 Ibid., I:23:I:487-8.
55 Ibid., I:23:II:885.

CHAPTER 16

"The Whole Rebel Army Is Marching Toward Harrisburg"

25 – 27 June 1863

Jefferson Davis wrote, on that 25th day of June, to both General Bragg and General Beauregard, asking if they could spare any more troops to reinforce Johnston in Mississippi. Neither one felt that they could.

Charles Dana wrote to Secretary Stanton that day, saying, "We have authentic information from Joe Johnston. He is between Canton, Bolton, and Bridgeport, and has made no movement of importance since that of Loring's [Division] back across the Big Black. The report from the spy of General Grant, which led to the sending out of Sherman on the 22d instant, was a mistake, though it must have had some foundation. Our present accounts indicate 35,000 as about the limit of the total troops of Joe Johnston. . . . Pemberton yesterday sent out to General Grant 4 men whom he has for several months held as hostages for the slaying of a Mr. White while concerned in a guerilla fight in Western Tennessee. Their release indicates the near surrender of Vicksburg. . . . From the best intelligence we can gain, the supply of food cannot be stretched to last more than a week longer. . . . Meanwhile our siege works are urged forward with great industry, though, if there was a better supply of engineer officers, the labor would be much more effectively applied. . . . The Marine Brigade has gone on an expedition, or rather a reconnaissance, to Delhi. The enemy are endeavoring to cut off the navigation of the Mississippi. They have planted a battery of six guns on Catfish Point, opposite Greenville, and have annoyed several boats on their way down. An expedition leaves to-day to clear them out. . . . The forces under Sherman still remain on Clear Creek and Bear Creek. No orders to return have been sent to them."[1]

The expedition that Dana mentioned, to clear away the Rebels that were annoying transports coming downriver, left Snyder's Bluff that afternoon under the command of Lieutenant Colonel Samuel J. Nasmith of the 25th Wisconsin. He had with him the 600 men of his own regiment (from Kimball's division, 16th Corps), the 4th Ohio Battery with four cannon, and 200 troopers of the 5th Illinois Cavalry. They proceeded to Young's Point, on the west bank of the Mississippi, where they were joined by three gunboats and one boat of the Marine Brigade, which was carrying 50 infantrymen and 100 cavalry. But they were detained there overnight waiting for coal for the boats.

Captain Hickenlooper's mine was completed that day. After the war he wrote that, "The main gallery was carried in 45 feet, and then a smaller gallery extending in on the same line 15 feet, while from the end of the main gallery two others were run out on either side at angles of 45 degrees for a distance of 15 feet. The soil through which this gallery was driven was reddish clay of remarkable tenacity, easily cut and requiring but little bracing." The powder was obtained from the Navy, brought up in barrels to the main sap and then transferred to 25-pound sacks. "These were taken upon the backs of the miners," he said, "who made the run over the exposed ground during the intervals between the explosion of the enemy's shells; and so well timed were these movements that, although it required nearly one hundred trips with the dangerous loads, all were landed in the mine without a single accident."[2]

His notes for the 25th say: "Last night during my temporary absence the miners became frightened at noise made in rebel counter-mine and quit work. Had to rush it ahead this a.m., and finished it before 9 o'clock. Deposited 1,500 pounds of powder in three different branch mines (500 in each), and 700 pounds in center; 2,200 pounds in all. Fuses so arranged as to explode them all at the same instant. Mine tamped with cross-timbers, sandbags, &c., and all ready to explode at 1 p.m. As per order, the mine was fired at 3.30 p.m."[3] (Charles Dana gave the time as just before 4 p.m., and various Confederates gave it as 5 p.m. or 5:30.)

In his post-war account, Hickenlooper (by then a brevet

brigadier general) said: "The commanding general having been advised on the day previous that the work would be completed before 3 p.m. of the 25th, general orders were issued directing each corps commander to order up the reserves and fully man the trenches, and immediately following the explosion to open with both artillery and musketry along the entire twelve miles of investing line; under cover of which the assaulting columns, composed of volunteers from the 31st and 45th Illinois, preceded by ten picked men from the pioneer corps under charge of the chief engineer, were to move forward and take possession of the fort. For an hour or two previous to the time of the explosion the scene from 'Battery Hickenlooper,' where General Grant and his subordinate commanders had taken their positions, was one of the most remarkable ever witnessed. As far as the eye could reach to the right and left could be seen the long winding columns of blue moving to their assigned positions behind the besiegers' works. Gradually as the hour of 3 approached the booming of artillery and incessant rattle of musketry, which had been going on all day, suddenly subsided, and a deathlike and oppressive stillness pervaded the whole command. Every eye was riveted upon that huge redoubt standing high above the adjoining works.

"At the appointed moment it appeared as though the whole fort and connecting outworks commenced an upward movement, gradually breaking into fragments and growing less bulky in appearance, until it looked like an immense fountain of finely pulverized earth, mingled with flashes of fire and clouds of smoke, through which could occasionally be caught a glimpse of some dark objects, – men, gun-carriages, shelters, etc. Fire along the entire line instantly opened with great fury, and amidst the din and roar of 150 cannon and the rattle of 50,000 muskets the charging column moved forward to the assault."[4]

"The effect," General Grant later wrote, "was to blow the top of the hill off and make a crater where it stood. The breach was not sufficient to enable us to pass a column of attack through. In fact, the enemy having failed to reach our mine had thrown up a line farther back, where most of the men guarding that point were placed. There were a few men, however, left at the advance line, and others working in the countermine, which was still being pushed to find ours."[5] Six Confederates, who were working in their countermine at the time of the explosion, were buried alive, but their shaft, being the path of least resistance, allowed much of the force of the explosion to escape, so not as much damage was done to the fort and its defenders as otherwise would have been done.

Where the fort had stood there was now a crater, 40 feet wide and 12 feet deep. "But little difficulty was experienced in entering the crater," Hickenlooper said, "but the moment the assaulting forces attempted to mount the artificial parapet, which had been formed by the falling debris about midway across the fort, completely commanded by the Confederate artillery and infantry in the rear, they were met by a withering fire so severe that to show a head above the crest was certain death. Two lines were formed on the slope of this parapet, the front line raising their muskets over their heads and firing at random over the crest while the rear rank were engaged in reloading. But soon the Confederates began throwing short-fused shells over the parapet, which, rolling down into the crater crowded with the soldiers of the assaulting column, caused the most fearful destruction of life ever witnessed under like circumstances. The groans of the dying and shrieks of the wounded became fearful, but bravely they stood to their work until the engineers constructed a casemate out of the heavy timbers found in the crater, and upon which the earth was thrown until it was of sufficient depth to resist the destructive effects of the exploding shells."[6]

According to Sergeant Tunnard, who was among the fort's defenders, not only artillery shells but purpose-made hand grenades were used in this fight. "These missiles," he said, "weigh about a pound, are an oval-shaped iron shell, a little larger than a hen egg and filled with powder."[7] Unlike the artillery shells, they did not have fuses; they were set off by a percussion cap being struck by a spring-loaded rod that would be driven in if the grenade landed on its nose. They had fins at the other end to make them, supposedly, fly right and land nose-first, but they didn't always do so. If they failed to detonate, the men on the receiving end would pick them up and throw them back, which they could also do with the artillery shells if their fuses were cut too long. However, the Rebels had the high ground and only had to throw or, in the case of the shells, roll them down on the Federals, whereas the latter had to throw them uphill – hard enough with the 1-pound grenades and even more difficult with the heavier shells.

Tunnard's 3rd Louisiana was soon reinforced by the 6th Missouri of Bowen's Division. This regiment's colonel was sick and should have been in bed, but, leading from the front, he jumped up on the top of the Confederate entrenchments and yelled for his men to come on. "They were his last words," Tunnard said, "for he was killed almost instantly by the deadly aim of the enemy's sharpshooters." And his men could not advance beyond the parapet. The battle soon resolved into a stalemate – the Confederates unable to push the Federals out of the crater; the latter unable to advance farther – but it raged on until dark, and beyond. "The day was very warm," Tunnard remembered, "and the sun sank below the horizon looking like a great ball of fire through the bluish haze – as if ashamed to shine bright and clear upon such a scene of butchery and bloodshed."[8]

"At dark the enemy had possessed himself of the ditch and slope of the parapet," Major General John Forney, commander of the Confederate division involved, reported, "and our forces retired to an interior line a few feet back."[9] They were soon reinforced by another regiment from Bowen's Division. "During the night," Grant said, "we made efforts to secure our position in the crater against the missiles of the enemy, so as to run trenches along the outer base of their parapet, right and left; but . . . we found it impossible to continue this work."[10] For the fight still continued all night and into the next day. Nevertheless, Hickenlooper, in his notes that day, termed his mine a "Perfect success. Troops rushed in and took possession of crater, and detail of pioneer troops went to work under my direction clearing away entrance to same."[11]

The next day, the 26th, Grant wrote a short dispatch to Halleck: "Yesterday a mine was sprung under the enemy's most commanding fort, producing a crater sufficient to hold two regiments of infantry. Our men took immediate possession, and still hold it. The fight for it has been incessant, and thus far we have not been able to establish batteries in the breach. Expect to succeed. Joe Johnston has removed east of the Big Black. His movements are mysterious, and may be intended to cover a movement from his rear into East or West Tennessee, or upon Banks. I have General Sherman out near his front on the Big Black with a large force watching him. I will use every effort to learn any move Johnston may make, and send troops from here to counteract any change he may make, if I can."[12]

Charles Dana sent a much longer report to Secretary Stanton at 10 a.m. on the 26th. After describing the fight of the day before he said, "We have made no progress in the work whatever, and have not been able either to plant a battery or open a rifle-pit, or even to ascertain what is the real practical value of the fort of which we have just got possession of one corner, and cannot tell whether the adjoining works are or are not enfiladed against fire from it. Our loss since the explosion to this hour is from 60 to 100 killed and wounded, including two lieutenant-colonels and 1 major. . . . [The Confederates reported their losses at 94 killed and wounded.] The siege works in front of Sherman are the most advanced, but have been delayed for two or three days by the effort to find a mine which the enemy . . . has run under our lines. General Grant this morning sent for Steele, who is in command there during Sherman's absence up Big Black, and directed him to push his approach with the utmost energy, and endeavor to crown the work to-day, if possible. F. Steele says it cannot be done before to-morrow. Similar orders have been sent to Ord, and every means will be taken to prevent the enemy from concentrating against McPherson.

"Steele's pickets, on the Mississippi, just above the wreck of the sunken gunboat Cincinnati, yesterday captured a rebel mail-carrier attempting to make his way through the Yazoo bottoms. Among his letters was one from General M. L. Smith and one from Major [W. T.] Withers, chief of artillery in Vicksburg. . . . All these letters agreed in saying that they were on short rations. . . . General Dennis, commanding at Young's Point, has thoroughly picketed the river front of Vicksburg (on the Louisiana side, of course), and began yesterday to keep the people from procuring water from the Mississippi by the fire of his sharpshooters. This he was also able to do to a great extent during the night. The rebels fired their water batteries at him, but up to this morning their shells have done him no damage."[13]

Captain Hickenlooper's notes for 26 June say: "Having orders to arrange crater for two guns, with proper protection for infantry support, commenced construction of covered gallery in center of crater, from which to lead mines or counter-mines, as the case might require. Finished it before dark, with a loss of 7 of pioneer company wounded. The rebels' hand-grenades (6 and 12 pound shells) being very destructive, the men were called back and placed behind rifle-pits, thrown up across center of crater, where they were perfectly protected against grenades thrown by the enemy, and still be able to hold the crater."[14]

Grant sent a report to Adjutant General Lorenzo Thomas that day, explaining in more detail why he had relieved McClernand from command. He sent along copies of the letters he had received from Sherman and McPherson complaining about McClernand's congratulatory order, a copy of that order and the correspondence relating to it, and a copy of his order replacing McClernand with Ord. "A disposition and earnest desire on my part to do the most I could with the means at my command," he said, "without interference with the assignments to command which the President alone was authorized to make, made me tolerate General McClernand long after I thought the good of the service demanded his removal. It was only when almost the entire army under my command seemed to demand it that he was relieved. The inclosed letters show the feelings of the army corps serving in the field with the Thirteenth Corps. The removal of General McClernand from the command of the Thirteenth Corps has given general satisfaction, the Thirteenth Army Corps sharing, perhaps, equally in that feeling with the other corps of the army."[15] The disposition to do the best he could with what he was given was one thing that set Grant apart from generals like McClellan and Rosecrans and endeared him to Halleck, Stanton and Lincoln. He didn't complain, he didn't demand, he made no excuses, he just got on with his job.

The expedition upriver got moving that day, leaving Young's Point about noon. That afternoon Colonel Nasmith disembarked his cavalry on the east bank, at the foot of Island No. 82, then proceeded on up to Greenville, where he personally left the boats and joined his cavalry, leading it farther up the river bank, while the infantry and artillery remained afloat. But he found no Confederates to fight.

Sherman issued detailed instructions to his forces guarding the rear that day in the form of Special Order No. 135. It sent out cavalry pickets from two regiments and cautioned them that they "must keep their horses saddled and their weapons well in hand, and a surprise will be certain ruin to the officer in charge." Divisions were assigned to defend specified ridges. "Re-enforcements must not be clamored for," the order said, "but each commander will fight back, along the ridge he is guarding, stubbornly, reporting facts and not opinions, that the general in command may draw his own conclusions."[16] But there was still no sign of Joe Johnston west of the Big Black River.

Johnston was writing to Kirby Smith, commander west of the Mississippi, that day: "You have probably learned before this reaches you of the critical aspect of affairs at Vicksburg. General Pemberton is closely invested with his garrison, numbering about 18,000 effectives. It is impossible with the force the Government has put at my disposal to raise the siege of the city. The most that I can do is possibly to extricate the army, leaving the place in possession of the enemy. If forced to the alternative, this is what I shall be compelled to do, however reluctantly. Our only hope of saving Vicksburg now depends on the operations of your troops on the other side of the river. General Pemberton says he has provisions for a fortnight; perhaps he has them for a longer time. Now, if you can contrive either to plant artillery on the Mississippi banks, drive beef into Vicksburg, or join the garrison, should it be practicable or expedient, we may be able to save the city. Your troops up to this time have done nothing. Placing the highest confidence in your intelligence, skill, enthusiasm, and appreciation of the mighty stake involved in the great issue now pending, I have earnestly to suggest that you will repair with all possible dispatch in person to the scene of action, and do whatsoever in your judgment you may deem best to accomplish the immense result of saving Vicksburg and our communications with you department." He added a postscript, saying, "An intelligent officer, who brought dispatches from General Pemberton, expresses confidence that if your troops could send in abundance of cattle, and themselves (8,000) join the garrison, the place would be saved."[17]

Kirby Smith did none of these things, most of which were impossible, but he had authorized another move, within his Trans-Mississippi Department, that could be of some use to the defenders of Vicksburg, as well as to his own department: namely an attack on Helena, Arkansas. This town, on the west bank of the Mississippi roughly one-fourth the way downriver from Memphis to Vicksburg, had been captured in June of 1862 by Union forces coming down from Missouri, but its garrison was now part of the 13th Corps in Grant's department. The Confederate commander in Arkansas, Lieutenant General Theophilus H. Holmes, said, "The possession of this place has been of immense advantage to the enemy. From it they have threatened at all times an invasion of Arkansas, thereby rendering it necessary that troops should be held in position to repel such an invasion. From it they have controlled the trade and sentiments of a large and important scope of territory. It has been to them a most important depot for troops in their operations against Vicksburg. In view of these great advantages to them, of the great embarrassment of my movements elsewhere, arising from the proximity of a large and threatening army, and of the deleterious effect on that portion of the State cursed by their presence, it was deemed of very great importance that they should be driven from this their only stronghold in Arkansas."[18]

Holmes had proposed to Kirby Smith back on 14 June that he be allowed to attack Helena, which he was sure he could take, and permission had quickly been granted, but it was taking time to assemble enough force. He had set this day, 26 June, as the day for Major General Sterling Price to have his division (two brigades of infantry) and Brigadier General John Marmaduke's division (two brigades of cavalry) at the village of Cotton Plant, some 60 or 70 miles northwest of Helena, and Brigadier General James F. Fagan to have his brigade of infantry at Clarendon, some 50 miles west of Helena, "whence," Holmes said, "by converging roads, the two columns would move in the direction of Helena." He already had a brigade of cavalry, under yet another general named Walker (Brigadier General L. M. Walker), in the Helena area, and this officer was ordered "to allow no ingress to the place." Holmes arrived at Clarendon on the 26th from his headquarters at Little Rock and found Fagan's brigade there, but Price's column, the major part of his force, was being delayed by "rain, high water, and wretched roads."[19]

One of Price's two brigade commanders, Brigadier General Dandridge McRae, wrote to him that night about the difficulties he was having in getting his command across the Cache River: "None of my commissary or regimental wagons and but two ordnance wagons have arrived. My battery is over all safe, except the battery wagon, which is mired. The way [on] this side of the bridge is entirely impassable for wagons until it is cross-laid, which cannot be done to-night, as my men are worn out. I have had 200 men on fatigue there since 6 o'clock. The mud is so deep on this side of the bridge that mules cannot stand up, and it is so dark in the bottom that men can neither see to work nor [to] drive [wagons]."[20]

Down at Port Hudson, on the morning of the 26th, a new battery the Federals had built to bear on the Confederate position known as the Citadel opened fire, as did every other Union battery and ship, in an attempt to overwhelm that position. Confederate return fire was quickly silenced. The fort's flag was repeatedly shot away, but each time a rebel artillery lieutenant would retrieve it and erect it again. The parapet was breached by the Union shells, but no assault was made, and the damage was repaired that night. Casualties were light.

The Confederate defenders were running low on ammunition, but they were collecting Union bullets and musket balls from the ground and melting and molding them to fit their own weapons, as well as collecting unexploded Union artillery shells that could be fired back at the Federals or used as hand-grenades or land mines. Many 8-, 10- and 13-inch mortar shells had been collected and planted, at night, in front of Fort Desperate. As at Vicksburg, the one necessity that could not be manufactured was food. As there, mule meat and horse meat were now common fare, but even that would run out soon. As at Vicksburg, the Federals were digging approach trenches, but they were not yet so close to the Rebel works, although Banks wrote to Admiral Farragut that day that "Our pickets are in possession of the mound before the citadel, and we hope to run our trenches to the enemy's rifle-pits, and may, perhaps, assault the citadel itself." But he complained that he did not have "a sufficient number of thoroughly trained, thoroughly disciplined soldiers, enlisted for the war and desirous to bring it to an end."[21] By this he meant that many of his regiments' enlistments were about up, and these men, being so close to making it home alive, did not want to risk too much now. Two lieutenant colonels in Dwight's division were arrested that day "for speaking in a discouraging manner of the prospects of this army before Port Hudson, and for habitually using such language as is likely to discourage and dishearten the troops of this division in the event of an assault upon the enemy works."[22] No charges were preferred against either officer, however, and Banks ordered their release; both were later promoted.

Although morale was thus running low on the Union side, it was still good inside the defenses. That day, a Confederate lieutenant and 30 volunteers from an Arkansas regiment raided the head of one Union sap, which was still some 200 yards out, captured 7 prisoners, 14 rifles, and several sandbags, while killing or wounding several Federals, for the cost of one man slightly wounded. But that night Captain Pruyn returned to Port Hudson after having gone to Jackson to communicate with General Johnston, bringing news that there was no hope that the latter would come to the garrison's rescue. The only real hope left was that General Taylor's threat to New Orleans would cause Banks to give up the siege in order to return to its defense. Taylor, himself, was on the way back up to Alexandria, but some of the troops that had taken Brashear City were advancing along the railroad toward New Orleans; others were on their way to attack a Union garrison at Donaldsonville and to interdict Union traffic on the Mississippi. At the request of General Emory, at New Orleans, Banks was holding one brigade at Port Hudson in reserve to send down the river to his assistance, if needed.

In Pennsylvania that day, the 26th, Carlisle remained in Union hands, as no Confederates advanced that far. However, a patrol of the Curtin Guards was ambushed near Stone Tavern, southwest of there, and one of its men was wounded and several captured, although one of them managed to shoot and kill two Rebels before giving up.

Heth's division of A. P. Hill's 3rd Corps passed through Chambersburg that day, turned east, and stopped near Fayetteville, just west of Greenwood, for the night. Anderson's Division got two miles beyond Greencastle. Longstreet's last units, Hood's and McLaws' divisions, crossed the Potomac that day, so all of Lee's army was now north of that river except most of the cavalry, a few regiments left to hold the Shenandoah Valley, and the units left in the Richmond area. Lee himself passed through Hagerstown, Maryland, that day, where, despite the fact that it was raining again, he was met by another contingent of ladies, one of whom asked for a lock of his hair. He declined on the grounds of a dwindling supply and suggested she take one from the younger and more bountifully supplied General Pickett, but this did not set well with either Pickett, who wanted to keep all his locks, or the young lady, who was more interested in the famous commander. Residents who had seen Lee on his first invasion of Maryland thought he had aged visibly during the intervening ten months. He was still a fine figure of a man, however, and one young lady of the Union persuasion, who waved a U.S. flag as he passed by, was heard to say, "Oh, I wish he was ours."[23] British Lieutenant Colonel Arthur Fremantle, traveling with the Confederate army to observe the war, described Lee as "the handsomest man of his age I ever saw. He is fifty-six years old, tall, broad-shouldered, very well made, well set up, a thorough soldier in appearance; and his manners are most courteous and full of dignity. He is a perfect gentleman in every respect."[24]

Lee rode on to Chambersburg, where he was met by Hill, and on out the pike running toward Gettysburg, stopping at a little grove that was a favorite picnic spot of residents of the area. Ewell, with Rodes and Johnson's divisions of his 2nd Corps, moved on up the Cumberland Valley that day and bivouacked near Shippensburg, driving Captain Boyd's small Union cavalry force beyond the town. "Maryland" Steuart's brigade of Johnson's division ended its two-day stay at McConnellsburg and marched east to Loudon, where it briefly gathered up more horses and cattle. When it marched out again, two Rebels who fell behind, probably still looking for loot, were captured by locals, including some recently discharged Union soldiers, and summarily shot. When Steuart approached Chambersburg, he learned that the rest of Ewell's 2nd Corps had moved on to Shippensburg, so he again made a loop to the west, collecting more supplies at Roxbury and camped near there that night. Captain Jed Hotchkiss, topographical engineer of Ewell's corps, noted, "The land is full of everything, and we have an abundance. The cherries are very fine.

Our men behave admirably. General Lee wrote to General Ewell that he thought the battle would come off near Frederick City or Gettysburg."[25]

If Lee did indeed believe that, it's hard to see why he was concentrating most of his army at Chambersburg instead at one of those places. But one battle did come off at Gettysburg that same day, although it probably wasn't what Lee had in mind. Jubal Early's division marched in that direction that morning, following the orders Early had received the day before from Ewell. The column of marching men, covered by the attached regiment and battalion of cavalry, was accompanied only by its ambulances (light two-wheeled wagons), plus one medical wagon per brigade, the regimental ammunition wagons, and fifteen empty wagons to carry whatever supplies would be "purchased" on its route. The rest of the division's wagons were sent to Chambersburg to join the corps train. Even officers were only allowed to bring what they could carry on their person or horse.

Two miles down the road, Early came to an industrial establishment known as Caledonia Furnace: forges, a rolling mill, coal house, shops, stables, sawmill, storehouse, a large charcoal-burning furnace, and a cluster of cottages for the workmen. It belonged to Thaddeus Stevens, a leader of the Radical Republicans in the U.S. Congress. At Early's order, his cavalry burned the furnace, sawmill, forges, rolling mill, office and store room. In addition, Stevens, who was in Lancaster at the time, later wrote a friend, they "took all my horses, mules and harness, even the crippled horses, that were running at large. Then they seized my bacon (about 4000 lbs.) molasses and other contents of the store – took about $1000 worth of corn in the mills, and a like quantity of other grains. . . . They even hauled off my bar iron, being as they said convenient for shoeing horses and wagons, about $4000 worth. They destroyed all my fences. . . . My grass they destroyed; and broke in the windows of the dwelling houses where the workmen lived."[26] Nevertheless, Stevens took a philosophical attitude to his loss, saying that everyone must expect to suffer from the war.

Six miles farther on, after having crossed South Mountain via Cashtown Gap, Early came to a road that forked off to the left, running due east through the villages of Hilltown and Mummasburg. Since he had heard that there was a Union force of unknown size at Gettysburg, he decided to use this road to bypass it with most of his division. About a mile down the road he stopped at a tavern, where he confiscated a map of Adams County displayed on the wall. He sent only the brigade of Brigadier General John Gordon on down the main road toward the town, preceded by White's cavalry battalion, to keep the Federals there from interfering with his main column. Or, should the force at Gettysburg be too large for Gordon and White to handle, Early could come in on its flank from the north with the rest of his division.

General Couch had already recognized that the numerous roads that converged at Gettysburg made that a point that the Rebels might eventually visit. He had, therefore, sent Major Granville O. Haller, of the Regular Army, to that town. For troops, he had only been able to give Haller the Philadelphia City Troop, the home guards known as the Adams County Cavalry (Gettysburg was the seat of Adams County), some civilian scouts, and the 26th Pennsylvania Volunteer Militia. This last unit was commanded by Colonel William Jennings, age 25, a friend of Governor Curtin. It had 743 officers and men, which was about twice the size of a veteran regiment, but it was also about as green an outfit as ever existed. It had only been mustered in on the 18th, had spent a couple of days at Harrisburg, receiving uniforms and equipment, and had then been put on a train bound for Gettysburg. About six miles from there, their train had run into a cow that had strayed onto the track, derailing several cars.

The men had bivouacked in the woods nearby, dining that night on hardtack and beef, both rather tough. Only about 100 of its men had ever fired their muskets, and these, designated as "sharpshooters," had been sent ahead to watch for any Rebels coming through Cashtown Gap, but a heavy rain had prevented them from proceeding beyond Gettysburg, and the rest of the regiment caught up with them there at about 9 a.m. on the 26th.

It was a familiar place to some of these men, for one company of the regiment was composed of students from Pennsylvania College, located there. The militiamen had a nice breakfast provided by the patriotic citizens, and at around 10:30 a.m. Major Haller sent them west on the Chambersburg pike to block any Confederate advance from Cashtown, despite the protests of Colonel Jennings that his men were too inexperienced to face any real Rebels. Then Haller headed east to Hanover to secure some government property there.

Jennings left a captain and forty men in the town to protect the railroad cars containing the regiment's baggage, then, preceded by the Adams County Cavalry, marched the rest westward in a drizzling rain to Marsh Creek, three and a half miles out of town. There they filed off to the right of the road and pitched their tents in a field of wet clover, with one company posted as pickets west of the stream. Then Jennings and Captain Robert Bell of the cavalry rode to the top of a ridge south of the pike, from which they could get a look around. Two miles up the road they could see several companies of cavalry in column, heading their way, and behind them a much larger column of infantry. And they weren't wearing Union blue. Jennings rode back to his regiment, got the tents struck and the men in ranks, and hastily marched them onto a dirt road that wandered off to the north and connected with the Mummasburg-Hunterstown road not far east of Mummasburg.

White's Rebel cavalry stopped to search the militia's campsite for plunder and to round up some of the pickets who had been left behind. Meanwhile, Bell's cavalry retreated to and through Gettysburg, where it was joined by the Philadelphia City Troop, the civilian scouts and the infantrymen left to guard the regiment's baggage. After riding down some of the Federals who couldn't get out of the way fast enough, White's Confederates soon rode into Gettysburg, "yelling and shouting," as a professor at the local college put it, "like so many savages from the wilds of the Rocky Mountains...."[27]

The militiamen who had been left to guard the baggage and

the Philadelphia cavalrymen had escaped to the east, taking with them a Rebel trooper they had captured. Many of White's men were soon drunk on beverages provided by the nervous civilians. Others searched the town for horses and for food. Then Gordon's Confederate infantry marched in from the west, in a drizzling rain. One resident of the town said that she "never saw a more unsightly set of men, and as I looked at them in their dirty, torn garments, hatless, shoeless, and foot-sore, I pitied them from the depth of my heart."[28]

General Early was amused to learn that the force of unknown strength at Gettysburg had turned out to be nothing but a bunch of militia that had run at first sight of his veterans. He left two of his brigades in camp on the west edge of Mummasburg and rode down to see Gettysburg for himself, dropping off another brigade about a mile northwest of the town. He assembled the town council and presented a demand for cash, rations and other useful supplies, but these worthies claimed to be unable to provide most of it. He had the town searched, but that didn't turn up much either, although he did take note of a shoe factory and sent word of it back to Chambersburg. Some 2,000 rations, meant for the 26th Pennsylvania, were found in some railroad cars on a sidetrack; these were issued to Gordon's men, and the cars and a small railroad bridge were burned. Early called off further search, satisfied that the locals, warned by refugees from the Cumberland Valley, had sent their movable property elsewhere. The innkeeper at the Globe Inn, which housed the headquarters of the Adams County Democratic Party, thought he recognized one of Early's aides as a man who had been a customer at his inn three weeks before.

The miscellaneous Federal units from Gettysburg continued on to Hanover, about 15 miles to the east. Major Haller reported to Couch from there that night that the Rebels' "advance guard" had caused Jennings to "fall back . . . without advising me or awaiting orders." He added later: "Rebels in Gettysburg. Ran our cavalry through town; fired on them; no casualties. Horses worn out. Ordered all troops to York, to rendezvous at Camp Franklin.

... Cavalry, officers and men, did well."[29] The same could not be said of the infantry.

Late that afternoon, the 17th Virginia Cavalry caught up with Jennings' 26th Pennsylvania at a spot about four miles north of Gettysburg called Bayly's Hill, where the east-west Mummasburg-Hunterstown road intersected the north-south Gettysburg-Middletown road. Seeing the Rebel troopers come over a ridge a few hundreds yards behind his column and spread out in skirmish formation, Jennings tried to form his regiment along a fence north of the road, but it wasn't easy. One militiaman said, "Such confusion I never saw – everyone gave orders and no one obeyed – we were all green and knew nothing about regular forming."[30] Even worse than their lack of formation was the fact that the powder in many of their muskets was wet and would not fire. Colonel William French, the Rebel commander, sent three companies forward dismounted and three others to turn the Federals' right flank, but, as one Rebel remembered, "the enemy only waited long enough to divest themselves of knapsacks, haversacks, canteens, blankets, and everything that would impede their flight and away they went soon crossing a stream."[31] French lost a few men to Union muskets that would fire, but managed to capture most of the rear-most company of militia.

Jennings finally managed to form a line on a hill some half-mile farther east. Calling the roll, he found that some 120 men were missing from his original 743. By then it was nearly night, and the Federals got away through the woods in the dark, convinced that the Rebels were hard on their heels, continuing on to the northeast until about 10 p.m. In fact, French had put his men in camp long since. Altogether, the Confederates captured about 174 men that day. General Early assembled them in the Gettysburg town square – known as the Diamond – and paroled them, telling them "You boys ought to be home with your mothers and not out in the fields where it is dangerous and you might get hurt."[32] Thus ended what we might call the first battle of Gettysburg.

Baldy Smith, as commander of the 1st Division of Couch's

department, was put in charge of all troops on the south/west side of the Susquehanna River near Harrisburg that day, relieving Couch of some of the problems of organizing a defense of the state capital. He inspected the units manning the new fortifications, had an artillery lieutenant on his staff correct some deficiencies in the placement of the guns, and put the troops to work clearing a field of fire and extending their trenches. That afternoon he sent two regiments of infantry four miles to the west to reconnoiter, but there was nothing to see and not much to do but steal cherries and otherwise annoy the civilians in the area. That evening it started to rain again, and the men took shelter in barns, except for a few nervous pickets left outside.

Major General Napoleon Jackson Tecumseh Dana, slated to be the commander of Couch's 2nd Division, if and when he ever had one, was put in command of the defenses of Philadelphia that same day. And Governor Curtin issued a call that day for 60,000 militiamen to repel the invasion. "They will be mustered into the service of the State for the period of ninety days," he said, "but will be required to serve only so much of the period of muster as the safety of our people and honor of our State may require."[33] This call met with a better response than the old call for a special corps. Eight regiments, including the 26th which fought that day at Gettysburg, were enlisted for the emergency or six months, and were designated Pennsylvania Volunteer Militia (PVM). All others, mustered in for either 60 days or 90 days, were known simply as Pennsylvania Militia (PM), and remained in state service, not Federal.

Joe Hooker was still trying to scrape up more troops for his army from Heintzelman's and Schenck's departments. At 7 p.m. on the 26th, he wired General Halleck from Poolesville, Maryland: "Is there any reason why Maryland Heights should not be abandoned after public stores and property are removed? I propose to visit the place to-morrow, on my way to Frederick, to satisfy myself on that point. It must be borne in mind that I am here with a force inferior in numbers to that of the enemy, and must have every available man to use in the field."[34] Hooker ordered General French, now in command at Harper's Ferry/Maryland Heights, to make a reconnaissance the next day toward Sharpsburg, Maryland. Meanwhile, he informed General Schenck that, with French in command, General Tyler's services could be dispensed with.

General Stahel sent some very good information to John Reynolds that afternoon from Frederick, Maryland: "I arrived at this place this afternoon, and have made the following disposition of my troops: I have one brigade and one section of artillery at Crampton's Pass, patrolling thoroughly on the other side, but without meeting with any enemy whatever; they are supported by one brigade and two sections of artillery of the Eleventh Corps. I have one regiment in South Mountain Pass, patrolling in that vicinity, but without meeting any of the enemy. One brigade and two sections of artillery are at Middletown, and two regiments about 2 miles from this place, on the road leading toward Lewistown. As was stated by telegraphic dispatch of last evening, there is no enemy in the neighborhood of any of the gaps, nor do they seem to have any intention of coming this side. There was a small force of rebel cavalry at Boonsborough this morning, but there are none of them there now.

"The whole rebel army is marching toward Harrisburg. Ewell's whole corps passed through Hagerstown and Smithsburg last Tuesday. Sixty-six pieces of artillery, belonging to this corps, passed through Hagerstown on Tuesday, and sixteen pieces belonging to the same corps passed through Smithsburg the same day. Their force is estimated at from 25,000 to 30,000. Both columns were marching in the direction of Greencastle. On Thursday, the 25th instant, Anderson's division, of Hill's corps, passed through Boonsborough about 6 a.m. They were three hours passing through the town. This column crossed at Shepherdstown. Ewell's corps crossed at Williamsport and Shepherdstown. I have sent out scouting parties of perfectly reliable men, who will endeavor to penetrate the enemy's lines and learn their strength and plans."[35] The only problem with this report was that it took 26 hours and 20 minutes for it to reach Reynolds, Stahel's excuse being that he didn't know where Reynolds' headquarters were. They were, in fact, a few miles southwest of him at Jefferson, Maryland.

Meanwhile, before receiving this report, Reynolds wrote to Butterfield that day: "The signal officers report that they can see nothing at Crampton's Pass. Howard [11th Corps] has moved up to Middletown.... General Birney [3rd Corps] is at Adamstown, and I have sent him orders to move up here to-morrow, and shall move Doubleday [1st Corps] forward to Howard.... The cavalry sent out by Stahel does nothing. They go into camp behind the infantry, and send out small squads from them."[36] This report might be at least part of what prompted an 8 p.m. wire from Hooker to Secretary Stanton, saying: "I would respectfully request that Major-General Stahel may be ordered by telegraph to report to General Couch, with a view to organizing and putting in an efficient condition any mounted troops that can be raised for service there. His presence here as senior major-general will much embarrass me and retard my movements."[37] Stahel's seniority meant that he outranked Pleasonton, who still had Hooker's confidence.

Pleasonton wrote to Butterfield and Secretary Stanton at 12:45 p.m. that day from Leesburg, Virginia: "Have just arrived. One division is covering the flank from Aldie to this place, by way of Mount Gilead. Three brigades of the Second Division are covering the three roads from Aldie and Gum Springs. All quiet toward the Blue Ridge. Very few cavalry pickets seen near Middleburg this morning. None in the Snicker's Gap pike. The telegraph operator of Hancock's corps reported, last night, a body of several thousand cavalry at Gainesville, from the direction of New Baltimore. My dispositions cover that. I shall remain here until the crossing [of the Potomac] is accomplished."[38]

That body of Rebel cavalry had been, of course, Jeb Stuart's three brigades. Stuart now faced a dilemma for which there was no good solution: with the Union army on the move and filling the roads he wanted to use, he would have to go even farther east if he wanted to get around it to reach the Potomac east of the Blue Ridge; but, if he turned back, he would have to spend at least one day just retracing the ride he had already made and might well find the Confederate infantry blocking the fords and roads he would need to cross the Potomac west of the Blue Ridge. Either way, he would be late in reaching Ewell, but by going on instead of turning back he might still do some damage to the Union rear. Stuart waited a full ten hours near Buckland, hoping to hear from Mosby but never did. Then he resumed his attempt to ride through or around the Army of the Potomac on the morning of the 26th, marching southeast to Brentsville and then east to Wolf Run Shoals on the Occoquan River, where the horses were allowed to graze again. By then he had been marching for two whole days and was still at least as far from Ewell as when he had started out.

The 2nd Vermont Brigade, which had recently abandoned the Wolf Run Shoals area, took to the roads again that day but was delayed by mud and by having to wait for two divisions of the 6th Corps to pass. It marched cautiously past Aldie, in case Rebel cavalry was still in that area, and made it only as far as Herndon Station, on the Hampshire & Loudon Railroad, that evening.

Down in southeast Virginia that day, Colonel Spear's Union cavalry moved up the south side of the Pamunkey River and its tributary, the South Anna, to the point where the Virginia Central Railroad crossed the latter. Ironically, Corse's Brigade of Pickett's Division, which had been stationed near there, at Hanover Junction, had just moved a day or two before over to Gordonsville and been replaced by a single regiment. As Spear later reported, when he reached the bridge: "I found a force of 125 men, under command of Lieut. Col. T. L. Hargrove, of the Forty-fourth North Carolina Infantry. I at once commenced the attack. He held the bridge manfully for over an hour, when, by stratagem, he found me in his rear, and his entire force captured. Nine were killed, and many so badly wounded I paroled them on the spot, by advice of my surgeon. I completely destroyed the bridge, and burned it till it fell into the river. It was fired above and below, and nothing is left. Lieutenant-Colonel Hargrove had sent to Hanover Junction for re-enforcements, and when they arrived, too late to support this attack, they at once went to the other crossing, [of the] Richmond and Fredericksburg Railroad, which rendered it impossible, with the loss of ammunition, and my fatigued command, to attempt to carry [that] bridge with prudence or safety. . . . This done, I countermarched, and found on arriving at Hanover Ferry (now a bridge) that General Wise would intercept me if I returned the same route, on the south side of the river. I crossed, took up the planks, and returned, via Newcastle, King William Court-House, &c., to White House, north side, where I reported in person to the major-general commanding."[39]

The colonel of the 44th North Carolina reported Hargrove's force as 50 men of Company A of that regiment, reinforced by 40 men from Company G. He said, "The fight with Company A must have been severe and close, as the men killed and wounded are cut with sabers, and some burned with powder from pistols."[40] But Spear reported, in addition to the killed and wounded, 94 enlisted men captured, plus Hargrove, the captains of both companies, and three lieutenants, as well as Brigadier General Rooney Lee and a Confederate naval officer. The young Lee was found at his father-in-law's plantation, Hickory Hill, recovering from a wound. He would be held as hostage against the fate of a Union prisoner, Colonel Abel Streight, who had been captured leading a raid down in Georgia and sent to Libby prison. The Confederates had refused to exchange him. Lee's younger brother, Robert Jr., who had been serving as Rooney's nurse, escaped capture by hiding in a hedge.

Spear added a postscript to his report, saying: "*En route* I met and captured a Government agent of the Confederate States, and took from him about $15,000, Confederate bonds. He was making a payment for purchased stores."[41] General Dix, in forwarding Spear's report to General Halleck a couple of days later, said: "A large number of slaves (men, women, and children) followed Colonel Spear's train. As they are desirous of remaining, I shall set the men to work, and send the women and children to Fort Monroe."[42]

In New York City, Admiral Foote died that day, making Admiral Dahlgren's command of the South Atlantic Blockading Squadron permanent.

Meanwhile, the Confederate Navy was not idle. *Archer*, the schooner taken over by the Rebels from the *Tacony*, having already captured 21 ships in 19 days, sailed right into Portland, Maine, late that afternoon and captured the revenue cutter *Caleb Cushing*. However, the Confederates were attacked by a collection of steamers and tugboats, and eventually the Rebels blew up the cutter and surrendered.

Out in Kentucky that day, the 26th, messages began passing back and forth between various Union commanders that Morgan's Confederate cavalry was reportedly entering that state and looking for a place to cross the upper reaches of the Cumberland River. The town of Burkesville, or fords in that area, were considered his likely crossing place, and yet the Federals did not go there to block him. In fact, Brigadier General Henry M. Judah, commander of the 3rd Division of the 23rd Corps (a mixed force of infantry, mounted infantry, and cavalry), had recently concentrated most of his division west of there and seemed reluctant to get too near. The plan, if there was one, seems to have been to let Morgan come north of the Cumberland, but not to let him get back, which did eventually work out, but only after a very long and difficult chase. General Burnside, from his headquarters at Cincinnati, wired General Hartsuff, commander of the 23rd Corps, at Lexington, that day: "Keep everything ready to move at a moment's notice. . . . All Judah's cavalry should be dashed at Morgan as soon as he gets well across, and, if possible, he should be broken to pieces."[43]

In Middle Tennessee that day, Rosecrans' complex plan continued to unfold. "On the 26th," he later reported, "most of the movements ordered for the 25th were completed, amid continuous rains. Generals Rousseau's, Reynolds', and Brannan's divisions [all from the 14th Corps] co-operated in a general advance on the enemy, who, after a short resistance, fled toward Fairfield, near to which place our pickets were advanced, while Reynolds' division and the baggage moved forward during the night toward Manchester, Wilder's brigade having seized Matt's Hollow early in the afternoon, and thus secured the passage."[44] But Wilder said, in his report, that his mounted brigade moved up a creek and overland to turn, or get around, "the strong position of Matt's Hollow; but on arriving at the Manchester pike, after it reaches the table-land, we found that the infantry column was passing, having met no enemy, they having retreated in the direction of Fairfield. We camped that night 6 miles from Manchester."[45] Rosecrans moved his own headquarters to Beech Grove, at the south end of Hoover's Gap, that afternoon.

Bragg was convinced that Rosecrans' main effort would come by way of Liberty Gap, farther west, where Hardee's corps was concentrating to hold against McCook's 20th Corps. Bragg met with General Polk at Shelbyville that afternoon and directed him to move north through Guy's Gap and then turn east to attack Rosecrans' right flank. Polk protested that the rough terrain and bad weather made such a move unworkable, but Polk never liked any idea that wasn't his own anyway, so Bragg ignored his complaint. However, soon after this meeting, while Polk was making his preparations, Bragg learned that a Union force, estimated to be as large as Hardee's entire corps, was moving through Fairfield, making for Manchester. He realized then that his entire line was being turned, for a Federal corps at Manchester would be about as close to his base at Tullahoma as Hardee was, and closer to the bridges over Elk River than Polk was. Bragg's chief of staff wrote to Polk at 4 p.m.: "Movement proposed for to-morrow is abandoned. Your corps must still be ready, with rations cooked, for prompt movement." Hardee wrote to Stewart: "The movement for to-morrow against Liberty Gap has been given up. If the enemy shows any disposition to press, withdraw your forces to Wartrace for a march on Tullahoma. Cleburne has been instructed to withdraw the two brigades he has near Liberty Gap to Bellbuckle early to-morrow morning."[46] At 11 p.m., Bragg ordered both Hardee and Polk to fall back behind the swollen Duck River to the entrenchments at Tullahoma.

General Buckner wired Bragg that day from Knoxville: "I learn of a large body of Federal cavalry near Jamestown [Kentucky], beyond Wartburg [Tennessee]; nevertheless, if they do not move before I do, I will join you. I start my troops as soon as I can get transportation for them. . . . Yours is the decisive point, and you may expect me."[47] Buckner's chief of staff wired General Samuel Jones, in southwest Virginia, that Buckner was going to reinforce Bragg and that he definitely wanted to borrow the 51st Virginia again, as he had done during Sanders' recent raid.

General Garfield wrote to General McCook at 11 p.m. on the 26th: "The general commanding directs you to move your [wagon] train forward to this place [Beech Grove] at 3 o'clock to-morrow morning, with orders to close up with General Thomas' train, now moving toward Manchester. At early dawn put your command in motion to this place, evacuating Liberty Gap as silently and secretly as possible. It may be best to move your force not holding the gap before that hour." Knowing that Major General Philip Sheridan's division was between army headquarters and McCook's, to speed things up he included directions for Sheridan to "read this dispatch, and act in obedience to it. He will forward it to any other division commander that may be in the route between him and General McCook."[48]

At midnight, Garfield sent orders to Stanley's cavalry to "feel the enemy in your front early to-morrow morning. General Granger's command will not advance farther than Guy's Gap. If it should appear that the enemy has fallen back beyond Duck River, General Stanley may advance to Shelbyville, if he deems it advisable. General Stanley will immediately send his baggage to the Manchester pike, and follow with his command as soon as the demonstration ordered above is made. He will leave one brigade of cavalry with General Granger; all the remainder must be brought to the front."[49] Garfield had already written to General Thomas at 10:15: "The general commanding desires to put this army on the south side of Duck River at the earliest practicable moment. He directs you to send General Reynolds' division forward at daylight to-morrow morning, with orders to cross the river at Manchester if the position of the enemy does not render it too perilous. At all events, he must endeavor to cover the crossing, and put everything in readiness to effect it as soon as practicable."[50]

The next day, Saturday the 27th, Wilder and his mounted brigade advanced again, cutting off a Confederate picket post, and, as he later reported, they "were in Manchester before the few rebels there knew of our approach. We captured about 40 prisoners."[51] Wilder immediately sent out pickets of his own, and as soon as Reynolds, his division commander, arrived, Wilder sent a detachment to destroy a trestle on the McMinnville railroad only four miles from Bragg's base at Tullahoma. In his official report, Rosecrans said: "June 27, headquarters reached Manchester, where General Reynolds' and part of Negley's division had already arrived. The remainder of Thomas' corps came in during the night. It was now manifest that the enemy must leave his intrenched position at Shelbyville, and that we must expect him at Tullahoma, only 12 miles distant. It was therefore necessary to close up our columns on Manchester, distribute our rations, and prepare for the contest. While this was progressing, I determined to cut, if possible, the railroad in Bragg's rear. Wilder's brigade was sent to burn Elk River Bridge and destroy the railroad between Decherd and Cowan, and Brig. Gen. John

Beatty, with a brigade of infantry, to Hillsborough, to cover and support his movements."[52]

Meanwhile, the Confederates marched south as best they could through the mud and rain. Cleburne, commanding one of Hardee's two divisions, had received orders during the night to retreat to Tullahoma at daylight on the 27th, "which I did without any loss," he later reported, "although my men were much wearied by the watching and fighting in front of the gaps, for it rained incessantly during most of the time. The men had no changes of clothing, no tents, and could not even light fires to dry themselves. Many had no shoes, and others left their shoes buried in the deep mire of the roads."[53]

With the Rebel infantry out of the way, the Union cavalry pushed through Guy's Gap on the 27th and collided with the Confederate horsemen trying to cover the retreat. "The enemy abandoned their position," Stanley later reported, "and fled toward Shelbyville, closely pursued by the First Middle Tennessee Cavalry [Union] . . . supported by the Fourth Regular Cavalry. . . . Immediately afterward I directed Colonel [Robert H. G.] Minty to support this movement with his whole brigade. The enemy in considerable force, consisting of [Brigadier General William T.] Martin's division and part of [Brigadier General John A.] Wharton's, all under command of Wheeler, made a stand at the fortifications 4 miles north of Shelbyville, where they commenced shelling our advance." Minty sent the 4th Michigan Cavalry to get on the Rebels' flank, and this caused the Confederates to mount up, preparing to fall back. Seeing this, the 7th Pennsylvania Cavalry, supported by the 4th U.S., charged up the pike and captured many of them before they could get away. Minty's entire brigade then pursued them to the edge of the town of Shelbyville, where Confederate artillery drove them back.

When he learned of this, Stanley sent word for Minty to charge the battery and capture it, and for Brigadier General Robert B. Mitchell to support Minty with his two brigades and a section of artillery. Then Stanley and Granger started for the front, but by the time they arrived the 4th Michigan, armed with

Colt revolving rifles, had driven the Confederates from the entrenchments. "The rebels fled to the town," Stanley reported, "where they attempted another stand on the line of the public square and railroad depot, but a part of Colonel Minty's brigade charging them on the pike, in the teeth of their battery, and Colonel [Archibald P.] Campbell's brigade [of Mitchell's division] cutting off their retreat at the upper bridge over Duck River, the enemy was overthrown, routed, his cannon and 591 prisoners captured, including 6 field officers, and a large number, estimated as high at 200, of the enemy killed, wounded, and drowned in Duck River. . . . The enemy threw away their arms in their flight, and two of their generals – Wheeler and Martin – escaped by swimming the river. Some five or six hundred stand of arms and a considerable amount of commissary and ordnance stores fell into our hands. . . ."

The reason that Wheeler made a stand at the river instead of destroying the bridge was that he had learned that Forrest's cavalry was planning to use it to cross the swollen river. That so many of his men were captured was at least partly due to the fact that a cannon or an artillery caisson overturned on the bridge, blocking traffic. Meanwhile, Forrest had realized that he couldn't reach that bridge in time and had found another crossing. "At midnight," Stanley said, "I learned from one of my scouts that Forrest's command, which had floundered in the mud all day between Unionville and Middleton, was crossing Duck River 4 miles below us, in great disorder, and endeavoring to escape to Tullahoma. I consulted General Granger as to the propriety of moving our whole force to attack and intercept him, but the general was of the opinion that the command was too much wearied to move in the night. As the matter turned out, I think it was very unfortunate that this attack was not made, as I think we could have completely routed this part of Forrest's force."[54] Nevertheless, considerable damage had been done to the mounted arm of Bragg's army. As one observer noted, the "finest cavalry of the rebellion found a grave in the mud and slime of Duck river. They never recovered from this defeat and its attendant horrors."[55]

Granger's infantry marched into Shelbyville at 6 p.m. He might have been surprised by the warm reception they received, for there was strong pro-Union sentiment in the town. "The Stars and Stripes floated from many windows and house tops," he reported to Garfield that night, "and we met a hearty welcome."[56] Probably no one was more happy to see the Federals march in than Pauline Cushman, who had been condemned for spying for the Union army and was being held at Shelbyville awaiting execution. She was seriously ill at the time, and a doctor recommended leaving her behind, as she couldn't live much longer anyway. However, she soon recovered from whatever illness, real or feigned, had postponed her hanging, and she was made an honorary major in the Union Army.

Bragg sent a brief report to Richmond from Tullahoma that day: "Yesterday the enemy in large force passed my right after skirmishing sharply along my whole front for two days. The line of Shelbyville being too long to be held successfully by my force, I to-day resumed my position in my intrenchments at this place to await the full developments."[57]

∽ Endnotes ∽

1 OR, I:24:I:108.
2 Hickenlooper, "The Vicksburg Mine" in B&L III:541-2.
3 OR, I:24:II:202.
4 Hickenlooper, "The Vicksburg Mine" in B&L III:542.
5 Grant, Personal Memoirs, I:551.
6 Hickenlooper, "The Vicksburg Mine" in B&L III:542.
7 Hoehling, Vicksburg: 47 Days of Siege, 228.
8 Ibid., 227-8.
9 OR, I:24:II:364.
10 Grant, Personal Memoirs, I:552-3.
11 OR, I:24:II:202.
12 Ibid., I:24:I:43.
13 Ibid., I:24:I:109-10.
14 Ibid., I:24:II:202. The shells would have been lighter than the weights given. They were shells for 6- and 12-pounder guns, but the terms 6-pounder and 12-pounder referred to the weight of the solid shot those guns threw; the shells, being hollow so as to hold gunpowder and fuse, would have

been quite a bit lighter.
15 Ibid., I:24:I:159.
16 Ibid., I:24:III:442-3.
17 Ibid., I:24:III:979, also I:22:II:885-6.
18 Ibid., I:22:I:408-9.
19 Ibid., I:22:I:409.
20 Ibid., I:22:I:886.
21 Ibid., I:26:I:599.
22 Ibid., I:26:I:600.
23 Douglas Southall Freeman, *R. E. Lee* (New York, 1934-5), III:54.
24 Schultz, *The Most Glorious Fourth*, 146.
25 Nye, *Here Come the Rebels!*, 302.
26 Ibid., 270.
27 Ibid., 274.
28 Scott L. Mingus, Sr., *Flames Beyond Gettysburg* (New York, 2011), 122.
29 OR, I:27:III:344, both messages.
30 Nye, *Here Come the Rebels!*, 276.
31 Mingus, *Flames Beyond Gettysburg*, 133.
32 Nye, *Here Come the Rebels!*, 277.
33 OR, I:27:III:347.
34 Ibid., I:27:I:58.
35 Ibid., I:27:III:334-5.
36 Ibid., I:27:III:335.
37 Ibid., I:27:I:58.
38 Ibid., I:27:III:333.
39 Ibid., I:27:II:796.
40 Ibid., I:27:II:797.
41 Ibid., I:27:II:797, italics in the source.
42 Ibid., I:27:II:794.
43 Ibid., I:23:II:469.
44 Ibid., I:23:I:406.
45 Ibid., I:23:I:459.
46 Ibid., I:23:II:886, both messages.
47 Ibid., I:23:II:887.
48 Ibid., I:23:II:463.
49 Ibid., I:23:II:465.
50 Ibid., I:23:II:467.
51 Ibid., I:23:I:459.
52 Ibid., I:23:I:406-7.
53 Ibid., I:23:I:587.
54 Ibid., I:23:I:539-40.
55 William B. Feis, "The Deception of Braxton Bragg" in *Blue & Gray Magazine*, X:1:51.
56 OR, I:23:I:534.
57 Ibid., I:23:I:583.

CHAPTER 17

"Tried and Condemned Without a Hearing"

27 – 28 June 1863

RICHARD TAYLOR WROTE TO Kirby Smith from Alexandria, Louisiana, on Saturday, the 27th: "I left Brashear City late on Wednesday night (24th instant), having made all the dispositions which were practicable, and arrived here a few hours ago. The receipt of communication from . . . General Johnston . . . induced me to hasten to this point, for the purpose of making such arrangements as are called for by the information contained in that communication. I have also received a report from Major-General Walker, in which he states that the unhealthiness of the locality in which his division has been operating has produced much sickness among his troops, which is daily increasing, and the effective men of the command are greatly reduced in number. Should the fall of Vicksburg occur, as predicted by General Johnston, Port Hudson must, of course, speedily follow, and thus a junction between the troops in the Washita and Upper Mississippi Valleys and those in the La Fourche would be attended with great difficulty. . . . I have ordered Major-General Walker's division to proceed immediately to Berwick Bay; thence I shall send it into the La Fourche country. . . . I feel confident that if Vicksburg should not fall shortly, the operations of our forces on the Mississippi coast between Baton Rouge and New Orleans will relieve Port Hudson."[1]

Meanwhile, operations near the west bank of the Mississippi continued, though perhaps not exactly as Taylor had planned or hoped. General Thomas Green, commanding the brigade of cavalry sent to capture Donaldsonville, Louisiana, wrote to General Mouton that day from a plantation about eight or nine miles from that place: "I have been all the morning collecting together all the information relative to the situation and strength of the defenses of Donaldsonville. After traveling all night, we arrived here at sunrise this morning. . . . I learn from citizens that the fort contains from 300 to 500 Yankees, and that there are five gunboats there now. The approach to the fort is through an open plain 900 yards, and the ditch around it is 16 feet wide and 12 feet deep, making it impossible to scale, except by having strong plank or suitable ladders. I have had a full consultation (which, by the way, is not the best thing to be governed by). They think that an attempt to storm will be attended with great loss and no adequate benefit, even if successful; and this is my opinion.

"The object of the expedition – being to annoy and take, if possible, the enemy's transports – can be better and more safely done by taking a position below Donaldsonville. I am making a bridge of sugar-coolers at this camp to cross one regiment, intending to swim the horses. I will push that regiment close upon Donaldsonville, throwing pickets up on the river. I am about sending another regiment down on this side near the fort, throwing pickets above, where the river can be seen. My pickets above and below will be able to see what number of gunboats there are at the fort, and I propose to fix the bridge during the day so that I can get artillery on the Mississippi. With one rifle section I can make the transports coming up retreat. Come down and take command. I want you badly, as I do not know fully what your views are, and would not like to take any steps in conflict with them. . . . I think now the fort can be rendered nugatory by taking a position below it. Adopting the latter view will induce the Yankees very probably to abandon the fort or come out and fight us."[2]

The Federals were aware of the Confederates' presence. An officer on General Emory's staff wired Donaldsonville's defenders from New Orleans that day: "Make a good fight. I will soon send gunboats to aid you."[3] In fact, Banks himself asked the Navy to send the ironclad *Essex* to aid in the defense of that place. Emory wrote to Banks that day saying he had not received acknowledgment of receipt of the messages he had sent regarding the fall of Brashear. "I need not remind the general," he said (but did anyway), "of the total inadequacy of the force left to guard the vast public interest here, if the enemy's force should be turned toward New Orleans."[4]

Meanwhile, General Halleck was writing to Banks that same day, and, in response to a previous report of trouble with the 9-months regiments, told him that, if troops were thought likely to refuse to charge, to place artillery behind them, loaded with cannister, with orders to fire on them "at the first moment of disaffection." He said that the reasons Banks gave for moving against Port Hudson were satisfactory, then added: "I regret exceedingly that we can get no more troops to send you. The discharge of nine months' and two years' men has so reduced our forces that we can hardly defend Washington and Baltimore. The effect of the Copperhead disaffection at the north has prevented enlistments, and the drafting has not yet been attempted. We have been forced to resort to State militia, most of whom refuse to be mustered into the service of the United States. Notwithstanding that Pennsylvania is invaded by a large army, the militia of that State positively refuse to be mustered. This is the work of the politicians."[5]

Up in Arkansas, the movement against Helena still wasn't moving, or at least not very fast, due to the rain and mud. Price's infantry had managed to get across the Cache River, but then came to Bayou de View and Caney Creek. Price wrote to General Holmes that day, saying: "The very heavy rains of yesterday and last night raised both the bayou and the creek so much as to sweep away the bridges, and to render the bottoms utterly impassable. Large working parties, limited only by the number of axes and tools in the command, have been kept constantly employed, and I am using every energy to the repair of the bridges and road. I hope to get over Bayou de View to-night or to-morrow. I shall have then to wait for the fall of Caney Creek, which is swimming, and which I have no means to bridge. The citizens of the vicinity inform me that it generally becomes fordable within twenty-four to forty-eight hours after the rains cease. I shall not depend upon its fall, however, but will do all that my limited means make possible to cross it."[6]

Meanwhile, the Federals at Helena had no idea that the Confederates were trying to get at them. General B. M. Prentiss, commanding there, wrote to Hurlbut, at Memphis, that day and said: "You mention that Price is at Jacksonport, building boats. I had information that he was there, but the latest intelligence from him is that he was moving toward Red River. My scouts have not been able for the past ten days to bring reliable information, further than that I am and have been threatened for weeks by a superior force of cavalry. Three full regiments are within 20 miles of this place, preventing communication with the interior. I have less than 4,000 men here, and of that number 600 are cavalry."[7]

On the other side of the Mississippi that day, Colonel Nasmith's expedition continued. "Searching the country to finds signs of the enemy," he later reported, "I arrived at Carter's plantation June 27, evening. The transports, with the infantry and artillery, came around by water. Not being able to find or hear of any enemy on this side of the river, I am satisfied, from information received from reliable sources, that there has been no enemy near Greenville, on the Mississippi shore, for nearly four weeks; previously to that time there was a small force encamped on Deer Creek, distant 10 miles from Greenville. We found at the foot of Island no. 83 embrasures cut in the levee for three guns, and across the point – 3 miles distant – for 2 guns; that a road had been cut across the point, connecting the two places; that they were in the habit of running the guns across the point while the boats were going round, and firing on the same boat at the two points."[8]

At Vicksburg that day, Grant was writing to Halleck: "Joe Johnston has postponed his attack until he can receive 10,000 re-enforcements, now on their way from Bragg's army. They are expected early next week. I feel strong enough against this increase, and do not despair of having Vicksburg before they arrive. This latter, however, I may be disappointed in. I may have to abandon protection to the leased plantations from here to Lake Providence, to resist a threat from Kirby Smith's troops. The location of these leased plantations was most unfortunate, and against my judgment. I wanted them put north of the White River."[9]

Halleck must have appreciated hearing from a general who thought he had enough troops, but this is a rare instance of Grant forwarding bad information. He had a very good intelligence system, run by General Grenville Dodge, up at Corinth, who employed numerous spies, both military and civilian. This particular idea came from one of those, as Charles Dana wrote to Secretary Stanton that day: "Spy from Canton, 25th, arrived at Haynes' Bluff on 26th. Troops of Joe Johnston (35,000) under marching orders; Joe Johnston personally in command; 10,000 from Bragg, viz, 5,000 from Polk and 5,000 from Hardee's corps, now on their way; will re-enforce Joe Johnston on or before 30th. Never saw so extensive a wagon train as that accumulated at Canton; mules all in good order; artillery very numerous, but of mixed sizes and characters. Whole body will move to attack Sherman early next week, just as soon as re-enforcements from the east arrive. All are zealous for fight; conscripts numerous in their ranks. They bring corn by rail from the country south of Granada.

"I was at Sherman's camp, on Bear Creek, yesterday afternoon, and found his amazing activity and vigilance pervading his whole force. The country is exceedingly favorable for defense, and he has occupied the commanding points; opened rifle-pits wherever they will add to his advantage; obstructed the cross-roads and most of the direct roads also, and ascertained every point where the Big Black can be forded between the line of Benton, on the north, and the line of railroad, on the south. By rapid movements of his forces, also, and by deploying them on all the ridges and open headlands, he produces the impression that his forces are ten times as numerous as they really are. He has moved but one division from Haynes' Bluff, and has General Parke's corps still encamped at Milldale, in front of Haynes' Bluff, where it was placed on its first arrival. His right, under Osterhaus, still rests on the railroad bridge across the Big Black. Scouts before mentioned say that Price and E. Kirby Smith combined are about to attempt to provision Vicksburg by way of Milliken's Bend, which they will try to capture. A vast number of small boats have lately been prepared in Vicksburg. Of the siege, there is nothing of importance to report since my last dispatch. McPherson has not yet succeeded in placing batteries or rifle-pits in the breach made by the explosion of the 25th. He is now busily engaged in mining the adjoining fort on the left of the one whose bastion he then blew up. [Signal] Rockets were thrown up in Vicksburg last night and night before last, and they were answered from a point on the Louisiana side opposite Warrenton."[10]

Sherman wrote a long dispatch to Rawlins that day regarding the situation between the Yazoo and Big Black, saying, "It was my purpose to come to headquarters yesterday, but the importance of knowing the ground in this quarter, so broken and complicated, induced me to continue what I had begun, and I continued my exploration. Big Black River is so easily passable at many points that I am forced to extend my lines to watch all. . . ." He went on to tell of a couple of families he had forcibly removed because they were suspected of passing information to the Rebels and apt to give details of his plans for defense should Johnston come his way, but added, "Not a sound, syllable, or sign to indicate a purpose of crossing Big Black River toward us, but I still enjoin on all that our enemy is too wary to give us notice a minute too soon. Every possible motive exists for them to come to the relief of Vicksburg, and we should act on that supposition rather than the mere signs of movements which are known only to Johnston, and will not be revealed, even to his own troops, till the last moment."[11]

Johnston received Pemberton's dispatch of the 23rd that day – the one in which Pemberton had suggested that Johnston should negotiate with Grant to see if he would allow the garrison to depart in exchange for the surrender of the city. Johnston told the captain who had brought the message and would carry the reply, that he was "in no condition to move in Pemberton's favor."[12] To Pemberton he wrote: "General E. K. Smith's troops have been mismanaged, and have fallen back to Delhi. I have sent a special messenger, urging him to assume the direct command. The determined spirit you manifest, and his expected co-operation, encourage me to hope that something may yet be done to save Vicksburg, and to postpone both of the modes suggested of merely extricating the garrison. Negotiations with Grant for the relief of the garrison, should they become necessary, must be made by you. It would be a confession of weakness on my part, which I ought not to make, to propose them. When it becomes necessary to make terms, they may be considered as made under my authority."[13] But Pemberton never received this message.

Meanwhile, the siege continued. Captain Hickenlooper's notes for 27 June say: "Entire force at work on left trench. Sent the detail of miners over to advanced work of General Ransom. Work progressing lively on Battery Archer, and small work for howitzer in front of rebel mortar."[14] On Sherman's part of the front facing the Vicksburg defenses, now commanded by Steele, the Confederates were the ones to explode a mine that day, "which," as Charles Dana reported to Stanton the next day, "destroyed those [that] Sherman's engineers had nearly finished, and threw the head of his sap into confusion generally. The engineers have gone back some 500 feet to run a new mine under the fort. The gully will not be less than one and a quarter hundred feet in length, and will require several days to complete."[15]

General McClernand wrote to Halleck that day from Springfield, Illinois: "In compliance with General Grant's order, I have the honor to report to Headquarters of the Army by letter for orders." He enclosed copies of various correspondence relating to his relief from command and briefly listed his accomplishments during the campaign, saying, "I ask, in justice, that I may be restored to my command at least until Vicksburg shall have fallen. Only two days before my banishment from the Department of the Tennessee, General Grant had increased my command by the positive addition of one division and by the contingent addition of two others, making it larger than the Fifteenth and Seventeenth Army Corps combined, and therefore cannot consistently object upon the score of distrust of my fidelity or ability."[16] No reply is on record, and probably none was sent. Halleck had great disdain for political generals and was, no doubt, quite happy to see this one put on the shelf.

In Virginia, General Dix wrote to Halleck from White House plantation that day: "I arrived here last night. General Keyes' column reached Cumberland, 5 miles below here, last evening, and will be here this morning. The roads are very bad. After weeks of continual drought, we have had three days of continual rain, which has probably swollen the waters of the Chickahominy greatly. The enemy had just finished a battery here, with a railway turn-table in it, for a railroad monitor, which mounts four guns. It was to have been in position yesterday, but Colonel Spear tore up the track the day before. I am expecting news from him this morning."[17]

Late that night (actually 1 a.m. on the 28th) Major General J. G. Foster, commander of the Union's Department of North Carolina, wired Halleck from Fort Monroe: "I have just arrived here with the last of the six regiments of Massachusetts militia that I was to send. I came in person to see that there was no delay in getting the transports across the Swash Channel and to this point. I have brought General [Henry] Prince to command the brigade of Massachusetts militia. General [Francis B.] Spinola's brigade, of Pennsylvania, was embarking at Beaufort, and should be here to-morrow. General [Henry M.] Naglee was telegraphed to be here, to take command of the division formed by these two brigades." Halleck replied a few hours later for the troops Foster had brought to be "turned over to General Dix for temporary duty. Judging from all reports received, nearly all the rebels troops have been withdrawn from North Carolina and Southern Virginia."[18]

In that, he was close to the truth. Confederate Secretary of War Seddon wrote to General D. H. Hill on the 27th: "You had better send here to-morrow [Micah] Jenkins' brigade and any other spare force you may have around Petersburg. The enemy are reported as concentrating about the White House, but I do not feel sure that there are yet more than some 6,000 there."[19] Hill wrote to Seddon from Petersburg that same day: "My adjutant, Major [Archer] Anderson, goes over to ascertain the condition of things below, so that I may know whether Colquitt should be ordered up. I think he ought not to come till the movement be fully developed. The North Carolina Railroad is of immense importance to us, and it can be cut when he is gone. On the other hand, if he is not here to take the place of Jenkins, this town could be taken by a handful of cavalry. So soon as the Yankees have abandoned their gunboats and fully developed their intentions, I think everything should be abandoned for the time being, Corse and Colquitt brought in, and an attack made upon the thieves. We can, for an emergency, bring together enough troops to make Dix the subject of the [prisoner exchange] cartel which he helped to frame."[20]

In reply, Seddon said: "Use your discretion about Colquitt. Some force, the number to be judged by yourself, should be left to prevent incursions in North Carolina. I think we may need all that can be spared." Later he added: "Positive information received that General Dix, with some 25,000 or 30,000 men, had concentrated at Yorktown. A real attack is doubtless intended. Your whole force will probably be needed, and you are requested to make disposition accordingly, without delay." Seddon also wrote to General Corse, whose brigade had been sent up to Gordonsville. "Reliable information is received that General Dix, with about 30,000 men, is below on the Peninsula, and will probably advance for a real attack on this city. If you have no positive intelligence of an [enemy] advance toward Gordonsville, hold yourself, with sufficient [railroad] cars, ready to return on call to

[Hanover] Junction, or, if need be, to this city."[21]

Jubal Early had his troops on the road at dawn on the 27th. He took three of his four infantry brigades and most of the 17th Virginia Cavalry along the road that passed north of Gettysburg through Hunterstown, New Chester, Hampton and East Berlin. Some of the men were still drunk and had trouble keeping up with the column. One hundred twenty-six paroled members of the 26th Pennsylvania Militia marched in the other direction, making for the railroad at Shippensburg. Led by two captured militia officers, Gordon's Brigade marched east from Gettysburg that morning out the York pike, screened by one company of the 17th Virginia Cavalry. Though the sky remained cloudy, the intermittent rain that had dogged them since the evening of the 25th finally ended that morning, the total, at Gettysburg, amounting to a bit over an inch and a quarter. The Rebels were all gone by 8 a.m., and at about 9:30 three Union scouts rode into town and captured two couriers whom General Ewell had sent to communicate with Early. The Confederates were highly impressed by the fertile and well cultivated country through which they marched and were pleased to discover that it was baking day for all the housewives along their route. Much of the resulting bread filled the Rebels' bellies, along with what one Georgian called, "milk, butter and cheese in the most extravagant abundance."[22]

White's cavalry battalion turned off to the southeast at New Oxford and stopped at the hamlet of McSherrystown to ask civilians whether there were any Union troops at Hanover, which was only another mile and a half down the road. The locals didn't know of any, and they were correct, for Major Haller and his home guard cavalry had already departed by then, making for York. But one civilian managed to ride ahead and warn the citizens of Hanover that the Confederates were coming that way. So when the Rebels rode into town and went "shopping" (with Confederate money) they found that most of the merchants had hidden their stock or shipped it farther east. They spent some time cutting telegraph wires and burning a few bridges, but around noon they rode out again, still heading east, and about 2 p.m. they came to Hanover Junction. Here the railroad to Hanover split off from the Northern Central Railroad, which connected Baltimore with Harrisburg. They chased away part of the 20th Pennsylvania Militia and burned railroad facilities, and late that afternoon they rode off to the north and bivouacked about three miles south of where Gordon's infantry stopped for the night, west of York.

After getting his other brigades into camp between East Berlin and Dover, Early rode down to confer with Gordon about the next day's march. Gordon informed him that word was that York was undefended. "If that proves true," Early told Gordon, "you will pass on through and move rapidly to the river to secure both ends of the Wrightsville-Columbia bridge."[23] Later that evening a civilian came in from York and asked Gordon for permission to inform the citizens there that the Confederates were coming. Gordon agreed on condition that the same man or a deputation of city officials would return to him early next morning and inform him whether there would be any resistance to his occupation of the town. That night Major Haller wired General Couch from York: "Off toward Wrightsville and Columbia. The enemy approaching with the Gettysburg force, about 4,000. Will respect private property if not resisted, and borough authorities wish no resistance."[24]

The other two divisions of Ewell's 2nd Corps moved on up the Cumberland Valley that day, Ewell with Rodes' Division taking a dirt road called the Walnut Bottom, which was muddy after overnight rains, and Johnson's Division, with the supply wagons and reserve artillery, following the macadamized turnpike. Most of Jenkins' cavalry led the way, although a company visited the town of Newville, on the railroad, looking for horses but didn't find many. However, they did find about 300 cattle, and one of the Rebels found his sister living there, and another found a man who had been his teacher down in Virginia not long before. One resident of the town thought that the Confederate commander, a Captain Priest, was "Quite a gentleman. He stood on one of our street corners talking politics with one of our citizens until nearly midnight."[25]

Around 10 a.m., Captain Boyd's Union cavalry passed through Carlisle, informing the citizens there that the Rebel cavalry would be along soon but that the Federal troopers would not try to defend the town, lest it be shelled. The town's burgess and his deputy rode out under a flag of truce and informed Jenkins that no resistance would be offered and asked that the Rebels not come dashing into town and scare the women and children. Jenkins agreed, and, at about 11 a.m., his men came in quietly but cautiously. He then demanded food for 1500 men and forage for his horses and left a detail to receive these while he led the bulk of his brigade on out the east end of town. Provost detachments patrolled the streets and searched for horses.

The Confederate infantry was not far behind Jenkins' cavalry, stripping the roadside orchards of great bunches of cherries, as they marched up the road. Rodes' Division came on into Carlisle, led by Ewell's escort, Company A of the 1st Maryland Cavalry. One brigade bivouacked on the campus of Dickinson College, where a professor noted that "Some had chickens under their arms, some loaves of bread, some onions, and some eggs in their pockets, captured in the fat valley of Cumberland."[26] Another brigade made camp on the east edge of town, and the others turned north to Carlisle Barracks, the Regular Army's primary facility for recruiting and training cavalrymen. Ewell had been stationed there after graduating from West Point. Now he took over the post commander's quarters. Rodes reported finding musketoons (short muskets used by cavalry before rifled carbines had become common), tents, rations and a great deal of grain for the horses. The town was searched for weapons, food, cooking utensils, and shoes, and doctors were required to turn over surgical instruments, medicines and chloroform for the military surgeons. A railroad bridge was destroyed, and a Rebel company serving as provost guard cut down and burned telegraph poles, using them to cook its supper.

A local teenager was impressed with the appearance of Rodes' men. "Knapsacks and the whole personal kit was in order," he said. "Arms were at every man's command. A significant touch to neatness was a toothbrush at hat band or buttonhole. The officers' uniforms were of light gray cloth, the garniture a brilliant gold galloon; the privates' a dark gray with a few martial frills. Further opportunity for inspection of the cavalry, infantry, artillery, and transportation service confirmed my first impressions of a fit, well-fed, well-conditioned army."[27]

Johnson's Division, marching behind Rodes', stopped short of Carlisle, making camp near Big Spring Creek at Springfield, about three miles to the west, where Maryland Steuart's Brigade finally caught up with it. At around 4 p.m., Ewell sent for Jenkins and gave him orders to scout ahead toward Harrisburg. He would be accompanied by Ewell's chief engineer and another officer of his staff, to gather information about crossings of the Susquehanna River, the stream's depth and current, and the availability of material for bridging it. The cavalry was to find out about the defenses of the city, strength of any Union forces there, their dispositions, and their morale. Jenkins started out before dark and bivouacked that night in fields near Hickorytown, about halfway to Mechanicsburg. All during the night, his pickets were harassed by the small mounted militia company called the Curtin Guards.

Of the two regiments that Baldy Smith had sent west from Harrisburg to reconnoiter the day before, one had gone to Shiremanstown (less than three miles east of Mechanicsburg) and hung around there during the 27th, doing about as good a job of plundering the civilians as any Rebels could do, and then withdrew to their camp west of Harrisburg that evening. The other regiment had camped about a mile west of Oyster Point, a crossroads where there was a hotel built by a man named Oyster. It had a brief scare that day when some of its men spotted a larger force approaching from the west, but this turned out to be General Knipe's small brigade, which had moved west from

Kingston that day, but only as far as Ironstone Ridge, and when Knipe had heard from Boyd that the Rebels were approaching Carlisle he had turned his men around and marched east again. Couch gave Smith authority over Knipe that same day. Counting Knipe's two, five regiments of New York and Pennsylvania militia camped near Oyster Point that night.

A. P. Hill's 3rd Corps of Lee's army continued to close up around Chambersburg that day; Anderson's Division marched through that town, turned east, and camped at Fayetteville, where it stayed until 1 July. Longstreet's 1st Corps also reached Chambersburg that day. Lieutenant Colonel Fremantle, the British officer who was tagging along with the Confederates to observe the war, was impressed with the troops of Hood's Division, though he called them a "queer lot to look at. They carry less than any other troops; many of them have only got an old piece of carpet or rug as baggage; many had discarded their shoes in the mud; all are ragged and dirty, but full of good-humor and confidence in themselves and in their general, Hood. They answered the numerous taunts of the Chambersburg ladies with cheers and laughter."[28]

Lee again conferred that day with General Trimble, who had lived and worked in Pennsylvania before the war, building railroads. According to Trimble, Lee unfolded a map of Pennsylvania and asked him about the area east of the South Mountain ridge. Trimble assured him that almost every square mile of it was well suited for maneuver and battle. "Our army is in good spirits," Lee told him, "not over fatigued, and can be concentrated at any one point in twenty-four hours or less. I have not yet heard that the enemy have crossed the Potomac, and am waiting to hear from General Stuart. When they hear where we are, they will make forced marches to interpose their forces between us and Baltimore and Philadelphia. They will come up, probably through Frederick, broken down with hunger and hard marching, strung out on a long line, and much demoralized when they come into Pennsylvania. I shall throw an overwhelming force on their advance, crush it, follow up the success, drive one corps back on another, and by successive repulses and surprises, before they can concentrate, create a panic and virtually destroy the army." Trimble said that Lee pointed to Gettysburg on the map and said, "Hereabout we shall probably meet the enemy and fight a great battle, and if God gives us the victory, the war will be over and we shall achieve the recognition of our independence."[29]

Such prognostications reported after the fact are suspect, of course. While the strategy sounds logical, the allusion to Gettysburg as the site of the coming battle does not jibe with the fact that when the two armies did collide at Gettysburg a few days later there was nothing about Lee's actions or words at that time to indicate he had anticipated such an event all along. Anyway, the problem with this strategy was that Lee now had no idea just where the Union army was. He was in the same state of ignorance that Hooker had been in after the two armies had marched away from Fredericksburg. The primary reason for this, of course, was that Stuart had taken his best cavalry off on what amounted to a raid, and the two brigades he had left behind were put strictly on the defensive, with no orders to keep track of the Federal army. "Ah! general," Lee told Hood that day, "the enemy is a long-time finding us. If he does not succeed soon, we must go in search of him."[30]

Down in Virginia, Jeb Stuart put his troopers on the road again that morning, crossed the undefended Occoquan at Wolf Run Shoals and headed north toward Fairfax Station, which was no longer Hooker's headquarters. Fitz Lee's brigade was sent farther east to cut the telegraph line and railroad tracks at Burke's Station. Hearing that there was no sizable Union force at Fairfax Station, Stuart went on ahead of his other two brigades and soon outdistanced even his small escort – and almost got captured by a squadron of the 11th New York Cavalry, which had been sent from Heintzelman's command to take over some supplies left behind by Hooker, and which thought it had run into Mosby's guerillas. Stuart managed to reverse course in time, and the pursuing Federals soon ran into Hampton's lead regiment, was surrounded, and lost 82 of their number, while only 18 made it safely back to camp. One Rebel officer described it as, "Without exception the most gallant charge, and the most desperate resistance that we ever met from the Federal cavalry...."[31] Stuart paroled those he had captured, most of whom were wounded or injured. Hampton's Brigade occupied Fairfax Court House while Fitz Lee's found the recently abandoned camp of the 6th Corps at Annandale after capturing a train of sutlers' wagons, full of all kinds of treats, and its small Union escort.

Stuart sent off another courier to Lee, with a duplicate of this message going to Richmond: "I took possession of Fairfax C.H. this morning at nine o'clock, together with a large quantity of stores. The main body of Hooker's army has gone toward Leesburg, except the garrison of Alexandria and Washington, which has retreated within the fortifications."[32] Again, the message reached Richmond safely, but was never received by Lee. The "stores" that the Rebels found included two large warehouses belonging to the same sutler whose wagons had been captured by Fitz Lee, and they were full of shoes, socks, gloves, hats, and all kinds of luxury foods, such as pickled oysters, canned fruits, and ginger cakes. Stuart let his troops rest for a few hours and treat themselves to the captured goods, then, still not having heard from Mosby, marched for Dranesville that afternoon, picking up a few stragglers from the 6th Corps in that area. Hampton led the way from there toward the river and met a friendly civilian who recommended Rowser's Ford – the very place he was heading for – as the best place to cross the Potomac.

Alarmed by the report of the encounter of two companies of his cavalry with Stuart's command at Fairfax Station, at 2:40 p.m. Heintzelman's headquarters informed the Union commander at Arlington House (property of General Lee's wife) that five more companies of the 11th New York Cavalry were being sent to him for the purpose of making a reconnaissance in front of the defenses south of the Potomac and that "Colonel Lowell, with five companies of cavalry, is at Poolesville. He will be ordered to make a reconnaissance in front of our works from Poolesville to Alexandria."[33] But Lowell's cavalry was no longer at Poolesville. In fact, Colonel Charles Russell Lowell of the 2nd Massachusetts

Cavalry had been watching the very stretch of river that Stuart was aiming for. However, as he reported that morning to General Heintzelman's headquarters, he had received orders the night before from Hooker's headquarters to proceed with his command and report to General Slocum at Knoxville, Maryland. "I have withdrawn all my pickets," he added, "and shall leave here at 9 a.m., this date." Heintzelman's assistant adjutant-general replied at 10:45 a.m. saying: "You will not obey any order from Major-General Hooker ordering you to move until you have instructions from these headquarters."[34] But it was too late; Lowell had already moved, the reconnaissance could not be made, and there was not a single Union picket at Rowser's Ford.

Even though the recent rains had caused the mile-wide Potomac to rise two feet at that crossing, it still could be waded by the horses, although with some difficulty. Vehicles, including the horse artillery, however, would be another matter. Stuart had another nearby ford examined, but it was found to be unsuitable. "I, however, determined not to give it up without trial," he later reported, "and before 12 o'clock that night, in spite of the difficulties, to all appearances insuperable, indomitable energy and resolute determination triumphed; every piece was brought safely over, and the entire command in bivouac on Maryland soil."[35] The artillerymen had used flatboats and hawsers to get their guns across, while each cavalryman carried a shell or shot over the river.

At 9 a.m. on the 27th, General Halleck received a dispatch from Hooker that said: "That there may be no misunderstanding as to my force, I would respectfully state that, including the portions of General Heintzelman's command, and General Schenck's, now with me, my whole force of enlisted men for duty will not exceed 105,000. Fourteen batteries of the Artillery Reserve have been sent to Washington. Of General Abercrombie's force, one brigade has just been sent home from expiration of service, and the others go shortly. One brigade of General Crawford's force has not reported with it. I state these facts that there may not be expected of me more than I have material to do with. My headquarters at Frederick to-night. Three corps at Middletown, one corps at Knoxville [Md.], two at Frederick, and the remaining infantry corps very near there to-night."

The 6th Corps and the cavalry were still crossing the Potomac at that time, but they would be over before the day was done and the bridges taken up. The 2nd Vermont Brigade crossed at about 3 p.m. – apparently the last Federals to do so – marched on a few more miles, and camped near Poolesville, just west of where Stuart's cavalry would cross that night. Dan Butterfield sent a message to Halleck not long afterwards: "General Hooker personally has just left here [Poolesville] for Harper's Ferry, where he will be about 11 o'clock, Point of Rocks about 10 a.m., and at Frederick to-night. Copies of all dispatches [to him] should be sent to Frederick and Harper's Ferry up to 11 a.m., and after that to Frederick. The staff are just leaving here for Frederick."[36]

One of the three corps that concentrated around Middletown that day was the 1st Corps. Men of the Iron Brigade in that corps, which had earned its name nearby the year before in forcing a passage through the gaps of South Mountain during the Antietam campaign, was thus afforded the opportunity to revisit the site of that action. One soldier wrote that "the grass has grown green over the graves of our . . . boys . . . The inscriptions on the head boards are already scarcely legible and with their destruction seems to go the last poor chance that the sacrifice these men have made . . . shall be recognized and commemorated."[37]

Hooker wired Butterfield at 10 a.m. from Point of Rocks: "Direct that the cavalry be sent well to the advance of Frederick, in the direction of Gettysburg and Emmitsburg, and see what they can of the movements of the enemy."[38] Since Gregg's division had been assigned the job of covering the crossing of the infantry over the Potomac, and Stahel's division was watching the crossings of South Mountain, this job was given to Buford's division.

At 10:30 a.m., Halleck replied to Hooker's request of the day before to abandon the last position near Harper's Ferry: "Maryland Heights have always been regarded as an important point to be held by us, and much expense and labor incurred in fortifying them. I cannot approve their abandonment, except in case of absolute necessity." But at noon he had more welcome news for Hooker: "Major-General Stahel is relieved from duty in the Army of the Potomac and will report to General Couch, at Harrisburg, to organize and command the cavalry in the Department of the Susquehanna. Lowell's cavalry is the only force for scouts in this department [of Washington], and cannot be taken from General Heintzelman's command."[39]

Another seemingly innocuous order that would soon cause problems was one sent that day by Brigadier General Rufus Ingalls, chief quartermaster of the Army of the Potomac, to a quartermaster in Washington: "Troops without transportation are being consolidated with this army. I fear I shall need more wagons. Send me one hundred and fifty without delay."[40]

Several reports came in to Butterfield, meanwhile, from various sources, military and civilian, all to the effect that all or almost all of Lee's army was in Pennsylvania. And John Reynolds forwarded the belated report from Stahel, just received, with the comment that he had "obtained the same information from [General] Howard nearly twenty-four hours ago. Stahel should have sent this information to Poolesville, as directed to send all other, as either you or I would be found there."[41] Some reports even included the information that Early's division had split off and was headed for Gettysburg.

At noon, General Schenck informed Halleck: "General Couch reports the rebels in possession of Gettysburg, and moving east, 5,000 strong. I expect to-day or to-morrow to hear of the Northern Central Railroad being cut. I directed Colonel [Robert S.] Rodgers [of the 2nd Maryland Eastern Shore Volunteers] to defend block-houses and stockades on my part of the line to the utmost. I have completed nearly all my line of defenses around this city [Baltimore], but have few guns for them. My infantry outside of the old forts are the Sixty-ninth New York [Militia], 462 men, and the Fifty-fifth New York [Militia], 210 men, with three small companies of Second Eastern Shore. Total, about 800, all raw. My cavalry are out as scouts on all the roads. The rest of my troops were sent, as ordered, to Monocacy, and are there or on the march."[42]

Schenck wired Butterfield that night asking that the section of artillery sent to the Monocacy with Lockwood's brigade be returned to him, and Butterfield replied at 10:27 p.m. that not only the artillery but the 6th New York Militia would be returned to and added: "Some of our batteries were sent into Washington, and could be sent to you for temporary duty in your defenses."[43] Fearing sabotage, Schenck also issued orders that day for the provost guard in Baltimore to take possession of the meeting house of a group called the Maryland Club, a Copperhead organization, and take the names of all its members.

Halleck received another message from Hooker at 2:55 p.m.: "I have received your telegram in regard to Harper's Ferry. I find 10,000 men here, in condition to take the field. Here they are of no earthly account. They cannot defend a ford of the river, and, as far as Harper's Ferry is concerned, there is nothing of it. As for the fortifications, the work of the troops, they remain when the troops are withdrawn. No enemy will ever take possession of them for them. This is my opinion. All the public property could have been secured to-night, and the troops marched to where they could have been of some service. Now they are but a bait for the rebels, should they return. I beg that this may be presented to the Secretary of War and His Excellency the President." Five minutes later came a follow-up message: "My original instructions require me to cover Harper's Ferry and Washington. I have now imposed upon me, in addition, an enemy in my front of more than my number. I beg to be understood, respectfully, but firmly, that I am unable to comply with this condition with the means at my disposal, and earnestly request that I may at once be relieved from the position I occupy."[44]

There has been, ever since, a suspicion that Halleck

intentionally maneuvered Hooker into asking to be relieved by his refusal to let him abandon Maryland Heights or by a whole series of refusals to give up troops that Hooker wanted from other commands, such as Lowell's cavalry and the 2nd Brigade of the Pennsylvania Reserves. There were good reasons for not letting him have these last two, of course, for Washington and its immediate surroundings were now highly vulnerable, and Stuart's cavalry was hovering nearby. But Hooker's contention that the troops on Maryland Heights could be better used elsewhere made good sense. The year before, when Lee had crossed into Maryland, the garrison of Harper's Ferry had not been withdrawn even to the nearby heights and Lee had surrounded and captured it without a fight, although in doing so he had divided his army and given General McClellan a chance to defeat him in detail (which chance McClellan frittered away so that the last Rebels from Harper's Ferry arrived on the field of Antietam just in time to foil a belated Union move against Lee's southern flank) – thus Hooker's remark that the troops there were useful only as bait for Lee.

At 8 p.m., Butterfield wrote to General Slocum: "Hold your command ready to march at 4 a.m. to-morrow. Colonel Lowell, with a regiment of cavalry, is ordered to report to you. Also two brigades from General French's command will join you at 6 a.m. at Harper's Ferry as you pass. Orders will reach you during the night." But a half-hour later he wrote again to say: "The order for your march toward Harper's Ferry countermanded. March your command to this point. Direct Colonel Lowell's cavalry to report to General French at 7 a.m. to-morrow." And at the same time, he wrote to French: "Colonel Lowell, with a regiment of cavalry, is ordered to report to you at 7 a.m. to-morrow. The general directs you to send all your cavalry to make a reconnaissance in the direction of Williamsport. The general suggests that you cross at Keedysville, looking into the rear of Sharpsburg."[45] What Hooker wanted was to join French's garrison to Slocum's 12th Corps and use the combined force to get south of Lee and cut him off from Virginia, but Halleck told General French, "Pay no attention to

General Hooker's orders."[46]

Five hours passed before Halleck replied to Hooker's last message, and then, at 8 p.m., he merely said: "Your application to be relieved from your present command is received. As you were appointed to this command by the President, I have no power to relieve you. Your dispatch has been duly referred for executive action."[47] Lincoln soon decided that Hooker had outlived his usefulness. According to Navy Secretary Welles: "The President said he had, for several days as the conflict became imminent, observed in Hooker the same failings that were witnessed in McClellan after the Battle of Antietam – a want of alacrity to obey and a greedy call for more troops which could not and ought not to be taken from other points."[48] Lincoln wanted the change made before the next big battle, which was obviously fast approaching, even though it saddened him personally. Newspaper correspondent Noah Brooks, an old friend of Lincoln, later wrote that the President had told him "that he regarded Hooker very much as a father might regard a son who was lame, or who had some other incurable physical infirmity. His love for his son would be even intensified by the reflection that the lad could never be a strong and successful man."[49]

The War Department issued General Orders No. 194 that day relieving Hooker and replacing him with Major General George G. Meade, who was the obvious choice, since most of Hooker's corps commanders had expressed a preference for him. Duplicate copies of the order were made, one addressed to Hooker and one to Meade, and both were entrusted to Brigadier General James A. Hardie, Stanton's chief of staff, who was a personal friend of both the old and the new commander. He was to make his way to Frederick, without disclosing his presence or purpose to anyone, and deliver Meade's copy first, and, to forestall any attempt by Meade to decline the honor, "give him to understand," as Charles F. Benjamin, a War Department functionary, later put it, "that the order for him to assume the command of the army immediately was intended to be as unquestionable and peremptory as any that a soldier could receive. He was then, as the representative of the President, to take General Meade to the headquarters of General Hooker and transfer the command from the latter to the former."[50]

A special train was ordered up to take Hardie on his mission. He found the city of Frederick to be without a provost guard and full of drunken soldiers, "many of them ripe for rudeness or mischief," as Benjamin phrased it, but Hardie managed to hire a buggy and a driver who knew the local roads, wend his way through wagon trains and straggling soldiers, and talk his way past sentries into Meade's tent at about 3 a.m. on the 28th, where he found that general asleep. He roused the general and informed him that he had been sent by the War Department and that he was there to give Meade trouble. Meade's first thought was that he was about to be arrested, but, as he later wrote to his wife, "my conscience was clear."[51]

As expected, after reading the order placing him in command, Meade protested that he didn't want the job, that he was totally ignorant of the positions of the other corps, and that Reynolds would be a better commander, but Hardie soon convinced him that he had no choice in the matter. (Benjamin said that Stanton was pleased when he later learned that it was no part of Meade's objections that Hooker should not be removed at all.) Finally, Meade said, playing upon his earlier idea that he was being arrested, "Well, I've been tried and condemned without a hearing, and I suppose I shall have to go to the execution."[52] Eventually Meade emerged from his tent to find his son, an aide on his staff, waiting for him. "Well, George," he said, "I am in command of the Army of the Potomac."[53]

About dawn, Hardie and Meade rode over to Hooker's headquarters. Hooker by then knew of Hardie's arrival and had surmised its purpose, so he was waiting for them in full uniform. "It was a bitter moment to all," Benjamin wrote, "for Hooker had construed favorably the delay in responding to his tender of resignation, and could not wholly mask the revulsion of feeling. General Butterfield, the chief of staff, between whom and General Meade much coldness existed, was called in, and the four officers set themselves earnestly to work to do the state some service by honestly transferring the command and all that could help to make it available for good. During the interview Meade unguardedly expressed himself as shocked at the scattered condition of the army, and Hooker retorted with some feeling. Tension was somewhat eased by Meade's insisting upon being regarded as a guest at headquarters while General Hooker was present, and by his requesting General Butterfield, upon public grounds, not to exercise his privilege of withdrawing with his chief; but Hooker's chagrin and Meade's overstrung nerves made the lengthy but indispensable conference rather trying to the whole party."[54]

At 7 a.m., long before the conference was done, Meade wrote to Halleck: "The order placing me in command of this army is received. As a soldier, I obey it, and to the utmost of my ability will execute it. Totally unexpected as it has been, and in ignorance of the exact condition of the troops and position of the enemy, I can only now say that it appears to me I must move toward the Susquehanna, keeping Washington and Baltimore well covered, and if the enemy is checked in his attempt to cross the Susquehanna, or if he turns toward Baltimore, to give him battle. I would say that I trust every available man that can be spared will be sent to me, as from all accounts the enemy is in strong force. So soon as I can post myself up, I will communicate more in detail."[55] When President Lincoln saw this message (he frequented the War Department telegraph office and read most of the important messages himself) he was pleased with his new general's show of initiative and promise of battle. "I think a great deal of that fine fellow Meade," he said.[56]

How fine he was remained to be seen. Meade was tall and spare and then 48 years of age but looked older, his hair and beard being flecked with gray, with bags under his rather bulging eyes, which were usually covered by glasses – not the sort of general to draw spontaneous cheers from his men, at least one of whom called him "a damned old goggle-eyed snapping turtle."[57] The snapping turtle part probably stemmed from Meade's irascible temper. One staff officer compared him to a firecracker whose fuse was always lit. In the pre-war Regular Army (West Point class of 1835 – two years ahead of Hooker) he had been an engineer, rising to the rank of major, and had never seen much combat. But in this war he had done well as a brigade and division commander. He had only been a corps commander for one battle, Chancellorsville, where he had done well enough but had not been involved in the heaviest fighting. Charles Dana, who would get to know him the following year, after Grant came east, said of Meade: "He was totally lacking in cordiality toward those with whom he had business, and in consequence was generally disliked by his subordinates. . . . He was an intellectual man, and agreeable to talk with when his mind was free, but silent and indifferent to everybody when he was occupied with that which interested him. As a commander, Meade seemed to me to lack the boldness that was necessary to bring the war to a close. He lacked self-confidence and tenacity of purpose. . . ."[58] (Those were two qualities that Grant had in full, as did Lee).

As Benjamin's quote, above, indicates, Hooker and Butterfield helped to bring Meade up to speed on the army's situation for much of the day. News soon spread throughout the army that it had a new commander. Most of the senior officers were pleased. John Sedgwick, commander of the 6th Corps, who was senior to Meade, seemed to be somewhat upset, spurring his horse into a furious gallop at the news, but soon settled down. Reynolds came over during the day to offer his congratulations to his friend and new commander, saying he thought the job had fallen to the right man and that he was glad not to have had the responsibility laid upon himself. Meade shared with him all he had just learned about the army's positions and movements, and the two friends set about making plans. Meade left Reynolds in command of the 3-corps wing Hooker had put him in charge of, and told him to bring all three corps to Frederick that day and encamp them there.

Keeping Butterfield on as chief-of-staff was not Meade's first choice, despite the former's knowledge of the army and its headquarters; he offered the job to Brigadier General Andrew

A. Humphreys, commander of the 2nd Division of the 3rd Corps, but that general "declined or deferred it."[59] Seth Williams and Gouverneur Warren both also declined to take on the job in addition to their existing duties, respectively, as assistant adjutant general and chief engineer.

That evening, Hooker and Hardie got into a wagon that would take them to the railroad station. "When all was ready for the start," Benjamin said, "the throng about the vehicle respectfully drew back as Meade approached with uncovered head; the two men took each other by the hand, some words passed between them in low tone, the wagon moved off, and Meade walked silently into the tent just vacated by his predecessor."[60] There was still much work to do. As he later told Congress's Joint Committee on the Conduct of the War: "My predecessor, General Hooker, left the camp a very few hours after I relieved him. I received from him no intimations of any plan, or any views that he may have had up to that moment, and I am not aware that he had any, but was waiting for the exigencies of the occasion to govern him."[61] Colonel George Sharpe, head of Hooker's – now Meade's – bureau of information, wrote that day that, "in the great game that is now being played, everything in the way of advantage depends upon which side gets the best information."[62]

Gathering information was, of course, one of the primary duties of the cavalry, and that arm of Meade's army was about to be reorganized somewhat. General Stahel departed that day, headed for his new job with Couch, and Seth Williams had signed an order in Hooker's name assigning his division to the Cavalry Corps, to be distributed however Pleasonton wanted. Meanwhile, the commander of Stahel's 1st Brigade, not yet aware that both he and Stahel were being transferred, reported to that general from Gettysburg at 2 p.m.: "We have just arrived with the column at this place, and find no enemy." He added a fairly accurate account of the size and movements of Early's division, and said "I have camped my men east of the city, where there is plenty of grass, and I think I can get grain for [the horses]. I shall picket the York, Chambersburg, and Hanover roads, and patrol communications between them."⁶³ This was not passed on to Meade until the following day. That evening the brigade received orders to withdraw from Gettysburg toward Emmitsburg, Maryland.

Before the day was out, Seth Williams signed another order, this time in Meade's name, assigning three brand-new brigadier generals to the Cavalry Corps. They were Elon J. Farnsworth, Wesley Merritt, and George Armstrong Custer. Until that morning, Farnsworth and Custer had both been captains on Pleasonton's staff. (Farnsworth's uncle was a U. S. Congressman and a friend of Lincoln's, but also a former brigade commander under Pleasonton.) Merritt had also been a captain and had previously been on the staff of Pleasonton's predecessor, Stoneman, but since then had been in command of the 2nd U.S. Cavalry in the Reserve Brigade. The promotion of the three young captains had been recommended by Pleasonton as a way to put some fight into his cavalry, and Meade had promptly complied, wiring Washington for approval. Cavalry Corps headquarters issued an order that day designating Stahel's old command as a new 3rd Division, with General Kilpatrick as its new commander. Farnsworth and Custer would command his two brigades. Merritt was ordered to report to Buford for orders and was given command of the Reserve Brigade. The order didn't specify a new commander for Kilpatrick's old brigade in Gregg's 2nd Division, so that fell to its senior officer, Colonel Pennock Huey.

There would soon be plenty of work for the cavalry to do. At 12:30 p.m. Halleck wired Meade: "A brigade of Fitzhugh Lee's cavalry has crossed the Potomac near Seneca Falls, and is making for the railroad to cut off your supplies. There is another brigade of rebel cavalry south of the Potomac which may follow. We have no cavalry here to operate against them. General Hooker carried away all of General Heintzelman's cavalry." Meade replied at 2 p.m. saying he had ordered two brigades of cavalry and a battery of artillery "to proceed at once in search and pursuit." That order went to David Gregg, whom Pleasonton told to send two brigades and a battery down the turnpike to New

Market and Ridgeville to scout in the direction of Ellicott's Mills and prevent the Rebel cavalry from injuring the railroad and telegraph lines. Meanwhile, Halleck had replied to Meade's first message at 1 p.m.: "I fully concur in your general views as to the movements of your army. All available assistance will be given you. General Schenck's troops outside the line of defenses will move as you may direct. General Couch is also directed to cooperate with you, and to move his forces as you may order. It is most probable that Lee will concentrate his forces this side of the Susquehanna."[64]

At that same hour of 1 p.m., Meade was writing to Halleck: "Am I permitted, under existing circumstances, to withdraw a portion of the garrison of Harper's Ferry, providing I leave sufficient force to hold Maryland Heights against a *coup de main*? Reliable intelligence leads to the belief Stuart has crossed at Williamsport, and is moving toward Hagerstown, in rear of Lee's army, and all accounts agree in giving Lee so large a force that I cannot believe he has left any considerable body on the south side of the Potomac. Please give me your views fully." Halleck replied at 3:30 p.m.: "The garrison at Harper's Ferry is under your orders. You can diminish or increase it as you think the circumstances justify."[65] Many historians have seen this message as giving Meade what Hooker had been denied and therefore proof that the denial was an intentional ploy for frustrating Hooker to the point where he would ask to be relieved. However, Hooker had asked if he could abandon Maryland Heights completely, Meade had merely asked if he could diminish its garrison while leaving enough force to hold it against a sudden attack – a somewhat different proposition. But it cannot be denied that the spirit of Halleck's answers to the two generals' requests was vastly different. Halleck neither liked nor trusted Hooker and later told Grant, "Hooker was more than a failure. Had he remained in command, he would have lost the army and the capital."[66]

At 2 p.m., Halleck wired Meade with more bad news about Confederate cavalry: "It is reported here that the supplies at Edwards Ferry and returning by the canal are left unprotected.

If so, Lee's cavalry will probably destroy them. It is reported that Lowell's battalion of cavalry, left at Poolesville, was sent to Sandy Hook, contrary to my orders. If so, there is not a cavalry picket on the line of the Potomac below Edwards Ferry, and we have none here to send out." In response, Pleasonton's headquarters told Gregg to detach one regiment from the two brigades sent after Stuart and send it to Edwards Ferry to cover the withdrawal of the supplies there. At 3 p.m., Halleck added more bad news: "It is just reported that your train of one hundred and fifty wagons has been captured by Fitzhugh Lee, near Rockville. Unless cavalry is sent to guard your communications with Washington, they will be cut off. It is reported here that there is still a considerable rebel force south of the Potomac."[67]

At that same hour, Meade was wiring Halleck: "Colonel Lowell has been directed to return to Poolesville. Do you consider the information at all to be depended upon concerning a force of the enemy south of the Potomac? All our information here tends to show that Lee's entire army passed through Hagerstown, the rear passing yesterday a.m." Meanwhile, Dan Butterfield wired Major Thomas T. Eckert, superintendent of the Military Telegraph, in the War Department: "The major-general commanding desires to know if any reliable information can be given as to the direction taken by the cavalry force that were at Rockville, the hour they left, the names of any generals or colonels, and the designation of any regiments. Did they return to recross the river, or proceed north, by what road, and when?"[68]

Sometime that day, quartermaster Ingalls wired the Quartermaster General of the Army, Brigadier General Montgomery C. Meigs, asking for 10,000 pairs of shoes and socks. He added, "General Meade is in command. The army has confidence in him. We must all support him." Meigs replied at 4:05 p.m. that the shoes and socks would be sent but could not help airing a complaint, without specifying who was at fault: "Last fall I gave orders to prevent the sending of wagon trains from this place to Frederick without escort. The situation repeats itself, and gross carelessness and inattention to military rule has this morning cost us 150 wagons and 900 mules, captured by cavalry between this and Rockville. Yesterday morning a detachment of over 400 cavalry moved from this place to join the army. This morning 150 wagons were sent without escort. Had the cavalry been delayed or the wagons hastened, they could have been protected and saved. All the cavalry of the Defenses of Washington was swept off by the army, and we are now insulted by burning wagons 3 miles outside of Tenallytown. Your communications are now in hands of General Fitzhugh Lee's brigade."[69]

Ingalls replied: "The cavalry that left before the wagon train has not been heard of here. Had the train been guarded by any ordinary force, the result would have been the same. Its starting was ill-timed and unfortunate. There is a powerful force of rebel cavalry between here and Rockville. Our own cavalry is in motion, and the army will march in the morning. We must and will fight to the end." Meigs replied to that at 10:30 p.m. that the Union cavalry in question, now estimated at 300, were troopers who had been sent to rejoin Pleasonton after going to Washington for new horses. "Had two skirmishes with Fitzhugh Lee's brigade, one on the river road, the other near Rockville. They returned with a loss of about 16, saving their own baggage train, and are in camp at Tennallytown. Had this cavalry escorted the wagon train and behaved as well as they did with their own, they would have saved it." He added a postscript: "A deserter reports that there are several brigades in all, including Fitzhugh Lee's, and that Stuart commands in person; 6,000 men and seven pieces of artillery."[70] Sometime that day Halleck ordered General Heintzelman to assume command of all the dismounted cavalry from the Army of the Potomac then at Washington, "have them mounted as soon as possible, and use them until further orders."[71]

It was 7:20 p.m. before Halleck answered Meade's query: "I doubt if there is any large force south of the Potomac; probably a few thousand cavalry, enough to render it necessary to have a strong rear guard, to protect the trains and picket the river. Lowell's command was ordered on the latter duty, but removed contrary to my positive order, which exposed your trains. We have no cavalry here excepting what we have picked up from Pleasonton's command."[72] At 7:25 p.m., Meade informed Halleck that scouts from the 11th Corps reported (incorrectly) that 5,000 of Stuart's cavalry had passed through Williamsport the day before. "My impression is that Stuart has divided his force, with a view of harassing our right and left flanks."[73]

At 8:15 p.m., Meade replied to Halleck's last message: "Colonel Lowell, as soon as your wishes were known, was ordered and will be left, and I shall intrust to him, through you, the guarding of the river. There seems to be no doubt that 3,000 of the enemy's cavalry have been on our right, between us and Washington, to-day. My intention is now to move to-morrow on three lines to Emmitsburg and Westminster, or as near there as we can march. This movement is based upon what information we have here of the enemy's movement. The army to-night as follows: First, Second, Fifth, Eleventh, and Twelfth Corps, with Artillery Reserve, within a few miles of Frederick; the Third Corps, 6 miles out toward Middleburg; the Sixth Corps, toward New Market, and expecting to reach there to-night. I have not decided yet as to the Harper's Ferry garrison. I should like to have your views as to the movement proposed."[74]

The Rebels who had captured Ingalls' wagons had, of course, been part of Jeb Stuart's force. It had been 3 a.m. on the 28th by the time his rear guard got across Rowser's Ford. "No more difficult achievement was accomplished by the cavalry during the war," Major McClellan later wrote. The men and horses were exhausted, and rest was essential. Consequently, as McClellan put it, "the sun was several hours high before the command left the Potomac for Rockville."[75] Meanwhile, some of the first men across had been put to work destroying boats, barges, and sluice gates on the Chesapeake & Ohio Canal, which paralleled the Potomac and drew water from it. More Union supplies were captured, including several barrels of whiskey, as well as about 300 Federal soldiers who had been en route to Washington in canal boats and 24 mules used to pull the boats. Stuart soon learned that Hooker had moved his headquarters to Poolesville, only some 15 miles west of where he stood, which meant that most of Hooker's army must be north of the Potomac. He also learned that it wasn't Hooker's army any more but was now commanded by George Meade. But he had no sure or quick way to get word of all this to General Lee.

Hampton's brigade again led the way that morning and easily scattered a small Union force at Rockville, which was only eight miles from Washington. The young ladies of a local female academy soon came out to flirt with the passing troopers, adding a touch of romance to the scene. The Confederates were greatly impressed by the difference between war-torn Virginia and untouched Maryland. It was past noon by the time Stuart got to Rockville, and, while the Rebels were busy rounding up supplies, including 28 wagons, and destroying the telegraph line, scouts brought word of Ingalls' approaching wagons.

The teamsters driving the wagons turned about when they spotted the Confederates and raced back towards Washington, chased by Virginians of Chambliss's brigade. One Rebel officer called it "a circus . . . that I have never seen paralleled."[76] The small Federal escort fired one long-range volley and fled. Captain William Blackford of Stuart's staff, with a lieutenant and a few men of Hampton's Brigade, then dashed along the whole length of the train – eight miles – which was brought to a halt by a pile-up of wagons caused when one overturned while negotiating a sharp turn in the road, within sight of Georgetown, D.C., and the unfinished dome of the Capitol building.

"The wagons were brand new, the mules fat and sleek, and the harness in use for the first time," the colonel of the 9th Virginia Cavalry recalled. "Such a train we had never seen before and did not see again."[77] The Confederates secured 125 wagons out of 140, and most of them contained oats intended for the horses of the Army of the Potomac – just what the Rebels needed for their own famished mounts. "It did one's heart good to see the way the poor brutes got on the outside of those oats," Captain Blackford remembered.[78] Other wagons contained food and drink more suitable for humans, which was also welcomed. The wagons that had been damaged beyond use were burned, but their mules and harness were taken along. To shorten the length of the train, Stuart had two mules detached from each team and collected in a herd with the extras.

As it turned out, the capture of these wagons was a big mistake, or at least Stuart's decision to bring most of them along was. Of course, part of his mission was to secure supplies, and here was a windfall of a large train of wagons filled with food and forage. But, as Major McClellan later said, "The time occupied in securing it was insignificant; but the delay caused to the subsequent march was serious at a time when minutes counted almost as hours."[79] Also, while the wagons and their contents were welcome, Stuart now had over 600 mules to feed. "We had scarcely set out from Rockville," one Rebel noted, "before many of us began to regret our capture, foreseeing that the train would impede our movements, and be very difficult to guard in passing through the enemy's country."[80]

Captain Thomas Nelson Conrad, an ordained minister and one of Stuart's best scouts, or spies, happened to be in Washington that day, where he made frequent forays, and he later recorded his impressions of the Federals' reaction to Stuart's presence just outside the city. "Every available soldier had been given to Meade," he said, "and the city was at the mercy of the 'rebel raiders.' The clerks from all the departments and the able-bodied men from every quarter were hurried to the entrenchments around the city for its defense. It was even said that a gunboat was detained at the navy yard to receive the cabinet and other high officials, with the most important papers, in the event of the rebel cavalry dashing into the city."[81] Conrad tried to ride out to Rockville to join Stuart and report, but he was delayed so many times by sentries and videttes that Stuart was gone before he could reach him.

Stuart briefly considered the desirability of attacking Washington, but he soon realized that it would be dark before he could get all his forces in place to do so, which would give the Federals time to call up local forces and bring in reinforcements. "To attack at night with cavalry," he later reported, "particularly unless certain of surprise, would have been extremely hazardous; to wait till morning, would have lost much time from my march to join General Lee without the probability of compensating results. I therefore determined, after getting the wagons under way, to proceed directly north, so as to cut the Baltimore and Ohio Railroad (now becoming the enemy's main war artery) that night."[82] Word of the Confederates' presence was telegraphed to General Schenk, in Baltimore, and he rushed what few troops he had left to protect the railroads in his department, including a squadron of the 1st Delaware Cavalry, sent to Westminster, Maryland, to keep an eye out for the Rebels.

Since Stuart's men and horses were still tired from their exertions in crossing the river, and Chambliss's brigade was badly scattered after chasing the wagons, his column went only another 10 miles up the road from Rockville that day and stopped at Brooksville, Maryland, about 6 p.m. Between the contents of the captured wagons and the offerings of pro-Confederate residents of the town, the Rebels ate well that night. There, also, began the laborious task of paroling some 400 captured Federals – taking their sworn promises not to take up arms again until properly exchanged – which involved a good deal of paperwork so that both armies could keep track of them. The only alternatives, however, were turning them loose to fight again, or bringing them along, which would require guarding them carefully.

The Rebels took to the road again after their supper, the advance drove off a few Federals at Cooksville who had themselves just captured one of General Lee's couriers (probably searching for Stuart), and the march continued all night. Colonel Lowell's 2nd Massachusetts Cavalry, having been ordered to return to Poolesville, came upon the Rebels' trail that night. "You may laugh and think it preposterous for one Battalion, three hundred strong, chasing three Brigades of the renowned cavalry," one of his men wrote, ". . . yet such is the fact, and we followed them up so close that at times our advance guard was not more than three quarters of a mile from the rebel column. We arrived at Rockville at 10 p.m. and saw a number of army wagons yet burning, having been set on fire by rebels."[83]

～ Endnotes ～

1 OR, I:26:I:211.
2 Ibid., I:26:I:226.
3 Ibid., I:26:I:601.
4 Ibid., I:26:I:602.
5 Ibid., I:26:I:603.
6 Ibid., I:22:II:888.
7 Ibid., I:24:III:445.
8 Ibid., I:24:II:516.
9 Ibid., I:24:I:43-4.
10 Ibid., I:24:I:110-11.
11 Ibid., I:24:II:246-7.
12 Hoehling, *Vicksburg: 47 Days of Siege*, 236.
13 OR, I:24:III:980.
14 Ibid., I:24:II:202.
15 Ibid., I:24:I:111.
16 Ibid., I:24:I:165.
17 Ibid., I:27:II:794.
18 Ibid., I:27:III:394-5, both messages.
19 Ibid., I:27:III:940.
20 Ibid., I:27:III:939.
21 Ibid., I:27:III:940, all 3 messages.
22 Mingus, *Flames Beyond Gettysburg*, 155.
23 Nye, *Here Come the Rebels!*, 279.
24 OR, I:27:III:363.
25 Nye, *Here Come the Rebels!*, 302.
26 Wingert, *The Confederate Approach on Harrisburg*, 64.
27 Nye, *Here Come the Rebels!*, 307.
28 Bowden and Ward, *Last Chance for Victory*, 141.
29 Schultz, *The Most Glorious Fourth*, 156.
30 Bowden and Ward, *Last Chance for Victory*, 141.
31 Eric J. Wittenberg and J. David Petruzzi, *Plenty of Blame to Go Around* (New York and California, 2011), 16.
32 Ibid., 20.
33 OR, I:27:III:359.
34 Ibid., I:27:III:358, both messages.
35 Ibid., I:27:II:693.
36 Ibid., I:27:I:59, both messages.
37 Alan T. Nolan, *The Iron Brigade* (Bloomington IN/Indianapolis, 1961), 229.
38 OR, I:27:III:349.

39 Ibid., I:27:I:59-60.
40 Ibid., I:27:III:355.
41 Ibid., I:27:III:351-2.
42 Ibid., I:27:III:360.
43 Ibid., I:27:III:361.
44 Ibid., I:27:I:60.
45 Ibid., I:27:III:354-5, all 3 messages.
46 Sears, *Gettysburg*, 121.
47 *OR*, I:27:I:60.
48 Sears, *Gettysburg*, 121-3.
49 Noah Brooks, *Washington, D.C. in Lincoln's Time* (Athens GA, 1989), originally published as *Washington in Lincoln's Time* (New York, 1895).
50 Charles F. Benjamin, "Hooker's Appointment and Removal," in *B&L* III:241-2.
51 Sears, *Gettysburg*, 123.
52 Benjamin, "Hooker's Appointment and Removal," in *B&L* III:243n.
53
Sears, *Gettysburg*, 123.
54 Benjamin, "Hooker's Appointment and Removal," in *B&L* III:243.
55 *OR*, I:27:I:61-2.
56 Schultz, *The Most Glorious Fourth*, 166.
57 Ibid., 165.
58 Dana, *Recollections of the Civil War*, 171-2.
59 *OR*, I:51:I:1064.
60 Benjamin, "Hooker's Appointment and Removal," in *B&L* III:243.
61 Schultz, *The Most Glorious Fourth*, 166.
62 Sears, *Gettysburg*, 133.
63 *OR*, I:27:III:377.
64 Ibid., I:27:I:62, all 3 messages.
65 Ibid., I:27:I:62-3, both messages.
66 Ibid., I:24:I:498.
67 Ibid., I:27:I:63, both messages.
68 Ibid., I:27:I:64, both messages.
69 Ibid., I:27:III:378.
70 Ibid., I:27:III:379, both messages.
71 Ibid., I:27:III:384.
72 Ibid., I:27:I:64.
73 Ibid., I:27:I:66.
74 Ibid., I:27:I:64.
75 McClellan, *I Rode With Jeb Stuart*, 323-4.
76 Wittenberg and Petruzzi, *Plenty of Blame to Go Around*, 33.
77 Ibid., 23.
78 Ibid., 35.
79 McClellan, *I Rode With Jeb Stuart*, 325.
80 Wittenberg and Petruzzi, *Plenty of Blame to Go Around*, 41-2.

81 Ibid., 40.
82 *OR*, I:27:II:694.
83 Wittenberg and Petruzzi, *Plenty of Blame to Go Around,* 40-1.

CHAPTER 18
"Move in the Direction of Gettysburg"
28 – 29 June 1863

A T 10 O'CLOCK ON SUNDAY morning, 28 June, Gordon's Brigade of Early's Division entered York, after being assured by the town's chief burgess that there would be no resistance. One regiment had already been sent ahead to act as provost guards; the others marched on through and stopped two miles east of town on the Lancaster pike. The rest of Early's Division marched to Weigelstown, from which point Early sent the 17th Virginia Cavalry to burn a railroad bridge at the mouth of the Conewago, and other bridges from there to York. Early's infantry then by-passed Dover and marched on to join Gordon at York. The leading brigade was commanded by Brigadier General William "Extra Billy" Smith, who was also the Governor-elect of Virginia, and who, upon seeing a crowd of curious on-lookers gather, could not resist the urge to make a speech, the gist of which was that the Rebels were gentlemen, not monsters, and were just there to get away from the heat of a Virginia summer. "Are we not a fine set of fellows?" he asked, with his hat in his hand and an umbrella tucked under his arm. "You must admit that we are." This drew a fine round of applause.

Jubal Early was not so pleased, however, and, after fighting his way through the crowd, grabbed Smith by the collar and almost screamed, "What the devil are you about? Stopping the head of the column in this cursed town!"[1] He sent Smith's brigade and one other to camp a couple of miles north of the town, while his remaining brigade took quarters at a large U.S. military hospital. Early made his headquarters in the sheriff's office and presented the town with a requisition for 2,000 pairs of shoes or boots, 1,000 hats, 1,000 pairs of socks, 165 barrels of flour or 28,000 pounds of bread, 3,500 pounds of sugar, 1,650 pounds of coffee,

300 gallons of molasses, 1,200 pounds of salt, 32,000 pounds of fresh beef or 21,000 pounds of pork or bacon, and $100,000 in cash, all to be delivered by 4 p.m. He got most of what he asked for, but only $28,610 cash. At about 3 p.m. Gordon conferred with Early, who repeated his previous instructions to seize the bridge over the Susquehanna that connected Wrightsville with Columbia. Gordon later claimed that, as he rode along the main street, a 10- or 12-year-old girl handed him a bouquet of flowers, in which was hidden a brief unsigned note informing him that the bridge at Wrightsville was defended only by militia.

That bridge was a large one, supposedly the largest covered wooden bridge in the world – well over a mile long. It carried both wagon and railroad traffic as well as a two-level tow path for a canal that crossed here from the northeast side to the southwest side of the river. Just downstream was a dam used to maintain a proper water level in the canal. Earthworks had recently been constructed for artillery to protect this dam, but defenses from which guns or infantry could protect the bridge had only been started that day. The bridge was being prepared for destruction, in case it could not be defended, by drilling holes in one span and filling them with gunpowder.

Major Haller, retreating from Gettysburg and York, had arrived the night before. He got tools from hardware stores in Columbia, on the east side of the river, and from the railroad, and distributed them to the militiamen that were charged with defending the area. Three companies from Columbia, having volunteered to fight, not to work, promptly returned home, and most of the men in the 27th Pennsylvania Militia, the largest unit of defenders, also declined the use of pick and shovel, so most of the work fell to a company of free blacks. Haller laid out a line of defense, with barricades in the streets as a back-up line. However, there were not enough troops to man everything properly; only something like 1,100 or 1,200, plus three guns. The latter were placed on the east side of the river, sited to cover the bridge, and were too far back to help the infantry.

At about 5:30 p.m., Confederate skirmishers, both mounted

and afoot, were seen approaching. Behind them came infantry regiments in solid formations. There was then a pause while the skirmishers disappeared into a field of tall grain and Gordon studied the situation through his field glasses. He couldn't tell how many Federals there were in the hastily built defenses, but there were pickets visible from the river above the town to a creek that flowed past the south end of town and into the river. There was an exchange of scattered shots for over an hour, while the Rebels got into position, then the Confederate artillery opened fire on both the defenses and the town while infantry probed towards the river both north and south.

Colonel Jacob Frick of the 27th Pennsylvania, the senior Union officer present, soon decided that the Rebels were too strong for him. He could not save the bridge, but he could keep the Confederates from using it. Major Haller agreed, but wanted to leave the militia on the west bank, thinking a destroyed bridge behind them would force them to stand and fight. Frick overruled him and ordered a retreat across the river. When he thought the last man was across, he ordered the gunpowder to be touched off. (Actually the Adams County Cavalry was still on the other side, but it got away safely and later crossed the river on a raft.) However, the charges were not powerful enough, and the span, though damaged, did not drop into the river.

But there was a back-up plan, as the timbers had already been soaked in kerosene and crude oil, and Frick had it torched. Soldiers and civilians tried to confine the flames to only a part of the bridge, so it could be easily repaired later, but they were not successful. Confederates also ran out on the bridge and tried to extinguish the flames, but they were soon driven back to the west bank. When the flames spread to Wrightsville, on the west side, civilians and Rebel soldiers worked together to put them out, but three houses, two lumber yards, and a foundry were burned. The glow of the fire, reflected off the clouds, was seen as far away as Harrisburg. Most of Gordon's brigade bivouacked for the night west of Wrightsville, but he and many of his officers spent the night in the town. A lady who lived in Columbia recorded that people who came over from Wrightsville said that the Rebels "were very much disappointed. They thought we would not have spunk enough to burn the bridge. They tried to flank our little force and capture them, and fifteen minutes more would have done it."[2]

The rest of Ewell's 2nd Corps remained at Carlisle that day. He and many of his officers and men attended Sunday services held by their own chaplains or at the local churches. A delegation from the Lutheran and Episcopalian churches asked Ewell if he would object if they included the usual prayer for the President of the United States. "Certainly not," he said. "Pray for him. I'm sure he needs it."[3] That afternoon, there was a ceremony at which the Confederate flag was raised over Carlisle Barracks, and several officers, even Ewell, made speeches, and a band played. It was a pleasant day for all, until a rain storm arrived.

Jenkins' cavalry, as ordered, moved on to Mechanicsburg that day, pushing the Curtin Guards before them. Under a flag of truce, Jenkins demanded the surrender of the town, saying no one would be hurt if there was no resistance, and the militia rear guard promptly got out of the way. The Rebels rode on through Mechanicsburg and stopped just east of town.

A citizen of Mechanicsburg did not find Jenkins' cavalry to be as well turned out as the boy in Carlisle had found Rodes' infantry. "Some were clad in the butternut uniforms, while the majority had no uniform on at all, many . . . having nothing but shirt, pants and hat. . . . They were armed with all sorts of weapons. Some with carbine, pistol and sabre, though the majority had nothing but muskets, while a few had double barreled fowling pieces. Their horses were generally very good, having been stolen from farmers in the upper end of the valley."[4]

Jenkins and his aides rode back into town, where he had lunch at the local hotel while carefully perusing the latest newspapers, which, being uncensored, contained a wealth of information about the Union army – some of it was even accurate – and demanded of the town's burgess 1,500 rations for his men and forage for the same number of horses. The food provided was both good and plentiful, but there wasn't enough forage, so Jenkins confiscated the contents of a couple of grain warehouses, which provided enough to feed his horses for several days.

Jenkins sent Lieutenant Colonel Vincent Witcher's 34th Virginia Cavalry Battalion and one of his two batteries north to Hogestown, where they turned east on the Carlisle Pike and soon came upon Knipe's small brigade, which had just moved west again from Oyster Point. Witcher had his artillerymen unlimber a couple of guns and open fire on this force, which outnumbered his lone battalion by 2 or 3 to 1 and was occupying some high ground called Sporting Hill. Knipe's battery returned fire, but the two forces were about a mile apart, and apparently no one was hurt except a Confederate horse, even though this long-range duel went on for about half an hour. When more Rebels were found to be moving east out of Mechanicsburg on a lower road, threatening his left flank, Knipe withdrew.

Jenkins, who had come over to see what the firing was about, rode with Witcher's force as far as Orr's Bridge, crossing a loop of Conodoguinet Creek, where Witcher had two guns unlimbered again. Then Jenkins rode down to the Trindle Road, running east out of Mechanicsburg, and rejoined his main force at Peace Church, just a bit west of Oyster Point, where he deployed his troops and guns while stopping to scan the area ahead. Thinking that he could see infantry pickets in the distance, he had his artillery open fire on some woods to see what was in there, and soon a Union cavalry patrol was seen to be falling back, and infantry pickets taking cover south of the pike. (Knipe's brigade had gone on closer to Harrisburg, but there were a couple of regiments of Pennsylvania Volunteer Militia near Oyster Point.)

All this activity convinced Jenkins that he was about to be attacked. He ordered his men to take cover, told some civilians to go to their cellar, out of harm's way, and ordered his artillery to blast those woods. Soon a battery of Union home guard artillery opened fire at long range in return, although without much accuracy. (One of its shots was intercepted by the Oyster Point Hotel.) The Confederate guns put several holes through a fence, but otherwise did no great harm.

Many residents of Harrisburg climbed to their rooftops to see what all the noise was about down the road, and the pastor of one church in that town led the male members of his congregation out with an assortment of weapons to reinforce the militia in the defenses across the river, where Knipe was now in command. But the Confederates came no closer. Then at dusk the Rebels withdrew.

The Federals did a good bit of stumbling around in the dark that night, trying to find the Rebels. Meanwhile, Jenkins assembled his senior subordinates to consider what to do next. Colonel Witcher suggested that the artillery bombard Oyster Point while his battalion feigned an attack, during which Jenkins could find a suitable position from which to get a look at Harrisburg, but Jenkins' scouts had already located such a spot: Slate Hill, not far to the southeast of Peace Church, near Shiremanstown. There is some evidence that Jenkins tried to slip some scouts through the lines for a closer look at Harrisburg. There was, for instance, another report of what looked like a man dressed in women's clothes, and two local men were arrested when they were thought to be sounding the depth of the Susquehanna.

Lee's 1st and 3rd Corps remained in camp around Chambersburg that day. Lee was also still there. But it was time to get moving again. "On the 28th, General Lee issued orders for the march upon Harrisburg," Longstreet later remembered.[5] According to Major Charles Marshall of his staff, Lee's plan was to use a threat to Harrisburg, the capital of Pennsylvania, to draw the Federals into his grasp. Ewell was to move directly on Harrisburg, and Longstreet would march to his support, while Hill was to follow Early's route, cross the Susquehanna south of Harrisburg, and cut the railroad between that town and Philadelphia. But all that was soon changed.

"After due preparation for our march of the 29th," Longstreet said, "all hands turned in early for a good night's rest. My mind had hardly turned away from the cares and labors of the day, when I was aroused by some one beating on the pole of my tent."

It proved to be one of his staff officers with a young man who had been arrested at the picket line. This turned out to be Henry Thomas Harrison, a civilian "scout" who had been sent out by Longstreet three weeks before with enough gold coins to support him behind Union lines for a while. "He had," Longstreet said, "walked through the lines of the Union army during the night of the 27th and the 28th, secured a mount in the dark of the latter day to get in as soon as possible, and brought information of the location of two corps of Federals at night of the 27th, and approximate positions of others. General Hooker had crossed the Potomac on the 25th and 26th of June. On the 27th he had posted two army corps at Frederick, and the scout reported another near them, and two others near South Mountain, as he escaped their lines a little after dark of the 28th." Longstreet sent him on to Lee's headquarters, but that general declined, at first, to see him. He had, as Longstreet termed it, a "want of faith in reports of scouts."[6] But, having heard nothing from or about Stuart, being in the dark about the location of the Army of the Potomac, and being reassured that Longstreet thought highly of Harrison, who had worked for him down in Southside Virginia, Lee finally heard the man's story.

It wasn't too surprising to learn that Hooker had crossed to the north side of the Potomac, but it was disturbing to only learn of it two or three days after the event. Harrison's additional observation that there wasn't a Confederate cavalryman to be seen anywhere in his travels only added to Lee's annoyance at not having heard from Stuart. Harrison also added one other tidbit of information: he had heard that Hooker had been fired and replaced by George Meade. Lee, of course, knew Meade from the old pre-war Regular Army. He respected him as a gentlemen, which is more than he thought of Hooker, but expected him to be cautious and that it would take him some time to get organized. Nevertheless, with the Union army north of the Potomac, it was time to concentrate his forces, so orders were sent that night for Ewell to join the rest of the army at Chambersburg.

If news was slow in reaching Lee, think of how Jefferson

Davis must have felt. It was only on the evening of the 28th that he received Lee's letter to him written on the 23rd (see Chapter 14) proposing the organization of a real or phantom army at Culpeper Court House. Davis wrote a reply that night complaining that "General Johnston continues to call for re-enforcements, though his first requisition was more than filled by withdrawing troops from Generals Beauregard and Bragg. General Bragg is threatened with attack, has fallen back to his intrenched position at Tullahoma, and called on Buckner for aid. General Beauregard says that no troops have been withdrawn by the enemy from his point since those returned to New Berne [North Carolina], and that his whole force is necessary to cover his line, this being in answer to a proposition to him to follow the movement of the enemy, said to be to the west, with all his disposable force, pointing him at the same time to the vital importance of holding the Mississippi, and communicating the fear that Vicksburg would fall unless Johnston was strongly and promptly re-enforced.

"D. H. Hill has a small force, part of which has been brought here. Clingman's brigade is near Wilmington; Colquitt's, Kinston [North Carolina]; Martin's nominally on railroad (Weldon, &c.). Cooke's, Ransom's, and Jenkins' have been brought here, the last two temporarily from the defense of Petersburg and country thereabouts. Wise's brigade is, as you left it, engaged in the defense of Richmond, and serving in the country to the east of the city. The enemy have been reported in large force at White House, with indications of an advance on Richmond. We are organizing companies for home defense, and the spirit of resistance is increasing. Corse's brigade, in accordance with your orders, left Hanover Junction. All the artillery, I am informed, was taken away, and the single regiment of infantry which constituted the guard for the bridges proved unequal to the duty, as you have no doubt learned. . . . It was stated that General W. H. F. Lee [Lee's son, Rooney] was captured . . . but I trust it will prove to be one of the many startling rumors which the newsmongers invent. . . .

"In yours of the 20th, you say, 'If any of the brigades that I have left behind for the protection of Richmond can, in your opinion, be spared, I should like them to be sent to me.' . . . Corse's brigade has gone, and Wise's is the only other left by you. Cooke's was in North Carolina, and Davis' brigade was sent to complete Heth's division in place of Cooke's. Ransom's and Jenkins' constitute the defense of the south side as far as Weldon [North Carolina], and are relied on for service elsewhere, from Wilmington to Richmond. General Elzey is positive the enemy intend to attack here, and his scouts bring intelligence which, if I believed it, would render me no more anxious for the city than at any former time. I do not believe the Yankees have such force as is stated, but that they have enough to render it necessary to keep some troops within reach, and some at Petersburg, at least, until Suffolk is truly evacuated. Do not understand me to be balancing accounts in the matter of brigades; I only repeat that I have not many to send you, and enough to form an army to threaten, if not capture, Washington as soon as it is uncovered by Hooker's army. My purpose was to show you that the force here and in North Carolina is very small, and I may add that the brigades are claimed as properly of their command."[7] This letter never reached Lee but was captured in transit by Union scouts, and, not being encrypted, provided valuable information to the Union War Department.

So far from sending more brigades to Lee, the Confederate authorities called to Richmond that day the only one that was being sent. Secretary Seddon wired General Corse, at Gordonsville: "If you have no reason to expect an advance of the enemy on Gordonsville, leave about 200 men, with some artillery, at that place, and with your brigade come down to this city."[8] General Dix, that same day, sent orders to the Union commander at Suffolk to destroy his entrenchments thoroughly and then to fall back to a new line near Portsmouth and Norfolk, as most of Dix's troops were being concentrated on the York River. Lee's oldest son, George Washington Custis Lee, an aide to President Davis recently promoted to brigadier general, called out the home guard companies of the Confederate War Department that day. "These," a War Department clerk recorded in his diary, "with the militia in the streets (armed by the government today), amounted to several thousand efficient men for the batteries and for guard duty. They are to rendezvous, with blankets, provisions, etc., upon the sounding of the tocsin. I learn that 8000 men in the hospitals within convenient reach of the city, including those in the city, can be available for defense in an emergency. They cannot march, but they can fight. These, with Hill's division, will make over 20,000 men; an ample force to cope with the enemy on the Peninsula."[9]

General Milroy, who had finally been arrested in accordance with Halleck's order, wrote to President Lincoln that day from Baltimore, protesting that "I had no orders to evacuate Winchester, I was told to get ready." Which he had done. "I love my country & the Union dearer than life, and God knows that every faculty of my soul & body has been devoted to its salvation. . . . I have never asked a leave of absence & have not been absent from my command a single day or night . . . until two days ago, I was suspended from command and placed in arrest by order of General Halleck, like a common fellon. I may have erred in judgment in remaining too long at Winchester . . . but without disobeying any orders or being guilty of any crime, I am deprived of command & made a prisoner. . . . Halleck hates me without cause . . . & I can ask or expect nothing but injustice from him, and I respectfully ask you sir, as a friend of our country, to suspend my arrest if only temporarily, during the present terrible crisis, and give my something to do, if it is only the command of a company in active service. If permitted I would freely resign my present commission, & take any command, or go into the ranks as a private, rather than remain idle at this critical period. After this crisis is passed, & my country is saved, Halleck may have me tried to his hearts content and hang me if he can."[10]

Down in Louisiana, General Green, after having recommended to Mouton that the Union garrison at Donaldsonville should not be attacked, went ahead and did it anyway. He spent the night of 27-28 June getting his men into position, and they attacked at about 2 a.m. on the 28th. The early hour was chosen to keep the gunboats in the river from spotting the Confederates' approach. One regiment of Texas Mounted Volunteers had been sent to circle around and come in along the bank of the Mississippi from the north; another was to follow Bayou La Fourche and attack from the south. Both regiments would be partially protected or hidden from the gunboats by a levee and by weeds along the bank. Both were to try to penetrate the Union position between the levee and the river, where there were only log stockades to bar entrance. Green's other three regiments were, as he later reported, "to envelop the works, moving up around them to the brink of the ditch, shooting down the cannoneers and their supporters from the ramparts at a distance of only 16 or 18 feet."[11] Inside the works were 225 Federals, including convalescents, commanded by Major Joseph D. Bullen of the 28th Maine. However, Green estimated them at 500 or 600 men.

The Confederates coming down the riverbank, despite fire from the fort and from two gunboats in the river, drove the Federals back from the stockade, and then crossed it themselves, helping each other over, or waded into the river to get around the end. The regiment coming up from the south, however, which was supposed to attack when it heard the firing begin on the north side, was delayed because the colonel was "unable to control his guide," and didn't get into the fight until it was almost over. Meanwhile, Green ordered "an advance of the whole line." One other regiment went around to the north and got into the fort at the stockade; another one never advanced because its commander was waiting for a guide, which Green had not sent, and never got into the fight at all; and the third "enveloped the ditch as directed."

Green later reported that "We were not repulsed and never would have been until we found, after getting into the stockade, there was yet a ditch to cross, running in front of and parallel with the river, and no means whatever on hand to cross it. At this ditch a most desperate fight ensued. . . . Our men here used brick bats upon the heads of the enemy, who returned the same. . . . At daylight I sent in a flag of truce, asking permission to pick up our wounded and bury our dead, which was refused, as I expected. My object in sending in the flag so early was to get away a great number of our men who had found a little shelter near the enemy's works, and who would have been inevitably taken prisoners. . . . The fort was much stronger than it was represented to be, or than we expected to find it. Had it fallen into our hands, I am satisfied, with a little work on it, we would have held it against all the gunboats below Port Hudson. Its capture and occupation would doubtless have caused great uneasiness and inconvenience to the Federal army besieging that fortress. In this view, much risk was justified in its attempted capture."[12]

Banks reported that "The garrison made a splendid defense, killing and wounding more than their own number, and capturing as many officers and nearly as many men as their garrison numbered."[13] Major Bullen, of course, asked for reinforcements, in case he was attacked again, but there weren't many available to send. Before the day was out General Emory, at New Orleans, issued an order authorizing the military governor of Louisiana to organize a brigade of infantry for Federal service for 60 days.

In Tennessee that day, the 28th, Rosecrans' army continued to struggle through the mud to concentrate at Manchester. Thomas's 14th Corps was already there; Sheridan's division of the 20th came in that day; the others were still en route. Stanley's cavalry fell back from Shelbyville to Guy's Gap to get resupplied with rations and ammunition. The Confederates had also been delayed by the mud and rain and didn't reach Tullahoma until that morning, the rear guard not arriving until after noon. (A Confederate staff officer wrote home that the name Tullahoma was of Greek origin: from *tulla*, meaning mud, and *homa*, meaning more mud.) Bragg would make his stand there, or so he told

Brigadier General St. John Liddell, a brigade commander in Cleburne's Division. But, when Liddell passed this word to one of his colonels, the colonel bet him an oyster dinner that Bragg would not stand and fight. At 3 p.m. Bragg, whose health was not good, held a conference with his corps commanders at which he did not seem very confident. Polk advised him to retreat before the Federals cut the railroad behind him, Hardee equivocated, and no decision was reached.

That morning, Wilder's mounted infantry brigade, as he put it in his report, "started to get in the rear of Tullahoma, to destroy the rebel communications. We moved rapidly to Hillsborough, leaving two companies . . . at that place, until relieved by a brigade of infantry, . . . and from thence toward Decherd; but on arriving at Elk River, found that the incessant rains had so swollen that stream that we could neither ford nor swim it, the current being so rapid that our horses were washed down stream. There was a bridge at Pelham, 6 miles farther up. We turned our course for that place, sending Colonel [James] Monroe, with eight companies . . . down Elk River, to destroy, if possible, the road and railroad bridges over Elk River at Estill Springs, with orders, if successful, to come down the railroad and join me at Decherd, or below. On his arrival at the railroad, he found a division of [Confederate] infantry guarding the bridges and a large wagon train. He immediately fell back to Hillsborough, finding it impossible to accomplish anything further, being pursued by a force of rebel cavalry, without any loss to himself, although skirmishing with and holding them in check for several miles." Monroe caught up with Wilder the next day, but, meanwhile, the latter kept moving.

"On leaving the direct road to Decherd," he later reported, "and going in the direction of Pelham, we were compelled to ford streams that swam our smallest horses, and compelled us to carry our howitzers' ammunition on the men's shoulders across the streams. When near Pelham, we learned that a party of rebels were at the bridge, with the intention of destroying it on our approach. I immediately ordered the advance . . . and about 30 scouts of the different regiments, to go forward on a run and prevent the destruction of the bridge. They dashed forward, not only saving the bridge, but taking 2 of the party prisoners, and capturing a drove of 78 mules, which were sent back to Hillsborough in charge of a company. We soon reached the South Fork of Elk River, and found the water deep enough to swim our tallest horses. The stream, though rapid, could, by crossing diagonally, be swum; and by tearing down an old mill, we made a raft that, by being towed with our picket ropes, floated our two mountain howitzers over. The crossing occupied about three hours.

"We immediately moved forward toward Decherd, half fording and half swimming another stream on the way. We reached the railroad at 8 o'clock in the evening, and immediately attacked the garrison of about 80 men, who, protected by a stockade and the railroad cut, made a pretty good resistance. We soon dislodged them, however, when they took a position in a deep ravine, with timber in it, completely protecting them, while our men had to approach over a bare hill to attack them, exposing themselves to sharp fire at 60 yards' range. I ordered up our howitzers, and a couple of rounds of canister silenced them and drove them out. We immediately commenced destroying the railroad track and water-tanks on the Nashville and Chattanooga Railroad, and blowing up the trestle-work on the branch road to Winchester. The railroad depot was well filled with commissary stores, which we burned. We also destroyed the telegraph instruments.

"A large force was by this time approaching from the north side, and, having destroyed about 300 yards of track, we left, after skirmishing with their advance guard and capturing some 4 or 5 prisoners, who, on being questioned separately, stated that six regiments of infantry were about to attack us. Believing that I would have but little chance of success in a fight with them, on account of the darkness and our total ignorance of the ground, we moved off in the direction of Pelham, and, after going about 6 miles, went off the road into the woods at 2 o'clock, and bivouacked without fires until daylight."[14]

Down in Mississippi, Charles Dana was writing to Secretary Stanton again that day, the 28th, and, after mentioning the mine that the Rebels had exploded under Sherman's lines the day before, said: "On McPherson's front nothing has been accomplished. An attempt is now being made to raise a cavalier work on the parapet of the crater formed by the recent explosion. Sand-bags are to be laid up, if possible, with loop-holes for sharpshooters, and short rifle-pits dug on each flank, with the design of driving the enemy from the interior of the fort; but this effort is of doubtful success, for the enemy maintain a most obstinate defense, and with their hand-grenades render it difficult for our working parties to remain in the crater at all. The wounds inflicted by those missiles are frightful. The working parties of Ord are also getting near enough to be checked by hand-grenades, while Lauman, while farther from the rebel lines, is almost nightly assailed by little sorties of the enemy. He loses one or two men every night, and sometimes more, generally by carelessness, and lately had one of his rifle-pits filled up by a party that made a dash upon him. Herron, too has been stopped for the last two nights by the brightness of the moonlight, which has enabled the enemy to fire at his men on fatigue duty. The heat of the weather, the unexpected length of the siege, the absence of any thorough organization of the engineer department, and the general belief of our officers and men that the town must presently fall into our hands without any special effort or sacrifice, all conspire to produce comparative inactivity and inefficiency on our part."[15]

Captain Hickenlooper's notes for the 28th say: "It being impossible to continue work on crater until rebels are driven from outer face of said work, we have concluded to spring another mine under parapet to left of crater, for the purpose of uncovering their work. Commenced work on said gallery, running northwest from covered gallery in crater."[16]

Admiral Porter wrote to Grant, that day, that "Two deserters came over yesterday. They say the town will surrender on the

4th of July after rebels fire a salute. Six days' quarter-rations left yesterday." General Herron also reported that day on receiving Confederate deserters, in his case six of them: "They are from Nineteenth Arkansas, stationed near center, and deserted under the impression that the town would be surrendered in a few days. They report a further reduction in rations and great dissatisfaction among men. . . . They say next Saturday will settle the question."[17]

General Hurlbut was writing to Rawlins that day from Memphis: "It is reported on pretty good authority that Marmaduke has occupied the crossings of the L'Augille River, 35 miles northwest of Helena, and that Price's whole force from Jacksonport is on its way down, threatening Helena, but, as I think, to come in at or near Milliken's Bend, and unite with Pemberton's force, escaping from Vicksburg by skiffs, &c., which my scouts inform me they have prepared for effecting a crossing, joining Johnston. One of our best spies, just from Jackson, reports that unless Johnston is re-enforced by Kirby Smith and Price, he will not be in condition to attack General Grant. The feeling throughout Mississippi is despondent, and they all talk of the line of the Tombigbee River as the next last ditch. Vicksburg and Port Hudson seem to be given up by everybody. Nothing now looks dark except the movement of Lee into Maryland and Pennsylvania. This would seem, from the papers, to be in very heavy force, and may be productive of very serious consequences."[18]

Henry Ginder, the civilian engineer inside Vicksburg, would not have agreed with that latter statement. He wrote that day, "I am almost sorry to hear of Lee's progress northward, for it looks as if the importance of Vicksburg were not understood. Our existence almost as a nation depends on holding this place. Why not then remain on the defensive and send troops hither, instead of employing them on useless expeditions which are only raids on a grand scale, having no decisive results. Our rulers seem to have gone clean daft."[19] Margaret Lord, wife of Vicksburg's Episcopal rector, wrote that day: "The siege has lasted 42 days and yet no relief – every day this week we have waited for the sound of General Johnston's guns, but in vain."[20] A Confederate chaplain wrote: "The sixth week was now closed and nothing from Johnston. Our fate seems to stare us in the face. Still we hear rumors that he is coming with a mighty army. . . . Can't our government send us relief? Shall Vicksburg fall for want of energy on the part of our government? Will all the blood be spilled in vain? For the first time, dark doubts cross my mind."[21]

General Pemberton wrote another message to Johnston that day: "Dispatches of 19th and 22d received. I am surprised that you have so small a force, but as the enemy has separated his so much and occupies so long a line, could not a combined, vigorous effort even yet raise the siege? The enemy occupies the peninsula opposite the city, and I think it would be entirely impracticable for General Taylor either to put in supplies or to cross the river, and equally so for me to cross the garrison over."[22] But this note was never sent, perhaps for lack of a messenger or of a way to get one through the lines.

A Union propaganda leaflet was circulating within the Confederate lines that day, telling the Confederates to "cave in," for there was no hope – that Sherman was after Johnston with 60,000 men and that Grant had them surrounded with 90,000 more (actually Grant's whole force, counting all reinforcements, might barely have reached 90,000), that the Rebels west of the Mississippi had been driven off, and that the garrison could not escape in boats. "Not one soldier of you will be heard of, as connected with the siege of Vicksburg," it said, "while your officers will all be spoken of as heroes. Your present form of Government crushes out the hopes of every poor man, distinction is kept for the aristocracy of the South. You have better friends on this side than on that, the friends of freedom."[23]

But perhaps the most effective piece of propaganda inside Vicksburg just then was an anonymous plea written that day, or night, signed "many soldiers," that found its way into Pemberton's headquarters. It began by saying that they thought he had done all, as their commander, that any man could have. "Everybody admits that we have all covered ourselves in glory, but alas! alas!

general, a crisis has arrived in the midst of our siege. Our rations have been cut down to one biscuit and a small bit of bacon per day, not enough scarcely to keep soul and body together, much less to stand the hardships we are called upon to stand. . . . Men don't want to starve, and don't intend to, but they call upon you for justice, if the commissary department can give it; if it can't you must adopt some means to relieve us very soon. The emergency of the case demands prompt and decided action on your part. If you can't feed us, you had better surrender us, horrible as the idea is, than suffer this noble army to disgrace themselves by desertion. I tell you plainly, men are not going to lie here and perish, if they do love their country dearly. Self-preservation is the first law of nature, and hunger will compel a man to do almost anything. You had better heed a warning voice, though it is the voice of a private soldier. This army is now ripe for mutiny, unless it can be fed."[24] The author, or authors, of this letter have never been identified, and there is some suspicion that it was another piece of Union propaganda. Admiral Porter was fond of such psychological warfare ideas and is known to have sent leaflets into Vicksburg on kites.

Farther up the Mississippi, Colonel Nasmith's expedition continued that day. "I embarked with the cavalry June 28," he later reported, "and proceeded across the river to Spanish Moss Bend, on the Arkansas shore. Arriving there, all the troops were ordered to disembark. . . ." The troops from the Marine Brigade, however, did not obey this order. Nasmith proceeded with the rest to Gaines' Landing, about 10 miles away. He had heard firing from there the night before and hoped to capture whatever force was in the area. After marching three miles he encountered Rebel pickets, who fell back before him all the way to Gaines' Landing, where they faded back from the river. By then it was dark, there were more roads leading inland than he could guard, and, unable to secure a local guide, Nasmith decided to return to his transports. "From what I deem reliable information," he reported, "the enemy had at Cypress Bend and Gaines' Landing, and points in the vicinity, from 4,000 to 5,000 troops, with eight pieces of artillery . . . two full regiments of infantry, and the balance of the force cavalry. . . . I also learned from good authority that all the forces in Arkansas, under Generals Price, Marmaduke, and other commanders, are ordered to the vicinity of Milliken's Bend. . . ."[25]

Actually, J. G. Walker's division was still lurking in that neighborhood, but Price and Marmaduke were not, of course, making for Milliken's Bend; they were still struggling through the mud trying to get at Helena. Price, having advanced five miles in two days, wrote to General Holmes again on the 29th from "Camp five miles east of Switzer's," saying: "I have delayed writing until I might inform you with some degree of certainty as to my future movements. I succeeded in getting all my trains across Caney [Creek] to-day, and both Parsons and McRae are now in camp at this place. I shall endeavor to make a move by to-morrow night, though it is possible that I may not be able to do so. I was compelled to make this detour in order to head an impassable creek to the direct road." He inclosed a message from Marmaduke that showed that "a part of to-morrow's intended march may be difficult." In fact, Marmaduke reported from the crossing of Flat Creek Bayou on the Helena road that the stream was "quarter of a mile wide, 50 yards of which is swimming water. The citizens say that this route cannot be passed by infantry[,] wagons and artillery under two days, and I do not think it can be bridged." The good news was that the civilians did tell him about an alternate route that could be forded and that crossed another stream, Flat Fork, near its head, and that "after crossing Flat Fork there is no creek or stream to obstruct the movement of your troops except one stream that is already bridged well enough to pass wagons and artillery."[26]

Down at Port Hudson that day, the 29th, Union soldiers began advancing toward the Confederate lines just north of the Citadel by rolling cotton bales ahead of them as portable breastworks.

They had almost reached the parapet of the defenses when the Rebels set the cotton bales on fire by hurling firebrands down on them, forcing the Federals to retreat. That night, the 6th Michigan and the 165th New York advanced from the head of a sap and attacked the Citadel itself. They hurled grenades into the defenses and then followed them into the trenches, fighting with clubbed muskets, but were soon caught in a deadly crossfire and forced out, although they made off with four prisoners, including a Rebel captain.

On that 29th day of June, President Lincoln sent a long reply to a series of resolutions of the Ohio Democratic state convention, a copy of which had been presented to him by a committee. Their major concern was the case of Vallandigham and his trial by a military commission. Lincoln pointed out that their position was mainly the same as the resolutions of the recent Democratic meeting at Albany, to which he had already replied publicly. "This response you evidently used in preparing your remarks, and I desire no more than that it be used with accuracy. In a single reading of your remarks I only discovered one inaccuracy in matter which I suppose you took from that paper. It is when you say 'The undersigned are unable to agree with you in the opinion you have expressed that the constitution is different in time of insurrection or invasion from what it is in time of peace & public security.' A recurrence to the paper will show you that I have not expressed the opinion you suppose. I expressed the opinion that the constitution is different, *in its application* in cases of Rebellion or Invasion, involving the Public Safety, from what it is in times of profound peace and public security; and this opinion I adhere to, simply because, by the constitution itself, things may be done in the one case which may not be done in the other." He said the only question was, who was to decide what the public safety requires, "and I think the man whom, for the time, the people have, under the constitution, made the commander-in-chief, of the Army and Navy, is the man who holds the power, and bears the responsibility of making it. If he uses the power justly, the same people will probably justify him; if he abuses it, he is in their hands, to be dealt with by all the modes they have reserved to themselves in the constitution.... You claim that men may, if they choose, embarrass those whose duty it is, to combat a giant rebellion, and then be dealt with in turn, only as if there was no rebellion. The constitution itself rejects this view. The military arrests and detentions, which have been made, including those of Mr. V. which are not different in principle from the others, have been for *prevention*, and not for *punishment* – as injunctions to stay injury, as proceedings to keep the peace – and hence, like proceedings in such cases, and for like reasons, they have not been accompanied with indictments, or trials by juries, nor, in a single case by any punishment whatever, beyond what is purely incidental to the prevention."

He said he had not been aware, until they themselves had informed him, that Vallandigham had been a candidate for governor of Ohio, but he pointed out that he "is known to you, and to the world, to declare against the use of an army to suppress the rebellion. Your own attitude, therefore, encourages desertion, resistance to the draft and the like, because it teaches those who incline to desert, and to escape the draft, to believe it is your purpose to protect them, and to hope that you will become strong enough to do so.... I can not say I think you desire this effect to follow your attitude; but I assure you that both friends and enemies of the Union look upon it in this light. It is a substantial hope, and by consequence, a real strength to the enemy. If it is a false hope, and one which you would willingly dispel, I will make the way exceedingly easy." He said he would revoke the order banishing Vallandigham if the members of the committee would publicly endorse these propositions: "1. That there is now a rebellion in the United States, the object and tendency of which is to destroy the national Union; and that in your opinion, an army and navy are constitutional means for suppressing that rebellion. 2. That no one of you will do any thing which in his own judgment, will tend to hinder the increase, or favor the decrease, or lessen the efficiency of the army or navy, while engaged in the effort to suppress the rebellion; and, 3. That each of you will, in his sphere, do all he can to have the officers, soldiers, and seamen of the army and navy, while engaged in the effort to suppress the rebellion, be paid, fed, clad, and otherwise well provided and supported." He said that he thought their doing so would more than compensate "for the consequences of any mistake in allowing Mr. V. to return; and so that, on the whole, the public safety will not have suffered by it. Still, in regard to Mr. V. And all others, I must hereafter as heretofore, do so much as the public safety may seem to require."[27]

The committee members declined to subscribe to these propositions. They said they had not been seeking a favor but demanding the recognition of a right, and they considered his offer "a mere evasion of the grave questions involved in this discussion, and of a direct answer to their demand."[28]

Lincoln also answered General Milroy's letter that day: "I have never doubted your courage and devotion to the cause. But you have just lost a Division, and *prima facie* the fault is upon you; and while that remains unchanged, for me to put you in command again, is to justly subject me to the charge of having put you there on purpose to have you lose another. If I knew the facts sufficient to satisfy me that you were not at fault, or error, the case would be different. But the facts I do know, while they are not at all conclusive, and I hope they may never prove so, tend the other way. First, I have scarcely seen anything from you at any time, that did not contain imputations against your superiors, and a chafing against acting the part they had assigned you. You have constantly urged the idea that you were persecuted because you did not come from West-Point, and you repeat it in these letters. This, my dear general, is I fear, the rock on which you have split."[29] (Milroy was eventually granted a court of inquiry, and in October Lincoln decided that Milroy had not disobeyed any order and that no court martial was necessary. He was returned to duty and served in the Department of the

Cumberland.)

The unfortunate town of Mercersburg, Pennsylvania, was invaded by Confederate troops for the fifth time that 29th day of June; this time by Imboden's brigade, belatedly following Lee's order to move along his army's left flank as it advanced along the Cumberland Valley. This was, perhaps, the harshest invasion yet. These Rebels not only plundered the town but all the surrounding farms, and found some 400 horses that had been hidden in the nearby mountains.

After issuing orders for Ewell and Early to join the rest of his army near Chambersburg, Lee changed his mind sometime during the night of 28-29 June. He was worried about Harrison's report that there were two Union corps near the passes of South Mountain in Maryland. This could indicate an intention – certainly the capability – of a sizable part of the Union army to move to the west side of the mountain ridge into the Cumberland Valley, between Lee and the crossings of the Potomac, cutting him off from Virginia. He was drawing all his food and forage from the Pennsylvania countryside, but he needed a secure supply line to obtain more ammunition, the one absolute essential his army had to have in order to fight. "By the report of the scout," Longstreet later wrote, "we found that the march of Ewell's east wing had failed of execution and of the effect designed, and that heavy columns of the enemy were hovering along the east base of the mountain. To remove this pressure towards our rear, General Lee concluded to make a more serious demonstration and force the enemy to look eastward. With this view he changed direction of the proposed march north, by counter-orders on the night of the 28th, calling [for] concentration east of the mountains at Cashtown, and his troops began their march under the last orders of the 29th."[30] In other words, Lee hoped to keep the Army of the Potomac east of the mountains by concentrating his own army on that side.

So, new orders were sent to Ewell. They are dated in the Official Records on the 28th, but obviously, from the content, were written early on the 29th. After mentioning the previous orders written "last night," Lee said: "If you have not already progressed on the road, and if you have no good reason against it, I desire you to move in the direction of Gettysburg, via Heidlersburg, where you will have turnpike most of the way, and you can thus join your other divisions to Early's, which is east of the mountains. I think it preferable to keep on the east side of the mountains. When you come to Heidlersburg, you can either move directly on Gettysburg or turn down to Cashtown. Your trains and heavy artillery you can send, if you think proper, on the road to Chambersburg. But if the roads which your troops take are good, they had better follow you."[31] (A footnote in the Official Records says of this message, "Noted in letter-book as copied from memory," which might account for the wrong date.) Longstreet's medical director remembered seeing the couriers and staff officers riding to and from Lee's headquarters that day in a flurry of activity and heard Lee tell those around him, "Tomorrow, gentlemen, we will not move on Harrisburg as we expected, but will go over to Gettysburg and see what General Meade is after."[32] Lee moved his headquarters that day to Greenwood, just ten miles west of Gettysburg on the Chambersburg pike.

Major Walter Taylor, of Lee's staff, replied that day to General Pickett's letter of the 21st complaining about his two lost brigades. "I am directed by the commanding general to say," Taylor wrote, "that he has repeatedly requested that the two brigades be returned, and had hoped that at least one of them (Corse's) would have been sent to the division ere this. There is no other brigade in the army which could be assigned to the division at this time. Though Corse's may not be expected immediately, he hopes that ere long it will be enabled to rejoin its division."[33] Lee, of course, did not know that Corse's brigade had been ordered back from Gordonsville to Richmond the day before.

The news that the Army of the Potomac had crossed its namesake river, combined with the absence of news from or about Stuart, prompted Lee to finally send for the two brigades of cavalry that had been left behind in Virginia under Beverly Robertson. Why he had not done so sooner is one of the unknowables of this campaign. Robertson had lost touch with the Union army and did not know that it had crossed the Potomac, so he had not yet followed the instructions Stuart had left him to, in that event, follow Lee's army north. He had also failed to keep in contact with Longstreet's infantry, as ordered. But on the 29th he and Grumble Jones met at Berryville and decided that there was no longer any sizable Union force threatening the gaps of the Blue Ridge and thus to make their move north at last. A courier from Lee met them at Martinsburg that same day with orders to do just that.

The three brigades with Stuart reached the Baltimore & Ohio Railroad early on the morning of the 29th, and spent several hours tearing it up along a stretch several miles long, further delaying their move north. Stuart was hoping to capture General Hooker as he made his way to Washington after being relieved of command, but the train carrying that general got word of the Confederate presence and turned back. By 10:30 a.m., the Rebels resumed their northward course, and, at about 4 p.m., the 4th Virginia Cavalry, leading the column, came under fire as it approached the town of Westminster, Maryland – terminus of the Western Maryland Railroad, which ran northwest from Baltimore – and was charged by the lone squadron of the 1st Delaware Cavalry that had been sent there by General Schenck the night before. The charge of this inexperienced squadron caught the head of the column in a narrow space and drove it back in some confusion.

Stuart had to take time to send out scouts to see what he was up against, and he was reluctant at first to believe that a single squadron would dare to take on his three brigades. But, once convinced that was all he was up against, he deployed 50 men at a road junction east of the town and sent a larger detachment to get around to the northwest side to cut off the Union retreat. The Federals tried to cut their way out by charging through the smaller detachment on the east side of town and would have succeeded, but Stuart counter-charged with the rest of the 4th Virginia and drove them back to the west again. There was a brief melee in the town, during which several Confederates went down, but, in the end, out of the 95 men in the Delaware squadron, 67 were killed, wounded, or captured, while the few survivors headed towards Baltimore. Their arrival there put that city in a panic, expecting a Confederate attack at any moment.

Stuart's Rebels also captured a lieutenant and ten men of the 150th New York Infantry who were guarding the railroad depot, and took over Westminster at about 5 p.m., where Stuart paused to care for the wounded, feed the horses, parole more prisoners and let his men and horses get some rest. About midnight Fitz Lee's brigade took the lead again, heading north. Late that night it came to Union Mills, just five miles from the Pennsylvania line, where young Lee spent the rest of the night sleeping under a tree in an orchard. Stuart is said to have slept in a chair on a sidewalk in Westminster.

Colonel J. B. McIntosh, commanding the two brigades of Gregg's Union cavalry that had been sent out after Stuart, failed to find him. McIntosh had been delayed by Union infantry using the road he needed. At 8 a.m., he reported from Ridgeville, Maryland, where the National Road and the B&O Railroad crossed Parr's Ridge, well west of the section of track that Stuart was then busily destroying. He said he had sent one regiment each to Cooksville, Lisbon, and Poplar Springs, all villages along the National Road and south of the railroad. A Rebel prisoner had told him that Stuart was supposed to camp at Cooksville, the more easterly of the three points, the night before, but McIntosh had not yet heard, at that time, from the regiment sent there. Gregg's division was thus slowly making its way toward Westminster, but wasn't expected to reach there until the night of the 30th, and meanwhile Pleasonton ordered Gregg to move his division the following day to Hanover Junction, Pennsylvania, "using your force to keep open communication with Baltimore by that railroad route. The infantry will move up and be in your rear. The enemy is at York, and you may meet some of them near that Junction. General Couch reports he is fighting at Columbia."[34]

Gregg's division was intended to cover the army's right flank as it advanced northward. A later message that night told Gregg to leave one brigade at Westminster until further orders, to cover the army's rear. Buford's 1st Division would cover the left flank. It started out to do so on the 29th from around Middletown, Maryland, west of Frederick. The Reserve Brigade, now under the newly promoted General Merritt, was detached and moved to Mechanicsburg, Maryland. Buford, with his other two brigades, passed to the west of South Mountain and went through Boonsborough, Maryland, and then back to the east of the mountains and encamped that night near Fairfield, Pennsylvania, just southwest of Gettysburg. Pleasonton, himself, was not allowed to accompany any of his units; Meade kept him at army headquarters, treating him more like a staff officer – his chief of cavalry – than a corps commander, and seemed to be considering him as a possible replacement for Butterfield as chief-of-staff.

Kilpatrick's new 3rd Division set out on the 29th heading for Hanover, by way of Littlestown, just across the Pennsylvania line. Farnsworth's 1st Brigade started the day at Frederick, Maryland, and marched to Littlestown. The 2nd Brigade, which had been at Gettysburg the day before and started this day at Emmittsburg, was, by the end of this day, split in half. Two of its regiments, the 5th and 6th Michigan Cavalry, camped that night at Littlestown, and the other two, the 1st and 7th Michigan Cavalry, several miles north of Hanover, at the village of Abbottstown. There, some time after sunset, this half of the brigade was joined by its new commander, Brigadier General George Armstrong Custer, who had graduated from West Point (at the very bottom of his class) in 1861, just in time to help cover the retreat from Bull Run as a brand-new 2nd Lieutenant of Cavalry. Now, two years later, and at just 23 years of age, he was the youngest general in the Union army. He had recently petitioned the governor of his home state, Michigan, to make him the colonel of either the 5th or 7th

Michigan Cavalry, which were then both in need of commanders, and had been flatly turned down. But now he commanded both of those regiments and two more besides.

In addition to being the youngest, Custer was no-doubt the most outlandishly dressed general in the Union army as well. He wore a short double-breasted jacket of black velvet, with five loops of gold braid on each sleeve and the large blue collar of a Navy seaman's blouse, with a white star in each corner, covering the jacket's collar; a matching pair of black velvet riding breaches, with two gold stripes down each leg, mostly covered by huge riding boots; a black hat with a huge brim, a gold cord, and another star, covering a head of long, wavy blond hair; and, most conspicuous of all, around his neck a bright red cravat. One of Meade's staff officers said Custer looked like "a circus rider gone mad!"[35] But there was method to his madness. He didn't want there to be any doubts that, despite his youth, he was a real brigadier general, and he didn't want anyone, least of all his own men, having any trouble finding him on a field of battle.

At 10:35 a.m., General Halleck wrote to Meade: "I have delayed answering your telegram of 9 p.m., received after midnight, in hopes of ascertaining something more of rebel forces on the Potomac; but there is nothing further that is reliable. The cavalry force in our front is said by some to be two, and by others three, brigades, with seven pieces of artillery. So far as I can judge, without a better knowledge of the enemy's positions, your proposed movement seems good." At 11 a.m., he wrote again: "Since my last telegram, I have heard from Lowell's cavalry, at Rockville. The rebel cavalry which destroyed the train left Brookville early this morning, apparently for the Relay Junction or Ellicott's Mills. They have with them the captured mules and part of the wagons. Your cavalry may be able to cut them off. [Major William H.] Fry's cavalry [from the dismounted cavalry camp near Washington] will be added to Lowell's, but they are too weak to do much."[36]

At that same hour, Meade was writing a long letter to Halleck: "Upon assuming command of the army, and after carefully considering the position of affairs and the movements of the enemy I have concluded as follows: To move to-day toward Westminster and Emmitsburg, and the army is now in motion for that line, placing two corps, First and Eleventh, at Emmitsburg; two corps, Third and Twelfth, at Taneytown; one corps, Second, at Frizellburg, and one corps, Fifth, at Union; Sixth Corps at New Windsor; my cavalry guarding my flanks and rear. If Lee is moving for Baltimore, I expect to get between his main army and that place. If he is crossing the Susquehanna, I shall rely upon General Couch, with his force, holding him until I can fall upon his rear and give him battle, which I shall endeavor to do. I have ordered the abandonment of Harper's Ferry, a detachment of not more than 3,000 to proceed with the property, by canal, to Washington, and strengthen your forces there against any cavalry raid; the remainder to move up and join me. The line from Frederick to Baltimore by rail will necessarily be abandoned. While I move forward, I shall incline to the right, toward the Baltimore and Harrisburg road, to cover that, and draw supplies from there, if circumstances permit it, my main objective point being, of course, Lee's army, which I am satisfied has all passed on through Hagerstown toward Chambersburg. My endeavor will be in my movements to hold my force well together, with the hope of falling upon some portion of Lee's army in detail.

"The cavalry force between me and Washington, as soon as I can learn sufficiently of their movement to pursue and fight without wasting the necessary force by useless movements, will be engaged by my cavalry. Stuart's cavalry, from my best information, have divided into two columns, one on my right, between me and Baltimore, and one on my left, through Hagerstown, to join their army. My main point being to find and fight the enemy, I shall have to submit to the cavalry raid around me in some measure.... I have hastily made up this dispatch to give you the information. Telegraphic communications have been cut off. I have no opportunity to receive a reply to mine asking your advice as to these movements, and upon my best judgment proceed to execute them. I can at present give no orders as to General

Schenck's department in Baltimore, or the Potomac in my rear; neither can I, in the absence of telegraphic communication, and on account of the great distance to Couch, exercise any influence, by advice or otherwise, concerning co-operation of that force. These circumstances are beyond my control. I send this by courier, with the hope and expectation that it will reach you safely. Headquarters to-night are at Middleburg, 3 miles from Uniontown and 13 from Westminster." A note in the Official Records, heading this letter, says, "Dispatch found on the body of a soldier, killed June 30, 4 ½ miles from Glen Rock."[37] It doesn't say whether the soldier was Union or Confederate.

The Federals were now having somewhat better luck locating Lee's main forces. John Reynolds wrote to Butterfield that afternoon from Emmitsburg, Maryland, very near the Pennsylvania line, southwest of Gettysburg. He had ridden there ahead of his marching troops, who were back at Mechanicsville, Maryland. He wrote to say he had just talked with one of Colonel Sharpe's scouts who had been at Gettysburg the day before, and he forwarded fairly accurate information, slightly dated, about the Confederates, saying that Early's division had passed through that town headed for York, another division was in the Cumberland Valley, Ewell with Rodes' division was near Carlisle, and A. P. Hill was said to be moving through Greencastle in the direction of Chambersburg.

Reynolds' 1st Corps and Howard's 11th both reached Emmitsburg that day, while Sickles' 3rd Corps reached Taneytown. Slocum's 12th Corps was delayed by Sickles' wagons and didn't quite reach Taneytown that night. Orders were late in reaching Hancock's 2nd Corps that morning, causing it to also fall short of its objective, Frizzelburg, even though it marched until well past midnight, and halted a mile east of Uniontown. This in turn caused the 5th Corps to fail to reach Uniontown, stopping at Liberty instead. Sedgwick's 6th Corps marched far into the night and camped some five miles southwest of Westminster. Meade was furious about the numerous foul-ups in the day's marching.

The large 2nd Vermont Brigade was still trying to catch up

with Reynolds. General Stannard ordered all officers' baggage removed from the wagons that day, to make room for men too exhausted to keep up the killing pace, and ordered that no one was to leave the ranks in search of water. But it was a hot day, and the roads were dusty, and many men did so anyway, often with the connivance of their officers. They reached Frederick, Maryland, at noon, just as the clouds let loose with a pouring rain, and heard a rumor there that Hooker had been replaced by Meade. They stopped for an hour or two, amidst several corps, but not the 1st, then marched on over the muddy roads for another twelves miles, to camp near Creagerstown, exhausted and hungry. Local citizens made a good bit of money selling them food, but the soldiers were happy to pay. "The price was high," one said, "but the food was the very best."[38]

At 9:30 p.m., Hancock sent word to Meade, at Middleburg, that local civilians reported Jeb Stuart to be at Westminster, seven miles to the east. Meade referred this to Pleasonton, who told Hancock that the civilians must be mistaken because Gregg's two brigades of cavalry were at Westminster. But they weren't; it really was Stuart, or part of his force, the rest being at Union Mills. With Kilpatrick at Littlestown, about seven miles northwest of Union Mills, Hancock seven miles west of Westminster, and Sedgwick just five miles southwest of it, the Federals missed a good opportunity to deal severely with Stuart.

Up near Harrisburg, Jenkins was still probing the defenses of that city on the 29th. His artillery began firing again that morning, evidently at nothing in particular. At about 11 a.m., one or two companies of his cavalry, accompanied by one cannon, charged into Oyster Point, where a few of the Rebels were wounded and one was captured by New York militiamen. The rest withdrew, temporarily abandoning their gun, but later came back and retrieved it. While this skirmish was going on, Jenkins and three officers from Ewell's staff, with an escort of 60 troopers, got a closer look at Harrisburg and its defenses. They made a favorable report to Ewell, who issued orders for Rodes to prepare to capture the city the next day, "a step," Rodes later reported, "which every man in the division contemplated with eagerness. . . ."[39] However, at about 3 p.m. a courier arrived with Lee's first order to Ewell, telling him to join the rest of the army at Chambersburg. Ewell was greatly disappointed to miss his chance to capture the capital of a northern state, but he promptly sent a staff officer to notify Early and another to order Johnson's Division, with the corps' supply wagons and reserve artillery, to head back down the valley.

Johnson's men were as disappointed as their corps commander. They had been ready all day to march on Harrisburg, and, as one officer put it, ". . . we were surprised to see the head of the column upon reaching the turnpike to file abruptly to the left instead of right, and we found ourselves retracing our steps of the 27th. Our disappointment and chagrin were extreme."[40] When another courier arrived with Lee's second message, telling him to stay on the east side of the mountains, Ewell decided not to recall Johnson; instead he sent him another message telling him to turn south at Greene Village, halfway between Shippensburg and Chambersburg, and take a road that would bypass the latter town and lead directly to Cashtown. It was then nearly dark, so he decided not to start Rodes' Division's march until the next morning, but it would follow the prescribed route to Heidlersburg. Jed Hotchkiss, 2nd Corps' topographical engineer, said later that Ewell was "quiet testy and hard to please the night of the 29th, because of disappointment, and had everyone flying around. I got up in the night to answer questions and make him a map."[41] Although it would have been logical to have Jenkins' cavalry precede Rodes' infantry on the march south through unfriendly territory, Ewell did not so order. Either in the confusion of suddenly changing objectives and directions or because of a reluctance to give up the threat to Harrisburg, Jenkins was not called in.

Down at Columbia, the Federals spent the day worrying that the Confederates might build rafts and cross the Susquehanna despite the lack of a bridge, but no such attempt was made. Instead, Gordon's Brigade marched back to York, where Early was busy gathering supplies and deciding what to burn, and then up the road toward Carlyle in anticipation of going on there to join the rest of Ewell's corps the next day. But, that evening, Early received a copy of Lee's first order to Ewell, and of Ewell's order to march west and rejoin the rest of the army "on the Western side of the South Mountain."[42] But the rest of Lee's army was already starting to move to the east side of the mountain ridge, and that day Heth's Division of Hill's 3rd Corps marched to Cashtown, just eight miles northwest of Gettysburg, and the other two divisions of the corps camped that night just west of the Cashtown Gap.

Meade found time that day to write a letter to his wife, in which he said, "We are marching as fast as we can to relieve Harrisburg, but have to keep a sharp lookout that the rebels don't turn around us and get at Washington and Baltimore in our rear. . . . I am going straight at them, and will settle this thing one way or the other."[43]

Endnotes

1 Nye, *Here Come the Rebels!*, 281.
2 Mingus, *Flames Beyond Gettysburg*, 263.
3 Nye, *Here Come the Rebels!*, 308.
4 Wingert, *The Confederate Approach on Harrisburg*, 87.
5 James Longstreet, *From Manassas to Appomattox* (Mallard Press reprint, New York, 1991), 344.
6 Ibid., 346-7.
7 *OR*, I:27:I:76-7.
8 Ibid., I:27:III:944.
9 John B. Jones, *A Rebel War Clerk's Diary*, 232-3
10 Basler, ed., *The Collected Works of Abraham Lincoln*, VI:309n.
11 *OR*, I:26:I:227.
12 Ibid., I:26:I:228-9.
13 Ibid., I:26:I:15.
14 Ibid., I:23:I:460-1.
15 Ibid., I:24:I:111.
16 Ibid., I:24:II:202-3.
17 Ibid., I:24:III:447-8, both messages.
18 Ibid., I:24:III:448.
19 Hoehling, *Vicksburg: 47 Days of Siege*, 238.
20 Ibid., 239.
21 Ibid., 240.
22 *OR*, I:24:III:981.

23 Hoehling, *Vicksburg: 47 Days of Siege*, 240-1.
24 *OR*, I:24:III:982.
25 Ibid., I:24:II:517.
26 Ibid., I:22:II:891, both messages.
27 Basler, ed., *Collected Works of Abraham Lincoln*, VI:300-6; italics in the source.
28 Ibid., VI:306n.
29 Ibid., VI:308.
30 Longstreet, *From Manassas to Appomattox*, 348.
31 *OR*, I:27:III:943-4. Nye (*Here Come the Rebels*, 345) thinks the next-to-last sentence probably originally said for Ewell to move directly to Cashtown or turn down to Gettysburg, but if the earlier part of the message was remembered correctly, and Lee really told Ewell to "move in the direction of Gettysburg" then the rest of it is probably accurate, as Cashtown had not previously been mentioned, and Gettysburg had been. Also, a move from Heidlersburg to Gettysburg would be a continuation of the march from Carlisle to Heidlersburg, while a move to Cashtown would be a "turn," not *vice versa*. Mosby, in writing a defense of Stuart against post-war charges that his ride around the Union army was the cause of Confederate defeat in Pennsylvania, even suggested in his memoirs (see bibliography) that Lee's first message to Ewell was written on the 27th and the second one, changing the concentration point, on the morning of the 28th, but this does not fit with other evidence.
32 Bowden and Ward, *Last Chance for Victory*, 146.
33 *OR*, I:27:III:944-5.
34 Ibid., I:27:III:399.
35 Gregory J. W. Urwin, *Custer Victorious* (East Brunswick NJ, 1983), 58.
36 *OR*, I:27:I:66, both messages.
37 Ibid., I:27:I:66-7.
38 Coffin, *Nine Months to Gettysburg*, 183.
39 *OR*, I:27:II:552.
40 Nye, *Here Come the Rebels!*, 346.
41 Ibid., 347-8.
42 *OR*, I:27:II:467.
43 Sears, *Gettysburg*, 142.

CHAPTER 19
"The Best Opportunity We Have Had"
29 – 30 June 1863

AT RICHMOND, ADJUTANT-GENERAL Cooper was writing to Lee on the 29th: "While with the President last night, I received your letter of the 23d instant [see Chapter 14]. After reading it, the President was embarrassed to understand that part of it which refers to the plan of assembling an army at Culpeper Court-House under General Beauregard. This is the first intimation that he has had that such a plan was ever in contemplation, and, taking all things into consideration, he cannot see how it can by any possibility be carried into effect." He went on to describe, as Davis had the night before, the threat to Richmond of the Union troops assembling at the White House plantation and the recent cavalry raid on the bridges, lamenting that if Corse's brigade hadn't been sent off to rejoin Pickett it could have dealt with the latter. "Every effort is being made here to be prepared for the enemy at all points," he said, "but we must look chiefly to the protection of the capital. In doing this, we may be obliged to hazard something at other points. You can easily estimate your strength here, and I would suggest for your consideration whether, in this state of things, you might not be able to spare a portion of your force to protect your line of communication against attempted raids by the enemy."[1] He was thus suggesting that, instead of calling on Richmond for reinforcements or for a new army to threaten Washington from the south, Lee should send some of his own troops back to help protect such things as the recently attacked bridges. Like Davis's letter to Lee of the day before, this message never reached Lee but was captured by Union cavalry, along with a copy of Lee's letter to Cooper of the 23rd to which this was a reply.

Threatened by Dix's troops gathering around White House

plantation, most of D. H. Hill's forces were being drawn north of James River to defend the Confederate capital. Secretary Seddon wrote to Cooper that day: "General D. H. Hill having come over from Petersburg, whence nearly all of his troops have been withdrawn for the defense of this city, applies for leave to command here. As the forces consist mainly of troops from his department, this seems to be reasonable, and you will issue an order giving him temporary command of the troops in the field for the defense of Richmond."[2]

Dix sent two telegrams to Halleck that day. In one he complained that most of the Massachusetts regiments sent up from North Carolina were useless, having many sick men, no tents or other camp equipment, and with poor arms, their good muskets having been taken from them before they left New Berne and replaced with unserviceable ones. In the other, he said he had that day convened a council of his generals. "I submitted to them the proposition whether it would be advisable, with the force I have, to make an attack on Richmond. Their opinion, without knowing mine, was promptly and unanimously given in the negative." He added that he concurred, but that he was planning "a very important movement, which will be made the day after to-morrow, and will occupy four days. A demonstration against Richmond will be made at the same time."[3]

He followed up with a letter: "The Massachusetts regiments have dwindled away to one piece . . . and the four Pennsylvania regiments, one of which has arrived, are very small. From information received to-day, I think the insurgents have gathered, exclusive of Pickett's division, some 8,000 troops. They have left nothing on the Blackwater, and only a company at Weldon. Their telegraph and railroad lines enable them to concentrate and move troops with great rapidity to different points in North Carolina and Virginia, to meet our movements. There was an operator here, and as our steamers approached he telegraphed our coming, so that it was probably known at Richmond, Weldon, Petersburg, Hanover Junction, and the Blackwater by the time we reached the landing. The enemy's force out of the intrenchments of Richmond are at Bottom's Bridge [on the Chickahominy River], ready to dispute our passage. I shall move a considerable body of troops down there on Wednesday morning, while I send a larger force in another direction. Colonel Spear's cavalry will not be ready to do very active service till then, having been a good deal jaded by their late hard work. My officers and men are very anxious to contribute to relieve the country from the disasters with which it is threatened in Maryland and Pennsylvania, and everything that is possible will be done here, if thought best to retain this position, to inflict injury on the enemy and keep his forces fully occupied. His losses from our late expedition are very severe."[4]

Down in Mississippi that day, Joe Johnston finally began to move. "On June 29," he later reported, "field transportation and other supplies having been obtained, the army marched toward the Big Black...."[5]

However, Sherman was ready for him. Grant wrote to Sherman that same day, saying he had received the order Sherman was promulgating for the distribution of his forces. "The dispositions you made are excellent," he said. "It will be impossible for Johnston to cross the Big Black River, north of the railroad, without being discovered and your troops ready for him. My only apprehensions are that Johnston, finding us so ready, may cover a movement south, and dash in at Baldwin's [Ferry] and south of that before troops can be got out to meet him. A move of this kind certainly could not be made for anything more than a diversion to relieve the Vicksburg garrison. It does not look to me as if Johnston would ever think of bringing his wagon train across Big Black River south of us. I had but little confidence in the blockading of the roads south of the Jackson road; something has been [done], however, and will help a little if Johnston should attempt to come in that way. Ord's cavalry watch all the ferries south of Baldwin's, and though they sometimes see rebel cavalry east of the river, yet they discover no signs of an attempt to cross. I sent out a scout, who traveled for some time east from Big Black River bridge and south of the railroad. He says no troops have gone south of the railroad. The same statement is made by a deserter from one of the Texas brigades stationed at Bolton Station; but this information is several days old. In the mean time Johnston may have changed his plans and position of his troops half a dozen times."[6]

Sherman's order, in addition to spelling out specific portions of the line for each command, said: "Each corps and division commander will proceed to entrench a position near his key-point, sufficient for two batteries and one brigade, commanding [drinking] water, and looking to the east and north. All roads to the rear should be improved; a double track for wagons made by opening fences and trimming out woods. Lateral roads should also be looked to, to facilitate concentration and lateral movements. Roads to the front should be obstructed, except such as are necessary for our guards and our own use."[7]

Charles Dana wrote to Secretary Stanton again that day: "Two separate parties of deserters from Vicksburg agree in the statement that the provisions of the place are near the point of total exhaustion; that rations have been reduced lower than ever; that extreme dissatisfaction exists among the garrison, and that it is agreed on all hands that the city will be surrendered on Saturday, July 4, if, indeed, it can hold on so long as that. Col. C. R. Woods, who holds our extreme right on the Mississippi, has got out five of the thirteen guns of the sunken gunboat Cincinnati, and this morning opens three of them from batteries on the bluff. The others, including those still in the vessel, he will place as rapidly as possible in a battery he has constructed on the river half a mile in the rear of his lines. Though this battery has no guns in it, yet the enemy has been firing its heaviest ordnance at it for several days past, and has done to the embrasures some little damage, easily repairable. It commands the whole face of the town. On McPherson's front a new mine is now nearly completed, and will at furthest be ready to spring at daylight to-morrow. It is intended to destroy internal rifle-pits with which the rebels still hold the fort whose bastion was overthrown by McPherson's former mine. If successful, it will give us complete possession of that fort, as the narrowness of the ridge on which it stands and the abruptness of the ravine behind it made it impossible that it should be defended by any third line in the rear of that now being undermined. The new line in Sherman's front will probably not be ready so soon, but the engineer's morning report has not been made. No news from Joe Johnston."[8]

No news, or false news, from Johnston, was one reason for failing morale among the defenders of Vicksburg. A newspaper reporter in the city noted at this time that "the citizens had almost despaired of ever seeing Johnston arrive. The couriers who ran the gauntlet through the enemy's lines, and arrived safely in Vicksburg, brought the most exaggerated reports possible of the strength and position of the army soon to march to our relief." Some reports said Johnston had as many as 60,000 men, leading the garrison and civilians to wonder why he did not attack Grant's rear with such a force. Other reports said that Johnston would not attack because if he should save the garrison it was prove he was wrong in having told Pemberton not to get shut up in the city in the first place. Another rumor said that Loring's Division had crossed the Big Black at Hankinson's Ferry, southeast of the city, and had been defeated by an overwhelming force. An addendum to this rumor said, yes, but then Breckinridge's Division had come to his rescue and routed the Federals and had taken 6,000 prisoners. The reporter added that "The brave men, nevertheless, still continued to bear up cheerfully against the hardships and sufferings they were then enduring, and there were but few who expressed any fear of our ability to hold the city, or who grew doubtful of final success."[9]

Sergeant Tunnard noted that "A large number of skiffs were constructed and conveyed to the lower portion of the town.... The conviction seemed finally to settle on every mind that a desperate attempt would soon be made to cross the river with the army, and escape into the Trans-Mississippi Department.... It would have been an insane enterprise in the presence of the enemy's gunboats and troops." Tunnard also noted that "The enemy were once more undermining the works held by the Third Louisiana Infantry, and the men went spiritedly to work digging a countermine. The laborers were so near each other that the strokes of the pickaxes could be distinctly heard, as well as the sound of the voices. Thus the deadly struggle went on."[10]

In Tennessee, Rosecrans' army continued to assemble around Manchester, "and all McCook's corps arrived," he later reported, "before the night of the 29th, troops and animals much jaded. The terrible rains and desperate roads so delayed Crittenden, who on the 26th got orders to march to Manchester with all speed, that it was not until the 29th that his last division arrived, badly worn."[11] Rosecrans then issued orders for Thomas's 14th Corps to occupy the center of a new line, with one division in reserve, McCook's 20th Corps to take the right with two divisions *en echelon* (meaning one to the right-rear of the other) and one in reserve, and Crittenden's 21st Corps on the left with one division on the front line and one in reserve (his other division still being back at Murfreesborough).

At about 5 a.m. on the 29th, Bragg received word that Federal forces were within five miles of Tullahoma. He met with General Polk at about 9 a.m. but, as usual, the two could not agree on what to do. Bragg wanted to stand and fight at Tullahoma, Polk thought it was too dangerous to do so with Winder's Federals tearing up his supply line. Nothing was definitely decided. Around noon Polk met with his fellow corps commander, Hardee, to pass on his fears, and at around 3 p.m. the two of them visited Bragg. The latter still wanted to stand and fight, saying that his cavalry, which had now arrived during the day, could protect his supply line. Polk said he didn't have enough cavalry to protect the railroad through the Cumberland Mountains and across Elk River, and if that line were cut the army would have to retreat to the southwest, through Fayetteville, Tennessee, and Decatur, Alabama, which would leave the way to Chattanooga open to Rosecrans and the Confederate army in danger of starving. While they talked, a telegram arrived saying that the damage Wilder had done to the railroad at Decherd was not as bad as originally thought and could be repaired in a few hours. At this Hardee agreed to the idea of holding on at Tullahoma for the present, but he still thought a retreat would be better. Polk still thought the army should fall back behind the Elk River. Again nothing was settled one way or the other, except to wait and see what developed. Throughout the day, while their generals dithered, the Rebels worked in the pouring rain to improve their entrenchments.

Meanwhile, Wilder's Lightning Brigade of mounted infantry continued its raid against Bragg's supply line. From its bivouac near Pelham, it started up the Cumberland Mountains again that day, determined to break the railroad below the town of Cowan. From part-way up the mountain they could see a considerable force of Confederate infantry and cavalry near Decherd. They came to a branch railroad running northeast to Tracy City, and from there Wilder sent a detachment of 450 men to destroy the main railroad at Tantalon while he took the rest of the brigade to do the same at the town of Anderson. However, he soon learned that there were three trains loaded with troops at Tantalon and two more at Anderson, both places could only approached by bridle-paths, and his pickets, left at the branch railroad, were being driven in by Confederate cavalry who were preceding yet another trainload of infantry. "They were," as Winder succinctly put it, "now on my track and in our rear."

He reassembled his brigade, except for a small rear guard whose job it was to skirmish with the Rebels and draw them down the mountain, away from the main force, which took the road toward Chattanooga. Fortunately for the Federals, what Wilder called "a tremendous rain" obliterated their tracks, and about eight miles down the road the brigade moved a couple of miles into the woods, where it was joined by most of the rear guard that had slipped away from the Confederates. "As soon as the rebel column had passed us," he said, "we struck through the mountains, without guides, in the direction of Pelham, and came out at the place we intended to strike, and reached the foot of the mountain, at Gilham's Cove, over a very rocky and steep road. We bivouacked at 10 p.m., and next morning at daylight started for Manchester, just getting ahead of Forrest, who, with nine regiments of cavalry and two pieces of artillery, aimed to intercept us at Pelham. We reached Manchester at noon, having been in the saddle or fighting about twenty hours out of each twenty-four for eleven days, and all the time drenched with rain, our men half-starved and our horses almost entirely without forage, yet our officers and men seemed willing and cheerful, and are now only anxious for another expedition, if by such they can accomplish any good. We did not lose a single man in our expedition to the rear of Tullahoma. If our course had not been impeded by the streams flooded beyond all precedent, we must have captured one or two railroad trains, one of them having General Buckner and staff on board. . . ."[12]

"It rained almost incessantly during the 30th," Rosecrans said, "but the troops, by dint of labor and perseverance, had dragged their artillery and themselves through the mud into position. It is a singular characteristic of the soil on the 'Barrens' that it becomes so soft and spongy that wagons cut into it as if it were a swamp, and even horses cannot pass over it without similar results. The terrible effect of the rains on the passage of our troops may be inferred from the single fact that General Crittenden required four days of incessant labor to advance the distance of 21 miles." While the new line was being formed, both Thomas and McCook sent brigades or regiments forward on several roads to reconnoiter the Confederate position. "These reconnaissances," Rosecrans said, "all returned and reported having found the enemy in force on all roads except the one leading to Estill Springs. Scouts all confirmed this, with the fact that it was the general belief that Bragg would fight us in his intrenchments at Tullahoma. . . . June 30, orders having been given General [James] Morton [his chief engineer] to ascertain the practicability of moving by column in mass in line of battle from our position to gain the rear of the rebel position at Tullahoma, and who reported favorably thereon, preparations were completed, and Crittenden's second division was moved into position."[13]

But, by the morning of 30 June, Bragg had decided to retreat. However, Elk River, behind him, was swollen by the rains and was unfordable. There were bridges at only three places near Tullahoma, and one of those, at Pelham, was in Union hands. The other two places were only a few miles apart, a road bridge at Bethpage and railroad and turnpike bridges connecting Estill Springs with Allisonia. Wilder was still threatening the entire line, and all that morning ominous reports came in: Large Union forces were pressing his pickets north of Tullahoma; a column of up to 10,000 Federals was within three miles of the Bethpage bridge; another Union column was reported on the road from Manchester to University Place, threatening the Chattanooga road. To keep from being cut off from his supplies, he would have to fall back behind Elk River after all, and do it quickly. The Estill Springs bridges were only eight miles from Tullahoma, but the roads were knee-deep in mud.

One small part of Bragg's army was moving in the opposite direction that day. Morgan's division of cavalry closed up to the Cumberland River, and one of its regiments, commanded by one of Morgan's brothers, Colonel Richard Morgan, began crossing it via two fords near Burkesville, Kentucky.

Down along the Mississippi, Colonel Nasmith's expedition continued. "On the morning of the 30th," he later reported, "I proceeded down the river. Hearing in the afternoon that they were fighting at Lake Providence, and needed help, I reported myself to the general commanding, who wished me to lie over night, fearing another attack in the morning."[14] The fighting Nasmith referred to was part of J. G. Walker's operations, designed to break up, as he reported, "the plantations engaged in raising cotton under Federal leases from Milliken's Bend to Lake Providence, capturing some 2,000 negroes, who have been restored to their masters, with the exception of those captured in arms, and a few the property of disloyal [to the Confederacy] citizens of Louisiana."[15]

Brigadier General H. T. Reid, commanding the garrison at Lake Providence, reported that the Confederates "came in near the Wilton plantation, at the Mounds, and made an attack there and at Goodrich's Landing, capturing two companies of the First Arkansas Volunteers (African descent) at the Mounds and burning every gin-house and negro quarter on their way toward this point. They also burned many of the dwelling-houses. Hearing through negroes that a fight was going on at the Mounds, I sent out the First Kansas Mounted Regiment to meet them, which they did 5 miles below town, in the woods, but found them too strong, and had to fall back. . . . Soon . . . a fleet of transports, with two gunboats, came in sight from above, but one of the Marine Brigade boats happened to be in advance, and could not be stopped at the landing, but fired one of its pop guns at the rebels, which frightened them off at once and prevented them being coaxed into the town, and also prevented the gunboats getting a chance at them."[16]

General Walker reported that "I consider it an unfortunate circumstance that any armed negroes were captured, but in the cavalry expedition which broke up the plantations below Lake Providence, Colonel [W. H.] Parsons, commanding two cavalry regiments from the District of Arkansas, acting under my orders, encountered a force of 113 negroes and their 3 white officers in a fortified position, and when the officers proposed to surrender upon the condition of being treated as prisoners of war, and the armed negroes unconditionally, Colonel Parsons accepted the terms. The position, upon a high mound, the sides of which had been scooped and otherwise strengthened, was of great strength, and would have cost many lives and much precious time to have captured by assault. Under these circumstances,

Brigadier-General Tappan, who came up before the capitulation was consummated, approved of the convention. . . . I had made all my arrangements to push the next day toward Providence and Ashton, some miles above, where I intended to establish my batteries for the annoyance of the enemy's transports. That night I received General Taylor's instructions to march my division to Berwick Bay. I immediately returned to [Delhi], and had embarked one of my brigades on the railroad train, when I received instructions from Lieutenant-General [Kirby] Smith to remain in this vicinity."[17]

Meanwhile, the siege of Vicksburg dragged on. Of that last day of June Sergeant Tunnard wrote: "The sun shone brightly, while groups of summer clouds floated across the heavens. The sharp-shooting was slow but constant – unceasing all day. The gunboats approached the terminus of the lines below, and poured a concentrated fire of shells into the entrenchments, doing little damage or injury. Across the river, the peninsula looked lonely and deserted. The general apathy in fighting appeared ominous, and a dull, leaden weight unaccountably oppressed the mind, giving a gloomy hue to every object."[18]

Charles Dana wrote to Secretary Stanton at 2 p.m.: "General Grant this morning held a council of war with his army corps commanders to take their judgment on the question of trying another general assault, or leaving the result to the exhaustion of the garrison. The conclusion of the council was in favor of the latter policy, and as General Grant had himself previously strongly inclined to that course, it will, no doubt, be adhered to. Captain [Cyrus] Comstock, chief engineer, reports to-day that in the present condition of the siege works, and the indisposition of the troops to work zealously in the trenches, it will require at least a fortnight to take the place by that means only; still, it is possible that the explosion of a new mine, now nearly finished, in the fort on McPherson's center, and another mine, under the rifle-pits on the front of Ransom, who holds McPherson's right, may give us advantages that will expedite the catastrophe. The first of these mines will be sprung within twenty-four hours."[19]

Confederate Major General John H. Forney, commander of one of Pemberton's divisions, later reported that on that last night in June, "Lieutenant [William] Allen, of the Second Texas Regiment, succeeded in burning the remaining [Union] sap-roller on the Baldwin's Ferry road. He used turpentine fireballs. At first the enemy pulled away the balls as fast as they were thrown against the roller; but the officer threw over a loaded shell wrapped in cotton, saturated with turpentine, which exploded the moment the enemy seized it. After this the roller was soon burned. The other sap roller had been previously burned by Lieutenant Burt, of Withers' artillery, who shot a piece of fuse into it from a musket. Since the burning of the sap-rollers the enemy seems to have given up extending his lines left of the Baldwin's Ferry road, and have begun what appears to be a mound, at which he is working industriously."[20]

Sherman wrote to Grant that day: "All quiet along the Big Black River. . . . All the troops are now in position. Please telegraph me if anything new. I feel uneasy about the affairs about Washington."[21]

Grant wrote to General Banks that day: "Feeling a great anxiety to learn the situation at Port Hudson, I send Col. Kilby Smith to communicate with you. Colonel Smith has been here during the entire siege of Vicksburg, and can inform you fully of the position of affairs at this place. I confidently expected that Vicksburg would be in our possession before this, leaving me able to send you any force that might be required against Port Hudson. I have a very large force here now – much more than can be used in the investment of the rebel works – but Johnston still hovers east of [Big] Black River. Whether he will attack or not, I look upon now as doubtful. No doubt he would, however, If I should weaken my force to any extent. I have sent into Louisiana to learn the movements of Kirby Smith, but as yet hear nothing definite. Should it be my fortune, general, to get into Vicksburg whilst you are still investing Port Hudson, I will commence immediately shipping troops to you, and will send such number as you may indicate as being necessary. The troops of this command are in excellent health and spirits. There is not the slightest indication of despondency either among officers or men. Hoping to hear favorable news from your field of operations by the return of Colonel Smith, I remain, very respectfully, your obedient servant, U. S. Grant."[22]

At Port Hudson that evening, the 6th Michigan and 165th New York again attacked the Citadel. With great courage and wild yells they leaped over the ditch and swarmed up the parapet, but were held there by the garrison until Confederate reinforcements could come up. Many of the Federals then tried to take shelter in the ditch only to be blown up by Union heavy artillery shells that the Rebels had planted there as land mines. The survivors eventually retreated to the protection of their sap under the cover of artillery fire.

Also that evening, Captain John McKowen, who was home from Virginia on leave, slipped through some loosened boards in the back fence of a plantation house some two miles from Port Hudson, where wounded Union Brigadier General Neal Dow was convalescing. The lady of the house had sent servants to loosen the fence boards and had made sure the hinges on the door to Dow's room were well oiled and wouldn't squeak. She guided McKowen to the general's room, and the captain slipped in quietly and shook the Federal awake with his pistol in his face. Dow was taken to the headquarters of Colonel John Logan's Confederate cavalry and was eventually exchanged for Rooney Lee.

Governor Richard Yates of Illinois, the man who had first given Grant a commission in this war, wrote to President Lincoln that day, 30 June: "Major-General McClernand arrived here on the 26th instant. He has been received by the people here with the greatest demonstrations of respect, all regretting that he is not now in the field. I desire to suggest that if General McClernand with some Western troops, was put in command of Pennsylvania, it would inspire great hope and confidence in the Northwest, and perhaps throughout the country."[23]

Supporters of other generals were also pressing their claims at this time. Lincoln received a telegram that day from influential citizens of New York asking for General William B. Franklin, a former corps commander in the Army of the Potomac, who had lost his command in attempting to get Burnside removed after the battle of Fredericksburg. But the greatest outcry was for McClellan. Some thought he should be restored to the command of the Army of the Potomac, others wanted him to have Couch's place, where his popularity would help recruiting and his organizational skills would be an aid in getting the militia and new volunteer units up to speed. There was some merit in this latter idea, but the problem would have been McClellan's inability or unwillingness to use the troops once he had raised and organized them. Lincoln responded that day to one such call, from the governor of New Jersey, saying: "I really think the attitude of the enemy's army in Pennsylvania presents us the best opportunity we have had since the war began. I think you will not see the foe in New Jersey. I beg you to be assured that no one out of my position can know so well as if he were in it the difficulties and involvements of replacing General McClellan in command, and this aside from any imputations upon him."[24]

To strengthen the defenses of the national capital, the War Department that day ordered the calling out of eight regiments of District of Columbia militia to serve for sixty days.

In Pennsylvania, two regiments of New York State National Guards went out looking for Jenkins' cavalry on the morning of 30 June, but returned to the defenses west of Harrisburg after failing to find the enemy. However, at about 1 p.m., before the men could settle back into their camps, their cavalry brought word that the Rebels had finally been located just beyond Sporting Hill. Reluctantly, they turned about and retraced their steps. Jenkins did not get word that Ewell's infantry had left Carlisle until around 2 p.m. on the 30th, just about the time that he learned that Union infantry was advancing on him. Somehow he got the idea that Couch was coming after him with 10,000 men, when actually it was only two large regiments of militia and one mounted company, totaling about 1,400 men, or about the same number as in his own brigade.

Jenkins hurried most of one regiment to Carlisle to hold that town, and the road through it, until he could extricate the remainder of his brigade, which was scattered throughout the area in small detachments. Witcher's battalion and battery were given rear-guard duties, and they held off the advancing militia, making good use of a sturdy barn at the northwest edge of Sporting Hill as a ready-made fort, until, sometime after 4 p.m., a Union battery arrived and put a shell through the side of the barn, after which "The Battle of Sporting Hill" degenerated into an artillery duel. It wasn't until around 6 p.m. that Witcher ordered a retreat. Just as his men were pulling out, artillery fire was heard to the south, where a single company of Rebel cavalry, with one artillery piece, was sparring with mounted militia around Mechanicsburg, but these Confederates soon received word from Witcher to fall back to Carlisle. The Federals did not pursue either Rebel force but retired to Oyster's Point to bivouac in a pouring rain.

Brigadier General Herman Haupt was the Union Army's officer in charge of railroads in the eastern theater. He had been planning to go to the Army of the Potomac to see what his old friend Meade needed, but found that Stuart's Rebels were in his way, so he had gone to Harrisburg instead, to check on things up there. He arrived late that evening and went to the capitol, where he conferred with Governor Curtin and his staff and with T. A. Scott of the Pennsylvania Railroad, who told him that the Rebels had begun to retreat, sometimes rather precipitately, which he attributed to the Federals' having fooled them into believing that Couch had a force of 60,000 men. Haupt said no, that wasn't it. "These movements do not mean retreat; they mean concentration. Retreat would not be made hastily with no enemy pushing; it would be done deliberately, foraging on the country on the route."[25]

When the first of Jenkins' men came into Carlisle they soon found some liquor that Ewell's infantry had somehow missed. Before long they were drunk and rampaging through the town, scaring the civilians. When the whole brigade had assembled, it eventually (after midnight) moved cautiously down the road south as far as Petersburg (now York Springs), two-thirds of the way to Heidlersburg, where it camped without unsaddling the horses. Rodes' infantry, preceding the cavalry, had reached Heidlersburg just at sunset, camping in the surrounding fields. Meanwhile, Johnson's Division had continued its march back down the Cumberland Valley on the 30th, pausing long enough for Johnson to order some Union prisoners being paroled to give their shoes to his men, then turned left at Greene Village, and made camp in a pleasant meadow.

At 4 a.m. on the 30th, Early's Division had marched out of York with flags flying and bands playing, apparently heading toward Carlisle, but, instead, had gone by way of Weigelstown toward East Berlin, with cavalry out front and watching the southern flank. The day was extremely hot, but the roads were good and the men's spirits were high. White's cavalry had a brush with a Union mounted patrol near East Berlin that day, which dashed in and captured one Rebel who was up in a cherry tree, and White thought these Federals were too bold and skillful to be mere militia. At East Berlin, Early received a message from Ewell saying that the latter, with Rodes' Division, was marching for Heidlersburg from the north and for Early to move to the same place.

Early put his men in camp three miles short of that town and rode on in to confer with Ewell, who informed him that the army was concentrating at Cashtown or Gettysburg – it wasn't clear which, but Ewell had a note from A. P. Hill saying that the latter's corps was already at Cashtown – and that the next day Early should go to Cashtown by way of a road farther south, through Hunterstown and Mummasburg, while Rodes would go pretty much due west via Middletown and Arendstville. Trimble, who had by this time joined Ewell's entourage, recommended, based on his previous discussions with Lee, that they go by way of Gettysburg (or so he later claimed), but Ewell was leery of that. However, he figured that when he got to Middletown he might be better able to judge whether to proceed west or turn toward Gettysburg, which was almost due south of Middletown. Ewell hated discretionary orders and vague directions. He always preferred to have clear unambiguous orders telling him exactly what to do. On this occasion he asked a rhetorical question that most likely has been echoed on many a battlefield throughout history: "Why can't a commanding General have someone on his staff who can write an intelligible order?"[26]

At Mercersburg, Pennsylvania, on that final day of June, General Imboden demanded that the town provide him with 5,000 pounds of bacon and 35 barrels of flour, as well as shoes, hats, and other items of clothing, all to be furnished by 11 a.m., otherwise, he threatened, his men would be quartered in private homes. Most of his demands were met, and he did not so quarter his troops, but he expressed a regret that he did not have the authority to burn the town and lay waste to every farm in the state as retaliation for Union depredations in Virginia.

Early that same day, Robertson's and Jones's cavalry crossed the Potomac at Williamsport, where there were long lines of wagons going in the opposite direction filled with forage gathered in Maryland and Pennsylvania. The progress of the two brigades was somewhat slowed by the provision in the order Stuart had left them about avoiding paved turnpikes to spare the horses' hooves.

Lee was still in the dark, not only about the location of the Union army but of his own cavalry. That day he talked with Captain James Power Smith, a 2nd Corps staff officer who was just rejoining the army after temporary duty in North Carolina. Lee asked Smith if he had "heard anything of General Stuart and his movements." Smith said that at Williamsport the night before, he had ridden "through the river with two cavalrymen who stated that they were couriers from Stuart's headquarters, and that they had left Stuart the day before somewhere east of the Blue Ridge and south of the Potomac. They had brought dispatches for detachments in the Valley, and had orders to follow the army trains into Pennsylvania." Lee was so astonished to hear that Stuart had still been south of the Potomac on the 28th that he had Smith repeat his story and later sent his chief of staff to hear it told a third time. "It was," Smith later wrote, "a great disappointment to General Lee, who expected that Stuart would have reported to him in Pennsylvania, and that Lee was troubled that his cavalry forces were not between him and the enemy, as he had expected them to be."[27]

Stuart and the three brigades with him were on the road north again at daylight on the 30th. Stuart, Fitz Lee, and their staffs had breakfast at Union Mills with the family of William Shriver, a Confederate sympathizer. They repaid their hosts by entertaining them with a sing-along, including an enthusiastic rendering of what might be called his theme song, "Jine the Cavalry." This was broken up by scouts coming in to report that there was veteran Union cavalry north of them, only seven miles away, at Littlestown, Pennsylvania, on the direct road to Gettysburg. Presumably these Federals had been sent out to deal with his column.

Stuart had no particular reason to go to Gettysburg, or Littlestown, except that the road he had been following (known at Gettysburg as the Baltimore Pike) led that way. He had not been able to learn the exact location of any part of Ewell's corps, with which he was supposed to make contact. Encumbered as he was with captured wagons and animals, and under orders to find and report to Ewell, he did not want to fight any sizable body of Union troops, so he would have to bypass them. His host's 16-year-old son volunteered to lead them around the enemy force by way of Hanover, about eight miles to the northeast. In return, Stuart promised the boy a free education at the Virginia Military Institute and a position on his own staff. After paroling the captured Delaware cavalrymen, at 8 a.m. Stuart left Union Mills, and five miles up the road he crossed the Mason-Dixon Line into Pennsylvania. Chambliss's brigade had the lead this day, followed by the horse artillery and the wagons; Hampton had the rear; Fitz Lee covered the column's left flank. Stuart's scouts assured him that the Federals were still at Littlestown, but when his first troopers came within sight of Hanover they could see a column of Union cavalry riding along the road from Littlestown to Hanover, and it would reach the latter town well ahead of the Confederates. "Both men and horses being worn out," a Virginia lieutenant later wrote, "all of us regarded the prospect of a fight with no little regret and anxiety."[28]

The Federal troopers at Littlestown were the 5th and 6th Michigan of Custer's brigade, left to cover Kilpatrick's rear and scout back toward Westminster. Custer, who had just taken command of his brigade the night before, was coming south from Abbottstown with his other two regiments, the 1st and 7th Michigan, and his attached battery of horse artillery, to unite his brigade at Hanover. The Union column just riding into Hanover from Littlestown was Kilpatrick with Farnsworth's brigade and another battery. Although he was aware of Confederate scouts off to the east, and had sent detachments from his rear guard to investigate them, Kilpatrick let the head of his column, the 1st Vermont Cavalry, after pausing in Hanover to receive food and cigars from the friendly villagers, proceed north toward Abbottstown while he listened to civilians tell him about the recent visit of Lige White's Rebels, and he examined a large map of the county found hanging on a resident's wall. He then proceeded north, intent on finding Early's infantry, and did not even know about Stuart's position south of him until he received a dispatch from Pleasonton saying that the Confederates were making for Littlestown. Five minutes after getting that message his rear guard was attacked.

One of the detachments his rear guard had sent out – about 40 troopers – had collided with about 60 Rebels at the village of Buttstown, where the road from Littlestown met the road from

Westminster, not far southwest of Hanover. The Federals charged right through the Confederates, who chased after them, only to be ambushed by more of the Union rear guard firing from behind roadside fences. These Rebels fell back, but soon others appeared. Stuart, seeing only this one Union regiment, bombarded it with a section of artillery, then sent one of Chambliss's regiments to charge its front and another to hit it in the flank. The booming of these guns got Kilpatrick's attention and that of every trooper in the vicinity. Kilpatrick's rear guard, the 18th Pennsylvania Cavalry, which was in its first fight, was routed, part of it retreating into Hanover, part of it making for McSherrystown, to the northwest. Stuart sent orders for Chambliss "to push on and occupy the town, but not to pursue them too far."[29] However, there were more Federals on hand than Stuart at first assumed, and Chambliss had bitten off more than he could chew. As the officer sent to deliver the order to Chambliss remarked, "We had apparently waked up a real hornet's nest."[30]

At the sound of this firing in his rear, Kilpatrick turned the head of his brigade around and galloped back to see what was going on. Meanwhile, the 5th New York Cavalry, which had been relaxing around Hanover's town square when the Pennsylvanians were attacked, formed up in a nearby vacant field and launched a counter-charge that was joined by the detachment of the 18th that had begun the fight and a squadron of the 1st Vermont Cavalry. They drove the Rebels out of the town but were stopped by a Confederate reserve regiment, the 9th Virginia Cavalry. The Federals were driven back in turn, but the Rebels were stopped by a line of dismounted troopers that extended beyond their right flank.

Soon thereafter, General Farnsworth reached the action and led the 5th New York Cavalry and parts of the 1st Vermont and the 1st West Virginia in another charge that captured the colors of the 13th Virginia Cavalry and wounded that regiment's commander. Another Confederate regimental commander, Lieutenant Colonel William Payne of the 2nd North Carolina Cavalry, was wounded and fell into a vat of dye in the yard of a tannery when his horse was shot. He was captured, his hair, face, and uniform all dyed a dark shade of brown, and his regiment was shot to pieces. Farnsworth's conduct of this, his first battle as a brigade commander, greatly impressed his men.

Stuart himself came up just in time to see his men fleeing from Farnsworth's charge and tried to stem the retreat and rally his men, but he soon had to flee for his own life, being saved only because his horse, a fresh one he had just changed to, was able to jump a 15-foot gully. Soon, however, the rest of Chambliss's brigade drove the Federals back to Hanover, where they dismounted and fashioned defenses for themselves out of hay bales, fence rails, packing crates, and overturned wagons. Custer's two regiments from the north arrived and formed on Farnsworth's right, and an artillery duel ensued between Stuart's one battery and Kilpatrick's two, which were positioned on high ground north of the town. Kilpatrick took position on the roof of a hotel and sent to Pleasonton's chief of staff, who by then was at Littlestown, to report that he was under attack, ask for reinforcements, and pass on a rumor that there was "a heavy infantry force at Berlin and Gettysburg," and that "Lee's headquarters are at Berlin." The idea of infantry at Berlin could have come from scouts spotting Early's Division passing near there, but how he got the idea that Lee was there is impossible to say. Pleasonton passed this supposed-information on to Meade, saying, "General Lee's being in Berlin is important."[31]

Hampton left the wagons and mules to shelter behind Fitz Lee's Brigade and finally brought his own brigade onto the field at about 2 p.m. Meanwhile, the 6th Michigan, from Littlestown, came up on Stuart's left flank and charged the 10th Virginia Cavalry of Chambliss's brigade, which was supporting a pair of Confederate guns. The charge drove back part of the Rebel regiment, but a counter-charge by another part drove the Federals back in turn. Then Fitz Lee's Brigade came up, and the lone Union regiment slipped away under the cover of a single squadron, which was cut off and didn't rejoin the regiment until the next morning. The 5th Michigan, also coming from Littlestown, came upon Fitz

Lee's Brigade at about 3 p.m., drove the Confederates back with a mounted charge, then followed them on foot and did not join the rest of their brigade until later that evening. This regiment was armed with Spencer repeating rifles, and thus often preferred to fight on foot.

Custer was conferring with Kilpatrick when the 6th Michigan reached Hanover, and Kilpatrick had Custer deploy it, dismounted, west of the town. In a single line about a mile long, these troopers crawled forward through brush and brambles to within 300 yards of a Rebel battery, beyond which, unknown to them, were the captured wagons and mules, parked in a clearing surrounded by woods. One battalion of this regiment, like the entire 5th, was armed with Spencer repeating rifles, and their volume of fire soon had the Confederate gunners running for the rear, but Fitz Lee sent reinforcements that drove the Federals back in turn. Custer moved up a second time, however, threatening Stuart's flank, and Fitz Lee was forced to use most of his brigade to hold off this lone regiment. Hampton made a feint against Kilpatrick's left flank, which caused the latter to bring his guns forward, off their hill. A lull in the artillery duel then followed, and both sides were content to merely skirmish and threaten each other. The captured, and stained, Lieutenant Colonel Payne may have convinced Kilpatrick that Stuart had 12,000 troopers on hand; at least that is what he told him. On the other side, Stuart was getting low on ammunition and had accumulated another bunch of prisoners to watch. He was also worried about the Union 12th Corps, at least one division of which was now at Littlestown.

"Our wagon train was now a subject of serious embarrassment," he later reported, "but I thought by making a detour to the right, by Jefferson, I could save it." About sundown Stuart started his wagons moving behind his lines, heading east toward Jefferson (over halfway to Hanover Junction). As soon as it was full dark, he followed them with his troopers, Fitz Lee's Brigade in the lead, with instructions to push through to York "and communicate as soon as practicable with our forces." So far as he knew, "the Army of Northern Virginia must be near the Susquehanna."

The day's fight had cost him yet another delay, and the detour to Jefferson would add an extra ten miles to his intended route. The only remedy was a night march. This was, as Stuart reported, "a severe tax" on his men's endurance. "Whole regiments slept in the saddle, their faithful animals keeping the road unguided. In some instances they fell from their horses, overcome with physical fatigue and sleepiness."[32]

Kilpatrick was content to let the Rebels go. He was still more concerned with Early's infantry than Stuart's cavalry. He mistakenly reported to Pleasonton that Stuart's force had gone in two different directions, one part toward York and the other toward Gettysburg. "As the enemy was reported to be advancing from the direction of Berlin, I made no further attempts to intercept Stuart's command. I have taken one battle-flag, a lieutenant-colonel, 1 captain, and 45 privates, and upward of 15 of the enemy have been killed. My loss is trifling. I have gone into camp at Hanover. My command will be in readiness to move again at daylight to-morrow morning. We have plenty of forage, the men are in good spirits, and we don't fear Stuart's whole cavalry."[33]

The Union 5th Corps, now under Major General George Sykes since Meade's elevation to army command, camped at Union Mills that night, and at 6:30 p.m. Sykes reported to army headquarters that Stuart, Fitz Lee and Hampton had all been there the previous night. "My troops are very foot-sore and tired," he complained.[34] Crawford's two brigades of Pennsylvania Reserves, from Washington, which had been assigned to this corps (they had previously been part of it as well as sometimes part of the 1st Corps), after months of garrison duty, were having an especially hard time with all the marching now being expected of them. Sykes figured they had marched some 25 miles that day but would still not reach his other two divisions that night. General Hancock of the Union 2nd Corps, wrote to army headquarters that night from his camp at Uniontown that "General Crawford is encamped immediately in my front. He has informed me that he will start his [wagon] train at 3 a.m., and that his command will march at 4.30 a.m. I notify you of these facts in order to show you that I will be considerably delayed if I am ordered to march in that direction."[35]

The 2nd Vermont Brigade of 9-months men was still trying to catch up with Reynolds, and had its hottest, hardest day's march yet, the sixth straight. "We were, as it seemed, marching faster and faster each day," one private wrote; "the regiment in the rear often had to double quick in order to keep up. The roads were now full of cavalry, artillery, infantry, ammunition trains, ambulances and frequently bunched and parked in such a manner as to impede our onward march, making our officers mad and progress slow and disagreeable. We reached Mechanicstown late in the afternoon and bivouacked for the night just south of Pennsylvania state line."[36] When they had reached Emmitsburg they had taken on the job of guarding the 1st Corps wagons, and it was 7:30 by the time they made camp. General Stannard proudly noted that all the stragglers eventually made it in except for two men.

For most of Lee's 1st and 3rd Corps, that final day of June was devoted to marching east toward or through South Mountain. The road was muddy due to recent rains, so the men marched along the side of the road, trampling whatever crops happened to be growing in the fields there. Colonel Porter Alexander of Longstreet's artillery talked to one Pennsylvania Dutchman who was shocked to discover that the horrors of war he had often heard about even included the trampling of his wheat, muddy footprints all over his porch, and his well being pumped dry by Confederate soldiers filling their canteens. Longstreet left Pickett's reduced division to hold Chambersburg and moved his other two divisions as far as Greenwood, about halfway between Chambersburg and the Cashtown Gap in South Mountain, except that Brigadier General Evander Law's brigade of Hood's Division, with a battery of artillery, was sent to New Guilford, southwest of Greenwood, to guard the southern flank, and Brigadier General Joseph Kershaw's brigade of McLaws' Division was left at Fayetteville, just west of Greenwood. Major General Dorsey Pender's division of Hill's corps closed up on Cashtown, and Major General Richard H. Anderson's division of the same corps camped that night at Fayetteville, with orders to proceed the next day.

Harry Heth's division had no marching to do that day, since it was already at Cashtown. Two of his regiments had been sent south from there on the road to Emmitsburg and had placed pickets near the village of Fairfield, and they had a brief encounter there with John Buford's Union cavalry on the morning of the 30th. Buford later complained in his official report that his camp at Fairfield on the night of 29-30 June was, as he later learned, "within a short distance of a considerable force of the enemy's infantry. The inhabitants knew of my arrival and the position of the enemy's camp, yet not one of them gave me a particle of information, nor even mentioned the fact of the enemy's presence. The whole community seemed stampeded, and afraid to speak or act, often offering as excuses for not showing some little enterprise, 'The rebels will destroy our houses if we tell anything.' Had any one given me timely information, and acted as guide that night, I could have surprised and captured or destroyed this force, which proved next day to be two Mississippi [sic] regiments of infantry and two guns."[37]

Heth was equally unaware of Buford's presence nearby, but he had heard that there were shoes to be had at Gettysburg, only eight miles down the road, so, with nothing better to do, he decided to dispatch one brigade to go there and search the town for shoes and any other useful items it could find. The brigade he chose was one of those recently sent up from North Carolina by D. H. Hill to replace a veteran brigade he was holding on to. It was commanded by scholarly Brigadier General J. Johnston Pettigrew. So far as Heth knew, there were no Union soldiers around except possibly some militia or home guards, such as those Early had encountered, but, just in case, he gave Pettigrew peremptory orders that if he should run into any part of the Army of the Potomac he was not to bring on a fight.

Pettigrew took only three of his four regiments plus a train of wagons to carry off any supplies he found. (His other regiment, the 52nd North Carolina, was one of the two Buford brushed with at Fairfield.) But five miles from Gettysburg he found the 55th Virginia, from Brokenbrough's Brigade, manning a picket line, and he ordered it to join his column. As he approached Gettysburg he was warned by Longstreet's spy, Harrison, as well as by a local Confederate sympathizer, that 3,000 Union cavalrymen were nearby. Pettigrew called a halt and sent this word back to Heth, asking for further instructions. Back came a repetition of the previous order: get the supplies but don't start a fight with anything stronger than a little militia. Pettigrew was somewhat lacking in experience but he wasn't stupid. The Union cavalrymen, some of whom were soon in plain sight, probing his skirmishers, certainly looked as if they knew their business. To proceed would most likely bring on a fight. Therefore, he turned around and marched his brigade back to Cashtown empty-handed.

That evening, when Pettigrew reported to Heth, Hill was also present, and the corps commander was sure that whatever Federals were at Gettysburg could not be part of the Army of the Potomac. "I am just from General Lee," he said, "and the information he has from his scouts corroborates what I have received from mine – that is, the enemy is still at Middleburg [Maryland] and have not yet struck their tents." Pettigrew called upon a staff officer who was well known to Hill to testify that the Union cavalry he had seen were too well-trained to be home guards, but Hill said that he still didn't believe it but that he hoped the Army of the Potomac was at Gettysburg, "as this was the place he wanted it to be."[38] Heth said that if there was no objection he would take his whole division to Gettysburg the next morning and get those shoes, and Hill said he had no objection, "None in the world."[39]

The cavalrymen that Pettigrew had encountered were, of course, from John Buford's force. His two brigades had moved out early that morning, heading for Gettysburg by way of Fairfield, but they had soon run into the two Confederate regiments stationed near there. Buford thought about attacking them but realized he would have to use artillery to dislodge them. So, as he later reported, he "Resolved not to disturb them, for fear cannonading from that quarter might disarrange the plans of the general commanding."[40] Besides, he was a few miles farther west than the road that had been assigned to him, so he just turned his column down toward Emmitsburg and took it on to Gettysburg.

Before the day was out, Buford reported to Pleasonton from Gettysburg: "I entered this place to-day at 11 a.m. Found everybody in a terrible state of excitement on account of the enemy's advance upon this place. He had approached to within half a mile of the town when the head of my column entered. His force was terribly exaggerated by reasonable and truthful but inexperienced men. On pushing him back toward Cashtown, I learned from reliable men that Anderson's division was marching from Chambersburg by Mummasburg, Hunterstown, Abbottstown, on toward York. I have sent parties to the two first-named places, toward Cashtown, and a strong force [south] toward Littlestown. Colonel Gamble has just sent me word that Lee signed a pass for a citizen this morning at Chambersburg. I can't do much just now. My men and horses are fagged out. I have not been able to get any grain yet. It is all in the country, and the people talk instead of working. Facilities for shoeing [horses] are nothing. Early's people seized every shoe and nail they could find." He added a postscript mistakenly saying that, "The troops that are coming here were the same I found early this morning at Millersburg or Fairfield. General Reynolds has been advised of all that I know." Pleasonton added an endorsement to this message, before passing it on to Meade, saying, "This information contradicts Kilpatrick's, of Lee being in *Berlin*."[41]

Buford had easily blocked the Rebels coming from Cashtown that day, but he assumed they would be back in greater force, probably as soon as the next day. That afternoon he let his two brigades and single battery of horse artillery rest just northwest of Gettysburg near a Lutheran Seminary, on a low ridge known forever after as Seminary Ridge. From there they could see the much higher South Mountain ridge some eight miles to the west. Buford rode around the town (population about 2,400), looking at the area from a military point of view. It was a vital hub of about a dozen roads leading in all directions, four of them paved turnpikes, and it was the western terminus of the Western Maryland Railroad, which connected the town with Hanover and Hanover Junction, and thence to points north and south. To Buford it seemed an important place to hang onto. The area around the town was mostly cleared for farming, with only an occasional woods to block vision or movement – much more open than most of the terrain the two armies had been fighting over in Virginia for the past two years. Near the southeast edge of town was a hill with a cemetery. Troops and guns there would have a commanding position. South of that hill, a slight ridge continued for a couple of miles, tapering off to nothing and then punctuated with two round, rocky hills. There were more such hills to the east of the cemetery.

But what evidently interested Buford most was the series of low ridges, such as the one with the seminary, on the west side of the town, each running roughly northeast-southwest and thus squarely across the path of any Confederates coming down the road from Cashtown, as Pettigrew's brigade had done that day. He moved his troops to the next of these ridges beyond Seminary Ridge (known to history as McPherson's Ridge), overlooking a small stream called Willoughby Run, with pickets on the next ridge (Herr Ridge), some three-quarters of a mile farther northwest. Colonel William Gamble's 1st Brigade was assigned the sector between the Chambersburg pike and the road running southwest to Fairfield, and the 2nd Brigade, under Colonel Thomas C. Devin, was placed farther north, between the Chambersburg pike and the Mummasburg Road, where it could keep an eye on both of those roads. His lone battery, under Lieutenant John Calef, was placed facing north near the Carlisle pike. That evening Colonel Devin told Buford he was confident that he could easily hold his position against any number of Confederates. "No you won't," Buford replied. "They will attack you in the morning and they will come booming – skirmishers three deep. You will have to fight like the devil to hold your own until supports arrive."[42]

At 10:30 that night, Buford wrote to General Reynolds, the commander of the nearest infantry corps, that he was satisfied that A. P. Hill's corps was massed just back of Cashtown; that enemy pickets were within four miles of Gettysburg; and that the road from Cashtown to Oxford, which bypassed Gettysburg to the north, was infested with Rebel cavalry. Also, one of his scouting parties had captured one of Lee's couriers near Heidlersburg that day – no message was found on him but he said that Ewell was crossing the mountains from Carlisle, with Rodes' Division at Petersburg – and that there were many rumors of Rebels advancing on him from York. Ten minutes later he sent the same information to Pleasonton and asked when the latter would return the Reserve Brigade to him. Pleasonton passed it on to Meade along with Kilpatrick's report, saying only, "Kilpatrick has done very well," but not commenting on Buford's report.[43]

However, Meade was not so impressed with Kilpatrick's fight. Seth Williams chided Pleasonton that day, saying, "The major-general commanding directs me to say that it is of the utmost importance to him that he receives reliable information of the presence of the enemy, his forces, and his movements.... To be able to find if [Lee's] army is divided, and to concentrate upon any detached portion of it, without departing from the instructions which govern him, would be a great object.... He looks to you to keep him informed of their movements, and especially that no force concentrates on his right, in the vicinity of York, to get between him and the Susquehanna, and also that no force moves on his left toward Hagerstown and the passes below Cashtown. ... Cavalry battles must be secondary to this object."[44] He ended by complaining that Gregg's division, which had been ordered to move parallel with Sedgwick's 6th Corps and cover its flank, had instead used the same road that corps had been assigned.

Williams also issued a circular saying that Meade wanted corps and other commanders to address their troops, "explaining to them briefly the immense issues involved in the struggle. The enemy are on our soil. The whole country now looks anxiously to this army to deliver it from the presence of the foe." He added, "Corps and other commanders are authorized to order the instant death of any soldier who fails in his duty at this hour."[45]

Yet another unnumbered order assigned objectives for the next day's march: "Third Corps to Emmitsburg; Second Corps to Taneytown; Fifth Corps to Hanover; Twelfth Corps to Two Taverns; First Corps to Gettysburg; Eleventh Corps to Gettysburg (or supporting distance); Sixth Corps to Manchester. Cavalry to the front and flanks, well out in all directions, giving timely notice of positions and movements of the enemy. . . . The commanding general desires you to be informed that, from present information, Longstreet and Hill are at Chambersburg, partly toward Gettysburg; Ewell at Carlisle and York. Movements indicate a disposition to advance from Chambersburg to Gettysburg. General Couch telegraphs, 29th, his opinion that the enemy's operations on the Susquehanna are more to prevent co-operation with this army than offensive. The general believes he has relieved Harrisburg and Philadelphia, and now desires to look to his own army, and assume position for offensive or defensive, as occasion requires, or rest to the troops." Another circular said, "The commanding general has received information that the enemy are advancing, probably in strong force, on Gettysburg. It is the intention to hold this army pretty nearly in the position it now occupies until the plans of the enemy shall have been more fully developed."[46]

Meade also had Williams issue an unnumbered order that day again putting or confirming Reynolds in command of the left wing of the Army of the Potomac, consisting of his own 1st Corps plus the 3rd and 11th. Reynolds had his headquarters that day at Moritz Tavern, a small building near Marsh Creek on the road between Emmitsburg and Gettysburg. About sunset, General Howard, commander of the 11th Corps, rode up to confer with Reynolds. They had known each other before the war, when Howard had been a young instructor at West Point while the somewhat older Reynolds had been the officer in command of the cadets there. Over the course of several hours, the two generals studied the reports and maps available to them and speculated on the battle they knew was coming soon. Howard eventually left to return to his own camp some six miles south, at Emmitsburg. It wasn't until after he left that Buford's message to Reynolds arrived. About midnight, Reynolds wrapped himself in a blanket and lay down to sleep on the floor of the tavern, some 60 miles west of his home in Lancaster. It was his last night on earth.

Meade wrote to Halleck at 4:30 p.m.: "Headquarters, Taneytown. Two corps between Emmitsburg and Gettysburg, one at Littlestown, one at Manchester, one at Union Mills, one between here and Emmitsburg, one at Frizzelburg. Pennsylvania Reserves can't keep up – still in rear. General Lockwood, with the troops from Schenck, still behind; these troops cannot keep up with the marches made by the army. Our reports seem to place Ewell in the vicinity of York and Harrisburg. The cavalry that crossed at Seneca Ford have passed on up through Westminster and Hanover, some 6,000 to 8,000 strong. The people are all so frightened that accurate information is not to be obtained. I shall push on to-morrow in the direction of Hanover Junction and Hanover, when I hope by July 2 to open communication with Baltimore by telegraph and rail, to renew supplies. I fear that I shall break down the troops by pushing on much faster, and may have to rest a day. My movement, of course, will be governed much by what I learn of the enemy. The information seems to place Longstreet at Chambersburg, and A. P. Hill moving between Chambersburg and York. Our cavalry drove a regiment out of Gettysburg this a.m. Our cavalry engaged with Stuart at Hanover this a.m. Result not yet known."[47] He sent a similar telegram to Couch an hour later.

As Meade's message to Halleck implies, his army had been marching hard and fast. "Our troops are making tremendous marches some of these days past," a Captain in the 2nd Corps wrote to his hometown newspaper; "and, if the enemy is anywhere, we shall be likely to find him and feel of him pretty soon."[48] Seasoned infantry could be counted on to make 20 miles a day, but on the 29th that corps had marched 32 miles in 18 hours. A soldier in Reynolds' 1st Corps calculated that he had marched 36 miles in just over 22 hours with only a 2-hour stop for rest. The marches were carefully planned by Meade, Butterfield, and the army's staff, but they were hard on the men who had to do the walking, carrying packs, rifles, ammunition, canteens, etc. through the heat, humidity and occasional showers of early summer. Many men fell out of ranks from exhaustion, their uniforms wet with sweat, their faces covered with dust, lips parched, feet blistered.

Meanwhile, Meade's attempt to draw reinforcements from the garrison of Harper's Ferry was not faring much better than Hooker's had. General French telegraphed Halleck from Harper's Ferry on the morning of the 30th, saying he couldn't telegraph the day before, the lines being down (due to Stuart's raid): "The immense amount of stores here cannot be removed under at least ten days. I shall be obliged to leave General [Washington] Elliott's brigade – 3,300 men – with artillery and engineer company. I commenced this morning to destroy ammunition. Some of the heavy guns will have to be left. I am in readiness to move with the remainder of my force, but will await your instructions. I cannot communicate with headquarters Army of the Potomac." Halleck replied at 2:15 p.m.: "No ammunition or stores should be destroyed, excepting in case of absolute necessity. These things should not be abandoned, but defended. You can now communicate with General Meade."[49]

At 11:30 that night, Secretary Stanton wrote to Meade to forward a message from General Haupt, who had written to Halleck that day to say: "Lee is falling back suddenly from the vicinity of Harrisburg, and concentrating all his forces. York has been evacuated. Carlisle is being evacuated. The concentration appears to be at or near Chambersburg. The object apparently a sudden movement against Meade, of which he should be advised by courier immediately. A courier might reach Frederick by way of Western Maryland Railroad to Westminster. This information comes from T. A. Scott, and I think it reliable." Stanton added:

"It is proper you should know that General French this morning evacuated Maryland Heights, blowing up his magazine, spiking the large cannon, and destroying surplus stores. A telegram from him, received this evening, indicates that he is still at Sandy Hook, waiting orders, and doubtful what he should do with his force. Please instruct him what you wish him to do."[50]

∼ Endnotes ∼

1 OR, I:27:I:75-6.
2 Ibid., I:27:III:945.
3 Ibid., I:27:III:412.
4 Ibid., I:27:III:413.
5 Ibid., I:24:I:244.
6 Ibid., I:24:III:449.
7 Ibid., I:24:III:450.
8 Ibid., I:24:I:112.
9 Hoehling, *Vicksburg: 47 Days of Siege*, 248-9.
10 Ibid., 245-6.
11 OR, I:23:I:407.
12 Ibid., I:23:I:461.
13 Ibid., I:23:I:407-8.
14 Ibid., I:24:II:517.
15 Ibid., I:24:II:466.
16 Ibid., I:24:II:450.
17 Ibid., I:24:II:466.
18 Hoehling, *Vicksburg: 47 Days of Siege*, 253.
19 OR, I:24:I:112-13.
20 Ibid., I:24:II:364-5.
21 Ibid., I:24:I:248.
22 Ibid., I:24:III:451-2.
23 Ibid., I:24:I:167-8.
24 Ibid., I:27:III:436-7.
25 Wingert, *The Confederate Approach on Harrisburg*, 136.
26 Harry W. Pfanz, *Gettysburg – The First Day* (Chapel Hill NC, 2001), 149.
27 Bowden and Ward, *Last Chance for Victory*, 152.
28 Wittenberg and Petruzzi, *Plenty of Blame to Go Around*, 67.
29 Ibid., 86.
30 Ibid., 88.
31 OR, I:27:I:987-8. Italics in the source.
32 Ibid., I:27:II:696.
33 Ibid., I:27:I:986-7.
34 Ibid., I:27:III:424.

35 Ibid., I:27:III:425.
36 Coffin, *Nine Months to Gettysburg,* 185.
37 *OR,* I:27:I:926.
38 Sears, *Gettysburg,* 137.
39 Freeman, *Lee's Lieutenants,* III:78.
40 *OR,* I:27:I:926.
41 Ibid., I:27:I:923. Italics in the source.
42 Longacre, *The Cavalry at Gettysburg,* 184.
43 *OR,* I:27:I:924.
44 Ibid., I:27:III:421.
45 Ibid., I:27:III:415.
46 Ibid., I:27:III:416, both messages.
47 Ibid., I:27:I:68-9.
48 Sears, *Gettysburg,* 144.
49 *OR,* I:27:III:428.
50 Ibid., I:27:I:69.

CHAPTER 20

"We Must Fight a Battle Here"

1 July 1863

At Vicksburg, Sergeant Tunnard wrote of the first day of July: "The hour had come that tried the souls of men. The dark cloud of disaster hovered over the devoted garrison.... Our batteries were very quiet.... The hospitals were sad scenes of agony, suffering and death, with their numerous occupants." One lady of Vicksburg said the entire town was "now like one vast hospital." And General S. D. Lee said that "Near 6,000 men were in the hospitals and ... I do not believe one-half of the men in the trenches could have stood up and fought had they been attacked by the enemy a few feet off and undermining the principal forts."[1]

General Grant was not yet prepared to risk another assault, but he was prepared to do some more undermining of forts. McPherson notified him that day that Captain Hickenlooper's second mine under the Confederate fort on the Jackson road was ready and that the Rebels were digging a countermine to try to intercept it before the fort could be blown up. "Should I explode it?" he asked. "And what disposition do you desire me to make of my troops; anything more than having the rifle-pits filled with sharpshooters?" Grant replied, "Explode the mine as soon as ready. Notify Ord the hour, so that he may be ready to make a demonstration should the enemy attempt to move toward you. You need not do more than have rifle-pits filled with sharpshooters. Take all advantage you can, after the explosion, of the breach made, either to advance guns or your sharpshooters." McPherson replied that "The mine will be exploded about 3 p.m. to-day."[2]

However, General Forney, who commanded that segment of the Confederate line, placed the hour "at about 1 p.m., when the enemy sprung his second mine, which was much heavier than the first. The result was the entire demolition of the redan, leaving only an immense chasm where it stood. The greater portion of the earth was thrown toward the enemy, the line of least resistance being in that direction. Our interior line was much injured. Nine men who had been countermining were necessarily lost, and a large number of those manning the works were killed and wounded. The enemy, however, made no attempt to charge, seeming satisfied with having materially weakened the position. I understand the amount of powder used by the enemy in this explosion was one ton."[3]

In an earlier report, Forney put the time as 1:30 p.m. and said: "Immediately after the explosion, the enemy opened his batteries upon the point mined, doing considerable damage. He also opened from what is supposed to be a Cohorn mortar, which throws its missiles among the men with great accuracy, killing and wounding many, and tending much to dishearten the men. At the time of the explosion, 1 white man (sapper) and 8 negroes are reported to have been countermining in the redan, who were, of course, lost."[4] Charles Dana, in reporting to Secretary Stanton the next day, said, "Six rebels were thrown into our lines by the explosion; all dead but one, a negro. The right flank fort was cleared off by it, so that Ransom's shells had free way into the work. Many rebels were killed, but McPherson has not yet got possession of the fort. In the absence of ordinary mortars, he has constructed several of wood, throwing 12-pounder shells effectively."[5] General Grant said that the one man who was thrown into the Union lines alive "was not much hurt, but terribly frightened."[6] When asked how high up he had gone the man said he didn't know, but thought about three miles. He soon became a servant at General Logan's headquarters.

Forney said another Union sap-roller was destroyed that night, near the Jackson road, by the use of fire-balls, "in the same manner as the one on Baldwin's Ferry road" the night before.[7] At any rate, Grant's engineers decided that "The hand-to-hand character of the fighting now showed that in the closer approaches little farther progress could be made by digging alone; the enemy's works were weak, and at ten different points we could put the heads of regiments under cover within from 5 to 100 yards of his line. The assault would be but little easier if we waited ten days more, and accordingly it was decided to assault on the morning of July 6."[8] Grant said, "The debouches were ordered widened to afford easy egress, while the approaches were also to be widened to admit the troops to pass through four abreast. Plank, and bags filled with cotton packed in tightly, were ordered prepared, to enable the troops to cross the ditches."[9]

General Ord was concerned that day about a report of Confederate troops crossing the Big Black River at Hankinson's Ferry, southeast of Vicksburg, but finally decided, as he told Grant, "I think it is likely the enemy has shown some force there, perhaps as a feint."[10] Grant told Sherman, "The enemy have shown some force this side of the Black, at Hankinson's Ferry. Ord sends out one brigade to-night to watch them. They may try a [diversion] to the south of the city, with the view of drawing as much force in that direction as possible. I will let you know all that takes place as early as possible."[11]

Grant also informed Sherman that "Our cavalry report, on information received from citizens east of the river, that 12,000 of Johnston's troops have passed south of Baldwin's Ferry. I place no great reliance in the information, but it may prove true." Sherman then told General Osterhaus, whose division was watching the army's rear along the Jackson road, "General Grant supposes Johnston to be feeling around toward the lower ferries. I don't think he will put his army in such a pocket. Yet it becomes us to leave nothing to conjecture." He therefore ordered Osterhaus to send out a spy named Tuttle "to go afoot up to the road about Auburn or Cayuga, to watch the road. If an army is passing or has passed, he can easily distinguish the fact by signs, or he may in his own way personate a straggler, and find out all from some farmer or negro. . . . We must discover the whereabouts of our enemy positively."[12] Johnston was, in fact, marching his army toward the Big Black that day, not down towards

Hankinson's Ferry, however, but northeast of Vicksburg, and, as he later reported, "on the evening of July 1 encamped between Brownsville and the river."[13] But he was running out of time.

"On July 1," General Pemberton later wrote, "I felt satisfied that the time had arrived when it was necessary either to evacuate the city and cut my way out or to capitulate upon the best attainable terms. My own inclination led me to favor the former. With this view, therefore, I addressed to my division commanders – Generals Stevenson, Forney, Smith, and Bowen – the following communication: . . . Unless the siege of Vicksburg is raised or supplies are thrown in, it will become necessary very shortly to evacuate the place. I see no prospect of the former, and there are many great, if not insuperable, obstacles in the way of the latter. You are, therefore, requested to inform me with as little delay as possible as to the condition of your troops, and their ability to make the marches and undergo the fatigues necessary to accomplish a successful evacuation. You will, of course, use the utmost discretion while informing yourself through your subordinates upon all points tending to a clear elucidation of the subjects of my inquiry."[14]

Lieutenant Colonel Nasmith's expedition was ending that day. "In the morning the cavalry marched through to Goodrich's Landing," he later reported, "seeing no enemy, but noticing the effects of what had been done the day before, the enemy having gone. Major [James] Farnan, commanding the cavalry, reports that the scenes witnessed by him in marching from Lake Providence to Goodrich's Landing were of a character never before witnessed in a civilized country, and the rebel atrocities committed the day before were such as the pen fails to record in proper language. They spared neither age, sex, nor condition. In some instances the negroes were shut up in their quarters, and literally roasted alive. The charred remains found in numerous instances testified to a degree of fiendish atrocity such as has no parallel either in civilized or savage warfare. Young children, only five or six years of age, were found skulking in the canebreak pierced with wounds, while helpless women were found shot down in the most inhuman manner. The whole country was destroyed, and every sign of civilization was given to the flames. The cavalry embarked at Goodrich's Landing, and the expedition, except the marine boat, came to Chickasaw Landing [on the Yazoo].... Before closing this report, it is proper that I should say that the portion of the Marine Brigade which accompanied me proved to be entirely worthless. At no time were my orders obeyed willingly, and the officer in command was disposed to find fault and cavil when any real service was required of them."[15]

In Tennessee on the first day of July, Bragg's Confederate army successfully retreated across the Elk River, the infantry all being across by noon while the cavalry delayed the Federal pursuit. "July 1, I received a dispatch from General Thomas," Rosecrans later reported, "that the enemy had retreated from Tullahoma during the night. Brannan's, Negley's and Sheridan's divisions entered Tullahoma, where the infantry arrived about noon. Negley's and Rousseau's divisions pushed on by Spring Creek and overtook the rear guard of the enemy late in the afternoon at Bethpage Bridge, 2 miles above the railroad crossing, where they had a sharp skirmish with the rebels occupying the heights on the south side of the river and commanding the bridge by artillery, which they had placed behind epaulements."[16]

The Rebel cavalry was across the river by nightfall and burned the Bethpage and Allison bridges behind them. Bragg sent a very brief report to Richmond that day from the town of Decherd: "Finding my communications seriously endangered by movements of the enemy, I last night took up a more defensible position this side of Elk River (which now, by reason of heavy rains, is impassable except at bridges), losing nothing of importance."[17] He issued orders that day designating Cowan as the place for his new supply depot. But Bragg was already thinking about another retreat. The water level in Elk River was already starting to fall, and soon it would be fordable in many places. Besides, the Union bridgehead at Pelham, as well as a number of roads converging on Decherd and Cowan, would make it relatively easy for Rosecrans to still cut him off from Chattanooga and points south. He had his engineers working on a line of retreat across the Cumberland Mountains to Chattanooga, and that night he sent notes to his corps commanders asking if they thought the army should fight where it was or retreat to Cowan. Both Polk and Hardee recommended retreat, at least partly because they knew that Bragg was in ill health. "I deeply regret," Hardee told Polk, "to see General Bragg in his present enfeebled state of health. If we have a fight, he is evidently unable either to examine and determine his line of battle or to take command on the field. What shall we do?"[18]

That same day, Rosecrans ordered Stanley to move with all his available cavalry to Pelham, by way of Hillsborough, and from there to reconnoiter over the mountains to discover the Confederate army's line of retreat and cut off a part of it if possible. At 7:15 p.m., believing that the Rebels were retreating to Winchester, to get behind another fork of the Elk, he followed this with an order for Stanley to move his whole command on the most direct route toward Decherd and to "Push your march to the utmost."[19]

Up at Knoxville, General John Pegram, who had been left in charge there by Buckner, wired General Samuel Jones of the Department of Western Virginia, saying, "I am directed by General Buckner to send nearly all my force immediately to Chattanooga, and to call upon you for re-enforcements. Please send the troops to this place immediately." But Jones's assistant adjutant general wrote back: "Cannot send re-enforcements. The Fifty-first Regiment is the only available one, and that is near the Salt-Works, on report of General Preston that the enemy is certainly advancing on that point."[20] The salt works in southwest Virginia were the Confederacy's main source of salt, which was needed for the preservation of meat for the army. Brigadier General Julius White's 4th Division of the 23rd Corps in Burnside's department was preparing to move against it at that time.

In Kentucky that day, Burnside informed General Hartsuff:

"The rebel Hines and his party of 10 or 12 men captured the passenger train on the Louisville and Lexington Railroad, at Christiansburg, 15 miles this side of Frankfort, this morning at 8.30 o'clock. He burned the baggage, one passenger car, and cut the telegraph lines. If there are any mounted men at Frankfort they should be sent after him, and at once. He is supposed to have gone to Owen County." Burnside added, "I think Captain [Greenberry] Reid, of Paris [Ky.], will be a proper person to send after him, and you may say to him that I will give him $1,000 if he will capture them and bring them to me."[21] However, Colonel E. W. Pierce, at Paris, informed Hartsuff: "I have not force so that I could send more than 50 men, but will do that at once, if you direct."[22]

Hines' commander, General Morgan, was continuing to cross the Cumberland River that day, near Burkesville, Kentucky. His 2nd Brigade of about 1,000 men got across that day, and his slightly larger 1st Brigade moved into positions from which it could cross the next day. Thirty-five miles away, at Tompkinsville, General Judah, commander of the 3rd Division of the 23rd Corps, found out about the Rebels' approach, reported it, and asked for a gunboat to prevent the river-crossing. He had one of his brigades watching the river in that area but made no move to reinforce it. The Cumberland River was above flood stage and over a half-mile wide, so Judah thought Morgan would have to wait for it to subside. But the Rebels rounded up every little boat they could find and connected them with planks to form rafts for their artillery and wagons. The troopers and horses swam over and soon drove off the few Union pickets in the area.

A state convention in Missouri adopted, on that first day of July, an ordinance declaring that slavery should cease in that state as of 4 July 1870. Farther south, in northeast Arkansas, Confederate forces were still struggling along muddy roads and over swollen streams trying to get to Union-held Helena.

Brigadier General M. M. Parsons, commander of one of Price's two infantry brigades, wrote to that officer's headquarters that evening to say that his troops had finally finished crossing the most recent stream. "Worked the men in water to their waists last night until 10; again this morning from daylight. Men much wearied; mules more so; they are without forage; not a grain to be had without pressing."[23] Price's boss, General Holmes, was also writing to him that day: "I deeply regret the difficulties that cause the delay in your march. I have used every precaution to prevent a knowledge of our approach from reaching the enemy, and have what I believe to be certain information that I had succeeded up to night before last. I fear these terrible delays will thwart all my efforts. Let me beseech you, therefore, to hasten forward as rapidly as possible consistently with the good order and efficiency of your command. . . . I think our prospects are flattering in the East and bright here."[24]

Even farther south, that day, in the northeast part of Indian Territory (now Oklahoma), a train of some 300 wagons carrying supplies to pro-Union Indians at Fort Gibson, in the Cherokee Nation, was blocked by about 2,000 Texans and pro-Confederate Indians under Colonel Stand Watie, a Cherokee. According to Colonel J. M. Williams of the First Kansas Colored Infantry, commanding the Union escort, "Nothing unusual occurred until about noon of the 1st instant, when we came upon the enemy, strongly posted upon Cabin Creek, completely commanding the ford." Major John A. Foreman's 3rd Indian Home Guards drove Confederate skirmishers across the creek, killing three and capturing three, and Williams brought up some of his artillery to bombard the far bank, under cover of which he had soundings made and found the stream, swollen by recent rains, was too high for the wagons to cross. He corralled the wagons on the prairie about two miles from the ford and "the forces were ordered into camp to await the falling of the stream. . . ."[25] Williams consulted with Foreman and with Lieutenant Colonel Theodore H. Dodd, commander of a mixed lot of cavalry companies, and they decided to unite as many of their forces the next day that could be spared from the immediate defense of the wagons and force a crossing. The three of them made a careful reconnaissance of the creek that evening and laid their plans for the next day's fight.

In southeast Virginia that first day of July, General Getty moved out at 8 a.m. from the left bank of the Pamunkey River, opposite White House plantation, with his own division of Dix's forces plus an extra brigade of infantry and part of another, as well as Spear's cavalry. His object was to seize and destroy the bridge of the Richmond, Fredericksburg & Potomac Railroad over the South Anna River and thus cut one of the primary links between Richmond and the Shenandoah Valley – and thus to Lee's army. The weather was, as Dix later reported, "intensely hot." As a diversion, to keep the Confederates around Richmond too busy to interfere with Getty, Dix sent General Keyes with three brigades "to advance on the Richmond road, and attack the enemy, who was understood to be in considerable force on the right [west] bank of the Chickahominy, a short distance from Bottom's Bridge."[26] Dix reported these moves briefly to Halleck at 8 a.m., and, three hours later, Halleck wired Dix that all the troops coming up from North Carolina who were "willing to continue in service will be sent to Baltimore, excepting those you have in the field. As soon as your forces return from the present expedition, report before sending out any more."[27]

The two brigades of Confederate cavalry that Stuart had left behind, Robertson's and Jones's, reached Greencastle, Pennsylvania, that day. Small groups of armed civilians nipped at their flanks, but did little harm. More discouraging to the Confederates was the sight of large numbers of military-aged men who were still not in the Union army. "This," one of Jones's troopers said, "had a rather depressing effect upon us, because it showed us that the North had reserves to draw from, while our men, within the age limit, were all in the army." These Rebels, like those who had passed this way ahead of them, were impressed with the Pennsylvania farms, and an artilleryman noted that "the barns look like churches," meaning that they were usually the best-made buildings around. The same gunner had an eye for more than farms and noted that there were some "beautiful, rose-cheeked, bonny lassies on the street in Greencastle, but they looked as sour as a crab apple, frowns an inch wide."[28]

Jeb Stuart's three brigades had ridden northward all night, and reached Jefferson, some 25 miles from Hanover, by the dawn of 1 July. Their horses were now going lame by the dozens. Stuart had obtained some newspapers along the way which confirmed his belief that Early occupied York, but when his first units reached the York pike only seven miles west of that town he found no evidence of a Confederate presence there. So he decided to continue moving north to Dover, which his column reached early that morning. There he paroled his prisoners and allowed his men and horses to rest but not unsaddle while scouts were sent out in several directions in a vain attempt to find Early's infantry. Local civilians claimed to be ignorant of the latter's recent movements, but, at Dover, Stuart found more recent newspapers, which related a rumor that the Confederates were concentrating around Shippensburg and that Early was probably headed there. He sent off Major A. R. Venable of his staff, with a detachment of 30 men, to try to find Early's route of march, and Fitz Lee later sent his own brother, a member of his staff, toward Gettysburg to see if there was any sign of their uncle's army in that direction.

Early's Division had, in fact, marched west from York the previous day and had passed through Berlin, thus leading to Kilpatrick's erroneous report. Early and his staff had stopped for lunch at a hotel along the road and afterwards had heard artillery fire but could not be sure of the direction or distance. It had, of course, been Stuart's and Kilpatrick's guns at Hanover, ten miles south. However, Early had concluded that it was mere militia skirmishing and does not seem to have wondered who the "militia" might have been skirmishing with, and he made no attempt to find out. Had he done so, he might have saved Stuart's cavalry another day's hard ride.

"I still believed," Stuart later reported, "that most of our army was before Harrisburg, and justly regarded a march to Carlisle as the most likely to place me in communication with the main army."[29] After four to six hours of rest, Stuart had his brigades on the road again, heading northwest toward Carlisle in two columns. To reach Carlisle, the Confederates had to cross the South Mountain ridge, a steep climb for exhausted men and horses, but, at the very least, this would bring them to an area where they could find more horses and some badly needed provisions, and they could still turn more to the west and go to Shippensburg if that rumor proved to be true.

Meanwhile, Pleasonton's chief of staff had shown up at Hanover during the fight the day before with about 40 troopers, having been sent out by his boss to find the Rebel cavalry, and he continued that assignment during the night and this day, taking fewer than 100 men to follow Stuart. But finally, at Rossville, northwest of Dover, they turned back with a few captured stragglers. Had Kilpatrick followed Stuart with his entire command he might have destroyed or captured Stuart's force completely, for when the Rebels reached Carlisle that evening they found it was in Federal hands.

Up near Harrisburg, on the morning of 1 July, Baldy Smith had issued orders for a Union advance on Carlisle. (A regiment of New York heavy artillerymen refused to serve as infantry, so General Couch sent them back to New York.) Captain Boyd's reinforced company of the 1st New York Cavalry were the first Federals to reach Carlisle that morning, but it rode on through to the west, following Johnson's Confederates. Next came the two New York National Guard regiments and attached battery that had fought with Jenkins the day before. They had advanced cautiously with skirmishers out front until well beyond Sporting Hill, at last assured by local civilians that the Rebels were long gone. The rain had stopped, the road was in good condition, and the scenery was beautiful, and all along the way women came out to offer them buckets of cool spring water and trays of bread plus the local staple, apple butter.

During a brief noontime stop at New Kingston, while they were consuming some of these offerings, the head of a column of four Pennsylvania regiments caught up with them and tried to pass. However, the New Yorkers refused to yield primacy of place, and even resorted to double-quicking for half a mile to keep their position at the front of the column. In fact, the spirit of competition grew until even the two New York regiments were vying with each other for the lead. But the militiamen were not used to long marches, and the day was humid, with intermittent thunder showers, and was growing increasingly hot, so that many men fell behind, unable to maintain the pace. Some were able to hitch rides in the supply wagons, and others hobbled along as best they could on sore and blistered feet, but some were too worn out to carry on at all. A newspaper correspondent who marched with a small rear guard said, "It was awful to see the boys drop out by the roadside, and lie there, too sick to move. In all cases they were taken into the nearest inhabited houses, the inhabitants of which were very hospitable."[30]

There were probably more New Yorkers strewn in the column's wake than remained with the colors when, at about 4 p.m., the head of the column reached Carlisle. The townsfolk were only too glad to see them, after the scare Jenkins' Rebels had given them the night before, and soon tables of all kinds of good food were set up in the town square. There was even hay, oats and water for the officers' horses. This impromptu picnic was broken up when reports came in, around 6 p.m., that the Confederates were coming back. Brigadier General John Ewen, commander of the two New York regiments, took his now-well-fed but still-weary men and part of their attached battery south to the top of a hill overlooking the Baltimore Pike, where many of them promptly fell asleep. Baldy Smith and his staff rode into town about a half-hour later.

The approaching Confederates were not Jenkins' brigade

returning for more plunder; they were Fitzhugh Lee's brigade of Jeb Stuart's command, still trying to find Ewell's infantry, and they came in from the east, by-passing Ewen's New Yorkers. There was some confusion at first, as some of the militia units wore gray uniforms, but Stuart soon figured out that the town was occupied by Federals. The Pennsylvania regiments and the rest of the battery attached to the New Yorkers were still resting and feeding in the town square when the first shell from the Confederate horse artillery came whizzing overhead. "At first not much attention is paid to it," a member of the Union battery remembered, "but five or six others arriving in rapid succession, several of which burst overhead, convinced the most confiding that the Rebels had again returned. There followed a scene of indescribable confusion, the soldiers running hither and thither to find their regiments; men, women, and children running about, each trying to find a place of safety. Tables loaded with crockery and food were upset, and piles of baggage were knocked over and strewn about. To add to all of this, two or three staff officers, ignorant of the position of the Rebels and their own duties, and feeling anxious that something should be done, ordered troops and guns into fifty different positions at the same time."[31]

A Confederate officer, with a white handkerchief tied to his saber and followed by a bugler, brought in a demand for surrender of the town and all its military forces, claiming that Fitz Lee had 3,000 men ready to attack. Various civilians crowded around, some advising Smith to surrender, other to fight, and Smith delayed his answer to give time for Ewen's New Yorkers to return to town – so long, in fact, that Stuart sent in another courier, informing Smith that if he didn't reply within three minutes the town would be shelled and burned. Smith told him to "Shell away."[32] Meanwhile, he sent off a volunteer aide to inform Knipe, who was to send on a report to Couch. Smith wanted Knipe to march his brigade to Carlyle at 3 the next morning (later changed to "immediately") but it was, instead, retained by Couch for the defense of Harrisburg.

Eventually, when the civilians and infantrymen were out of

the way, the four guns in the square were deployed, with two facing east and two facing south, but Smith soon ordered them to cease fire, as all they were accomplishing was to attract counter-battery fire. Colonel William Brisbane's four Pennsylvania regiments were broken up into companies and scattered among various houses, ready to repel an assault on the town, but after a half-hour or so they were reassembled and sent out the main roads to lie on their arms until morning. The two New York regiments and their two attached guns defended the southern part of town, some facing south, some east, and five companies of home guards, backed up by two companies of New Yorkers, manned a forward skirmish line along Letort Creek, east of town.

Fitz Lee had served at Carlyle right out of West Point and felt that he had many friends there, but he reluctantly bombarded the town with his attached battery. His exhausted cavalrymen were in no condition to attack even inexperienced militia, and, in fact, many of them were so tired that they fell asleep despite the roaring guns. Stuart saw one trooper fall asleep in the middle of climbing over a fence, one leg on each side. But Stuart needed rations for man and horse, and hoped to frighten the militia into surrendering or retreating. Smith refused to return fire, saving his ammunition to repel any assault. At about 11p.m., the Rebels set fire to the cavalry barracks outside of town, and at about midnight Stuart sent in another demand for surrender, but the same answer was given. By 1 a.m., most of the firing had ceased, and by 3 a.m. on 2 July, Smith got word that the Confederates were leaving. Not much damage had been done to the town, but its natural-gas purifying house had been burned, in addition to the barracks. Some 17 Federals had been wounded, some of them only slightly, one mortally, and one Confederate. Stuart had finally heard, through Major Venable and Captain Lee, that General Lee was at Gettysburg, for which place he wanted Stuart to proceed at once.

At 7 a.m. on the first day of July, Meade had written a short note to Halleck (not received until 3:40 p.m.) from nine miles east of Middleburg: "Dispatch of June 30, 11.30 p.m., received. French was ordered to send 3,000 of his force to Washington, with all his property, then to move up and join me with the balance." At the same hour, he sent Halleck a longer message (received at 4 p.m.) "Dispatches of General Couch and General Haupt received. My positions to-day are, one corps at Emmitsburg, two at Gettysburg, one at Taneytown, one at Two Taverns, one at Manchester, one at Hanover. These movements ordered yesterday, before the receipt of advices of Lee's movements. Our cavalry, under Kilpatrick, had a handsome fight yesterday at Hanover. He reports the capture of 1 battle flag, a lieutenant-colonel, 1 captain, with 15 or 20 of the enemy killed. The point of Lee's concentration and the nature of the country, when ascertained, will determine whether I attack him or not. Shall advise you further to-day, when satisfied that the enemy are fully withdrawn from the Susquehanna. If General Couch has any reliable force, I shall call upon him to move it to aid me."[33]

Unknown to Meade, a battle was to begin in just a few minutes of those messages that would eventually draw in the entirety of both armies, his and Lee's. The 2nd Vermont Brigade, at Emmitsburg, received an order from Reynolds early that morning to hurry forward, as he expected to need every man he could get that day. "The morning of July 1 was cloudy and gloomy," one Vermonter remembered, "all was commotion and confusion and the vast army all about was moving forward in the direction of Gettysburg, cavalry, artillery, infantry, a grand and impossing spectacle." Another noted that "About 11 a.m. passed over Mason & Dixon under a drenching rain storm and more than ankle deep in mud."[34] An hour later, General Stannard received an order to leave two regiments to guard wagons and hurry forward with his other three. "The forenoon was misty and rainy," yet another Vermonter noted, "but later the sun came out, and during the afternoon the heat was oppressive."[35] The Vermonters didn't know it yet, but up ahead, the battle was raging. They finally caught up with the 1st Corps that night, too late to participate in that day's fight. Nor did they do much the next day; but on the third day they did more than most veteran units to put an end at last to Lee's year-long string of victories.

At noon on 1 July, Meade still did not know what was going on at Gettysburg, for he wrote to Halleck again at that hour: "Dispatch sent last night giving my position at Emmitsburg, Gettysburg and Hanover. Ewell is massing at Heidlersburg. A. P. Hill is massed behind the mountains at Cashtown. Longstreet somewhere between Chambersburg and the mountains. The news proves my advance has answered its purpose. I shall not advance any [farther], but prepare to receive an attack in case Lee makes one. A battle-field is being selected in the rear, on which the army can be rapidly concentrated, on Pike [Pipe] Creek, between Middleburg and Manchester, covering my depot at Westminster. If I am not attacked, and I can from reliable intelligence have reason to believe I can attack with reasonable degree of success, I will do so; but at present, having relieved the pressure on the Susquehanna, I am now looking to the protection of Washington, and fighting my army to the best advantage." He added a postscript at 1 p.m.: "The enemy are advancing in force on Gettysburg, and I expect the battle will begin to-day."[36]

Seth Williams sent out a long circular that day, at Meade's command, to all corps with detailed instructions on how the army would move to take up position along Parr Ridge and behind Pipe Creek, which ran from near Manchester past Union Mills and Middleburg to join the Monocacy River not far west of the latter place. The line was too long to properly man it all, but it was good defensive terrain and covered his supply base at Westminster well. Forces could have been shifted about once it was known Lee was approaching any particular part of it.

The circular began: "From information received, the commanding general is satisfied that the object of the movement of the army in this direction has been accomplished, viz, the relief of Harrisburg, and the prevention of the enemy's intended invasion of Pennsylvania, &c., beyond the Susquehanna. It is no longer his intention to assume the offensive until the enemy's movements or position should render such an operation certain of success. If the enemy assume the offensive, and attack, it is his intention, after holding them in check sufficiently long to withdraw the trains and other *impedimenta*; to withdraw the army from its present position, and form line of battle with the left resting in the neighborhood of Middleburg, and the right at Manchester, the general direction being that of Pipe Creek." Details of routes and destinations for the various commands followed, beginning with instructions for Reynolds to "withdraw the force at present at Gettysburg. . . ."

Although the plan was detailed and elaborate about routes and objectives, "The time for falling back," it said, "can only be developed by circumstances. Whenever such circumstances arise as would seem to indicate the necessity for falling back and assuming this general line indicated, notice of such movement will be at once communicated to these headquarters and to all adjoining corps commanders."[37] Thus Meade was authorizing any corps commander to decide when the time had come to implement this plan. But events had already made it obsolete. Meade had intended for this circular to go out the previous afternoon, and he later complained bitterly about the slowness of his staff. He said he "had arranged for a plan of battle, and it had taken so long to get the orders out that now it was all useless."[38]

A copy of this Pipe Creek Circular, as it has come to be known, was sent to General French for his information, and in a covering letter Williams told him that Meade "directs that you will hold Frederick, camping your troops in its immediate vicinity; also the Monocacy bridges, both rail and turnpike. You will also guard the Baltimore and Ohio Railroad from Frederick to a junction with General Schenck, to whom you will communicate your instructions. In the event of our being compelled to withdraw and retire before the enemy, you will be in readiness to throw your command by rail, or march, as may be most practicable and speedy, into the Defense of Washington. He desires that for the present you will hold the line of communication to Frederick.

Keep it open, and send up from Frederick all stragglers, keeping the town clear and in good order."[39] French wired Halleck that night at 5:30 from Frederick that his troops were just going into camp there. He also sent a longer message to Seth Williams, acknowledging receipt of his instructions and notifying him of his arrival with 5,000 infantry, 700 cavalry, and three batteries of 3-inch rifles, after leaving 4,000 men at Harper's Ferry under Brigadier General Washington Elliott. He added that he had picked up 200 stragglers from the Army of the Potomac, whom he would forward as soon as possible.

Seth Williams also wrote a long dispatch to Reynolds sometime that first day of July saying, "The commanding general cannot decide whether it is his best policy to move to attack until he learns something more definite of the point at which the enemy is concentrating. This he hopes to do during the day. Meanwhile, he would like to have your views upon the subject, at least so far as concerns your position. If the enemy is concentrating to our right of Gettysburg, that point would not at first glance seem to be a proper strategic point of concentration for this army. If the enemy is concentrating in front of Gettysburg or to the left of it, the general is not sufficiently well informed of the nature of the country to judge of its character for either an offensive or defensive position." He said Meade thought the two armies to be about equal in numbers, and if French's troops joined him, as ordered, he might have a slight advantage, but that he had not had time to check into the state of the troops' morale or their true numbers compared to the most recent returns, considering possible straggling on the hard marches of late. "He feels you know more of the condition of the troops in your vicinity and the country than he does," and suggested that Reynolds might consult with General A. A. Humphreys, a division commander in the 3rd Corps, whom "the general considers an excellent adviser as to the nature of the country for defensive or offensive operations." He reiterated that Meade would like to have Reynolds' views and added, "The movement of your corps to Gettysburg was ordered before the positive knowledge of the enemy's withdrawal from Harrisburg and concentration was received."[40] But this letter also went out too late; the battle was already underway; half of Meade's army was even then converging on Gettysburg; and Reynolds was dead, shot while leading his troops forward against A. P. Hill's Rebels.

General Lee had spent the last night of June near Greenwood, camped at a deserted sawmill. He wrote to Imboden from there on the morning of 1 July. That general's brigade was expected to arrive at Chambersburg during the day, and Lee told him to take over the defense of that place from Pickett, who would then advance to Greenwood. "You must turn off everybody belonging to the army on the road to Gettysburg," he said. "The reserve trains of the army are parked between Greenwood and Cashtown, on said road, and to-morrow I desire you to move up to this place, establish yourself so as to command the cross-roads and roads leading into town. . . . It will be necessary for you to have your men well together and always on the alert, and to pay strict attention to the safety of the trains, which are for the present placed under your charge, and upon the safety of which the operations of this army depend. . . . Send word to General Pickett at this place to-morrow, which is 8 miles from Chambersburg, the hour when you will arrive here, in order that he may be prepared to move on your arrival. My headquarters for the present will be at Cashtown, east of the mountains."[41]

Lee had received a report from Hill the night before about Pettigrew's foray to Gettysburg and back, and Hill's intention to advance this morning to see what was in his front. Lee had sent Major Taylor to Hill, telling him to make the reconnaissance but "without forcing an engagement."[42] However, as far as Lee knew, the Army of the Potomac was still down in Maryland. Harry Heth had his division on the road early that morning, heading for Gettysburg; Pender's Division followed later. Anderson's Division passed through Greenwood early that morning, on its way to join Hill. The day was mostly sunny where Lee was, and there was a gentle breeze blowing as he set out for Cashtown. "He was in his usual cheerful spirits on the morning of the 1st," Longstreet later remembered, "and called me to ride with him. My column was not well stretched on the road before it encountered the division of E. Johnson (Second Corps) cutting in on our front, with all of Ewell's reserve and supply trains. He ordered the First Corps halted, and directed that Johnson's division and train should pass on to its corps, the First to wait.... After a little time General Lee proposed that we should ride on, and soon we heard reports of cannon. The fire seemed to be beyond Cashtown, and as it increased he left me and rode faster for the front."[43]

At Cashtown Lee found General Hill just risen from bed, pale and apparently ill. The two spoke briefly about the distant artillery fire, which seemed to be growing ever heavier, but Hill knew no more than Lee. Hill mounted up and rode off to find out about it, and, around noon, Lee called for General Anderson, whose division had now reached Cashtown. "I found General Lee intently listening to the fire of the guns, and very much disturbed and depressed," Anderson later told Longstreet. "At length he said, more to himself than to me, 'I cannot think what has become of Stuart. I ought to have heard from him long before now. He may have met with disaster, but I hope not. In the absence of reports from him, I am in ignorance as to what we have in front of us here. It may be the whole Federal army, or it may be only a detachment. If it is the whole Federal force, we must fight a battle here. If we do not gain a victory, those defiles and gorges which we passed this morning will shelter us from disaster.'"[44] Lee ordered Anderson to take his division forward to join the rest of Hill's corps, and then he rode on in that direction himself, heading for Gettysburg and the battle that had already started without him.

∽ Endnotes ∽

1 Hoehling, *Vicksburg: 47 Days of Siege*, 256, all three quotes.
2 *OR*, I:24:III:456, all three messages.

3 Ibid., I:24:II:368.
4 Ibid., I:24:II:365.
5 Ibid., I:24:I:113.
6 Grant, *Personal Memoirs*, I:552. Grant places this incident at the explosion of the first mine, on 25 June, but Forney's and Dana's reports, written much closer to the event, make it clear that it happened at the 1 July explosion. Hickenlooper's notes agree.
7 *OR*, I:24:II:365.
8 Ibid., I:24:II:175.
9 Grant, *Personal Memoirs*, I:555.
10 *OR*, I:24:II:209.
11 Ibid., I:24:III:457.
12 Ibid., I:24:III:458, both messages.
13 Ibid., I:24:I:244.
14 Ibid., I:24:I:281.
15 Ibid., I:24:II:517-18
16 Ibid., I:23:I:408.
17 Ibid., I:23:I:583.
18 Cozzens, *This Terrible Sound*, 19.
19 *OR*, I:23:II:497.
20 Ibid., I:23:II:896, both messages.
21 Ibid., I:23:I:632.
22 Ibid., I:23:II:502.
23 Ibid., I:22:II:900.
24 Ibid., I:22:II:899-900.
25 Ibid., I:22:I:380.
26 Ibid., I:27:II:821.
27 Ibid., I:27:II:818.
28 Longacre, *The Cavalry at Gettysburg*, 234.
29 *OR*, I:27:II:709.
30 Wingert, *The Confederate Approach on Harrisburg*, 141.
31 Ibid., 145-6.
32 Ibid., 151.
33 *OR*, I:27:I:70, both messages.
34 Coffin, *Nine Months to Gettysburg*, 187.
35 Ibid., 186-7. All three quotes.
36 *OR*, I:27:I:70-1.
37 Ibid., I:27:III:458.
38 Sears, *Gettysburg*, 150.
39 *OR*, I:27:III:462-3.
40 Ibid., I:27:III:460-1.
41 Ibid., I:27:III:948.
42 Bowden and Ward, *Last Chance for Victory*, 149.
43 Longstreet, *From Manassas to Appomattox*, 351-2.
44 Ibid., 357.

EPILOGUE

THE CANNON FIRE LEE HEARD was, of course, the result of the collision between Harry Heth's Confederate infantry and John Buford's Union cavalry. The battle that was thus joined soon drew in first Pender's Division and then Ewell's two divisions on the Rebel side and Reynolds' 1st and Howard's 11th Corps on the Federal, and eventually the entirety of both Lee's and Meade's armies; it lasted for three days of extremely violent all-out conflict, and is generally regarded as the greatest battle ever fought on the North American continent. It was a classic case of what strategists call a meeting engagement: two armies on the march running into each other and neither willing to back off.

Neither Lee nor Meade intended to bring on a battle that day at that place. The decision was made for them by subordinates: Heth, Hill, and eventually Ewell on the Confederate side; Buford, Reynolds, and eventually Hancock, on the Union side. As Lee later explained to Jefferson Davis: "It had not been intended to fight a general battle at such a distance from our base, unless attacked by the enemy, but, finding ourselves unexpectedly confronted by the Federal Army, it became a matter of difficulty to withdraw through the mountains with our large trains. At the same time, the country was unfavorable for collecting supplies while in the presence of the enemy's main body, as he was enabled to restrain our foraging parties by occupying the passes of the mountains with regular and local troops. A battle thus became, in a measure, unavoidable."[1] Meade expressed similar sentiments when he reported briefly to Halleck on the night of 1 July and said, "I see no other course than to hazard a general battle."[2]

Based on the sluggish movements of the Army of the Potomac since its inception up to that time, Lee evidently expected that he could ramble around in Pennsylvania for most of the summer without fighting a major battle, or that he could pick off chunks of the Union army if and when it came after him. Two major factors prevented this: the replacement of Hooker with Meade; and the separation of Stuart with the best part of his cavalry from the main body of Lee's army. Meade showed considerably more initiative and drive between his assumption of command and the actual fighting than any of his predecessors had ever shown. And Stuart's attempt to ride around or through the Union army had the misfortune to begin just as that army started to move north. Had it begun a day or two earlier, or had Hooker been content to remain in camp behind the Bull Run mountains a day or two longer, Stuart might well have joined Ewell in Pennsylvania in time to resume his function of screening the army's movements and observing the enemy's. But, as it was, Lee was without the eyes and ears of his army just when he needed them most. D. H. Hill, who was, soon after this, transferred to Bragg's army, said, "The want of information at General Bragg's headquarters was in striking contrast with the minute knowledge General Lee always had of every operation in his front."[3] But in the final days of June 1863 Lee knew far less about his enemy's movements than his enemy knew about his.

So the most positive result of Pleasonton's attacks on Stuart in the Loudoun Valley, although unintended, had been to pin Stuart and his best cavalry to that area, defending Lee's right and rear as he advanced down the Shenandoah Valley. As a result, Lee's infantry marched into enemy territory ahead of his best cavalry, and the only way the latter could get around in front again was either to follow the infantry and overtake it, or find a different route. Stuart suggested the latter and Lee acquiesced. In retrospect, it would have been better for the cavalry to have followed the infantry and overtaken it, but that was not so easily discernible at the time. Also, in retrospect, Lee or Ewell might have made better use of Jenkins' and White's cavalry in the absence of Stuart, and Lee might have called Robertson's and Jones's brigades north earlier, or at least one of them, and with more urgency than he did, and sent them out east of South Mountain to watch for the Federal army.

As for Lee's decision to invade the North in the first place, it was, from the standpoint of his theater of operations, the best move available. He had the Confederacy's largest and best army, a force with a proven track record of success. He skillfully withdrew from his Fredericksburg position into the Shenandoah, inflicted a stinging defeat on the Union forces there, relieved Virginia from the ravages of war, and subsisted his army at Federal expense for almost a month. Further, as we shall see in the next volume of this series, he came much closer to a major victory at Gettysburg than he has generally been given credit for. But was it the correct move from a larger, grand-strategic, point of view? Many Confederates claimed later – or even claimed to have felt at the time – that it was the wrong move. D. H. Hill later wrote that, "The drums that beat for the advance into Pennsylvania seemed to many of us to be beating the funeral march of the dead Confederacy."[4]

The largest question mark of all was: what should have been the Confederacy's response to Grant's threat to Vicksburg. As Joe Johnston pointed out, it was Jefferson Davis's responsibility to decide whether it was worth risking the loss of Middle Tennessee (and consequently exposing East Tennessee) in order to make it more likely that Johnston could save Vicksburg, the Mississippi Valley, and communication with the trans-Mississippi. Likewise, it was up to Davis to decide whether to let Lee take the offensive or to send a major portion of Lee's troops to the West. However, Davis let things drift, making, or at least announcing, no decision. Not wishing to interfere with his commanders on the spot, he left each one to his own devises instead of orchestrating them in aid of each other. Bragg was left with most of his army intact facing off against the (so-far) inactive Rosecrans, Lee was allowed to march off on his great raid/invasion north of the Potomac, and Johnston was left to accomplish an impossible task with too small a force. However, if Johnston really believed it was the right thing to do, he could have, in the absence of any orders from Davis to the contrary, ordered the movement of Bragg's army himself – if not before 10 June, certainly afterwards, when he had been informed that he had the authority to do so. Which was more important, saving Vicksburg and its garrison or allocating the responsibility to the proper authority? Such a decision, if it proved wrong, could ruin Johnston's career, but, then, what was that career worth if the country he served was conquered?

However, once Pemberton had retreated into the defenses of Vicksburg and Grant had established a secure supply base on the Yazoo, the fall of Vicksburg could only be prevented by driving him away from that base. But the destruction Grant had wrought in and around Jackson, Mississippi, would have made it very difficult for the Confederacy to supply and maneuver a large army in that area even if it had sent one there, and the Big Black River served as a moat protecting Grant's rear. About the only way that the Confederates could have dislodged him was by attacks on his supply line, namely the steamers coming down the Mississippi. The Rebels west of the river eventually saw that as a viable strategy but applied it too weakly and too late. Johnston never seems to have considered it. The presence of numerous Confederate batteries along the Mississippi, say at or near Greenville, backed up by Johnston's 25,000 or 30,000 troops, would have posed a considerable problem for Grant. Likewise, the best hope of shaking Banks loose from Port Hudson was an attack on his supply line up the Mississippi, including, possibly, an attempt to retake New Orleans. Again, the Confederates eventually tried this, but too late and with not-quite-sufficient force.

As it turned out, for a lack of decision about which was more important – saving Middle Tennessee, saving Vicksburg, or invading Pennsylvania – all three were failures, and Johnston's army of roughly 30,000 men sat around accomplishing nothing. Since it was too small to take on Grant's reinforced army alone and too lacking in wagons and supplies to undertake an offensive elsewhere, it would have been better sent, instead, to reinforce either Bragg or Lee. Had it gone to Tennessee, and Johnston with it to supercede Bragg, it's possible that the Confederates might have retained possession of Middle Tennessee – if for no other reason than that Rosecrans might not have advanced against a larger, better-led enemy. This would have been of considerable strategic advantage, but hardly decisive. Had the forces sent to Johnston from Bragg and Beauregard been sent to Lee instead, Gettysburg might well have ended in a Confederate victory. Whether even that would have won the war or even have offset the certain fall of Vicksburg is another question and all depends on just how decisive the victory turned out to be. But such, with the advantages of hindsight, would appear to have been a better Confederate option.

As it turned out, the battle at Gettysburg, for all its size, all its heroic moments, and all its death and destruction, was not a decisive battle, and the war continued for another two years. It could have been a decisive victory for either side, but neither army was able to overcome its own mistakes of commission and omission to the extent necessary to deliver a knock-out blow. Just why this was so, will be examined in the next volume of this series.

Endnotes

1. *OR*, I:27:II:308.
2. Ibid., I:27:I:72.
3. Daniel H. Hill, "Chickamauga – The Great Battle of the West" in *B&L* III:640.
4. Ibid., 639n.

THE ARMIES

★ UNITED STATES ARMY ★

Commander-in-Chief – President Abraham Lincoln
Secretary of War – Edwin M. Stanton
General-in-Chief – Major General Henry W. Halleck
Quartermaster General – Brigadier General Montgomery C. Meigs
Adjutant General – Brigadier General Lorenzo Thomas

DEPARTMENT of the EAST (New York, New Jersey and New England):
Commanding General – Major General John E. Wool

MIDDLE DEPARTMENT (8th Army Corps): (as of 31 May)
Commanding General – Major General Robert C. Schenck

    1st Separate Brigade: Brigadier General Henry H. Lockwood
    2nd Separate Brigade: Brigadier General William W. Morris
    3rd Separate Brigade: Brigadier General Henry S. Briggs
    4th Separate Brigade: Brigadier General William W. Averell

    1st Division: Brigadier General Benjamin F. Kelley
    1st Brigade: Brigadier General John R. Kenly
    2nd Brigade: Brigadier General William H. Morris
    3rd Brigade: Colonel Benjamin F. Smith
    4th Brigade: Colonel Jacob M. Campbell
    5th Brigade: Colonel James A. Mulligan
    6th Brigade: Colonel Nathan Wilkinson

    2nd Division: Brigadier General Robert H. Milroy
    1st Brigade: Brigadier General Washington L. Elliott
    2nd Brigade: Colonel William G. Ely
    3rd Brigade: Colonel A. T. McReynolds

    3rd Division: Brigadier General E. P. Scammon
    1st Brigade: Colonel Rutherford B. Hayes
    2nd Brigade: Colonel Carr B. White

DEPARTMENT of WASHINGTON (22nd Army Corps): (as of 31 May)
Commanding General – Major General Samuel Heintzelman

    Artillery Camp of Instruction: Brigadier General William F. Barry
    Provisional Brigades: Major General Silas Casey
    Corps of Observation (Poolesville and Seneca Locks, Md.):
      Colonel Albert Jewett

    Abercrombie's Division: Brigadier General J. J. Abercrombie
    1st (Me.) Brigade: Colonel Frank Fessenden
    2nd (Vt.) Brigade: Brigadier General George J. Stannard
    3rd (N.Y.) Brigade: Brigadier General Alexander Hays

    District of Alexandria: Brigadier General J. P. Slough

    Defenses South of the Potomac: Brig. Gen. Gustavus A. De Russy

        Pennsylvania Reserve Corps: Brig. Gen. Samuel W. Crawford
        1st Brigade: Colonel William McCandless
        3rd Brigade: Colonel Joseph W. Fisher

        Cavalry Division: Major General Julius Stahel
        1st Brigade: Brigadier General Joseph T. Copeland
        2nd Brigade: Colonel R. Butler Price
        3rd Brigade: Colonel Othneil De Forest

    District of Washington: Brigadier General J. H. Martindale

    Defenses North of the Potomac: Lieut. Colonel Joseph A Haskin
    1st Brigade: Colonel Augustus A. Gibson
    2nd Brigade: Colonel Lewis O. Morris
    3rd Brigade: Colonel Alexander Piper

ARMY of the POTOMAC (as of 31 May)
Commanding General – Major General Joseph Hooker
Chief of Staff – Brigadier General Daniel Butterfield
Chief Engineer – Brigadier General Gouverneur K. Warren
Chief of Artillery – Brigadier General Henry J. Hunt
Quartermaster General – Brigadier General Rufus Ingalls Assistant
Adjutant-General – Brigadier General Seth Williams
Provost-Marshal-General – Brigadier General Marsena R. Patrick

    Engineer Brigade: Brigadier General Henry W. Benham

1ˢᵀ Army Corps: Major General John F. Reynolds
Artillery Brigade: Colonel Charles Wainwright

1st Division: Brigadier General James S. Wadsworth
1st Brigade: Colonel Edward B. Fowler
2nd Brigade: Brigadier General Lysander Cutler
3rd Brigade: Brigadier General Gabriel R. Paul
4th (Iron) Brigade: Brigadier General Solomon Meredith

2nd Division: Brigadier General John C. Robinson
1st Brigade: Colonel Samuel H. Leonard
2nd Brigade: Brigadier General Henry Baxter

3rd Division: Major General Abner Doubleday
1st Brigade: Brigadier General Thomas A. Rowley
2nd Brigade: Colonel Roy Stone

2ᴺᴰ Army Corps: Major General Winfield Scott Hancock
Artillery Brigade: Captain John G. Hazard

1st Division: Brigadier General John C. Caldwell
1st Brigade: Colonel Edward Cross
2nd (Irish) Brigade: Colonel Patrick Kelly
3rd Brigade: Colonel Orlando H. Morris
4th Brigade: Colonel John R. Brooke

2nd Division: Brigadier General John Gibbon
1st Brigade: Colonel Turner G. Morehead
2nd Brigade: Brigadier General Joshua T. Owen
3rd Brigade: Colonel Norman J. Hall

3rd Division: Major General William H. French
1st Brigade: Colonel Samuel S. Carroll
2nd Brigade: Colonel Thomas A. Smyth

3ᴿᴰ Army Corps: Major General David B. Birney
Artillery Brigade: Captain George E. Randolph

1st Division: Brigadier General J. H. Hobart Ward
1st Brigade: Colonel Andrew H. Tippin
2nd Brigade: Colonel Philip Regis de Trobriand
3rd Brigade: Colonel Samuel B. Hayman

2nd Division: Brigadier General A. A. Humphreys
1st Brigade: Brigadier General Joseph B. Carr
2nd (Excelsior) Brigade: Colonel William R. Brewster
3rd Brigade: Colonel William J. Sewell

3rd Division: Brigadier General Charles K. Graham
1st Brigade: Colonel A. Van Horne Ellis
2nd Brigade: Colonel Samuel M. Bowman
3rd (Sharpshooter) Brigade: Colonel Hiram Berdan

5TH ARMY CORPS: Major General George G. Meade

1st Division: Brigadier General James Barnes
1st Brigade: Colonel William S. Tilton
2nd Brigade: Colonel Jacob Sweitzer
3rd Brigade: Colonel Strong Vincent

2nd Division: Major General George Sykes
1st (Regular) Brigade: Brigadier General Romeyn B. Ayres
2nd (Regular) Brigade: Colonel Sydney Burbank
3rd (Zouave) Brigade: Colonel Patrick H. O'Rorke

6TH ARMY CORPS: Major General John Sedgwick
Artillery Brigade: Colonel C. H. Tompkins

1st Division: Brigadier General Horatio G. Wright
1st (New Jersey) Brigade: Colonel William H. Penrose
2nd Brigade: Brigadier General Joseph J. Bartlett
3rd Brigade: Brigadier General David A. Russell

2nd Division: Brigadier General Albion P. Howe
2nd (Vermont) Brigade: Colonel Lewis A. Grant
3rd Brigade: Colonel D. D. Bidwell

3rd Division: Major General John Newton
1st Brigade: Colonel Silas Titus
2nd Brigade: Colonel Henry L. Eustis
3rd Brigade: Brigadier General Frank Wheaton

11TH ARMY CORPS: Major General Oliver Otis Howard
Artillery Brigade: Captain Michael Wiedrich

1st Division: Brigadier General Francis C. Barlow
1st Brigade: Colonel Gotthilf Bourry
2nd Brigade: Brigadier General Adelbert Ames

2nd Division: Brigadier General Adolph von Steinwehr
1st Brigade: Colonel Adolphus Buschbeck
2nd Brigade: Colonel Orland Smith

3rd Division: Major General Carl Schurz
1st Brigade: Colonel George von Amsberg
2nd Brigade: Colonel Wladimir Krzynawski

12TH ARMY CORPS: Major General Henry Slocum
Artillery Brigade: Captain Michael Wiedrich

1st Division: Brigadier General Alpheus S. Williams
1st & 2nd Brigades: Colonel Archibald L. McDougall
3rd Brigade: Brigadier General Thomas H. Ruger

2nd Division: Brigadier General John W. Geary
1st Brigade: Colonel Charles Candy
2nd Brigade: Colonel George A. Cobham, Jr.
3rd Brigade: Brigadier General George S. Greene

CAVALRY CORPS: Brigadier General Henry Pleasonton
Artillery: Captain James M. Robertson
Regular Reserve Brigade: Brigadier General John Buford

1st Division: Colonel Benjamin F. "Grimes" Davis
1st Brigade: (Colonel Benjamin Franklin "Grimes" Davis)
2nd Brigade: Colonel Josiah H. Kellogg

2nd Division: Colonel Albert N. Duffié
1st Brigade: Colonel Horace B. Sargent
2nd Brigade: Colonel John Irvin Gregg

3rd Division: Brigadier General David M. Gregg
1st Brigade: Colonel Calvin S. Douty
2nd Brigade: Colonel Percy Wyndham

Artillery Reserve: Brigadier General Robert O. Tyler

Regular Division: (no commander mentioned)
1st Brigade: Captain Dunbar R. Ransom
2nd Brigade: Captain John C. Tidball

Volunteer Division: Major John A. Tompkin
1st Brigade: Major Freeman McGilvery
2nd Brigade: Major Thomas W. Osborn
3rd Brigade: Captain Richard Waterman
4th Brigade: Captain Robert H. Fitzhugh

DEPARTMENT of VIRGINIA: (as of 31 May)
Commanding General – Major General John A. Dix

4TH ARMY CORPS: **Major General Erasmus D. Keyes**
Reserve Artillery (Yorktown): Captain James McKnight

1st Division (Yorktown): (no commander named)
Advance Brigade: Colonel R. M. West
King's Brigade: Brigadier General Rufus King

2nd Division (West Point, Va.): Brig. General George H. Gordon
1st Brigade: Colonel William Gurney
2nd Brigade: Colonel Burr Porter

7TH ARMY CORPS: **(Major General John A. Dix)**
Norfolk: Brigadier General Egbert L. Viele

Post of Suffolk: Major General John J. Peck
Artillery: Captain F. M. Follett

Peck's Division: Brigadier General Michael Corcoran
1st Brigade: Brigadier General Henry D. Terry
2nd Brigade: Colonel Robert S. Foster
3rd Brigade (Irish Legion): Colonel Mathew Murphy

Getty's Division: Brigadier General George W. Getty
1st Brigade: Colonel W. R. Pease
2nd Brigade: Brigadier General Edward Harland
3rd Brigade: Colonel A. H. Dutton
Reserve Brigade: Brigadier General I. J. Wistar

DEPARTMENT of NORTH CAROLINA (18th Army Corps) (as of 31 May)
Commanding General – Major General John G. Foster

Post of New Berne: Brigadier General Innis N. Palmer
Jourdan's Brigade: Colonel James Jourdan
Lee's Brigade: Colonel Francis L. Lee
Cavalry Brigade: Lieutenant Colonel S. H. Mix

    1st Division (New Berne): Colonel T. J. C. Amory
    1st Brigade: Colonel C. L. Holbrook
    2nd Brigade: Colonel George H. Peirson

    District of the Albemarle: Brigadier General Henry W. Wessells

    District of Beaufort: Brigadier General F. B. Spinola

    District of the Pamlico: Brigadier General Henry Prince

DEPARTMENT OF THE SOUTH (10th ARMY CORPS) (as of 31 May)
Commanding General – Major General David Hunter
Chief of Staff – Brigadier General Truman Seymour

    Folly Island: Brigadier General Israel Vogdes

    Seabrook Island: Brigadier General Orris S. Ferry
    Stevenson's Brigade: Brigadier General Thomas G. Stevenson
    Guss's Brigade: Colonel Henry R. Guss

    2nd Division, Detachment 18th Corps: Brig. Gen. C. A. Heckman
    1st Brigade: Colonel J. J. De Forest
    2nd Brigade: Colonel J. B. Howell
    3rd Brigade: Colonel T. O. Osborn

    Hilton Head Island: Colonel John L. Chatfield

    Port Royal Island: Brigadier General Rufus Saxton

    Fort Pulaski, Georgia: Colonel William B. Barton

DEPARTMENT of the GULF (19th ARMY CORPS) (as of 31 May 1863)
Commanding General - Major General Nathaniel P. Banks
Chief of Staff – Brigadier General George L. Andrews

    1st Division: Major General Christopher Colon Augur
    1st Brigade: Colonel Charles J. Paine
    3rd Brigade: Colonel Nathan A. M. Dudley

    2nd Division: Brigadier General William Dwight
    1st Brigade: Colonel Thomas S. Clark
    3rd Brigade: Brigadier General Frank S. Nickerson
    Artillery: Captain William Roy

3rd Division: Brigadier General Halbert E. Paine
1st Brigade: Colonel Timothy Ingraham
2nd Brigade: Colonel Hawkes Fearing, Jr.
3rd Brigade: Colonel Oliver P. Gooding
Artillery: Captain Richard C. Duryea

4th Division: Brigadier General Cuvier Grover
2nd Brigade: Colonel William K. Kimball
3rd Brigade: Colonel Henry W. Birge
Artillery: Captain Henry W. Closson

Provisional Division: Brigadier General Godfrey Weitzel
2nd Brigade, 1st Division: Colonel Stephen Thomas
1st Brigade, 4th Division: Colonel Joseph S. Morgan

Cavalry: Colonel Benjamin H. Grierson

Corps D'Afrique: Brigadier General Daniel Ullmann

Defenses of New Orleans: Brigadier General William H. Emory
2nd Brigade, 2nd Division: Colonel Thomas W. Cahill

District of Key West and Tortugas: Brig. Gen. Daniel P. Woodbury

District of Pensacola: Colonel Isaac Dyer

DEPARTMENT of the TENNESSEE: (18 May - 4 July 1863)
Commanding General - Major General Ulysses S. Grant
Chief of Staff – Lieutenant Colonel John A. Rawlins

Unattached Cavalry (brigade): Colonel Cyrus Bussey

Herron's Division: Maj. Gen. Francis J. Herron (from Mo. 11 June)
1st Brigade: Brigadier General William Vandever
2nd Brigade: Brigadier General William W. Orme

District of Northeast Louisiana: Brig. General Elias S. Dennis
Detached Brigade: Colonel George W. Neeley
African Brigade: Colonel Isaac F. Shepard
Post of Milliken's Bend: Colonel Hiram Scofield
Post of Goodrich's Landing: Colonel William F. Wood

9ᵀᴴ Army Corps: Major General John G. Parke (from Ky. 14-17 June)

1ˢᵗ Division: Brigadier General Thomas Welsh
1ˢᵗ Brigade: Colonel Henry Bowman
3ʳᵈ Brigade: Colonel Daniel Leasure

2ⁿᵈ Division: Brigadier General Robert B. Potter
1ˢᵗ Brigade: Colonel Simon G. Griffin
2ⁿᵈ Brigade: Brigadier General Edward Ferrero
3ʳᵈ Brigade: Colonel Benjamin C. Christ

13ᵀᴴ Army Corps: Major General John A. McClernand
 (Major General E. O. C. Ord from 19 June)

9ᵗʰ Division: Brigadier General Peter J. Osterhaus
1ˢᵗ Brigade: Brigadier General Albert L. Lee
 (Colonel James Keigwin from 19 May)
2ⁿᵈ Brigade: Colonel Daniel W. Lindsey
Artillery: Captain Jacob T. Foster

10ᵗʰ Division: Brigadier General Andrew Jackson Smith
1ˢᵗ Brigade: Brigadier General Stephen G. Burbridge
2ⁿᵈ Brigade: Colonel Willism J. Landran

12ᵗʰ Division: Brigadier General Alvin P. Hovey
1ˢᵗ Brigade: Brigadier General George F. McGinnis
2ⁿᵈ Brigade: Colonel James R. Slack

14ᵗʰ Division: Brigadier General Eugene A. Carr
1ˢᵗ Brigade: Brigadier General William Benton
 (Colonel Henry Washburn from 31 May)
2ⁿᵈ Brigade: Brigadier General Michael K. Lawler

4ᵗʰ Division, 16ᵗʰ Corps (attached to 13th):
Brigadier General Jacob Lauman
1ˢᵗ Brigade: Colonel Isaac C. Pugh
2ⁿᵈ Brigade: Colonel Cyrus Hall
3ʳᵈ Brigade: Colonel George E. Bryant
 (Colonel Amory Johnson from 22 June)
Artillery: Captain George C. Gumbart

15ᵗʰ Army Corps: Major General William Tecumseh Sherman

    1ˢᵗ Division: Major General Frederick Steele
1ˢᵗ Brigade: Colonel Francis H. Manter
       (Colonel Bernard Farrar from 13 June)
2ⁿᵈ Brigade: Colonel Charles R. Woods
3ʳᵈ Brigade: Brigadier General John M. Thayer

    2ⁿᵈ Division: Major General Francis P. Blair, Jr.
1ˢᵗ Brigade: Colonel Giles A. Smith
2ⁿᵈ Brigade: Colonel T. Kilby Smith
       (Brigadier General A. J. Lightburn from 24 May)
3ʳᵈ Brigade: Brigadier General Hugh Ewing

    3ʳᵈ Division: Brigadier General James M. Tuttle
1ˢᵗ Brigade: Brigadier General Ralph Buckland
       (Colonel William McMillen from 22 June)
2ⁿᵈ Brigade: Brigadier General Joseph A. Mower
3ʳᵈ Brigade: Brigadier General Charles Matthies
       (Colonel Joseph J. Woods from 1 June)
Artillery: Captain Nelson T. Spoor

Detachment, 16ᵀᴴ Army Corps: Maj. Gen. Cadwallader C. Washburn

    1ˢᵗ Division: Brig. Gen. William Sooy Smith (from Tenn. 12 June)
1ˢᵗ Brigade: Colonel John M. Loomis
2ⁿᵈ Brigade: Colonel Stephen G. Hicks
3ʳᵈ Brigade: Colonel Joseph R. Cockerill
4ᵗʰ Brigade: Colonel William W. Sanford
Artillery: Captain William Cogswell

17ᵀᴴ Army Corps: Major General James B. McPherson

    3ʳᵈ Division: Brigadier General John A. Logan
1ˢᵗ Brigade: Brigadier General John E. Smith
       (Brigadier General M. Leggett from 3 June)
2ⁿᵈ Brigade: Brig. Gen. M. Leggett (Col. Manning Force from 3 June)
3ʳᵈ Brigade: Brigadier General John D. Stevenson
Artillery: Major Charles J. Stolbrand

6th Division: Brigadier General John McArthur
1st Brigade: Brigadier General Hugh T. Reid
2nd Brigade: Brigadier General Thomas E. G. Ransom
3rd Brigade: Colonel William Hall
        (Colonel Alexander Chambers from 6 June)
Artillery: Major Thomas D. Maurice

7th Division: Brigadier General Isaac F. Quimby
        (Brigadier General John E. Smith from 3 June)
1st Brigade: Colonel John B. Sanborn
2nd Brigade: Colonel Samuel A. Holms
        (Colonel Green B. Raum from 10 June)
3rd Brigade: Colonel G. Boomer
        (Colonel H. Putnam 22 May, Colonel C. Matthies 2 June)
Artillery: Captain Frank C. Sands

District of Western Tennessee & 16th Corps (as of 30 June):
Major General Stephen Hurlbut

District of Memphis (5th Div.): Brigadier General James C. Veatch
1st Brigade: Colonel Charles D. Murray
2nd Brigade: Colonel William H. Morgan
3rd Brigade: Colonel John W. Fuller
4th Brigade: Colonel David Moore

District of Columbus (6th Division): Brig. Gen. Alexander Asboth
Cairo, Illinois: Brigadier General Napoleon B. Buford
Columbus, Kentucky: Colonel George E. Waring
Paducah, Kentucky: Colonel James S. Martin

Left Wing, 16th Corps: Major General Richard J. Oglesby

District of Corinth (2nd Div.): Brig. Gen. Grenville M. Dodge
1st Brigade: Brigadier General Thomas W. Sweeny
2nd Brigade: Colonel August Mersy
3rd Brigade: Colonel Moses M. Bane
3rd Brigade, 3rd Division: Colonel James M. True
4th Cavalry Brigade: Lieutenant Colonel Bazil D. Meek

Cavalry Division: Colonel John K. Mizner
1st Brigade: Colonel Lafayette McCrillis
2nd Brigade: Colonel Edward Hatch
3rd Brigade: Colonel Florence M. Cornyn

District of Eastern Arkansas: Major General B. M. Prentiss

13th Division of 13th Corps: Brigadier General Frederick Salomon
1st Brigade: Colonel W. E. McLean
2nd Brigade: Colonel S. A. Rice

DEPARTMENT OF THE CUMBERLAND: (as of 30 June)
Commanding General – Major General William S. Rosecrans
Chief of Staff – Brigadier General James A. Garfield

Artillery Reserve (Nashville): Captain Warren P. Edgarton
Clarksville, Tenn.: Colonel Sanders D. Bruce
Camp Spears (Nashville): Colonel Alvan C. Gillem
Gallatin, Tenn.: Colonel Benjamin J. Sweet
Pioneer Brigade: Brigadier General James St. Clair Morton

14TH ARMY CORPS: Major General George H. Thomas

1st Division: Major General Lovell H. Rousseau
1st Brigade: Colonel Benjamin F. Scribner
2nd Brigade: Colonel Henry A. Hambright
3rd (Regular) Brigade: Brigadier General John H. King
Artillery: Colonel Cyrus O. Loomis

2nd Division: Major General James S. Negley
1st Brigade: Brigadier General John Beatty
2nd Brigade: Colonel William L. Stoughton
3rd Brigade: Colonel William Sirwell
Artillery: Captain Frederick Schultz

3rd Division: Brigadier General John M. Brannan
1st Brigade: Colonel Moses B. Walker
2nd Brigade: Brigadier General James B. Steedman
3rd Brigade: Colonel E. Van Derveer
Artillery: no commander named

4th Division: Major General Joseph J. Reynolds
1st (mounted) Brigade: Colonel John T. Wilder
2nd Brigade: Colonel Albert S. Hall
3rd Brigade: Brigadier General George Crook
Artillery: no commander named

20ᵗʰ ARMY CORPS: Major General Alexander M. McCook

1ˢᵗ Division: Brigadier General Jefferson C. Davis
1ˢᵗ Brigade: Colonel P. Sidney Post
2ⁿᵈ Brigade: Brigadier General William P. Carlin
3ʳᵈ Brigade: Colonel Hans C. Heg
Artillery: no commander named

2ⁿᵈ Division: Brigadier General Richard W. Johnson
1ˢᵗ Brigade: Brigadier General August Willich
2ⁿᵈ Brigade: Colonel Joseph B. Dodge
3ʳᵈ Brigade: Colonel Philemon P. Baldwin
Artillery: Captain Peter Simonson

3ʳᵈ Division: Major General Philip H. Sheridan
1ˢᵗ Brigade: Brigadier General William H. Lytle
2ⁿᵈ Brigade: Colonel Bernard Laiboldt
3ʳᵈ (Illinois) Brigade: Colonel Luther P. Bradley
Artillery: Captain Henry Hescock

21ˢᵗ ARMY CORPS: Major General Thomas L. Crittenden

1ˢᵗ Division: Brigadier General Thomas J. Wood
1ˢᵗ Brigade: Colonel George P. Buell
2ⁿᵈ Brigade: Brigadier General George D. Wagner
3ʳᵈ Brigade: Colonel Charles G. Harker
Artillery: Captain Cullen Bradley

2ⁿᵈ Division: Major General John M. Palmer
1ˢᵗ Brigade: Brigadier General Charles Cruft
2ⁿᵈ Brigade: Brigadier General William B. Hazen
3ʳᵈ Brigade: Colonel William Grose
Artillery: Captain William E. Standert

3ʳᵈ Division: Brigadier General Horatio P. Van Cleve
1ˢᵗ Brigade: Brigadier General Samuel Beatty
2ⁿᵈ Brigade: Colonel George F. Dick
3ʳᵈ Brigade: Colonel Sydney M. Barnes
Artillery: Captain Lucius H. Drury

Reserve Corps: Major General Gordon Granger

1st Division: Brigadier General Absalom Baird
1st Brigade: Colonel Smith D. Atkins
2nd Brigade: Colonel William P. Reid
3rd Brigade: Colonel William L. Utley

2nd Division (at Nashville)**: Brigadier General James D. Morgan**
1st Brigade: Colonel Robert F. Smith
2nd Brigade: Colonel Daniel McCook
3rd Brigade: Colonel Charles C. Doolittle

3rd Division (HQ at Nashville)**: Brig. General Robert S. Granger**
1st Brigade (at Fort Donelson): Colonel William P. Lyon
2nd Brigade (various garrisons): Brigadier General William T. Ward

Cavalry Corps: Major General David S. Stanley

1st Cavalry Division: Brigadier General Robert B. Mitchell
1st Brigade: Colonel Archibald P. Campbell
2nd Brigade: Colonel Edward M. McCook

2nd Cavalry Division: Brigadier General John B. Turchin
1st Brigade: Colonel Robert H. G. Minty
2nd Brigade: Colonel Eli Long

DEPARTMENT OF THE OHIO: (as of 30 June)
Commanding General – Major General Ambrose E. Burnside

District of Ohio: Brigadier General Jacob D. Cox
Columbus: Brigadier General John S. Mason
Camp Dennison: Lieutenant Colonel George W. Neff
Cincinnati: Lieutenant Colonel Seth Eastman

District of Illinois: Brigadier General Jacob Ammen

District of Indiana and Michigan: Brig. Gen. Orlando B. Willcox

23rd Army Corps (Kentucky): Major General George L. Hartsuff

1st Division: Brigadier General Samuel D. Sturgis
1st Brigade (inf., mtd. inf. & cav.): Brig. General Samuel P. Carter
2nd Brigade (inf., mtd. inf. & cav.): Colonel Samuel A. Gilbert
3rd Brigade (cavalry): Colonel August V. Kautz

2nd Division: Brigadier General Jeremiah T. Boyle
1st Brigade (inf., mtd. inf. & cav.): Brig. Gen. James M. Shackelford
Munfordville, Ky. (inf.): Colonel Charles D. Pennebaker
Bowling Green, Ky. (inf. & cav.): Colonel Cicero Maxwell

3rd Division: Brigadier General Henry M. Judah
1st Brigade (inf. & cav.): Brigadier General Mahlon D. Manson
2nd Brigade (inf. & cav.): Brigadier General Edward H. Hobson
3rd Brigade (inf. & mtd. inf.): Colonel Joseph A. Cooper

4th Division: Brigadier General Julius White
1st Brigade (inf., mtd. inf. & cav.): Colonel Daniel Cameron
2nd Brigade (inf. & cav.): Colonel Samuel R. Mott

DEPARTMENT OF THE MISSOURI: (as of 30 June)
Commanding General – Major General John M. Schofield

District of Central Missouri: Brigadier General Egbert B. Brown

District of Northeastern Missouri: Brig. General Odon Guitar

District of Northwestern Missouri: Brig. General Willard P. Hall

District of Rolla: Brigadier General Thomas A. Davies
1st Brigade: Lieutenant Colonel John T. Burris

District of Saint Louis: Brigadier General William K. Strong
Benton Barracks: Colonel Benjamin L. E. Bonneville
St. Louis: Colonel Henry Almstedt

**District of Southeastern Missouri (1st Cavalry Division):
Brigadier General John W. Davidson**
1st Brigade: Colonel Lewis Merrill
2nd Brigade: Colonel John M. Glover
Cape Girardeau: Colonel John B. Rogers
Pilot Knob: Major James T. Howland

District of Southwestern Missouri: Colonel William F. Cloud
Newtonia: Colonel John F. Philips
Springfield: Colonel John Edwards

**Eighth District (Enrolled Missouri Militia):
Brigadier General Thomas J. Bartholow**

District of the Frontier: Major General James G. Blunt

District of Nebraska: Brigadier General Thomas J. McKean

District of Colorado: Colonel John M. Chivington

DEPARTMENT of the NORTHWEST: (as of 30 June)
Commanding General – Major General John Pope

District of Wisconsin: Brigadier General T. C. H. Smith

District of Minnesota: Brigadier General Henry H. Sibley

District of Iowa: Brigadier General Benjamin S. Roberts

District of Dakota: Brigadier General Alfred Sully

DEPARTMENT of NEW MEXICO:
Commanding General - Brigadier General James H. Carleton

DEPARTMENT of the PACIFIC
Commanding General – Colonel George Wright

★ CONFEDERATE STATES ARMY ★
Commander-in-Chief – President Jefferson Davis
Secretary of War – James Seddon
Adjutant and Inspector General – General Samuel Cooper

DEPARTMENT and ARMY of NORTHERN VIRGINIA: (as of 2 June)
Commanding General – General Robert Edward Lee
Chief of Artillery: Brigadier General William Nelson Pendleton

Northwest Virginia Brigade (Cav. & Mtd. Inf.):
Brigadier General John D. Imboden

Valley District: Major General Isaac Trimble
Jenkins' (Va.) Cavalry Brigade: Brigadier General Albert G. Jenkins
The Maryland Line (Inf., Cav. & Art.)

Cavalry Division: Major General J. E. B. Stuart
Hampton's Brigade: Brigadier General Wade Hampton
Fitz. Lee's (Va.) Brigade: Brigadier General Fitzhugh Lee
W. H. F. Lee's (Va. & N.C.) Brigade: B. Gen. W. H. F. ("Rooney") Lee
Jones's (Va.) Brigade: Brigadier General W. E. ("Grumble") Jones
Robertson's (N.C.) Brigade: Brigadier General Beverly Robertson
Horse Artillery Battalion: Major Robert F. Beckham

1ST ARMY CORPS: Lieutenant General James ("Pete") Longstreet

Reserve Artillery, 1st Corps: Colonel James B. Walton
Washington Artillery Battalion: Major Benjamin Franklin Eshelman
Alexander's Artillery Battalion: Colonel Edward Porter Alexander

McLaws' Division: Major General Lafayette McLaws
Kershaw's (S.C.) Brigade: Brigadier General Joseph B. Kershaw
Barksdale's (Miss.) Brigade: Brigadier General William Barksdale
Semmes' (Ga.) Brigade: Brigadier General Paul Jones Semmes
Wofford's (Ga.) Brigade: Brigadier General William Tatum Wofford
Cabell's Artillery Battalion: Colonel Henry Coalter Cabell

Hood's Division: Major General John Bell Hood
Law's (Ala.) Brigade: Brigadier General Evander McIvor Law
Texas (Tex. & Ark.) Brigade: Brig. Gen. Jerome Bonaparte Robertson
Rock (Ga.) Brigade: Brigadier General Henry Lewis Benning
Anderson's (Ga.) Brigade: B. Gen. George Thomas ("Tige") Anderson
Henry's Artillery Battalion: Major Mathias Winston Henry

Pickett's Division: Major General George Pickett
Armistead's (Va.) Brigade: Brigadier General Lewis ("Lo") Armistead
Kemper's (Va.) Brigade: Brigadier General James L. Kemper
Garnett's (Va.) Brigade: Brigadier General Richard Brooke Garnett
Corse's (Va.) Brigade (left in Virginia): B. Gen. Montgomery D. Corse
38th Virginia Light Artillery Battalion: Major James Dearing

2ND ARMY CORPS: Lieutenant General Richard Stoddert Ewell

Reserve Artillery, 2nd Corps: Colonel John Thompson Brown
1st Virginia Artillery Battalion: Captain Willis Jefferson Dance
Nelson's Artillery Battalion: Lieutenant Colonel William Nelson

Early's Division: Major General Jubal Anderson Early
Gordon's (Ga.) Brigade: Brigadier General John Brown Gordon
Hoke's (N.C.) Brigade: Colonel Isaac Erwin Avery
Hays' (Louisiana Tiger) Brigade: Brig. Gen. Harry Thompson Hays
Smith's (Va.) Brigade: Brig. General William ("Extra Billy") Smith
Jones's Artillery Battalion: Lieutenant Colonel Hilary Pollard Jones

Johnson's Division: Major General Edward ("Allegheny") Johnson
Steuart's (N.C. & Va.) Brigade: B. Gen. George ("Maryland") Steuart
Stonewall (Va.) Brigade: Brigadier General James Alexander Walker
Jones's (Va.) Brigade: Brigadier General John Marshall Jones
Nicholl's (2nd Louisiana) Brigade: Colonel Jesse Milton Williams
Latimer's Artillery Battalion: Major James W. Latimer

Rodes' Division: Major General Robert Emmett Rodes
Daniel's (N.C.) Brigade: Brigadier General Junius Daniel
Doles' (Ga.) Brigade: Brigadier General George Pierce Doles
Iverson's (N.C.) Brigade: Brigadier General Alfred Iverson, Jr.
Ramseur's (N.C.) Brigade: Brig. General Stephen Dodson Ramseur
Rodes' (Ala.) Brigade: Colonel Edward Asbury O'Neal
Carter's (Va.) Artillery Battalion: Lieut. Col. Thomas Henry Carter

3RD ARMY CORPS: Lieutenant General Ambrose Powell Hill

Reserve Artillery, 3rd Corps: Colonel Reuben Lindsay Walker
McIntosh's Artillery Battalion: Major David Gregg McIntosh
Pegram's Artillery Battalion: Major William Johnson Pegram

Anderson's Division: Major General Richard Herron Anderson
Wilcox's (Ala.) Brigade: Brigadier General Cadmus M. Wilcox
Mahone's (Va.) Brigade: Brigadier General William Mahone
Perry's (Fla.) Brigade: Colonel David Lang
Posey's (Miss.) Brigade: Brigadier General Carnot Posey
Wright's (Ga.) Brigade: Brig. Gen. Ambrose Ransom ("Rans") Wright
11th Georgia ("Sumpter") Artillery Battalion: Major John Lane

Heth's Division: Major General Henry ("Harry") Heth
Pettigrew's (N.C.) Brigade: Brig. General James Johnston Pettigrew
Davis's (Miss. & N.C.) Brigade: Brig. General Joseph Robert Davis
Brockenbrough's (Va.) Brigade: Colonel John Mercer Brockenbrough
Archer's (Ala. & Tenn.) Brigade: Brigadier General James Jay Archer
Garnett's Artillery Battalion: Lieutenant Colonel John J. Garnett

Pender's "Light" Division: Major General William Dorsey Pender
McGowan's (S.C.) Brigade: Colonel Abner Perrin
Lane's (N.C.) Brigade: Brigadier General James Henry Lane
Scales' (N.C.) Brigade: Brigadier General Alfred Moore Scales
Thomas's (Ga.) Brigade: Brigadier General Edward Lloyd Thomas
Poague's Artillery Battalion: Major William Thomas Poague

DEPARTMENT of WESTERN VIRGINIA: (as of 31 May 1863)
Commanding General – Major General Samuel Jones

1st (Va.) Brigade: Brigadier General John Echols
2nd (Va.) Brigade: Brigadier General John S. Williams
3rd (Va.) Brigade: Colonel G. C. Wharton
4th (Va.) Brigade: Colonel John McCausland
Cavalry (Va.) Brigade: (Brigadier General Albert G. Jenkins)
  (much of it in the Valley)

DEPARTMENT of RICHMOND: (as of 20 June 1863)
Commanding General – Major General Arnold Elzey

Wise's (Va.) Brigade: Brigadier General Henry A. Wise
Cooke's (N.C.) Brigade: Brigadier General J. R. Cooke
Rhett's Command: Colonel T. S. Rhett
Artillery Defenses: Lieutenant Colonel J. M. Maury
Naval Detachment: Captain Sidney Smith Lee

DEPARTMENT of NORTH CAROLINA: (as of 30 June 1863)
Commanding General – Major General Daniel Harvey Hill

Colquitt's (Ga.) Brigade (near Kinston): Brig. General A. H. Colquitt
Ransom's (N.C.) Brigade (at Richmond, Va.):
  Brigadier General Mathew W. Ransom
Clingman's (N.C.) Brigade (near Wilmington):
  Brigadier General T. L. Clingman
Martin's (N.C.) Brigade (guarding Weldon RR):
  Brigadier General J. G. Martin
Jenkins' (S.C.) Brigade (at Richmond, Va.): Brig. Gen. Micah Jenkins
Moseley's (artillery) Battalion: Major E. F. Moseley
Boggs' (artillery) Battalion: Major F. J. Boggs
Branch's (artillery) Battalion: Major J. R. Branch

District of Cape Fear: Major General W. H. C. Whiting

DEPT. OF SOUTH CAROLINA, GEORGIA, AND FLORIDA:
Commanding General – General P. G. T. Beauregard (as of 25 May 1863)

    1st **Military District of S. Carolina: Brig. Gen. Roswell S. Ripley**

    2nd **Military District of S. Carolina: Brig. Gen. Johnson Hagood**

    3rd **Military District of South Carolina: Brig. Gen. W. S. Walker**

    District of Georgia: Brigadier General H. W. Mercer

    District of Middle Florida: Brigadier General Howell Cobb

    District of East Florida: Brigadier General Joseph Finegan

TRANS-MISSISSIPPI DEPARTMENT
Commanding General – Lieutenant General Edmund Kirby Smith

    District of Arkansas: Major General Theophilus Holmes

    Price's Division: Major General Sterling Price
    Fagan's (Ark.) Brigade: Brigadier General James F. Fagan
    McRae's (Ark.) Brigade: Brigadier General Dandridge McRae
    Parson's (Mo.) Brigade: Brigadier General Mosby M. Parsons

    Steele's (Cavalry Division): Brigadier General William Steele
    Cooper's (Indian & Tex.) Brigade: Brigadier General D. H. Cooper
    Cabell's (Ark. & Tex.) Brigade: Brigadier General W. L. Cabell

    Marmaduke's (Cavalry) Division: Brig. Gen. J. S. Marmaduke
    Burbridge's (Mo.) Brigade: Colonel John Q. Burbridge
    Shelby's (Mo.) Brigade: Colonel Joseph O. Shelby
    Greene's (Mo.) Brigade: Colonel Colton Greene

    Frost's Division (Defenses of Lower Arkansas): (as of 31 May)
    1st (Ark.) Brigade: Colonel John B. Clark, Jr.

    District of West Louisiana: Major General Richard Taylor

    Carter's (Tex.) Brigade (of Marmaduke's Div.): Col. George W. Carter
    Polignac's Brigade: Brig. Gen. Camille Jules Marie, Prince de Polignac
    Speight's (Tex.) Brigade (at Shreveport): Colonel J. W. Speight

Forces South of Red River: Brig. Gen. Jean Jacques Alfred Mouton
Mouton's (La.) Brigade: (Brig. General Jean Jacques Alfred Mouton)
1st (Tex. & La.) Cavalry Brigade: Brigadier General Thomas Green
2nd (Tex.) Cavalry Brigade: Colonel James P. Major

Walker's (Texas) Division: Major General John G. Walker
McCulloch's Brigade: Brigadier General Henry E. McCulloch
Hawes' Brigade: Brigadier General J. M. Hawes
Randal's Brigade: Colonel Horace Randal
Tappan's (Ark.) Brigade (of Price's Div.): Brig. Gen. James C. Tappan

District of Texas, New Mexico & Arizona: Maj. Gen. John B. Magruder

Western Subdistrict (1st Division): Brig. General Hamilton P. Bee
1st Brigade: (no commander mentioned)
2nd Brigade: Colonel S. P. Bankhead

Eastern Subdistrict (2nd Division): Brigadier General W. R. Scurry
1st Brigade: Colonel P. N. Luckett
2nd Brigade: Colonel X. B. Debray

☆ *DEPARTMENT OF THE WEST** ☆

Commanding General – General Joseph E. Johnston

Loring's Division: Major General W. W. Loring (as of 30 May)
1st (Tilghman's) (Miss.) Brigade: Colonel A. E. Reynolds
2nd (Miss.) Brigade: Brigadier General W. S. Featherston
3rd Brigade: Brigadier General Abraham Buford
Maxey's Brigade: Brig. General S. B. Maxey (temporarily attached)

Walker's Division: Major General W. H. T. Walker (as of 26 May)
Gist's Brigade: Brigadier General States Rights Gist
Ector's Brigade: Brigadier General M. D. Ector
Gregg's (Tenn. & Tex.) Brigade: Brigadier General J. Gregg
McNair's Brigade: Brigadier General E. McNair
Wilson's Brigade: Colonel C. C. Wilson
Adams' (mounted) Brigade: Brigadier General John Adams
Ferguson's (sharpshooter) Command: Colonel Samuel W. Ferguson

Breckinridge's Division:
Major General John C. Breckinridge (as of 3 June)
Adam's (La. & Ala.) Brigade: Brigadier General Daniel W. Adams
Helm's (Ky. & Ala.) Brigade: Brigadier General Ben. Hardin Helm
Stovall's (Fla. & N.C.) Brigade: Brigadier General M. A. Stovall
Evans' (S.C.) Brigade: B. Gen. Nathan G. Evans (with Loring 30 May)

French's Division:
Major General Samuel G. French (created 21 June 1863)
Evans Brigade (from Breckinridge's Division, see above)
Maxey's Brigade (from Loring's Division, see above)
McNair's Brigade (from Walker's Division, see above)

Cavalry Division: Brig. Gen. W. H. "Red" Jackson (as of 4 June)
1st (Miss.) Brigade: Brigadier General George B. Cosby
2nd (Tex.) Brigade: Brigadier General J. W. Whitfield

DEPARTMENT of MISSISSIPPI and EASTERN LOUISIANA
Commanding General – Lieutenant General John C. Pemberton

1st Military District (N. E. Miss.): **Brigadier General Daniel Ruggles**

2nd Military District (Vicksburg): **Major General Carter L. Stevenson**

Stevenson's Division: (Major General Carter L. Stevenson)
1st (Ga.) Brigade: Brigadier General Seth Barton
2nd (Ala.) Brigade: Brigadier General Stephen D. Lee
3rd (Ga.) Brigade: Brigadier General Alfred Cumming
4th (Tenn.) Brigade: Colonel A. W. Reynolds
Waul's (Tex.) Legion: Colonel T. N. Waul

Forney's Division: Major General John H. Forney
Moore's (Ala.) Brigade: Brigadier General John C. Moore
Hebert's (Miss.) Brigade: Brigadier General Louis Hebert

Smith's Division: Major General Martin Luther Smith
1st (La. & Miss.) Brigade: Brigadier General W. E. Baldwin
Vaughn's (Tenn.) Brigade: Brigadier General J. C. Vaughn
3rd (La.) Brigade: Brigadier General Francis A. Shoup
Mississippi State Troops: Brigadier General John V. Harris

Bowen's Division: Major General John S. Bowen
1st (Mo.) Brigade: Colonel Francis M. Cockrell
2nd (Ark.) Brigade: Brigadier General Martin E. Green

Loring's Division: Major General W. W. Loring
1st Brigade: Brigadier General Lloyd Tilghman
2nd (Miss.) Brigade: Brigadier General W. S. Featherston

3rd Military District (Port Hudson):
Major General Franklin Gardner (19 May)

Beall's Brigade: Brigadier General W. N. R. Beall
Left Wing Heavy Batteries: Lieutenant Colonel P. F. De Gournay
Miles' Command: Colonel W. R. Miles
Cavalry Brigade (Clinton, La.): Colonel John L. Logan

4th Military District (Jackson): (Major General John C. Breckinridge)

5th Military District (N. W. Miss.): Brig. General James R. Chalmers

1st (Cavalry) Brigade: Colonel Robert McCulloch
2nd (Cavalry) Brigade: Colonel W. F. Slemons
3rd (Partisan) Brigade: Brigadier General J. Z. George

DEPARTMENT of the GULF: (as of 8 June 1863)
Commanding General – Major General Dabney H. Maury

Slaughter's Brigade: Brigadier General J. E. Slaughter
Powell's Brigade: Colonel W. L. Powell
Post of Pascagoula: Colonel J. H. Marshall
Eastern Division: Brigadier General James Cantey

DEPARTMENT OF EAST TENNESSEE: (as of c. 31 May 1863)
Commanding General – Major General Simon Bolivar Buckner

1st Brigade: Brigadier General William Preston
2nd Brigade: Colonel Robert C. Trigg (probably)
3rd Brigade: Brigadier General Archibald Gracie, Jr.
4th Brigade: Brigadier General Alfred E. Jackson
5th Brigade: Brigadier General John W. Frazer
1st Cavalry Brigade: Brigadier General John Pegram
2nd Cavalry Brigade: Colonel John S. Scott (probably)

DEPARTMENT No. 2 and ARMY OF TENNESSEE
Commanding General – General Braxton Bragg
Chief of Staff – Brigadier General William W. MacKall

> Artillery Reserve: Colonel James Deshler
> District of Northern Alabama (Cav. Brigade):
>   Brigadier General Philip D. Roddey
> Jackson's Brigade: Brigadier General John K. Jackson
>
> **Forrest's Cavalry Division: Brigadier General Nathan B. Forrest**
> 1st Brigade: Brigadier General Frank C. Armstrong
> 2nd Brigade: Colonel James W. Starnes
> Artillery: Major John H. Rawle

1ST ARMY CORPS:[24] **Lieutenant General Leonidas Polk**

> **Cheatham's Division: Major General Frank Cheatham**
> Maney's (Tenn.) Brigade: Brigadier General George Earl Maney
> Smith's (Tenn.) Brigade: Brigadier General Preston Smith
> Wright's (Tenn.) Brigade: Brigadier General Marcus Joseph Wright
> Stewart's (Tenn.) Brigade: Colonel Otho French Strahl
>
> **Withers' Division: Major General Jones Mitchell Withers**
> Anderson's (Miss.) Brigade: Brigadier General J. Patton Anderson
> Deas' (Ala.) Brigade: Brigadier General Zachariah Cantey Deas
> Walthall's (Miss.) Brigade: Brigadier General E. C. Walthall
> Manigault's (Ala.) Brigade: Brigadier General A. M. Manigault

2ND ARMY CORPS: Lieutenant General William J. Hardee

> **Cleburne's Division: Major General Patrick R. Cleburne**
> Wood's (Ala.) Brigade: Brigadier General Sterling Alexander Wood
> Churchill's (Tex./Ark.) Brigade: Brigadier General T. J. Churchill
> Liddell's (Ark.) Brigade: Brigadier General St. John R. Liddell
> Polk's (Tenn./Ark.) Brigade: Brigadier General Lucius E. Polk
>
> **Stewart's Division: Major General Alexander P. Stewart**
> Jackson's (Tenn.) Brigade: Brigadier General Bushrod R. Johnson
> Brown's (Tenn.) Brigade: Brigadier General John C. Brown
> Bate's Brigade: Brigadier General W. B. Bate
> Clayton's (Ala.) Brigade: Brigadier General H. D. Clayton

Cavalry Corps: Major General Joseph Wheeler

Wharton's Division: Brigadier General John A. Wharton
1st Brigade: Colonel Charles C. Crews (probably)
2nd Brigade: Colonel Thomas Harrison (probably)

Martin's Division: Brigadier General William T. Martin
1st Brigade: Colonel James Hagan (probably)
2nd Brigade: Colonel A. A. Russell (probably)

Morgan's Division: Brigadier General John Hunt Morgan
1st Brigade: Colonel Basil W. Duke
2nd Brigade: Colonel Adam R. Johnson

* Included all the organizations listed below it.

BIBLIOGRAPHY

ALL BOOKS AND ARTICLES CITED in chapter notes are listed below, as well a few others that were consulted but not quoted. As with the previous volume of this series, my chief reliance has been on the Official Records, actually titled *War of the Rebellion*. Again, Long's *Civil War Day by Day* provided an excellent starting place, and Boatner's *Civil War Dictionary* provided many useful facts about various generals. Dana's *Recollections,* Grant's *Personal Memoirs,* Longstreet's book and Porter Alexander's, and *Battles and Leaders* all added useful first-hand accounts. Hoehling's day-to-day recounting of the siege of Vicksburg was extremely useful and saved me from having to find individual first-hand accounts of it such as he collected. I thank my fellow former employees of the old Fallbrook *Enterprise* for the gift of it. Hewitt's and Cunningham's two books on Port Hudson helped me make sense of a campaign that has received far less attention than it deserves. And my chief guide for Confederate doings in Maryland and Pennsylvania leading up to the battle of Gettysburg was Nye's *Here Come the Rebels!,* without which this volume would have been much the poorer.

Books

Alexander, Edward Porter. *Military Memoirs of a Confederate.* Da Capo Press edition, New York, 1993.

Basler, Roy P., editor. *The Collected Works of Abraham Lincoln.* 8 volumes. New Brunswick NJ., 1953-1955.

Bearss, Edwin C. *Forrest at Brice's Cross Roads and in North Mississippi in 1864.* Dayton OH, 1979.

Beymer, William Gilmore. *Scouts and Spies of the Civil War.*

Lincoln NB, 2003.

Boatner, Mark Mayo III. *The Civil War Dictionary*. New York, 1959.

Bowden, Scott and Bill Ward. *Last Chance for Victory: Robert E. Lee and the Gettysburg Campaign*. Conshohocken PA, 2001.

Bradley, Michael R. *Tullahoma: The 1863 Campaign for the Control of Middle Tennessee*. Shippensburg PA, 2000.

Brooks, Noah. *Washington, D.C., in Lincoln's Time*. Athens GA, 1958 – originally titled *Washington in Lincoln's Time*, New York, 1895.

Carter, Samuel III. *The Final Fortress: The Campaign for Vicksburg 1862-1863*. New York, 1980.

Catton, Bruce. *Grant Moves South*. Boston, 1960.

Coddington, Edwin B. *The Gettysburg Campaign: A Study in Command*. New York, 1969.

Coffin, Howard. *Nine Months to Gettysburg: Stannard's Vermonters and the Repulse of Pickett's Charge*. Woodstock VT, 1997.

Coggins, Jack. *Arms and Equipment of the Civil War*. Garden City NY, 1962.

Cornish, Dudley Taylor. *The Sable Arm: Black Troops in the Union Army, 1861-1865*. Lawrence KS, 1987.

Cozzens, Peter. *This Terrible Sound: The Battle of Chickamauga*. Urbana IL and Chicago, 1992.

Cunningham, Edward. *The Port Hudson Campaign, 1862-1863*. Baton Rouge LA, 1963.

Dana, Charles A. *Recollections of the Civil War*. First Collier Books edition, New York, 1963.

Doubleday, Abner. *Chancellorsville and Gettysburg*. New York, 1882.

Douglas, Henry Kyd. *I Rode With Stonewall*. Mockingbird Books pocket edition, Atlanta, 1974.

Emilio, Luis F. *A Brave Black Regiment: History of the Fifty-fourth Regiment of Massachusetts Volunteer Infantry 1863-1865*. Bantam Books edition, New York, 1992.

Faust, Patricia, editor. *Historical Times Illustrated Encyclopedia of*

the Civil War. New York, 1986.
Feis, William B. *Grant's Secret Service: The Intelligence War from Belmont to Appomattox*. Lincoln NB, 2002.
Field, Ron. *American Civil War Fortifications (3): The Mississippi and River Forts*. Oxford UK, 2007.
Fishel, Edwin C. *The Secret War for the Union: The Untold Story of Military Intelligence in the Civil War*. Boston and New York, 1996.
Freeman, Douglas Southall. *Lee's Lieutenants*. 3 volumes, New York, 1942-4.
----------, *R. E. Lee: A Biography*, 4 volumes, New York, 1934-5.
Grant, Ulysses S. *Personal Memoirs of U. S. Grant*. 2 volumes. New York, 1885.
Greene, Francis Vinton. *The Mississippi*. New York, 1882.
Hewett, Lawrence Lee. *Port Hudson, Confederate Bastion on the Mississippi*. Baton Rouge, 1987.
Hoehling, A. A. *Vicksburg: 47 Days of Siege*. New York, 1969.
Horan, James D. *Confederate Agent: A Discovery in History*. New York, 1954.
Johnson, Robert Underwood and Clarence Clough Buel, editors. *Battles and Leaders of the Civil War*. 4 volumes. New York, 1888 (Castle Books edition, New York, 1956).
Jones, Archer. *Confederate Strategy from Shiloh to Vicksburg*. Baton Rouge, 1961.
Jones, John B. *A Rebel War Clerk's Diary*. Sagamore Press condensed edition. New York, 1958.
Jones, Virgil Carrington. *Ranger Mosby*. Chapel Hill NC, 1944.
Josephy, Alvin M., Jr. *The Civil War in the American West*. New York, 1991.
Kegel, James A. *North with Lee and Jackson: The Lost Story of Gettysburg*. Mechanicsburg PA, 1996.
Lesser, W. Hunter. *Rebels at the Gate: Lee and McClellan on the Front Line of a Nation Divided*. Naperville IL, 2004.
Long, E. B., with Barbara Long. *The Civil War Day by Day: An Almanac 1861-1865*. Garden City NY, 1971.
Longacre, Edward G. *The Cavalry at Gettysburg*. Lincoln NB,

1986.

----------- *Grant's Cavalryman: The Life and Wars of General James H. Wilson.* Mechanicsburg PA, 1972.

Longstreet, James. *From Manassas to Appomattox: Memoirs of the Civil War in America.* Mallard Press edition, New York, 1991.

Marszalek, John F. *Sherman: A Soldier's Passion for Order.* New York, 1993.

McClellan, H. B. *I Rode With Jeb Stuart.* Da Capo Press edition, New York, 1994.

McDonough, James Lee and James Pickett Jones, *War So Terrible: Sherman and Atlanta.* New York, 1987.

Miers, Earl Schenck. *The Web of Victory: Grant at Vicksburg.* Baton Rouge, 1955.

Mingus, Scott L., Sr. *Flames Beyond Gettysburg: The Confederate Expedition to the Susquehanna River, June 1863.* New York, 2011.

Monaghan, Jay. *Civil War on the Western Border 1854-1865.* New York, 1960.

Mosby, John S. *Gray Ghost: The Memoirs of Colonel John S. Mosby.* Bantam pocket edition, 1992. Originally published in 1917 as *The Memoirs of Colonel John S. Mosby.*

Nichols, Edward J. *Toward Gettysburg: A Biography of General John F. Reynolds.* Pennsylvania, 1958.

Nolan, Alan T. *The Iron Brigade: A Military History.* Fourth edition. Bloomington IN and Indianapolis, 1961.

Nye, Wilbur Sturtevant. *Here Come the Rebels!* Baton Rouge LA, 1965.

Palmer, Michael A. *Lee Moves North: Robert E. Lee on the Offensive.* New York, 1998.

Pfanz, Harry W. *Gettysburg – The First Day.* Chapel Hill NC, 2001.

Ramage, James A. *Rebel Raider: The Life of General John Hunt Morgan.* Lexington KY, 1986.

Schultz, Duane. *The Most Glorious Fourth: Vicksburg and Gettysburg, July 4, 1863.* New York, 2002.

Sears, Stephen W. *Gettysburg.* New York/Boston, 2003.

Sherman, William T. *Memoirs of General William T. Sherman.* Da Capo Press 1-volume paperback edition, New York, 1984.

Starr, Stephen Z. *The Union Cavalry in the Civil War.* 3 volumes. Baton Rouge, 1979-85.

Still, William N., Jr. *Iron Afloat: The Story of the Confederate Ironclads.* Nashville, 1971.

Thompson, John W., Jr. *Jeb Stuart.* New York, 1930.

Trotter, William R. *Ironclads and Columbiads: The Civil War in North Carolina: The Coast.* Winston-Salem, 1989.

Trudeau, Noah Andre. *Gettysburg: A Testing of Courage.* New York, 2002.

Urwin, Gregory J. W. *Custer Victorious: The Civil War Battles of General George Armstrong Custer.* East Brunswick NJ, 1983.

U.S. War Department. *The War of the Rebellion: a Compilation of the Official Records of the Union and Confederate Armies.* 70 "volumes" in 128 parts. Washington, 1891-1895. National Historical Society reprint, Harrisburg PA, 1971. Cited in notes as OR.

West, Richard S., Jr. *Mr. Lincoln's Navy.* New York, London and Toronto, 1957.

Wingert, Cooper H. *The Confederate Approach on Harrisburg: The Gettysburg Campaign's Northernmost Reaches.* Charleston, 2012.

Wise, Stephen R. *Gate of Hell: Campaign for Charleston Harbor, 1863.* Columbia SC, 1994.

Wittenberg, Eric J. And J. David Petruzzi. *Plenty of Blame to Go Around: Jeb Stuart's Controversial Ride to Gettysburg.* New York and California, 2011.

～ Articles ～

Benjamin, Charles F. "Hooker's Appointment and Removal." In *Battles and Leaders of the Civil War,* Vol. 3.

Feis, William B. "The Deception of Braxton Bragg." In *Blue &*

Gray Magazine, Vol 10, Issue 1 (October 1992).

Hickenlooper, Andrew. "The Vicksburg Mine." In *Battles and Leaders of the Civil War,* Vol. 3.

Hill, Daniel H. "Chickamauga – The Great Battle of the West." In *Battles and Leaders of the Civil War,* Vol. 3.

Stuntz, Margaret L. "Lightning Strike at the Gap." In *America's Civil War,* July 1997.

Index of Names

A

Abercrombie, John J. 272, 404, 474
Abrams, Alexander 103, 104, 262, 268
Adams, Wirt 106
Alexander, E. Porter 83, 85, 110, 170, 320, 552
Allen, William 540
Ames, Adelbert 146, 158, 163, 203
Anderson, Archer 466
Anderson, Ephraim 44, 96
Anderson, Richard H. 83, 156, 185, 250, 278, 313, 360, 437, 445, 471, 552, 555, 581, 582
Andrew, John A. 69
Andrews, George L. 56, 59
Augur, Christopher C. 15, 32, 50, 51, 52, 56, 59, 60, 188, 219
Averell, William W. 157, 254
Aylett, W. R. 127

B

Babcock, John C. 332, 333, 350, 406
Baird, J. P. 154, 173
Balfour, Emma 38, 45, 48, 64, 76, 88, 104
Banks, Nathaniel P. 1, 5, 6, 7, 8, 14, 15, 20, 28, 32, 33, 36, 41, 43, 46, 49, 50, 51, 56, 59, 60, 61, 77, 79, 81, 92, 93, 94, 95, 96, 101, 112, 113, 114, 115, 128, 134, 147, 149, 178, 187, 188, 192, 209, 218, 219, 222, 258, 299, 338, 339, 369, 375, 392, 431, 436, 437, 459, 460, 506, 540, 587
Barnes, James 352
Bartlett, Frank A. 135, 147
Bartlett, William F. 60
Bate, William B. 389, 390
Beall, N. R. 51, 57

Beatty, John 452
Beauregard, P. G. T. 46, 68, 183, 184, 349, 376, 377, 381, 385, 413, 414, 415, 426, 502, 529, 588
Bell, Robert 441
Benham, Henry W. 204
Benjamin, Charles F. 479, 480, 482, 483
Bevier, R. S. 129, 130
Birge, Henry W. 220
Birney, David 204, 446
Bixby, A. H. 307
Blackford, William 489
Blair, Francis P., Jr. (Frank) 47, 49, 74, 78, 93, 105, 106, 107, 130, 190, 301
Blair, Francis P., Sr. 49
Blair, Montgomery 49
Blythe, Green L. 364
Bowen, John S. 31, 104, 430, 566
Bowles, William A. 319
Boyd, William H. 218, 238, 239, 247, 248, 329, 330, 361, 396, 397, 418, 438, 469, 471, 573
Bragg, Braxton 11, 31, 32, 44, 65, 68, 75, 91, 101, 102, 108, 109, 150, 151, 153, 173, 177, 178, 183, 191, 192, 193, 194, 197, 198, 205, 206, 208, 212, 228, 263, 293, 298, 299, 305, 336, 339, 340, 345, 367, 380, 381, 382, 383, 385, 386, 413, 415, 420, 421, 423, 426, 450, 451, 452, 454, 455, 461, 462, 502, 506, 507, 534, 535, 536, 537, 567, 568, 585, 586, 587, 588
Brannan, John M. 421, 450, 567
Breckinridge, John C. 31, 98, 102, 150, 192, 224, 382, 533
Brisbane, William 576
Brooks, W. T. H. (Bully) 172, 186, 187, 231, 283, 310, 331
Buckner, Simon Bolivar 145, 152,

263, 298, 299, 327, 336, 367, 368,
413, 415, 423, 451, 502, 536, 568
Buford, Abraham 158
Buford, John 17, 71, 119, 123, 146,
158, 159, 160, 162, 163, 165, 167,
168, 186, 307, 315, 335, 354, 355,
475, 484, 521, 553, 554, 555, 556,
557, 559, 584
Burnside, Ambrose 42, 68, 75, 76,
91, 92, 98, 102, 108, 115, 145, 173,
190, 192, 196, 209, 228, 261, 263,
264, 283, 299, 320, 321, 322, 336,
367, 368, 403, 413, 415, 450, 542,
568, 569
Butler, Benjamin 47
Butterfield, Daniel 19, 70, 119, 146,
168, 185, 203, 204, 212, 213, 233,
234, 253, 293, 308, 309, 335, 350,
402, 404, 405, 408, 409, 410, 411,
446, 475, 476, 477, 478, 480, 481,
482, 486, 521, 524, 560
Byrd, R. K. 337

C

Cadwalader, George 276
Calef, John 556
Campbell, Archibald P. 454
Carter, Thomas H. 242, 243
Chalmers, James R. 43, 364, 365
Chambliss, John R. 250, 278, 287,
288, 307, 315, 316, 352, 354, 355,
408, 489, 491, 547, 548, 549
Chapin, Edward P. 59, 60
Chase, Salmon P. 19
Cleburne, Patrick 421, 451, 453, 507
Collins, Charles R. 100, 121
Colquitt, Alfred H. 466, 502
Comstock, Cyrus 539
Connolly, James A. 388, 389, 390
Conrad, Thomas Nelson 490
Cooke, John R. 156, 377, 502, 503
Cooper, Samuel 174, 183, 299, 328,
377, 529, 530
Corse, M. D. 328, 347, 377, 447,
466, 502, 503, 518, 529
Couch, Darius 18, 172, 186, 187,
205, 231, 252, 256, 269, 270, 271,
276, 280, 282, 283, 293, 310, 311,
328, 329, 330, 331, 332, 350, 351,
362, 379, 399, 400, 403, 404, 409,
418, 440, 442, 443, 444, 446, 468,
471, 476, 483, 485, 521, 523, 524,
542, 543, 558, 559, 573, 575, 577
Cox, Jacob D. 264
Crane, C. R. 311
Crawford, S. W. 378, 404, 411, 412,
475, 551
Crittenden, John J. 384
Crittenden, Thomas L. 384, 387,
421, 534, 536, 537
Cullum, G. W. 20
Curtin, Andrew G. 204, 214, 231,
232, 234, 251, 283, 397, 399, 437,
440, 444, 470, 498, 543
Curtis, Samuel 33, 34, 35
Custer, George Armstrong 158, 162,
291, 484, 521, 522, 547, 549, 550
Custis, George Washington Parke
417

D

Dabney, Frederick Y. 46
Dahlgren, John A. 22, 294, 343, 449
Dahlgren, Ulric 22, 146, 164, 273,
286, 295, 343
Dana, Charles A. 24, 25, 26, 27, 28,
36, 72, 79, 92, 94, 102, 103, 104,
106, 107, 130, 131, 132, 133, 138,
141, 148, 150, 177, 191, 193, 208,
223, 260, 266, 299, 303, 323, 325,
365, 366, 384, 385, 426, 427, 431,
462, 464, 482, 509, 532, 539, 564
Daniel, Junius 418
Davis, Benjamin Franklin (Grimes)
158, 161, 162
Davis, Hasbrouck 417
Davis, Jefferson 11, 12, 29, 31, 42,
47, 85, 86, 97, 98, 99, 126, 127,

144, 179, 249, 263, 298, 299, 327, 328, 334, 339, 340, 375, 381, 413, 414, 426, 501, 502, 503, 529, 584, 586, 587
Davis, Jefferson C. 153
Davis, Joseph, jr. 185, 503
Davis, Joseph, sr. 339
Dennis, Elias S. 137, 138, 141, 147, 190, 366, 373, 432
Denver, James William 95
Devin, Thomas C. 158, 162, 355, 556
Dix, John A. 67, 68, 87, 119, 122, 125, 181, 182, 186, 202, 229, 256, 284, 312, 377, 378, 416, 417, 449, 465, 466, 503, 529, 530, 571
Dodd, Theodore H. 570
Dodge, Grenville 462
Douglas, Henry Kyd 309
Dow, Neal 57, 58, 541
Dow, Tristam T. 337
Duffié, Alfred N. 159, 160, 164, 165, 167, 288, 291, 292, 306, 307, 309
Duke, Basil 183
Du Pont, Samuel 20, 112
Dwight, William 50, 52, 54, 56, 80, 188, 219, 338, 436

E

Early, Jubal 82, 119, 214, 232, 237, 241, 242, 247, 248, 250, 277, 278, 279, 309, 312, 313, 360, 379, 397, 419, 439, 440, 442, 443, 467, 468, 476, 483, 495, 496, 500, 517, 518, 524, 526, 527, 544, 547, 549, 551, 553, 555, 572
Eckert, Thomas T. 486
Ellet, A. W. 266
Ellet, Charles 78, 80
Elliott, Washington 245, 560, 580
Ely, William G. 246
Elzey, Arnold 67, 127, 128, 212, 328, 413, 503
Emory, William H. 50, 338, 437, 459, 506
Everett, P. M. 229
Ewell, Richard S. 82, 83, 85, 119, 121, 126, 154, 155, 168, 179, 185, 200, 201, 202, 212, 213, 214, 216, 217, 218, 230, 231, 232, 233, 234, 235, 236, 237, 239, 241, 242, 244, 247, 248, 249, 250, 252, 270, 272, 278, 279, 293, 309, 312, 314, 327, 347, 350, 352, 357, 359, 360, 374, 375, 379, 395, 397, 398, 399, 401, 407, 411, 419, 438, 439, 445, 447, 467, 468, 469, 470, 498, 500, 501, 517, 518, 524, 525, 526, 527, 543, 544, 545, 546, 557, 558, 559, 575, 578, 582, 584, 585
Ewen, John 328, 574, 575

F

Fagan, James F. 435
Farnan, James 566
Farnsworth, Elon J. 484, 521, 547, 548, 549
Farragut, David G. 20, 49, 50, 52, 218, 222, 338, 436
Finnie, J. Orr 265
Foote, Andrew H. 112, 184, 207, 259, 343, 375, 449
Foreman, John M. 570
Forney, John H. 430, 540, 563, 564, 566
Forrest, Nathan B. 65, 192, 218, 380, 382, 383, 454, 536
Foster, Henry C. 225
Foster, J. G. 158, 332, 465
Foster, W. L. 262
Franklin, William B. 542
Frayser, Richard E. 121
Freeman, Fletcher 311, 312
Fremantle, Arthur 438, 471
Fremont, John Charles 47
French, S. G. 72
French, William [Confederate] 443
French, William H. [Union] 400,

401, 411, 445, 478, 560, 561, 577, 579, 580
Frick, Jacob 497
Fry, James B. 320
Fry, William H. 522

G

Galligher, James A. 282
Gamble, Hamilton R. 34
Gamble, Richard H. 34, 35
Gamble, William 307, 315, 316, 355, 555, 556
Gantt, E. W. 208
Gardner, Franklin 15, 32, 33, 46, 51, 54, 60, 81, 188, 219
Garfield, James 154, 173, 205, 207, 451, 452, 455
Getty, G. W. 76, 416, 571
Gibson, William H. 422
Gillis, James H. 127
Gillmore, Quincy A. 20, 112, 207, 258, 259
Gilmor, Harry 395, 396
Ginder, Henry 150, 210, 265, 510
Gist, States Rights 45, 46
Gordon, George H. 87, 312
Gordon, John B. 237, 241, 440, 442, 467, 468, 495, 496, 497, 526
Gorgas, Josiah 156
Granger, Gordon 153, 383, 384, 385, 386, 387, 421, 452, 453, 454, 455
Grant, Ulysses S. (Sam) 1, 5, 6, 7, 8, 9, 10, 11, 12, 14, 15, 17, 24, 25, 26, 27, 28, 31, 32, 33, 35, 36, 39, 40, 42, 43, 44, 46, 47, 48, 49, 51, 65, 68, 74, 77, 78, 79, 80, 81, 91, 92, 93, 94, 95, 96, 97, 98, 101, 102, 104, 105, 106, 107, 108, 109, 113, 114, 115, 128, 129, 130, 131, 132, 133, 135, 140, 145, 147, 148, 149, 150, 152, 176, 177, 179, 189, 190, 191, 192, 197, 205, 206, 208, 209, 210, 211, 212, 223, 260, 261, 263, 264, 266, 267, 301, 302, 303, 304, 305, 323, 324, 338, 339, 342, 345, 365, 366, 367, 372, 373, 378, 381, 383, 385, 392, 426, 428, 430, 431, 432, 433, 434, 461, 462, 463, 464, 465, 482, 485, 509, 510, 511, 531, 533, 539, 540, 541, 563, 564, 565, 586, 587
Greeley, Horace 69
Green, Thomas 369, 458, 504, 505
Gregg, David M. 71, 146, 159, 160, 162, 163, 164, 165, 166, 167, 168, 186, 288, 292, 307, 315, 335, 353, 354, 355, 356, 407, 475, 484, 486, 520, 521, 525, 557
Gregg, J. Irvin 307, 315, 353, 354
Grierson, Benjamin 32, 41, 43, 44, 93, 95, 113, 114, 115, 128
Grimes, Absalom 134
Grover, Cuvier 50, 51, 54, 56, 59, 188, 220

H

Halleck, Henry W. 20, 22, 33, 35, 47, 66, 68, 77, 87, 91, 95, 101, 102, 107, 108, 112, 113, 115, 122, 123, 124, 149, 157, 158, 176, 178, 180, 185, 192, 193, 197, 200, 201, 202, 208, 213, 214, 229, 230, 231, 252, 253, 254, 255, 258, 259, 269, 271, 272, 273, 274, 275, 276, 280, 282, 283, 286, 293, 303, 309, 312, 313, 314, 320, 323, 331, 332, 334, 344, 350, 368, 373, 377, 399, 400, 401, 402, 403, 405, 409, 410, 411, 412, 413, 416, 417, 431, 433, 444, 449, 460, 461, 462, 464, 465, 474, 475, 476, 477, 478, 479, 481, 484, 485, 486, 487, 488, 504, 522, 530, 559, 560, 571, 577, 578, 580, 584
Haller, Granville O. 440, 441, 442, 467, 468, 496, 497
Hall, Richard R. 63
Hampton, Wade 155, 162, 163, 166, 250, 278, 308, 316, 352, 353, 354,

356, 358, 398, 408, 472, 473, 489, 547, 549, 550, 551
Hancock, Winfield S. 18, 233, 234, 252, 400, 407, 408, 418, 446, 524, 525, 551, 584
Hardee, William J. 212, 381, 382, 383, 386, 389, 450, 451, 453, 462, 507, 534, 535, 568
Hardie, James A. 479, 480, 483
Hargrove, T. L. 447, 448
Harrison, Henry Thomas 501, 517, 554
Hart, James 166
Hartsuff, George L. 75, 91, 92, 109, 336, 368, 450, 568, 569
Harvie, E. J. 339
Hatch, Edward 43, 364
Haupt, Herman 543, 560, 577
Hawes, J. M. 139, 140
Hays, Harry 217, 241
Heintzelman, Samuel P. 124, 125, 271, 272, 402, 403, 404, 410, 412, 413, 444, 472, 473, 474, 476, 484, 487
Herron, Francis J. 176, 177, 191, 192, 209, 223, 260, 261, 365, 372, 509, 510
Heth, Henry (Harry) 83, 121, 185, 250, 278, 437, 503, 527, 553, 554, 581, 584
Hickenlooper, Andrew 48, 65, 73, 77, 88, 104, 109, 115, 129, 132, 134, 150, 175, 193, 224, 262, 268, 300, 304, 323, 325, 343, 366, 374, 392, 427, 428, 429, 430, 432, 464, 509, 563
Hill, Ambrose Powell (A. P.) 74, 82, 83, 85, 121, 126, 127, 156, 170, 182, 185, 202, 232, 233, 235, 249, 250, 253, 255, 270, 272, 275, 278, 279, 293, 313, 327, 335, 350, 351, 352, 359, 360, 375, 397, 399, 419, 420, 437, 438, 445, 471, 500, 524, 527, 544, 552, 554, 557, 558, 559, 578, 581, 582, 584

Hill, Daniel Harvey (D. H.) 72, 83, 85, 86, 91, 155, 214, 328, 348, 349, 363, 385, 415, 416, 466, 502, 530, 553, 585, 586
Hillyer, William S. 94, 95
Hines, Thomas H. 229, 263, 297, 305, 306, 319, 368, 569
Holmes, Theophilus H. 434, 435, 460, 513, 570
Hood, John B. (Sam) 66, 67, 72, 83, 86, 110, 122, 154, 155, 157, 185, 312, 313, 420, 437, 471, 472, 552
Hooker, Joseph 12, 13, 16, 17, 18, 19, 21, 22, 23, 65, 66, 67, 69, 70, 71, 72, 86, 87, 99, 100, 101, 110, 119, 122, 123, 125, 146, 156, 159, 163, 164, 168, 172, 180, 181, 182, 185, 186, 201, 202, 203, 212, 213, 214, 217, 229, 230, 231, 232, 233, 234, 235, 249, 252, 253, 254, 255, 269, 270, 271, 272, 273, 274, 275, 276, 279, 280, 286, 288, 293, 294, 295, 307, 308, 309, 313, 314, 332, 333, 334, 335, 343, 350, 351, 358, 359, 363, 374, 378, 379, 393, 399, 400, 401, 402, 404, 405, 408, 409, 410, 411, 412, 413, 444, 445, 446, 472, 473, 474, 475, 476, 477, 478, 479, 480, 481, 482, 483, 484, 485, 488, 489, 501, 503, 519, 525, 560, 585
Hotchkiss, Jed 438, 526
Houston, David C. 299
Hovey, Alvin P. 47, 191
Howard, Oliver O. 202, 204, 309, 403, 408, 446, 476, 524, 558, 559, 584
Huey, Pennock 407, 484
Humphreys, Andrew A. 482, 580
Hunter, David 20, 111, 112, 183, 184, 375
Hunter, Sherod 369
Hurlbut, Stephen 6, 10, 27, 28, 31, 42, 43, 77, 80, 91, 93, 94, 101, 108, 177, 191, 211, 364, 373, 461, 510

I

Imboden, John D. 21, 84, 144, 145, 239, 281, 282, 326, 327, 330, 352, 360, 517, 545, 581
Ingalls, Rufus 293, 314, 476, 486, 487, 488, 489
Irwin, Richard B. 49, 51, 61, 188

J

Jackson, Andrew 49
Jackson, Thomas J. (Stonewall) 12, 13, 17, 65, 82, 83, 84, 85, 111, 135, 159, 185, 231, 234, 278, 348
Jackson, William H. (Red) 102, 109, 382
Jenkins, Albert G. 21, 84, 144, 145, 146, 157, 161, 200, 214, 215, 216, 237, 239, 240, 242, 243, 244, 247, 248, 250, 276, 277, 281, 282, 309, 329, 330, 333, 347, 351, 352, 358, 359, 360, 361, 362, 379, 395, 396, 397, 418, 419, 468, 469, 470, 498, 499, 500, 502, 503, 525, 526, 542, 543, 544, 348, 573, 574
Jenkins, Micah 348, 349, 416, 466
Jennings, William 440, 441, 442, 443
Jewett, A. B. 402, 404
Johnson, Amory K. 74, 105, 106, 107
Johnson, Andrew 76
Johnson, Bushrod 390
Johnson, Edward (Allegheny) 82, 83, 214, 237, 242, 245, 246, 247, 248, 278, 279, 309, 361, 395, 397, 438, 468, 470, 526, 544, 573, 582
Johnson, Richard 391
Johnston, Joseph E. 9, 10, 11, 12, 28, 29, 31, 32, 33, 43, 44, 45, 46, 47, 48, 49, 50, 65, 68, 72, 74, 77, 78, 80, 81, 88, 91, 93, 94, 96, 97, 98, 101, 102, 107, 108, 109, 113, 114, 115, 125, 128, 130, 133, 134, 149, 150, 151, 152, 153, 158, 177, 178, 183, 188, 189, 191, 192, 193, 195, 197, 198, 206, 207, 208, 209, 211, 212, 223, 224, 228, 261, 263, 267, 268, 298, 305, 322, 338, 339, 340, 341, 345, 364, 365, 366, 367, 372, 373, 381, 382, 392, 415, 426, 431, 433, 437, 458, 461, 462, 463, 464, 502, 510, 511, 531, 532, 533, 540, 565, 586, 587, 588
Jones, Samuel 145, 327, 415, 423, 451, 568
Jones, William E. (Grumble) 21, 22, 66, 160, 161, 162, 163, 164, 166, 239, 250, 278, 280, 316, 352, 354, 355, 398, 399, 419, 519, 545, 571, 585
Judah, Henry M. 449, 450, 569

K

Keifer, J. Warren 237
Kelley, Benjamin F. 157, 216, 231, 234, 238, 254, 281, 282, 326, 330, 399, 400
Kershaw, Joseph 552
Ketchum, W. Scott 334
Keyes, Erasmus D. 67, 87, 126, 284, 393, 416, 465, 571
Kilpatrick, Hugh Judson 67, 68, 70, 100, 110, 288, 289, 290, 291, 292, 315, 352, 353, 354, 356, 484, 521, 525, 547, 548, 549, 550, 551, 555, 557, 572, 573, 577
Kimball, Nathan 42, 106, 107, 115, 130, 132, 133, 149, 267, 427
Knipe, Joseph F. 329, 351, 360, 361, 363, 396, 397, 418, 470, 471, 499, 500, 575

L

Lauman, Jacob G. 28, 107, 191, 209, 260, 261, 365, 509
Law, Evander 552

Lee, "Captain" 576
Lee, Fitzhugh (Fitz) 154, 162, 168, 250, 287, 288, 408, 472, 473, 484, 486, 487, 520, 546, 547, 549, 550, 551, 572, 575, 278
Lee, George Washington Custis 503
Lee, Robert E. 1, 12, 13, 14, 16, 17, 18, 21, 22, 38, 47, 66, 67, 68, 72, 74, 82, 83, 84, 85, 86, 87, 97, 99, 100, 110, 111, 119, 120, 121, 122, 123, 124, 125, 126, 127, 144, 145, 154, 155, 156, 157, 158, 159, 168, 172, 179, 180, 181, 182, 183, 185, 192, 195, 200, 202, 203, 209, 212, 214, 217, 218, 229, 230, 231, 232, 235, 236, 239, 244, 248, 249, 250, 252, 253, 254, 269, 271, 273, 277, 278, 279, 280, 283, 287, 293, 308, 309, 310, 312, 313, 314, 326, 327, 328, 332, 333, 334, 335, 347, 348, 350, 356, 357, 358, 359, 362, 374, 375, 377, 378, 381, 397, 399, 400, 403, 408, 411, 413, 415, 420, 437, 438, 439, 471, 472, 473, 476, 478, 482, 485, 486, 489, 491, 500, 501, 502, 503, 510, 517, 518, 519, 523, 524, 526, 527, 529, 545, 546, 549, 552, 554, 555, 557, 560, 571, 576, 577, 578, 581, 582, 584, 585, 586, 587, 588
Lee, Robert, jr. 448
Lee, Stephen D. 45, 563
Lee, W. H. F. (Rooney) 126, 162, 167, 168, 250, 278, 287, 417, 448, 502, 541
Leggett, Mortimer 134
Liddell, St. John R. 507
Lily, Eli 389
Lincoln, Abraham 10, 15, 18, 19, 20, 24, 31, 34, 35, 42, 47, 49, 65, 68, 75, 76, 98, 100, 101, 104, 111, 122, 123, 125, 149, 180, 182, 194, 199, 203, 213, 229, 230, 231, 232, 233, 234, 235, 251, 254, 255, 269, 270, 271, 272, 273, 274, 275, 276, 303, 304, 324, 348, 374, 399, 413, 433, 479, 481, 484, 504, 514, 516, 541, 542
Littleton, J. K. 393
Lockett, Samuel 45
Lockwood, Henry H. 405, 409, 477, 559
Logan, John A. [Union] 47, 268, 564
Logan, John L. [Confederate] 81, 113, 114, 189, 541
Lomax, Lundsford 354
Long, A. L. 145
Longstreet, James 66, 72, 76, 83, 85, 86, 110, 125, 154, 155, 168, 185, 202, 212, 213, 217, 232, 233, 235, 249, 250, 254, 270, 272, 275, 278, 279, 287, 293, 310, 313, 327, 334, 348, 350, 351, 355, 356, 357, 358, 375, 397, 398, 399, 417, 420, 437, 471, 500, 501, 517, 518, 519, 552, 554, 558, 559, 578, 582
Lord, Lida 341
Lord, Margaret 10, 510
Lord, Willie 151, 300
Loring, W. W. 9, 10, 11, 45, 158, 261, 267, 426, 533
Loughborough, Mary 341
Lowell, Charles Russell 186, 473, 474, 476, 478, 486, 487, 488, 491, 522
Lyon, Hylan B. 188

M

Major, James P. 306, 338, 369
Mallory, Stephen 296
Marmaduke, John 435, 510, 513
Martin, William T. 167, 453, 454, 502
Maxey, Samuel B. 32
McArthur, John 78
McClellan, George B. 13, 273, 326, 333, 348, 361, 385, 433, 478, 479, 542
McClellan, Henry B. 120, 154, 155,

162, 165, 166, 169, 398, 488, 490
McClernand, John A. 6, 8, 9, 24, 25, 26, 27, 35, 36, 47, 48, 49, 79, 80, 88, 190, 209, 210, 260, 261, 300, 301, 302, 303, 304, 323, 366, 374, 432, 433, 464, 541
McClure, Alexander 251
McCook, Alexander 384, 387, 391, 420, 421, 450, 451, 534, 536
McCown, J. P. 102, 192
McCulloch, Henry E. 136, 137, 138, 139
McCulloch, Robert 365
McEntee, "Captain" 286, 287, 288
McGuinness, William 225
McIntosh, J. B. 520
McKowen, John 541
McLaws, Lafayette 83, 110, 350, 355, 420, 437, 552
McPherson, James B. 6, 8, 9, 25, 47, 48, 72, 80, 134, 190, 224, 225, 260, 299, 302, 303, 365, 431, 432, 463, 509, 532, 533, 539, 556, 563, 564
McRae, Dandridge 435, 513
McRae, Lucy 37, 342
McReynolds, A. T. 200, 215, 216, 217, 218, 237, 239, 245, 246, 253
Meade, George G. 18, 70, 100, 101, 119, 164, 185, 186, 204, 209, 308, 309, 335, 378, 408, 479, 480, 481, 482, 483, 484, 485, 486, 487, 488, 489, 490, 501, 518, 521, 522, 524, 525, 527, 543, 549, 551, 555, 557, 558, 559, 560, 577, 578, 579, 580, 581, 584, 585
Meade, George, jr. 480
Meigs, Montgomery C. 486, 487
Merritt, Adoniram J. 150
Merritt, Wesley 167, 168, 323, 357, 392, 484, 521
Miles, William R. 51, 57
Milroy, Robert 157, 200, 201, 214, 215, 216, 217, 218, 230, 231, 232, 235, 236, 238, 239, 240, 241, 242, 244, 245, 246, 247, 248, 249, 252,

253, 254, 270, 282, 326, 329, 330, 331, 332, 334, 350, 362, 363, 379, 395, 396, 403, 409, 420, 504, 516
Minty, Robert H. G. 453, 454
Mitchell, Robert B. 386, 387, 453, 454
Monroe, James 507
Montgomery, James 112, 184, 259
Moore, Alpheus S. 337
Moorman, Robert B. 362
Morgan, John Hunt 173, 183, 228, 229, 262, 263, 297, 305, 319, 336, 343, 367, 368, 382, 383, 449, 450, 537, 569
Morgan, Joseph S. 188
Morgan, Richard 537
Morris, Robert 163
Morton, James 536
Morton, Oliver P. 75
Mosby, John S. 66, 84, 186, 307, 308, 313, 358, 359, 398, 408, 447, 472, 473
Moss, Hugh 176
Mouton, Alfred 178, 187, 188, 458, 504
Mower, Joseph A. 78, 106, 107, 130, 147, 190, 192, 342, 343
Munford, Thomas 162, 250, 278, 287, 288, 289, 290, 291, 307, 316, 352

N

Naglee, Henry M. 465
Nasmith, Samuel J. 427, 461, 512, 537, 566
Negley, James S. 452, 567
Nelson, John A. 55, 56
Nickerson, Franklin S. 58

O

O'Brien, James 60
Oldroyd, Osborn 176, 224, 304, 322, 342

Ord, E. O. C. 209, 299, 300, 302, 303, 323, 366, 378, 431, 432, 509, 531, 563, 565
Osterhaus, P. J. 48, 79, 365, 463, 565

P

Paine, Halbert E. 50, 52, 54, 128, 134, 188, 220, 221, 222
Palfrey, John C. 299
Palmer, Charles A. 248, 387
Parke, John G. 261, 267, 304, 365, 463
Parsons, M. M. 513, 570
Parsons, W. H. 538
Patrick, Marsena 293, 314
Payne, William 548, 550
Peck, John J. 87, 186, 375
Pegram, John 367, 368, 568
Pemberton, John C. 8, 9, 10, 11, 12, 14, 29, 31, 32, 33, 36, 37, 44, 45, 46, 47, 65, 76, 80, 81, 87, 96, 98, 101, 104, 109, 113, 128, 129, 134, 150, 152, 178, 207, 209, 210, 211, 223, 224, 261, 268, 298, 305, 322, 340, 341, 342, 364, 372, 426, 433, 434, 463, 464, 510, 511, 533, 540, 566, 587
Pender, Dorsey 83, 170, 250, 278, 552, 581, 584
Pettigrew, J. Johnston 121, 127, 128, 185, 377, 553, 554, 556, 581
Piatt, Donn 200, 201, 216, 239, 254
Pickett, George 66, 67, 72, 83, 87, 100, 110, 121, 122, 127, 156, 185, 249, 328, 347, 348, 350, 377, 416, 417, 419, 438, 447, 518, 529, 530, 552, 581
Pierce, E.W. 569
Pitcher, T. G. 311
Pleasonton, Alfred 17, 18, 23, 70, 71, 146, 158, 159, 160, 162, 163, 164, 165, 167, 168, 180, 181, 185, 186, 202, 203, 204, 212, 229, 232, 233, 234, 235, 252, 253, 254, 269, 276, 286, 287, 288, 291, 293, 307, 308, 309, 315, 334, 335, 351, 352, 356, 403, 405, 407, 411, 417, 446, 483, 484, 486, 487, 488, 520, 521, 525, 547, 549, 551, 555, 557, 573, 585
Polk, Leonidas 381, 382, 383, 420, 450, 451, 462, 507, 534, 535, 568
Porter, David Dixon 7, 9, 11, 27, 37, 64, 77, 78, 95, 109, 130, 140, 177, 193, 266, 342, 366, 392, 509, 512
Prentiss, Benjamin M. 43, 461
Preston, William 263, 568
Price, Sterling 81, 108, 115, 211, 266, 373, 435, 460, 461, 463, 510, 513, 570
Prime, Frederick E. 40
Prince, Henry 465
Pruyn, Robert 188, 437

Q

Quinby, Isaac F. 48, 268, 343

R

Ransom, Matthew 349, 416, 502, 503
Ransom, T. E. G. 48, 65, 88, 262, 300, 323, 343, 464, 539, 564
Rawlins, John A. 25, 27, 31, 42, 43, 77, 106, 132, 133, 177, 190, 267, 302, 373, 463, 510
Reid, Greenberry 569
Reid, Hugh T. 174, 190, 538
Reynolds, J. J. 387, 390, 421, 450, 452
Reynolds, John F. 18, 100, 101, 186, 203, 204, 209, 212, 213, 234, 378, 379, 385, 405, 406, 411, 445, 446, 476, 480, 482, 524, 525, 552, 555, 557, 558, 559, 560, 577, 579, 580, 581, 584
Riggin, John Jr. 43, 79, 94, 149
Robertson, Beverly 21, 161, 162,

164, 165, 250, 278, 287, 307, 315, 316, 335, 352, 353, 354, 398, 399, 519, 545, 571, 585
Rodes, Robert 83, 119, 200, 214, 215, 216, 242, 243, 244, 248, 249, 277, 279, 310, 314, 333, 361, 362, 397, 418, 438, 468, 469, 470, 498, 524, 525, 526, 544, 545, 557
Rodgers, John 295, 296, 297
Rodgers, Robert S. 476
Rosecrans, William S. 1, 33, 34, 65, 68, 75, 91, 92, 93, 101, 102, 108, 109, 152, 153, 154, 177, 193, 197, 205, 207, 211, 212, 223, 263, 264, 269, 326, 336, 344, 367, 380, 382, 383, 384, 385, 386, 387, 388, 390, 410, 420, 421, 433, 450, 452, 506, 534, 535, 536, 567, 568, 586, 588
Rosser, Tom 289, 290, 291, 316
Rousseau, L. H. 450, 567
Routh, S. M. 136, 139
Ruggles, Daniel 364
Russell, D. A. 146, 159, 165, 167, 203

S

Sanders, William P. 223, 228, 297, 298, 321, 336, 343, 364, 368, 379, 382, 423, 451
Schaff, Philip 395, 420
Schenck, Robert C. 125, 201, 216, 218, 230, 231, 234, 238, 253, 254, 269, 270, 274, 280, 282, 310, 331, 332, 334, 350, 362, 363, 379, 399, 402, 403, 404, 409, 410, 444, 445, 474, 476, 477, 485, 519, 524, 559, 579
Schofield, John M. 33, 34, 102, 108, 115, 320
Scott, T. A. 234, 251, 543, 560
Seddon, James 100, 128, 151, 155, 178, 208, 212, 261, 268, 305, 338, 348, 363, 415, 466, 503, 530
Sedgwick, John 13, 204, 482, 524, 525, 557
Seymour, Horatio 251, 252
Sharpe, George H. 65, 286, 333, 350, 378, 406, 483, 524
Shaw, Robert Gould 111, 184
Sheridan, Philip H. 207, 451, 506, 567
Sherman, Thomas W. 33, 50, 51, 52, 54, 56, 57, 58, 59, 60, 188
Sherman, William Tecumseh 6, 7, 9, 11, 25, 28, 33, 45, 47, 49, 63, 64, 72, 73, 78, 80, 102, 103, 104, 106, 149, 189, 190, 223, 260, 261, 267, 299, 301, 302, 303, 304, 324, 365, 366, 372, 373, 384, 392, 426, 431, 432, 433, 462, 463, 464, 509, 511, 531, 532, 533, 540, 565
Shingler, W. P. 393
Shriver, William 546
Sickles, Daniel 19, 524
Sigel, Franz 47
Sinclair, George T. 296
Skelton, L. H. 423
Slocum, Henry W. 18, 308, 309, 350, 356, 405, 408, 474, 478, 524
Slough, John P. 412
Smith, A. J. 299, 372
Smith, B. F. 238, 239, 240, 243
Smith, E. Kirby 79, 81, 96, 97, 114, 138, 150, 174, 178, 187, 209, 339, 364, 392, 433, 434, 435, 458, 462, 463, 464, 510, 539, 540
Smith, James Power 545, 546
Smith, Martin Luther 103, 432, 566
Smith, T. Kilby 138, 540, 541
Smith, W. F. (Baldy) 403, 443, 470, 471, 573, 574, 575, 576
Smith, William (Extra Billy) 495
Smith, William Sooy 95, 189, 209, 223, 267
Spear, Samuel P. 378, 417, 447, 448, 449, 465, 531, 571
Spinola, Francis B. 465
Stahel, Julius 71, 72, 186, 212, 270, 272, 308, 316, 351, 375, 378, 401,

404, 405, 411, 412, 445, 446, 475, 476, 483, 484
Stanley, David S. 384, 388, 421, 451, 452, 453, 454, 506, 568
Stannard, George 379, 406, 407, 412, 525, 552, 577
Stanton, Edwin M. 22, 24, 25, 26, 28, 36, 65, 66, 71, 72, 92, 94, 112, 123, 130, 131, 133, 138, 148, 172, 191, 193, 204, 205, 208, 223, 229, 231, 232, 234, 251, 252, 256, 260, 264, 266, 271, 276, 283, 303, 310, 323, 334, 350, 362, 365, 366, 426, 431, 433, 446, 462, 464, 479, 480, 509, 532, 539, 560, 564
Starr, Samuel H. 356
Steedman, I. G. W. 46, 51, 52
Steele, Frederick 31, 47, 431, 464
Steuart, George H. (Maryland) 395, 396, 420, 438, 470
Stevenson, Carter L. 37, 209, 566
Stevens, Thaddeus 439
Stewart, A. P. 389, 390, 451
Stoneman, George 17, 21, 22, 67, 71, 110, 159, 169, 417, 484
Streight, Abel 448
Stuart, J. E. B. (Jeb) 21, 71, 83, 84, 85, 86, 100, 119, 120, 123, 126, 146, 154, 155, 157, 158, 160, 161, 162, 163, 164, 165, 166, 168, 169, 170, 180, 181, 202, 217, 235, 249, 250, 252, 253, 254, 278, 279, 287, 288, 291, 292, 306, 307, 308, 309, 310, 312, 315, 316, 327, 334, 335, 351, 352, 353, 354, 356, 357, 358, 359, 360, 374, 375, 397, 398, 399, 403, 407, 408, 411, 446, 447, 471, 472, 473, 474, 475, 478, 485, 486, 487, 488, 489, 490, 491, 501, 519, 520, 523, 525, 543, 545, 546, 547, 548, 549, 550, 551, 559, 560, 571, 572, 573, 575, 576, 582, 585
Sykes, George 551
Szink, Jacob 395, 396

T

Tappan, James 147, 178, 539
Taylor, Richard 81, 96, 97, 135, 136, 138, 139, 140, 147, 173, 174, 178, 187, 364, 437, 458, 511, 539
Taylor, Walter 518, 581
Taylor, Zachary 135
Tevis, C. Caroll 126, 127, 128
Thomas, George H. 207, 383, 384, 385, 387, 390, 421, 451, 452, 506, 534, 536, 567
Thomas, Lorenzo 15, 432
Trimble, Isaac R. 84, 85, 145, 234, 347, 471, 472, 545
Tunnard, William 96, 104, 116, 134, 150, 175, 176, 193, 225, 262, 265, 304, 325, 367, 429, 430, 533, 534, 539, 563
Tuttle, James M. 190, 365
Tyler, Daniel 201, 216, 217, 231, 232, 237, 238, 239, 243, 253, 254, 271, 272, 275, 280, 281, 286, 329, 331, 332, 334, 403, 409, 410, 445
Tyler, R. O. 407

V

Vallandigham, Clement C. 42, 75, 76, 98, 99, 194, 196, 368, 514, 515
Van Dorn, Earl 382
Venable, A. R. 572, 576
Venable, Charles 168
Vincent, Strong 352, 353, 354, 356
Vogdes, Israel 259, 260

W

Walker, John G. 81, 97, 135, 136, 137, 138, 139, 147, 178, 187, 458, 513, 537, 538
Walker, L. M. 435
Walker, W. H. T. 93, 94, 97, 133, 189
Wallace, W. W. 396
Warren, Gouverneur K. 230, 400,

405, 483
Washburn, Cadwallader C. 36, 148, 149, 189, 191, 261, 267
Washburne, Elihu 148
Washburn, W. M. 176
Washington, George 384, 417
Watie, Stand 570
Webb, William A. 296, 297
Weitzel, Godfrey 46, 50, 51, 52, 56, 59, 188, 220, 222
Welles, Gideon 343, 479
Wharton, John A. 453
Wheeler, Joseph 228, 262, 305, 336, 382, 383, 453, 454
Whelan, Henry 163, 164
White, E. V. (Lige) 280, 327, 419, 440, 441, 442, 467, 544, 547, 585
White, Julius 568
Whiting, Charles 158
Wickham, William C. 121, 289
Wilder, John T. 387, 388, 389, 390, 391, 420, 450, 452, 507, 535, 537
Williams, J. M. 570
Williams, Seth 23, 71, 203, 286, 351, 356, 357, 401, 403, 404, 405, 407, 417, 418, 483, 484, 557, 558, 578, 579, 580
Willich, August 391, 421, 422, 423
Wilson, James Harrison 26, 27, 107, 267, 299, 302, 303
Wise, Henry A. 127, 128, 393, 448, 502, 503
Witcher, Vincent 499, 500, 543
Withers, W. T. 432, 540
Wood, S. A. M. 211
Woods, C. R. 532
Wyndham, Percy 166

Y

Yates, Richard 541

Printed in Great Britain
by Amazon